Individuality
in Clothing Selection
and Personal Appearance

Individuality

in
Clothing Selection
and
Personal Appearance

A Guide for the Consumer

4th Edition

Mary Kefgen
California State University, Long Beach, California

Phyllis Touchie-Specht
Mt. San Antonio College, Walnut, California

Macmillan Publishing Company
New York

Collier Macmillan Publishers
London

Copyright © 1986, Macmillan Publishing Company, a division of Macmillan, Inc.

Printed in the United States of America

Earlier editions copyright © 1971, 1976, and 1981 by Macmillan Publishing Co., Inc.

Macmillan Publishing Company
866 Third Avenue, New York, New York 10022

Collier Macmillan Canada, Inc.

Library of Congress Cataloging in Publication Data

Kefgen, Mary.
  Individuality in clothing selection and personal appearance.

  Bibliography: p.
  Includes indexes.
  1. Clothing and dress.   I. Touchie-Specht, Phyllis.
II. Title.
TT507.K36   1986   646'.3   85-10585
ISBN 0-02-362560-0

Printing: 345678   Year: 789012345

ISBN 0-02-362560-0

For those we love:

Jasmine

Katmandu

Mayo

Cinco

Rodney

Chester

Autom

William

Jeffrey

Alice

Paul

George

Louise

Karl

Betty

Preface

Dressing is not so much a choice of being right or wrong, of being correct or incorrect—for there is no one right way to dress. It is more a choice of being able to produce a desired effect, which is psychologically, sociologically, and physiologically comfortable for the individual. The design principle that sums up this goal is unity. In order to achieve unity, we must know ourselves, the expectations of others, and what is appropriate for our age and body conformation, and for the time, the place, and the event. When all these factors are in harmony, then the desired effect of dress can be achieved by the individual.

The purpose and content of the fourth edition of *Individuality* is summarized in its subtitle, *Clothing Selection and Personal Appearance, A Guide for the Consumer.* The book is designed as an introductory-level course in clothing analysis for college, university, and vocational programs. It can be used in a variety of classes that explore clothing, society, and the individual. Special efforts were made to make this text appeal to the broad spectrum of men and women that compose today's college clientele.

Each of the major subjects covered in previous editions has been carefully edited and updated. Many new photographs have been added to illustrate current fashion developments and to add depth to the design and cultural sections. Favorite photographs of historical or cultural interest have been retained. Suggested Readings have been updated. Suggested Activities have been revised and are included for use by the instructor and the student. These activities are intended to be a springboard for class planning and discussion. The writing style is modern and direct. Unisex terms are used. Where feasible, both the metric and English systems of measurement have been included. Throughout the book the authors have drawn from the fields of art, anthropology, economics, history, psychology, physiology, and sociology.

The text has been divided into four parts which can be presented in the order that pleases the individual instructor. Part I deals with the psychological and sociological influences of dress. The importance of appearance in first impressions and a discussion of the dimensions of individuality introduce this section. Reasons for wearing clothing are analyzed. The discussion of clothing as a communicator of culture helps to build a wide base for accepting and understanding individual differences, a base that is of particular importance in view of world political situations and the migration of so many of the world's varied people. Fashion is broadly defined to include the phenomena of all the social institutions that affect men and women at a particular time, with clothing only one aspect of the subject.

Part II covers the physical aspects of appearance. The premise for this section is that clothing selection must be realistically based on body formation. The individual is helped to understand how personal body conformation relates to the fashion figure used to merchandise clothing in the marketplace and in advertising. The new diet patterns for the United States, including the *Basic Four Plus One* are included, and these are related to individual health and appearance. The physiological composition of skin, hair, and nails is presented to be used as a basis of making consumer decisions.

Part III presents the principles of design and the design elements and relates them to clothing selection and personal appearance. Each of the design elements is illustrated with many photographs to clarify concepts. The dimensions of color are carefully explained. Several color systems have been introduced. A discussion of methods of the color consultant is included. The Color Key Program has been retained because it is the "granddaddy" of all the new glamor color systems. Methods for students to determine their own personal color patterns are emphasized.

Part IV is devoted to consumer information. Wardrobe strategies are designed to help individuals develop wardrobes that will fit their lifestyles and careers. Shopping and advertising techniques are explored to help consumers become aware of selling pressures exerted on them in the marketplace. Buying guides for various family members have been included. Correct fit of many types of garments either for ready-to-wear or self-creation are presented. Updated legislation pertaining to textiles is included. A new stain-removal chart adds depth to the care and maintenance methods of all wardrobe items that are stressed so that clothing dollars may be stretched because clothes will last longer.

The last chapter looks into the future, using the present problems of energy, population growth, and advancing technology as a basis from which to predict social changes and fashion in the twenty-first century. The history of self-adornment is related to human behavior as part of this prediction.

The appendices contain tables and charts for additional information and clarification. Addresses for various resources are also included. A glossary has been added to help students enhance reading and understanding of the text.

We are indebted to many people who have contributed, both knowingly and unknowingly, to the content of our book. They have helped us in many ways. Our families and friends have contributed moral support and understanding as well as their talents and ideas. Students have inspired us and helped us keep pace with our changing society. Colleagues have recommended picture sources and references and have shared ideas. Many educators have used our text in the United States and in many countries abroad. We want to thank each one.

We must give special acknowledgments to several individuals who gave generously of their time and talents to help us create this edition: Judy Argyres for her superb typing and preparation of our manuscript; Clem Inskeep, photographer; the Tournament of Roses Association for the fashion review of the T of R courts; and Pat Solderboum for her essay. We deeply appreciate the generous assistance of Rodney Jones and the Ameritone Color Key Corporation. Special thanks go to Betty and Karl Kessler, Jo Ann Crist, Newt and Gloria Le Baron, Josephine Schultz, James W. Peters, John J. Shaak, Heidi Kessler, and W. Stanley Larsen for photographs.

We wish to thank our editors, Peter C. Gordon and Julie Levin Alexander, for their support and encouragement. We are grateful to our production editors Hurd Hutchins and Janice Marie Johnson, our copy editor Frances Long, and our book designer Harold Stancil, for making our fourth edition a reality. To Chester J. Specht for his love and understanding we are forever indebted. We are most grateful to each of you.

MFK

PT-S

About the Authors

Mary F. Kefgen is a Professor of Home Economics at California State University, Long Beach, California. She received a BS in Home Economics from Iowa State University and an MA in Home Economics from New York University. She also studied at Oregon State University, Traphagen School of Fashion, and the Fashion Institute of Technology. She has done textile research in India and in South East Asia. She was the recipient of a Ford Foundation Grant to participate in the Oklahoma State University Project in Bangladesh (East Pakistan). She was selected to teach in Ethiopia with the Agency for International Development Teacher Corps. Other overseas teaching includes Germany and France. Miss Kefgen is a member of the Costume Council of the Los Angeles County Museum of Art, the Textile Group of Los Angeles, Omicron Nu Honor Society, and the American Home Economics Association. She is a former member of the Executive Board of the Western Region Costume Society of America. Currently she is a member of the Executive Board of the Association of College Professors of Textiles and Clothing, Western Region.

Phyllis Touchie-Specht received her BS in Home Economics from Oregon State University and her MA in Home Economics from California State University, Long Beach. She has done additional study at University of California, Los Angeles; University of Southern California; Temple University; California State University, Los Angeles; Chapman College; and Fashion Institute of Technology. She did nutritional research at Oregon State University. She modeled professionally for John Robert Powers. She had a daily fashion/food/talk show for KIEM-TV, Eureka, California. Mrs. Touchie-Specht is a faculty member at Mount San Antonio College, Walnut, California and past Faculty Senate President. She is past president of Foothill District, California Home Economics Association, American Home Economics Association. Currently she is a member of several Executive Boards including: Costume Society of America, Association of College Professors of Textiles and Clothing, Western Region; Costume Council; Los Angeles County Museum of Art; and The Fashion Group.

Contents

Appendices   **565**

Glossary   **589**

Selected Readings   **596**

Author Index   **599**

Subject Index   **602**

I

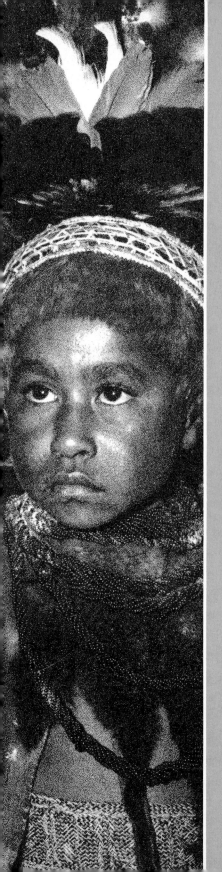

Psychological and Sociological Influences of Dress

1 *Impact*

Impact! Impression! In the same length of time that it takes to read those two words we can come in contact with a stranger and make an impression. The reflex of a first impression is automatic and instantaneous. We take the measure of strangers and decide if they are friendly or threatening; if they are worthy of more attention or not. This speedy inventory is categorized and the ensuing behavior is ordered based on the combinations of the first assessments. If a stranger appears nonthreatening but not very interesting the impression will probably not even register. If the stranger is threatening, more attention is certainly in order and various physical actions will follow to alleviate the fear. If the stranger is friendly and worthy of more attention, again attention is focused and the first impression is recorded and remembered.

As individuals in a highly competitive society, we are repeatedly judged in the course of our daily lives. These assessments come in the form of first impressions, and the impact of these first impressions can change our destiny. They can mean the difference between success and failure, not only in our interpersonal relationships but also in our educational pursuits and professional careers.

The marketplace is jammed with items that are packaged to make a calculated first impression. If the package design does not transmit a visual message that attracts and sells the consumer, then the packaging is manipulated until a satisfactory visual impact is achieved, or the product is withdrawn from the market. An inadequate wrapper around the product has been responsible for the bankruptcy of many business ventures. The packaged product has to look "good" to the consumer or it will not be purchased. The product that does not have the "right look" fails.

The composition of our society puts people into the same kind of supermarket competition. We must be "packaged" to make the "right" visual impact or we are out of the action. Our packaging includes the clothing and decorative accessories we wear, the grooming we practice, and the scents we select, as well as our facial expressions and our body movements.

How Dress Affects Behavior

This section of your text stresses the importance of the impact of clothing on individual and group behavior. The function of apparel communication is a vital part of everyday social interaction.

3

The study of clothing related to individual behavior and group behavior is based on psychology (the study of individual behavior) and on sociology (the study of group behavior). Social psychology studies the influence of group behavior on the individual. The social psychology of clothing, then, is concerned with both individual and group behavior.

There are numerous influences that affect clothing choices. By studying dress from the perspective of social psychology we can begin to understand:

why we dress as we do
why we prefer certain clothes and reject others
how our behavior is affected by what we wear
how our clothing choices affect others
what we communicate with our clothing
how we use clothing cues to understand others

First Impressions

First impressions are a vital form of communication in an urbanized society. During this initial contact many cues are received, categorized, and acted upon. The rapidity and completeness of the first impression are astonishing (Figure 1-1). Observers note that clothing gives cues to others about our social status,

1-1 First impressions are a vital form of communication. During this initial contact many cues are received, categorized, and acted upon. What is your first impression of this couple? (Courtesy Folkwear, Inc.)

occupation, and destination. The first things we notice in a brief encounter are age, sex, race, and physical appearance, including the clothing of the other person. Although these may seem to be superficial qualities, they are important factors that determine one's personal reaction to another.[1]

A first impression is always a correct impression *if* there is no second impression. Many times we have only one chance to present ourselves. We win approval or we are rejected; there is no second encounter. This happens in social situations, in school competitions, and in job interviews. If we win approval, we can have other opportunities to reinforce our first impression or alter the initial judgment or perhaps change it completely. If we are rejected, we may never have a second chance to make an impression.

Today, most of us cover great distances in our lives. We commute to school, to jobs, and for recreation. We frequently move from one residence to another, sometimes across town but often across country. This wide geographical range is populated with people. Parties, tours, clubs, schools, and other kinds of group contact throw people together quickly and randomly. The need for understanding effective first impressions is a very real one.

Nonverbal Communication

Clothing has been called a *silent language*. As a silent language it has a silent vocabulary which takes the form of symbols (signs, cues, or icons) that are used by individuals as tools for social interaction. This form of nonverbal communication is very informative. For by our dress we "tell" others:

what kind of a person we are
   or
what kind of a person we think we are
   or
what kind of a person we would like to be
   and
what we think about the person we represent (Figure 1-2)

A noted scholar of nonverbal communication explained "Dress is not what we wear, dress is what we think we wear and what we think others will see."[2]

When we speak a language and we say something that is misunderstood or say something we did not mean, we can usually retract our words immediately and attempt to clarify our intent. The silent language of our clothing however cannot be as easily retracted, although it can be completely revised at the next meeting,

---

[1] Leonard Bickman, "Clothes Make the Person," *Psychology Today*, April 1974, p. 49.
[2] Charles M. Galloway, Ph.D., "Non-verbal Communication," Combined Proceeding ACPTC 1979, p. 70.

1-2 Clothing has been called a silent language. What messages are the clothing symbols in this photo sending you? (Courtesy Hartmarx Corporation)

if there is one, which may make our intent clear or confuse the issue to even greater extent.

It is good to use clothing to please ourselves and to be attractive to others. No matter what our taste in garments is at the moment, no matter whether we use clothes to camouflage, to reveal, or to conceal, we should be aware of the impression we make.

Reading Clothing Messages

Clothing symbols are useful because they express meaning and they provide information to others. People can respond to clothing symbols when they understand their message. However, if the observer is to understand the clothing message, the meaning that the wearer attaches to the clothing must be the same message that the observer reads. For example, the wearing of "the old school tie" will have special meaning only for an alum of the same institution. Any person will have difficulty interpreting the clothing symbols when they differ from those with which he or she is familiar. Therefore, it is important to remember that clothing symbols do not hold the same meanings for all. People read the silent language of clothing messages from the alphabet they have learned and understand.

The symbols of dress are not always static. They assume different meanings depending upon:

where the clothing is worn
when the clothing is worn
how the clothing is worn
who wears the clothing

These factors all can alter the message significantly. Some examples: A skimpy beach outfit carries a different connotation when worn on the city street than it does when worn at the club pool. A low-cut satin dress may be appropriate at a nightclub but out of order at the office. Winter boots worn with light summer clothing on a hot day appear ludicrous. Parts of military uniforms may be worn as symbols of protest at disarmament rallies, but when they are worn by the active military they carry an entirely different message. Some consider it natural to see females going topless at the beach, but only if they are under five years of age. The wearing of skirted garments by American males (unless they are Scots) is generally considered a social embarrassment. Active sportswear including jogging suits, tennis outfits, leotards with leg warmers, and ski togs are worn by a large segment of our population; the wearers of these garments often use them for activities other than those intended, leading the observer to make false assumptions about their participation in sports activities.

1-3 Among the clothing clues that are most obvious in their meaning are T-shirt illustrations and slogans although the messages will not always be the same for all who view them. (Courtesy Camp Beverly Hills)

Among the clothing cues that are most obvious in their meaning are T-shirt illustrations and slogans. Representing a myriad of ideas such as product advertising, political leanings, school and fraternity loyalties, geographic wanderings and great humor, T-shirt messages are visual symbols for all to see and interpret. Again, the message will not always be the same for all (Figure 1-3).

All types of uniforms including those of police, military, medical, school band, flight attendant, fast-food server, Cub Scout, and Brownie present obvious clothing symbols. Uniforms sometimes represent power and authority, sometimes represent rank and privilege, sometimes identification or belonging, and often a combination of these and other connotations. The clothing messages that the uniform communicates vary with the observer and the circumstances under which the uniform is being observed.

Each of us has preconceived ideas of what various clothing symbols represent. We hold a storehouse of interpretations from which we draw to identify a particular cue or set of cues. Our impressions and the behavior that follows them is based on this individual response to the clothing symbols. Interpretations of clothing symbols are based on past experiences and personal values rather than drawn from any scientific study. We must be aware that these judgments are subjective and because of this they do vary from person to person. To illustrate, what messages do these clothing symbols have for you, your classmates, your friends, or your family?

designer clothing ———ethnic clothing
jogging shorts ————sweat suits
army uniform ————navy uniform
reading glasses ———sunglasses
attaché case ————book bag
high-heeled pumps ——barefoot sandals
punker dress ————preppie dress

How many of these clothing symbols were perceived the same by you and by the others you discussed them with and how many were perceived differently? Can you think of other examples that would be more controversial? This exercise supports the concept that we each speak our own silent clothing language through the way we dress. The symbols that we use are not always understood by others nor do we always find the language that others use intelligible to us.

A clothing researcher recommends using objective judgments to understand others through their clothing clues. When individuals share with others their interpretation of common symbols in an ongoing process we can attempt to learn as much as possible about these meanings and the consequences of these meanings in human interaction. We need to increase our awareness and objectivity in our observations of others.[3] It is not always possible to understand the meaning that individuals may be intending to communicate with their clothing cues, but if we are aware of our shortcomings in this regard, we are less likely to prejudge others and hinder meaningful communication (Figure 1-4).[4]

Sending out Unintended Messages

As author Emily Cho observed:

Animals wear the same clothing every day. The color and markings of their bodies trigger specific responses in other creatures, and they are not surprised by the effect that their clothing creates. However, as the only animals who choose their own plumage, we human beings are far less expert at articulating our needs and our intentions. Too frequently, our clothing sends a message contrary to our intent, and when a roomful of people start sending out messages about themselves that are unintended or incorrect, chaos ensues. . . .

Each of us has to discover exactly how clothing can express our needs and desires, how it can communicate who we *are* and what we *want*. Throughout much of human history, this whole plumage business has been largely a matter of hit or miss because we lack a highly developed instinct to guide us. However, although we are clumsy at designing our own messages, we intuitively pick up the unintended messages of others. We know when something is frightening or repellent or exciting to us. The ability to judge another creature is, after all, an instinct essential to our survival so we react strongly to the way others

---

[3] Susan B. Kaiser, *Social Psychology of Clothing and Personal Adornment* (New York: Macmillan, 1985).
[4] Ibid, Chapter 1.

1-4 We need to increase our awareness and objectivity in our observations of others. When we share the interpretation of common clothing symbols we can learn more about human interactions. (Courtesy Altra)

dress. Sometimes that reaction is conscious and other times subconscious, but it is always important. You may think that you "never rely on first impressions" but that is not so; our reaction to a person's clothing is instinctive and involuntary.[5]

One Set of Feathers Isn't Enough
Everyone needs a variety of clothing this author continued:

The messages we humans communicate to one another are so complex and so varied that one set of feathers is not enough. In fact, we need a whole closetful. For we dress to demonstrate many things—to show our social origin, our artistic bent and our sexual makeup. We dress to show our politics. We dress to protest or emulate, to attract or to intimidate. We dress to be accepted, to find security and identity in a group. Our clothing is an attraction and a distraction, a security blanket and a fantasy. Often it reveals and conceals at the same time.

If everyone understood the clothing language and was able to use it to advantage, life would be simple, for all of us would understand at a glance where everyone else stood and where they were headed. However, far from being expert at the nuance of clothing language—though we react instinctively—most of us speak a halting pidgin clothing at best. Frustrated by our inability to communicate ourselves, we even resort to message T-shirts, simply spelling out our messages across our chests for all to read. Slogans such as "My Body Belongs To Me," "Grouch" or "Unemployed Artist" may be a little crude, but they are effective and speak out loud and clear.

Trying to avoid the whole issue, people often think they can stay out of trouble by dressing in a nice neutral sort of way. Unfortunately, it is not possible to dress in a neutral way; whatever you wear makes a statement of some kind. Every time you dress, you're making choices and even an "I-don't-care" message is a clear statement.

[5] Emily Cho and Linda Grover, *Looking Terrific* (New York: Pulman, 1978), pp. 20–21.

9

In nature, careful grooming is basic to survival. An animal that displays a shabby coat is immediately marked as easy prey. In the same manner, when we encounter another person who is poorly dressed, we tend to discount his worth. When we see he is not up to par, we may treat him badly and degrade him even further. If you have ever been depressed and let your appearance show it, you may have experienced this phenomenon yourself.[6]

Nonverbal Communication and Verbal Communication

The Halo Effect

A concept of first impressions which is based on physical appearance is called the *halo effect*. The halo effect results from the impression we get from the first encounter with a person. It may become a lasting and unchanging impression regardless of any future encounters with that person.

People who are positively impressed with a person at the first meeting often credit that person with talents and traits that may not have any relationship to the first encounter or to the individual. For example, a teacher who likes the way a student looks and acts in the first class meeting may assume the student is smart. All the classwork this student produces is subjected to the halo effect and the student makes excellent grades, which are not always earned.

The reverse is true also. When a poor first impression is made, the halo effect can influence opinions negatively. When this happens, the future conduct or performance of the individual does not alter the original negative impression.

Examples of this can also be found in the classroom setting. When the halo effect is operating in a negative manner, it makes no difference how successful or talented the student proves to be. The teacher's evaluation may always be critical, and when grading is subjective this student receives lower marks than he or she has earned.

The halo effect is an important phenomenon to understand. It can be a critical factor in job interviews, sales presentations, and business transactions, as well as in social situations.

The First Four Minutes

Initial human contact is established or reaffirmed in a very short period of time. A study revealed that the average length of time during which strangers in a social situation interact before they decide to part or continue their encounter was four minutes. This length of time was established by careful observation of hundreds of people at parties, offices, schools, homes, and in recreational settings. Four minutes, which was approximately the minimum breakaway point, was the length of contact that was considered socially acceptable before a shift of conversational partners could occur.

[6] Ibid., p. 22.

The researcher believes that the four-minute concept applies appropriately to both first impressions and to the ongoing contacts, such as husbands and wives on awakening or at day's end, children and parents, and with anyone you know well and greet often. Whether with strangers, friends, or intimates, contact goals are basically similar. They are to create response and involvement, to give and take, to talk and to listen . . . to communicate.[7]

Assumptions in First Impressions

Assumptions are opinions or ideas that we take for granted as true or factual. What and how you assume can be of critical importance in the formation of first impressions. At the time of initial contact with strangers, instant assumptions are developed. Some of these impressions are valid, others will be discarded in due time. This is the *assumptive world*. It infiltrates behavior at different levels of awareness and influences a wide range of activities.

Assumptions are made as a normal part of life. Assumptions run the gamut from fantasy to routine habitual conclusions. In the latter category, we presuppose an order in our thinking about ourselves and the world around us. We plan our hours, days, and life assuming that the sun will rise and set as usual, the institutions that serve us will remain intact, the society in which we live will continue. We base our lives on a highly complex blend of experience, knowledge, and assumption.

In the area of first impressions, our assumptions, especially those called up by the sight, smell, and sound of others, always involve emotional reactions along with intellectual estimation.

Since everyone operates at one time or another on assumption, it is important to recognize how assumptions affect behavior. In first impressions it is difficult not to over- or underestimate an individual or a group. We should recognize that assumptions do exist and that they are vulnerable. Through a process of time and growing perception, some assumptions will become fact and others will not. By learning to predict the results of action and understanding, we can gain more realistic perspectives and enjoy more success in relationships. Flexible people can learn to examine their assumptions as they register them during contact with others, and if there seem to be contradictions, they can learn to make spontaneous revisions.[8]

Assumptions are based upon:

Emotional reactions + Intellectual judgments = Stereotyping
   Sound   and experiences
   Sight
   Smell
   Physical characteristics

---

[7] Leonard Zunin, M.D., with Natalie Zunin, *Contact: The First Four Minutes* (Los Angeles: Nash, 1972), p. 8.

[8] Zunin, op. cit., pp. 19–29.

Stereotype

A stereotype may be defined as a standardized mental picture that is held in common by members of a group. It is used to categorize and sort information. Stereotypes represent an oversimplified opinion or an unethical judgment that can influence the understanding of others. They are simplistic in nature, and often convey special meanings. In first impressions they are used as instant mental shorthand. They may be related to age, sex, ethnicity, politics, religion, or physical appearance.

It is not unusual for us to form stereotypes based upon appearances. An example of this was given the authors by a student who claimed she was able to select a brilliant lab partner for her science classes with a high degree of accuracy. She said she would choose a boy she believed looked and dressed "quite average" and "middle of the road." Her reasoning:

A boy with an extreme hair style was questionable and difficult to predict.
A homely boy would have "hang-ups" because of his appearance.
A boy who was very good looking would not be too smart as he would be getting through life on his looks.
A boy who dressed too smartly was not seriously interested in academia.
A sloppily dressed boy was uncertain about himself and not a good student.

Cultural stereotyping can affect our judgments of others (Figure 1-5). Some stereotypes of this kind are these:

All South Sea islanders wear grass skirts.
All blacks have rhythm and are good dancers.
All whites have round eyes.
All Latins are lovers.

All Poles like jokes.
All Orientals get good grades.
All Irish like green.
All Africans look alike.

When we receive further information regarding a person that conflicts with the stereotype, we do not revise our assumptions but rather hold to the stereotyping, prejudice results.[9]

An interesting study stereotyping footwear presents opinions reached by the respondents concerning four groups of shoes. The first group, "young and casual," included among others, clog, earth sandal, thong, topsider, casual sandal, and desert boot. This group of shoes was seen as young, casual, with few sexual connotations and not particularly good for trying to make a positive social or professional impression. The second group of masculine shoes included loafer, cowboy boot, jogging shoe, wing tip and black lace-up. These shoes were considered comfortable, appropriate for work or leisure and they made a positive social or professional impression. The third shoe group, "feminine and sexy,"

[9] Kaiser, op. cit., Chapter 8.

1-5 *Stereotyped societal uniforms such as these grass skirts are often associated with people of the South Seas. Here Tahitian dancers greet tourists at an air terminal, thus promoting such typing. (Courtesy Qantas)*

included black, slinky high-heel sandal, high boot and two-toned pump. The high-heeled slinky sandal was considered as most feminine, most formal, most fashionable, most sexy, most prestigious, most inappropriate for work and most uncomfortable. The last group, "asexual or dowdy" women's shoes, were a nursing shoe and a classic career pump. This group was described as casual, conservative, unsexy, comfortable, and appropriate for work. The researchers noted "this suggests an interesting dilemma for the career woman who wants to make a positive impression (not with respect to sexiness). It also suggests a double standard with regard to men's and women's shoes. In order for women's shoes to be considered attractive, they should also appear sexy and uncomfortable. This relationship does not hold for men's shoes."[10]

Personal Appearance

Our physical appearance is the one personal characteristic that is obvious and accessible to others in first impressions as well as in almost all social interactions. Researching social psychologists have compiled a fascinating work on the effect and influence of physical appearance on interpersonal relationships and social phenomena. Their work was the study of *morphology*, which they defined broadly as the study of the physical, structural aspects of the organism as well as the externally observable and objectively measurable attributes of the person including aesthetic attractiveness (Figure 1-6).

They reported that physical attractiveness was measurable and that although hard to define, when photographs were used in the study, a consensus of what was attractive could be obtained. They noted that personal attractiveness has an important impact upon our lives and that its influence starts very early. Teachers from nursery school through high school and college admitted that they ranked pupils by appearance. The most attractive children were assumed to be the smartest. Peers tended to do the same kind of ranking so that the most attractive children were also usually the most popular. Parents followed the same pattern; not only were the most attractive children smart and popular but they were thought to be better behaved than unattractive children.

The investigators found that college students, when considering physical attractiveness and popularity, ranked intelligence, friendliness, and sincerity first. Further investigation revealed that many of the students, when publicly polled, believed it vulgar to judge others by physical appearance. But in actual practice, it was demonstrated that they did rate physical attractiveness first. Men, more often than women, admitted valuing beauty.

In another study, the authors found that young adults thought that good-looking persons were generally more sensitive, kind, interesting, strong, poised, modest, sociable, outgoing, and exciting than less-attractive persons. Attractive persons were expected to lead happier, more fulfilling lives and marriages and have better jobs.[11]

In our society we prefer to believe that it is what is behind the mask of appearance that really counts. But as the morphological research develops it ap-

---

[10] S. B. Kaiser, H. G. Schultz, and J. L. Chandler, "Sex Roles, Social Cognitive Perceptions and Shoe Stimuli." *Ms.*, 1983, cited in Kaiser, op. cit., Chapter 8.

[11] Ellen Bersheid and Elaine Walster, *Advances in Experimental Social Psychology* (New York: Academic Press), Vol. VII (1973).

pears more frequently that in first impressions more favorable judgments are made on the physically attractive. Attractiveness has its primary influence on first meeting. On subsequent meetings we are judged by other factors. Research has shown that we rely less on physical appearance for our evaluations as we get to know a person. It must be understood that physically attractive people are not necessarily happier or better adjusted than others.[12]

Common sense helps us realize that the man or woman who relies completely on physical attractiveness, to the exclusion of the development of the other as-

[12] Chris L. Kleinke, *First Impressions* (Englewood Cliffs, N.J.: Prentice-Hall, 1975), p. 15.

1-6 Physical attractiveness is hard to define. When photographs are used a consensus can be obtained. Do you consider these children physically attractive? (Courtesy Qantas, Warrem Clarke photograph)

pects of his/her being, will have serious difficulty adjusting to life. For our purposes, it should be firmly established that physical attractiveness is a significant standard by which we form our first impressions.

> Beauty is a greater recommendation than any letter of introduction.
> Aristotle
> 4th century B.C.

Perceptions on First Impression Situations

The social functions of clothing play an important part in first impressions. Clothing can be used:

    to communicate
    to motivate
    to attract
    to separate
    to show discipline
    to show rebellion

How the clothing is perceived depends entirely on the frame of reference of the person making the judgment. As we have seen, different people, because of their own unique background, will evaluate clothing cues in their own manner. People dressing in a similar manner are generally approving of each other and critical of those dressing in a different manner. The wider the variation of dress, often the harsher the criticism.

Recently there has been a proliferation of books, magazine and newspaper articles, seminars and workshops devoted to information on the "art of dressing for success." Men and women invest in advice to assure themselves of first impression sartorial success. Whether their goals are for:

    securing the right job
    finding a good mate
    contending in a political campaign
    winning a case in court

Men and women have become more aware that in addition to what they have to say, their clothes communicate strong messages.

In the Courtroom

The social psychology of dress has found its way into the legal profession. Because the courtroom presents a first-impression situation, legal dress has become a style issue. Lawyers worry that their clients might look too rich, too nonconformist, or too messy, and thus adversely influence the jury. Attorney F. Lee Bailey advises all of his clients to avoid flashy dress. Attorney Marvin Belli believes that going to court is like going to church, "you dress up for it." He advises his clients to avoid wearing wild neckties or suits, fancy hairdos, jewelry, dark glasses, white shoes, message T-shirts or sweat shirts. He also cautions them against gum chewing. Palimony attorney Marvin Michelson advises clients against ostentatious dress, too much makeup, sexy outfits, and "jewelry dripping from the hands." In the notorious John DeLorean trial, Christina Ferrare, who was not legally involved, dressed to help her husband by appearing in court in conservative clothing selected specifically for the trial.

In a Washington case a woman seeking compensation for a back injury received a smaller award than expected. The jurors noticed that during the trial she wore sandals and changed her toenail polish three times. They reasoned that her back didn't hurt her that much.[13]

It was reported that the judges who wear sports coats to Hinds County Justice Court in Jackson, Mississippi, say they've had enough of informality—they want robes, just like other judges. "In improving the image of the Justice Court, we feel the need for robes to maintain a proper decorum," said a letter from three of the five Justice Court judges to the county authorities.... "Anytime you go into a courtroom, you're sitting on a bench, you've got a flag. You need a robe."[14] Throughout the United States, other judges are following this lead and requesting that lawyers wear their academic robes when appearing in court.

On the Job

The impact of dress in the job interview is revealed in this statement:

That first split-second impression that your clothes make on the personnel director can determine whether or not you make it to the interview. Clothes may not make the man, and they may not be a legitimate job requisite under the Fair Employment Practices Act, but they do communicate. Veteran recruiters say that clothes can be as reliable a placement indicator as a battery of psychological tests (Figure 1-7).[15]

In order to test the influence of the dress of female job applicants for middle-management positions, 77 personnel administrators evaluated 4 applicants. Each was dressed in 4 different costumes representing 4 levels of yangness (masculinity). The analysis was used to estimate the following personality types: forceful, self-reliant, dynamic, aggressive, and decisive. The moderately masculine costume portrayed the personal characteristics better than the most masculine costume. However, the more masculine costume tested better than the least masculine costume for the desired management characteristics.[16]

[13] Gary Abrahams, "Taking the Case to Court: Do Clothes Really Affect the Verdict?" *Los Angeles Times*, July 1, 1983, Pt. V, p. 1.

[14] *Los Angeles Times*, October 4, 1984, Pt. I.

[15] Mary Lou Luther, "Work Clothes," *West*, October 8, 1972, p. 25.

[16] Sandra Monk Forsythe and Mary Frances Drake, "Influence of Female Applicants' Dress on Interviewer's Perception of Personal Characteristics for Middle-Management Positions," ACPTC Combined Proceedings, 1981, pp. 112–113.

1-7 *The first split-second impression that your clothes make on the personnel director can determine whether or not you make it to the interview. (Courtesy Hartmarx Corporation)*

In the Classroom—Reading the Teacher

Several studies of student reaction to the dress of their teacher clearly show how clothing symbols translate to instruction capability. One investigation concluded that the quality of a teacher's work was rated significantly higher when the teacher was fashionably dressed than when he was unfashionably dressed (Figure 1-8).[17]

In another study, students classified teachers who were dressed formally as the most organized, best prepared and knowledgeable. Teachers who were dressed informally were rated highest in fairness, friendliness, flexibility, and sympathy. While no form of dress proved to create a most favorable overall impression, the evidence suggested that teachers could use clothing to create the image they wanted to project. (This test utilized photographs of clothing of teachers from the neck down.)[18]

At the high school level, similar testing was done to learn whether the dress of female teachers affected the students' view of the teacher. Wearing feminine,

[17] Peggy Englebach and Mary Lapitsky, "The Fashionability of Clothing: Its Effect on Perceptions of an Educator," ACPTC Combined Proceedings, 1978, p. 92.

[18] Ernestine N. Reeder and Anita C. King, "Are Teachers Dressing for Success?" *Illinois Teacher*, May–June 1984, p. 212.

18

dainty dress the teacher was ranked highest in favorable characteristics, most likely to offer assistance and most approachable. The teacher dressed in a tailored, skirted suit was judged as most capable of maintaining classroom order, most desired for a homeroom teacher, one with whom the student could discuss personal problems. The teacher who wore the most masculine pant suit received the lowest rankings as having the least desirable traits. (The test consisted of transparencies of various dress using identical head and hair styles.)[19]

In an investigation which supported the old adage "clothes make the man," two college psychology instructors appeared for their first classes wearing the garb of Catholic priests. They appeared in other classes in suits and ties. Students in the classes where they had appeared in the priestly attire rated them significantly more moral, reputable, unusual, and also more withdrawn than did the classes where they had appeared in regular suits and ties.[20]

In another college classroom situation, students rated pictures of physically attractive male and female psychology professors as being warmer, more sensitive, better able to communicate, more knowledgeable of the subject matter than the less attractive professors.[21]

[19] Ibid, pp. 212–213.
[20] Chris L. Kleinke, op. cit. p. 11.
[21] J. P. Lombardo and M. E. Tocci, "Attributions of Both Positive and Negative Characteristics of Instructors as a Function of Attractiveness and Sex of Instructor and Sex of Subject," *Perceptual and Motor Skills*, **48**, 1979, pp. 491–494.

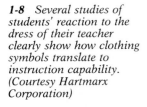

1-8 *Several studies of students' reaction to the dress of their teacher clearly show how clothing symbols translate to instruction capability. (Courtesy Hartmarx Corporation)*

Dressing the Part

In contemporary patterns of dress it is not so easy to make predictions about people from the clothes they wear. Although it is often possible to make assumptions about their employment because of a uniform or style of dress associated with certain types of work, confusion can arise because some institutions require employees to wear conservative dress, when in their private lives they prefer a casual style of dress (Figure 1-9).

There is some reasonable evidence that nonconformity in dress indicates a casual lifestyle that implies a personal freedom. Other patterns of dress that reveal lifestyle include extreme fashion conformity, participant sports attire, bare body clothes, and ethnic costumes. Clothing cues are not always infallible, since taste may be influenced by the current fashion, rather than reflecting the individual's values.

The colors of clothing, as well as design can signify the ease or seriousness with which one takes oneself. Most of us have color preferences and color dislikes. Much of culture has been rich in color associations. We may be "in the pink, red with shame, green with envy, black with despair, a yellow coward, having the blues, or seeing the world through rose-colored glasses." Flags, emblems, religious rituals, customs, and superstitions use color. Color fills our language, reflects our feeling, and portrays our emotions.

Every color and mode of dress can influence the first impression regardless of whether or not the assumptions we make are correct. Researchers emphasize that since we dress to please our own self-image as well as to influence the impression that others will have, choice of clothing is important. It tells others a great deal about our tastes, which are an integral part of our personalities. Today we are not bound by narrow standards of dress. There is an enormous variety of styles that allow both men and women the opportunity for self-expression and individuality in dress.

What you usually wear can be a portrait of your self-concept. Clothing tells others who you are or what you would like to be. Style does telegraph messages, daring or conservative, fashionable or funky, fun or functional, plain or fancy, drab or colorful—all offering instant impressions to and from others. Any distinct type of dress or grooming meets with immediate associative response from others that is partly assumptive. A researcher observed:

In our minds is a fat file of cultural conditioners and personal experiences that call up associations through which we label and categorize. We all make fast references to that mental file; the point is not to be overly dependent on it.[22]

Contrary to what we may imagine, people observing us are not generally looking to see if we are physically perfect. They are not really looking to see if we are wearing last season's fashions. What they are looking for is a harmonious whole. Whether they know it or not, they are looking to see if everything about the other person fits together. If the parts add up to a whole, the person is judged in a positive manner, if they do not, negative or critical judgments are made.

[22] Zunin, op. cit. pp. 107–111.

1-9 *It is not always easy to make predictions about people from the clothes they wear for work because some institutions require employees to wear conservative dress, when in their private lives they prefer a casual style of dress. (Courtesy Hartmarx Corporation)*

Grooming

Grooming is how we care for ourselves. It includes that which we apply to our faces and bodies, and the way we arrange our hair. Physical attractiveness cannot be applied, but it can be enhanced. Healthy skin, styled hair, and clean manicured nails are all plainly desirable and complete the picture you present.

How you look affects how you feel. It is psychologically pleasing to look your best. Sociologically it is demanded.

Perfumes, lotions, mouthwashes, toothpastes, underarm deodorants, hairspray, and other fragrances or odors are a part of the nonverbal language of first impressions. If one is to make contact effectively, it is important to exude socially acceptable fragrances.

Scents can convey meanings that, it is hoped, are consistent with (or perhaps slightly ahead of) verbal and body communication. The presence or absence of your grooming, dress, and aromas make a statement about you in each first impression. Remember, we never get a second chance to make a good first impression.

Body Movement

An important component of surface language is body movement. Our posture, our walk, our smile or our frown, and the many other gestures that we use all contribute to the initial impression and the halo effect that influences others' estimation of ourselves (Figure 1-10).

We need also to consider how the surface language of others is computed in our own minds. For as others are judging us, we are judging them. We arrive at

1-10 Our posture, smile, and many other gestures that we use contribute to the initial impression and the halo effect which influences others' estimation of us. What do the warmth of his smile and the casualness of his pose tell you about Willi Smith, designer of WilliWear? (Courtesy WilliWear)

our own first impressions from the messages we receive, both verbal and non-verbal, from the facts that we know, and from the assumptions we make. Frequently the judgments we make of others are greatly influenced by our own patterns of dress and grooming. It should be noted that our personal friends generally dress in a manner of which we approve.

Suggested Activities

The following exercise was patterned after a form used at a University of California, Los Angeles, class entitled "Contact!" presented by Leonard Zunin, M.D. It is an excellent tool to use the first day of class. Following the completion of the form, students are asked to give it to the person observed. The group members are then asked to discuss the experience, the degree of accuracy of the first impressions, and to reveal the surface language clues that led them to their assumptions.

Instructions
1. Read and follow these instructions. If you have a question, raise your hand.
2. Do not speak, whisper, or giggle.
3. Observe one person who is a stranger to you.
4. Silently complete this form answering the questions as best you can.
5. When you finish the form, relax and silently wait for the class to resume with additional instructions.

Estimated age _____ Place of birth _____ Month of birth _____
Marital status: married ___ separated ___ divorced ___ single ___ widowed ___
Children: yes _____ no _____ ages of children _____
Nationality _____ Race _____
Year in school _____ Occupation other than student _____
Education major _____ Education minor _____
Economic status: lower ___ low middle ___ middle ___ upper middle ___ upper ___
Position in family: oldest _____ youngest _____ middle _____ only _____

Interests (use answers: yes, no, maybe or other appropriate term):

spectator sports (name) _____	participant sports (name) _____
music (type) _____	movies (type) _____
reading (type) _____	artistic and creative _____
gourmet _____	community activities _____
favorite food _____	school activities _____
dancing _____	writing _____
camping _____	hiking _____
travel _____	politics _____
sewing _____	cooking _____
television _____	gambling _____

Organization memberships (name them):

Religious belief: first guess _____ second guess _____
　　　　practice: strong _____ moderate _____ little _____ none _____

Personality traits:

leader _____	follower _____	soft _____	tough _____
aggressive _____	passive _____	naive _____	jaded _____
patient _____	impatient _____	flamboyant _____	plain _____
trusting _____	distrustful _____	fashionable _____	casual _____
tactful _____	blunt _____	sarcastic _____	humorous _____
extrovert _____	introvert _____	sad _____	happy _____
shy _____	outgoing _____	up-tight _____	relaxed _____
friendly _____	aloof _____	rough _____	gentle _____
frilly _____	tomboyish _____	thoughtful _____	rude _____
liberated _____	dependent _____	quick _____	slow _____
talkative _____	quiet _____	romantic _____	realistic _____
intelligent _____	dumb _____	in love _____	free-lancing _____

After completing the form pass it to the person observed. Discuss with person observed the accuracies and inaccuracies of the observation. What clues led to the impressions given? What part did grooming play? Clothing? Body language? Did you answer all the questions honestly? If not, why not?

1. First Four Minutes. Arrange to observe classmates (unacquainted, if possible) in conversation for four minutes. At the end of time ask them to "freeze." Observe their body language. Discuss this experience. Be aware of the first four minutes of each renewed association with family and friends. How does this time experience change your relationships?
2. Does the first impression you have of people generally prove to be accurate? What aspects of a person do you focus upon in a first impression situation?
3. Recall some personal experience with the "halo effect." Was it a positive or negative experience?
4. Write out your personal T-shirt slogan. Do not sign the front of your paper. Post it on the board. What do they each reveal about the writer?
5. Decide why you are wearing what you are wearing right now. What are the social reasons for your garb? How would you rate your personal appearance right now? What impact would you have on a total stranger?
6. Write a brief paper defining your personal philosophy of dress. Include: (a) How you feel about clothes; are they important or not? (b) What guides you in selecting or rejecting particular styles? (c) What do you feel about the changing fashions? (d) What portion of your income is spent on clothing and personal appearance?

Keep this paper for review at the end of course. Indicate whether or not you think your feelings toward clothing will be changed during the class.

2 Individuality—A Search for Identity

Individuality is the personification of characteristics that make each of us distinctive. Each person is a special human being. This uniqueness is what sets us apart from others and makes each of us what we are, individual.

The term *individuality* is often used but seldom understood. In order to understand the implications of the word individuality, think of a friend or a person who stands out in your mind as being very distinctive. Try to describe *what* makes this person different from everyone else. Could the special qualities of this person be singled out and seen in a crowd? If not, the uniqueness of the friend probably is not in the nature of physical appearance but in personal qualities not visible. Next, try to describe yourself to someone you do not know well. Do not use biographic or physical information, but try to describe yourself as a person. What distinctive adjectives would you use that would make it possible for the stranger to identify you from all others? Younger people may find this exercise more difficult than older people because their individuality is still in the formative stage. Yet, when you think about it, small children, even babies, have distinctive qualities that set them apart.

A part of individuality is:

uniqueness
originality
personal signature
daring to be yourself
doing your own thinking, and saying "no" when you do not agree
rejecting styles that are in fashion when they are not "you"
refraining from wearing the same style garments, hair, and jewelry just because
   everyone else is wearing them
not using the latest "in" words and phrases that everyone else is adopting
being true to yourself

Individuality also means having exclusive or distinctive characteristics or qualities that no one else has. This may be a work of nature such as a dimple in your chin, freckles on your nose, or a crooked tooth. It may be a personalized physical feature such as a hair style or manicure.

Individuality can be expressed by something you wear such as distinctive

2-1 *Individuality means identifying your talents and developing them to the utmost. (Courtesy Danskin, Inc.)*

jewelry, or unusual eyeglass frames. It can be the use of color or texture or unique fabric design in your clothing. It can be garments that are unusual or are worn with uncommon flair.

Individuality also means identifying your talents and developing them to the utmost. It means pursuing your own interests and developing a special expertise in something such as building furniture, doing creative needlework, collecting miniature animals, or playing the banjo. These interests will add dimension to your character, be satisfying to you, be of interest to others and add to your specialness (Figure 2-1).

The opposite of individuality is conformity. There are periods of one's life when conformity is an important and necessary part of personal growth. As we progress through childhood to adulthood, we go through stages in which peer group identification is extremely significant. This need is particularly strong in grade school. At this point in development, each child wants to be part of "the gang"; to be ostracized, for any reason, is most painful. This strong desire to be part of the group usually extends into the teen-age years when the uncertainties of adolescence are often coped with by group membership. One of the most overt symbols of this type of socialization is dress. Each generation has produced a "teen look" that is easily identified. Look through high school and college annuals that date

25

back ten, fifteen, twenty, or thirty years, and you will be able to observe this dress phenomenon in action. As each man and woman leaves this adolescent period of maturation for adulthood, the importance of peer group identification should lessen and emphasis should be placed on achieving individuality.

Careful understanding of oneself is vital to the expression of individuality. One must strive to develop this self-knowledge so that the person you develop is the real you, and not the someone you or someone else thinks you should be. This is an important part of maturity. Understanding of oneself is indeed difficult and takes much time, thought, and self-analysis. The search for identity includes seeking the answers to such questions as these:

Who am I?
What are my commitments?
What are my obligations and responsibilities?
What are my guiding values?
What are my interests?
What are my priorities?
What are my expectations?
What lifestyle makes me comfortable?
What pleases me?
What kind of people do I admire?
What are my goals?
What are my strengths?
What are my weaknesses?
What do I want from life?
What am I going to give in return?

If, in your lifetime, anyone is to understand you, shouldn't it be you? This kind of self-knowledge is the cornerstone of mental health and is essential to the expression of true individuality.

Personal Awareness

Each individual is composed of many parts. The physical composition of the individual is observable and can be most adequately measured and described. Later chapters deal at length with the physical self. The *nonphysical properties* of the individual are much more difficult to assess. Each individual interprets these nonphysical qualities in his own frame of reference, or on his own "personal computer." The sum of the physical and nonphysical qualities reveals a unique human being—one of a kind. It is the purpose of this chapter to help you understand the nonphysical qualities that are so great a part of the real you.

Certain terms, such as personality, self-concept, values, and attitudes, are used to describe the nonphysical qualities of the individual. Discussion of each of these should help you in considering various facets of yourself.

Personality

The term *personality* is frequently used to describe the individual. The dictionary supplies a number of definitions of personality for the layman, yet research shows that professionals disagree on an exact definition. Variation of interpretation for the term comes from the theoretical preference of the person making the definition. The psychologist, physician, sociologist, biologist, and philosopher all use the term in their own way. It becomes obvious that "personality" covers a multitude of definitions.

For our purpose a simple definition is best. We are concerned with a relationship between personality and clothing and personal appearance. Therefore, we define *personality* as "The distinctive individual qualities of a person." We perceive another's personality from the visible aspects of his character.

Each person is an embodiment of a collection of qualities. Personality is influenced by abilities, temperament, talents, physical structure, emotional tendencies, ideas, ideals, skills, motives, memories, goals, values, moods, attitudes, feelings, beliefs, habits, and behavior. These qualities, all of which are highly individualized, make up personality. The influences of heredity, social and cultural contacts, learning, and experience also contribute.

Many attempts have been made to classify personalities into types in an effort to assist people to express their individual characteristics. These classifications have included personality type labels such as romantic, athletic, ingenue, dramatic, and macho. This typing is based on components that include physical build, coloring, voice, mannerism, temperament, and behavior. These types were devised by collecting composites of various personalities; they were not individuals but groups of many people. Personality types are artificial classifications.

This theory of personality typing assumes that individuals will fit into rigid groupings. Certainly it is possible to type people in some respects, but the many facets that make up our individuality cannot be pigeonholed into a simple classification that fits a large number of the population. Allport stated, ". . . each is of a type only with respect to some one segment of his nature . . . in reality types are valid only for a limited characteristic; they embrace a segment of individuality, but never the total individual."[1]

Personality is sometimes described by trait names. A *trait* is the term used to describe a consistent manner of behavior, and the individual possesses a composite of many and varied traits. When we describe a person as being aggressive, friendly, artistic, or austere, we are describing traits of behavior that are frequently observed in him. Again, personality traits do not fall into easily categorized types. It is impossible to put a variety of people into a filing system and expect results that will give an accurate definite type.

Your personality is your very own. To describe it or any other personality, groups of descriptive words must be used. Each individual interprets another's personality within his own personal frame of reference. Therefore, your personality becomes many-faceted as it continually changes as you mature and evolve

[1] G. W. Allport, *Personality, A Psychological Interpretation* (New York: Holt, 1937), p. 15.

and as it is comprehended by others. Your personality is a vital expression of your individuality.

Many people make personal judgments on the basis of appearance. Hair styles, grooming, and clothing have a particularly strong influence on these judgments. Further cues are presented by the way we walk, talk, and move both face and body. The manner in which we present ourselves certainly does reflect how we feel about ourselves and others. It reflects the values placed on dress and appearance and expresses a personal philosophy.

In spite of the difficulty in doing so, we should attempt to express our personality in dress. By striving for better understanding of ourselves, we can discover who we are and delimit the image we wish to present to others. The study of clothing and fashion can expand our knowledge of the symbolism of dress. By combining our self-understanding with the knowledge of clothing, we can present the image we desire.

Rosenbaum expressed it this way:

Until recently, it was easily possible to meet a man or a woman and from their clothes deduce their occupations, economic level, and social status. The world was divided into blue-collar and white-collar workers. The rich looked rich and the poor looked poor. Everybody had a place and knew it, and everybody had a role and dressed for it. Now, although it is not so simple to tell occupation and status, it is easier to look for personality traits. People are no longer hiding behind a façade of costume; they are expressing themselves more directly.

You express yourself every day when you get dressed. You show other people something about yourself and your emotions. You reveal a glimpse of your true self and express hidden wishes.

You and your clothes are an important part of your ability to be happy. If you have a sensible attitude toward clothes, it means that you have a sensible attitude toward life, and being at ease with your choice of clothes means that you are also at ease with your own personality. Not only can your mirror tell you how you look in your clothes, it can also tell you what your mood is and how you really feel about yourself.[2]

How Personality Is Expressed with Clothing

If we use our definition of personality, we can make it applicable to dress. Clothes and combinations of garments present visible characteristics that give them personality (Figure 2-2). A study of commercial advertising pictures will show that different garments combined with accessories and grooming communicate a variety of feelings; they also suggest where and when they should be worn. Some clothing may be classified as formal, casual, sophisticated, businesslike, unisex, feminine, masculine, dramatic, and so on. The degree of expressiveness that clothing possesses varies with the person making the obser-

---

[2] Jean Rosenbaum, M.D., *Is Your Volkswagen a Sex Symbol?* (New York: Hawthorn, 1972), pp. 105–106.

vation and the person wearing the clothes. The personality of clothing makes some garments unsuitable for particular persons. It is important to become aware of the impact of matching clothing characteristics to personality qualities. A shy, reserved man is overwhelmed by bold-colored and body-revealing clothing. A very soft, gentle woman looks and may be uncomfortable in severly tailored tweeds. On the other hand, a person with an effervescent personality looks superb in bright-colored, attention-grabbing clothing. A sophisticated worldly person would appear miserable when dressed to fade into the crowd. The personality of your clothing should complement your own personality.

The messages that we convey with our clothing should harmonize with the other aspects of our personality and with the general setting. If conflicting messages are being sent, as by a mature adult dressed as a child; an aggressive athlete dressed in frills and bows; or an efficient bank clerk dressed in feathers and sequins, then other people are going to sense the confusion and they may tune out, either because of mistrust or because they don't want to take the trouble to clarify the ambiguities. If you build up certain expectations with your clothing, but your actions run contrary to your clothes—or if your identity turns out to be different from what was "advertised"—people tend to become disconcerted or possibly even angry with you for disrupting their system. For example, if you look like one of the employees, and you're actually the boss, you may incur the hostility or disrespect of those who mistake your identity.

2-2 *Garments present visible characteristics that give them personality. What adjectives would you use to describe the personality of this outfit? (Courtesy Catalina)*

As each individual is a complex personality and engages in many activities, clothing for differing moods and occasions is almost a necessity. Clothes for school may be representative of local campus customs. Some days one may feel like being the "Joe Cool" on campus and will dress and behave in a manner that may differ greatly from that worn on the day the same "Joe Cool" goes in to see the professor about failing grades. Clothing for employment will be determined by the job and the philosophy of the employer. Applicants for positions in merchandising, advertising, and interior design must pay more attention to fashion of their clothing than one who opts to work in a research laboratory. People who apply for work in traditionally conservative business firms will find it expedient to dress conservatively. Clothing for dating or social life should be appropriate for the occasion, the location, and the other people involved. What might look extreme in one group or setting or geographic location might be considered conservative in another. People engaged in community service, political campaigns, or local causes in the community have learned the importance of image in projecting their causes. Gloria Steinem, a feminist leader, gives this advice on dressing for impact:

> In a political sense it is better to send a woman in a print dress and pearls rather than blue jeans to a meeting of the Democratic National Committee. Even if they say the same things, the woman in the dress has more of a chance for acceptance; therefore it is more subversive.[3]

Self-concept—Self-image

Self-concept or *self-image* is the general notion that each person has of himself. The terms are interchangeable. Used here, they encompass the idea we have of ourselves both as a physical person and as a psychological person. We each have a mental concept of how we look and how we behave.

Our self-concept is formed very early in life from the feedback or response we receive from others. Some of these responses are based upon our clothes and appearance. The notion we have of ourselves often changes from continuing feedback. This feedback is received in the form of direct verbal comments about ourselves including clothing, appearance, behavior or conversation and/or in the form of nonverbal responses such as stares, frowns, smiles, or gestures. Feedback may come as a lack of response, that is, no comments, no looks, no gestures, "no nothing" but a complete "ignore." This too is information. We evaluate any input based on how reliable or important we feel the source to be.

We also obtain information about ourselves from photos and sometimes from seeing what is before us in a mirror. We may evaluate what we see by comparing ourselves with others. After we decide how we wish others to see us, we attempt

[3] Truchia Kushner, "Finding a Personal Style," *Ms.*, February 1974, p. 45.

2-3 *One's self-concept may not be realistic.*

to select a pattern, including speech, movement, dress, and actions, that will reinforce our self-image or be consistent with the image we wish to project.

For many, this self-image may be a very incorrect assessment of either the physical or the psychological self, or both. This is a kind of "mental myopia" that allows us to see ourselves only as we wish to be seen. What others see may differ from what we know of ourselves (Figure 2-3).[4]

The image we have of our bodies affects how we feel about ourselves. The feeling of satisfaction or dissatisfaction we experience is shaped by current fashion ideals or by real-life models in our society. One of the body ideals continuing from the 1960s is thinness. "Less is more," less weight is more desirable. This ideal is epitomized by skinny fashion models, fashion illustrations, dancers, and actors/actresses.

Our clothing choices reflect our self-concept. The examples of clothing that are easiest to understand in relationship to self-image seem to be negative ones. For example, you have observed a chubby person poured into tight pants that outline every bulge. You have probably wondered how a person could appear in public

[4] Camile M. Anderson, "The Self-Image, a Theory of the Dynamics of Behavior," *Mental Hygiene,* **36,** 1952, pp. 227–244.

in such unbecoming garb. An explanation for that clothing selection may be the individual's self-image. The person may not perceive himself as overweight; instead, his self-image allows him to believe that he appears slim, trim, and attractive in pants. When we have a true assessment of our self-image we can more accurately select clothing that reflects the concept of who we really are.

We all have favorite articles of clothing, ones that are extremely comfortable and pleasing to us. These garments offer something more than physical comfort. They give us a *psychological* comfort because they are so closely related to our personal characteristics. These favored garments express our self-image. Psychological comfort or lack of this kind of comfort in clothing may be closely related to how well the garments express our individual self-image.

We all have reasons for not wearing certain garments; some are out of fashion, others fit poorly or are the wrong color. Still others may be difficult to maintain or are not in keeping with our lifestyle. Yet, some garments are continually pushed to the back of the closet for no apparent reason. It is possible that we choose not to wear these garments because the image that these garments reflect is incompatible with the image we wish to project. They are not psychologically comfortable.

Some people have a variety of clothing that is representative of various images. Their wardrobes are a potpourri of diverse themes. There is no strong underlying feeling of the clothes that would identify them to a particular personality. Gergen, in his studies of the self-concept, found that his subjects projected different self-images in different situations. He was convinced that "multiple self-images are the healthy rule rather than the sick exception." He believes that each of us should not be defined by a consistent character type. Gergen pointed out that William James also believed that man has as many clearly identifiable social selves.[5]

The author of *Your Erroneous Zones*, believes that we have many self-images and that they vary from moment to moment. We have the feelings about ourselves that are many—physical, social, intellectual, and emotional. We have opinions about our abilities in athletics, art, music, writing, and so on. Our self-portraits are as numerous as our activities.[6]

Ryan noted another theory of self-image that postulates that it is normal for people to develop a consistent sense of identity, and it is unhealthy for them not to do so. Once a sense of identity is fixed, it will remain stable. This situation makes a person predictable. We can anticipate his behavior in any situation. As an individual progresses toward maturity, he develops more definite clothing choices. The wardrobe of the mature person expresses predictable themes. Less diversity in clothing choices is the result of earlier experimentation, plus a focused self-image. Ryan cited Ditty's study that reported individuals who rated high in social maturity were more consistent in their clothing choices than were those rated socially immature.[7]

[5] Kenneth J. Gergen, Ph.D., "The Healthy, Happy Human Beings Wear Masks," *Psychology Today*, May 1972, pp. 31–66.
[6] Dr. Wayne W. Dyer, *Your Erroneous Zones* (New York: Avon Books, 1976), pp. 42–43.
[7] Mary Shaw Ryan, *Clothing: A Study of Human Behavior* (New York: Holt, 1966), p. 94.

2-4 *Whatever theory of the self-image is favored, the current fashion and social practices allow individuals to wear clothing that is expressive of self. Outside of business dress requirements most people are enjoying a variety of styles, textures, and colors in their garments and freely using self-adornment to express themselves.*

Whatever theory of the self-image is favored, the current fashion and social practices allow individuals to wear clothing that is expressive of self. Both women and men are no longer following the dictates of the fashion designers, the fashion media, or other arbiters of fashion. Many have turned away from trying to follow the dress axioms of their families and friends. Outside of business dress requirements most are happily enjoying a variety of styles, textures, and colors of their garments. Many people are freely using self-adornment to express themselves (Figure 2-4).

Values, Attitudes, and Interests

Values, attitudes, and interests each affect personality. We reflect our individuality by the values we esteem, the attitudes we express, and the interests that intrigue us. Values are derived from attitudes and interests; yet values are broader and more basic in concept.

We learn values from our culture, environment, family, associates, and individual experiences. Mass media, especially television and advertising, have influenced value patterns. Some values are commonly held by all members of a specific culture. There may be a wide variation in the application of cultural values. An example of this is the value of education in the United States. As a culture, we value free education for the young; the amount of education deemed necessary by different segments of the population may vary from the basic reading and writing skills to advanced degrees. Individual experience is responsible for such a range in application of this value.

Height and Schley composed the following lists as kinds of values that individuals may hold. You may wish to add other values that are important to you to their list. You may find it interesting to rank your five top values.

INDIVIDUAL VALUES:

I value beauty.
I value being challenged.
I value a close marriage relationship.
I value recognition.
I value being feminine.
I value professional commitment.
I value personal integrity.
I value social skills.
I value individuality.
I value new experiences.
I value parental love.
I value emotional maturity.
I value openness.
I value being successful.
I value influencing others.
I value helping others succeed.
I value doing things that are
   important.
I value giving love.
I value being protective.
I value emotional security.
I value time.
I value comfort.
I value happiness.

I value financial security.
I value receiving love.
I value nature.
I value health.
I value the spiritual.
I value family.
I value solitude.
I value independence.
I value freedom.
I value people.
I value knowing.
I value helping others to be happy.
I value being masculine.
I value harmony with others.
I value close friendships.
I value achievement.
I value wisdom.
I value equality.
I value sexual attractiveness.
I value physical attractiveness.
I value money.
I value perfection.
I value being respected.[8]

Values are a directive or motivating force in behavior and decision making. Research has established that values that direct other choices also will direct clothing choices. If one holds aesthetic values highest, then clothing will be selected for its attractiveness of line, beauty of fabric, or personal satisfaction of being well dressed. If economic values are highest, clothing purchased may reveal

[8] Mildred E. Height and Robert A. Schley, *Self-Actualization by Group Process* (San Jacinto, Calif.: Mount San Jacinto College, 1973), pp. 10–11.

the utility, quality, and price as most important; or the clothing selected may make a statement about financial status (high or low).

Creekmore developed the following relationships between clothing behavior and values rated high.[9]

Clothing Behavior	Value Rated High
Management of clothing	Economic
Experimenting in clothing	Exploratory
Status symbol	Political
Appearance	Aesthetic
Conformity	Social
Fashion	Political
Modesty	Religious

Understanding the influences of values on clothing choices is not always easy. Values often conflict, and there is a compromise on the part of the wearer. For example, a girl with a modest income may value conformity with her peer group, but if the family budget will not allow this, she must make some kind of value compromise. Often a conflict of values leads to serious altercation between parents and children. Amount of cosmetics, length of hair, closeness of fit, décolleté of neckline have all been debated in many families. This happens when the values of the parents conflict with those of their offspring.

Horn found that "the importance of clothing as a means of achieving approval and acceptance is paramount in the value configuration of the adolescent, but this value appears to decrease in favor of aesthetic or economic considerations for those with greater maturity and/or self-confidence."[10] This may explain the wide variety of clothing found on the cosmopolitan college campus as contrasted to the small town high school. As we mature, we are able to express more individuality in our clothing selection.

Over a period of time values may change. Group value change becomes a cultural change. This is particularly true in a technical society. The individual must change with the times. An economic value that has changed drastically is the method most of us use to pay for our clothing. The credit card with all of its ease and temptation is in diametric opposition to the Puritanical belief that indebtedness is sinful. Several social values have changed as the result of understanding the need for physical fitness in men, women, and children. As science made discoveries concerning nutrition and physiology, ideas about diet and exercise changed. The clothing requirements demanded by active sports resulted in value changes of how much body exposure was socially acceptable.

Spranger's six ideal types can be used as theoretical guides to aid in understanding people. These ideal types are value directed. Spranger believed that

[9] Ryan, op. cit., p. 103.
[10] Marilyn J. Horn, *The Second Skin* (Boston: Houghton, 1968), p. 81.

people are best known through a study of subjective values. In daily life a person meets with many situations that call for such evaluative judgments.[11]

Even though these types are isolated, Spranger concluded that one type would not exist in one man but that every value attitude can be found in all personalities in varying degrees.[12] Spranger believed that every person is best characterized by the things he considers of highest value.[13] These values reveal themselves in personalities in the areas that the individual considers to be of greatest importance.

Spranger's value profile is used for testing in the Allport, Vernon, Lindzey *Study of Values* to indicate major areas of endeavor most important to the individual.[14] This test, along with others using Spranger's values, is often used to relate personal values to clothing.

The following table is an adaptation of Spranger's values as applied to clothing. The authors have based the brief descriptions of value upon suggestions from Allport[15] and Hartmann.[16] The relationship of these values to clothing has been made by the authors.

Spranger Value	Description of Value	Relationships to Clothing
Theoretical	Discovery of truth, facts, and information; judgments regarding beauty and utility are not regarded.	Honest use of materials; wears only real jewelry, furs, and leather rather than simulated material; clothing probably of little importance; would look for fiber content and care label.
Economic	Usefulness important; practical; accumulation of much wealth; luxury often confused with beauty; commercial.	Comfort, easy to maintain and use; examines carefully to get true dollar value for purchase; comparative shopper; gets best for least cost; abhors waste. Invests in precious stones and jewelry.
Aesthetic	Design; fit; beauty; harmony; individualism; mass production a threat to him; expressiveness; creativeness.	Clothing must be attractive, well-designed; texture and colors pleasing; individuality; hates uniforms; favors handwoven, hand-wrought jewelry.

[11] P. E. Vernon and G. W. Allport, "A Test for Personal Values," *Journal of Abnormal and Social Psychology*, **26**:231 (1931).

[12] Ibid., p, 236.

[13] George W. Hartmann, *Educational Psychology* (New York: American Book, 1941), p. 25.

[14] G. W. Allport, P. E. Vernon, and G. Lindzey, *Study of Values* (Boston: Houghton, 1960).

[15] G. W. Allport, op. cit., p. 278.

[16] George W. Hartmann, "Clothing: Personal Problem and Social Issue," *Journal of Home Economics*, **41**:297–298 (1949).

Spranger Value	Description of Value	Relationships to Clothing
Social	Concern for welfare of people; kind; unselfish (concern for providing clothing that would better all people).	Dresses appropriately; would not offend others by wearing what would make them feel uncomfortable; dresses like those in his group; wishes to feel confident in order to make others comfortable; would not try to dress better than others.
Political	Power; leadership; dominating people; vanity; enhancement of self; esteem; wants admiration.	Dresses to impress others and to show he is better than others; would wear status clothing, lodge and fraternity/sorority pins, school rings, designers' labels or logos.
Religious	Mystical, relates himself to entire universe as a complete and orderly system; sees the divine in every event.	Appreciation of God-given gifts of fibers; simplicity is the ideal; no definite texture, no elegance; modesty important; uniforms acceptable.

Evaluative judgment of a suit by six different people is given in the following example. One person may look at a bathing suit and would evaluate its fiber content (*theoretical* value); another person would evaluate its colors and design (*aesthetic*); a third person would consider the care needed for the garment (*economic*); a fourth person might judge if it would be similar, suitable, and approved by other people (*social*); a fifth person would evaluate it by its new and different design that would impress people (*political*); and the sixth person might consider it as being highly immodest (*religious*).

A study made by Lapitsky confirmed that there is a positive relationship between clothing values and corresponding general values. This study used the same general values as given by Spranger, but she added a second value, that of being accepted by others. The Spranger social value was based upon concern for others. Lapitsky dropped the theoretical and religious values because it was her belief that these values are not related to clothing interest.[17]

Studies among adult women show high clothing values to be aesthetic and economic whereas appearance and status were most important among college women. Values rated highest among male college students were economic whereas social and aesthetic were the lowest.[18]

[17] Ryan, op. cit., p. 117.

[18] Elizabeth A. Richards and Ruth E. Hawthorne, "Values, Body Cathexis and Clothing of Male University Students," *Journal of Home Economics*, Vol. 68, No. 3 (March 1971), pp. 190–193.

The Value of Attractiveness—And Its Impact

Among the readers of this book, there may be some who feel that trying to make a good impression by improving personal appearance would be dishonest, or a showing of false values. "People should like me (judge me) for what is on the 'inside,' not for my looks." This reasoning is often used as an excuse for not spending time on oneself. The thinking is idealistic, not realistic. People may never get to know what is on the inside if they are not attracted by what is on the outside. Some of the very brief encounters that we have with others may be highly significant to the relationships that follow.

Making a poor personal presentation can be interpreted in many ways. The individual may be judged as:

lacking personal pride
having little respect for others
feeling physically ill
being mentally ill
reacting negatively to the values of society
experimenting to get reactions from others
ignoring social conventions
being rude or ignorant

Matthews confirmed that attractive personal appearance is important in our culture. The visual impression that we make can be of profound significance both to ourselves and to others. Physical attractiveness, as it is related to feelings of self-worth, dating, marriage, and children, has been the favored subject of much investigation. The findings of this research support the theory that personal attractiveness is most important in social interaction. We often seem to reject this knowledge because it violates the American concept of democracy that all people are created equal.[19] In a study to determine whether people in our culture actually do attach value to physical appearance, subjects were given photographs of people ranging in all degrees of physical attractiveness. The results revealed that interpersonal attraction was greater toward the physically attractive strangers, regardless of their sex, than toward the unattractive ones. This showed that people in our culture do attach value to physical appearance.[20] Just what constitutes physical attractiveness? Variations as to what constitutes physical attractiveness do occur. Sex and race differences regarding standards were found in a study of facial beauty. Adult male faces were rated higher by female observers than by male observers. Black observers gave higher ratings to both black and

---

[19] Dr. Lillian B. Matthews, speech, 6th Annual Meeting, Assoc. of College Professors of Textiles and Clothing, Portland, Oreg., June 19–22, 1974.

[20] Donn Byrne, Oliver London, and Keith Reeves, "The Effects of Physical Attractiveness, Sex and Attitude Similarity on Interpersonal Attraction," *Journal of Personality,*1968, pp. 36, 259–271.

2-5 *Studies found that children and adults generally agree on who is attractive. Both use the same criteria in judging physical appearance. (Courtesy Health-tex Inc.)*

white faces than the white observers. Young female and adolescent faces received higher ratings than male and older faces.[21] Cavior and Lombardi's study found that children (from age seven) and adults generally agree on who is attractive. Both use the same criteria in judging physical appearance.[22] Although there are individual differences on specific aspects of physical appearance there is a tendency for general agreement on who is and who is not attractive among people within the same culture (Figure 2-5).[23]

Courses in personal improvement are held in many of the women's correctional institutions in the United States. In some women's penal institutions, traditional prison garb has been replaced by attractive clothing. The inmates have been encouraged to improve self-image and to use makeup and have their hair styled.

[21] J. F. Cross and J. Cross, "Age, Sex, Race and the Perception of Facial Beauty," *Developmental Psychology*, 1971, **5**, 433–439.

[22] Norman Cavior and David A. Lombardi, "Development Aspects of Judgment of Physical Attractiveness in Children," *Development Psychology*, 1973, pp. 8, 67–71.

[23] Chris L. Kleinke, *First Impressions* (Englewood Cliffs, N.J.: Prentice-Hall, 1975), p. 2.

Self-improvement classwork has been credited with helping to rehabilitate these women. In West Germany, women prisoners are issued attractive pants suits, bright dresses, and sweaters. The German prison officials have adopted the theory that "a certain measure of vanity is healthy and serves to bolster the damaged self-confidence of women convicts."[24] A prison social worker felt that improved personal appearance helped the women overcome feelings of indifference and resignation. Records reveal that women who have taken self-improvement courses while incarcerated return to prison at the rate of only 5 percent, as contrasted with the national rate of recidivism of 40-60 percent.[25]

A Beverly Hills, California, plastic surgeon donates his services to female inmates of the Los Angeles Sybil Brand Institute who need their self-esteem reconstructed. Dr. Harry Glassman reasoned that plastic surgery must benefit women coming out of jail because it would bolster their self-esteem and confidence. He has rebuilt a nose that was crushed in an auto accident, enlarged a chin, reduced a nose, altered scars, and removed tattoos. Of the sixteen cases he has worked on, only two of the women have been rearrested. Glassman hopes that his work will heal psychic as well as physical scars by showing that somebody cares. He says, "Increased self-confidence can be temporary but it can get you stepping in the right direction."[26]

The John Roberts Powers Modeling School in Carson, California, has given scholarships for a course in self-improvement to delinquent young women (ages 13-18). The course teaches girls to sit, walk, dress, and behave according to society's standards in the hope of improving their self-image and their ability to cope with the world at large. Probation officers who have watched the dozens of girls go through the program believe strongly in its benefits.[27]

Personal appearance of men is equally important. In 1984, the California Youth Authority officials adopted a policy to encourage young offenders to discard bizarre clothing and get regular haircuts, groom scraggly beards and moustaches. This policy is designed to discourage gang and delinquent subculture identification and to make the CYA's 6,300 incarcerated wards more employable when they are released. Research has shown if the young men are able to get and keep jobs they will be less likely to commit crimes. However, it was found that a lot of the youths going on parole were rejected by prospective employers because they did not "look right" when they were seeking jobs (employer's value judgment). This grooming policy is designed to encourage the wards to learn to "look right" before they leave the institutions. Failure to comply to this dress policy will affect privileges and release dates.[28]

[24] "Women Jail Images Get Bright Garb," *Los Angeles Times*, January 23, 1973, Pt. I-A, p. 10.
[25] Matthews, op. cit.
[26] Betty Liddick, "Reconstruction of Self-Esteem," *Los Angeles Times*, Pt. IV, p. 1, January 25, 1977.
[27] Bettijane Levine, "Charm Is Power for Delinquents," *Los Angeles Times*, Pt. X, p. 1, February 8, 1976.
[28] *San Francisco Examiner*, September 30, 1984, p. 7.

Other studies established that values or characteristics are attributed to people who are rated physically attractive (halo effect). Among these are such qualities as being poised, modest, and sensible; also having better character, higher-status occupations, and generally being more interesting.[29]

As an indication of how people attribute values to a good appearance, Matthews gave the example of a woman who received help in personal improvement before appealing for parole. Her hair was styled, her grooming was improved, and her clothing was selected. When the woman appeared before the court, the judge observed that she did not look like the kind of a woman who would commit a criminal act. The jury seemed to be influenced by the judge's remarks and reduced her sentence. This supports the findings that "those who meet our stereotyped image of attractiveness do receive different responses from others."[30]

Attitudes in Relation to Clothing

Attitudes can be expressed by how we feel, think, and behave. Attitudes are individualistic. They are often learned from parents and family. As we mature, we tend to mold our attitudes based on societal, familial, and educational experiences. Attitudes about clothing are concerned with comfort, utility, conformity, economy, fashion, self-expression, and status. We reflect our attitudes about specific garment styles by what we wear.

Individual attitudes are closely associated with value patterns. A person who has strong aesthetic values will probably choose clothing for its interesting design, exciting texture, or pleasing color. A person who has strong political values will probably select clothing that is acceptable to a special interest group (this type of motivation often leads to choices that are fashionable, but not becoming to the individual). A person who has strong economic values may display more interest in construction, durability, and maintenance requirements than in the style of the garment. Individual application of values may be thought of as attitudes.

A study of male university students correlated the relationship between attitudes and values. It was revealed that men who held religious values high had strong attitudes toward economy. Those with high social values (concern for the welfare of people) showed low regard for status clothing. The men who had high political values gave economy little importance.[31]

The concept of attitude has been divided into three components. The *affective component* refers to the feelings or emotions associated with a given object or

[29] Ellen Bersheid and Elaine Walster, *Advances in Experimental Social Psychology* (New York: Academic Press), Vol. VII (1973).
[30] Matthews, op. cit.
[31] Richards and Hawthorne, op. cit., pp. 192–193.

entity. Clothing choices can create a wide variety of feelings or emotions for both men and women. For example:

Feeling or Emotion	*Clothing Choices*
sexuality	body-revealing
happiness	fun-fashion, bright color
sadness	somber hue, body-concealing
youthfulness	current teen-age fads
sophistication	understated, severe, cosmopolitan
superiority	expensive, high-fashion, use of expensive symbols, jewelry, club insignia
inferiority	sleazy, worn, inappropriate, or too perfect
self-confidence	appropriate style for the function

The *cognitive aspect* of attitudes concerns the beliefs held about clothing. A woman may believe that clothing is unimportant, that it is just a nuisance, to be tolerated, because of the dictates of her society. A man may feel that clothing is the key to social status, and that, by acquiring a large, flamboyant wardrobe he will gain status and recognition. We may believe that persons wearing conservative business dress are politically conservative (Figure 2-6).

The *behavioral component* of attitude is inferred from what the person actually does. A girl may stay home from a party because she does not have the right dress. A man may hide behind a voluminous coat because he is fat. A student may be an exhibitionist, flouting propriety with nudity.

Attitudes explain how we feel, what we think, and how we behave. In relationship to clothing, attitudes are expressed by the clothing selected and the behavior exhibited while wearing that clothing. Attitudes are personal expressions or interpretations of the values held by each individual.[32]

Feelings of self-confidence are linked to clothing choices. A study considered whether well-dressed individuals would present themselves in a more positive manner than those poorly dressed. The subjects were 32 male undergraduates. They were told that they would be interviewed and the interviews would be taped. Half of the subjects were told to wear a coat and tie. The other half were not given dress instructions and appeared in casual campus clothing. The study revealed that the group that dressed in coat and tie felt more positive about themselves than those casually dressed. The research showed that feelings of self-confidence in presenting oneself are linked to the clothing one wears.[33] Another way to state the findings of this study: The me I see, is the me I will be.

[32] Horn, op. cit., p. 77.
[33] D. J. Schneider, "Effects of Dress on Self-Presentation," *Psychological Reports*, 1974, **35**, 1, 167–170.

2-7 Interest in clothing is expressed in many ways including experimenting with different "looks." (Courtesy WilliWear)

2-6 We reflect our attitudes about specific garment styles by what we wear. Many believe that persons wearing conservative business dress are politically conservative. (Courtesy Hartmarx Corporation)

Interests in Relation to Clothing

Interest may be defined as appeal, concern, or intrigue. Interest is the opposite of indifference or dislike. One may be interested in a class of things such as rocks, animals, or flowers. One may be interested in a field of study such as astronomy, anthropology, or mathematics. Usually, the stronger the interest in a subject, the more effort is put into the study of that subject.

Clothing interest is expressed in many ways:
attention to personal appearance
concern with the selection of the wardrobe
experimenting with different "looks"
reading fashion magazines
attending fashion shows
attention to wardrobe care and maintenance
frequent shopping for clothing
awareness of clothing practices of others (Figure 2-7)

Another type of interest in clothing is shown by people who are interested in clothes in an impersonal manner. Designers, fashion buyers, clothing manufacturers, and sales representatives are among those who have an awareness in clothing from a merchandising point of view exclusive of any application to themselves.

Lifestyle

Throughout a lifetime, interest in clothing varies. Clothing is used to meet certain social and psychological needs of the individual. Clothing is related to the development of the personality and the satisfaction of emotional needs. The following examines the impact of clothing as related to interest, the satisfaction of emotional needs, and the development of the personality at various stages of life. The pattern by which we live is known as *lifestyle*. The lifestyle we are currently experiencing may not be permanent. During a life span we may try several lifestyles. One may choose abruptly to change his lifestyle by changing his employment and/or residence. The harried corporation officer living in the middle of a huge cosmopolitan city who moves to the wilderness to write books has made such a drastic change. It is more common for changes of lifestyle to evolve as one experiences life. The child lives a lifestyle selected by family; as the child grows into adulthood he is able to choose more and more the pattern of his life. The completion of education and the acquiring of the first professional job often marks a change in lifestyle.

Lifestyle is determined by the value system of each individual. Changes in lifestyle can be responsible for shaping some values. It can also reshuffle the priority of our value system. Because the lifestyle adopted is dependent on individual choice, it cannot be universal.

Some of the choices that shape lifestyles include the following:

family unit	recreation
financial status	clothing
housing	leisure
education	values
occupation	attitudes
employer	interests
geographical location	food patterns
transportation	friends
hobbies	colleagues
travel	

The style of living in which one finds oneself is shaped by the things that are of concern to the individual at that particular time. College students generally have a lifestyle that is centered around their college. This collegiate lifestyle could include all the choices listed as selected by each student and very possibly could change in some degree with each school year. The couples who choose to become parents discover that their lifestyle changes with each stage of development of their offspring. When children leave home to create a lifestyle of their own, parents often make drastic changes in their lifestyle that may include changing housing, occupation, and geographical locations along with devoting more time to education, hobbies, recreation, and travel.

We identify others by their lifestyle. We are accepting or rejecting in this classification. The outward signs such as clothes, homes, cars, and jobs help us link with others that share the same interests and similar values (Figure 2-8). If we disapprove of the lifestyle signals, we attempt to avoid the people embracing

2-8   We identify others by their lifestyle. The outward signs such as clothes, homes, cars, jobs, and hobbies helps us link with others that share the same interests and have similar values. (Courtesy Allied Corporation)

this pattern of living. Rosenbaum, in his delightfully titled book, *Is Your Volks-wagen a Sex Symbol?* continues this theme to explain how your lifestyle is revealed by the items most of us choose, including our cars, dwellings, clothing, pets, and colors.[34]

Silberman observed that clothing is the most portable of lifestyle signs. He wrote:

> For an increasing number of Americans, the clothes they wear are not simply material objects; on the contrary, they are viewed with almost mystical fervor as the most basic expression of lifestyle, indeed, identity itself.[35]

The lifestyle, whether or not it is arrived at consciously, establishes a kind of order in our pattern of consumption. In *Future Shock*, Toffler demonstrated the choicemaking procedure of a young couple who selected their first piece of furniture. The choice was singled out from the thousands available. Their selection of the Tiffany lamp was made because the couple had a set of pre-established values. The selections of rug, table, and so on that followed the lamp choice were related to their first choice. This was a demonstration of personal style. This procedure is followed as the couple choose ideas and friends.

Toffler explained how mannerisms and dress choices reveal lifestyle:

> The American male who wears a button-down shirt collar and garter-length socks probably also wears wing-tip shoes and carries an attaché case. If we look closely, chances are we shall find a facial expression and brisk manner intended to approximate those of the stereotypical executive. The odds are astronomical that he will not let his hair grow wild in the manner of a rock musician. He knows, as we do, that certain clothes, manners, forms of speech, opinions and gestures hang together, while others do not.
> The black-jacketed motorcyclist who wears steel-studded gauntlets and an obscene swastika dangling from his throat completes his costume with rugged boots, not loafers or wing-tips. He is likely to swagger as he walks and to grunt as he mouths his antiauthoritarian platitudes. For he, too, values consistency. He knows that any trace of gentility or articulateness would destroy the integrity of his style.[36]

Lifestyle helps us make choices from the vast array of alternatives we face each day. Once we have embraced a lifestyle, the decisions are narrowed or automatic. The way we live, the friends we keep, the food we eat, the clothes we wear, the vocations we seek, the philosophies we adopt, the books we read, the schedules we maintain, the vocabulary we use, the items we cherish, and the joys we experience are among the facets of our lives that are determined by our individual lifestyle.

For a comparison of the vast changes in lifestyles of public school teachers read the following exchange, which appeared in the "Dear Abby" newspaper column:

[34] Rosenbaum, op. cit.
[35] Charles E. Silberman, "Identity Crisis in the Consumer Market," *Fortune*, March 1971, p. 95.
[36] Alvin Toffler, *Future Shock* (New York: Bantam Books, 1970), p. 307.

DEAR ABBY: I am a 29-year-old schoolteacher (female). I teach 10th grade students in a public school. I love my work and wouldn't want to do anything else.

I also feel that I am entitled to live the kind of life-style I feel is right for me.

Now, my problem: I have fallen in love with a man and we want to live together. Neither one of us wants to get married right now—or maybe ever.

I dislike lying but I doubt that I could continue my teaching job in this city while living with a man who is not my husband.

Do you know of any community that is sufficiently sophisticated to permit their schoolteachers the freedom to live as they wish?

NAMELESS, PLEASE

DEAR NAMELESS: No. But that doesn't mean there isn't one. We have come a long way in the last 60 years. As proof, I submit a piece from *Quote* magazine. I hope you are able to read it without cracking up. I couldn't.

"Truly, the life-style of a schoolteacher has changed radically in the last 50 or 60 years. For example, a 1915 teacher's magazine listed the following rules of conduct for teachers of that day:

1. You will not marry during the term of your contract.
2. You are not to keep company with men.
3. You must be home between the hours of 8 P.M. and 6 A.M. unless attending a school function.
4. You may not loiter downtown in ice cream stores.
5. You may not travel beyond the city limits unless you have the permission of the chairman of the board.
6. You may not ride in a carriage or automobile with any man unless he is your father or brother.
7. You may not smoke cigarets.
8. You may not dress in bright colors.
9. You may under no circumstances dye your hair.
10. You must wear at least two petticoats.
11. Your dresses must not be any shorter than two inches above the ankle.
12. To keep the schoolroom neat and clean, you must sweep the floor at least once daily; scrub the floor at least once a week with hot, soapy water; clean the blackboards at least once a day; and start the fire at 7 A.M. so the room will be warm by 8 A.M."[37]

Life Stages and Clothing Behavior

Children, as well as adults, have their favorites in clothing. They may also have definite dislikes for certain garments. Their tastes tend toward primary, saturated colors. Boys and girls from the ages three to ten prefer red to any other color.[38] Decorative features such as ornaments and appliquéd designs in the form of flowers and animals appeal to children. Velvety and furry textures such as fleece, terrycloth, and fur are often stroked and patted. A definite dislike is shown to

[37] Abigail Van Buren, "Dear Abby," *Los Angeles Times*, March 23, 1975, Pt. X, p. 5.
[38] Ryan, op. cit., p. 213.

2-9 Preschoolers are not usually concerned about keeping clothing clean. Here the painting is more important than the smock being dragged through it. (Courtesy Australian Consulate, W. Peterson photograph, Education —Play Centers.)

harsh and scratchy textures; these should be avoided as they can irritate a child's delicate skin.

Children like garments that are familiar to them. Often it is difficult for them to give up a garment that is no longer wearable because they have a strong attachment to it.

Qualities of becomingness, appropriateness, durability, conformity, size of wardrobe, cleanliness, and neatness often are important to mothers but not to their offspring[39] The fact that a garment may be unattractive on, or that a party dress is inappropriate for rough play, is usually of no concern to youngsters. Generally they do not recognize having a large or a limited wardrobe or if their clothing consists of "hand-me-downs." Frequently what is most important to them is a liking for the garment itself, regardless of the source.

Preschoolers

Very young boys and girls are not aware that their clothing conforms to that of their playmates. It is not known at what exact age the desire to conform in dressing occurs. The need to dress as others do becomes evident when the child refuses to wear something that differs from what the other children are wearing.

[39] Ryan, op. cit., p. 216.

Preschoolers who are interested in mud puddles and dirt care nothing about getting mud and dirt on their clothing. It is not normal for a child to be overly concerned about keeping clean. The child who does care often has difficulty in group adjustment.[40] Mothers who are too anxious about their children getting dirty may restrict a child's attitude concerning play. Part of being a child is experimenting in water, clay, paints, and other messy media. These are learning experiences for children, and they should not be hampered by adults who are overly concerned with cleanliness (Figure 2-9).

Does clothing have an effect upon the mood and behavior of a child? Observation of preschool girls' clothing as it related to play behavior showed that there was not a significant difference in their play behavior whether they were wearing pants or frilly dress.[41]

Children 6–12

Clothing is important for the social and emotional development of the child between the ages of 6 and 12. Pronounced ideas about what should be worn appear sometime during this period. These ideas will be related to what the child's playmates and schoolmates wear. There is a strong need for children to dress like their group (Figure 2-10). The "gang" is a significant part of their lives, and the feeling of group belonging is strong. One of a child's greatest fears is that of being ridiculed by his peer group. Clothing may be an object of ridicule when it differs from what friends are wearing. Dressing differently may give rise

[40] Ryan, op. cit., p. 16.
[41] S. B. Kaiser and Rudy M. Byfield, *Role of Clothing in Sex-Role Socialization: Person Perception vs. Overt Behavior*, 1983. Manuscript submitted for publication.

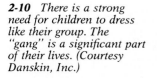

2-10 *There is a strong need for children to dress like their group. The "gang" is a significant part of their lives. (Courtesy Danskin, Inc.)*

to feelings of inferiority and insecurity. For many children the dislike of wearing "hand-me-downs" may be that such clothing does not conform with what the group wears more than the fact that the garments have been used by others.

Because of the need for conformity in dressing as their friends do and the fact that children now have some definite ideas about how they want to dress, it may be helpful to them and to you to take them shopping when buying their clothing. Often children can derive a sense of importance and freedom if they are allowed to help select their clothing.[42] For younger children, a preselected sample of clothing could be presented from which they can make their selection. This age group is not so concerned with whether the garment looks attractive on them as they are with "Are the other kids wearing it?"

A back-to-school merchandising campaign was launched to promote designer labels in children's clothes. Traditional denim and corduroy pants, classic knit and woven shirts, and certain brands of underwear had conspicuously placed designer names to spell prestige to parents and sophistication to kids. The clothes looked remarkably like the nondesigner styles sold as standard rough-and-tumble school and play clothes. The designer-label children's clothes cost from 25 to 30 percent more than similar merchandise without designer labels. An informal

2-11 *For some conspicuously placed designers' labels spell prestige and sophistication. (Courtesy Levi Strauss & Co.)*

survey of merchandise managers and buyers at major Los Angeles retail stores revealed that the executives really believed that kids have absorbed their parents' status consciousness like blotters. They also believed parents would be impressed enough with the labels to pay higher prices for them (Figure 2-11). Sales confirmed the merchandisers' belief. The designer-labeled clothing sold very well in spite of the price difference.

Another informal survey taken at Roxbury Park in Beverly Hills, California, indicated that the only status names the children responded to were those of superheroes. One child announced she "liked long sleeves in winter and short sleeves in summer." Other comments from the kids indicated their most important needs are "material that doesn't scratch," pleasing colors, and "nothing too tight."[43]

Activities such as baseball leagues and scout troops give children the opportunity to belong to organized groups. The wearing of uniforms, pins, and badges visually identifies them with a group. Most children enjoy wearing these uniforms and look forward to the days on which they can be worn (for some children, this is every day) (Figure 2-12).

Interest in what is worn does not always extend to appearing neat and well groomed. Children need to be trained by their families to be well groomed and to take responsibility in clothing care, such as hanging up garments, reporting needed repairs and preparing soiled garments for laundry.

Opinions and attitudes that are formed early in childhood are often lasting; therefore, it is important in our society to teach children the value of looking their best in clothing that has been selected to enhance them. Developing taste in clothing can begin by dressing children attractively, comfortably, and appropriately for their activities; exposure to good examples is a way of learning that can be easily understood by a child.

Growth in body width may alternate with growth in length. The selection of lines that will minimize the problems of skinniness or chubbiness may help to reduce a child's feelings of self-consciousness that can arise from these problems of growth. Shy children should not be overdressed or dressed in loud colors since this can add to their discomfort. Drawing attention because of their clothing may cause shy children to withdraw even more.

The Teen-age Years

During the teen-age years, clothing continues to be a significant factor in the satisfaction of emotional and social needs. Vitally aware of how they look, teenagers are often extremely critical about clothing and personal appearance. Self-confidence is increased when teen-agers know that they are well-dressed by their peer group standards. Some boys and girls will change clothing several times before they arrive at a look that satisfies them. The often worry about their bodies, facial features, skin, hair, and teeth. The clothes they wear affect how they feel

[42] Walter Neisser, "Your Child's Sense of Responsibility," New York Public Affairs Pamphlet No. 254 (1957), p. 14.

[43] Bettijane Levine, "Labels to Kid Around In," Fashion 79, *Los Angeles Times*, p. 1, August 3, 1979.

2-12 *Club activities give children the opportunity to wear uniforms, pins, and badges that visually identify them with a group. (Courtesy Bettmann Newsphotos)*

and how they act. Clothing satisfaction has a significant effect upon their moods and actions. A study by Wass and Eicher revealed that high school girls believed that they act differently in school on days that were designated as "dress up." Over two-thirds of the students felt that they acted more grown-up, and better behaved on these days. Over 80 percent of the students felt that some styles of dress influenced the way they acted in some way.[44] In a recreational situation Tharin studied the relationship between clothing and behavior at roller rinks. On evenings when dress codes were enforced there were fewer confrontations, fewer accidents, and less noise. Skaters wearing more covered clothing had fewer

[44] B. Wass and J. Eicher, "Clothing as Related to Role Behavior of Teen-Age Girls," *Quarterly Bulletin*, 1964, **47**(2), 206–213.

52

accidents and made less noise.[45] These reasons are often cited by authorities in schools that have dress codes or require uniforms.

Social approval is of great concern to the teen-ager. One of the most important factors in the selection of teen-age clothing is that it conform with what is worn by the peer group. Very often this does not meet the same standards that have been established in the family. Often parents need to reshuffle their value priorities in order to be more tolerant and understanding of teen-age dress during this traumatic adolescent period. Angelino reported that a study on clothing disagreements has shown that conflicts between teen-age girls and their parents are most often due to differences in opinion about personal appearance, habits, and manners. The areas of clothing disagreement in the upper-status families concerned the selection of formals, shoes, coats, suits, jeans, shorts, and accessories. In the middle-status families, the disagreements were over formals, shoes, and grooming. In the lower-status families, the disagreements were over undergarments. Most teen-agers feel a strong need to conform in order to avoid teasing and possible ostracism from the group.[46]

Dress of teenagers, such as the punk/heavy metal/bag lady styles of the early 1980s, is often adopted to deliberately create a negative reaction from parents and others in authority. This situation requires adult understanding of the young persons needs to express himself and/or to dress for peer identification. For many this is a rite of adolescence and soon passes.

In families where the teen-agers' dress behavior is completely unacceptable, parents should try to help the young people understand the underlying reasons of why they wish to dress in a different manner. Teen-agers should be made aware of the possible negative reaction, and the consequences of this reaction, from others. Sharp criticism or sarcastic ridicule from adults will often produce more antagonism. A diplomatic approach to the problem usually brings the happiest results.

The relationship between personal appearance and popularity was the subject of an interesting study reported by Hendricks *et al*. The results revealed that a girl's popularity was influenced by her clothing. Students listed the same girls as being "best-dressed" and the most popular. The same study also demonstrated that appraisal of a new student was first derived from dress. After students got to know the new girl, her personality, general attitudes, and beliefs were considered.[47]

Teen-agers usually own large wardrobes. Individuality is rarely expressed in their dress because peer group identification is more important than self-expression. Clothing is very important to this stage of development. Quantity

[45] L. Tharin, *The Effect of Dress Codes on Behavior in Roller Rinks*, unpublished manuscript, University of California, Davis.

[46] H. Angelino, L. Barnes, and C. Shedd, "Attitudes of Mothers and Adolescent Daughters Concerning Clothing and Grooming," *Journal of Home Economics*, December 1956, p. 799.

[47] Suzanne H. Hendricks, Eleanor A. Kelley, and Joanne B. Eicher, "Senior Girls' Appearance and Social Acceptance," *Journal of Home Economics*, **60**:167–171 (March 1968).

rather than quality is the general preference for most young people.[48] The building of self-confidence and "being in fashion" are dominant factors in teen-age clothing decisions.[49]

College and Career Years

The late teens and early twenties are the periods of highest interest in clothing. It is a time when the "follow the herd" tendencies of the previous years begin to depart and individuality is more often expressed. This expression of the unique self is often found in dress and self-adornment. Following fads at this time is done more often for the fun of it rather than for the necessity of peer group identification.

Horn cites that college students are the most conscious of any group of outdated and outmoded styles. This attitude means frequent wardrobe replacement.

This period represents a change in lifestyle. Whether it is entering college, dating, getting married, or beginning a career, it is a phase that has new wardrobe demands. Both a high interest in personal appearance and assumption of new roles makes these years the most costly in terms of clothing expenditures (see Chapter 15).[50]

The Middle Years

Most men and women are interested in clothing. Clothing is always a good topic of conversation when making small talk. Even those who announce no interest in clothing usually have several opinions to state. The degree of interest in clothing is related to age. As people mature, their interest in clothing generally becomes less emphatic, probably because so many other facets of life develop. The clothing interests of middle-age people emphasize either the aesthetic or the economic. Members of this group often express individuality in clothing and are concerned about price, lasting qualities, and maintenance problems. Although the interest in clothing may be dormant at times in an adult's life, it is usually revived by a special invitation—and the familiar question: "What shall I wear?"

The Senior Years

The special clothing needs of the senior years are finally being recognized. As this group of our population expands, more interest by both the researcher and the merchandizer is evidenced. The clothing needs of older men and women are being identified, and although they are unique to this group in detail, they fall into the same categories as the needs of other groups. The clothing concerns of the aged are physical and psychological. There is also the added problem of availability. This results from a lack of commercial interest in producing and merchandising clothing for this special group. As the aged are linked to the

---

[48] Horn, op. cit. p. 77.
[49] K. Gibbons, "Communication Aspects of Women's Clothes and Their Relationship to Fashionability," *British Journal of Social and Clinical Psychology*, 1969, **8**, pp. 301–312.
[50] Marilyn J. Horn, *The Second Skin* (Boston: Houghton, 1975), p. 405.

2-13 *People in their senior years have special clothing needs. The physical changes that take place during aging must be satisfied by clothing styles that are appropriately designed to comply with body changes.*

handicapped, the current legislation to mainstream the handicapped into society may change clothing availability.

Although the psychological clothing needs of the senior citizen remain as individual as they are for any age, the physical needs are shared by large numbers of this group. These physical requirements must be satisfied by clothing styles that are appropriately designed to comply with body changes that take place with advanced age (Figure 2-13). Some of the physical changes that take place during the aging process are these:[51]

Height decreases.
Head tilts forward and lowers.
Shoulders curve forward.
Arms and legs become thinner and bent.
Bust/chest sags.
Waistline thickens, abdomen protrudes.
Hip and pelvic area widens.
Spine curves.
Feet become deformed.
Muscle tone becomes flabby.
Skin wrinkles, shows pigment changes.
Hair color fades or changes; hair thins or balds.
Body heat regulation changes.
Mobility is impaired.
Vision, hearing, are impaired.
Flexibility is impaired.

These physiological changes result in problems of fit, comfort, and function related to clothing. Senior citizens often wear garments that have been in their wardrobes a long time, or buy ready-to-wear off the rack. These garments are often too narrow in body circumference, have improperly placed darts, waistline, and sleeves, are too long in front and too short in back. Improperly fitted clothing is uncomfortable as well as unattractive.

Studies reveal some of the shopping and style likes and dislikes of the aged consumer. Some of these are[52,53]:

Shopping—Prefer mail order, telephone order, or department stores.
       Find shopping malls tiring, feel they cater to youth.
Styles preferred—Body-concealing, long-sleeved, adequate length.
       Round necklines, V necklines. (Better coverage and V necklines accommodate head tilt.)

---

[51] *Tips and Topics*, Texas Tech.. Vol. 8. No. 1 (November 1972), p. 4. and other sources.

[52] Pam Sears, "Clothing Needs of the Aged," Student survey, California State University at Long Beach, 1978.

[53] Phyllis Carol, "Clothing Preferences and Problems of a Selected Group of Women Sixty-five Years of Age and Over Living in Tallahassee, Florida" (Tallahassee, Fla.: Florida State University, 1975).

3/4 to long sleeves (for warmth, cover, appearance of arms).

Raglan sleeves, full yokes with pleats, gathers. (Allow for shoulder, spine curve.)

Pockets. (Carry personal belongings, free hands.)

Sweaters and jackets (for warmth, body covering).

Washable fabrics (easy, inexpensive care).

For men, solid color pants, colorful shirts, coordinating sweaters, jackets.

For women, pants suits with overblouses, jacket covering hips. (Conceals body and legs.) Prints rather than solids. One-piece dresses without waistlines.

Style dislikes—Body-revealing clothing.

High-neck or turtle neck. (Does not accommodate head tilt.)

Back zippers (impossible for some).

Infantile styles.

The senior citizen is just as interested in clothing as anyone else. If this interest has been high in earlier life, it will remain so as long as health permits. The beauty and barber shops in retirement centers are often busier than those elsewhere. Getting coiffed (styled, colored, and combed), manicured and pedicured are events that are enjoyed by both aged men and women. It is often the last outing to be given up to the infirmities of old age. Today it is recognized that the longer senior citizens can participate in family and community the healthier and happier their last years will be. "Looking good" is closely related to "feeling good." It remains as important for the old as it was for the young.

The Physically Disabled

People with physical disabilities have many clothing problems. The exact problems are related to the type of disability and are very individualistic. However, many of the social, psychological, and physical requirements of clothing for the physically limited are commonly shared. Clothing attractiveness, safety, comfort, independence, durability, and availability are basic concerns of all.

The social and psychological aspects of clothing for the physically disabled are especially important. As emphasized previously, improved appearance increases self-confidence and helps one gain social acceptance. Being "in fashion" is important. Being "out of fashion" is another way in which the physically handicapped can be set apart. Clothing carefully selected for its design, color, and fabric can be used to enhance the individual and minimize the appearance of the handicap.

Some considerations of the physical needs of clothing for the physically disabled are these:[54]

---

[54] Clarice L. Scott, *Clothing for the Physically Handicapped Homemaker*, Agricultural Research Service, U.S.D.A. Home Economics Research Report No. 12 (June 1961).

Safety:

Limit excessive fabric, which can impede movements, get in the way of crutches, wheelchairs, walkers.

Select flameproof, flame-retardant fabrics.

Select shoes with handicap in mind, low heels, nonslip soles.

Select gloves with palm reinforcement to prevent slipping, friction burns from walkers, wheelchairs.

Select 3/4-length or cuffed sleeves.

Comfort:

Stretch and knit fabrics accept more strain, have more "give" than others; absorptive, soft, smooth textures are kinder to skin.

One-piece garments, when easy to put on, can eliminate waistline separation.

Slippery linings help garments slide on or off.

Collars that are cut to fit low on neck do not ride up.

Shoulders that are built up in undergarments prevent slipping of straps.

Arm movement is eased with released pleats in back and sides of garments.

Armholes should be cut high for crutch walkers to prevent ride up; should be cut low for wheelchairers for reach ease.

Waist fit should be easy for abdomen and hip movement.

Wheelchair users need garments with extra width in lap area.

Wrap garments often good.

Short jacket prevents sitting on extra fabric.

Pants cut high in back rise and low in front adapt to sitting positions, offer less bulk.

Independence:

Select all garments with exact physical impairment in mind.

Garment openings must be accessible and easy to manipulate: long front openings, large flat buttons, zippers with large pull rings, "Velcro."

Pants and skirts can wrap or have full-length leg openings.

One-piece garments (dresses, jumpsuits) may be easier to get in and out of for some.

Shoes that slip on are easy to get into; avoid ties, buckles.

Pockets attached to wheelchairs, crutches, and clothes help carry things.

Durability:

Strong, closely woven fabrics will take abrasion.

Reinforce areas that rub against prosthesis with iron-on patches, iron-on interfacings.

Reinforce seams, select flat-felled, overlocked seams.

Protective garments, such as bibs and aprons, reduce maintenance.

Appearance:

Clothing is in fashion and similar to what others are wearing.

Clothing does not call attention to the disability.

Fabric designs of overall prints distract the eye and conceal wrinkles, spots, and stains.

Proper fit is essential for appearance as well as safety.

Aids for the Physically Disabled

The following is a list of clothing aids and information for the physically disabled.

Sears Home Health Catalogue—available at no charge at Sears catalogue counter.

Measurements Guidelines and Solutions by Kay Caddel
Kay Caddel
Rte. 8, Box 12T2
Lubbock, Tex. 79407

Clothing for the Handicapped: An Annotated Bibliography and Resource List by Naomi Reich, Patricia Otten, and Marie Negri Carver.
University of Arizona, distributed by The President's Committee on Employment of the Handicapped, Washington, D.C. 20210

"Clothes to Fit Your Needs," Cooperative Extension, University of California, Berkeley, Calif. 94720.

PTL Designs
P.O. Box 364
Stillwater, Okla. 74074

FashionABLE
Rocky Hill, N.J. 08553

Head Coverings (for loss of hair due to chemotherapy)
"Hide & Chic" booklet
Marebar, Inc.
P.O. Box 547
Marleton, N.J. 08053

Closet Comments

Discovery of self may be approached by studying an extension of that self, that is, clothing. An objective analysis of your wardrobe may help you discover your individuality, personality, values, attitudes, interests, and lifestyle. Trying to read the messages contained in your clothing may help you to understand the impressions your clothes give to others and what your clothes may say about the kind of person you are. If you cannot be objective, get someone to help you. Perhaps several opinions will make the message even stronger. Completing this exercise will help you know what your clothes are saying about you.

Procedure:

Open your closet as though you were seeing the clothing collection for the first time. Imagine that the wardrobe belongs to someone you have never met. You want to learn as much as possible about this individual. The only clues you have are the garments and accessories before you.

1. Look at the *arrangement* of the clothes, shoes, and other items in the closet. What is your first impression.?
2. Consider the *order* of the closet and the clothing. What does it suggest?
3. Look at the *garments*. What do they express?
4. What *colors* are the garments. What do they express?
5. Would you *rate the wardrobe* as that of a fashion leader, follower, or creative individual?
6. Does the *clothing show* thought, planning coordination, or impulse buying?
7. What *activities* do the clothes suggest?
8. What clothing *values* are revealed by this collection of clothes?
9. What *attitude* does the owner have toward clothing?
10. What *interests* does the owner have?
11. What *lifestyle* would you associate with this wardrobe?
12. Briefly describe the kind of *person* that you feel would own this wardrobe.
13. Does this collection of clothing make a statement that accurately fits your *self-concept*? Explain this answer.

Suggested Activities

1. Collect advertisements from magazines that show personality of dress. Post on a bulletin board. Describe how lifestyle is projected by the dress and adornment of the advertisements.
2. Name celebrities with physical defects that have become a personality signature.
3. Have each class member remove three items from his/her wallet or handbag. Ask each one to explain why the items are important to him/her. Relate the verbal responses to the list of values in this chapter. Discuss how our individual value system is revealed by the things we feel to be important.
4. Consider your tolerance of another's clothing or patterns of dress. Do you stereotype? Do you make assumptions? Give specific examples.
5. Recall any examples from your personal experiences of wearing a style of garment that projected an image that was not your real personality. What were the reactions of others? How did you feel wearing it?
6. Have you ever been mistaken for someone else? A store clerk? A male or female? A mother or father? What were the false cues given by your dress?
7. Identify some of your favorite garments. Try to determine why they are your favorites. Are they physically comfortable? Are they psychologically comfortable? What image do they project? Is this how you think of yourself?

8. Identify some garments that you dislike. Do you often put these garments on but change them before leaving home? Do these garments fit you physically? Do they fit you psychologically? What image do they project?

9. Do the Closet Comments Assignment.

10. Read the following article. How does it relate to expressing individuality? Is the article timely or dated? What messages does it have for you?

The Secret of the Well-Dressed Woman[55]

The art of dressing is an art as complex and elusive as all the others. It, too, has its principles and traditions, known only to persons of taste because they harmonize with their inmost feelings. This art has little in common with money. The woman whose resources are limited has no more cause for being dowdily dressed than the woman who is rich has reason to believe she is beautifully gowned. Except insofar as money can procure the services of a good dressmaker, of an artist who can judge his customer's style and garb her accordingly, the wealthy woman stands no better chances of being correctly dressed than the woman who must turn every penny before spending it.

The contrary is very often true. Whereas the rich woman can satisfy her least caprice in a most haphazard fashion, the woman of average means, simply because she is actually forced to *think* about her wardrobe, is more apt to realize what is suitable to her and what is not. She learns how to choose and what to select. She acquires the art of dressing well.

And it is not an easy art to acquire. It demands a certain amount of intelligence, certain gifts, some of them among the rarest, perhaps—it requires a real appreciation of harmony of lines, of colors—ingenious ideas, absolute tact, and above all, a love of the beautiful and clear perception of values. It may be résuméd in two words—good taste.

Taste is by no means developed by riches; on the contrary, the increasing demands of luxury are killing the art of dressing. Luxury and good taste are in inverse proportion to one another. The one will kill the other as machinery is crowding out handwork. In fact, it has come so far that many persons confuse the two terms. Because a material is expensive they find it beautiful; because it is cheap they think it must be ugly.

To give you an example. All women whose wealth may be measured beyond a certain figure invariably appear with a string of pearls around their necks. Pearls are essentially becoming to certain types only, and cannot possibly be suitable to all women, but they seem to have become a visible sign of social caste. To how many women does a pearl necklace add beauty? How many women choose their pearl necklaces for reasons of good taste and style, that is to say, in order to set off the beauty of their coloring?

At the theater, in restaurants, you see hundreds of women more adorned than Indian idols. The most sparkling with jewels, the most expensively garbed, are never the most beautiful. Quite the contrary. Those who are most loaded down with precious stones, necklaces, bracelets, and rings rarely attract my attention. Sometimes I try to force myself to admire them. But it is impossible for me to feel anything more for them than for the dazzling setting of a jeweler's window, and the women who appear thus dressed in their fortune only would not appear one whit less attractive to me if they wore it in their hair as curling papers made out of banknotes!

The well-dressed woman is the one who picks out her gown, her adornments, simply because they make her appear more pleasing, not because other people are wearing that style or because it will be a palpable proof of her husband's bank account. Because one

---

[55] By Paul Poiret, a designer, who lived from 1880 to 1944. This article appeared in *Harper's Bazaar* when he was at the height of his influence just prior to World War I. It is reprinted by courtesy of *Harper's Bazaar* from *Harper's Bazaar: One Hundred Years of the American Female* (New York: Random, 1967).

woman chooses to emphasize the purity of her Grecian profile by winding a band of gold around her hair, why should twenty the next day and five hundred the day after that do their hair in the same style? But that is the way fashion sways women today. The only well-dressed women are those who dare and create original ideas, not those who servilely follow fashion.

In order not to appear entirely out of harmony with her surroundings and the place where she lives, a woman is obliged to follow fashions to a certain extent. But let that be within certain bounds! What does it matter if tight skirts be the fashion if your figure demands a wide one? Is it not more important to dress so as to bring out your good points rather than to reveal the bad? Can any idea of being fashionable make up for the fact of being ridiculous?

I dined the other day in a fashionable restaurant. At the tables around me I noticed at least half-a-dozen women whose hair was dressed in exactly the same way, with the same number of puffs and switches. All were dressed in equally expensive goods, although I was not able to judge of the colors because they were all equally overloaded with beading, embroideries, gold, silver, or steel ornaments, with laces and fringes.

These women, who, I imagine, were neither sisters nor friends, were all shaped in the same mold, that is to say, in the same kind of corsets, and they all wore jewels, pendants, and necklaces that, if not exactly alike, were at least of the same type. Every woman had adapted her body, her movements, and her taste to the commonplace desire of being fashionably dressed. And in looking at them I could not help thinking that in case of a panic their husbands or brothers or friends would be perfectly justified in mistaking one for the other.

Instead of hiding their individuality, why did not each woman try to bring out her personal type of beauty? One woman would have been more attractive without the puffs and switches; another would have been more beautiful in black; jewels were out of place on the third.

But, curiously enough, women fear being called original or individual, but never hesitate to make fools of themselves in following the latest fashion. A woman will submit to any torture, any ridicule, if she believes she is worshipping the absurd goddess Fashion. Every year a certain very limited number of types of styles are seen, and almost all women may be classified under one of them. Only those who do not fit in under any particular heading are worthy of being called well dressed.

I cannot help feeling a vague contempt for those who ask at the beginning of the season, "What is to be the favorite color?" Choose the color that suits you, madame, and if someone tells you that red is to be worn, dare to wear violet and consider only *what is suitable to you*, because there is only one single rule for the well-dressed woman, and the old Romans expressed it in one word—*decorum*—which means "that which is suitable." *That which is suitable!*

Choose whatever is suitable to the time, the place, the circumstance, the landscape, the place you are staying, whether it be a large city, a village, or a watering-place!

Choose whatever is most in harmony with your character, for a dress can be the expression of a state of mind if you but try to make it. There are dresses that sing of joy of life, dresses that weep, dresses that threaten. There are gay dresses, mysterious dresses, pleasing dresses, and tearful dresses.

3 Reasons for Wearing Clothes

Why do we wear clothes? Many theories have attempted to explain the motivation for human beings to cover and decorate all or parts of their body. The basic reasons behind this motivation appear to be the physical, the psychological and the sociocultural needs of all mankind.

The Batterberrys pose the question:

Why do people wear what they wear? Why, indeed, have human beings chosen to transform themselves in such astonishing ways? For the sake of the flesh or the spirit? For themselves or the eyes of the beholders? What has driven them? Lust? Ambition? Fear? Piety? Shame? There is and can be no single adequate response . . . it might be helpful to pause briefly and ponder the most plausible reasons for adorning the naked person, whether with a scrape of loincloth and a daub of clay or a blaze of tiara and a twenty-foot train. To our minds, clothes have traditionally served four basic functions: to protect the body, to exalt the ego, to arouse emotions in others, and to communicate by means of symbols.[1]

Evans stated in *Man the Designer* that of all the arts, designing his costume is one of man's most personal expressions. She listed the following motivations for dress:

comfort and protection from the elements of heat, sun, and other cosmic elements providing
    the modesty prescribed by a society
ritual and ceremony (wedding regalia)
decorations and embellishment
conspicuous consumption to display wealth and status (designer logos)
identification and recognition: royal crowns, clerical vestments, uniforms
differentiation of the young from the older (skirt lengths, see-throughs, tight pants)
extension of one's self: billowing gowns, resplendent crowns (platform shoes)
transformation or change of personality: hats, wigs, hairstyle
satisfaction of the urge to create
revealing one's body structure for enhancement
self-expression: "The apparel oft proclaims the man. . . ."—Shakespeare
attraction of the opposite sex
uncovering: Salome's dance, Gypsy Rose Lee and the art of striptease
social protest
competition with one's own sex
fun and recreation
escape from boredom

[1] Michael and Ariane Batterberry, *Mirror, Mirror* (New York: Holt, 1977), p. 8.

securing attention
convention (dress code)
satisfying a desire for change
bringing one's body into closer alignment with an idealized image of a particular culture—
     shaping as well as covering
displaying technological changes[2]

In reviewing the literature, the explanations most often cited for the use of clothing are protection, modesty, and self-adornment. The physical need for protection of the body from weather, animals, insects, vegetation, and enemies, both human and the unseen evil spirits, make body covering seem essential to man's survival in a harsh and hostile environment. The psychological need for modesty is brought about by cultural conditioning. The need for modesty seems to be present in some form in most societies; it is the area of anatomy to be concealed that creates the wide range of different customs. The psychological need for adornment includes many motives, such as self-expression or status, to depict age, group membership, for ritual, or for the attraction of the opposite sex.[3]

The following discussion is presented to help the student understand the numerous forces that have led man to create body coverings and adornment. As you peruse this material, perhaps you can add your own observations to those of the authors and better answer the question: Why do we wear clothing?

Clothing of Early Man

Prehistoric cave paintings have preserved the images of the clothing and adornment of early man. One of the oldest depictions is in the caverns in the French Pyrenees known as *Trois Frères*. These have been dated as being created twenty to thirty thousand years ago. The cave paintings show a man wearing animal skins and a headpiece. It appears that he was taking part in a ritual or was a hunter disguised as an animal.

In Eastern Spain at Cogul, the Late Paleolithic and Mesolithic cave drawings depicted naked men. The women of these illustrations are shown wearing long bell-shaped skirts or straight shifts. Their hair seems to be braided and adorned with a bonnet (Figure 3-1).

The Stone Age warriors drawn in the Gasulla Gorge in Eastern Spain are wearing headdresses, some of which are feathered. Skeletons of the Upper Paleolithic Age found in Europe were discovered wearing necklaces, bracelets, legbands, and headpieces. These ornaments were made of bone or shell.

Articles of early clothing were found at a Siberian site of the Upper Paleolithic Age. Included in this group were interestingly crafted beads and pendants of

[2] Helen Marie Evans, *Man the Designer* (New York: Macmillan, 1973), pp. 303–307.
[3] John Carl Flugel, *The Psychology of Clothes* (London: The Hogarth Press, Ltd., 1930, reprint 1950), p. 16.

3-1 *Rock-shelter paintings in Cogul, eastern Spain. Late Paleolithic period. Women are depicted wearing bell-shaped skirts and straight shifts. Men in the same cave drawing appear naked. (Drawing courtesy Betty Kessler)*

ivory and bone, and a statue of a man wearing a hood, a closely fitted body garment, and trousers with fur on the outside (Figure 3-2).

These ancient cave and gravesite findings support the theory that clothing was a concern of early man. Of course, we cannot completely understand the significance of the dress relics, but the evidence seems to suggest the idea that the clothing of early man was used for rituals and for ornamentation as well as for protection.[4]

Between 4500 and 4000 B.C., Western civilization had its beginning. The cradle of this civilization was located in the area of the Mediterranean Sea. Artifacts show that the two great river valleys of the Near East, the Tigris-Euphrates in Mesopotamia and the Nile in Egypt, became the permanent home of wandering tribes. The oldest of these tribes is now known as Sumerian; it evolved into the Babylonian, the Assyrian, the Phoenician, and the Egyptian, as well as other civilizations in the area west of India and Afghanistan and south of the Black Sea. What set these people apart from their ancestors was the fact that they remained in one location for a long period of time and they developed into military, religious, and civil societies. They formulated laws for the protection of citizens and property, divided labor, thus creating the first industries, and even fostered the arts, including clothing (Figure 3-3).[5]

Pistoles and Horsting described the Sumerians and their dress in this manner:

From rare examples of their costume, we are able to deduce that the Sumerians were a refined, slender, and elegant people who took extremely good care of their person and their attire.

Both men and women wore plain but finely woven tunics, which the women usually draped over the left shoulder. Slaves of both sexes were naked above the waist, but their skirts were often multitiered fringes or petal-shaped pieces of cloth.

3-2 *Statuette from Mal'ta, Siberia, Upper Paleolithic period. Man wearing a hood with fitted body garment and trousers of skins with fur worn on the outside. (Drawing courtesy Betty Kessler)*

[4] Jacquetta Hawkes and Sir Leonard Woolley, *Prehistory and the Beginnings of Mankind* (New York: Harper, 1963), pp. 161–165.

[5] Rosana Pistoles and Ruth Horsting, *History of Fashions* (New York: Wiley, 1970), pp. 1–2.

64

Men wore shallow, bowl-shaped hats and women embellished these for themselves by adding coiled decorations. For the male of this period, long beards and long hair were elements of refinement. Finally, women sometimes created dresses by employing a unique *volant* wrapped spirally around the entire figure, up to the necks.[6]

Clothing for Protection

From the most ancient times until the very day you are reading this, psychological protection has been an important function of clothing. Some scholars theorize that the origin and primary function of adorning the body of early man was the need to defend himself from spiritual powers that will bring harm. Belief in the power of supernatural forces to cause floods, earth tremors, drought, illness, and death prompt man to adorn himself for protection. Superstitions, fear of the unseen, belief in evil spirits and demons, and "luck" have all been responsible for the use of certain garments, jewelry, and other body adornment. Some examples are these:

Cowrie shells protecting women from sterility in many Pacific cultures (Figure 3-4).
Bridal veils to protect the bride from evil spirits (Figure 3-5).
Evil-eye beads to protect children and animals from unseen powers in the Near East.
Lucky charms, jewelry, coins, clothing, shoes and hats to bring good luck (Figure 3-6).[7]

The climates in which early civilizations flourished were tropical or semitropical. The temperatures were warm or hot and the air was very dry. (This was a vital factor in the preservation of their artifacts.) Clothing for warmth was rarely necessary. Clothing for protection from the hot sun would seem more important, but from what we know of their styles this was not often a consideration. Our knowledge of the clothing practices of the Sumerians and their neighbors the Egyptians reveals that dress was used to show rank, wealth, and status, for ritual and individual ornamentation, more than for protection.

The Yaggans from the vicinity of Tierra del Fuego at the tip of South America live in the world's most severe climate. The weather is cold, damp, and stormy. Snowfall is common even in summer. The winter mean temperature is 34.7°F (1.5°C) and the summer mean temperature is 50.2°F (10.1°C). These people developed brief clothing in the form of a small cape made of fox, sea otter, or sealskin worn with the fur side out. This cape covered only the shoulders; it did not reach to the waist. In winter the people sometimes wore moccasins and

3-3 *A Sumerian statuette (c. 2000–1500 B.C.) shown wearing a Kaunakes or Pagne-skirt of tufted or woven material. (Courtesy Trustees of the British Museum, London)*

[6] Ibid., p. 3.
[7] Batterberry, op. cit. p. 9.

3-4 *Cowrie shells are believed to protect women from sterility in many Pacific cultures. (Courtesy Department Library Services American Museum of Natural History)*

3-5 *Modern bridal veils evolved from a belief that they protect the bride from evil spirits. (Courtesy Priscilla of Boston)*

3-6 Left: *The Hmong (Miao), a northern Thai hill people, embellish their clothing with fine appliqué and embroidery for magic purposes. Baby carrier is decorated to prevent evil spirits from attacking the baby from the back. Right: An ornate headdress is decorated with metal spangles and colorful beads. Around the child's arms, neck, and other joints are bracelets to prevent the child's soul from leaving the body. This jewelry serves to attach the child's soul to the child. (Courtesy Heidi Kessler)*

leggings. The head was generally bare. Some body warmth might have been retained by their practice of smearing the head and body with animal grease.[8]

When Charles Darwin, the biologist and author of *Origin of the Species*, visited this area he gave the people some red cloth. Instead of using it to wrap the body to provide warmth, the people tore it up into strips and used it for decorative purposes, despite their nakedness in the bitter Antarctic cold.

The aborigines of Australia live in temperatures that range between 23°F (5.0°C) and 117°F (52.7°C). They create the scantiest shelter and sleep in the open air curled around a fire. They wear only brief loincloths. They use grease and ochre to decorate their bodies. This ornamentation is solely for ceremonial purposes (Figure 3-7).[9]

[8] L. H. Newburgh, ed., *The Physiology of Heat Regulation and the Science of Clothing* (New York: Hafner Publishing Co., 1968), p. 30.

[9] Daisy Bates, *The Passing of the Aborigines* (New York: Pocket Books, 1973), pp. 25–26.

The Alaskan Eskimo has fashioned boots, breeches, and parkas from the fur and skins of the animals that provide his food. These garments offer both warmth and protection. It is interesting to note that the Eskimo has also enlisted body chemistry to assist him in his environmental survival. By eating a high fat and protein diet, the Eskimo has developed a high rate of metabolism that raises the amount of heat produced by his body.[10] His winter garments consist of two layers, using fur on the inside as well as the outside, to help trap and hold warmth next to his body (Figure 3-8).[11]

Whether man adjusts to his environment through biological or genetic alteration or by cultural adaptation is debatable. There is question whether climatic conditions, such as cold, actually bring about permanent genetic alterations. Many scientists believe that this type of physiological adjustment is a temporary adaptation. Downs and Bliebtreu wrote as follows:

In general, research suggests that man, whatever race or population, whether he lives at Arctic sea level or in the freezing winds of the Himalayas or the Andes or the fringes of South America at Tierra del Fuego or in explorer's camps in the Antarctic, is not biologically adapted to retain heat but accomplishes this through a series of cultural devices. The somewhat higher rate of metabolism of the Eskimos is the only possible exception, and even that is questionable because when an Eskimo is put on a European diet for an extended period, his metabolic rate drops.[12]

[10] James F. Downs and Hermann K. Bliebtreu, *Human Variations: An Introduction to Physical Anthropology* (Beverly Hills, Calif.: Glencoe, 1969), p. 202.
[11] Newburgh, op. cit., p. 9.
[12] Downs and Bliebtreu, op. cit., p. 202.

3-7 *Australian aborigine of the Northern territory painted for a funeral ceremony. Temperatures in Australia range from 23°F to 117°F yet the briefest of clothing is worn. Body ornamentation such as this is used only for ceremonial purposes. (Courtesy Qantas)*

3-8 *The Alaskan Eskimo makes clothing from fur and skins which offer warmth and protection. (Courtesy Josephine Schultz)*

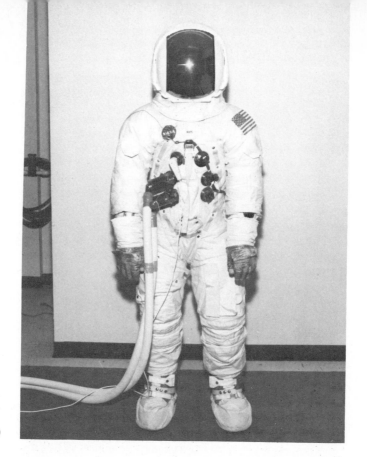

3-9 *Man has always adapted his clothing to his habitat. The latest example of this is found in the spacesuit. (Courtesy NASA)*

When astronauts leave the Earth's atmosphere for space, their lives depend upon the technological expertise of man. A part of this incredible feat is the design of the spacesuit. This garment is carefully constructed to make the Earth's atmosphere portable. It also includes life-support systems. The spacesuit is truly a triumph of modern man's scientific ingenuity. The spacesuit was developed to protect the wearer and to support his/her very life (Figure 3-9).

Most of us wear clothing that is related to the geographical location and climatic conditions in which we live. Many individual wardrobes have clothing suitable to meet a range of temperatures and weather conditions (Figure 3-10). We tend to layer clothing for warmth and peel it off for cooling. Most people use common sense and experience to regulate clothing to the weather (see Chapter 15).

There are times when both common sense and experience are ignored and fashion or peer group identity sways our judgment. For example, consider traditional business dress for men, a suit, a long-sleeved, collared shirt, and a tie are often mandated on the hottest day; consider, too, coatless and sweaterless high schoolers waiting for school in the shivering early dawn; high boots worn by girls and boys on scorching summer city streets; young children going barefoot almost anytime.

And yet, examples of many kinds of protective clothing are easy to find. The fire-fighter wears garments that do not catch fire or melt and protect from heat and debris both falling and underfoot. Police officers often wear bulletproof vests

3-10 Protective clothing in both hemispheres of America serves the same purpose. Left: North American children wear water-resistant nylon lined in pile. (Courtesy Allied Corporation) Right: A young girl from the high altitudes of Cuzco, Peru, keeps body warmth with layers of wool clothing. (Courtesy Josephine Schultz)

of strongly woven filaments that stop or slow down bullets. Industrial workers use goggles, gloves, and especially designed garments that protect them in their dangerous jobs, such as the stainless steel wire mesh suit created for electric pylon operators who are exposed to extremely high voltages of electricity.

Less sophisticated kinds of protective clothing are such items as baby bibs and diapers, knee and elbow patches, dress and pant shields. Clothing used for various sports has protective devices built in such areas as the shoulder, knee, shin, chest, crotch, elbow, and hand. Wet suits and diving gear protect the wearer under water. Thermal socks and underwear, water and windproof pants and jackets, hoods, muffler, helmets, visors, boots and gloves or mittens protect the wearer against cold. Hats, "cover-ups," and sunglasses protect against sun and glare.

Clothing for Modesty

Is modesty the primary motive that led man to develop clothing for his body? In order to arrive at some kind of answer to this question, we need to examine several ideas and practices showing the relationship between clothing and modesty.

It cannot be denied that many among us wear clothes for purposes of modesty. In fact, expressions of modesty are found among all cultures. The anthropologist Conrad says, "... all people have rules about modesty that relate to their bodies."[13] There is, however, a lack of agreement as to what constitutes modesty. There is even disagreement found among the same cultural group. "Your neckline is too low," "That swimsuit is too scanty," "Your pants are too tight." These typical admonitions are often heard by American young people within their own immediate family.

Different concepts of modesty are found in different cultures as well. The covering of the body or the lack of it is considered improper or immodest because of cultural interpretation (Figure 3-11). In the Japanese public bath, both sexes bathe together and their nudity is not considered immodest, but for any other social situation, the conventional Japanese apparel for both men and women is body enveloping. A brief bikini worn on an American beach is not usually considered immodest, but the same garment would be considered indecent if worn on a business street. The Botocudo of the Amazon are nude except for ear and lower lip plugs. It has been observed that when the plugs were removed for purposes of trade, these people fled into the jungle in shame.[14] This concept was best stated in the play *Teahouse of the August Moon*. "Pornography [is a] matter of geography."

Conventions of modesty change from time to time in the same culture. In the nineteenth century concealing the leg was a manifestation of modesty; even the

[13] Jack Conrad, *The Many Worlds of Man* (New York: Crowell, 1964, Apollo ed., 1968), p. 117.
[14] E. Adamson Hoebel, *Man in the Primitive World* (New York: McGraw-Hill, 1958), p. 240.

3-11 *There is a lack of agreement as to what constitutes modesty.* Left: *A bikini at poolside USA. (Courtesy Jantzen)* Right: *This Balinese mother would consider it highly immodest to show her legs.*

3-12 *Isfahan, Iran. Three teen-age Moslem girls wear a body-enveloping shawl, the chador; they would consider themselves immodestly dressed if they appeared on the street without the wrap. Short Western style skirts and white cotton blouses comprise the costume under the shawl.*

word was taboo. If one had to refer to "that" part of the body, it was called a limb. (Even the legs of furniture had been covered by dust ruffles.) By the early 1980s the French cut bathing suit revealed most of the female anatomy. Among the Comanche, as late as 1936, elder males felt a sense of discomfort and indecency if they went without a G-string, even though they were fully clothed in American-type pants and shirts.[15]

From these examples it is clear that cultural learnings determine what is modest, and immodesty is breaking of a cultural custom (Figure 3-12). There is not an inborn feeling or instinct of body shame. Young children do not have an innate sense of modesty. Feelings of immodesty are learned and are often accompanied by fears and anxieties resulting from the possible consequences of the sanctions imposed by each society.

Modesty does not necessarily mean the covering of the sexual parts of the body. Highly developed civilizations, such as those found in ancient Egypt, Crete, Greece, Cambodia, and India, had clothing customs that exposed the genitalia. Yet they too had customs of decency. Modesty is often equated in terms of gestures, facial expressions, and body posture.

James Laver, in his book *Modesty in Dress*, says of the dilemma concerning modesty versus adornment:

Modesty is an inhibitory impulse directed against either social or sexual forms of display. It is opposed both to the wearing of gorgeous clothes, and to the wearing of too few clothes. It aims on the one hand, at prevention of disease or satisfaction (social or sexual), and on the other at the prevention of disgust, shame or disapproval.[16]

[15] Ibid., p. 240.
[16] James Laver, *Modesty in Dress* (Boston: Houghton, 1969), p. 13.

72

The intention of clothing the body for purposes of modesty is in direct opposition to the intention of clothing the body for adornment. Modesty seeks to hide and divert attention, whereas adornment seeks to attract. Some clothes do not always conceal or make unnoticeable the sexual areas of the body. On the contrary, they may, by their conspicuous nature, attract rather than hide. Examples of this are uplift bras, tight pants with ornamented hip pockets, and body-hugging sweaters. That which is concealed is a mystery; thus fashion may seize upon that feature as a breach of modesty. Flugel noted:

The real point to bear in mind is that modesty is essentially correlated with desire. Its purpose is to fight desire, but in so doing it rekindles it, so that a circular process is inevitably set in motion.[17]

Fashion calls attention to one part of the body until that gets wearisome or boring and then covers that part and exposes another part. This exposure and concealment have covered and uncovered almost the entire body at one time or another. Almost all parts of the human body have been considered indecent or immoral at some time.

The wearing of clothes may be titillating. An art professor cited the fact that a completely nude female model produced no disturbing effect upon his male students. However, when the same model appeared wearing either a hat or a pair of stockings, the male students became restless. The professor felt that their restlessness was caused by erotic feelings aroused by the partly nude model.

Hoebel, professor of anthropology, says,

The use of clothing does not rise out of any innate sense of modesty, but that modesty results from customary habits of clothing or ornamentation of the body and its parts.[18]

It is generally believed by scholars of clothing that modesty was not the primary motive in the development of clothing. How can modesty in dress exist if clothes are not the custom of the culture?

Clothing for Adornment

Man's pursuit of personal adornment is universal. All societies have adorned themselves in some form. It is interesting to consider that except for pierced ears, tattooing, and cosmetic surgery, most of modern man's form of adornment is temporary. Clothes are added or removed and cosmetics or hairstyle changed, creating temporary alterations in appearance. Fashion dictates changes in adornment. The nature of fashion is change.

However, some people do use permanent forms of adornment. Their styles of ornamentation form lasting cultural practices. If, in their society, little or no

[17] Flugel, op. cit., p. 192.
[18] Hoebel, op. cit., p. 240.

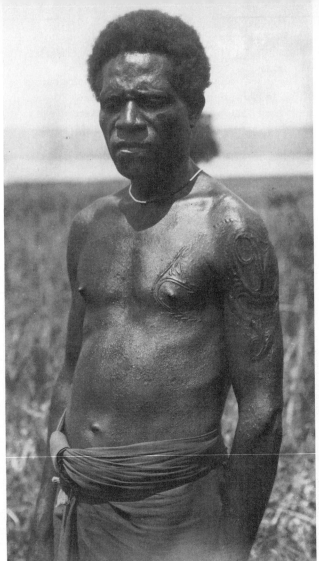

3-13 Scarification, Mandang, New Guinea. Intricate curvilinear designs adorn the arm and chest of this young man. (Courtesy Department Library Services American Museum of Natural History)

3-14 An African pygmy with his teeth filed to points. This practice has religious meaning. (Courtesy Department Library Services American Museum of Natural History)

clothing is worn, they frequently adorn their skin. If the skin is of a light enough tone, tattooing may be used. If tattooing is not visible, scarification may be used (Figure 3-13).

Other forms of permanent adornment are foot-binding (China), extension of ear lobes and lips (Africa), filing or removal of teeth (Figure 3-14), and perhaps most dramatic of all, cranial deformation (Figure 3-15). This latter practice has been used in many parts of the world. Anthropologists believe reasons for this practice include the following:

To signify noble birth
To look more formidable
To improve health and vigor
To distinguish one's children from those of the masses

74

3-15 *A high-domed skull was a form of permanent body adornment of the Pacific Northwest coast Kwakiutl Indian (before 1895). It was produced by head flattening. (Courtesy Smithsonian Institution National Anthropological Archives)*

To achieve cranial deformation, pressure is applied to the child's head soon after childbirth and continued for months or years.[19]

The universal practice of adornment is an ancient one. The earliest evidence of adornment was found on bones in mid-Paleolithic Neanderthal burial sites where ochre clays were found.[20] On the cave floors in Europe, Paleolithic peoples left bone and antler containers with stoppers that contained cosmetic pigments mixed with fats, yellow and red iron oxides, and black manganese oxides.[21] What were the motivations for the use of cosmetics by early man? Perhaps protection from unseen evil forces, sexual attraction, ritual ceremonies, status symbols, or to frighten the enemy.

A statuette known as the *Venus of Willendorf* over twenty thousand years old, was made in the Aurignacian epoch (Figure 3-16). This prehistoric fertility figure, whose face has been ignored by her creator, wears an elaborate and detailed hairstyle. Other statuettes from prehistory, such as the woman's head from *Grotte*

[19] Spencer L. Rogers, *Artificial Deformation of the Head*, San Diego Museum Papers #8, pp. 1–5.
[20] Justine M. Cordwell and Ronald A. Schwartz, "Uncovering the Secret Vice," in Justine M. Cordwell and Ronald A. Schwartz, eds., *The Fabrics of Culture* (The Hague: Mouton Publishers, 1979), p. 25.
[21] Ibid., "The Very Human Arts of Transformation," p. 49.

3-16   Cast of the statuette Venus of Willendorf, a fertility figure over 20,000 years old, wears an elaborate and detailed hairstyle. (Original in Natural History Museum, Vienna, Austria. Courtesy American Museum of Natural History)

de Pane at Brassempouy, France, also show care in the styling of the hair (Figure 3-17). From these early times to the present, man has been preoccupied with adornment of the hair. In early times hair adornment often served as a social status symbol (Figure 3-18).[22]

In what is considered the most elaborate Ice Age burial yet found, the skeleton of a middle-aged woman buried in 23,000 B.C. at Sungir, near Moscow, revealed early civilization's incredible concern with adornment. Her skeleton was embellished by 13,500 beads of mammoth ivory and bone. Most of the beads appeared to have been sewn to clothing at the time of the burial. It has been estimated that it took more than 1,000 hours to carve the beads. Each of her arms was adorned with 25 thin ivory bracelets interspersed with beaded bracelets. Archeologists who reconstructed the woman's apparel believed it to be a pull-over skirt of fur or hide and trousers that had moccasins sewn to them. An outer mantle and cap were decorated with 20 teeth of the silver fox.[23]

Personal adornment has served many other motives: to frighten the enemy, to repel evil spirits (Figure 3-19), to gain approval, to attract the opposite sex, to indicate age, to express self, to extend the image, and to show economic position (Figure 3-20). Langer noted that man from earliest times has worn clothes to overcome his feelings of inferiority and to achieve a conviction of his superiority to the rest of creation. Clothing is worn to win admiration and assure man that he belongs (Figures 3-21, 3-22).[24] In support of Langer's observations consider the popularity in the United States of America of brand-name clothing. The identifying name, insignia, or logo makes this status clothing. The status may be within a small clique, a large group, national, or even international. The symbols make a statement for all to read and interpret.

[22] Hoebel, op. cit., p. 245.
[23] Exhibit, "Ice Age Art," American Museum of National History, May 1978-January, 1979. Alexander Marshack.
[24] Lawrence Langer, *The Importance of Wearing Clothes* (New York: Hastings House, 1959), p. 12.

3-17   A statuette from Grotte de Pape at Brassempouy of the Aurignacian-Perigordian period (C. 20,000–30,000 B.C.) shows care in the styling of the hair, a preoccupation of man from early times to the present. (Drawing Courtesy Betty Kessler)

3-18 *When Balinese women take offerings to the temple, they adorn themselves, as well as their food offering, with fresh flowers. (Courtesy Qantas)*

Protection, or Modesty, or Adornment?

Of the three basic reasons for covering the body—protection, modesty, adornment—there is some disagreement as to the primary motive. Flugel believed that decoration was the primary motive for the adoption of clothing. The protective and modesty functions of dress came later once the wearing of clothing became habitual.[25] In his essay "Uncovering the Secret Vice," Schwartz examines the

[25] Flugel, op. cit., p. 17.

origins and functions of clothing. He recalls that Hirn in 1900 *(Origins of Art)* examined all the available ethnographic evidence and reviewed all the theories of adornment and concluded that there was no possibility of deciding with any certainty the reason why man began to decorate himself. Schwartz believes that little has been uncovered since that time to modify Hirn's conclusion.[26] Although proof is not within our grasp, and some scholars opt for a particular theory, most agree that "a combination of environmental, psychological and sociocultural factors are involved in the origin and evolution of clothing, and that motives for continued use of an item may be rather different from those which led to its adoption."[27]

[26] Cordwell and Schwartz, op. cit., p. 24.
[27] Ibid., p. 25.

3-19 *Personal adornment serves many motives—to frighten the enemy, to repel evil spirits. A Bird of Paradise headdress crowns a New Guinea Western Highlands tribesman. (Courtesy Qantas)*

3-20 *Cuna Indians, San Blas Islands, Panama. Adornment of the Cuna woman indicates economic position. Jewelry in the form of beaded leg and arm bracelets, silver or gold nose rings, earrings, and necklaces serves as a status symbol. (Courtesy Panama Government Tourist Bureau)*

3-21 *A shaven head is a sign of beauty to the Masai women of Kenya. It sets off to advantage the beaded ornaments that adorn their heads and necks. (Courtesy Gloria Le Baron)*

3-22 *Clothing is worn to win admiration and assure man that he belongs. (Courtesy Qantas)*

Suggested Activities

1. Read over the list of motivations for dress found in this chapter. Add to this list, if you can.
2. Consider the clothing that you are wearing at this time. For what reasons did you select the clothes you are wearing today?
3. Arrange a bulletin board showing clothing for protection, modesty, and self-adornment. Use this as a basis for class discussion. Do all class members agree on the functions being performed by the various garments?
4. Find examples of clothing representing different fashion periods. Determine the function of these garments.
5. Watch various television programs or movies to see the clothing theories of protection, modesty, adornment, exemplified in the clothing of the actors and actresses. Also note how clothing is used to identify various roles.
6. Discuss how the concept of modesty was changed in our own country. Use history and costume books to illustrate this transition.
7. Collect news articles and pictures illustrating how a person's dress became worthy of a news item.

80

4 Clothing, the Communicator of Culture

From prehistoric days when man first came home from the hunt with blood smeared on his body to the sophisticated cultures that have since evolved, man has adorned his body with clothing and ornaments in some form. Although clothing is used to fulfill personal needs, it also communicates the human conditions, traditions, and values of a society. Clothing and all other varieties of body adornment, because of their personal and portable nature, reflect the lifestyle and social group to which the individual belongs.

The study of dress of varying geographic locations and differing cultures reveals how man has solved the problem of the special need to be clothed. An infinite variety of forms of body coverings and enrichments has evolved and is continually being expanded. Groups and individuals within groups differ in their ideas of what is appropriate, attractive, or fashionable.

Culture

Each society has found methods for meeting the needs for obtaining food, shelter, and clothing. These solutions are referred to as a *culture*. Therefore, culture can be defined as a product of the creative human response in meeting the needs of the group. Brown defines culture as accepted and patterned ways of behavior. "It is the sum total of the organization or arrangement of all the groups ways of thinking, feeling and acting. It includes the physical manifestations of the group as exhibited in clothing, shelter, tools, and so on."[1]

Cultural traditions provide formulas for dress patterns. For example, some groups derive texture from fibers and weaves while others use scarification of the skin. The methods used depend on the customs or traditions of the society (Figure 4-1). Cultural traditions also impose limitations upon clothing. Traditions determine what is appropriate. "Proper dress" had been debated down through the centuries. Opinions vary with time and tradition. In 700 B.C. it is recorded that Isaiah denounced the women of Israel for wearing fine linen, veils, ankle bracelets, and nose jewels. Somewhat later, the young men of Rome in the fourth century A.D. were defying both the Roman government and their fathers by wear-

---

[1] Ina Corrine Brown, *Understanding Other Cultures* (Englewood Cliffs, N.J.: Prentice-Hall, 1963), p. 3.

81

4-1 Cultural traditions provide formulas for dress patterns. The methods used depend upon the customs of the society. A young Moravian girl from Czechoslovakia wears her native costume for a spring festival. (Courtesy Cedok)

ing *braccos*, a trouser worn by the invading Barbarians. From these early times until now and probably continuing into the future, journalists authoritatively explain what is right or wrong about our manner of dressing.

The mores (prevailing uses and traditions) of a society exert pressure on individuals to conform. The mores thus furnish sanctions of dress. These social pressures very often make the majority of the group conform so that the welfare of the society is preserved (Figure 4-2).

As commerce, exchange, and communication between groups increases, acculturation of ideas takes place. Among other things, similarities of dress become evident. Adaptations are made and the uniqueness that at one time demarked the costume of the group is diminished or disappears. As expressions of cultural conditions by means of dress become vague, political beliefs, religious ideas, sex differentiation, and marital status become more difficult to determine. Mass production, as seen in Western dress,[2] blurs the cultural expression of occupation, religion, and social status. Fairservis, in his book, *Costumes of the East*, postulated that as Westernization of dress takes place throughout the world, we can expect conformity of cultures, standardization of laws, politics, and educational policy, mass values, and, in general, undermining of cultural traditions. The result of this will be "... one nation, one people, one government, one belief, and, of course, one costume repertory" (Figure 4-3 a,b,c,d).[3]

In many parts of the world Western dress has already replaced traditional folk dress because of a desire of the people to be modern and a part of the twentieth century. This influence of Western style of dress and grooming is considered a potential cultural threat in areas striving to maintain their unique identity. When Pathet Lao took command of Laos, his first command ordered teen-agers to give up their Western fashions and cut their hair. Jeans, lipstick, and nail polish were forbidden since they were regarded a threat to their cultural traditions.

[2] Western dress is defined as the clothing of Western Europe since the industrial revolution and particularly that of the United States of America.

[3] Walter A. Fairservis, Jr., *Costumes of the East* (Riverside, Conn.: Chatham, 1971), p. 28.

4-2 The mores of a society exert pressures on individuals to conform. The mores thus furnish sanctions concerning dress. These social pressures often make the majority of the group conform so that the welfare of the society is preserved. Note the resting position of the man on the far right. Although it is seldom seen in the Western world, it is a common stance elsewhere. (Courtesy John J. Shaak)

4-3a,b,c,d *As communication between groups increases acculturation of ideas takes place. Adaptations are made and the uniqueness of the costume diminishes or disappears. (a) New Guinea native chief (Courtesy Qantas); (b) Fiji policeman (Courtesy Qantas); (c) South African woman (Courtesy South African Tourist Corporation); (d) South Indian men (Author).*

World travelers have been embarrassed, intimidated, and barred from some countries because of official restrictions on dress. Those wearing long hair, blue jeans, and having an unkempt look are kept out of Malaysia, Singapore, Thailand, and Burma. These forms of dress are associated with drug users and irresponsible persons. In an attempt to reduce street crime and drug use among their own youth and tourists as well, dress regulations are in practice.

In the African Republic of Malawai, an airport barber is ready to trim male locks if the immigration officials deem that they are not a "reasonable" length. Women are forbidden to wear minis or shorts or pants except at resorts or for sports. In Saudi Arabia women travelers showing arms or legs violate Islamic law. The king has ordered police to punish violators. In Israel, a very orthodox area called Mea Shearim has a multilanguage sign warning women visitors not to wear sleeveless dresses, short skirts, or pants at the risk of stoning.[4]

The victors of the 1978 Iranian revolution lead by the Ayatollah Khomeini, a fanatic Moslem, ordered women to wear the traditional chador (body covering veil) at all times in public, even while swimming. Khomeini also ordered segregation of sexes at schools, forbade music, and called for a prompt return to the strict Islamic laws.[5]

To help the student understand the amazing variety of clothing that man has created, examples of dress from many cultures and times including our own are cited. A brief discussion of how these body coverings were used within the society to achieve cultural purposes is included. The terms *clothing, dress, costume,* and *body covering* include anything that is put on the body such as a covering, textile, or jewelry and anything that is done to or applied on the body such as hair arrangement, painting, tattooing, disfiguring, or scarring.

Clothing Communicates

Clothing communicates the cultural conditions of a society. These comprise:

economic position
social situation and identification
social status/rank
international identification
sex differentiation
age

marital status
political beliefs
religious ideas
technical changes
aesthetic ideals

Because of the overlapping and interweaving of the meanings and use of dress, it must be kept in mind that the functions of dress may communicate several

[4] "Immodest Dress Latest Religious Issue in Israel," *Los Angeles Times,* August 25, 1977, Pt. I, pp. 1 and 11.

[5] "According to Code," *Los Angeles Times,* August 2, 1979, p. 1.

cultural conditions. For example, Chinese foot binding: was this practice an example of economic position, social status, attitudes toward women, or aesthetic ideal? The custom of foot binding fits under all these categories; this becomes evident as one understands the entire breadth of the meaning of this practice. So although the authors have attempted to group clothing customs under headings for ease of study, the student may have insights into the costuming that places it in several categories.

Economic Position

In 1899, Thorstein Veblen, an economist, wrote the classic *Theory of the Leisure Class*. In explaining how dress was used as an expression of personal financial worth he stated

Expenditure on dress has this advantage over most other methods, that our apparel is always in evidence and affords an indication of our pecuniary standing to all observers at first glance.[6]

Both quality and quantity are indicators of economic position. A wealthy *begum* of metropolitan New Delhi, India, wears saris of rich brocaded silk. Her neck and wrists are adorned with heavy lustrous gold. The *Gujarat* farmer's wife of Northwest India is garbed in brightly embroidered cotton skirts and blouses with veils of tie and dye. Heavy bracelets of silver circle her wrists and ankles. In both cases, jewelry is the common means of investment and the woman's body serves as a bank or repository (Figures 4-4, 4-5, 4-6).

The prosperous Hausa chief of Northern Nigeria wears a "layered look." He wears as many as twelve embroidered robes one on top of the other. Quantitative display of wealth is more important than creature comfort in this extremely hot climate.

In ancient times the wealthy Chinese grew their fingernails to inordinate lengths, thus affirming to all that they did not perform lowly manual tasks. To further enforce the inactivity of their hands, they wore robes with very long sleeves that completely covered the fingernails. Any work involving the hands was impossible.

At the end of the nineteenth century, the English businessman of wealth and power wore a high, tight, white collar with his heavy, stiff Edwardian suit. Physical exertion of any kind was inhibited and would probably have caused difficulty in breathing, if not strangulation. Thus the term *white-collar worker* came into use. This term, as well as the clothing practice, denoted both economic success and status above that of the manual laborer, who usually wore a soft-collared, blue shirt.

These examples reinforce Veblen's statement:

Our dress, therefore, in order to serve its purpose effectually, should not only be expensive, but it should also make plain to all observers that the wearer is not engaged in any kind of productive labour (Figure 4-7).[7]

[6] Thorstein Veblen, *The Theory of the Leisure Class* (New York: Modern Library, 1931), p. 167.

[7] Ibid., p. 170.

4-4 *South Cotabato, Mindanao, Philippines. Layers of garments and jewelry are indications of economic status. (Courtesy Philippines Department of Tourism, Manila)*

4-5 *Heavy silver earrings and ivory bracelets on this woman proclaim that she is from a wealthy Indian family. (Courtesy John J. Shaak)*

4-6 *A richly brocaded sari of silk and neck and wrists adorned in heavy gold jewelry express the economic wealth of this Bengali bride in Bangladesh.*

4-7 *This Ndebele woman with her neck, arms, and legs encircled in brass rings makes it plain to all that she is not engaged in physical labor. (Courtesy South African Tourist Corporation)*

In Cuba, economic conditions restricted the amount of clothing a person was allowed under the Castro government in the early 1970s. Only 27 yards of fabric were allowed each individual per year. Ingenuity extended this amount to cover all clothing needs. Designs were created involving such ideas as patchwork and very short, tight skirts. Students from Cuba told of shortages of shoes, stockings, shampoos, and cosmetics. Nylons were worn until they no longer resembled the original stockings, but took on incredible designs of darns and mends. When a supply of hair coloring arrived, it was usually only one color, so many women had the same color hair.

Within China, orders went out in late 1984 from Communist Party officials stating that "Our leading cadres should take the lead to dress more fashionably. We should liberalize our minds a bit, make life more beautiful, and stop viewing fancy clothes as exotic," a reversal from the previous philosophy of drab, baggy uniforms, no-nonsense dressing and the old saying that a person should wear each item of clothing for 9 years—the first 3 years, new, the second 3, old, and the final 3, patched and mended. China is in the process of transforming to a consumer society, anxious to develop and expand its industry. Vice Premier Tian asked, "How are we going to develop our textile industry if everyone keeps wearing the same garment for 9 years?"[8]

In the United States of America, economic position is often displayed by dress. Among some social groups, conspicuous display of rare furs, precious jewels, and

[8] "China Out to Be Consumer Society," *Los Angeles Times*, October 29, 1984, Pt. IV, p. 3.

88

expensive fabrics has always been practiced. Other groups have rejected this form of ostentation by wearing apparel that lacks the traditional symbols of economic abundance. It is probable that this phenomenon could happen only in affluent societies and become fashionable only among those who are financially secure. The 1960s' rebellion against such values as material success, work, status, and grooming was epitomized by the "hippie" lifestyle. The "jeans look" symbolizes this revolution. At that time the more faded, worn, ragged, patched, and body-conforming the jeans, the greater was the status (Figure 4-8).

During the early 1970s many high school and college students' wardrobes of jeans represented reverse snobbism. They paid high prices for recycled, faded, patched, and embellished jeans. A rhinestone-studded jeans outfit sold for as much as $300.00.[9] To meet the volume of the demand for prefaded blue denim, mills in France, England, Yugoslavia, Hong Kong, and the United States all swung into production. The faded, used, worn look was achieved by laundering the indigo-dyed fabric a minimum of four times or until it took on the desired fade. Hang tags noted that any defects in the garments were intentional. For those affecting this recycled style, accessories for the jeans were carefully selected. Among the wealthy, jeans were teamed with the Gucci shoe, a Hermès scarf, a Cardin shirt, and a Vuitton handbag. Covering this ensemble was a fragile suede jacket, which left no doubt about the economic position of the wearer.

[9] *Parade*, July 7, 1974, p. 5.

4-8 *In recent fashion history the more faded, worn, ragged, and patched the greater the status.*

Sportswear, a classification of dress, is an immense industry in the United States, where it was developed, nourished, and finally exported all over the world. Economic conditions were responsible for the development of sportswear. Until the early part of the twentieth century, participation in active sports was a privilege of the wealthy upper class exclusively. Others had neither the leisure time nor the money for such pursuits. As working conditions improved, shorter working hours, education, and economic security became available to a large part of the American population. More and more people had the time, learned the skills, and could afford to participate in sports. As most sports involve special dress, the sportswear industry was born. (Research has revealed that products and services related to sports activities have totaled over $100 billion per year.[10]) Parallel to the development of participant sports apparel was the creation of spectator sports clothing that evolved into the wardrobe of the post-World War II suburban wife, children, and finally, husband. The spectator sports wardrobe now wears the label "sportswear" or "athleisure" and it is the preferred clothing style of many enjoying a casual lifestyle (Figure 4-9).

4-9 *Sports apparel evolved into the wardrobe of the post-World-War-II suburban family. (Courtesy Jantzen)*

[10] "Women's Lob, or Who's Leading the Sporting Life Now," *Clothes, Apparel Statistics* (New York: PRADS, Inc., 1972), p. 25.

Social Status: Identification and Rank

Very often economic condition and social status are bases for clothing selections. We generalize that the wealthy have money and, therefore, have the resources to buy both rank and any wardrobe they choose, whereas graduation of income downward lessens both status and the amount of money available for clothing. Both of these ideas are faulty. In many circles it is impossible to guess financial success or social status by the clothing selected. Sometimes the wealthiest people choose to limit their clothing expenditures and their wardrobes appear very small, even old and eccentric. At the opposite end of the money scale, many desiring to appear prosperous spend the majority of their income on apparel. It has been stated that mass production of clothing has been the common denominator of our society. As the volume of clothing in the marketplace became greater the prices have been lowered and a wider selection of fashionable clothing has been made available to all.

Clothing makes an ideal object for communicating social rank. Clothing is portable, and most forms of dress can be carried by the wearer wherever he goes and be an integral part of his person. Raiment is easily seen. A great variety of differentiation is possible by cut, texture, trim, color, symbols, and surface enrichment. Clothing can be quickly changed or replaced as custom or laws change. It can be mass produced of cheap and easily obtained materials, or it can be exclusive one-of-a-kind made of the most expensive, rare substances. Some of the forms of clothing used to present social rank have been

4-10 *Indentification of rank and status is evident in the dress of a Tswana chief's daughter by the quantity of beads and volume of fabric. (Courtesy South African Tourist Corporation)*

Quantity or volume:	layers of garments, numbers of beads and necklaces, rows of bracelets, both leg and arm (Figure 4-10)
Size or scale:	lengths of sleeve, pants, or trains, large and small headgear, reduction/extension of shoe (Figure 4-11)
Quality:	metals, jewels, fabrics, furs (Figure 4-12) "off the rack" or "custom"
Workmanship:	construction techniques of garments, tattooing or scarification
Color:	the rarest dyes being the most exclusive/laws limiting use to population groups

Sumptuary Laws and Clothing

A study of historical and cultural dress reveals a very interesting aspect of clothing that is related to legal code. Restrictions, called sumptuary laws, have regulated style and personal expenditure of dress in many societies and have perpetuated distinctions in social class. A discussion of these laws in several cultures will help the student understand this influence on self-adornment.

Many examples of sumptuary laws can be found in Western Europe. As the business classes gained wealth they were able to challenge the status of royalty. The bourgeoisie could purchase the opulence of the royal courts. So sumptuary

4-11 *Social status can be expressed by size or scale. Shoes worn by an American woman contrast with the shoes once worn on the bound foot of a Manchu woman. (Courtesy JoAnn Crist)*

laws were enforced. Legal restrictions were placed on individual clothing choices by color, motif, and style that designated rank, class, and position within the society. These laws maintained class distinctions. Fairservis noted that until the end of the nineteenth century styles of the peasant changed slowly, whereas royal dress made vast changes with each century (Figure 4-13).[11]

[11] Fairservis, op. cit., p. 23.

4-12 *The leopard cloak, a royal garment, is worn by a chief of the Southern Sotho of Lesotho (formerly called Basuto). The tall tufted stick is a symbol of rank and authority. Hats also indicate rank or status. The hat of this chief, in matching leopard, is bedecked with plumes. (Courtesy Information Service of South Africa)*

4-13 *Until the end of the 19th century peasant styles of dress changed slowly whereas royal dress made vast changes with each century. (Courtesy Cedok)*

Sumptuary laws have often promoted excesses and exaggerations that are carried to extreme before the style dies. During the early part of the fourteenth century, French court dress was rich and opulent. Footwear was used to show social status. Shoes known as *poulaines* had long pointed toes. Eventually the length of the toe became so extended that Philipe IV decreed that the points for the common people could be no longer than six inches, for the wealthy bourgeoisie, twelve inches, and for the princes and men of rank, twenty-four inches. Such extreme lengths of toes impeded walking so greatly that chains were attached to the point of the shoe and secured to the ankle or the knee.[12]

Sumptuary laws have always chafed the people who had to obey them. Even though these laws were strictly enforced by death or long imprisonment, people found ways to circumvent them. This is one reason why magnificent creative stitchery appears on so many regional peasant costumes. The cut and cloth of these garments were decreed by law; the surface enrichment did not break the law and yet expressed individuality. Other examples can be found in the paintings of the Dutch masters showing wealthy businessmen and their families. The clothing is austere, but marvelously elegant petticoats peep out from under skirts and beautiful ermine and mink pelts adorn capes and tunics.

Sumptuary laws were also part of the many Asian cultures. For more than four thousand years the Chinese had rigid rules that governed the ornamentation of robes indicating both social and political position. The first recorded use of such symbols dates back to 206 B.C.[13]

[12] Mary Evans, *Costume Through the Ages* (Philadelphia: Lippincott, 1950), p. 38.
[13] Edmund Capon, "Chinese Court Robes in the Victoria & Albert Museum," *Victoria & Albert Museum Bulletin Reprint 14* (1970), p. 5.

In the year 1759, the emperor, annoyed with the abuses of dress, drew up a set of regulations for costumes and accessories to be used at ceremonies. These rules affected the emperor, the empress, princes, concubines, nobles, the military, and civil servants. Each member of the hierarchy had robes appropriate to rank. The basic garments were the same, the color and decorative detail determined rank. The emperor's robe was embellished with the twelve imperial symbols including the sun, moon, mountain, ax, water, weed, and flame. Each symbol had a specific position on the robe. The dragon, a benevolent creature, was the chief feature of the robe. The emperor's dragon had five claws and faced front. The robes of nobles of lesser rank had four-clawed dragons that were shown in profile. Civil servants had symbols showing varying ranks that were worn in designated positions on the front and back of the surcoat (Figure 4-14).[14]

Most of the recorded history of Japan includes the use of sumptuary laws. The development of the Japanese *kimono* was completely dominated by these laws. It was the end of the *Tokugawa* period, during the *Tenna* era, that the most extreme sumptuary laws were passed. Two devastating fires, one in Edo, in 1657, and the other in Kyoto, in 1661, destroyed the possessions of most Japanese. To replace the *kimono* lost in these fires, the weavers and dyers were forced to develop quicker and more simple methods. *Kimono* designs became bold, flowing, and abstract. In this period of recovery, the merchants became extremely affluent. Dress became very elaborate as merchants' wives vied with each other for fashion leadership. So keen did the competition become and so extravagant the dress that the merchant class outshone the *Daimyo*. This curious situation prompted *Shogun Tenna* to enforce a series of sumptuary laws that eventually placed all citizens in the most sober attire. Laws controlled wearing apparel as to fabric, color, and decorative design. The *samurai*, all *Noh* dancers (Figure 4-15), artists,

[14] A. C. Scott, *Chinese Costume in Transition* (Singapore: Donald Moore, 1958), pp. 22–28.

4-14 *China 19th-century* K'ossu *Technique. Official rank was denoted by an ornamental badge,* p'u tzu. *The badge on the right was worn on the front opening of the robe and the badge at the left was attached to the back. Designs differed for rank of the civil and military officials. The white crane motif was worn by a first-grade civil servant.*

4-15 *Elaborate costumes of a past age are seen today in the Noh drama of Japan. (Courtesy Japan National Tourist Organization)*

and *Daimyo's* servants as well as the merchants were included in these edicts. The penalty for violation of these laws was usually death. These sumptuary laws brought sweeping change in decoration of the *kimono*. As the price of the *kimono* was controlled, new methods of weaving, dyeing, and decorating had to be developed. The solid embroidery was replaced by appliqué and embroidery was used only as an outline. A stencil painting called *tayu-kanoko* imitated the tied *kanoko* and became the rage. Another substitute, known as *uchidashi-kanoko*, developed a tufted texture. Gradually small motifs were allowed on the *Edo kimono*. The style remained simple and the dyers continued to improve their techniques. The fashions after *Tenna*, which evolved because of his laws, looked very modest but often were really more costly because of the newer decorative techniques.[15]

Although we do not have sumptuary laws as such in the United States, we do cling to certain traditions of dress that show rank or position. In some places a form of prescribed dress occurs.

[15] Helen B. Minnich, *Japanese Costume* (Rutland, Vt.: Tuttle Co., 1963), pp. 191–199.

Throughout our history uniforms have been used to identify the wearers as members of a specially designated group. The user of a uniform substitutes individuality for a type of behavior expected of the group. Uniforms most often identify the position which the wearer holds within the group. In the military, badges and medals distinguish the corporal from the commander. Caps and gowns worn at college graduation ceremonies indicate the academic degree, school, and area of study. Fire and police personnel, food servers, and sports team members among many groups wear uniforms to eliminate confusion when identification is essential.

The business suit is a form of prescribed dress for both men and women. This conservative, traditional attire is preferred by many, so much so that many clothing consultants insist that job promotion is definitely related to compliance with this clothing tradition (Figure 4-16).

School dress codes might, in a way, be considered a form of sumptuary law. These are often imposed when dress behavior results in disruptive conduct. Anti-punk dress codes enforced at a Junior High School in Fontana, California, included a ban on Mohawk haircuts, spiked or colored hair, earrings through the nose, and other punk fashion looks. The ban resulted from incidents in which punks exchanged obscenities and punches with students who were hostile to their appearance.[16]

[16] Bettijane Levine, "From Rags to Riches: Children Shaping Their Own Dress Codes," *Los Angeles Times*, December 1983, Pt. V, p. 1.

4-16 *The business suit is a form of prescribed dress. This traditional attire is preferred by many companies as standard wear. (Courtesy Hartmarx Corporation)*

Among the 6,000 known active neighborhood gangs in south central Los Angeles, two-thirds of them affiliate with one of two sides in their gang wars. These groups are known as the "Bloods" and the "Crips" or "Cuzz." The "Bloods" are identified with the color red, the "Crips" with blue. Members dress in the clothing color of the gang affiliation. Shoelaces, shirts, trousers, headbands, and schoolbook covers in the identifying color visually communicate gang affiliation. Even youths who are not gang members will wear the colors of the group that is dominant in their neighborhood in order to blend in; otherwise, they may be unwittingly inviting a gang attack. When a gang heads for a fight they "dress down" in their gang color, a sign that serious trouble is about to happen.[17]

International Identification by Dress

The practice of identifying nations by dress has been historically a very important one. Wealth and power as well as national characteristics have been displayed with personal adornment. Whereas the clothing of the majority of the world leaders has become increasingly Westernized, the display of wealth and power with clothing continues. When international meetings are held the appearance of the various heads of state and all members of their entourage are duly noted. If the head of state is male, the details, and especially the cost, of the wardrobe of his spouse is of particular interest.

The First Lady of the United States often has a problem with this demand of her station. Each of our First Ladies has handled it differently. Since we are a democracy, it is important for her to dress in a manner that does not set her too far apart from other citizens. On State occasions, it is necessary for her to dress to impress the people of other nations with the wealth and power of the United States of America. The messages sent by the appearance of the President and his spouse are understood the world over. It has been noted that a multithousand dollar gown worn by the First Lady to an official function is more important on the international scene than supplying guests at that function with an itemized printout of intercontinental missiles.

The opening ceremony of the 1984 summer Olympics held in Los Angeles provided a significant display of the character of many nations. Anthropologist John MacAloon remarked that the pageantry represented "ritual performances of the world order." By this he explained that the way athletes conducted themselves during the ceremony was quite significant. Many of the athletes from emerging nations wore formal costumes and marched in solemn ranks. In contrast, the U.S. athletes wore casual warm-up suits, and whimsical sunglasses, and they tossed Frisbies into the crowd. He pointed out that for the smaller nations, participating in the opening ceremonies was of great significance because it demonstrated to the world who was a nation and who was not. The U.S. athletes did not seem to take the ritual so seriously because they were conscious of representing a superpower.[18]

[17] T. W. McGarry, *Los Angeles Times*, October 28, 1984, Pt. II, p. 1.

[18] *Los Angeles Times*, August 5, 1984, Pt. I, p. 18.

Sex Differentiation with Clothing

Sitting on the beach, for example, it is much easier to determine if the figure approaching in the distance is female if she is wearing a swimsuit. If she is nude and really well-tanned, you will figure it out by the motion of her walk before you can confirm it by anatomical sightings.[19]

This quote appeared in the *Los Angeles Times* shortly after an ordinance was presented to allow nude bathing at a beach in Venice, California. The author neatly expressed the dilemma of sex differentiation when clothing clues are absent. Dress is used to identify sex in most societies. True, in some societies the male-female attire appears identical, but close observation will show differences. For example, the sarong, or wrapped skirt, of Indonesia is worn by both male and female. The *kapala* or decorative panel which runs from the waist to the hem of the skirt is the feature that indicates masculinity or femininity. The *kapala* is worn in the front or back of the body, depending upon local custom (Figures 4-17a,b).

In Palestine, around the first century of the Christian era, the robes of the men and women were of the same cut but differed in the application of a band on the lower edge of the garment. The woman's robe had a *gamma* band (L-shaped), whereas the man's garment had a short, notch-shaped band. In the fifth century, this subtle difference went unnoticed by the creators of the magnificent mosaics found portraying biblical figures in the Italian cities of Rome, Naples, and Ravenna. The garments of the mosaic figures of the male show the *gamma* band, the ancient symbol of woman.[20]

In societies where little or no clothing is worn, some form of body adornment serves to distinguish between the sexes. Hairstyles, tattooing, scarification, body painting, and mutilation of ears, nose, or head, along with a wide variety of body jewelry, are used to make the differentiation between men and women.

Renbourn described biblical admonitions regarding the clothing of men and women during the time of Moses:

From the earliest times the Jews had somewhat separate clothing for men and women, although being of a robe-like character, the differences were, from a point of view of design, not well marked. Nevertheless, these differences had to be maintained. In Deuteronomy, Moses insisted: "A woman shall not wear that which pertaineth unto a man; neither shall a man put on a woman's garment, for all that do so are an abomination unto the Lord thy God." This injunction may have been introduced because of the transvestite (sexual exchange of garments) rituals of the Babylonians, Assyrians and even closer neighbors.[21]

Today, many feel as strongly about the sexuality of clothing as Moses did. In each culture this anger is vented against different forms of personal adornment.

---

[19] C. T. Powers, "Anatomy of a Beach Happening," *Los Angeles Times*, July 4, 1974, Pt. IV, p. 4.

[20] Yigael Yadin. *Bar-Kokhba* (London: Weidenfeld and Nicolson, 1971), p. 79.

[21] E. T. Renbourn, *Materials and Clothing in Health and Disease* (London: H. K. Lewis and Co., 1972), p. 515.

4-17a *An Indonesian woman wears a batik sarong in the marketplace. The towel wrapped like a doughnut is worn on the head to support a heavy load. (Courtesy Qantas)*

4-17b *The batik sarong of Java, Indonesia, is worn by both men and women. The decorative panel at the right, called a* kapala, *runs from the waist to the hem. The way the* kapala *is worn gives the garment its masculinity or femininity. The* kapala *is worn in the front or the back of the body depending on local custom.*

In various periods in the United States people have been upset by many forms of dress.

Consider hair. At the turn of the century both men and women wore long hair. The men usually had facial hair in the forms of beards, moustaches, and sideburns; it was considered effeminate not to do so. World War I brought in the Prussian military influence and men cut their hair quite short and shaved their faces. In the period of the 1920s and women's suffrage, women bobbed their hair to show their emancipation. Women's hair was so short that the horrified protested that you could not tell the women from the men. Skirts also got very short during this period. During the 1930s skirts got long, but women's hair stayed short.

The World War II days saw the crew cut and whiskerless face . . . the "clean-cut look." Women began to grow their hair, perhaps as a sign of femininity during that austere time. Post-World War II skirts got long and women's hair was shortened in the form of the "Italian Cut," the "Poodle Cut," and the "Ducktail." High school boys picked up the same hairstyles and "going steady" often meant going to the same barber and wearing the same style as "your girl." Again the cry arose that, you could not tell the he's from the she's. . . .

The 1960s saw hair influenced by "rock and roll" stars led by Elvis Presley and the Beatles. Hippies and flower children grew hair to set themselves apart and display their protest. Parents were horrified to have "sissy" sons with hair longer than their daughters'. It had become increasingly difficult to tell the boys from the girls. The musical/movie *Hair* captured the genesis of the hair-styling phenomena that resulted in the 1970s being labeled "the Hair Generation."

Many young women joined the hair display by growing hair as long as possible. Waist-length hair was the goal and if the hair grew past this magic length it was marvelous. Most simply parted their hair in the center and let it hang. Hand movements and body language involving pushing hair from face became habits. The hair also had to be straight to accommodate this style. Beautiful curls, after

4-18 Custom or tradition establishes the sex of a garment. For centuries men have worn skirts in many parts of the world. An Egyptian male stands before the temples of Karnak near Luxor. (Courtesy Qantas)

4-19 *Tradition determines the sex of a garment. An Arabian man wears a body-enveloping garment that is protective from the blowing desert sands. (Courtesy Department Library Services American Museum of Natural History)*

a long happy reign, were now viewed with disdain. Straightening, or pressing hair (literally with iron and ironing board) became the grooming necessity for those cursed with curls. The older generation was again appalled as faces were obscured by incredible displays of hair.

The 1960s civil rights movement lead by Dr. Martin Luther King inspired the motto "Black is Beautiful." Taking pride in their racial heritage, black men and women styled their hair in "Afros," some of amazing proportions. Interestingly, this is a style not commonly worn in Africa. The first to wear the "Afro" were viewed with apprehension and labeled agitators or revolutionists. But by the late 1970s the "Afro" was commonplace. The frizzy permanent that approximates the "Afro" had been adopted by many nonblacks, and blacks had moved on to "corn-rowing" (a series of French braids done in elaborate geometric patterns over the entire scalp, often enhanced with beads and feathers).

The end of the 1970s saw hair styles greatly modified. Hairstyling was firmly established for both men and women. Extremely long or extremely short hair usually identified the wearer as being out of step with the times, a religious fanatic, or new service recruit. The dramatic play *Zoot Suit*, based on California Mexican racial prejudices of the 1940s, inspired hairstyles of that period. Women cut their hair to resemble the "pachuco."

In the 1980s, sales of hair-care products and services are at an all-time high. Men and women, boys and girls, enjoy their hair and have fun expressing their personal points of view with it. What hairstyles will be next is anyone's guess. What is certain is that what some consider a personal expression of their individuality will upset and anger those who regard it as "an abomination" that "pertaineth" to the opposite sex.

Sex of Garments

Custom or tradition establishes the sex of a garment (Figures 4-18, 4-19, 4-20, 4-21). In the Western world we have learned to think of pants as masculine and skirts as feminine. Why? Distinct dress differences for males and females were based upon role differences. Roach explains this phenomenon:

Traditional roles for men and women in Western society have been largely defined on the basis of life patterns developed in its nonindustrial past when women's energies were directed toward nurturing children they had borne and caring for their homes and men's to sustenance and protection activities requiring considerable physical strength. The dress of each sex tended to be more or less useful in fulfilling these types of roles—at least not so hindering as to prevent role performance.

Once distinctions between the dress of the sexes have existed for a long time, as they have in Western society, their continuation is supported by custom even though the tasks that men and women perform may change. People are simply used to distinctions—they expect men to dress in one way, women in another; they experience shock and social unease if their expectations are not fulfilled. In addition, through time a complex set of meanings becomes attached to the traditional dress of each sex, and sanctions develop that discourage behavior inconsistent with meanings.[22]

[22] Mary Ellen Roach, "The Social Symbolism of Women's Dress," in *The Fabrics of Culture*, Justine Cordwell and Ronald Schwartz, eds., (The Hague: Mouton Publishers, 1979), p. 416.

4-20 *Policemen in Fiji direct traffic in a skirt serrated at the hem. (Courtesy James W. Peters)*

4-21 *Wide, calf-length trousers are part of the traditional dress of the men of Santiago, Atitlán, Solola, Guatemala. (Courtesy Guatemala Tourist Commission, Rodolfo Reves Juárez photo)*

4-22 Amelia Bloomer, among the first women to join the movement to reform dress, wore a trouser costume in the mid-1800's in spite of the ridicule which she had to endure. (Courtesy The Bettmann Archive)

In the nineteenth century women organized several movements for the purpose of reforming dress. They were striking out against dress that made them dependent on men, adorned as a sex object, and subject to health hazards. In 1851 a short dress and trouser costume was introduced by Elizabeth Smith Miller. Amelia Bloomer (Figure 4-22), among others, adopted the costume. Most of the women gave up wearing it after a couple of years as the ridicule was too much for them. Plucky Mrs. Bloomer wore the style six to seven years.[23]

One of the more illustrious pioneers of pant dressing, a U.S. Civil War surgeon and the only woman ever to win the Medal of Honor, was Dr. Mary Walker. Regardless of the harassment she received from General William Tecumseh Sherman, Dr. Walker persisted in wearing trousers through her military career up until the last days of her life, after World War I. As a "preliberationist" (a century before this term was used), she devoted her energies to liberating herself and others "from the bondage of all that is oppressive."[24] Two of her goals were to obtain women's right to vote and achieve dress reform that would do away with constricting and unhygienic clothing. Both of these causes were found in the "Mutual Dress Reform and Equal Rights Society." Much to the ire of her contemporaries, Dr. Walker adopted the straight, tailored, masculine trouser rather than the ankle-length pantaloon of Amelia Bloomer. She was often arrested and made the butt of humorists' writings (Figure 4-23). One labeled her "a self-made man." Her colorful defense included castigating the corset as a "coffin with iron bands" and the hoop skirt as an invention of the prostitutes of Paris.[25]

By 1870, Dr. Walker appeared in topcoat and trousers by day and full male evening dress by night, as she had by then given up female dressing. She wore her hair in curls to keep her female identity. In her later years she found it difficult to earn a living—evidence that she was discriminated against owing to her unusual mode of dress.

In the late nineteenth century, thanks to the accent on health, the gymnasium became popular, and sports involving physical activity demanded unencumbering dress. Amelia Bloomer's bloomers were "waiting in the wings," and they were just the style needed. Popularity of the new invention, the bicycle, made bloomers "respectable." By the 1920s women's dress and women's suffrage had undergone revolutionary changes. In the 1930s Marlene Dietrich scandalized the movie-going public by wearing a man-tailored suit in the film *Morocco*. Slacks soon became respectable for leisure wear. Known as "beach pajamas," this garment was worn at country clubs and boating events and as casual at-home wear. As "Johnny" marched off to World War II, many women marched off to salaried work for the first time. The symbol of this new woman was "Rosie the Riveter." As women filled the wartime needs of industry, they also quite nicely filled out the trousers of the workmen they replaced. Teen-age girls of this time adopted the jeans and dress shirts their fathers, brothers, or boyfriends had shed for a

[23] Ibid., p. 419.
[24] Alison Lockwood, "Pantsuited Pioneer of Women's Lib, Dr. Mary Walker," *Smithsonian Magazine*, March 1977, p. 113.
[25] Ibid., p. 113.

4-23 A pioneer of pant dressing, Dr. Mary Walker devoted her life to dress reform. As a Civil War surgeon she was the only woman to win the Medal of Honor. (Courtesy The Bettmann Archive)

uniform. Pants were then considered appropriate work and play garments for women. They were not, however, considered appropriate for street wear or most social functions. Most schools and colleges banned them from both classroom and campus. Women's pants suits were introduced into European high fashion in the middle of the 1960s. The "hippie" movement found impetus about the same time. Betty Friedan's classic *The Feminine Mystique* also gained status during this period. The result was a revolution in dress and social movement, a part of which is "Women's Lib." Johnston stated,

Of course jeans, T-shirts and knits are not the exclusive property of the woman's movement. They're inseparably part of the larger clothing revolution that has been forced by many social factors. But I do think that changing attitudes towards and by women are what have forced the most dramatic and basic changes in clothes, specifically the coming together of the dress of the sexes . . . and women in pants.[26]

Two factors joined to force the acceptability of pants for American women. The "pants suit," designed with a top or tunic long enough to cover the hip-thigh region, put most women, including "Grandma," into pants. This style, coupled with the complete breakdown of dress traditions caused by the "hippie" rebellion of the 1960s, created a unisex wardrobe of jeans and T-shirts, which was adopted universally by youth and youth-oriented adults. As fashion is a part of social movement, the wearing of pants by women of all walks of life for all kinds of occasions, from marriages to funerals, was interpreted as a push for women's freedom among certain groups of our population. "Women Libbers" chose the panted costume for their "uniform" and used examples of the skirted female throughout history as a symbol of the oppression of their sex.

Developing during this same time was the change in attire for men. The male fashion leaders were the "rock and roll" stars of the 1960s, who dressed flamboyantly. Their young fans adopted these styles and soon men of all ages and socioeconomic levels were caught up in their peacock kaleidoscope of fashion. First came color. The white dress shirt that had been standard for the businessmen who were required to wear a suit and tie to work became colored and patterned. Among the first to wear these shirts were the self-employed, particularly those in artistic fields. Christmas of 1967 was the turning point; many men received a colored shirt as a gift. Only the bravest wore their bright shirts at first, but within two or three months the colored dress shirt had pushed the traditional "white collar" to the back of most closets.

Bell-bottomed trousers came next. As the popularity of jeans for everyone spread, new designs developed. "Hip huggers" and "bell bottoms" were called "low rise" and "flares" and were adapted to the business suit. It is interesting to note that many of these pant styles were worn at first by homosexuals, especially the tight, body-revealing styles. The universal use of body-conforming jeans made tight pants fashionable for all men. Because the close fit of these trousers eliminated pockets, some men began to carry an attaché case, or purse.

[26] Moira Johnston, speech, "Cutting the Corset Strings," 65th Annual Meeting, American Home Economics, Los Angeles, Calif. (June 25, 1974).

Shirts with ruffles, lace and see-through fabrics joined the ethnic Mexican wedding, and African *buba*, to bring shirts of all imaginable styles to male acceptance. The fabrics used for pants included crushed velvets, satins, and suede and leather. The jet-setter and American tourist brought clothing back from the marketplaces of the world. The Black, the Latin, and the Oriental demonstrated pride in their cultural heritages by wearing the costumes of the countries of their ancestry. The *caftan* or *jalapa* have even put some men into skirts. Traditions were broken and for the first time many men felt free to wear the clothing of their choice. They were able to select clothing that was both physically and psychologically comfortable for them as individuals.

Androgynous Dressing

While men's clothing was moving from a very narrow conservative choice to a much wider freedom in color, design and informality, another bastion of nineteenth- and twentieth-century masculinity, the natural face, was quietly being changed. The rock and roll celebrities, led by Elvis Presley, in the late 1950s, began to use eyeliner, mascara, cheek blusher, and lip gloss. David Bowie and Alice Cooper, joined by the thousands of music groups that created the rock videos for MTV continued this practice through the 1960s and '70s. During this time period, the "punkers" appeared in England and their fashion influence moved in many directions to influence dress and adornment. In the early 1980s two male superstars from two very separate directions brought male makeup to an abrupt climax. The two were England's Boy George and America's Michael Jackson. Both wore full makeup on and off stage. Boy George cross-dressed in complete feminine attire. Michael Jackson wore a band uniform type of costume of battle jacket and trousers of brightly colored satins covered with sequins, and one white glove. His facial features, makeup, and hairstyles were feminine in appearance. Young people who were devoted to MTV, its music and these superstars developed a new look and easily adapted the makeup practices to their own faces. By 1984 many young men were wearing facial makeup and feminine-appearing garments.

Fashion writers found a then unfamiliar word to describe the fashion phenomenon . . . *androgynous*. Androgynous is defined as having the characteristics of both male and female. Unisex dressing is as old as the oldest civilization, but the unisex look has most often taken on the appearance of the male attire, for example, jeans and T-shirts. Now there was something new in our culture. Men were dressing like women. Other writers called those devoted to this new style, the third sex, and noted it was their intention to neuter the gender of clothes.

The hot new designer from Paris who brought the androgynous look to high fashion was Jean-Paul Gaultier. He wore a skirt and used male, female, and transexual models dressed in bandeaus and sarongs, earrings and skirted suits. Foremost among Gaultier's beliefs is that men and women can dress alike and still look different. "Masculinity is not a question of a skirt or a trouser," he says. "It is in the head."[27]

[27] "Clashing with Convention," *Newsweek*, October 29, 1984, p. 136.

Dr. Gregory W. Brock, of the United States International University, San Diego, California, observed:

Society's acceptance of androgyny is a positive cultural development and unless the way girls are brought up is changed, they may not grow up to be as creative in sex roles as the boys. Our future survival depends on our creativity. As our culture evolves, and we become a more service-oriented society, the question of sex roles will become more and more irrelevant. I think androgyny is very positive. We're going to need more deviation from the two-sex role scheme if our culture is to survive.

He continued:

Parents fear the notion of androgyny because they see it as a unification of the male and female sex roles. It's actually the possibility of both sexes choosing from many roles.

Is androgyny really the harbinger of the future of dress? Will men wear skirts as commonly as women currently wear pants? Will as many men as women wear makeup daily or for special occasions? Only the future will tell.

We do know that this is a very fundamental change in our cultural tradition and formula for dress patterns. We can predict that for men to wear skirts and elaborate makeup, the mores of our society will not change quickly. Much pressure will be exerted to discourage this radical change in attire. The men who adopt androgynous dress in the feminine extreme will be subject to sanctions comparable to those suffered by the women who pioneered male attire for women. Our society will struggle to preserve its cultural dress traditions.

As we approach the year 2000, and the twenty-first century, perhaps cultural upheaval is necessary to the survival of our society. Perhaps the westernization of dress of the twentieth century will be replaced by androgynous dress which allows the talents of all people to be utilized to the maximum, and never again will our society know the discriminization of a talent such as Dr. Mary Walker's because of clothing preferences.

Age Differentiation

Certain customs are observed for the sake of fashion, beauty, status, religion, or lifestyle that change the human form. These changes involve, at the minimum, inconvenience and discomfort, and at the maximum, mutilation and continuing pain.

Many of these changes begin with ceremonies to mark the transition from childhood into adulthood. Commonly known as puberty rites, these traditions often involve body alteration such as tooth removal, tooth filing, scarification, or tattooing. Included also is revealing or draping the body with clothing and changing the appearance of the head and face with ornamentation or hair arrangement (Figure 4-24). For those outside of a particular culture, it is difficult to appreciate and understand how certain practices evolved. One wonders whether the people affected have ever rebelled against these practices or if they have willingly accepted them with pride in what tradition has destined for them. Role

4-24 *When a young Zulu woman is ready for marriage the sign is a decorated hair style. Head bands are worn to show respect for the father-in-law. Beadworked rectangles, which hang from the neck, are ornaments indicating an engagement. The color and pattern of the beads have meaning and express the girls' wishes. These ornamented pieces are similar to love letters. (Courtesy South African Tourist Corporation)*

expectations for both sexes have been involved with "coming of age" rites. Usually the male was expected to demonstrate extreme physical strength and endure suffering to prove his manhood. Women, too, have had their share of pain during these rites.

Chinese Foot-binding

Foot-binding of China began in the 10th century and was practiced into the 20th. Try to comprehend these rituals:

These are the words of a Chinese woman at the end of the nineteenth century talking about having her feet bound, a practice that usually started at the age of five.

When I was nine they started to bind my feet again. My feet hurt so much that for two years I had to crawl on my hands and knees. Sometimes at night they hurt so much I couldn't sleep, and I stuck them under my mother so that they hurt less. By the time I was thirteen, they were finished. The toes were turned under so that I could see them on the inner and under side of the foot. Two fingers could be inserted in the cleft between the front of the foot and the heel. My feet were very small indeed.[28]

[28] Moira Johnston, speech, "Cutting the Corset Strings," 65th Annual Meeting, American Home Economics, Los Angeles, Calif. (June 25, 1974).

Towl elaborated on this custom in her article, "The Golden Lotuses of China," by stating that folklore attributes this custom to court dancers, whose small feet were admired by all. At the beginning, only the court ladies and the upper classes adopted this status symbol that impeded walking. These ladies could afford to be carried in their sedan chairs and supported by servants whenever they moved about. In A.D. 1130, the scholar *Chang Pang-Chi* recorded that bound feet were not uncommon. The conservative *Sung* Dynasty with its puritanical values encouraged the spread of this practice as it kept women in their "proper place." In the twelfth century, the governor of the *Fukien* province required all women of nobility to bind their feet so tightly that they would have to walk with a cane.[29]

Scott, in *Chinese Costume in Transition*, pointed out that

Formerly, Chinese women were expected to remain inconspicuous in their homes and devote their lives acquiring knowledge suitable for their duties as wife and mother. They were not supposed to be seen in public, mingle in common society or take part in outside affairs of any description. Women's dress of the period symbolized this social background to a great extent, the long gowns and robes which exposed no part of the body, and the bound feet were indicative of those who led a secluded life both mentally and physically and who took no part in the world beyond their own threshold.[30]

Another factor responsible for the continuation and popularity of the three- to four-inch foot fetish related to the marriageability of the young girl. During the bargaining procedure, a dainty, embroidered slipper was presented to the prospective groom. To arrange a "good" marriage, a small-footed bride was essential.

In the thirteenth century, the Mongol conquerors of China encouraged the practice of foot-binding as they believed that the crippled woman would produce a weakened Chinese race, one that would be easier to handle. The Chinese continued to promote the ritual as they felt it separated them from their barbarian invaders.

The custom of foot-binding was such an important part of the Chinese culture that it was very difficult to terminate. The *Manchu* ruler in the *Ching* Dynasty issued royal edicts to stop foot-binding. They were unsuccessful. It was not until 1911, and the establishment of the Republic of China, that foot-binding was outlawed. However, it was practiced as late as 1935 (Figure 4-25).[31] In 1974, Americans living in Taiwan, Republic of China, reported seeing several old women with bound feet. The ladies, who were very petite in stature and obviously wealthy, were observed around the temples. They were surrounded by younger women, appearing to be relatives and servants, who supported them. The old women wore elaborate embroidered shoes measuring three to four inches in length. They were pleased to pose for pictures and seemed to enjoy the attention their bound feet brought them.[32]

[29] Diane Grady Towl, "The Golden Lotuses of China," *Echo Magazine*, December 1973, pp. 25–28.

[30] Scott, op. cit., p. 77.

[31] Towl, op. cit., p. 57.

[32] Statement by Mr. and Mrs. Newt Le Baron, Personal Interview, Pasadena, Calif., July 1974.

4-25 *Although footbinding was outlawed in 1911, it was practiced as late as 1935. Visitors to China today will see some old women with bound feet. (Courtesy JoAnn Crist)*

Samoan Tattooing Ritual

A very elaborate and festive coming-of-age ceremony takes place in Samoa when the young are initiated into manhood at a tattooing ritual. If a chief's son is to be tattooed, it is an especially important occasion. Other boys, who are about eighteen years old, can be tattooed at the same time, saving individual families expense, as the chief pays for the whole production.

The eldest son of a Samoan chief gave this description of the ordeal of tattooing:

A great feast is prepared, a special house is erected and the artists are called in. The normal time allotted for the tattooing is about a week. If a boy thought that he could endure the pain, the whole operation might take place in one day, but due to a great amount of blood loss and the possibility of serious infection this was not common.

In Samoa, the tattoo distinguishes rank. The greater the rank the more numerous the tattoos. Thus, the District Chief has the most, followed by the County Chief and lastly, the village chief.

The dye is made from the oily soot collected from burned "lama" nuts (*Aleurites moluccana*). This is mixed with water. The first design, an outrigger, is sketched on the back, just above the waist. (The outrigger symbolizes their ancestors who arrived in Samoa by this boat.) The tattooing is done with an instrument made from pigs' teeth which are needle sharp, tied to a stick. The teeth are dipped into the dye, the instrument is placed on the skin, and the end of it is struck with a mallet to force it beneath the surface of the skin in order to produce the design.

During this entire process a woman sings to the boys "to keep them from crying." The males are tattooed from their calves to their navel and, depending upon their rank, the upper parts of their bodies.[33]

[33] Statement by Tusiitoga Ta'ase Mamea, Sr., Personal Interview by Mary Archibald, Long Beach, Calif., May 12, 1974.

4-26 *Tattoo of the Nukahiwa. In a society where little clothing is worn people may adorn their skin with tattooing if the skin tone is light enough. Where tattooing is not visible, scarification is used. (Courtesy Department Library Services American Museum of Natural History)*

Mead says that women are tattooed lightly on their arms, legs, and the area above the groin. Tattooing for females does not have the significance it has for the males as the women would not be barred from any activity if they were not tattooed. Men, on the other hand, if not tattooed would be segregated in a society of untitled men. They would not be allowed to make *kava* or *tafolo*, the sacred drinks.[34]

It is interesting to note that many of the designs on *tapa* cloth[35] are the same as those found in tattoos. The majority are of geometric motifs (Figure 4-26).

Coming of Age in—

In New Guinea, along the Sepik River, a ritual is performed to cast out from the male the inferior "mother blood." The village elders cut the adolescent boy's skin in many tiny slashes and rub ash and oil into the wound so that permanent welts are formed. This ceremony is a focal point in the religious and social life of the village.[36]

---

[34] Margaret Mead, *An Inquiry into the Question of Stability in Polynesia* (New York: A.M.S. Press, 1969), pp. 78–79.

[35] Tapa cloth is made from the bark of trees, most often the mulberry tree.

[36] Malcolm S. Kirk, "Change Ripples New Guinea's Sepik River," *National Geographic*, September 1973, p. 359.

110

The Cuna Indians of the San Blas Islands, Panama, mark the adolescent girl's womanhood with a ceremony that includes cutting the hair. The long tresses are removed and the hair is never allowed to grow long again.

Among Southeast Asian areas, including Bali, a tooth-filing practice defines age. Tooth filing is performed in order to ward off the six evil qualities of human nature: laziness, indifference, indecisiveness, love of worldly goods, sexual pleasure, and love of luxury and splendor.

In Japan the color of the *kimono* is used to show age. Young children and marriageable young women wear brightly colored and gaily patterned *kimonos*. Dark *kimonos* of a solid color are for the mature, including married women (Figure 4-27).

In the United States in the past, a dress ritual marked adulthood for both boys and girls. Young ladies knotted their hair up on their heads and lengthened their skirts. Boys graduated from short pants to knickers and finally to full-length trousers. These practices have been abandoned by fashion. At present, the clothing of young and old is very much alike. Currently such events as high school proms, graduations, fraternity and sorority installations, military inductions, Bar Mitzvahs, and religious confirmations require a change of dress. Although such ceremonies are often of short duration, they do mark growing up.

4-27 In Japan the young women wear bright, colorful, patterned kimonos *while the mature and married women wear solid colors in dark shades. The manner in which the* obi *is tied also indicates marital status. (Courtesy Japan National Tourist Organization)*

Marital Status

Visible means of recognizing marital status is a common practice among many different cultures. Hair arrangements have often been used for this purpose. Among the Hopi Indians the young unmarried girls wore their hair in large spirals on either side of their head as a symbol of the immature squash blossom (Figure 4-28). After marriage, the hairstyle was changed to two long braids worn down the back. The braids were symbolic of the mature squash vine.[37]

Traditional Japanese hairstyling was stiffened into sculptured shapes with camellia oil. Unmarried girls wore one large puff in front and a smaller one behind, whereas married women wore just one puff placed on top of the head (Figure 4-29 a,b).

To mark a change of staus, widows in Cambodia have traditionally worn white garments and shaved the hair on their heads. Similarly, in the past, women who entered Catholic convents had their hair cut very short or shaved as a symbol of shedding the vanities of this world to become a bride of Christ.

Clothing is used to indicate marital status. In Japan, the *kimono* is held together with an *obi*. The *obi* is a band of decorated cloth about five yards long and a foot wide. The way the *obi* is tied explains the wearer's marital state. On her wedding day the bride wears the *obi* tied in a butterfly bow straight across the back or at an angle as young girls do. As a married woman, she ties her *obi* in a flat knot across the back. The sleeve of the *kimono*[38] is also used to show marital state.

4-28 *The young Hopi Indian girls wear their hair in large spirals on either side of their head. These represent the immature squash blossom. (Courtesy Department Library Services American Museum of Natural History)*

[37] Jack Conrad, *The Many Worlds of Man* (New York: Crowell, Apollo ed., 1964), p. 117.
[38] The term *kimono* as used in Japan means clothing, not a particular article of dress.

4-29a *Traditional Japanese hair styling stiffened into sculptured shapes with camellia oil. (Courtesy Japan National Tourist Organization)*

4-29b *A Japanese beauty salon creates traditional hair styles which indicate marital status. (Courtesy Japan National Tourist Organization)*

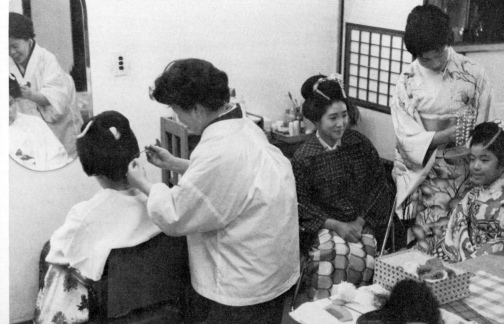

4-30 *Portions of two cloths made by the warp ikat technique in Sumba, Indonesia. Intricate motifs are dyed into the warp yarns before weaving. An offer of marriage is accompanied by a gift of an ikat weaving.*

Young girls wear a *kimono* having long swinging sleeves. The married woman's *kimono* is called the *kosode* and has a small short sleeve.

Exchange of clothing or jewelry is often a part of marriage ceremonies. Sometimes this includes the giving of women's garments to men for the purposes of wearing them ceremonially. The Masai warrior of Kenya wears the clothing of the bride and carries a distaff[39] instead of a spear. Renbourn said of this custom:

Although the disguise may primarily have represented a protection of the man against magic, it apparently later became rationalized into the symbolic possession of the woman by her man.[40]

In Sumba, an island in the Sunda Straits east of Bali, textiles play an important part in the marriage contract. This area is noted for *warp ikats* of astounding beauty. These cloths are distinguished by their design arrangement of horizontal bands running the length of the cloth. Intricate motifs connected with ancestor worship feature human forms, animals, and florals that are dyed into the yarns before weaving (Figure 4-30). The offer of marriage is made to the bride's family

[39] Distaff is a staff with a cleft end for holding wool from which the thread is drawn in spinning by hand. This use of a distaff exhibits complete role reversal by the warrior.
[40] Renbourn, op. cit., p. 481.

113

4-31 *The Ndebele women of the Transvaal Veld shave their heads completely to represent the beginning of a new venture—marriage. The woman wears a symbol of married women, the* mapoto, *an apron of goatskin covered with beads. (Courtesy South African Tourist Corporation)*

accompanied by a gift of an *ikat* weaving and a woman's skirt. This is equal to a marriage contract.[41]

Rings are popular in many cultures as symbols of marriage. The placement of the ring varies. For some the rings are worn on the right hand and some the left. Various fingers are also used. Sometimes the ring is placed in the nose and sometimes even on the toes. In some cultures bracelets worn on the arms and ankles also take on this symbolism (Figure 4-31).

Political Beliefs

Political causes have been supported and suppressed by dress. During the Roman Empire the "Phrygian" style cap was worn by slaves who were given their freedom. This same cap was worn by the French Revolutionists and the American Revolutionists as a symbol of freedom. In the American Revolution it was known as the liberty cap. Perhaps the most famous political garment was the *sans-culotte*, which became the battle cry of the French Revolution of 1789. *Sans-culottes* were the rough trousers worn at that time by French farmers and sailors that were adopted by shopkeepers and laborers as a visible symbol of the Revolution. When the Revolutionists stormed the gates of the Versailles Palace demanding *Liberté, Egalité, Fraternité,* they were wearing *sans-culottes.* The aristocrats inside the palace were dressed in their elegant brocades, hose, and em-

[41] M. Adams, *System and Meaning in East Sumba Textile Design* (New Haven: Yale University, 1969, Southeast Asia Studies, Cultural Report Series No. 16).

114

broidered breeches called *culotte dorée*, which translates, gilded or golden breeches. As the revolution continued, anyone dressed in the finery of an aristocrat was in danger of death by *guillotine*. Soon peasant and aristocrat alike wore the *sans-culotte*. The use of this garment continued for all after the revolution and became the symbol of equality.[42]

In 1745, the Battle of Culloden Moor took place between the Hanovers, who were in control of the British throne, and the Scots, supporters of the Stuarts. The Scots were badly defeated and lost their claim to the British throne. In an effort to destroy the spirit and political ambitions of the Scots, the British passed a series of Acts in 1746, which forbade the Scots to wear their national costume, including the *tartan*. Contrary to the intent, the prohibition united the clansmen more solidly. The *tartan*, symbol of national pride, was credited as the unifying force. Men defiantly wore both a kilt and shawl of their clan *tartan*. Women wore a shawl.[43]

In Gambia, Africa, before an election, fabric imprinted with the faces of the political candidates is sold. The Gambian women create garments from this cloth and thus become walking billboards advertising their political choice. Harrington quoted a local Gambian shopkeeper who considered his political-motived fabric educational. He said

Most Gambians are illiterate. But they recognize a picture and are drawn closer to their leaders and name spellings. The same when flags are on dresses and maps and slogans.[44]

Examples can also be cited in Cuba, in the Peoples' Republic of China, and Germany during the Nazi regime, where the clothing of the people, particularly the young, has been controlled by the political leaders. This technique is one that has proven useful in controlling a population and in enforcing a political doctrine, by rewarding those who are most supportive to the government with badges, symbols, and uniforms.

In the United States, particularly during election campaigns, supporters wear buttons, badges, or hats proclaiming their party or candidate. More frequently, T-shirts are used to exhibit personal causes, including political opinions.[45]

Religious Ideas

Clothing and religion have been intertwined throughout history. Many examples of clothing rules and regulations are available in the wide range of religious practices from ancient to current times. In a walk across a large, metropolitan city or college campus the dress requirements of several religious sects may be observed. The special qualities of clothing, such as identification, sim-

[42] Christie Harris and Moira Johnston, *Figleafing Through History* (New York: Atheneum, 1971), p. 206.
[43] John Teller Dunbar, *History of Highland Dress* (Edinburgh: Oliver and Boyd, 1962), p. 3.
[44] Richard Harrington, *Parade*, September 19, 1966, p. 14.
[45] "The American T Party," *Time*, September 16, 1974, p. 72.

4-32 *Amritsar, India. The faithful Sikh abstains all his life from cutting his hair. (Courtesy John J. Shaak)*

4-33 *An orthodox Sikh of India wears a* kara, *a metal bangle. (Courtesy John J. Shaak)*

plicity, propriety, reserve, and adornment, contribute the enduring relationship between clothing and religions.

Tenets of the Islamic faith prohibit the wearing of garments of pure silk. However, weaving of silk combined with cotton creates a fabric that is allowed to be worn. Followers can accept this compromise with reality while still adhering to the letter of the law.

The faithful orthodox Sikh of India proclaims belief in his religion by observing the five K's or kakkars:[46]

1. kesh—uncut hair. He abstains for life from cutting his hair and beard. A 15-foot coiled and pleated turban covers his head, and a fine mesh net encases his beard (Figure 4-32).
2. kachh—short pants.
3. kara—metal; bangle worn on his wrist (Figure 4-33).
4. kanga—a wooden comb.
5. kirpan—an iron-handled knife around which the hair is rolled.

[46] Sir Arthur C. Lothian, *A Handbook to India and Pakistan, Burma and Ceylon* (London: J. Murray, 1959), p. xivii.

116

The East Indian woman is adorned with a red or saffron *tika* mark on her forehead to show that she has made her offering at the temple. The *tika* symbol is of *Hindu* origin. It has now become fashionable for the non-*Hindu* East Indian also to wear a *tika*. The ultramodern East Indian girl has replaced the traditional *tika* with a sequin to match the color of her *sari*.

In some of the Islamic countries, women wear a veil that covers them from head to toe when they leave their homes. The wearing of this veil, or *burka* as it is known in Pakistan, is a condition known as being in *purdah* (Figures 4-34, 4-35, 4-36). In Chad, the Muslim women are covered even more completely; they may expose only one hand and one eye. Saudi Arabian women follow rigid practices in covering their bodies. The Moslem women of Indonesia, Malaysia and Egypt do not wear such a garment. The holy book of the Moslems, the Koran, does not spell out rigid rules pertaining to body covering. It does not instruct women to veil their faces; rather, the Koran provides guidance by these words:

> Say to the believing men that they should lower their gaze and guard their modesty: that will make for greater purity for them. And say to the believing women that they should lower their gaze and guard their modesty; that they should not display their beauty and ornaments except what must ordinarily appear thereof; that they should draw their veils over their bosoms.[47]

Thus each country interprets this guidance according to its tradition. Societies with a tradition of rigid male domination interpreted the Koran in a strict sense, while others were more tolerant.

[47] Quaran, sura (Chapter) 24, aya (verse) 30.

4-34 *In some Moslem countries women wear a garment which shields them from the eyes of others. The bright red-orange silk garment of Afghanistan has tiny knife pleats. A fine mesh grille permits the wearer to see her way.*

4-35 *Tangier, Morocco. Moslem women wear a veil around the head and another below the eyes as a shield from the sight of others. (Courtesy James W. Peters)*

4-36 *The Saudi Arabian woman keeps her face as well as her body covered while shopping in the market. (Courtesy Karl G. Kessler)*

The custom of enveloping women in a veil actually began before Islam. Ancient Persians wore such a garment. Traditionally it was worn by Moslem women in Arab and Eastern countries although Christians, Jews, Hindus, have worn the garment without the face veil.[48]

The reverse of this practice of covering the body is found among some of the Algerian Muslims. The Tuareg male of Algeria wears the veil while his wife goes unveiled. This male veil is not removed for any purpose, even eating or drinking.

In a small mountain village in eastern Bali, a very complex type of woven cloth is attributed magical powers. It is the *grinsing*, which translates "freedom from illness." The cloth is created by the *ikat* method. Designs of human figures are arranged to indicate sex, marital status, and other social designations of the wearer. The design is formed by resist dye methods. The unwoven yarns of both the warp and the weft are tied off in desired patterns and then dyed. So complex is this process that the dyeing alone takes six years. The work on the *grinsing* is begun on a date established by a priest. The *grinsing* is worn by all men and women for religious ceremonies (Figures 4-37a,b,c,d).

Holy men of many faiths are distinguished by their dress. The *sadhus* of India are wandering holy men who devote their entire life to meditation. Their naked bodies bear a minimum of clothing to show their ascetic condition. On their foreheads lines of colored ashes indicate the signs of the Hindu deities.

The saffron-robed monks of the Buddhist faith do not blend in with the dress of the Buddhist followers. Their specially draped garment of an intense yellow-orange color sets them apart from the masses (Figure 4-38).

In the United States many religions are identified by dress. The *Rama Krishna* groups have adopted a yellow robe similar to that of the Buddhist monk. Their heads are shaved except for the crown hair that is braided into a long queue. The *Amish* cling to a farm dress that was popular in the days of "Tom Sawyer." The men wear work clothes or black suits, black felt hats; their faces are bearded. The women wear somber-colored, body-concealing dresses that cover both arms and legs; sunbonnets often cover their heads. Their children are dressed in a manner similar to that of the adults. The people of this faith avoid such modern devices as buttons and zippers. They prefer horse-drawn vehicles to motorized ones.

The clothing of Catholic nuns has gone through a period of change and transition. Some nuns are identified by the traditional medieval habit, another member of the same order may be dressed very fashionably. A third member of the order may be dressed in a combination of traditional and modern, head veiled, somber-colored midcalf-length skirt, and a large visible crucifix. Catholic priests generally wear the Roman collar and dark suit that makes them easy to identify. For services, they wear the garment style used by the laymen of the Roman Empire, not the dress of biblical priests as is often believed.[49]

[48] Doreen Yarwood, *The Encyclopedia of World Costume* (New York: Scribner, 1978), p. 73.
[49] Renbourn, op. cit., p. 233.

4-37a *Front view of the* grinsing *as worn by a young woman and her brother at* Tenganan, Bali.

4-37b *Back view showing* kris, *a sacred knife worn in the back waistline. The male wears his* grinsing *over a batik sarong.*

4-37c *A simple back-strap type of loom is used to weave the* grinsing.

4-37d *Tenganan Bali, Indonesia. A Balinese woman holds a portion of the* grinsing *(freedom from illness), a double ikat cloth, showing the design motif (note the two figures in each design unit).*

4-38 The saffron-robed monk of Thailand wears a garment that sets himself apart from his fellowman.

Technical Changes and Industrialization

In a technical and highly industrial society, clothing styles change rapidly. This has been true in the United States. The earliest settlers were farmers who were often able to produce a surplus of their crops that could be marketed. Cotton was one of these crops. (George Washington grew it on his Virginia plantation.) To process the cotton, textile mills were built. The mills produced great amounts of fabric. Factories to mass produce clothing followed. The United States has been in the clothing business since this early period. To keep this industry growing, changes of fashion have been important.

A study of the history of dress in the United States reveals continued changes in styles. (For example, note the Tournament of Roses section in Chapter 5.) Technical advancement and vast industrialization and merchandising have created the tremendous clothing industry in this country. To support this giant, changes of styles and planned obsolescence are necessary. Nontechnical, nonindustrial, and tradition-bound societies show few style changes in dress over the years. Countries such as India, Ceylon, Bhutan, and Burma have clung to their own patterns of dress for centuries (Figure 4-39 a,b,c,d).

4-39a *Nonindustrial, nontechnical, and tradition-bound societies show few style changes in dress over the years.(Courtesy Heidi Kessler)*

4-39b *In nontechnical, agrarian, and tradition-bound societies, little change in style of dress has taken place over the centuries. The usual everyday dress of a woman living in Nepal. Garments similar to this are also worn by the women of Sikkim and Tibet. (Courtesy John J. Shaak)*

4-39c,d *These photographs of Korean women were taken thirty years apart. Subtle style differences have taken place over the years. However, the basic garment has changed little. Sleeve fullness, skirt length and fullness, tie length, and jacket length show change. (Courtesy (left) W. Stanley Larsen, (right) Korea National Tourism Corp.)*

121

4-40a,b,c *Economic and technical growth brings about changes in clothing patterns. Western styles have made an impact on these young boys in Saudi Arabia, whereas their grandfathers hold to traditional dress. (Courtesy Karl G. Kessler)*

As societies become technically oriented, style changes become frequent. Fashions are adopted and discarded following patterns of economic and technical growth. Western styles have made an impact. Increased communications, travel, films, television, and foreign student exchange have affected dress patterns that have been relatively stable for so long (Figure 4-40 a,b,c). The dress of the Punjab area (and worn elsewhere) is the *shalwar-kameez*. The *shalwar* is a long pant full in the leg and tight at the ankle. The *kameez* is, by tradition, a long, loose blouse

4-41 *The Indian* sari *was traditionally wrapped to conceal the body. These women from southern India make their living from reeling silk from the cocoons. (Courtesy Josephine Schultz)*

ending at the knee area. The changes that have taken place in the pant show Western influence. This garment has been styled into full, narrow, and straight-legged pants that have followed Western pants fashions.

The traditional *sari* (Figure 4-41), a draped garment that was traditionally wrapped to conceal the body, has undergone changes that now reveal the body. It is worn wrapped low over the hip leaving a broad bare expanse to the blouse, which ends just below the bust. These *saris* are aptly called "hipsters." Blue jeans are also being worn by the East Indian *avant garde* youth of both sexes.

It is sometimes humorous to find a product of a technical society put to use by a nontechnical society in an unusual manner. Such was observed in August 1973 at the "sing-sing" of the stone-age tribe living in the Wahgi Valley, New Guinea (Figure 4-42). The Papuan warriors were dressed in feathered headdresses made from the Bird of Paradise and smeared with protective pig fat. The big bone that traditionally extended through their noses was replaced with ballpoint pen casings.[50]

[50] "Stone-Age Papuan Warriors Compete in Primitive Festival," *Los Angeles Times*, August 5, 1973, Pt. I, p. 1.

4-42 *Bird of Paradise headdress as worn in the Western Highlands of New Guinea. (Courtesy Qantas)*

Similarly, Masai tribesmen of Kenya have been seen with packages of cigarettes or beer cans extended in their punctured ear lobes. The beer can replaced the customary beaded finery. Perhaps they found the cans more of an individualistic expression.

Japan, a nation which has become highly technical, industrialized, and affluent, provides a study in change of clothing patterns. The traditional Japanese *kimono* is centuries old. It is a very practical and very beautiful garment. It can be worn by either sex. All body sizes and shapes can be accommodated. It is easily stored and maintained and it is almost ageless. It can be adjusted to be warm or cool. It is physically comfortable both for touch and movement. It can be very simple in fabric and surface enrichment, or extremely ornate. The garment price can range from inexpensive to costly.

The Japanese were first introduced to Western dress in the early 1600s by the Dutch, who were allowed to establish a trading post at Hirado near Nagasaki. Early fascination with this new form of costume is reflected in Japanese art of that period.[51] By the early 1900s a very serious movement to adopt Western dress in Japan was made by the military and business communities. Many problems

[51] Bradley Smith, *Japan History in Art* (Garden City, N.Y.: A Gemini-Smith Book published by Doubleday, 1964), pp. 194–200.

124

were involved in this change. The Japanese had to learn to wear tightly fitted garments made of heavy fabrics. These garments were subject to rapid changes of style because of the fashion decrees of the Western world. Although the Western dress allowed the Japanese who traveled abroad to adapt himself to Western ways, the garments did not lend themselves to Japanese architecture and furniture. The most graceful Japanese found such Japanese customs as kneeling, floor sitting, and shoe removal all awkward in Western dress.[52]

In spite of the reasons one can advance for the Japanese *not* adopting Western dress, the desire to be part of the sophisticated community of industrial nations appears to have triumphed. Isao Nakauchi, president of the Dai'ei, Inc., Japan's largest retailing operation, reports that clothing in Tokyo is now 90 per cent Westernized. He stated that although most of this clothing is produced in Japan, most of the designs are French.

The Japanese also seem to be in the process of recapturing their heritage. In 1972, a renewed interest in the *kimono* was noted. Sales increased 40 per cent over the previous year. This boom skyrocketed the price of raw silk so greatly that the government shut down the raw silk exchange for two weeks. Prices for the raw material were inflated from $7.50 to $26 per pound. This renewal of interest brought about another problem. Many women did not know how to wear the *kimono*. Because of the chaos of World War II, several generations of Japanese women previously did not have the time, the money, or the lifestyle required by the *kimono*.

In 1973, over one thousand schools opened in Japan to teach the art of wearing the *kimono*. The course takes four months and at a cost of $20 to $30 teaches the arts and skills necessary to wear the *kimono* and wrap the *obi*. Use of this traditional dress is now most often confined to ceremonial or festive wear. The renewed interest, especially by the young, reflects an awareness of their rich cultural traditions of the past.[53]

Aesthetic Patterns

Ideals of beauty are part of each culture. We learn what is considered beautiful in our society. Because ideals of beauty differ with each group, it is sometimes difficult to appreciate the art forms of another culture. The standards for judging what is beautiful vary as widely as the geographic locations of the different societies. The customs of body covering and adornment reflect the vast array of that which is considered aesthetic. To illustrate this point, let us create an imaginary international beauty contest. Each contestant will display the ideals of beauty of her own society that exist today or in the past. (These are cultural ideals of beauty. Many of the costumes worn are not commonly seen today.) It must be pointed out that our contest would be impossible to rate because judges could not avoid making decisions in terms of their own cultural standards of

[52] Bernard Rudofsky, *The Unfashionable Human Body* (New York: Doubleday, 1971), pp. 193–195.
[53] "Japanese Maidens Go to School to Learn How to Wear a Kimono," *Los Angeles Times*, June 6, 1973, Pt. VI, p. 8.

4-43 *San Blas Islands, Panama. Under the elaborate necklace the Cuna women wear a* Mola, *a blouse featuring appliqué and reverse appliqué. (Courtesy Panama Government Tourist Bureau)*

beauty. Our purpose is to show the wide differences in what is considered beautiful and to illustrate that there is no *right way* for all people to be beautiful.[54]

The first contestant is Ms. Jivaro of the primitive tribe of the same name. Because she is of marriageable age, she has a lip plug of cane inserted in a hole just below the lower lip. Her gown is formed of a simple rectangle of woven cloth that is wrapped around her body under the left arm and two corners fastened with a wooden pin on the right shoulder. Both arms and the left shoulder are bare. Her waist is defined by a belt that hangs down below the knee.[55]

Next, Ms. Cuna, from the San Blas Islands, Panama. She is dressed in the distinctive *mola*, an elaborate blouse displaying the finest handwork. Motifs on the blouse are created by appliqué and reverse appliqué of numbers and letters representing her primary education. She wears gold nose ring, ear plates, necklaces, and arm and leg bracelets (Figure 4-43). Her short hair is covered with a headscarf. She is one of the most petite contestants: she stands only 4'8", the average height of women on her island.[56]

---

[54] The authors found this idea suggested by Henry Pratt Fairchild in his *Race & Nationality* but have substituted their own contestants. Henry Pratt Fairchild, *Race & Nationality* (New York: Ronald, 1947), p. 89.

[55] Edward Weyer, Jr., *Primitive Peoples Today* (New York: Dolphin Books, 1961), p. 103.

[56] Ibid., p. 90.

Ms. Lolo has had the most difficult journey to our contest. Her home is in the mountainous region in the Western part of China betwen Mongolia, Tibet, Burma, and Thailand. She had to cover the first part of her trip on foot down narrow mountain trails because there are no roads. Her robe is of dark brown wool and is fastened with a silver brooch. Her giant headdress is outstanding. It contains one hundred feet of cloth and weighs over six pounds. Her ears are hung with over a dozen fine chains. She occasionally puffs on her five-foot pipe.[57]

Ms. Hottentot is the next entry (Figure 4-44). She won the right to represent her South African area in a regional contest in which the beauties were lined up, and judged by the most protruding buttocks. This strategically located cushion of fat is steatopygia, or the overdevelopment of the subcutaneous fat that covers a woman's hind parts and upper thighs. Both the Hottentots and Bushmen find this physically more attractive than the prominently cantilevered bosom of Western cultures.[58,59]

The contestants are moving quite quickly. Miss Namba, from New Hebrides, is wearing a wig of purple-dyed pandamus leaves. Her broad smile reveals that she is a woman of status by the absence of her two front teeth.

From northern Japan, representing an ancient Caucasoid tribe, is Mrs. Ainu. Her mouth tattoo was started by her family in her childhood and completed after marriage by her husband. The area around her lips is encircled in a smoky-colored hue (Figures 4-45, 4-46).

4-44 *Hottentots and Bushmen find overdevelopment of buttocks and thighs attractive in their women.*

[57] Ibid., p. 211.
[58] Ibid., p. 99.
[59] Carleton S. Coon, *The Living Races of Man* (New York: Knopf, n.d.), pp. 113–114.

4-45 *Chief of an Ainu village and his wife stand before their thatched, semi-subterranean pit home. The practice of mouth tattooing was abandoned years ago. (Photo 1951, courtesy W. Stanley Larsen)*

4-46 *In former times, married Ainu women of Northern Japan and their mouths tattooed. (Courtesy Department of Library Services American Museum of Natural History)*

It is impossible to see Ms. Zig of Morocco, as her Islamic faith prevents her from displaying herself in public. She is enshrouded in a long, black robe that covers her from head to toe; she has a very small peephole to see her way.

From northern Burma comes Ms. Padung. She is taller than many of the contestants. Her coil-bound neck and legs are encircled with more than fifty pounds of metal coils.

Ms. Sumbawa, of Sumbawa, Indonesia, flashes a smile showing teeth encased in gold and filled with colored enamels. This elaborate dentistry signifies that her father is a wealthy farmer.

The last contestant is from the United States. She is tall, lean, and athletic. Her legs appear quite long. Her breasts are nearly exposed by her brief bathing suit. Her entire body seems to be hairless and deeply suntanned; even her hair looks sunstreaked. She is wearing intense color around her eyes, on her mouth, and the nails of both her hands and feet. Her ears are pierced and ornamented. She is wearing a metal necklace, finger rings of metal and precious stones, and on one arm she is wearing a small clock.

After the runway show, the contestants were interviewed. Many of the women explained the traditions behind the folk dresses they were wearing. Many said that they only wear these costumes for ceremonial occasions. Others stated that their life revolves around the production and maintenance of their garments. Many, including the representatives of Thailand, the Philippines, Indonesia, Kenya, Ethiopia, Turkey, Brazil, Mexico, Japan, England, and France and the United States find that their travel and casual clothing is very much alike. They all agree that international travel, study, television, magazines, and the movies had brought a conformity to dress and broken down many cultural patterns and helped all appreciate the ideals of beauty of differing peoples (Figure 4-47 a,b).

Conrad, in his book *Many Worlds of Man*, has this to say of ideals regarding clothing practices:

To speak of superior and inferior practices in clothing and ornamentation is impossible as far as beauty, modesty, and status are concerned. There is and can be no universal best way to be beautiful or modest or show one's position in society. Each society has its own rules and these are right for it. Cultural learning alone determines our preference for a plaid shirt rather than a chest tattoo, for pierced ears rather than pierced lips.[60]

Suggested Activities

1. In this chapter, clothing has been related to the way it communicates the cultural aspects of various societies. You should now be able to expand upon this subject: What influences the type of clothing we wear? Think of ideas not discussed in this chapter: for example, attitude of my family, size of my community, current events, and so on.

[60] Conrad, op. cit., p. 118.

4-47a,b *Note the differences between the clothing of the men and women from the Guatemalan villages of Solola (left) and Santiago Atitlán (right). As is often the case, the men and sometimes the children are the first to wear Western-style clothing. Although the male garments are tailored, they utilize traditional details and fabrics that characterize their village. The women's garments, on the other hand, are nontailored blouses woven on a hip strap loom as shown. (Courtesy Rodolfo Reyes Juarez, Guatemala Tourist Commission)*

2. The year is one thousand years from now. An archaeologist has dug down through the rubble to our civilization. He has unearthed your wardrobe. He summons his friend the anthropologist for an interpretation of the culture through this wardrobe. Your clothes are the only available remaining clue to our civilization. How could your wardrobe be interpreted as an index of this era?

3. Find a picture of clothing of another culture. If possible, clip it out; if not, photocopy or make a sketch. Mount it and give source and page number. Read something about that culture to learn why the people dress as they do or why they decorate their bodies as they do. Consider the reasons for wearing clothes and the influences on the choice of clothing. Write a summary and share it with your class.

4. Find a picture of a dress of historical interest of the Western world. Clip it or trace or photocopy it. Mount it and give source and page number. Read about the period to learn the influences that brought about the particular fashion. Write a brief summary of your research.

5. Study your family history for its national costume. If possible, model the costume for the class; if not, present pictures of the costume. Read about the garment in costume books to discover how the dress communicates the culture of the people who wore the costume.

6. Invite foreign students to class to model their national costume and discuss clothing traditions in their home countries. Ask them to explain the socioeconomic conditions of their country as these relate to current dress practices.

5 *Fashion*

Fashion has a strange fascination. It can be habit forming. Those who study, create, or simply enjoy it find that fashion piques a consuming interest. Basic to giving in to the fascination of fashion, is an academic understanding of all that it encompasses and the impact that fashion has exerted on the world in which we live. The study of fashion is an outstanding example of interdisciplinary collaboration. The methods of economics, psychology, sociology, social psychology, anthropology, and ethnology (animal and human) converge in the study of fashion. Fashion is a wide-ranging social phenomenon that requires a wide range of perspectives for its understanding.

The noted German sociologist René König observed that fashion is as profound and critical a part of the social life of man as sex and is made up of the same ambivalent mixture of irresistible urges and inevitable taboos. Fashion is not merely superficial; it is an important regulator and means of expression within the human community. König elaborated by explaining that man's status in his community, his manner of expressing himself, even his own self-image have depended from the beginning of his existence as a species to an amazing extent on that mysterious force we simply call fashion.[1]

It is difficult for some to accept this thesis. During the 1960s and 1970s we experienced a period in which it was fashionable to be unfashionable. It was appropriate to discuss lifestyles, including clothing, in terms of comfort, convenience, practicality, ease, simplicity, naturalness, and, perhaps, fun but important to avoid the term and the state of fashion. A very studied effort to be antifashion was the fashion. Examples of this can be found in every fashion publication dated from the early 1960s to the late 1970s. The same curious taboo that promoted antifashion among consumers has been at work for a much longer period of time among scholars. John Carl Flugel (*The Psychology of Clothes*, London: Hogarth Press, 1930) and others did some outstanding work in this area of study early in this century. However, until most recently, the field has been abandoned. Louis Auchincloss, the novelist, has been credited with explaining the lack of research in the area of fashion by observing that academic writers seem to find the courage to write about society in terms of fashion only from a great distance—either from across an ocean or across a gulf of a century or more in time and preferably both.[2] At the present time there is renewed interest in fashion. Individuals are delighting in wearing fashionable clothing and acquiring

---

[1] René König, *A La Mode, On the Social Psychology of Fashion* (New York: Seabury, 1973), p. 17.
[2] Ibid., p. 19.

130

fashionable possessions. Researchers and writers are recognizing fashion as an index to the behavior of man. In this critical period of accelerating social change, all available tools are needed to assist man to adjust to a future that may not have much relationship to the past. Fashion is such a tool.

Fashion Discussed and Defined

Fashion, in its broadest definition, is a general social phenomenon that affects and shapes man as a whole. Fashion is a universal, formative principle in civilization. It can affect and change the human body and all modes of its expression. Fashion is not limited to clothing or personal adornment. Clothing can be considered an active expression of the fashion of a particular period, but clothing is only a small part of the entire fashion concept.

Each period of civilization known to us has exhibited the force of fashion. Each group of people developed a lifestyle that was suitable to their particular needs. They established patterns of family, housing, eating, speaking, working, playing, governing, and dressing. Historical drama (theater, movies, television), when accurately researched, can give us insights into the fashion of the period portrayed. Historical novels, music, dance concerts, and museum exhibits can help recreate the flavor of passed fashion eras. Study of popular design (form-shape-space, line, color, and texture) of any fashion period reveals fascinating relationships. For example: The Greeks of the Archaic and later periods wore complicated draped garments that played an important role in Greek art and are found duplicated in Greek architecture. Gothic clothing and decoration were based on doting attention to delicate detail as revealed in the period's tapestries and jewelry. The length of Gothic clothing corresponds in form and spirit to the heights of Gothic architecture. The spire of the steeple suggested the hennin; the pointed arches of doors and windows were echoed in the pointed toes of shoes and pointed sleeves; the slim, soaring rib of the Gothic cathedral found a counterpart in the narrow, tightly covered human body, the magnificent beauty of stained-glass windows compared to the finely set Gothic jewelry (Figure 5-1a,b,c,d,e).

In the Renaissance period clothing was designed to broaden the body. The wide, rectangular necklines, padded shoulders with detachable sleeves, and the bulky shapes of short cloaks echoed the massive forms of Renaissance architecture (Fig. 5-2a,b,c,d,e,f).[3] Such comparison can be found in contemporary fashion. The efficiency of modern buildings, transportation, communication, entertainment, and language is repeated in many of the sleek body-revealing garments that are fashionable. Most modern clothing is easy to get into, easy to care for, and permits comfortable, natural body movement.

[3] Michael and Arlane Batterberry, *Mirror, Mirror* (New York: Holt, 1977), pp. 34–127.

5-1 *Each period of history has exhibited a trend in fashion. Interesting relationships can be found between the fashionable patterns of clothing, architecture, and furniture, and also between the patterns found in its literature, work, play, and dance.*

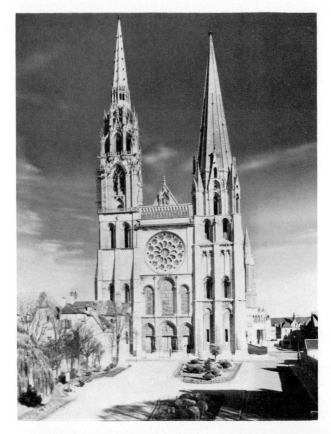

5-1a *Chartres Cathedral is a good illustration of 15th-century architecture. Note the long, narrow vertical shapes and the lines that form the doors, windows, and spires, and the overall proportions of the facade. (Religious News Service Photo)*

5-1b *A 15th-century manuscript illustration vividly portrays the clothing of the men and women of this period. The overall silhouette was made up of elongated vertical lines. (Courtesy Bibliothèque Nationale, Paris)*

5-1c *This 15th-century chest has space divisions which respond to the configuration of the spires and the pointed arches of the doors and windows of the cathedral. (Courtesy The Metropolitan Museum of Art, Rogers Fund, 1905)*

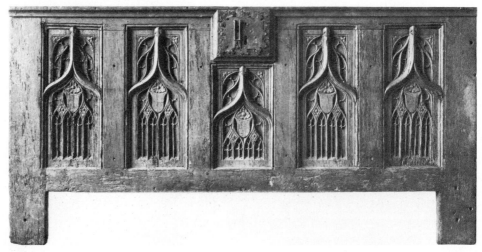

5-1d *The vertical lines in this 15th-century chair form the pointed arch, a distinctive decorative feature characteristic of this period. (Courtesy The Metropolitan Museum of Art, Rogers Fund, 1907)*

5-1e *Portrait of a knight and his lady, early 15th century, as depicted on their tomb giving us a picture of the clothing fashions of the period. Note characteristics that relate to the furnishings and architecture illustrated. (Courtesy Victoria and Albert Museum. Copyright of The Crown)*

In the 16th century the Renaissance brought many modifications to the fashions of the previous period. Lines and shapes changed from being predominantly vertical to horizontal.

5-2a *The interior of a 16th-century Dutch room shows the use of predominantly horizontal lines. Features such as the lowered, flat ceilings, breaking the wall height with wainscoting, and low room dividers produce a wide and spacious appearing interior. (Courtesy the New York Public Library)*

5-2b *The lines used in architecture, furnishings, and clothing created wider, flatter, and lower shapes. In this early 16th-century Flemish building we see the change taking place. The windows are nearly square in shape. Note the flattened arch at the main entrances. The silhouette of the building has a less lofty feeling than 15th-century Gothic structures. (Courtesy the New York Public Library)*

5-2c   The structural details of this 16th-century French table show the use of flattened and widely spaced arches. A sturdy appearing base and the overall proportions of the table produce a broad horizontal appearance. (Courtesy The Metropolitan Museum of Art, Bequest of Michael Friedsarn, 1931. The Friedsarn Collection)

5-2d   Compare the features of this Renaissance chair to those of the 15th-century chair. Note the thick, solid looking structural shapes in the 16th-century model at the top of the back, base of the seat, arms and base at the legs. The decorative features used at the chair back again reflect the flattened rounded arch. (Courtesy The Metropolitan Museum of Art, Gift of George Blumenthal, 1941)

5-2e,f   These portraits illustrate the extreme use of horizontal line popular during the 16th-century. Yards of thick, heavy fabrics were used to create garments of great dimension. Additional volume was achieved by layering, padding, slashing, stuffing, wiring, and underproping. (Top: Courtesy New York Public Library. Bottom: Courtesy The Metropolitan Museum of Art, Gift of J. Pierpont Morgan, 1911.)

Primitive man was also subject to fashion. Too often anthropologists have a tendency to freeze in time the group of people they are studying. Fashion changes occur with these groups just as with all other cultures. The Australian aborigines exhibited a fashion change as they adopted a form of clothing. When the group was first found, they were completely naked. Later they began to wear a waist bracelet, or string. Next, cloth was draped from the waist in front and back in the form of a small apron. Sometime later, it was recorded that the apron had been drawn between the legs into the form of a loincloth.[4]

Fashion can be defined as the style accepted by a large group of people at a particular time. Fashion encompasses all facets of a lifestyle.

Fashion is said to be the code language of status. Those within the group fully understand the meaning; those outside can only guess. Each stratum of status may have its own variations of fashion that cause many subdivisions. For example, on a college campus, striations of status can be found among the students living in fraternities, dormitories, apartments, or with parents. Campus activities, scholastic standing, economic position, employment, and ethnic background, as well as educational major, may be other subdivisions of status. We make broad status confessions every day in our response to fashion. We reveal our own self-image with the fashion we select.[5]

Fashion constitutes an important regulator and means of expression within the community of man. Our daily lives are affected by an abundance of social rules and standards that help us understand our expected behavior. Fashion has established not only the rules but also the sanctions that follow if the prescribed behavior is ignored.[6]

Fashion cannot exist in seclusion. It needs a broad stage on which to be displayed. It must be seen, and it needs time to be adapted. Ostentation and demonstration are two essential features of fashion. Only with exposure can fashion stimulus change the dominant behavior patterns and customs and replace them with new ones. Only when a large number of people have been affected by the change will a fashion be created.[7]

Fashion must be novel. It is the desire for change that is responsible for the continued acceptance of the movement of fashion. At certain periods fashion becomes nostalgic, but it never returns exactly to the earlier period. Current fashion may have characteristics reminiscent of another time, but closer examination will reveal that the current fashion is new and different.

The sudden standing still of fashion is a difficult-to-explain phenomenon. Among the North American Indians, for instance, the women of the Navajo and Apache adopted the colorful velvet blouse of the Spaniards and they have retained it ever since. Other examples of "fossilized fashions" include many peasant costumes, the monk's habit, the academic regalia, and the Spanish bullfighter's

---

[4] König, op. cit., p. 92.
[5] König, op. cit., p. 27.
[6] König, op. cit., p. 40.
[7] König, op. cit., pp. 54–57.

dress. No specific reason can be given for this sudden freezing of fashion except that often folk costumes do not grow among people, but are granted by rulers[8] (sumptuary laws) (Figures 5-3, 5-4).

Other factors that are responsible for fashion are a desire for decoration and distinction. Wearing a display of trophies or wealth demonstrates how one has met the competition and succeeded. Recognition is a product of fashion, not because of the visible characteristics of the fashion so much as because those who are able to sustain the rapid change of fashion set themselves apart from others by showing they "belong."

Fashion is responsible for introducing beauty into the lives of the masses. Within the confines of the regulatory forces of fashion, there is a great freedom for self-expression.[9] Perhaps this has always been the most important aspect of fashion. Through the creative expression of a few men and women, great strides in science technology have been made. The self-expression of people has produced

[8] König, op. cit., pp. 88–89.
[9] König, op. cit., p. 225.

5-3 *This relief, probably of Hermes, was taken from an Athenian temple of c. 520 B.C. The shirt resembles the modern tank-top or undershirt in cut and texture. This is an example of fossilized fashion. (Photo Karl G. Kessler, permission Acropolis Museum, Athens)*

5-4 *Missionary Sisters of the Immaculate Heart of Mary model the old and new habits. The traditional garb on the left represents a fossilized fashion worn by the order for 67 years. This habit, including coif, gown, apron, and waistline rosary can be traced to medieval times. The new habit was adopted to make the nuns seem more a part of the mainstream of our contemporary society. The styles are classic, but not fashionable. (Courtesy UPI/Bettmann Newsphotos)*

the world we know today. The roles and controls of fashion combined with this freedom of individual expression may lead us into the world of tomorrow.

Each person takes a fashion position. Those who reject the current fashion are labeled either *old-fashioned* or *antifashion*. Those who are extremely far ahead of fashion are called the *avant-garde*. In each community, and each subgroup of the community, there are *fashion leaders*, who quickly adopt new styles, and *fashion followers*, who wait for fashions to be completely established before embracing them. Fashion leaders are sometimes considered liberals whereas fashion followers are labeled conservatives. As one moves through daily activities and social groups, one can move from the position of fashion leader to fashion follower or from fashion follower to fashion leader. One's fashion position is defined by association. To be comfortable in your fashion period is a desirable condition. How one copes with fashion is another expression of individuality.

Fashion is shaped by society. Stella Blum, while director of the Costume Institute of the Metropolitan Museum of Art, observed, "A fashion is no accident. It will always suit a situation, time and place. Fashion is really a matter of evolution. It has a natural life. . . ."[10]

Fashion in Clothing

Fashion is a continuing process of change in the styles of living. A specific fashion is a defined style that is accepted by a large group of people at a particular time. This is the general definition of fashion and it is most often applied to clothing. To illustrate this definition, consider the antebellum fashion of bouffant, crinoline-supported hoop skirts popular with American Southern women prior to the Civil War; the elaborately trimmed military uniforms worn over corsets by western European men during the reign of Napoleon; and the unisex sweatsuit chic of the 1980s.

Accompanying each of these garment style periods was the style prescribed by fashion for the total spectrum of human activity, including all social activities, manners, and morals. In other words, the manner of living, eating, talking, walking, dancing, and behaving of the antebellum period was appropriate to that period as was the style of dress. The same is true for each of the other style periods mentioned and it would be true for every other period of human existence. For fashion historians, it is easier to recall the mode of dress than the code of etiquette of the same period. Clothing is easier to preserve and to evaluate. Fashion represents the total style of human activity accepted by a large group of people at a specific time. The style of clothing is only one aspect of fashion but a most important one.

The magnanimity of the impact of fashionable clothing is demonstrated in the complex, multibillion-dollar, worldwide industry created to produce and distribute apparel and accessories for men, women, and children. The production and sale of garments would be greatly simplified if the fashion mystique did not exist. For the clothing industry, upon closer inspection, is revealed to be the fashion industry. The unknown link in the clothing business is the unpredictable consumer, who can accept or reject the products of this vast industry. The consumer's final decision is subject to the capricious whims of fashion.

[10] Batterberry, op. cit., p. 14.

As Melinkoff stated:

> To stay in fashion is to go with the flow. If we women are the pragmatists that we are so often touted to be, it affects our dress too. Once a new style is on a roll, we know it's best not to be too firmly attached to the old look. And while we have been able to call a halt to, or at least redirect, a few fashions, we know that we are not in total control. At best, we have only a veto power, which we exercised with the sack and the midi. We are able to nix a new style and stick with what we have been wearing, but for the most part, we cannot create a new one. Lace tights, stretch pants, bikinis, pea jackets—like every thing else we have worn—were offered for our consideration. Years ago, we didn't realize we could say, "No, thank you." Designers became accustomed to having unquestioned authority, and when we finally refused to wear one of their dictates, the sack, they were stunned.
>
> Despite our newfound tongues, we still wait for the new looks to be announced each year, the cut of jeans, the width of lapels, the newest shades. Some of us have been playing this fashion game for thirty years or more and we still go with the flow.[11]

Fashion Terminology

In order to be able to communicate effectively, it is necessary to understand the vocabulary of the technical area and the connotation of the terms applied. This is also true in the field of clothing. Textbook authors and fashion reporters often attach personal meaning to the words used that may result in confusion in the mind of the reader. The following definitions and explanations are made to clarify the terms used in this text and should serve as a point of reference when reading the various chapters.

Style. Style is a distinctive characteristic or way of expression. There are styles of houses, styles of cars, styles of refrigerators, styles of life, and styles of speaking. Style in dress describes the lines that distinguish one form or shape from another. The pleated skirt, the A-line skirt, and the straight skirt are styles because they have characteristic shapes and lines.

A style remains a style whether it is currently fashionable or not. The bow tie, the saddle shoe, and the T-shirt are examples of apparel styles. Each has distinguishing or identifiable characteristics. They are not necessarily "in fashion" at this time.

Style creates an impression that reflects the outlook of the times. The mood or feeling created by particular styles is an emotional quality that reflects the outlook of a person or a group of persons during a certain period of time.

We often hear the expressions, "Chet has style" or "Joyce dresses in a stylish manner." This is a misuse of the term. Every person is clothed in a style because of the distinguishing characteristics of the garments worn. Style should not be equated with the words *taste*, *chic*, or *elegance*. Style is a general term used to

[11] Ellen Melinkoff, *What We Wore, An Offbeat Social History of Women's Clothing, 1950–1980* (New York: Quill, 1984), p. 14.

5-5 *A style remains a style whether it is currently fashionable or not. The styles included in this picture are a beret, his and her smocks, jeans, knickers, boots, pumps, and pageboy hairstyle.*

describe the details of a garment. Fashion includes style but expresses the acceptance of the style at a given time (Figure 5-5).

Fashion. A continuing process of change in the styles of living, including dress and behavior, that is accepted or followed by large groups of people at any given time and place. A specific "fashion" is the particular style that is accepted by a large group of people at a particular time (Figure 5-6).

Anti-Fashion. Against current fashion. Combining styles which show rejection of contemporary fashion.

Fashionable. A person who conforms to fashion.

Fashionmonger. A person who studies, follows and helps to popularize the current fashion.

Fashion Plate. A picture showing the prevailing or new style in clothes. *Colloquial:* A person who consistently wears the latest style in dress.

Old-Fashioned. Clinging to styles of the past.

141

5-6 *Fashion represents the total style of human activity that is accepted by a large group of people at a specific time. The style of clothing is only one aspect of fashion. These sketches of men's clothing are examples of fashions of different periods.*

Beginning of Christian era   Englishman of 1640   Two symbols of the French Revolution: culotte-dorees above, sans-culottes at right.

Englishman circa 1800   Gentleman of 1826   19th Century Mexican   1922 fashion plate

1930 "bags"   1940's zoot suit   1970   1980   1985

Campus Fashion. Styles including clothing that are distinctive to a particular school or campus. These change with the passing of each generation. Junior high and high school students often create a "look" that they cling to through college. Often campus fashion clothing is casual and comfortable and not a manner of dress that is acceptable away from the campus in city or business life. This is not always true. Sometimes campus fashion is the same as the prevailing fashion or even ahead of it.

High Fashion—Haute Couture. High fashion refers to new garment styles. Because high fashion is created to inspire fashion change, it has several identifiable characteristics. It is very expensive because of the specialness of the design, the quality of the fabric, and the excellence of workmanship. It is extreme sometimes to the point of being startling. This piques interest in the design and the designer but limits the appeal of the garment to those who can and will wear it. Some high-fashion designs may be too impractical to meet the needs of the demands of varied lifestyles. High fashion remains high fashion only until the newness wears off. If a high fashion gains acceptance and is mass produced, it then becomes fashion. High fashion is important because it is a source of some fashion inspiration (Figure 5-7).

Couture. An establishment devoted to the creation of fashion where the designer, rather than working to meet the requirements of the individual customer, develops his own ideas. The *couture* sells clothing to an exclusive clientele.

5-7 This white chiffon dress with white Chantilly lace represents high fashion or haute couture. It has the characteristics of being expensive, extreme, limited in appeal, and somewhat impractical. The accessories, facial ornamentation, and hairstyle of the mannequin show how the couturier presents the mood or total look of the new design. (Courtesy Christian Dior)

acceptable ot all the time

here today gone tommorow

Couturier. *Couturier* is the French term for designer.

Classics. Classics are styles that endure. They continue to be accepted by a large segment of the buying public because of their timeless quality and because they meet the lifestyle needs of many. *Classic* is a term used to describe many things including cars, movies, music, books, as well as clothing. The cardigan sweater is a classic; it may go through minor variations such as the addition of sequins, fur, or embroidery, but the style remains basic. Cowboy shirts and boots, boxer shorts, trench coats, shirtwaist dresses, and tuxedos are classic. Classic clothes are designed with clean, uncluttered, body-conforming lines. A key to understanding what is classic is simplicity of design. If the design of the article is good, it is always pleasing and therefore timeless or classic (Figure 5-8).

Fad. A fad is a fashion that is short-lived. Fads usually have quick acceptance by a relatively small group of people. An interesting phenomenon of fads is their speed of movement. They leave the scene with almost the same speed with which they arrive (Figure 5-9).

Some fads of recent years are slogan T-shirts, leg warmers, plastic shoes, single earring/multiple earrings, layered socks, billed caps, and mirrored sunglasses. Accessory fads often occur in jewelry, purses, shoes, and gloves. Analyzing fads

5-8 *Classics are styles that endure. They continue to be accepted by a large segment of the buying public because of their timeless quality and because they meet the lifestyle needs of many. (Courtesy Levi Strauss & Co.)*

to determine why they are so short-lived reveals that they are usually too flashy, poorly designed, easily available, inexpensive, and extreme or exaggerated.

Fads may be confined to a particular locale or they may sweep the country, as Cabbage Patch dolls and Trivial Pursuit did. A fad may appeal to a certain group or subgroup. Teen-age magazines often promote fads because young people are more accepting than adults. Fads may be bizarre or flamboyant and noticed by all, or extremely subtle and known only by an in-group (Figure 5-10).

5-9 *Fads are fashions that are short-lived. Fads usually have quick acceptance by a relatively small number of people. Fads may be confined to a particular locality or may sweep the country. Safari dressing for both men and women was considered a fad in the mid-1980s. (Courtesy Camp Beverly Hills)*

5-10 *Punker dress featuring unique hairstyles, colorful makeup, bizaare dress with a flavor of violence was a fad which developed on the streets of London and spread around the world. (Courtesy Alon Reininger/Contact)*

Custom. Custom means made for the individual. Custom clothing is cut and fitted to the body so that correction may be made to fit body contours. These garments are also called "made-to-measure." The custom clothing market today is very limited because of high labor costs and the availability of a large variety of ready-to-wear in all price ranges.

Taste. Taste is a subjective judgment of what we think is appropriate or beautiful. Because of the individualness of this judgment, standards of taste are not universal. What one person considers to be "good taste," another does not. Our taste is a result of (1) how we see things aesthetically; (2) the scope of our experience, both educationally and culturally; and (3) our own values and attitudes. As we mature, our tastes grow more varied and often broaden. Taste makes us reject certain styles and accept others. Rejection may evolve into acceptance as we become more familiar with the style.

Tournament of Roses Pictorial Review

The following section includes pictures of the Tournament of Roses queens and courts for the past eighty years. Study the sequence pictures to see how the fashion of clothing has evolved. Notice the details of the garment styles as well as those of makeup and hair arrangements. Try to determine which styles are classics and which were fads. Observe changes in grooming practices over the years. Find styles from the earlier pictures that have returned to fashion. Remember that the selection of a queen is a matter of taste. The ideals of beauty change with fashion so that some of the queens may have been selected because of attributes not currently *in vogue.*

If possible, share this selection with a person who can reminisce about some of the fashion periods illustrated by the Tournament of Roses pictures. Perhaps you can even find someone who attended some of the New Year's festivities sponsored by the tournament. Ask that person to recall other aspects of the various fashion periods such as the dating customs, the fashion of men's garments, the kinds of dances that were popular, some of the music of the period, and other forms of social practices.

The Tournament of Roses selects seven girls each year to reign during the New Year's festivities and throughout the year. These finalists are chosen from several hundred senior high and junior college students in the Pasadena, California, area. From the time the first announcement of the finalists is made until their first official appearance, the girls are groomed for their public. The wardrobes, makeup, and hairstyles selected for them are promoted as the trends in fashion by department store sponsors. The Tournament of Roses queen and her court represent a fashionable look at California schoolgirls for the year that they reigned (Figure 5-11).

5-11 *The Tournament of Roses Parade is an American tradition. Every New Year's Day since 1901, the parade has rolled down Colorado Boulevard in Pasadena, California. With the development of movies and television the Rose Parade has gained worldwide recognition. The members of the Tournament serve as goodwill ambassadors throughout the world and claim that the film of the current parade is shown every day of the year in some part of the world. Thus the Rose Parade is one facet of America that contributes to the Westernization of dress and the perception that others have of the American people.*

The following photos present a unique pictorial review of fashion as it has evolved during the twentieth century. Study each photo in detail to see how the styles of clothing evolved. Note how classics remained, with subtle changes and how fads faded. Remember, had you been a part of the generation depicted, you probably would have dressed in a very similiar style. (All Tournament of Roses photos courtesy Pasadena Tournament of Roses Association)

Hallie Woods was selected the first Tournament of Roses Queen, in 1905. Her ornate hat, upswept hair style denoting maturity, fresh face, and high-necked, lacy dress represented the latest fashion.

Here comes the parade! The first Rose Parade, January 1, 1901. Spectators are attired in the fashions of the day which appear rather formal today. Skirts swept the unpaved streets, women's hair was long and pinned up to show maturity. Both men and women wore hats for public appearances. The bicycle was a rather new and exciting mode of transportation which allowed women to wear bifurcated skirts.

In 1904, a 16-year-old miss won the U.S. Tennis Championship. In 1908, she reigned as Queen of the Tournament of Roses. Here she displays a daring tennis outfit consisting of shirtwaist and bifurcated skirt which shows the ankles. Note weight of tennis racket. In the early 1970s this same woman, May Sutton Bundy, was still competing, playing the Senior Olympic doubles championships—a true sports pioneer.

In 1925 women had won the right to vote, bob their hair, and show their legs as demonstrated by this Tournament of Roses court. Think of the generation gap between these girls and their grandparents shown at the first Rose parade.

1930 was depression time. This court reflects some of the uncertainty of the times in the wide variety of their hemlines.

A close-up of the 1931 Rose Queen reveals marcelled hair, plucked eyebrows, and a cupid bow mouth.

In times of stress, clothing often becomes more protective as illustrated by the 1937 court. Finger waves were popular hairstyles and eyebrows were pencil thin. The movies had strong impact on fashion at this time.

By 1939 skirts were back to knee length and the tailored look was popular.

In 1939 Lathrop Leishman was president of the Tournament of Roses; in 1979 he was Grand Marshal. The 1939 court reassembled to honor him. Can you match the faces after 40 years?

A face portrait of the 1939 Rose Queen reveals the natural all-American look. Note brows and emphasized mouth. Longer hair was popular. The elaborate sleeve treatment was typical of the period.

By 1940 the big bands were touring the country. Many girls danced to this music in formals such as these worn by the 1940 court. The shapelessness of the bodice is not due to a lack of feminine curves, the uplift bra had not been invented.

1942 and America was just entering World War II. A patriotic mood gripped the country. The luxurious satin gowns with square shoulders, long sleeves, and peplums were the ultimate in fashion. A fresh scrubbed face, dark red mouth, casually styled hair, comprised the collegiate look of the day.

1946—a tailored look prevailed, each college woman built her wardrobe around a suit. Shortages of stockings made the "bobby sox" a favorite.

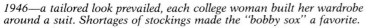

Bob Hope reigned as Grand Marshal twice. In 1968 he reminisces with his 1947 queen. Women's styles between the two periods changed greatly, but Mr. Hope's classic herringbone tweed sports jacket must be studied carefully before it can be determined whether he is wearing the same jacket in both photos.

1948—the military shoulders were an influence of World War II. The suit was a basic item in most women's wardrobes. Makeup emphasized the mouth.

Nylon tulle came to the Tournament of Roses in 1954. This new textile made possible many new effects in clothing. The strapless formal was almost a uniform for most coeds.

The influence of Dior's "New Look" is shown by the skirt lengths in this 1957 Rose Court. The style was introduced in France in 1947 but it took time to become a fashion accepted by the young in the U.S. Movie star Grace Kelly's white glove signature had become an important accessory at this time. The classic business suit with tie, white shirt, and handkerchief dominated male fashions.

1959—dressmaker suits with natural shoulders and long slender skirts and pearl chokers represent the fashion of this period. Note new stiletto-heeled pumps. As skirts get shorter, heels get higher. The tight pageboy was an important hairstyle.

1968 Rose Bowl court. The "Jackie look" was fashionable. It included pill box hat, masses of teased, sprayed hair, striped coat, short skirts, and low-heeled shoes.

Above, 1973—the mini-skirt began to yield to the classic sporty look as demonstrated when the short-skirted past queen presented roses to the longer skirted new queen.

The "Mod" or mini-skirt was firmly established in 1971. The Queen of the Rose Tournament was allowed to reign in past shoulder-length-hair for the first time in the history of the pageant.

Reunion pictures demonstrate the fashion changes dramatically. The 1954 Tournament of Roses Court posed again in 1971. The line-ups are the same in both pictures.

The 1967 court in formal ballroom attire.

The 1967 court met again in 1971 and posed for this picture. Mini-and maxi-skirts were both appropriate for this type of social function.

The 1975 court shows the fashion trend to longer skirts, shorter hair, and higher heels. Note how the classic pump has been modified with a round toe and very thick heel. Knit sweater and dress combinations were very popular. Eye makeup dominated the face.

A gathered cummerbund accents the waistline and reveals the feminine curves of the 1978 Court. The textural softness of the folds of the polyester gowns is achieved by modern technology.

1960

Twenty years of fashion and maturing beauty are represented in these pictures of the Rosecourt of 1960. The positions of each court member are the same in each photo. Notice how each woman adapted her personal style signature to remain fashionable. The central figure, Queen Margarethe Bertelson, appears with the 1985 Rose Queen in the last photo in this section giving the student a twenty-five year study of a lovely woman.

1970

158

1975

1980

Top: *The 1982 Court on the day of their selection. Their garments, accessories, hairstyles, and makeup reveal their individuality. Their body positions reveal untrained postures.*

Bottom: *The 1982 Court at an official function. They have been schooled, polished, and styled to present a poised unit to represent the Tournament of Roses for the calendar year.*

The 1985 Rose Queen, Kristina Smith, poses with Queen Margarethe Bertelson 1960, and Queen Holly Halsted 1930. This photo shows the healthy vitality and beauty of women of a wide age span.

Historical Overview of French Fashion Leadership

Since the middle of the seventeenth century, when the court of Louis XIV were the tastemakers, France has been in a position of fashion leadership. Why has this phenomenon been true? France, and particularly Paris, has maintained the reputation of "Fashion Capital of the World" because of the continued fostering of a climate and atmosphere that encourages creativity and inspiration. Paris has continued to be a meeting ground for all of the arts. It is the city to which the world's aspiring musicians, writers, and artists are attracted by the magnetism of the creative climate that abounds for each of the arts. The architecture, parks, monuments, and the very layout of the city present unequaled expressions of beauty along the winding river Seine.

Fashion is regarded as a national industry in France, and as such it is fostered, protected, and financed. The artists of fashion design find inspiration in the priceless collections of art found in the hundreds of museums. In 1986 the *Musée*

5-12 *Section of Toile de Jouy, "Le Ballon de Gonesse"—design by Jean Baptiste Huet. Jouy, France, 1784–5. Copper plate printing on linen. This technique of fabric printing was an innovation in printing technology. It was developed to replace Indian hand-painted and printed fabrics which were much in demand from the beginning of the 17th century. (Courtesy Los Angeles County Museum of Art)*

des Arts de la Mode (MAM) became the national French museum of fashion. It combines two separate costume collections: the *Musée des Arts Décoratifs*, which consists mostly of accessories, textiles, and historical costumes dating back to the eighteenth century, and *Union Centrale des Arts Décoratifs*, which is strongest in the nineteenth and twentieth centuries and has a rich fund of fashion magazines, photographs, and designer drawings. The new museum will occupy a nine-floor building in the Louvre complex located at 109 Rue de Rivoli, Paris. Exhibits are planned to present all of the arts of fashion including not only clothes but all accessories, jewelry, combs, hair curlers, shoes, mirrors, buttons, canes, handkerchiefs, ribbons, hats, umbrellas, underwear, wigs, handbags, and fans. Also showcased will be the people who produced these items and how production proceeds from sketch to completed garment, including sewing, pressing, and photographing. The purpose of MAM goes beyond exhibiting fashion as an aspect of the national culture; it aims toward an economic goal. This museum and the way it will be operated is designed to help Paris and France to regain their leadership in the fashion world.[12]

Dressmaking is a most honorable profession in France; legions of well-trained seamstresses are available to execute a designer's work. A great spirit of cooperation exists among the allied trades; for example, buttonmakers will provide just the exact fastener that the designer requests or needs. Entire cities such as Alençon, Chantilly, Valenciennes, and Calais exist to support the fashion industry with their products of exquisite laces and trims.

The various French textile manufacturers cooperate by providing fabrics to the designer free of charge for the first model. The silk and textiles industry has been given financial assistance by the French government since the fifteenth century. Because of this subsidy, production continues and the beautiful cottons, lovely silks, and fine wools of France are known and treasured throughout the world. *Toile de Jouy*, the printed fabric made in the town of Jouy, was developed by an engraver-designer named Oberkampf during the time of Napoleon (Figure 5-12). Oberkampf was awarded the French Legion of Honor for his contribution to the French textile industry.

The trade association, *Chambre Syndicale de la Couture Parisienne*, founded in 1868, has protected the French designer ever since. The general function of this organization is to serve its membership in all branches of fashion. The *Chambre Syndicale* acts as adviser and counselor in such matters as interpretation of laws and taxes, employment relationships, and business management. It coordinates the dates for showing each designer's collection and offers protection from "idea pirates." A series of identifying photographs of each design is registered with the *Chambre Syndicale*, so that any pirating of designs can be prosecuted. The *Chambre Syndicale* also conducts a school to train personnel for the needle trades, thus assuring a continued supply of these vital workers.

[12] Leon Harris, "Museum of Chic," *Connoisseur*, June 1985.

The emphasis placed on clothing by French women has also had an impact on the fashion industry. Historically, Madame de Pompadour and Madame du Barry, both mistresses of Louis XV, are credited with setting the pace for court attire by arraying themselves in magnificent clothes. Marie Antionette symbolized the epitome of fashion impact in her day. She spent most of her time and the fortunes of the king on her personal adornment and introduced many innovations that became fashion. So powerful was Marie Antoinette and so strong was her interest in clothing that she made her dressmaker, Madame Bertin, Minister of Fashion.

The first *haute couture* salon was opened in Paris in 1860 by an Englishman, Charles Worth. He designed show pieces for his wife and then escorted her to the most important social functions. In this manner he attracted the attention of Empress Eugénie, wife of Napoleon III, and became her dressmaker. This relationship with the empress secured his position as the "father of the *couture*." (A House of Worth has been in continued existence to this date; its importance in fashion has been very minor in recent times.)

Soon, other houses were established, and royalty both supported and encouraged them. Most memorable of the early *couturieres* were Madame Cheruit and Madame Redfern in 1881, Jeanne Lanvin in 1890, and the House of Callot Soeurs in 1895. As the status of royalty changed with political events, the clientele of the *couture* of necessity expanded to include the very wealthy, the international set, actresses of the stage and later the films, and finally society women and wives of political and business leaders. Magazine and newspaper coverage given to these famous women in their various activities helped to spread the favored styles. Fashion magazines were created with the specific purpose of spreading the fashion news to even a wider public. Fashions were copied by "little dressmakers" or home seamstresses everywhere. This, in turn, gave rise to an entirely new facet of fashion, the pattern industry.

A new concept in fashion was initiated when Paul Poiret, who had worked in the House of Worth, opened his own salon. Poiret designed gowns that for the first time released women from the constricting corsets and allowed them to breathe freely (Figure 5-13). Walking was free and easy in this new style, so Poiret innovated his scandalous culottes and walking skirt, the *trotteur*. Paul Poiret became an "ambassador of fashion" by traveling around the world with his mannequins advertising French fashion. He was the first *couturier* to create a perfume. In 1914, Poiret sadly closed his house and went to serve his country in World War I. He reopened his salon after the war but was not able to regain his former fame. In the war years fashion had changed, and Poiret seemed unable to understand or appreciate the new trends. Paul Poiret, who had contributed so much to the world of fashion, died in poverty in 1944.

In 1914, Madeleine Vionnet opened her house which was soon closed by World War I. She bravely reopened in 1919 and made tremendous contributions to fashion. Vionnet was *art nouveau* before there was such a period. Her sketches and designs are collectors' items of this intriguing art form. She was the first to design asymmetrical necklines, skirts with handkerchief points, dresses to be worn without underwear, and costumes with the coat lining and dress fabric the

5-13 Paul Poiret was a French designer who was first responsible for the change in women's dress in the 20th century. He did away with the corset, relaxed the waistline, and freed the body from clothing constrictions of almost a hundred years. The dress here shows oriental influence. (Courtesy Los Angeles County Museum of Art)

same. Her greatest innovation was the use of bias. If you can imagine, no one had used the bias cut before Vionnet.

In 1918, Gabrielle "Coco" Chanel established her house. This designer may well be regarded as one of the "wonders of the world," as she has been a dynamic force in fashion ever since. Her designs are popular today. Her designs and innovations have become classics. It is really safe to say that the wardrobes of all women in the Western world have felt the impact of Chanel.

In 1919, Chanel shocked the fashion world by using wool knits in suits and coats. Until that time this fabric had been used only for underwear. The popularity of wool knits today illustrates Chanel's farsighted approach to fashion. The *chemise* dress, featured in her 1924 collection, became fashionable at all social levels, so much so that it could be regarded as the "uniform of the day." Chanel has always shown a great understanding of fabric and fit. Her garments seem so simple in design, yet they use fabric to its best advantage. A Chanel design is reputed to be the most comfortable of all clothes to wear. The "Chanel Suit" is a common fashion term used to describe any suit with a collarless, cardigan jacket. Her perfume Chanel No. 5 is probably the one best known throughout the world. It was named for her favorite number.

Because of Chanel's pleasure in jewelry, a whole new concept of jewelry has evolved. Chanel has always loved extravagant ropes of pearls; large, bright pins and bracelets; colorful earrings. Until she featured this costume jewelry in her 1920 collection, it was not socially accepted. The only kind of jewelry regarded as proper was made of precious metals and stones. Think of how limited your jewelry collection would be if this were still true. Chanel's penchant for jewelry gave us the wide variety of costume jewelry we all enjoy today.

Chanel closed her house in 1939; both the coming of World War II and a certain indifference to fashion prompted this. In 1954 she made a triumphant return. Although Chanel never married, her life was filled with romance and color. A Broadway show "Coco," was based on her life. She died in 1971, and her name is now franchised to others.

Elsa Schiaparelli entered the fashion world because of economic necessity. She had many wealthy, socialite friends to whom she sold her latest designs. Her first effort was a trimmed cardigan sweater that is now regarded as a classic. Her feeling for design in some ways is comparable to Chanel's, in that she stressed comfort and movement in her clothing. Among her contributions to fashion were shoulder emphasis, use of scarves as accessories, use of synthetic fabrics, chic tailored evening dresses, and *shocking pink*, the fashion color. Schiaparelli is also credited with removing class distinction from clothing through simplicity of designs that were suitable for mass production.

Many other designers, too numerous to mention here, left their impact on fashion during these times. Each made a romantic and important contribution to *haute couture*. The student is urged to pursue an interest in this historical costume period in other references.

Current French Couture

After World War II, Christian Dior created the fashion coup to date by introducing the *New Look* (Figure 5-14). Skirts plunged toward the ankles; the natural shoulder and the nipped-in waist displayed feminine curves in a manner that delighted both sexes. The lifting of rationing and wartime restrictions plus the mood of the times made this phenomenon of fashion possible. It is doubtful if any other designer will ever be able to duplicate this feat. Within four years the New Look had completely swept the fashion world. Every woman with the ability

5-14 Christian Dior's "New Look." Presented immediately after World War II, it is rated the fashion coup of all time. (Courtesy Christian Dior)

and means to do so had completely replaced her wardrobe, if not with Paris originals, with mass-produced copies or home-crafted creations. The New Look pumped new blood into French fashion and was instrumental in revitalizing the *couture.* The houses of Balenciaga, Givenchy, La Roche, and Chanel flourished. New darlings arrived, including Fath, Cardin, Balmain, St. Laurent, Courrèges, Bohan, Valentino, and Ungaro.

The last strongest statement to be made by French couture in the traditional manner was made by Courrèges in the early 1960s. He engineered garments that picked up the *mod* look of the London kids. Miniskirts and go-go boots sounded the death knell for traditional *couture.* As with any other atavism, it would take years for this homage to fade in terms of retail presentation.[13]

Times have changed. To most, French *couture* seems like a relic of the opulent past. Economic pressures, the changes in lifestyle, the rise of a large and influential middle class, the mass of youth, all have affected *French couture.* Still, twice a year costly collections are presented to a dwindling clientele. The international jet set now represents the bulk of the Paris *couture* business. Although

[13] "Celebrities: Center Stage," *Retailweek*, September 1, 1979.

many American store buyers have stopped buying *couture*, their places at the houses have been taken by wealthy Arab princesses with "virtually bottomless pocketbooks." Another new group of *couture* patrons are the wealthy, and sometimes royal, young including Olimpa de Rothschild, Princess Caroline, and Princess Diana.

A typical *couture* collection costs over $400,000 to produce. Prices of the individual garments range, but all are high. A daytime suit costs between $5,000 and $15,000, a daytime dress over $3,000, and evening gowns start at $5,000, and can cost up to $60,000. A designer Russian Lynx coat was sold for $150,000 in 1985.

Many of the famous old-name houses have closed. Twenty-four *couture* houses remain in Paris. To survive, these establishments have had to diversify and change their methods of operation. Most have entered the high-profit market of cosmetics, accessories, perfumes, and *prêt-à-porter* (ready-to-wear), for both men and women. In Paris, the exclusive *couture* salon upstairs is most often supported by the street level *boutique* catering to "walk-in" customers. *Couturier boutiques* have been franchised and are found on the fashionable boulevards throughout the world.[14,15]

Many designers are in the licensing business. That is, they lend or license their names on a royalty basis to producers who manufacture and market merchandise that will be sold under the designer's name or logo. The house of Christian Dior is involved in a licensing program that includes over one hundred and forty contracts for over thirty different products, which are sold in eighty different countries. Pierre Cardin licenses everything from packaging for candy to furniture and electronic items. Givenchy even licensed his name to the interior of a Lincoln-Continental automobile. The income from these business transactions helps subsidize their *couture*.[16,17]

In August 1985, the Paris *couture* collections opened for the two hundred and sixty-sixth time. Although some people complained that the whole system was out-dated and urgently needed a face-lift, the atmosphere of extravagant elitism was still strong. Most couturiers, who barely break even on the collections, shudder at the thought that this ancient, twice-a-year ritual will ever come to an end. The reasons for preserving the *couture* delineates the primary functions of these famous houses. These are best summed up by the designers themselves:

YVES ST. LAURENT—The *couture* is the essence of designing, of creating clothes. It provides the standards, the craftsmanship that makes fashion possible. It should always exist.

[14] Patrick McCarthy and Edwina La Farge, "Paris Opens: Still Elite, Extravagant," *Women's Wear Daily*, July 23, 1979, pp. 1, 6, 7.

[15] "Paris Couture: Extravagant Elitism," *W*, August 3–10, 1979, p. 6.

[16] Marion McEvoy, "Behind the Doors at House of Dior," *Women's Wear Daily*, September 17, 1977, p. 8.

[17] Nancy Yoshihara, "U.S. Playing the Pucci, Gucci Kootchy Coo," *Los Angeles Times*, December 18, 1977, p. 8.

JEAN-LOUIS SCHERRER—The *couture* establishes the image. It is the promotion and the publicity for all the rest, from sunglasses to ready-to-wear.

MARC BOHAN of Christian Dior—All my major ideas come from the *couture*. The ready-to-wear couldn't be shaped the way it is without the *couture*. It is that simple.[18]

BERNARD LANVIN, grandnephew of Jeanne Lanvin, who founded the House of Lanvin in 1888—Of course our *haute couture* clients are not enough to support our whole operation. Nobody today can build a business out of just *couture*. We think of it as a "plus"—the prestige end of our operation. If we did not also have ready-to-wear and the fragrances, we would not survive. [*Haute couture* sales presently account for about one tenth of his entire business.] Of course, this varies enormously depending on many things. For example, an Arab came into the men's shop a few weeks back and bought himself 1,200 custom-made shirts, including 57 tuxedo shirts. [Total cost $156,000.] Who knows? That could be the sale of the century. Or, another man could walk in tomorrow and order twice as many shirts, if you see what I mean.[19]

In the late fall of 1984, Jean Paul Gaultier, a young French designer made popular a new buzz word in the fashion vocabulary: *androgyny*—having the characteristics of both male and female (Figure 5-15a,b) Eloise Salholz and Ruth Marshall described the scene:

> . . .the models came into view—men in sarongs or trouser skirts, women in layered vests and jackets that made a mockery of the traditional man's suit—and removed all doubt. This was cross-dressing, couture style.
>
> Gaultier, thirty-two, is high fashion's latest bad boy, a quirky, talented designer who transforms the rags of bag ladies and street urchins into humorous, richly textured and, needless to say, expensive ($840 for a sweater) clothes. Foremost among his inconoclastic beliefs is that men and women can dress alike and still look different. "Masculinity is not a question of a skirt or a trouser," he says. "It is in the head." His fashion shows are theatrical events that invariably attract hordes of groupies and serious buyers as well; his more celebrated fans include Isabelle Adjani, David Bowie, and Prince. Often, he uses amateur models because they are more natural than professionals. "He puts clothes together in a bizarre way to show that fashion need not be taken too seriously," says Dawn Mello, president of Bergdorf Goodman, which [fall of 1984] presented Gaultier's fall line in a circus tent in lower Manhattan.
>
> For such an original Gaultier invites plenty of comparisons. His playful irreverence reminds some observers of a young Kenzo. For others, his creativity and deft tailoring hold the promise of an Yves Saint Laurent. "People thought Saint Laurent was crazy at first because he was so daring," says stylist Cathy Lempert. "Now Gaultier, too, is creating a library for other designers." Several recent trends—notably, clashing paisleys with plaids and layering cropped jackets over longer shirts—began on his drawing board. "He is one of the biggest influences in ready-to-wear," says *Vogue* fashion editor Polly Mellen. "In the shows, he takes on an eccentric quality but underneath the fun and games, there are real clothes, wonderful clothes."

[18] McCarthy, op. cit., p. 6.
[19] Jennifer Seder, "Promise Her Anything?" *Los Angeles Times*, October 5, 1979, p. 1.

5-15 *In the fall of 1984 the new buzz word in the fashion vocabulary was* androgyny—*the state of having both male and female characteristics. Cross dressing became part of the fashion scene.*

Gaultier was born to middle-class French parents, but weaned on more exotic stuff: as a child, he lived for a time with his grandmother, a faith healer and fortune teller whom he credits with forming his odd sensibility. By the time he was fifteen, Gaultier was drawing his own *haute couture* collections, writing glowing reviews of them for his private amusement. ("It was a very Parisian collection and we loved it.") On his eighteenth birthday, Pierre Cardin, to whom he had submitted some sketches, offered Gaultier a job. After a brief stint *chez* Cardin and several years at Jean Patou, Gaultier struck out on his own, staging shows with characteristic outrageousness: at one, he had Edwige, a reigning Paris punk, dress up in ostrich feathers and vinyl to sing a wicked parody of Frank Sinatra's hit "My Way."

It was an apt anthem for a designer who finds conventional good taste depressing. "I prefer something awful to nothing," says Gaultier. "People, even if they have no money, should be individualistic."[20]

[20] *Newsweek*, "Clashing with Convention," October 29, 1984, p. 136.

International Designers

Fashion is now international. *Couture* has not been limited to France for many years. Designers from all over the world contribute inspiration to the fashion picture. Many governments have encouraged and subsidized designers because of the important economic benefits for their country. In England, Mary Quant, Jean Muir, and Zandra Rhodes have all been recognized for their contribution to the fashion industry and its monetary benefits to the country. Sybil Connolly, of Ireland, has revived a fashion interest in Irish tweeds and linens through her designs. For this, she has been granted official recognition and financial support by her government.

Italy now enjoys a reputation for technical leadership in knits and woven fabrics, creative *couture* and quality *prêt à porter*. It is the biggest European exporter of wearing apparel. American buyers attend fashion showings in Milan, Florence, and Rome. *Couturiers* working in Italy include Valentino, Andres Laug, Mila Schön, Basile, Roberta di Camerino, and Gianni Versace. Missoni is known for superb knits. Gucci and Ferragamo are longtime leaders in leather handbags and shoes. Fendi creates innovative furs and clothing. Giorgio Armani has been credited with worldwide impact in menswear, particularly the unstructured look.

The list of international fashion designers and contributions could go on and on. A stroll through any American department store will reveal how very international our tastes have become. For fashion this can only be a romantic adventure forward. As each designer makes his unique contribution from his corner of the world, inspiration is excited in another land. Thus, we have the Tyrolean-inspired embroidery gracing a Japanese fabric, the mandarin neckline on a Mexican peasant shirt, and Javanese batik print on an African *burnoose* for American loungewear. The desire of women and men for something different, unique, and exciting creates the impetus for the international market of fashion.

American Designers

During World War II, France was occupied by Nazi Germany, and from 1940 to 1945 the French fashion industry ceased to function. Many of the great houses closed rather than serve the conqueror. Fashion designers became national heroes and vital Paris underground workers rather than submit to Hitler's plan to move the Paris *couture* to Germany. Hitler knew how strong the economic force of French fashion was and felt it should be a part of postwar Germany.

It was during this time that American designers moved into prominence. Among these early designers were Norman Norell, Claire McCardle, Mainbocher, Howard Greer, and Charles James. Gilbert Adrian, the man who probably had the most influence, designed for the movies when Hollywood was at its zenith and the neighborhood theater of every town and hamlet was the social and cultural mecca (Figure 5-16). Adrian's work has been recently "discovered." It seems very compatible with the wide shoulders and narrow-skirted styles of the 1980s. Nola Ewing, of the Textiles and Costume Department of the Los Angeles County Museum of Art, believes Adrian was one of the world's greatest designers.

He did things that had never been done before. He created a new triangular silhouette. Because much of his work was done during the fabric rationing of World War II, he often worked with such fabrics as cotton gingham and rayon crepe, yet he created masterpieces for both the screen and his private *couture* clientele. His influence was felt in every showroom and store in this country; his trim suits and slinky dresses were reproduced in every price bracket. To judge by his imitators, he was the most influential designer in their copybooks. For them he took the place of Paris during the war years. His untimely death robbed the world of a great creative talent which was changing the face of fashion.[21]

Listing early American designers is difficult, as they did not have the recognition of the European designer. Often American designers worked for large

[21] Nola Ewing, Preparator, field trip presentation, Textiles and Costume Department, Los Angeles County Museum of Art, January 7, 1979.

15-6a,b *Gilbert Adrian was a Hollywood designer who established a couture house in Los Angeles in 1939. He designed for many of the famous Hollywood film stars including Marlene Deitrich (shown here), Joan Crawford, and Katherine Hepburn. He is considered one of the world's greatest designers. The Los Angeles County Museum of Art has featured his work in several exhibits. (Courtesy John Engstead)*

manufacturers rather than the small houses and thus their reputations were overshadowed. Some of the important pioneer American designers were independent and patterned their business operations after those in Paris. Among the best known are James Galanos, Pauline Trigere, Norman Norell, Bonnie Cashin, Ben Zuckerman, Sidney Wragge, Rudi Gernreich, Halston, Anne Fogarty, Bill Blass, Geoffrey Beene, and Anne Klein. Probably the greatest contributions of Americans have been in sportswear, particularly swimwear. Standardization of size and the engineering of design of American foundation garments have no equals in the world. American textile research and production have made possible whole new concepts for the designer. American mass production has made fashion a commodity available to all, and its innovation of planned obsolescence helps to keep fashion vital, alive, and on the move. Current American designers include Norma Kamali, Bob Mackie, Perry Ellis, Liz Claibourne, Bill Blass, Adolfo, Halston, Donna Karan, Louis Dell'Olio, Willi Smith (Figure 5-17), Calvin Klein, Ralph Lauren, and Mary McFadden. (Figures 5-18, 5-19)

Kennedy Fraser, a fashion writer, summed up the strength of American style:

After all, it is the jogging suits, leotards, T-shirts, even the ubiquitous polyester double knits—and not Joan Crawford's shoulder pads—that are the source of the perennial strength of truly indigenous American style.[22]

[22] Kennedy Fraser, "On and Off the Avenue," *New Yorker*, June 11, 1979, p. 153.

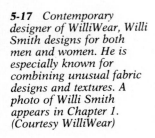

5-17 Contemporary designer of WilliWear, Willi Smith designs for both men and women. He is especially known for combining unusual fabric designs and textures. A photo of Willi Smith appears in Chapter 1. (Courtesy WilliWear)

5-18 *Merle Norman underwrote a design competition as a sponsor of the 18th Century Woman exhibit at the Metropolitan Museum of Art. Here Albert Capraro shows how he captured the drama and opulence of the 18th century in a blush rose silk taffeta gown with a full skirt and deep v-neck. The sleeves are puffed to the elbow and adorned with silk roses. (Courtesy Fashion Institute Design and Merchandising)*

5-19 *Arnold Scaasi shows his 18th century-inspired ballgown with this silver, pink-voile, and gray brocade with ruching around the deep decolletage. The gray velvet cloak is collared and cuffed in sable-dyed fox and lined in pink-violet taffeta. (Courtesy Fashion Institute Design and Merchandising)*

The Designer—Creator of Fashion Inspiration

The creators of new fashion ideas are the designers (or *couturieres*) who initiate the styles that the buying public accepts or rejects. Designers must continually provide innovations in style because of the demands of the consumer. Designers often develop classic designs that are the backbone of their collections. Chanel did this with her suits, Balenciaga with the little black dress, Givenchy with his coats, and Balmain with his fabulous ball gowns. These are the designers' specialties, yet to remain competitive they must continually devise variations of these staples as well as create fresh designs.

Designers often show a similar trend each season, and it is commonly thought that they work together to form a conspiracy that will direct the public acceptance of their work. This is not true. Designers work independently. Actually, they are most jealous of their collections and work in utmost secrecy. Seamstresses, mannequins, custodians, and other personnel who have access to workrooms and designs are carefully policed so that they will not pass "trade secrets." Many designers do not complete a garment until moments before the mannequin presents it for the first time.

The successful designers must be in constant touch with the times. They must understand the people for whom they design, their interests, attitudes, and values of dress, modes of living, and occupations. Designers must also be aware of political affairs.

Popular newspapers and magazines, museums, books, plays, television, motion pictures, sports, and music all have a direct influence on fashion. A designer must be sensitive to such influences and be able to translate into fabric the feeling of the times. Style of clothing, as much as any other criteria, represents the era. As the famous French philosopher Anatole France observed when noting what literature he would choose as an index to a culture a hundred years after his death:

I would simply take, my friend, a fashion paper to see how women dressed a century after my decease. Their ribbons and bibbons would tell me more about future humanity than all the philosophers, novelists, preachers and men of science.[23]

Brockman qualified this thinking and applied it more directly to the modern designer by stating: "The trend setter is the designer who expresses the essence of an era with the greatest fashion awareness."[24]

This explains why designers tend to show similar trends each year. They are each affected by the same influences, which in turn make fashion. They read the same magazines and newspapers; see the same films, plays, and television shows; and react to the same triumphs and tragedies of mankind. When the current

[23] Jean Brousson, *Anatole France Himself*, trans. J. Pollock (Philadelphia: Lippincott, 1925), p. 106.
[24] Helen L. Brockman, *The Theory of Fashion Design* (New York: Wiley, 1965), p. 74.

events focus on a particular person or place, designers translate these happenings into clothing styles.

Small changes in fashion seem to occur very quickly as compared to basic changes in the silhouette that take place over a period of years. It would appear that small changes in fashion are affected by fashion leadership, whereas the major changes are affected by political, economic, and cultural factors.[25]

In every collection, buyers in the industry look for the one or two models that may become trend setters. Originals may often vary only slightly from last year's styles, but a subtle change in sleeve fullness, neckline cut, waist placement or hem length may be just what the makers of fashion desire. Store buyers purchase those garments that show new trends and those that can be adapted for American ready-to-wear.

Buyers can purchase *couture* models for copy purposes only. The originals may not be resold but must be returned by a specified date. Replicas of the original are sold. These gowns are limited in number, and less expensive models called *toiles* may also be purchased. These are made of muslin, and full directions for making them are included. These become the designs for ready-to-wear. Often adaptations must be made so that the garment may be manufactured in certain price ranges. If a *toile* is reproduced without variation, it is expensive.

As fashion becomes more international, the role of the Paris *couturier* will continue to be challenged. Whether as a group they can continue to influence the press and buyer remains to be seen. Pierre Cardin has acknowledged that there is creative fashion talent all over the world and not just in Paris.

Fashion Promotion—From Designer to Closet

Before a new style becomes fashion, a feeling of familiarity must be established. The first of a long line of publicity begins when a new collection is presented by the designer. As each model is presented at the showing, it is labeled with a name such as "Rodeo," "fluid look," or "futuristic." This helps to establish the mood the designer is developing in his line.

As buyers make their selections, fashion writers and editors appraise the collection and send stories and sketches to their newspapers and magazines. Established or prestige customers also attend the openings, and their individual purchases are noted and revealed to the general public by the fashion writers. The first news releases appear in the fashion section of the daily newspapers and, therefore, quickly reach the public. Often the fashion reporter selects the most extreme and bizarre models, as these make good copy. Magazine writers select

[25] Jeanette Jarnow and Bernice Judelle, *Inside the Fashion Business* (New York: Wiley, 1966) p. 15.

the models of the collection that they feel will appeal to their particular reading audience. *Women's Wear Daily, the* publication of the garment industry, is closely read by those interested and involved in fashion, both in and out of the trade. Although it does sometimes get a bit frivolous in its gossip, it continually reflects the fashion action. To maintain the position of leadership on the fashion scene, *WWD* maintains a resident staff in all the major cities in the United States and abroad. *W* is a condensation of *WWD*. It is a fashion magazine with a newspaper format, so it often "scoops" other fashion magazines.

Women's fashion magazines carry the collection news about two months after the opening presentations. They cater to all ages, purses, and tastes and do much to promote trends. Editors in this medium have the power to make or break either a design or a designer. These editors can and do exert much influence in the fashion world. Some magazines have the policy of promoting their advertisers through their editorial sections. This type of cooperative promotion is highly desirable and thus very profitable to the magazine.[26] A single advertisement in a magazine is very costly. Actual rates vary with the circulation of the magazine.

High-fashion magazines for women that are currently popular are *Vogue, Harper's Bazaar, Town & Country,* and *Black Enterprise.* European high-fashion magazines such as *L'Officiel* from either Paris or U.S.A. and *Linea Italiana* from Italy reflect a slightly different approach and are interesting to compare with the American magazines. Fashion magazines directed toward the college or career girls are *Mademoiselle* and *Glamour.* Both of these publications present youthful, *avant-garde* fashions. *Seventeen* presents less sophisticated styles for a seventeen-to twenty-four age group. *Gentlemen's Quarterly, M,* and *Esquire* are men's fashion magazines. Combined, these publications exert tremendous influence on fashion and fashion trends.

A child once commented that high-fashion magazines were in reality comic books for adults; many would agree with this astute observation. Yet once the purpose of the high-fashion magazine is understood, it becomes an important reference for fashionable people. By picturing the latest work of the designers, high-fashion magazines present to a wide audience the new ideas that will become fashion. The astute person can learn to discern fashion trends from these magazines.

Fashion illustrations capture the essence of the new style image. Fashion photography is an art form that has become a multimillion dollar business. It uses as its setting every geographical location from the outposts of the Sahara to the deltas of the Ganges to publicize high fashion. The mannequins used in fashion photography are more representative of the fashion figure than the average male or female. That is, they have long, drawn-out, slender bodies, often with very few womanly curves or manly muscles. The poses used in fashion illustrations are oftentimes grotesque. The purpose of this generally is to create an art image, pique the interest of the reader, or show the mood of the garment. It should always be remembered that high-fashion illustrations should never be copied exactly since they are too bizarre and exotic for everyday living.

[26] P. Levine, *The Wheels of Fashion* (Garden City, N.Y.: Doubleday, 1965), pp. 92–93.

Cooperative advertising by textile mills and clothing manufacturers that was formerly directed to the trade has lately been going more directly to the consumer by national media—newspapers, magazines, and television. The high cost of this advertising is often shared when related manufacturers join forces. A textile firm and a garment manufacturer may cooperate to publicize both companies and often extend this type of advertising further to tie in local merchants throughout the country.

At the community level, stores feature new designs in their advertising. Individual designers or lines are promoted in fashion shows throughout the local stores and restaurants. Mail order catalogues and flyers, enclosed with the monthly statements, reach the patron directly.

The Designer and the Celebrity

In the good old days the creation of *couture* celebrities was the exclusive right of Paris. America could provide its own singers, comedians, actors, athletes, or industrialists for the celebrity status, but when it came to excellence in the art of decorating the body, that was exclusively a function of the French. By the late 1960s a change had begun to occur. A whole new group of European designers ushered in *prêt-à-porter* and in the process pushed the established *couturiers* into designing lines in men's ready-made clothing. Strong egos made it impossible for the old names, at that moment in time, to join the *prêt* bandwagon. But New York retailers such as Bloomingdale's and Bendel's welcomed the change and highlighted certain of the new names as a means to attract consumer attention. For the retailer, it was a new reason for being.

As time passed, some of the French *couturiers* began to realize that it was far more profitable to toss their egos aside and follow the way of the new European designers. So they re-entered the woman's fashion world with ready-to-wear in order to partake in the exploitation by the New York retailers of their newly discovered consumer. Most of America's top name designers followed suit.

Meanwhile, the world continued to push on. The move by the upper-middle class from the cities to the suburbs gained momentum, and more and more people left the nightclubs and formal balls behind. They now were forced to live their lives around the automobile, and they dressed accordingly. For women the pants suit became the fashion of the day.

Following a different drummer, out of the depths of Seventh Avenue came Anne Klein, prepared to offer the New York retailer better sportswear to fill the growing need. New York retailers took their cue. Slowly, the Green Rooms and the Crystal Rooms were retired into fashion history, while Anne Klein and the designers who followed her footsteps moved into the limelight. Floor space was appropriated for the better sportswear designers, and the individual designers were promoted.

With their names in public view, these designers took their places alongside the Hollywood movie stars who were billed on the lighted marquees of theaters across the country. The designer had become a celebrity.

What is a celebrity? It is a person who has been accepted by a notable percentage of the masses as being over and beyond them in terms of life's accomplishments. In other words, a celebrity is really created by the public's perception. Celebrities ranging from political figures to video stars often find their pictures plastered on the front pages of newspapers and magazines whenever the camera happens to catch them. Celebrities are an industry unto themselves. The only rational assessment that can be made of their success or failure is how long they last in the limelight. Consider the tenures of Bob Hope, Brooke Shields, Michael Jackson, Liz Taylor, John Forsythe, Van Halen, and Eddie Murphy.

The designer celebrities gave the New York retailer a new handle for selling exclusive merchandise at a comparatively affordable price. The splash that the New York retailers made with their newly found designer celebrities caught on quickly, for when New York gets excited, the rest of the country, not wanting to be thought of as provincial, follows New York's lead.

From this beginning, the industry knew where its next dollars would come from. It was time to exploit celebrity names in the promotion of moderate-priced apparel. In the designer category, Calvin Klein, Bill Blass, Ralph Lauren, and Halston were ripe enough to be picked, and their names were well-known enough to retailers to be used as means to attract attention outside of better sportswear.

The upper-middle-class youth, who in the late 1960s and early 1970s dressed down to prove a point, were now beginning to join the "establishment." They would continue to wear jeans, but the jeans were no longer a symbol of the 60s. Instead they carried a visible label and were a part of the new world of celebrity fashion.

To confirm the fact that the celebrity was of growing importance to Americans, all the retailer needed to do was to look around and notice that the apparel industry was not alone in the exploitation of the stars. Prior to the television boom, the Hollywood celebrities were known to the public only through motion pictures. But by 1960 the majority of U.S. households owned a TV set and viewing a celebrity became an everyday occurrence.

For a number of years the majority of Hollywood stars were camera shy when it came to produce endorsement. But by the late 1970s, with sports stars leading the way, Hollywood celebrities knew that associating their names with a product was not so demeaning—especially in light of the fact that a 30-second spot could earn them from $25,000 to millions of dollars depending on their celebrity status.

What this Hollywood star endorsement game seemed to prove was that America was bored with commonplace merchandise but might be intrigued if the product was approved by a celebrity. As more and more stars jumped on the endorsement bandwagon, it became apparent that for the most part stars could move merchandise.

The success or failure of a celebrity runs more or less like the introduction of a new line in packaged goods. There are no formulas for success or failure. The Gloria Swanson line of dresses flopped. The Calvin Klein jeans and skirts in denim and corduroy took off like a skyrocket. There is probably no better example than Gloria Vanderbilt. Who is she? Does anyone really know? Probably not. Nevertheless, in terms of retailing she was the number one celebrity in 1980. Why? Nobody knows.

In the typical pattern of fashion movement, the designer/celebrity-labeled clothing was exploited to the maximum and it became property of the masses. Sears Roebuck negotiated a lucrative contract with top model Cheryl Tiegs to use her name for a line of clothing exclusive to them. In the fall of 1984, 12 million Americans received the Sears catalogue with its cover picture of Cheryl Tiegs wearing her designer-wear sweater, skirt, and blouse. Inside the catalogue other big names including Arnold Palmer, Joe Namath, Diane von Furstenberg, Johnny Carson, and Evonne Goolagong, labeled fashionable goods. In a multimillion dollar deal J. C. Penney Company signed Halston to design the Halston III collection for their exclusive use. Other designer-labeled clothing was available everywhere from the smallest to the largest shopping mall, the swap meets, and the roadside vendor. When a fashion becomes available to all, its cycle is near completion. Designer status labels no longer have status. It was time to move on.

A new group of celebrities have moved into fashion prominence. They are the stars of the TV soaps. Their influence is probably going to be felt for a long time for reasons comparable to those affecting the influence of movie stars in the 1940–1950 era.

People describe the soap look several ways. Bullock's Wilshire fashion director Rosemarie Troy noted,

Women shop with an idea of how they should look, and the subliminal suggestion for it comes from the TV series. It's a very finished look, with hats, gloves, and hosiery. The store buyers are picking up on it too. One showed me an outfit with a beautiful silk shirt and nice pants and said, "This is my Linda Evans look."

Nolan Miller, who designs all the costumes for *Dynasty*, describes the soap approach to fashion in one word: glamorous. He started designing costumes in the 1950s. He dressed such stars as the late Joan Crawford (whom he calls "the most glamorous star I've ever known"), June Allyson, and Dick Powell, Jaclyn Smith, Bette Davis, and Barbara Stanwyck. Such stars spoiled him, he says, when it comes to appreciating modern actresses.

They walk like truck drivers and wear nothing but sandals and blue jeans, haven't set foot in a pair of high-heeled shoes in their life and have been brainwashed by designer labels. . . . An outfit can look terrible on them, but if it's by a designer they've seen in a fashion magazine, they think it looks great. It seems no matter what character they play, they want to dress the way they dress anywhere else, and they come from a generation of junk-shop dressers.

He cited a young actress who wanted to wear a miniskirt and pink hair to the Academy Award presentations. He said, "This night is supposed to have some dignity to it. Thirty years from now you'll really be sorry."[27]

[27] *Los Angeles Times*, "Costumes on TV Soaps Channel Their Way to Viewers' Closets," June 17, 1984.

Jack Smith, observer of human foibles, summed it up this way:

Did you happen to read the story in our Newsmakers column the other day about the two young women in Albuquerque who have launched a prospering little business in what they call "resigner jeans"—for the woman who has resigned herself to what the story discreetly called "a full figure"?

They call their product "Lardashe Resigner Jeans," and they are being sued by Jordache, the makers of Jordache designer jeans, who claim that the new trademark is too much like their own.

I don't wish to provoke whatever court may have the jurisdiction in this matter, but I hope the young women—Susan Duran, 34, and Marsha Stafford, 32—prevail over their celebrated and, I imagine, well-heeled competitor.

He continued:

You can't blame any manufacturer for wanting to protect a trademark, but I doubt that *Jordache* is likely to fall into the general language, the way *aspirin* and *linoleum* have, for example. *Denim jeans* is the generic term, and the only trademark in danger of becoming generic is Levi's.

I suppose *Lardashe* may be disdained as a vulgar echo of the common slang term for "full figure," but at the same time it also echoes the tony *Jordache*, and there is sauciness about this double pun that makes it amusing and forgivable.

It certainly inspired my colleague DeWayne Johnson in writing the item in Newsmakers:

"The Lardashe jeans feature reinforced seams, a high waist and an appliqued pig peering over the back pocket. Not wanting to hog the market, they started cautiously but fear the suit by Jordache Enterprises may kill their fledgling business. The women said they had sold more than 600 pairs to buyers who have gone hog wild over them."

I'm not sure that I like the idea of the appliqued pig. It seems to me that the name *Lardashe* would be concession enough for a woman of full figure to make to the humor of her problem, but that is Duran and Stafford's business, and they seemed to be doing all right until Jordache squealed.

I should think Jordache would welcome the appearance of Lardashe. At least people will know now how to pronounce their name. I never knew whether it was Jord-ake or Jord-ack.

And now I know it rhymes with Lardashe.[28]

Fashion Leadership

Early each year the press presents featured picture stories on resort-wear fashions. These are the designs that promoters believe will be big sellers later in the season. The purpose of the emphasis on resort-wear fashions at this time is to feel out the market and get some indication of how the later spring and summer sales will go. Resort-wear fashions are made available in January for wear in the southern playgrounds such as the French Riviera, the Greek Islands, the Bahamas, Florida, and Southern California. These testing grounds have been proven

[28] Jack Smith, *Los Angeles Times*, November 22, 1984, P. V, p. 1.

to give an indication of the success or failure of a new style. The growing popularity of skiing and other snow sports has somewhat lessened the impact of resort wear.

As the new designs become available, who are the first to pick them up? Generally, this *avant-garde* group is comprised of the wealthy, the socially prominent, actresses or actors, political and business leaders or their spouses, and other persons who are widely recognized and publicized. These people must have money and the opportunities to display their wardrobes. They must have the self-confidence to wear and show their new creations to advantage. They must have a strong desire to be identified with high fashion and the courage to dress differently from the masses.

Fashion leadership can be found at all social strata. The men and women who innovate new styles in their own local social groups can thus be categorized. Excellent examples of fashion leadership are to be found on college campuses. Each social group seems to have a member or two who lead the way in new styles of dress. These also are fashion leaders. Jarnow pointed out:

Today, however, fashion is not a matter of imitating any particular social or economic class. Fashions seem to emerge spontaneously; if style offerings are appropriate and acceptable, they need not wait for the approval of an elite in order to become the fashion. . . .[29]

After the fashion leaders introduce the new style, the followers take it up. Followers are basically imitative and need to become familiar with the new style to feel confident in it. Followers also need the assurance that the new style has gained the approval of a number of fashion leaders.

The duration of popularity of any fashion varies. Classics remain fashionable over a long time period. Fads flit in and out of fashion quickly. When people tire of a fashion, they discard it. As soon as the fashion has been accepted by the masses, the fashion leaders tire of it and experiment to find the next trend. This pattern appears to be followed by all but the very highest and the very lowest socioeconomic groups.

Understanding this movement of fashion is important to the expenditure of the clothing budget. Buying clothing on the outgoing phase of its popularity is more expensive than buying new fashion as it comes in, because the old will be discarded more quickly. This caution should be particularly applied to sale merchandise, as sometimes it is already obsolete or soon will be.

Who Really Makes Fashion?

It is very simple to decide what was fashion one hundred or more years ago. It is not too difficult to explain what is fashion today. But it is absolutely im-

---

[29] Jarnow and Judelle, op. cit., p. 6.

possible to predict accurately what will be fashion at any time in the future. Although fashion does depend on many detectable influences and forces, it also seems to have a capricious mind of its own. Fashion may be practical, comfortable, and convenient to its time or it may just as likely be the opposite. Examples of this may be found in every recorded fashion history. During the Depression years of the 1930s, the fashionable styles included expensive plumed hats, sequined and beaded garments, precious jewels, furs, and luxurious fabrics. These same costly items returned to fashion early in the 1980s, in a period of economic inflation, recession, unemployment, and international turmoil.

It has been determined that fashion is influenced by a number of components, which may work singly or in concert. Fashion is influenced by the era or the time in which it exists and by the current events of that time. New technical developments create products from which fashion may be innovated. The lifestyles practiced either by governmental decree or by free choice create the background against which fashion will be used and displayed. Fashion trend-setters are usually prominent people; today these are often entertainers, sports stars, or superheros, whereas in the past they were royalty or the very rich. It is acknowledged that the real arbiters of fashion are the people, for it is the consumer who must buy and display the styles of the marketplace. Returning to our definition of fashion, understand that it is only when enough people have adopted a style that it becomes fashion. It is this free choice of the people that makes fashion so unpredictable.

Fashion Adoption Theories

Fashion theories help explain the phenomenon of fashion. These theories may be operating separately or concurrently. Each is easier to identify after the style has become fashion than to predict. Fashion merchandisers must develop some sense of fashion movement; many are very skilled, but all will admit that no theory of predicting the general acceptance of a style, which makes it fashionable, is foolproof.

Trickle-down Theory

Centuries ago the setters of fashion were royalty. The nobility copied the royalty and they in turn were copied by the middle class. At this time the lower class was prohibited by sumptuary laws from copying anyone. In time, royalty was replaced by the fashion leadership of the families of business—men who had climbed to the top of the economic and social ladder and wanted to display their wealth and power. It became important for others in business to adopt the dress, activities, and appearances of the fashion leaders. Those scattered along the socioeconomic scale found it safe to copy what "they" wore rather than lead in fashion experimentation. Thus, fashion *trickled down* from higher to lower echelons. As fashions were adopted by the masses, new styles were introduced at the top. It was during this period that the *couture* was in its most prestigious position.

This *trickle-down theory* of fashion evolvement was identified and accepted by the nineteenth-century economists John Roe, Caroline R. Foley, and Thorstein Veblen, and by the sociologist George Simmel, who published a step-by-step description of the theory in 1904.

Kaiser applies this theory to the classic fashions of the early 1980s. Business wear for women imitates the classic blazer and classic blouse worn by the upper classes a long time before women entered the business world en masse. The polo style pullover shirt follows a classic style worn by the upper classes for leisure time wear for over two decades. She reminds us that the upper, upper classes do not set fashions, it is the classes immediately below them, that is, the lower-upper and upper-middle that set the fashions. The upper, upper classes are not concerned with fashion.[30]

The trickle-down theory of fashion is applicable in the contemporary scene. Examples of trickle-down fashion are the designer clothes, customized ski boots, foreign sports cars, Perrier Mineral Water, Mediterranean and Caribbean cruises, and Princess Di hats.

Trickle-across Theory

As the twentieth century progressed, fashion no longer was created by imitating any specific social or economic class. Heroes and heroines from all walks of life became the fashion leaders. Movie stars, television personalities, campus celebrities, folk heroes, sports stars, and other figures captured the public's fancy and gave impetus to fashion. The *trickle-across theory* of fashion was proposed by Charles W. King in 1963. He acknowledged that each group or segment of society has its own leader or leaders of fashion. The approval of these local leaders is required before a fashion can be adopted by the group.[31]

Recent examples of the trickle-across theory include the gloved hand inspired by Cyndi Lauper and Michael Jackson, boxer shorts and jogging shoes and suits lifted from athletes, and the Mary Lou Retton haircut adopted after her Olympic triumph.

Bottom-up Theory

The *bottom-up theory* explains that fashions filter up from youth to age and from lower to upper socioeconomic groups. The idea behind this theory is that lower-income youths have little social position and thus fewer inhibitions. They

[30] Susan B. Kaiser, *Social Psychology of Clothing and Personal Adornment* (New York: Macmillan, 1985), Chapter 12.
[31] Jarnow and Judelle, op. cit., pp. 9–10.

are freer to create new dress patterns. Those from upper socioeconomic groups are secure in their positions and feel free to adopt novel dress patterns. Those in the middle socioeconomic groups are often more conservative but can accept clothing styles emerging from lower and upper socioeconomic groups.

Some examples of the bottom-up theory are these:

The *mod look* of the 1960s came from the poor boys and girls of London and put wealthy ladies into miniskirts and their husbands into Edwardian-cut suits. The protective black leather outfits of the motorcycle club elite became the uniform for many in the wealthy "Jet-Set" where it evolved from black leather to pastel suede. The T-shirt-jeans uniform of the earliest "hippies" swept the world, and became the uniform of the young and the would-be young all over the world. The exotic use of makeup, extreme haircuts and color, and the flamboyant dress of the London punker spread through the world and was caught up by high fashion in the mid-80s.

A new form of TV music videos picked up the punker's theme and added the individuality of each group. Stars like Michael Jackson, Madonna, and Cindy Lauper joined by thousands of other performers gave teen-agers a different perspective on clothing and personal adornment. These ideas were combined with the endless reruns of "Leave It to Beaver," "Father Knows Best" and "I Love Lucy," which are docu-dramas of how life was supposed to be in the 1950s, the teen years of many of today's parents. The result was a time warp of fashion.

Mom's strapless prom dress or facsimile in nylon tulle and lace with fitted waistline and bouffant skirt was combined with high-top "tennies," neon socks, denim jacket, and long lace gloves. Clash with class was "it" in the teen-age world. Taking something traditional and combining it with the direct opposite made a new statement that shocked the "older generation." The combination of thrift store clothing, accessories, and distressed hair styles was described by many as weird. The cross-pollinization of fashion time zones gave the video its spunk and a whole new generation its very own look. This look moved up to influence the whole fashion world.[32]

Another example of the bottom-up theory of fashion movement, and perhaps the most enduring, may be referred to as Third World wear. As interpreted by Westerners, it is often a collage of many different national styles and costumes. Third World wear is often worn by the young or economy minded; it is also worn by the well-traveled, the cultured, and the affluent. Third World wear manifests itself in simple, "timeless" elements, such as Indian cotton, three-button undershirts worn under denim jackets and "organic" trousers, which wrap around the waist without zippers or buttons. This school of costume is perhaps the most persistent of all and is likely to remain so[33] (Figures 5-20, 5-21).

---

[32] Bettijane Levine, "Prom Time: A Spunky Spectacle of Fantasy Highlighted by Funk," *Los Angeles Times*, November 30, 1984, P. V, p. 1.
[33] Peter Carlsen, "Costumed As We Are," *Gentlemen's Quarterly*, August 1979, p. 69.

The Fashion Industry

The fashion industry is the largest employer in the world. Millions of people are employed in the production of textiles, clothing and accessories and in the staffing of stores that sell this merchandise. Consumer consumption is continually sending this figure higher. Apparel manufacturing alone employs more people than the entire printing and publishing field, and the chemical and drug industries combined.[34]

Because of the size of this industry, it is obvious that the prediction of fashion is a very serious aspect of the business. With the understanding of fashion and the technological capacities of computers, this prediction is based more and more on reliable information. The clothing merchant who ignores these new research methods will not last long in this highly competitive business. The makers and sellers of fashion merchandise have their own methods for studying trends in

[34] Robert Beaulieu, The Costume Society of America 11th Annual Symposium, Fashion Institute of Technology, New York, New York June 12, 1985.

5-20 *Leisure-wear wardrobes include Third World-inspired garments such as this Tunisian-style tunic. (Courtesy National Cotton Council)*

5-21 *Third World clothing manifests itself in simple, timeless elements. This shirt has East African origins. (Courtesy Simplicity Pattern Company)*

consumer preferences. They use their past successes for clues as to what will work in the current market, and they study today's fashion activity for clues to what will happen tomorrow.

The more one understands the dynamics of fashion, the more obvious it becomes that fashion is not imposed on the public by a controlling industry. Fashion in apparel is a phenomenon that must be analyzed and interpreted into clothing designs. Of the many thousands of clothing styles that are promoted, only a few actually become fashion. A style is never a fashion if it is worn by only a few people, no matter who they may be. Fashion is not a matter of opinion but of actual count.[35]

Givenchy, the French designer, stated, "A designer cannot dictate change . . . fashion today is so capricious."[36] Norman Norell, one of America's most successful designers, acknowledged, "Fashion is what is accepted and worn by the general public. When it reaches that point, you know the design is a good one."[37]

Perhaps the best summation of fashion was made by an astute observer of fashion who wrote:

A history of fashion is a history of life: To be out of fashion is to be out of life. The way people dress is truly a reflection of their times, as well as their class, economic status, and of the weather.

—Anonymous

Suggested Activities

1. As you watch television or movies, become aware of the fashion of speech, music, dance, manners, morals, body movement, architecture, furniture, and clothing. Contrast today's fashion with the historical portrayals of fashion you see.
2. Invite guest speakers representing some aspect of the fashion industry to class to discuss the industry today.
3. Survey your campus for fashions. Start a pictorial record of campus fads that can be used in coming years to illustrate the changing nature of fashion in your local area.
4. Determine whether styles are on the way in or out by doing a fashion count. Decide what you are going to count, where and when you will count. Do at least 50 samples. Repeat at different times and places. Analyze the data and discuss it with the class.
5. Read the following humorous essay by Art Buchwald and consider its fashion influence. What is revealed by the article? If possible, discuss the article with your class.

[35] Jarnow and Judelle, op. cit., p. 17.
[36] "Givenchy Means Never Having to Say You're Sorry," *Los Angeles Times*, September 16, 1974, Pt. 4, p. 1.
[37] *Business Week*, September 11, 1964, p. 64.

Plumage on the Potomac

Art Buchwald

WASHINGTON—The new summer fashions for American tourists visiting Washington have recently been released, and from all indications the clothes are going to be more formal than in previous years.

The source of this information was Sophie Glutz, the famous Washington tourist fashion expert, who said, "It appears now that women will be wearing more stretch pants than Bermuda shorts when visiting the public monuments."

"Does this mean that women tourists visiting this town will no longer be wearing blue jeans and sweat shirts?"

"Oh, I wouldn't rule that out completely. In the daytime you may find a certain number of women in blue jeans and sweat shirts, as well as shorts, but in the evening they will probably change into slacks, stretch pants and blouses."

"Is it true that the short shorts are out?"

"They are after 4 o'clock. Of course, many tourists will still visit the White House and the Lincoln Memorial in short shorts, but we're recommending longer shorts for the Senate and House of Representatives."

"I think that's wise," I said. "What about skirts?"

"Skirts are awfully dressy for sight-seeing in Washington, but some women will wear them with halters and bare midriffs and open-toed sandals."

"What about dresses and suits for women?"

"Heaven forbid. A woman tourist wouldn't be seen dead in a dress or suit. All the other tourists would laugh at her."

"What about styles?"

"Keeping your hair in curlers while sight-seeing still seems to be the rage. The large colored plastic curlers which stick out all over your head are coming back in again."

"How about face cream?"

"It's optional. Many women tourists prefer it to suntan oil as suntan oil doesn't show up as well."

"I suppose socks and stockings are out?"

"They have been for some time now, unless you're going to a state dinner at the White House."

"What's new in colors?"

"In shorts, we're recommending plaids for women who weigh more than 150 pounds. They look so much better from the rear. Also, stripes are back in, at least as far as sweat shirts are concerned. The simple black toreador pants of a few years ago are definitely out."

"What about men's tourist fashions?"

"There hasn't been too much change in men's fashions this year. They'll still wear Army fatigues, bright-colored sports shirts, sneakers and baseball caps."

"And children?"

"We're not laying down any hard and fast rules on what children should wear in Washington. The National Gallery of Art has asked that children not wear bathing suits when visiting it, but you have to remember that the gallery is a very stuffy institution."

"I'm delighted to see how the standards in clothes have gone up in the nation's capital this year," I said.

"Yes, it's amazing how clothes-conscious Americans are when they visit Washington these days. It's as though they know that they're on display."[38]

---

[38] Permission granted, courtesy of author.

II

Physical Factors Influencing Appearance

6 *Your Body*

The human body comes in an infinite variety of forms. People vary in height, weight, shape, posture, carriage, and bearing. The basic factors responsible for such variety are heredity, nutrition, and environment.

One of the most individual features about you is your body structure. Unless yours was a multiple birth that resulted in identical siblings, you are the only person with your body design. The bone structure that you have inherited has been influenced by your racial background and your ancestral heritage. This frame is one thing you cannot change (there are some rare exceptions). If you are tall or short, small boned or large boned, accept it. This is you. This is part of your individuality.

Your nutritional status in early years has had a tremendous influence on your body development. Malnutrition in utero, infancy, or childhood, whatever its causes, affects the conformation of the body. Some evidences of nutritional deficiencies are stunted growth and misshapen limbs.

Environment and culture also influence growth patterns. In the United States, Westerners are generally larger than Easterners. Sunshine and outdoor exercise could be responsible for this. Cultural ideas of attractiveness have a tremendous influence on body development. In a culture where bosoms are a beauty symbol, women strive to develop the bust. In a culture where tall men are admired, height is emphasized. Prevailing fashion influences the body (Figure 6-1).

Another element closely related to the presentation of the figure is individual self-concept (self-image). The people who have a confident, positive attitude relate this in the manner in which they carry their bodies. Individuals who are less

6-1 *Female body distortion dictated by fashion.*

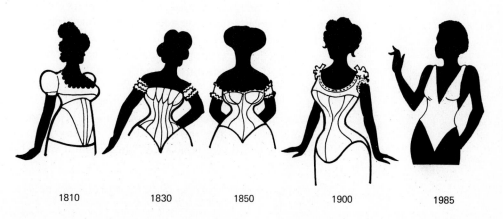

1810	1830	1850	1900	1985

sure of themselves often make this statement in their carriage. Oftentimes when posture is slumped and slovenly, it appears to be an apology for taking up floor space.

Analyze your body as objectively as you can. List the assets and the problems. If you can make corrections, try to do so. If you cannot make changes, decide to accept this as part of your uniqueness. It helps to keep in mind that no one is absolutely perfect, and it is the imperfections that give one individuality. (Designing personal appearance to cope with body imperfections is covered in Part 3.)

Body Image

We each have our own body image. Body image is the individual's perception of his own being.

William James, one of the first to concern himself with the self-concept, defined the "empirical me," or the self, as being composed of the material me, the social me, and the spiritual me. In respect to the material me, he postulated: "The body is the innermost part of the material me in each of us; and certain parts of the body seem more intimately ours than the rest. The clothes come next."[1]

Jersild suggested that appearance and physical ability play an important role in one's approach to life. Body image beliefs are formed early in life. The self is a subjective system through which experiences are interpreted and given meaning. Jersild stated:

The self is a composite of many psychological states, impressions and feelings. It includes the perceptions the adolescent has of himself; the impressions he has of his body, the image he has of his physical appearance and the tangible properties of his person.[2]

The body image may be a distortion of reality. Some overweight people see themselves as slender. Some slender people see themselves as heavy. Because of inaccurate body image, clothing that exaggerates irregularities may be selected rather than clothing that conceals. Examples of this are the very thin woman who does not see herself as skinny and wears clothing that exaggerates her boniness; the portly man who does not visualize himself as heavy and wears skintight clothes which reveal each bump and bulge.

To have a true concept of one's physical self requires complete objectivity. An honest body analysis must be made with the mind as well as the eye. If an accurate body image can be achieved, clothing decisions can then be made that will enhance the assets and camouflage the problems.

Warschaw observed that changes in body image generally occur slowly and imperceptibly. Since the body image is many years in the making and involves crucial experiences in one's life, one does not vary this attitude in a brief period

[1] William James, *Psychology* (New York: Holt, 1880), p. 177.
[2] A. Jersild, *In Search of Self* (New York: Teachers College, Columbia University, 1952), p. 3.

of time. She concluded that *any* change in body image that is more accurate should be considered a success.[3]

Body Types

The human body has been categorized according to similarities into *three basic somatotypes* (body types). These are the *endomorph*, the *mesomorph* and the *ectomorph* (Figure 6-2).

The endomorph frame has a relatively prominent abdomen and generally tends toward certain softness or roundness of the body parts. Muscular development does not appear prominent, although the person may be very strong. The endomorph has a genetic tendency toward softness in outline. An extreme or exaggerated endomorph would have a sizable round body, which might be described as portly or queen-size. The neck and limbs are short. The upper arms and thighs are fleshy. A relatively larger amount of overall body fat may be present, but this alone does not determine the endomorphy. It is possible for an underweight person to be considered an endomorph.

The mesomorph frame is bonier, more angular, and more muscled. It is often called an athletic build. The appearance of the musculature is the body's most visibly pronounced feature. The mesomorph has large shoulders and chest, well-developed arm and leg muscles, and a minimum of body fat. The mesomorph can be overweight. Mesomorphy, like the other somatotypes, is a natural tendency, which may not be fulfilled. Although muscle can be developed on all body types through exercise, if an individual is not born a mesomorph, true mesomorphy cannot be attained.

The ectomorph frame is long and lean. The muscular development is lineal. The body is tall and narrow, the limbs are long and thin, there is very little body fat. While in the natural state, the ectomorph appears underfed. If the ectomorph becomes overweight the body appears puffy or blown-up. The avoirdupois would make the skeletal frame virtually disappear.

In life, assigning people to one of the three somatotypes is not always simple because we are the offspring of random mating and not cloning. The somatotype theory does not presuppose that all people can be definitively typed. Some people may be combinations of the three types. The hypothesis is that men and women come in all shapes and sizes with many variables, but all human forms can be analyzed against the three prototypes. This theory also helps people understand why no matter how hard they try there are some body types that are impossible for each individual to achieve.[4]

[3] Tessa Albert Warschaw, "The Development and Evaluation of a Personal Management Program and Its Effects Upon the Self-Concept and Perceived Locus of Control of Blind Adolescent Females," doctoral dissertation, University of Southern California, June 1973, p. 121.

[4] Charles Hix with Brian Burdine. *Dressing Right* (New York: St. Martin's Press, 1978), pp. 16–21.

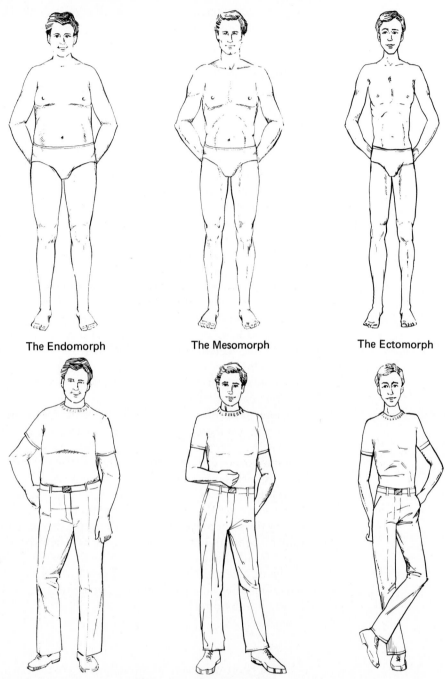

The Endomorph   The Mesomorph   The Ectomorph

6-2 *The human body has been categorized according to similarities into three basic somatotypes. These are the endomorph, the mesomorph, and the ectomorph.*

Physical Fitness

There is no rigid medical definition of *physical fitness*. Most authorities agree that physical fitness means being strong and flexible enough and having adequate endurance to do the tasks you want to do. For a person who manages a home with small children, it signifies being able to lift and carry, to bend and reach, and to work at a certain rate all day without fatigue. For a person working at a desk, it denotes being able to sit and work for a period of time without strain or muscle soreness. Fitness depends on your individual needs, your unique body type, your daily activities and the manner in which you perform them.[5]

Laurence E. Morehous, Ph.D., Professor of Exercise Physiology at UCLA, distinguishes among fitness, health, and performance. Fitness is the ability to meet the demands of your environment. Health is freedom from disease. Performance is how well you do something. He defines levels of satisfactory fitness: the irreducible minimum, below which your physical condition deteriorates; general fitness, which includes a safe margin for adaptation to change and emergency; and preparation for fairly strenuous recreational or occupational activity. Morehous stresses that most people maintain the minimum fitness simply by performing the normal tasks of everyday life. By slightly increasing daily activities, fitness reserves can be strengthened.[6]

James Z. Nicholas, M.D., founder and director of the Institute of Sports Medicine and Athletic Trauma at Lenox Hill Hospital in New York, states:

There is much more to fitness and there are many more ways to get fit and stay fit than people realize. In its fullest sense, fitness is an integrated system which involves your body, mind and soul. It is a state of health, of looking and feeling good. It helps keep your figure trim and your posture right, and it minimizes fatigue. It helps your body respond to unusual demands and ward off disease. It is the key to a longer and healthier life. So what we emphasize at the Institute is the importance of lifetime sports—fitness as an integral part of your daily life.

Nicholas and his colleagues have studied the movement in seventy sports. They have found that most sports use six different motions in varying combinations. These six basic ways of moving are jumping, throwing, kicking, running, walking, and stance.[7] They recommend these basic movements be incorporated in any physical-fitness regime. Physical fitness is imperative to good health and attractive appearance. Most children and teen-agers exercise strenuously as part of their daily lives. As we mature, our daily activities usually grow less strenuous, and although we experience tiredness, it is usually induced by boredom or mental fatigue rather than by strenuous exercise.

The body needs strenuous exercise to maintain tonus and strength, burn off

---

[5] "How to Get In Great Shape," *Harper's Bazaar*, January 1979, pp. 68–69, 135–136.

[6] Laurence E. Morehous, Ph.D., and Leonard Gross. *Total Fitness* (New York: Pocket Books, 1975), pp. 17–34.

[7] "Fitness," *Vogue*, April 1979, p. 233.

6-3 *The body needs strenuous exercise to maintain tone and strength, burn off food intake, and help in the functioning of the vital organs and circulatory system. (Courtesy Jantzen)*

food intake, and help in the functioning of the vital organs such as the heart, lungs, and circulatory system. Physical exertion, if incorporated into a lifelong plan, will also slow down the aging process and add grace to your movements. There are various kinds of exercises. Each kind of exercise produces a certain type of result (Figure 6-3).

Body Exercises

Isometrics (Literally, "Equal Measures")

Isometric exercises contract one set of muscles without producing movement or demanding large amounts of oxygen. They tense one set of muscles against another or against an immovable object. Examples of isometric exercises are pushing against opposite sides of a door jamb or pushing toes hard against the floor. Isometrics are capable of increasing the size and strength of individual skeletal muscles. They can firm and tone these muscles, and this is what they should be used to do. Let no claim of "physical fitness in only sixty seconds a day" mislead you. This is truly impossible. Although isometrics are great for developing muscles, they have little significant effect on the pulmonary or cardiovascular systems.

Isotonics (Literally, "Equal Tension")

Isotonic exercises contract muscles and produce movement. Popular isotonics are calisthenics and weight lifting including workouts on Nautilus-type equipment; games such as shuffleboard, archery, and pitching horseshoes are in this category. As a form of exercise, isotonics are preferable to isometrics because they exercise muscles over a range of motion. Isotonics also develop the skeletal muscles. They have very little effect on the pulmonary and cardiovascular systems because this type of exercise is not sustained over a long enough period of time. These exercises are fine for firming and toning the body. The biggest problem with them is maintaining vigor and enthusiasm while doing them. For some zealots isotonics are great exercise, but for others they are just too monotonous (Figure 6-4).

Aerobics (Literally, "with Oxygen")

Aerobics are the exercises that demand oxygen and can be continued over a long period of time. The exercises in this category are running, jogging, dancing, skating, swimming, cycling, walking, race walking, and stationary running, and exercise routines which include the movements of these activities. The participant sports such as golf, tennis, racketball, and volleyball are aerobic. These exercises are the ones that should be the basis of any fitness program. The physical effects produced by aerobics are roughly these: your lungs begin processing more air and with less effort; your heart grows stronger, pumping more blood with fewer strokes; the blood supply to the muscles improves; and your total blood volume increases. In short, you are improving your body's capacity to bring in oxygen

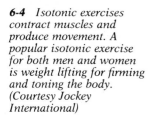

6-4 *Isotonic exercises contract muscles and produce movement. A popular isotonic exercise for both men and women is weight lifting for firming and toning the body. (Courtesy Jockey International)*

6-5 *Aerobic exercises demand oxygen and can be continued over a long period of time. Running, jogging, and walking are excellent aerobic exercises which should be a part of a lifelong fitness program. (Courtesy Allied Corporation)*

and deliver it to the tissue cells, where it combines with food to produce energy (Figure 6-5).

If you are interested in firming and reshaping the body, a combination of all three types of exercises, isometrics, isotonics, and aerobics, could be used in a program to speed results. For a lifetime of physical fitness, one of the aerobic exercises should be incorporated into your pattern of living (at least 20 minutes four days per week). Choose the things you really like to do. If you feel self-conscious, find a friend to do them with you. Walking a dog is a most compatible aerobic exercise and one that can be enjoyed completely by both parties. (See the section Dressing for Exercise, in Chapter 17.)

Eastern Philosophies

Eastern philosophies have always dealt with the need for unity of mind and body. The stylized movements of the martial arts, of the Japanese Aikido, and the Chinese Tai Chi Chuan attempt to free the body by causing it to relax until it presents no obstacle to the energy flow of nature.

Aikido recognizes the mind and body as one and holds that if the body is relaxed the mind will be calm and perceive more clearly. The calm mind is never housed in a tight, rigid body.

Tai Chi Chuan is a method of giving up tensions, of learning to know one's own body so well that by extension one can know another's. The double-edged wooden sword is the literal extension with which students sense out their opponents. When not dueling, students work singly, standing in rows as would a *corps de ballet*. The gestures and jumps and pivots are done slowly in a prescribed manner.

Yoga has many variations. Basically yoga is a school of Hindu philosophy advocating and prescribing a course of physical and mental disciplines for attaining the union of self with a supreme being or ultimate principle.

Fashionable Fitness

The 1980s will be remembered as the decade of physical fitness. Great numbers of people of all ages have made fitness part of their lifestyle and are participating in group exercise classes, working out at gyms, and playing games such as tennis, golf, and volley ball. Individuals can be seen at all times of the day and night walking or jogging along county roads or busy city streets. Memberships in health clubs and spas are at an all time high. These clubs have become *the* social center much in the manner of the Roman baths and the Greek gymnasiums. An incredible number of businesses have spun off from this fitness fashion.

Clothing fashions reflect the fitness emphasis. Jogging suits can be found in the closets of many and the designer versions of the lowly sweat suit have been worn to some of the fanciest parties around. Jogging shoes are worn by many

6-6 The fashion industry has developed a new category called athleisure *to merchandise clothing that was developed for active sports, but is now being worn during leisure time. The sweat suit and jogging shoe are athleisure gear. (Courtesy Jockey International)*

6-7 Job applicants who are in top physical condition are usually hired by corporations over other applicants. College years are good years to develop the body along with the mind. (Courtesy Jantzen)

for work, for play, and all times in between. Headbands, leg warmers, leotards, and tights are among the clothing articles originated for athletic pursuits which have been made fashionable by fitness. The fashion industry labels these clothes *athleisure*. Evidently even those who do not participate want to look as if they are part of the physical fitness scene (Figure 6-6).

In 1968, Americans spent $58 billion on health care. By 1983, the total figure had swelled to $355 billion. Health and medical costs were 11 percent of the Gross National Product in 1984.[8] Big business throughout the world is reacting to the high cost of medical care and the importance of employees' well-being by providing exercise facilities.

Fitness for business executives has taken on a new meaning. Workout sessions in health clubs and fitness centers produce not only personal fitness but an opportunity to make deals and business contacts. "There is absolutely no doubt about it. All other things being equal, the job applicant who is in top physical condition will be chosen by a corporation over the other applicants."[9] (See Figure 6-7.)

---

[8] "Fitness Boom," *News Flash*, Fashion Group, New York, September 14, 1984, p. 1
[9] "Make Way for the New Spartans," *Time Magazine*, September 19, 1983, pp. 90–92.

Health clubs have long been the haven for the young and social and they continue their importance while health spas have become the preferred vacation spots for families as well as singles. Celebrities of all ages with youthful, healthy bodies have become our new role models.

Whereas fitness is fashionable and most people are knowledgeable about its benefits, a recent survey by the National Center for Health Statistics reported that only 49 percent of adult Americans engage in a regular exercise program. Some fitness authorities believe the actual number of faithful exercisers is even lower, perhaps only 10 or 15 percent of the population. Other studies show that those who do begin an exercise program often abandon it during the first twenty-one days.

Robert Hopper, an exercise physiologist who teaches the fine art of fitness fidelity for Health Management Associates recommends that people wanting to maintain a fitness program change their attitudes from thinking of exercise as work or the "sweat ethic," to regarding exercise as fun. He recommends:

Choose a lifetime sport, an activity you enjoy and think you'll enjoy for years. Supplement it with an exercise program that will enhance your performance in the lifetime sport. For example, a lifetime sport of tennis could be supplemented by swimming, which will improve endurance on the court.

Find a coach, someone who will inspire continued participation. A coach helps you set goals, pats you on the back and teaches you correct techniques.

Join a team. A team provides camaraderie, fun, competition and models to copy. Teams do not have to be formally organized; they can consist of the people with whom you enjoy exercising.

Make fitness appointments. Block out time for workouts. Consider these appointments as important as a business meeting or doctor's appointment.[10]

Safety of Exercise

People are often concerned about the safety of exercise, particularly if they feel they are not in very good condition or have never participated in athletic activities. Kenneth H. Cooper, M.D., M.H.P., the man who started the world jogging and founder of the Institute for Aerobics Research in Dallas, Texas, recommends the following guidelines:

1. Have a checkup by a physician.
2. Prepare with a proper diet, proper clothing, and equipment, and proper work-out conditions.
3. Warm up thoroughly, stretch adequately.
4. Choose your proper performance objective, and avoid overexertion.
5. Cool down thoroughly.
6. Monitor your exercise and recovery pulse regularly.[11]

[10] "Staying Fit by Playing the Role of Olympians," *Los Angeles Times*, July 17, 1984.
[11] Kenneth H. Cooper, M.D., M.P.H., *The Aerobics Way* (New York: Pocket Books, 1977), pp. 50–56.

Muscles Versus Fat

Muscles are the underlying tissues in your body that alternate contracting and relaxing to make you move. Muscular contractions contour and tone the muscles. Contoured muscles give the body shape. The condition or shape of the muscle, not the size, is determined by its use. Muscles that are not used will waste away or atrophy. An atrophied muscle appears loose and flabby.

Some women worry that exercised muscles will create a masculine appearance. This does not happen. Exercise affects only the condition of the muscles. The size of muscles is determined by heredity, body chemistry, and sex. Female and male hormones are responsible for the variation between male and female muscle appearance. The predominantly male hormone, testosterone, is responsible for the mass and bulkiness of muscles. This hormone is present in women but in very small amounts, which do not affect the muscle mass.

Male muscle contains more fibers than the female muscle, which means the female has less potential for strength development. A man and woman of the same size, weight, and physical conditioning would never have equal muscle strength.

A woman has a thicker layer of fat deposited around her muscles. This gives her a softer appearance and feel. Men's muscles are better defined under the skin and are firmer.[12]

Posture

Posture is the term used to describe the position of the limbs and the carriage of the body as a whole. It is the structural basis of the body and contributes to the proper functioning of several physiological processes within the body. Correct posture is an important factor in general good health. It should be maintained while standing, walking, and sitting (Figure 6-8). An individual's posture, or presentation of the body, also makes a nonverbal statement about how one feels about oneself.

A body that is aligned correctly is truly beautiful. It shows pride and self-confidence. It wears clothing well. To observe good posture, tune in your television set or go to the movies or theater. Actors and actresses are among the best-postured citizens around. Those who have made a success in the theater have learned to walk, stand, and sit correctly—except, of course, when appearing in a character role for which it would be inappropriate to do so. For them, correct walking, standing, and sitting are a part of their craft, for they cannot afford to be seen from any angle at less than their best. Can you?

Most of us have been told all of our lives to "stand up straight." But most of us really do not know exactly what that means. "Good posture" involves aligning the body from head to toe. The weight should be distributed from front to back and from side to side through the center of gravity of the total body. The place-

[12] Linda Garrison, Phyllis Leslie, and Deborah Blackmore, *Fitness and Figure Control: The Creation of You* (Palo Alto, Calif.: Mayfield Publishing, 1974), pp. 30–31.

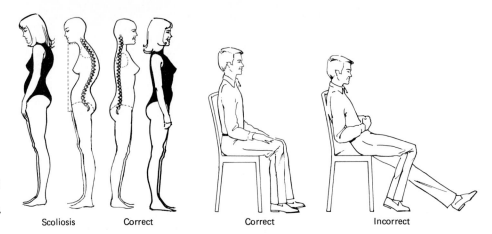

Scoliosis   Correct   Correct   Incorrect

6-8 *Correct posture is an important factor in general good health. It should be maintained while standing, walking, and sitting.*

ment of various parts of the body is important in creating postural balance. Garrison *et al.*, recommended the following for balanced posture:

Feet: parallel with toes straight ahead. The ankle and foot should meet squarely at right angles indicating even distribution of weight directly through the ankle (check the soles of your shoes, especially the heels, for signs of uneven wearing . . . this indicates poor distribution of weight).

Knees: neither flexed (bent) nor hyperextended (locked), but loose and held straight.

Seat and abdomen: hips tucked down and forward, stomach pressed in as in holding a deep breath (this is the basis for straightening the curves in the lower back and eliminating protruding stomachs and seats).

Shoulders and chest: upright yet relaxed, chest and rib cage lifted but not exaggerated by an arch in the back.

Head and neck: centered squarely above the shoulders, the head balanced evenly with the chin parallel to the floor. (Avoid tucking chin in or pushing head forward.)[13]

When a person is poorly aligned at any one of these checkpoints, the body weight is unevenly directed to the body's base of support. The result of this "poor posture" is a strain on muscles, bones, and joints, which leads to fatigue. Over the years, "poor posture" stress takes its toll; many of the health problems of the middle and senior years can be attributed directly to the posture habits of a lifetime.

Walk

A great walk. It is one of the best assets a body can have. The way the body is held and moved reflects a positive attitude. The head should be lifted high, the arms move in easy rhythm with the body, the legs stride freely, the step is light and in proportion to body height. Long legs are an asset for such a walk, but not

[13] Ibid., pp. 23–27.

a necessity. The way you walk and stand creates the impression of your size and shape, of your looks and health, of your age and style. The smallest person can dominate a room by the dignity of his or her movements. An older person can retain a youthful appearance. Men and women of any age can reflect a zest for life and good health and fitness through their walk and body presentation.

Poor carriage negates good looks. Correct posture and a good walk affect your health, the way your clothes look, what people think of you, and what you think of yourself.

When walking, the same posture is maintained as in standing: the knees lead with the buttocks tucked under and following. At each step the heel goes down first; it is followed by the outer border of the foot. The weight should never go on the inner side of the foot, which was not made to support it.

To check your walk study yourself as you walk toward a full-length mirror. Try to catch a glance of yourself in the glass display store windows as you walk down the street. If possible, carefully analyze your walk in home movies or on closed-circuit TV. Study the wear pattern on the sole of your shoe. Test your walk by walking with a book on your head and by walking with your hands placed on the buttocks, fingers pointed downward to see if the motion you feel is forward or side to side. When your body is in perfect alignment the book will stay on your head and there will be no bounce or pendulum swing to your walk, only smooth, graceful movements.

Fashion affects body movement (see Current Fashion Body Ideals, later in this chapter). Remember the shoe styles you wear have a great deal to do with the pattern of your walk. The "jogging shoe" produces a loping effect; platform soles a tottery, unbalanced look; slip-ons a shuffle; high heels a mincing step; flat sandals a relaxed casual step. When buying new shoes consider the effect the style of shoe has on your style of walk.

Walking encourages good health. The President's Council on Physical Fitness and Sports lists some of the biggest benefits of brisk walking as improved circulation, increased lung power, stabilized weight, firmer muscles, and a spiritual lift. The recommended amount of time is 30 to 60 minutes a day at least four days a week.[14]

Body Control by Artificial Devices

Corsets, girdles, trusses, waist-cinchers, elastic body suits, and other such devices have long been used by both men and women to achieve a trimmer body. Although many of these items are viewed by some as unfashionable, even archaic, it is surprising the number of them that are still a part of many wardrobes. If you challenge this statement, check the advertisements on television, in the newspapers, in magazines and catalogues, or take a trip through the men and women's underwear section of any large department store. Interestingly, it is the sale of men's girdles and body stockings that is on the rise.

[14] Craig, Miss, *Feel Younger and Live Longer.* (New York: Rand McNally, 1974), pp. 43–49.

These articles of apparel are a substitute for strong muscles that should support the area of the body doomed to confinement. Overweight, and the desire to appear fashionably slim, are reasons for their popularity. A few people psychologically enjoy or require the tight, structured feeling that these restraining garments create.

A light, supportive garment is fine. Often it makes clothing fit more smoothly and more attractively. However, dependence on supportive garments does weaken the muscle structure and can cause health problems. For women, weakened abdominal muscles are very common. These cause complications during pregnancy and inhibit the regaining of a youthful figure after pregnancy. Men also have a problem with weakened abdominal muscles. For them a "pot" or bulging stomach is a most common problem. Depending on a girdle to support this area can be a very foolish practice. Exercise, concentrating on abdominal muscle development, is a much more healthful solution.

Cooper's Droop

One supportive garment that most women should not go without is the properly fitted brassiere, according to Dr. Mary Schreiber of the California State University, Los Angeles. Today's liberated braless women are running the risk of being tomorrow's "Cooper's Droopers." By not wearing a bra or wearing an incorrectly fitted one many women stretch the ligaments that support the mammary glands, which are called the *Ligaments of Cooper.* Not wearing a brassiere or wearing an unsupportive bra causes the breasts to sag, and once the ligaments are stretched ("Cooper's Droop"), they cannot be restored to their original tautness except by surgery.[15]

Dr. John H. Wulsin of the University of Cincinnati College of Medicine warned that the lack of mammary support may lead to the development of pendulous breasts ". . . the fibrous attachments that support the breast stretch under the influence of gravity, more so in some women than in others, and especially in those breasts that are naturally large or fat and pregnant or lactating. Once lengthened by tension, these fibrous connections do not resume youthful dimensions and, despite hopeful legend, no amount of exercise will restore a pristine mammary profile." He added that exercise may, by improving posture and the thickness of the underlying pectoral muscle, push forward and thereby embellish breast contour, sagging or otherwise.

Wulsin continued by recommending proper support for the breasts in the form of a well-fitted brassiere. This garment can be expected to minimize stretching of the intrinsic mammary connective tissue. When asked if the AMA should issue a warning about the effects of bralessness, he said ". . . this calls for special finesse of judgment in the realm social rather than scientific. To the unfettered female of today, her unbuttressed drooping breast may evoke greater peace of mind and cosmetic elan than the traditional projecting hemisphere so idealized by artist and female fantasy."[16]

[15] "Braless Invite Droop," *Los Angeles Times*, May 28, 1972, Pt. 4, p. 1.

[16] "They Find the No-Bra Look Unsupportable," *Los Angeles Times*, February 10, 1972, Pt. 4, p. 1.

Glamour magazine's answer to the braless dilemma was to devise a pencil test to help readers decide if they could or should go braless. The test was simply to place a pencil under the breast. If it dropped to the floor, the braless fashion was recommended. If the pencil was held in place by breast tissue, the braless look was not recommended (see Fitting a Bra, Chapter 16).

Body Communication

The way you move and use your body is a distinct part of your individuality. From a distance, friends and family can see and recognize you only by your body movements, not by your facial features. Therefore, any analysis of your body should include consideration of your movements and gestures.

Your body movements combine with your voice, language, and emotional expressions to communicate your messages to others. One method of communication serves to emphasize the other; however, each can express meaning separately. *Kinesics* is the name of the science based on the behavioral patterns of nonverbal communication. *Body language* is the lay term associated with this science. Fast said, "Body language can include any nonreflexive or reflexive movement of a part, or all of the body, used by a person to communicate an emotional message to the outside world (Figure 6-9)."[17]

[17] Julius Fast, *Body Language* (New York: Pocket Books, 1971), p. 2.

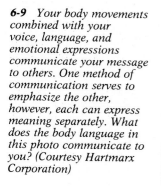

6-9 *Your body movements combined with your voice, language, and emotional expressions communicate your message to others. One method of communication serves to emphasize the other, however, each can express meaning separately. What does the body language in this photo communicate to you? (Courtesy Hartmarx Corporation)*

Social scientists have been studying body movement as a key to better human understanding for over thirty years. At present, in the behavioral sciences there are two schools of thought about body behavior. In the psychological school, "nonverbal" communication is considered to be the expression of the emotions. Anthropologists and ethologists view the behaviors of posture, touch, and body movement in relationship to social processes such as group cohesion and group regulation. The way people hold their bodies and move their limbs and facial features tell a great deal about what is going on both within the individual and within groups of two people or more.

Body language is related to both cultural and environmental differences. In describing cultural difference, Scheflen observed:

When two people come together for a communicational exchange they address each other, greet, and take *vis-à-vis* positions. Then they will adjust the distance between themselves according to their ethnicity, their level of intimacy, their prior relations, their business together, and the available physical space and circumstance.

Often the participants come from different cultures or have different ideas about their twosome, so they do not find the same interpersonal distance comfortable. In such cases, they may do a "spacing dance" until they come to some compromise.

People of North European derivation, like the British and British-Americans, tend to use large interpersonal distances. They stand just beyond easy tactile range and do not use much touch in a conversation. But Latin peoples, the French, and Eastern-European Jews stand closer, within easy range for touching each other. Jewish culture is highly tactile.[18]

Nierenberg and Calero noted that observing and becoming aware of gestures is fairly simple, but interpreting them is difficult.[19] They further stated that the art of thoroughly seeing nonverbal communications is a learned process. This skill is almost as difficult to acquire as fluency in a foreign language. They recommended that the student who wishes to perfect this skill should learn to maintain a conscious awareness of his own gestures and the meaning that is being conveyed by them to an audience. They also advised that the student set aside at least ten minutes a day to consciously "read" the gestures of others.[20]

The best way to observe your own body movements is to see yourself as others do. The eyes of a camera can help achieve this. Since home movies and closed-circuit television are common, you may wish to arrange to have yourself filmed. Candid photographs of yourself can also be helpful. However, when the pictures are taken, they should be unposed if they are to be an accurate portrayal of body movements. The subject should be relaxed and should not feel self-conscious or uncomfortable.

Watching others on campus, on city streets, at airports, and other such places will help you to develop an awareness of body-movement communication. Teach-

[18] Albert E. Scheflen, M.D., with Alice Scheflen, *Body Language and Social Order* (Englewood Cliffs, N.J.: Prentice-Hall, 1972), p. 28.

[19] Gerard I. Nierenberg and Henry H. Calero, *How to Read a Person Like a Book* (New York: Pocket Books, 1973), p. 24.

[20] Ibid., p. 26.

ers, ministers, politicians, and television hosts are also good subjects for studying body language. A collection of candid pictures from newspapers and magazines can add to the understanding of this nonverbal communication.

Graceful Body Presentation

People perceive others by the way they manage their bodies in relationship to themselves, to other individuals and to the furniture and other surroundings. In times past children were given very serious lessons in body movement including:

carriage or body posture: standing repose
motions: changing from one position to another that is, walking, sitting, dancing
manners: performing social rituals
address: bearing of the body during conversation

Upper-class standards of movement originated in seventeenth-century France during the reign of Louis XIV. They were continually regarded as the epitome of courteous behavior and elegant movement until the French Revolution. From the time they could walk, upper-class boys and girls were tutored by French-trained dancing masters who regularly visited the fashionable homes of their charges to teach the latest bows, curtsies, and dances. Between visits each child was expected to practice the lessons daily in front of a mirror. A child learned very early how much effort it took to appear effortless, in much the same way as does a classical ballet dancer today.

During this class-conscious era, movement was the ultimate status symbol. As the emerging middle-class moved upward it carefully adopted the movement of the upper-class. "Movement became the final rung on the eighteenth-century social ladder. It was one art which could not be purchased; it had to be learned—a painstaking process requiring time and practice. There were rules for every conceivable type of movement—from entering a room to passing someone on the street, fighting a duel, dancing a minuet, or drinking a cup of tea. These rules were gleaned from three main sources: dancing masters, etiquette books, and costumes. By the end of the century, all three sources were being directed toward furthering the upward mobility of the middle classes."[21]

The influences of this period of very proper manners and prescribed conduct has continued to be felt by many groups as a study of social history will reveal. In the United States, the social revolution of the 1960s broke down many of the cultural traditions of behavior and a casualness of dress and a relaxation of movement prevailed. Young people growing up during this period scoffed at etiquette and did things "their way." By the mid-1980s the fashion changed in clothing styles, business practices, and social functions. Elegance and sophisti-

[21] Alicia M. Annas, "The Elegant Art of Movement," in Edward Maeder, *An Elegant Art, Fashion and Fantasy in the Eighteenth Century* (Los Angeles: Los Angeles County Museum of Art, 1983), pp. 35–37.

cation returned to people's lifestyles creating a new demand for refinement and a return to traditional social graces.

The guides that helped the citizens of the eighteenth-century are valuable today. Dancing lessons are a wonderful way to get in touch with your body and its movement. Modern etiquette books have advice for all situations. Clothes will tell you exactly what behavior is expected by their informality or formality. Watching others, whether on the TV screen or in person, can show you the movements that modern life requires. Schools, classes, publications, all have advice to help you complete the part of your individuality that gracefully presents your body at all times. Keep in mind this kindly advice:

One should always put the best foot foremost. One should please, shine and dazzle, wherever it is possible.[22]

Current Fashion Body Ideals

Body ideals are cultural and change with fashion. Although the anatomy remains the same, it is often forced into a variety of positions and shapes by the prevailing fashion body ideals of a culture.

The Western world has, in turn, admired solid, hefty women, emaciated women, ample hips, large breasts, tiny waists, small hands and feet, flat chests, slender hips, short legs, long legs, and various combinations of these physical formations. When a style of body becomes fashionable, many try to attain it. When Twiggy was the top fashion model in the late 1960s, many coeds dieted and starved to attain her adolescent-boyish figure of 5'7" and less than 100 pounds. Great-grandmothers to these same young ladies might have been among those women who had ribs removed to achieve the hourglass figure that was popular at about the turn of the century. The children of the "Twiggy" generation are often bulimic or anorexic.

The conformation of men has also evolved through many fashion changes in the Western world. Areas of male anatomy that have been admired at differing times include the well-turned leg, the small waist, the large abdomen, the barrel chest, the overdeveloped muscle structure, and the bulge of the genitals (Figure 6-10).

Bigelow wrote,

As clothing forms and fashions of each age changed, figure emphasis areas and pose patterns developed. There has been a direct relationship between the part of the figure receiving focus of attention and the resulting posturing, pose pattern or movement. During the Egyptian period the head and shoulders received emphasis and were elaborately decorated with wigs and large collars of beads or jewels. In more modern times when the posterior

[22] Lord Chesterfield, 1752, as quoted in ibid., p. 35.

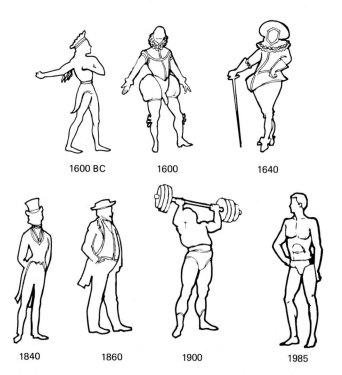

1600 BC   1600   1640

1840   1860   1900   1985

6-10 Areas of male anatomy that have been admired during various fashion periods.

was given importance, the bustle and train were added to the costume. The Greeks emphasized the body as a whole and swathed it in the draped *chiton*. This demanded that the wearer learn to walk with a graceful, gliding step, a walk which in turn brought attention to the emphasis area, the entire body. Ancient cultures of Egypt, Greece and Rome treated the human figure *in puris naturalibus* but without the sexual considerations or implications of the plastic garb of the 1960s which was apparently devised to deny the Puritan ethic. The body, thus clothed, however, had none of the grace or dignity of the figure seen beneath the gossamer gala gown of the Egyptian era. The many different costume details that evolved also controlled the posturing and activity patterns of the wearer. For example, maneuvering of the beruffled train of the late nineteenth century required activity skills and demanded specific pose patterns. The ruffs of the sixteenth century, the *paniers* of the eighteenth century, the hoop skirts of the nineteenth century, and the fringed chemises of the early twentieth century are other illustrations. Ruffs doubtless limited the gesturing movements of the head. *Paniers* caused ladies to use a swaying step, leading first with one side then the other to avoid colliding with nearby objects. The geometric construction of fashions of the late nineteenth century demanded posturing that defied the hinge and ball construction of the human body. Details like coiffures, eyebrows, and lips; fans, gloves, and walking sticks; capes, skirts, and bodices combined to direct attention to parts of the figure considered the most significant during a particular fashion period.[23]

The current body ideal for both men and women is a naturally curved, slender, strong, physically fit form. Greatest emphasis for conformity is on weight control.

[23] Marybelle S. Bigelow, *Fashion in History, Apparel in the Western World* (Minneapolis, Minn.: Burgess, 1970), p. 4.

Fashions in clothing reveal and move easily with the body. Both the National Bureau of Standards and the U.S. Department of Agriculture have statistics that show that today's young people are taller, heavier, and measure more in "body landmarks" such as upper arm, waist, thigh, and hip.

We are in a period that stresses individuality so why should we even consider the current body ideals? There are several good answers: first, the satisfaction of personal curiosity to see how we compare to the body conformation that is popular; second, because body ideals are the prototypes used in both designing and promoting clothing. If we understand how our body varies from these ideals it will be easier to make decisions concerning clothing selection.

At this time, the ideal body conformation for men is prototyped after the youthful athlete such as the swimmer, the runner, the tennis player. The overall image is tall and slender. The muscles of the shoulders are broad and well developed. The torso tapers to a slender waist. The abdomen is flat. The hips are narrower than the width of the shoulders. The arms and legs are slender and well muscled. Head, hands, and feet are proportionate to body size.

The ideal body conformation for women is based on a tall, slender figure also. Because there has been more interest in figure analysis of the female, more exacting standards have been established. The shoulder and hip width (front face) silhouette measurement is the same. The circumference measurement of hips and bust should not differ more than two inches. The circumference of the waist is nine to eleven inches smaller than the hips and bust. The abdomen is flat. The arms, hands, and fingers are long and tapered smoothly. The legs curve smoothly from ankle to knee. The ankle is measured just above the protruding bone. The calf of the leg measures four to six inches larger than the ankle. The thigh is six to seven inches larger than the calf.

Accurate measurements cannot be taken by oneself. The correct position for measuring is the same as for correct body alignment, described in this chapter. The head must be up with eyes looking straight ahead. The weight should be equally distributed on both feet. All circumference measurements should be taken so that the measuring tape is parallel to the floor. The tape should not be drawn tightly to the body but should fit snugly enough not to slip out of position. The measurements are most accurate when taken at the fullest part of area, if not otherwise indicated.

Racial Body Conformation

Among the many differences between races, variations in body size are especially conspicuous. In some groups males average close to six feet (180 cm), but in other populations the average male stature is nearer five feet (150 cm). Garn found that *fat-free* body weight of American males approximates 135 pounds (60.75 kg) (some go as high as 190 pounds [85.50 kg]), whereas the comparable fat-free weight in other groups may average as little as 105 pounds (47.25 kg).

Garn noted that large size has advantage. Among other things, the bigger man can cover more territory, he is speedier, he can tackle bigger game and bring it home. Not too surpising, the hunting peoples of North America and Europe have all been tall on a world scale. Given large animals to hunt, Garn believed that size is adaptive.

Garn continued to point out that size and massivity have their disadvantages. Larger sizes require more calories merely to keep alive, as many Americans, Dutchmen, and Englishmen learned during World War II in Japanese concentration camps. Larger size requires more calories to grow so that the genetically large child is at a particular disadvantage when food is scarce. The large man, although more efficient at heat regulation in cold weather, is less efficient in hot weather.

Garn observed that for small size, the advantages and disadvantages reverse. Size is of no advantage when tending a trap. The less food there is the more advantages there are to being small. On short rations the genetically small child has a better chance to live, mature, and reproduce. In the extremes of heat, the small man is favored, as he is during violent exercise even at moderate temperatures.

Garn stated that the small peoples of the world tend to be found nearer the equator. There is a marked negative correlation between the mean annual temperature and weight; that is, as temperature rises weight drops.

Within each geographical race there is a range of sizes small to large. This range can best be explained in terms of the selective forces such as temperature and food supply. Documentable as these generalizations are, Garn found that they did not explain such racial variations as the short size of the Ituri Forest Pygmies or the fatness of the Papago Indians of North America.[24]

Mead *et al* pointed out that literature on racial typologies of earlier historical periods in America indicates that both scientific and popular racial classification reflect the prevailing sociopolitical conditions. Thus, changes in political status of some ethnic groups have led to a rappraisal of the "racial" characteristics by which they were defined. Because of the continuing movement of peoples and expansion of population, it is difficult to establish and maintain racial guidelines.[25]

Coon presented an outstanding pictorial review of circumpolar peoples, which he introduced by observing,

Before the end of the last glacial period the circumpolar regions were almost entirely uninhabited. Both Caucasoid and Mongoloid peoples migrated northward and eastward. As we move to the east from Lapland to Greenland, we find the Circumpolar peoples starting out Caucasoid and ending up Mongoloid with many stages of transition.

Coon included twenty-five plates of Africans. He continued,

[24] Stanley M. Garn, Ph.D., *Human Races* (Springfield, Ill.: C. C Thomas, 1962), pp. 56–59.
[25] Margaret Mead, Theodosius Dobzhansky, Ethel Tobach, and Robert E. Light, *Science and the Concept of Race* (New York: Columbia U. P., 1968), p. 157.

Africa is the home of the Bushman. The origin of the Pygmies and the Negroes is unknown. As early as 13,000 years ago, Caucasoids invaded North Africa from Europe and Western Asia. Some of the invaders crossed the Sahara and mixed with the peoples they found beyond it. It is quite evident from these pictures as it is from genetic studies that the African Negroes have long been partly Caucasoid.[26]

Some or a combination of these many racial characteristics are yours. This genetic inheritance combined with your environment and nutritional status make up the unique you.

There is not another model exactly like yours anywhere on the face of the earth. Your body is a very important part of your individuality.

It is amazing to consider that with all the possible forms of human anatomy, a rather brief range of clothing patterns can be adjusted to fit a wide variety of shapes. Clothing manufacturers do not particularly cater to differences in body conformation. Extremely short and tall; extremely fat or thin; long arms, short arms, long legs, short legs; wide bodies, narrow bodies; and all possible combinations manage to find garments to cover and adorn.

Body Proportion

Proportion is the relationship of all parts to each other and of the parts to the whole. For the body, proportion includes the size of each part of the body compared to every other part and the relationship of individual parts of the body to the total body mass. That is, proportion includes the size relationship of the head to the torso, to the arms, to the hands, to the legs, and to the feet, and the relationship of each mentioned part of the anatomy to the entire body conformation.

A vertically well-proportioned human body may be divided into four even parts. The distance from the top-of-the-head to the underarm is one quarter of the total length of the figure. From the underarm to the hip is two quarters, or one half, of the total length of the body. The waist divides the underarm-to-hip section in half. From the hip to the knee is three-quarters to the total length of the body. From knee to bottom-of-the-foot is the fourth quarter of the total body length (Figure 6-11).

You may determine your body proportions by several means. You may wish to measure a photograph taken in body-revealing clothing such as a bathing suit or body suit. You may wish to have someone outline your body on a large piece of paper and then measure "body landmarks." (See Body Analysis at end of this chapter for complete instructions.)

By learning how your body is proportioned, you can better understand how your body relates to the fashion ideal. (Proportion is also discussed in the design chapters.)

[26] Carlton S. Coon, *The Living Races of Man* (New York: Knopf, 1965), plates 1–128.

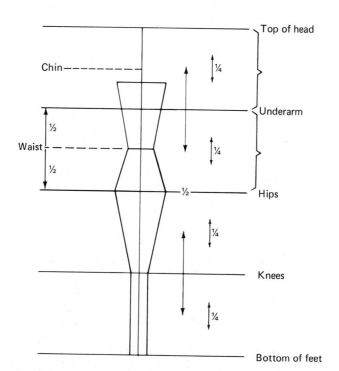

6-11 *A well-proportioned body may be divided into four equal parts.*

Height-Weight Distribution

In body analysis it is fundamental to consider the distribution of weight on the body frame. The actual weight is not so important as the way it is arranged to create the shape of the body (Figure 6-12). Weight charts can give you an idea of what you should weigh, but when reading any weight chart remember to acknowledge that these are not precise and that your best weight may be somewhat above or below the recommendation.

Understand how your body mass is distributed on your skeletal frame. The body mass should be distributed evenly from the center core of the body or the spine as the body is viewed from the front, back, and side. The bust/chest mass should balance the buttocks mass as the body is viewed in profile.

Because clothing is designed to hang as cylinders from the shoulders or from the waist, it is important to analyze your body in profile position. Using a profile photo of yourself taken in body-revealing clothing, draw a straight line that connects the center of your ear lobe to the center of your ankle bone. This line represents the center of your body. Study the distribution of your weight along this line. Next draw a line straight down from the fullest part of bust/chest to the floor. Draw a second line straight down from fullest part of stomach to floor. Study these two lines. Wherever the lines touch the lower part of the body so will clothing. On the back side of the body draw a line straight from the fullest part of the shoulder area to the floor. Draw a second line from the fullest part of the buttocks to the floor. Wherever these lines touch the body so will clothing (Figure 6-13).

6-12 *In body analysis it is important to consider the distribution of weight on the body frame. The actual weight is not as important as the way it is arranged to create the shape of the body.*

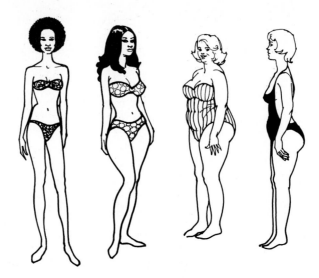

6-13 *Some clothing is designed to hang as cylinders from the shoulders or from the waist. These plumb lines work for both men and women.*

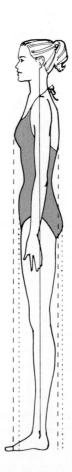

The purpose of drawing the two lines on the front and back of your profile is to demonstrate how different garments will hang from your body. Clothing designed to hang from the shoulder, such as shirts, coats, jackets, fits the body from the shoulder to the fullest parts of the bust/chest. From this point the garments are often designed to hang straight. If the abdomen protrudes farther than the bust/chest, the clothing design will be distorted. In the back if the buttocks protrudes farther than the shoulder blades, the garment will be distorted.

Garments that are designed to hang from the waist, such as pants and skirts, generally fit the body from the waist to the stomach in front. If the thigh protrudes farther than the stomach the garment design is distorted. In the back these garments generally are fitted from the waist to the buttocks. If the calf of the leg protrudes farther than the buttocks the garment design is distorted. The preceding discussion refers to straight-cut garments. Many design details are used to camouflage these body conformation problems (see Chapter 16).

A pleasing distribution of flesh over the body is most desirable. The current fashion ideal is slender, that is, neither plump nor gaunt. Although Babe Paley of the "best-dressed-jet-set" has been quoted as saying, "No woman can be too thin, or too rich," it is possible for both men and women to look too emaciated to be attractive.

A more common problem is the deposits of *avoirdupois* tissue in certain areas of the body. For women, fat often accumulates in the thigh, hip, abdomen, midriff, and upper arm. For men, fat tissue most often collects in the abdomen and kidney area. A person may have a very good distribution of flesh on his frame except for these areas. It is common for family members to inherit a tendency toward fat deposits in certain locations. The best remedy for such fat deposits is exercise (sometimes accompanied by a reducing diet). A variety of exercises have been designed to eliminate fat deposits wherever they occur. This type of body control takes a great deal of time and work. The fat deposit may never be remedied completely, but it can be reduced.

Reasonable Body Weight

A general guide for establishing a reasonable body weight is presented here. Reasonable body weight is based on the current medical recommendations, that is, slightly higher than previously presented. It has been agreed in the medical community that the reasonable body weight at age twenty-five is the body weight to maintain for a lifetime.

Body Weights: Rules of thumb for people less than 25 years of age (down to 18 years of age)
Men:
For 5 feet, consider 110 pounds a reasonable weight.
For each inch over 5 feet, add 5 pounds.
Example: A man 5'8" tall would start at 110 pounds, add 40 pounds and arrive at a reasonable weight of 150 pounds.

Women:
For 5 feet consider 100 pounds a reasonable weight.
For each inch over 5 feet, add 5 pounds.
For each year under 25 (down to 18 years), subtract 1 pound.
Example: A woman 21 years old, 5'4" tall would start at 100 pounds, add 20 and subtract 4, arriving at a reasonable weight of 116 pounds.[27]

Ideal Weight Chart

The ideal weight charts included here are based on today's fashion ideal body conformation. They vary from other weight charts because (1) they are based on the ideal rather than statistical averages of an overweight population, and (2) they are for height measurements *without* shoes and weight *without* clothing. The ideal weight chart for women is closely aligned with many of the desired requirements for flight attendants and fashion models. The men's ideal weight chart is based on the concept of the tennis player, swimmer, or track-man body conformation, which has replaced the football player and wrestler-weightlifter ideal.

Ideal Weight

1. These charts (Tables 6-1 and 6-2 following) are designed to produce a more nearly ideal figure according to the current fashionable standards.
2. Weight must come close to the range given for height and body frame size.
3. To determine your body frame size (women only—not yet developed for men), use the wrist measurement. Measure circumference just below wrist bone (away from the hand) on arm that you use least.

Body Frame Size Wrist Measurement
small frame $4\frac{1}{2}''$ to $5\frac{1}{8}''$ (11.25 cm to 12.81 cm)
medium frame $5\frac{3}{8}''$ to $6\frac{1}{8}''$ (13.43 cm to 15.31 cm)
large frame $6\frac{1}{4}''$ to $6\frac{3}{4}''$ (15.63 cm to 16.88 cm)

4. Measure height accurately. Barefooted. If you fall between a height range, add $1\frac{1}{3}$ pound (.6 kg) for each $\frac{1}{4}$ inch (.62 cm).
   Example: medium frame, $5'6\frac{1}{2}''$ (166.25 cm) ideal weight = 122 pounds (54.90 kg)
5. For weight range add and subtract five pounds from your ideal weight.
   Example: ideal weight 122 pounds (54.90 kg)
   weight range 117 to 127 pounds (52.65–57.15 kg)
6. There are always exceptions to any standard. Both the wrist measurement and ideal weight chart will work for most, but there may be variations.

[27] Eleanor N. Whitney and Eva M. N. Hamilton, *Understanding Nutrition* (St. Paul, Minn.: West Publishing, 1984), back inside cover.

Suggested Activities

1. Arrange with the campus audiovisual center to videotape class members as they walk, sit, and stand in conversation groups. Show tapes several times so students may observe. Repeat taping at later date, if possible, to show improvements. Discuss the experience of being taped as well as the body language shown by the tape.
2. Collect several pictures from newspapers and magazines that show body language. Write captions for pictures and use as basis of class discussion.

Table 6-1. Women's Ideal Weight Chart

Height*	Small Frame**	Medium Frame**	Large Frame**
4'8"–140.0 cm	65 lb–29.25 kg	70 lb–31.50 kg	75 lb–33.75 kg
4'9"–142.5 cm	70 lb–31.50 kg	75 lb–33.75 kg	80 lb–36.00 kg
4'10"–145.0 cm	75 lb–33.75 kg	80 lb–36.00 kg	85 lb–38.25 kg
4'11"–147.5 cm	80 lb–36.00 kg	85 lb–38.25 kg	90 lb–40.50 kg
5'0"–150.0 cm	85 lb–38.25 kg	90 lb–40.50 kg	95 lb–42.75 kg
5'1"–152.5 cm	90 lb–40.50 kg	95 lb–42.75 kg	100 lb–45.00 kg
5'2"–155.0 cm	95 lb–42.75 kg	100 lb–45.00 kg	105 lb–47.25 kg
5'3"–157.5 cm	100 lb–45.00 kg	105 lb–47.25 kg	110 lb–49.50 kg
5'4"–160.0 cm	105 lb–47.25 kg	110 lb–49.50 kg	115 lb–51.75 kg
5'5"–162.5 cm	110 lb–49.50 kg	115 lb–51.75 kg	120 lb–54.00 kg
5'6"–165.0 cm	115 lb–51.75 kg	120 lb–54.00 kg	125 lb–56.25 kg
5'7"–167.5 cm	120 lb–54.00 kg	125 lb–56.25 kg	130 lb–58.50 kg
5'8"–170.0 cm	125 lb–56.25 kg	130 lb–58.50 kg	135 lb–60.75 kg
5'9"–172.5 cm	130 lb–58.50 kg	135 lb–60.75 kg	140 lb–63.00 kg
5'10"–175.0 cm	135 lb–60.75 kg	140 lb–63.00 kg	145 lb–65.25 kg
5'11"–177.5 cm	140 lb–63.00 kg	145 lb–65.25 kg	150 lb–67.50 kg
6'0"–180.0 cm	145 lb–65.25 kg	150 lb–67.50 kg	155 lb–69.75 kg
6'1"–182.5 cm	150 lb–67.50 kg	155 lb–69.75 kg	160 lb–72.00 kg
6'2"–185.0 cm	155 lb–69.75 kg	160 lb–72.00 kg	165 lb–74.25 kg

*Height without shoes.
**Weight without clothing.

3. Find several fashion advertisements that use sketches rather than photos. Measure the total body by the head length. How many heads tall are the fashion sketches? Why do the clothes look so different on the human body than they do in the sketches?
4. Repeat the above exercise using the head length measurements of store mannikins and fashion models (magazine pictures or actual models). What do you discover about body proportion? What do you discover about mannikins and fashion models? How can you use this information when purchasing clothing?
5. Analyze your own body by the methods suggested in the chapter.

Body Analysis

Method 1. Body pictures

1. One of the most effective tools to employ to see yourself as you really are is a series of full-length photographs taken in a body-revealing outfit, such as a bathing suit or leotard. Do not wear shoes. These pictures should be taken so that the body level is not distorted. The weight should be equally distributed on each foot; the hands and arms should not interfere with the body silhouette. The "bench-marks" of the body can be indicated by tieing contrasting string or tape around under arm, waist, hip, the knee and ankle, as well as the shoulder width (place around arm socket). The hair should be pulled to back of head so that ear lobe and neck-shoulder conformation are revealed.

   Take at least three pictures. Body front, body back, and body profile. Be certain that your photographer does not take an artistic pose. Head and feet must be in the photo.

2. Study your body pictures carefully. Decide what you like about your body.

3. *On front and back full-view photos* draw a vertical line that bisects the body. Compare right side with left side (remember photo is your body reversed). Determine any difference between the two sides.

4. *On front and back full-view photos* draw a horizontal line across shoulders, waist, hip, and knee. Study each of these areas. Are the horizontal lines level?

5. *On front and back full-view photos* draw straight lines on each side from shoulder to hip (along silhouette). *For women*, these lines should be parallel, that is, the silhouette measurement should be the same for shoulder and hip. *For men*, these lines should taper from shoulder to hip (the shoulders should be wider than the hip).

6. *On profile-view photo*, draw a vertical line from ear lobe to ankle. Determine the distribution of your body mass on both sides of this line (see Fig. 6-13). Rate your posture (Fig. 6-13). Is your body in good alignment? Study shoulder and stomach areas carefully. Compare profile posture with full-view, front, and back posture. Examine your full-length weight distribution.

7. *On profile-view photo*, face side, draw a vertical full-length line that just touches the widest of bust/chest silhouette. On the back side, draw a vertical full-length line that just touches the widest part of the shoulder blade. Study these lines carefully. Remember any garment designed to hang from the shoulders will follow these lines (coats, jacket, shirts) (see Fig. 6-13). How does your body conformation correspond to this clothing design requirement?

8. *On profile-view photo*, face side, draw a vertical line from fullest point of stomach silhouette to the floor. On back side, draw a vertical line from the fullest part of the buttocks to the floor. Study these lines carefully. Remember any garment designed to hang from the waist (skirts, pants) will follow these lines (see page 214). How does your body conformation correspond to this clothing design requirement?

9. Complete the checklist Body Picture Analysis.

Table 6-2. Man's Ideal Weight Chart

Height*	Small Frame**		Medium Frame**		Large Frame**	
5'1"–152.5 cm	112–120 lb	50.40–54.00 kg	118–129 lb	53.10–58.05 kg	126–141 lb	56.70–63.45 kg
5'2"–155.0 cm	115–123 lb	51.75–55.35 kg	121–133 lb	54.45–59.85 kg	129–144 lb	58.05–64.80 kg
5'3"–157.6 cm	118–126 lb	53.10–56.70 kg	124–136 lb	55.80–61.20 kg	132–148 lb	59.40–66.60 kg
5'4"–160.0 cm	121–129 lb	54.45–58.05 kg	127–139 lb	57.15–62.55 kg	135–152 lb	60.75–68.40 kg
5'5"–162.5 cm	124–133 lb	55.80–59.85 kg	130–143 lb	58.50–64.35 kg	138–156 lb	62.10–70.20 kg
5'6"–165.0 cm	128–137 lb	57.60–61.65 kg	132–147 lb	59.40–66.15 kg	142–161 lb	63.90–72.45 kg
5'7"–167.5 cm	132–141 lb	59.40–63.45 kg	138–154 lb	62.10–69.30 kg	147–166 lb	66.15–74.70 kg
5'8"–170.0 cm	136–145 lb	61.20–65.25 kg	142–156 lb	63.90–70.20 kg	151–170 lb	67.95–76.50 kg
5'9"–172.5 cm	140–150 lb	63.00–67.50 kg	146–160 lb	65.70–72.00 kg	155–174 lb	69.75–78.30 kg
5'10"–175.0 cm	144–154 lb	64.80–69.30 kg	150–165 lb	67.50–74.25 kg	159–179 lb	71.55–80.55 kg
5'11"–177.5 cm	148–158 lb	66.60–71.10 kg	154–170 lb	69.30–76.50 kg	164–184 lb	73.80–82.80 kg
6'0"–180.0 cm	152–162 lb	68.40–72.90 kg	158–175 lb	71.10–78.75 kg	168–189 lb	75.60–85.05 kg
6'1"–182.5 cm	156–167 lb	70.20–75.15 kg	162–180 lb	72.90–81.00 kg	173–194 lb	77.85–87.30 kg
6'2"–185.0 cm	160–171 lb	72.00–76.95 kg	167–185 lb	75.15–83.25 kg	178–199 lb	80.10–89.55 kg
6'3"–187.5 cm	164–175 lb	73.80–78.75 kg	172–190 lb	77.40–85.50 kg	182–204 lb	81.90–91.80 kg
6'4"–190.0 cm	168–178 lb	75.60–80.10 kg	177–195 lb	79.65–87.75 kg	187–209 lb	84.15–94.05 kg

*Height without shoes.
**Weight without clothing.

BODY PICTURE ANALYSIS

Front full-view photo reveals:

Shoulders .... parallel _____ right high _____ left high _____

Waist .... parallel _____ right high _____ left high _____

Hips .... parallel _____ right high _____ left high _____

Knees .... parallel _____ right high _____ left high _____

Feet .... parallel _____ toes out _____ toes in _____

Back full-view photo reveals:

Shoulders .... parallel _____ right high _____ left high _____

Shoulder blades ..... balanced _____ protruding _____ too flat _____

Spine .... vertical _____ moves right _____ moves left _____

Waist .... parallel _____ right high _____ left high _____

Hips .... parallel _____ right high _____ left high _____

Knees .... parallel _____ right high _____ left high _____

Feet .... parallel _____ toes out _____ toes in _____

Profile-view photo reveals:

Head .... balanced _____ forward _____ back _____

Body line .... balanced _____ forward _____ backward _____

Knees .... flexed _____ hyperextended _____ too fixed _____

Abdomen .... contracted _____ protruding _____ too flat _____

Back curve .... balanced _____ hollow _____ flat _____

Chest .... balanced _____ high _____ flat _____

Shoulders .... balanced _____ round/forward _____ back _____

PROPORTION STUDY

Width Proportions

Shoulder width compared to hip width

wider _____ the same _____ narrower _____

    If you did not check "the same" it is because your

        _____ shoulders are wide

        _____ shoulders are narrow

        _____ hips are wide

        _____ hips are narrow

Thigh compared to hip/abdomen

balanced _____ protrudes to front _____ protrudes to back _____

Calf compared to hip/abdomen

balanced _____ protrudes to back _____

Length Proportions

Top-of-head to chin compared to chin to tip-of-bust (chest) length

longer _____ the same _____ shorter _____

    If you did not check "the same," it is because you have

        _____ an elongated head

        _____ a shorter head

        _____ are high-busted (chest)

        _____ are low-busted (chest)

Elbows compared to waist

longer _____ the same location _____ shorter _____

    If you did not check "the same," it is because your

        _____ upper arm is long

        _____ upper arm is short

        _____ waist is high

        _____ waist is low

Wrist compared to crotch

higher _____ the same location _____ lower _____

    If you did not check "the same," it is because your

        _____ forearm is long

        _____ forearm is short

        _____ crotch is high

        _____ crotch is low

Waist/knee length compared to knee/heel length

longer _____ the same _____ shorter _____

    If you did not check "the same," it is because your

        _____ thighs are long   _____ buttocks are long

        _____ thighs are short   _____ buttocks are short

        _____ calves are long   _____ calves are short

Head/wrist length compared to wrist/foot length

longer _____ the same _____ shorter _____

    If you did not check "the same," it is because your

        _____ arms are long

_____ arms are short
_____ legs are long
_____ legs are short

Body Analysis

Method 2. Body Proportion Drawing
Equipment needed:
    Shelf paper (longer and wider than you are), pencils, felt pen, 12-in. ruler, 36-in. ruler, string, body-contour-revealing clothing.

1. Crease paper in half lengthwise to establish a center line. Mark center line with felt pen. Fasten paper to a flat wall or door. Crease paper at floor level and tape to floor. (Paper must extend onto floor.)
2. Secure string around waistline, full hip, and other body "benchmarks."
3. Center your body along the vertical centerfold line of the paper. Stand so your body is relaxed but straight. Shoeless feet should be together. Do not move while someone else marks the following measurements on your paper.
4. Using a straightedge, mark these points on paper:

    top of head, not top of hair
    tip of chin
    base of neck (height, width)
    tip of shoulder (height, width)
    under arm (height, width)
    crown of bust, woman (height, width)
    widest part of chest, men (height, width)
    waistline (height, width)
    hip line (height, width)
    knee line (sides and centers) (height, width)
    ankles (sides and centers) (height, width)
    feet at floor line (width)

5. After all marking is completed, fold paper in half across the width, matching the floor line with the top-of-the-head line. Fold each half in half dividing your body length into four equal sections. Open paper out and match under-arm crease (top $\frac{1}{4}$ line) to hip-line crease ($\frac{3}{4}$ line) and press in a new crease, which will indicate waistline level. Mark dotted line at all fold lines with felt pen.
6. Draw your body. To do this draw horizontal lines connecting width points at the levels indicating:

top of the head	waistline
chin	knee line
shoulder line	ankle line
under arm	floor line

Comparison of Body Proportions Based on Head Length Measurement

Length	Female Fashion Model	Self	Male Fashion Model
Top of Head to	(Head Lengths)	(Head Lengths)	(Head Lengths)
Chin	1	1	1
Base of neck	$1\frac{1}{3}$		$1\frac{1}{4}$
Shoulder	$1\frac{1}{2}$		$1\frac{1}{2}$
Bust/chest	2		$2\frac{1}{8}$
Waist	$2\frac{5}{8}$		3
Full hip	4		4
Knee	6		$6\frac{1}{4}$
Ankle	$7\frac{1}{2}$		$8\frac{1}{4}$
Floor	8		$8\frac{1}{2}$
Width			
Shoulder	$1\frac{1}{2}$		2
Waist	$\frac{3}{4}$		$1\frac{1}{8}$
Full hip	$1\frac{1}{4}$		$1\frac{1}{2}$
Knee	$\frac{2}{3}$		$\frac{3}{4}$
Ankle	$\frac{1}{3}$		$\frac{5}{8}$

7. Connect with diagonal lines:

> base of neck to shoulder
> shoulder to waist
> waist to hip
> hip to knee
> knee to ankle (inside and outside)
> ankle to floor (inside and outside)

8. Measure your body in head lengths. To establish head length unit for measuring, take a separate piece of paper and measure the length of your head on your paper body drawing. Be exact. Trim off excess paper. Fold the exact head length measure into fractions and mark carefully each fraction with the actual number. Measure body drawing lengths and widths with your own head length unit measure, using paper exactly as you would use a ruler. Record head lengths on chart on this page. Using scale 1 head length = 1 inch, draw your body in indicated area (Figure 6-14).

9. Compare your body proportions to fashion model body shown in Figure 6-14 and body-proportion body (Figure 6-11).

Body Analysis

Method 3. Silhouette Drawing

Another method for measuring body proportions is to have your body silhouette drawn on a large sheet of paper fixed to the wall. The outline of both front and side view should be drawn. Be careful to make exact size. Comparisons to the fashion figure can then be made.

Figure comparison   Scale: 1 head length = 1/2 inch

Female Fashion Model   My Figure   Male Fashion Model

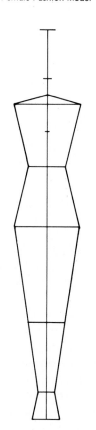

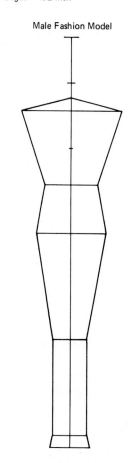

6-14 *The scale shown here is 1 head length = ½ inch, but when the student reproduces this exercise for body comparison, it is recommended that he/she use a larger scale of 1 head length = 1 inch.*

7 *Your Diet*

Body conformation of both male and female is closely related to eating habits, food intake, and nutritional status. The student of clothing selection and personal appearance must have an understanding of how the body shape may be maintained, controlled, and contoured by diet as well as by exercise. Body shape is a determining factor for both the selection of garments and the presentation of the individual. The body form is fundamental to the way we dress and the way we are perceived by others.

This chapter does not attempt to cover the science of nutrition in depth. It is designed to present information that often seems to be misunderstood or is not readily available. References are included for those who desire further study.

No one, no matter what age, can ever reach his health potential without a well-balanced diet. We are what we eat. Hair, skin, nails, teeth, plus good health and emotional stability, all reflect the food habits of the individual. Each age of development, from embryo to elderly, has special nutrient needs.

Food patterns vary from one culture to another just as they do from one family to another. Before World War II, the Japanese were of very small stature. Nutritional improvements since the end of World War II have helped many Japanese to reach their growth potential, which corresponds to that of North Americans. The same phenomenon is being noted among newly immigrated Vietnamese, Cambodians, Koreans, and Chinese. Food habits of families are often obvious and are exhibited by overweight or underweight tendencies of the family members.

An abundance of food does not necessarily mean that the nutritional needs of the individual will be met. This is because the individual makes the food choices, and these selections may not supply adequate nutrition. Many factors influence food patterns or choices. A discussion of these will help you analyze and understand your own diet pattern.

Basic Influences of Individual Eating Habits

Basic influences on eating habits may be grouped as follows:

Food supply. This refers to the amount and variety of food available, which vary tremendously from one area of the world to another. People who depend

224

7-1 *Social customs of sharing food with friends such as the British practice of afternoon tea, may be based on ancient rites. (Courtesy The Joseph & Feiss Company)*

on their own resources to raise and provide their own food often have very limited supplies. Others who live in cosmopolitan centers usually have a great variety and volume of foodstuffs from which to choose.

Economic status. Economic status is the ability of the individual or family to afford the foods that are available. However, recent studies have revealed that those with the most limited resources often make the poorest utilization of their food money; that is, they often buy high-cost items of low nutritional benefit.

Family eating habits. Family meal patterns may be deeply rooted in racial, religious, national, or regional customs. Family food habits are also developed over generations. Individual food habits are derived from these family practices.

Social customs. Attitudes and practices of sharing food with friends and strangers may be based on ancient rites. Peer-group practices further influence food choices (Figure 7-1).

Emotional associations. Situations that generate emotions, such as pleasure, annoyance, or frustration, may result in strong attitudes. Often, there is a strong carry-over from childhood in these emotional associations. The practice of some families of forcing the child to always "clean up his plate" has been responsible for adult aversion to many foods. Candy or dessert given as a reward to a child has created a strong association between good behavior and sweets.

Sensory reactions. The individual's response to the smell, flavor, appearance, and/or texture of various foods may result in acceptance or rejection of it.

Educational influences. The study and application of the principles of basic nutrition can act as a guide to the selection and preparation of foods. Through education many food prejudices may be broken down. By practicing the basic concepts of nutrition, the individual can establish the patterns of eating to meet the daily requirements of the body of optimum health.

Relate these influences to your own dietary habits. Try to analyze why you eat as you are eating. Do you have food prejudices? What are they? Do they affect your nutritional status? What part does food play in your life—is it very important or not so important? If, by the end of this chapter, you find fault in your eating habits, are you going to be willing to change them? Do you use food in a capacity other than for nourishment; that is, as a reward or emotional release? How does your appearance reflect your nutritional status?

Individual Body Conformation

Many factors are responsible for individual body shapes; among these are environment, heredity, posture, cultural ideals, fashion, and eating customs and habits.

Throughout the world the ideals of body shape vary a great deal. In some cultures extremely overweight men or women are prized because they exhibit wealth and success. Other cultures esteem overweight in certain areas such as the hips, thighs, abdomen, or breasts. A study of historic costume will illustrate how fashion has decreed changes in body shape ranging from the stout Henry VIII of England, the stiffly farthingaled Queen Isabella of Spain, the wasp-waisted, mono-bosomed Lillian Russell, the bulging-muscled Arnold Schwarzenegger to the firm, svelte Jane Fonda. All have had the same basic body structure. Many extraneous forces have mandated alteration of this body form throughout the world.

For now, fashion and nutrition have come together to decree that the slender, natural, strong body is "in." The current ideal is a very healthy, fit body (Figure 7-2).

How you think of your body shape is a very personal perception. Studies have

7-2 *Fashion and nutrition have come together in the 1980s to decree that the slender natural body is "in." The current ideal as a very healthy, fit body. (Courtesy Catalina)*

demonstrated that only a few people actually have a clear or accurate body image. Sometimes the slender see themselves as fat and the fat see themselves as even fatter. (In the U.S. 70 percent of the women think of themselves as overweight).[1] Most people are not pleased with their body conformation and the majority desire a change.[2]

Take stock of how you look. Stand nude in front of a full-length mirror; with another mirror, study your body from all angles. Try jogging in place to see if anything jiggles. Try the "pinch test" on any fatty area of the body. Start by using the triceps area of the upper arm. With the arm bent slightly, pinch the skin halfway between the shoulder and the elbow on the underside of the arm, drawing it away from the bone. The "pinch" will be a double fold of tissue; the thickness of the fold should be between $\frac{1}{2}$ inch to 1 inch. If the "pinch" is greater than one inch, you are fat. This test may be tried in other areas of the body such as the abdomen, thigh, or back of calf. The pinch test is a good guide, but it is not always accurate because of the variety of structural differences in body forms.[3,4]

You may like the way you look. Great! Your problem will be to maintain this body shape for a lifetime. This can be a very difficult task. Often the skinny child or young adult becomes the overweight middle-ager. High school class reunions held after ten or twenty years very often reveal that the weight ratio has changed. The skinny kids are fat and the fat ones have become skinny. One explanation of this weight shift is that often the overweight youngsters learned their nutrition lessons and have spent a lifetime eating a properly balanced diet, whereas those who were slender when young have very often ignored healthful food practices and, because of this, have added pounds with the years. Too often a slender body is maintained by malnutrition; this is a foolish practice which soon leads to serious health problems.

Perhaps you think of yourself as being too thin. Very often thin young people find that the years help to overcome this problem since weight gain is easier for adults. If you are impatient, it would be wise to consult your physician, to study your food habits, and to develop a sensible pattern of eating designed to help you eat a variety of healthful foods in the amounts that will add weight.

You may be one of a large majority who have the problem of extra weight. This should be of continuing concern to you. You, also, would be wise to follow the advice: Consult your physician, study your food habits, and develop a healthful eating pattern designed to help you lose, and then to maintain your weight at the desired amount. As designer Edith Head observed, "I can't control growing older, but I can control my weight and how my body looks."[5]

[1] *U.S. News and World Report*, August 30, 1982, pp. 47–48.

[2] "Body Images—The Happy American Body," *Psychology Today*, November 1973, pp. 119–131.

[3] Ronald M. Deusch, *The Family Guide to Better Food and Better Health* (Des Moines: Meredith Corporation, 1971), p. 102.

[4] Theodore Berland, *Rating the Diets* (Skokie, Ill.: Consumer Guide, 1974), p. 12.

[5] Edith Head speech at Designer lecture series, Los Angeles County Museum of Art, February 18, 1979.

Nutrition in Brief

The subject of nutrition deals with the food we eat. Man has long been fascinated with this study and yet has only in a relatively recent period of time begun to develop an understanding of the relationship of the food intake to the body functions. Although much is now known, there is still a great deal to be learned in the field of nutrition.

Nutritional ingredients that make up all foods are the chemical substances called carbohydrates, proteins, fats, vitamins, minerals, and water. Our body is a gigantic collection of living cells. These cells are continuously born, fulfill their role, and die. Our bodies are healthy as long as the cells composing it are healthy.

Every single cell in our body is an elaborate, dynamic chemical factory. Each cell has the ability to take chemicals into itself, to change its size or shape as required, and to create chemicals that are passed along to other cells. Many kinds of cells comprise the body: muscle cells, brain cells, blood cells, and so on. Each cell has a vital job to do.

From these three observations come the three fundamental concepts underlying the science of nutrition. These concepts are:

1. Human cells are small factories that must be fed the right chemicals so they may perform their assigned tasks.
2. Human beings can be healthy only if their cells are fed the right chemicals.
3. The science of nutrition is concerned with the study of the body cell chemicals and their function.[6]

Our discussion is limited to the food chemicals that are essential for good health and life itself. These six essential nutrients are carbohydrates, proteins, fats, vitamins, minerals, and water. A knowledge of the six classes of essential nutrients will assist in forming a better understanding of the importance of the inclusion of each in the daily diet. There is some overlapping in the role of the various nutrients, but they may be classified as follows:

1. Body building, maintenance, and repair
   Proteins   Minerals
   Vitamins   Water
2. Body fuel for energy and heat
   Carbohydrates
   Proteins
   Fats
3. Regulation of body processes
   Vitamins
   Minerals
   Water

[6] John Leonard, J. L. Hofer, and N. Pritkin, *Live Longer Now* (New York: Grosset, 1974), p. 87.

228

Carbohydrates. Carbohydrates, along with proteins and fats, are responsible for body heat and energy. They are not body builders but are necessary for the health and function of every cell in your body. The cells of your brain and nervous system depend solely on carbohydrates, when broken down into glucose, for their energy. There are two large groups of carbohydrates, namely, sugars and starches. The sugar groups include cane and beet sugars and sugar products; honey, candies, desserts, frostings; preserves, jams, and jellies. The starch groups include bread, crackers, pasta, and cereals. Fruits and vegetables are also carbohydrates and fit in both sugar and starch classsfications, depending on the variety and age of the fruit or vegetable.

When digested, all carbohydrates are broken down into simple sugars. Thus, a diet high in starches is really high in sugars. Sugars are necessary for heat and energy and should not be eliminated from the diet. Excessive carbohydrates in the diet are easily converted to fats and stored in the body.

Although sugars are necessary for body heat and energy, they must not be eaten in such large amounts that they replace the body-building foods. Too much of the refined sugar foods not only lowers the intake of proteins, minerals, and vitamins but also promotes dental caries. Complex carbohydrates (starches) offer many health benefits and should be increased in many Americans' diets.

Proteins. Proteins are essential to the building and maintenance of body tissues. Meat, eggs, legumes, cheese, milk, nuts, grain, and fish are sources of protein.

Proteins are part of every living cell, and life without them is not possible. The body wears out cells every second. These cells, blood, bone, muscle, nerve, and connective tissue must be rebuilt and repaired through protein-bearing foods. Protein will be burned as fuel if the diet supplies too little of the carbohydrates and fats to meet the energy needs. When this happens the body building, maintenance and repair function of protein ceases.

Proteins, through the process of digestion, are converted into building units called *amino acids.* Some proteins contain all the essential amino acids and are called "complete" proteins; others contain only a few amino acids and are referred to as "incomplete." The incomplete proteins need to be supplemented by other protein-bearing foods in order for the body to obtain the necessary amino acids. In general, proteins of animal origin are complete proteins, whereas vegetable proteins are usually incomplete or partially complete.

Protein is not stored in the body, so a daily supply is needed. One pint of milk, or milk substitute (such as cheese or ice cream), and two servings of protein food, of which one should be another complete protein, are recommended daily for upkeep of the adult body, In cooking, proteins are hardened and toughened by high temperatures. Proteins are most tender and readily digested when cooked at low temperatures.

Fats. Fats also supply body heat and energy. In addition, they serve as carriers of the fat-soluble vitamins. Some unsaturated fatty acids are necessary for healthy skin.

Fats do not conduct heat, but the layer of fat beneath the skin helps conserve the body heat. Fats are stored in the body. Excessive fat stored on the body may be injurious to health. Fats supply a little over twice as many calories per gram as carbohydrates and proteins.

Vitamins. Vitamins are compounds that occur in minute quantities in foods. They are necessary for normal growth and development of the body and for the maintenance of health. All vitamins are found in food sources, and some are synthesized or produced in the body.

Nutritional-deficiency diseases such as pellagra, beriberi, scurvy, and rickets may be eliminated by incorporating vitamins in the diet. These diseases are thought by many to be relegated to history, yet it is not uncommon to find symptoms of them in modern society, not only among the indigent who lack food resources but also among the legions of do-it-yourself dieters.

Vitamin potency is diminished in storage and often oxidized by exposure to air. Much vitamin value may be lost in food preparation (including the thawing of frozen foods).

Vitamins can be made synthetically, as is done in pills and food additives. Some vitamins are stored in the body and can become toxic causing a condition known as hypervitaminosis. The use of vitamin supplements should be discussed with a personal physician.

Foods are the natural sources of vitamins. Very few foods contain all the known vitamins. Foods that come directly from nature to the table unprocessed are the highest in vitamin content. Dairy products, lean meats, whole grains, fruits, and vegetables are the chief sources of vitamins. A daily diet containing a sufficient supply of all vitamins is needed for optimum health and attractiveness.

Minerals. The body contains many minerals that must be replaced daily by foods containing them. Minerals are essential for normal growth, body mainte-nance, and body-regulating processes. Minerals are constituents of bones, teeth, and soft tissues, and they give elasticity to muscles and nerves. In the American diet, the minerals most often supplied in insufficient amounts are calcium, iodine, and iron. Interestingly, when these three minerals are adequately supplied, it generally is found that the other minerals are also in sufficient amount.

Some minerals are water soluble, which means that they are absorbed from foods by liquids. In cooking, very little water should be used. If liquid is left after food is removed, it should be utilized in soups or sauces, since discarding this liquid means a loss of minerals.

The role of each mineral is continually being investigated and better under-stood. Minerals in adequate supply are vital to life itself. The use of mineral supplements should be discussed with a personal physician.

Water. Every cell in our body is surrounded by fluid which is made up mostly of water. One half to three-fourths of our body weight is water. Our circulation, digestion, and elimination systems all require large amounts of water. Whenever fluids are lost from the body they must be replaced. So essential is this nutrient that a 5 percent loss causes dehydration and a 10 percent loss death. Most people are negligent in the amounts of water they drink. Six to eight glasses of water a day, which is often recommended, sounds like a tremendous amount, particularly if consumed all at once. Half a glass every hour during the active day seems much more acceptable—a drink every time you pass by a fountain, even easier. Soups and beverages also contribute to the amount of water consumed.

Calories/Kilocalories/Kcalories/Kcals

When food is consumed, digested, and utilized in the body, energy is released. Heat is a by-product of energy. Although the body is definitely not a machine, it is sometimes easier to grasp the relationship between food and body when it is associated with fuel and the engine. Food ingested produces, among other things, the energy needed to allow the body to function.

The term *calorie* is the name given to the unit of measurement used to describe the amount of heat generated when food is burned by the body. The scientific definition of calorie is the unit of heat that will raise the temperature of one kilogram of water one degree centigrade. Food energy is measured in kilocalories (thousands of calories), abbreviated *kcalories or kcals* or capitalized: Calories. Most people, even nutritionists, speak of these units simply as calories, but on paper they should be prefaced by a k. (The pronunciation of "kcalories" ignores the k.) A calorie is not a nutrient. It serves simply as a convenient measurement of the yield of energy from nutrients—proteins, fats, carbohydrates. The energy or kcaloric measurements of separate nutrients of many foods and food combinations have been determined by special tests devised for this purpose. The objective of this work has been to determine the kcalorie values of foods as potential sources of energy for the body. The results of this work are presented in kcalorie charts.

The kcalorie chart is simply another kind of tool to use in food planning. In studying the kcalorie values of various foods, it is easy to see that foods high in fat are high in calories. Actually, one gram of fat yields more than twice as many calories as one gram of either protein or carbohydrates. Removal of fat lowers the kcaloric count of a food. Nonfat milk has about half the number of kcalories as whole milk. Lean steak with the fat trimmed away is dramatically lower in kcalories than the untrimmed, well-marbled meat.

Kcalorie values of food vary greatly, and fat content is one of the prime reasons for this variation. But kcalories themselves do not vary in value; the unit of measurement always remains the same. Therefore, no food can be more "fattening" than any other food. Kcalories merely count up faster in foods that are high in fat.

The use of kcalories in weight control can sometimes simplify the task. Food intake becomes simple arithmetic. To gain, increase the intake of kcalories; to lose, decrease the intake of kcalories; to maintain, keep the same intake of kcalories. In this manner various favorite foods, even though high in kcalorie count, may be enjoyed if the daily totals are observed. It should be noted that one pound of fat equals 3,500 kcalories. To gain one pound, eat 3,500 kcalories that are not burned up with activities. To lose one pound, reduce food intake 3,500 kcalories below number of kcalories required for body functions while maintaining the same level of activities. A combination of kcalorie reduction and added exercise will speed weight loss.[7]

Study a table of nutritive values of foods and read labels on food products. Understand the contribution each food makes to your diet. Learn which foods fall into the category of "empty calories," that is, those that are high in calorie count but low in food value. Food is too essential to our well-being not to be fully understood. Start getting full nutritional value for calorie value.

The USDA's Daily Food Guide[8]

The United States Department of Agriculture, in cooperation with several of its agencies including the Science and Education Administration, the Human Nutrition Center, and the Consumer and Food Economics Institute, has developed a Daily Food Guide often referred to as Basic Four or Basic Four Plus One based on the kinds and amounts of foods that make up a nutritious diet. This guide lets *you* make the food choices to fit your eating style and physical requirements. The guide is based on current nutritional information and American eating customs.

The guide divides commonly eaten foods into *four groups* according to the nutritional contributions they make. By following the Guide you will be able to choose foods for their essential nutrient value as well as their calorie content.

The suggested number of daily servings in the Guide average about 1,200 calories, and provide adequate protein, carbohydrates, fats, vitamins, and minerals. By using the USDA's Daily Food Guide to plan and evaluate your daily food consumption you can be assured of a healthful and well-balanced diet (see Figure 7-3).

Making the Guide Work for You

You can personalize the USDA's Daily Food guide by fitting it to your calorie needs. All foods, except water and noncaloric drinks have calories. There are not "good calories" or "bad calories" nutritionally, but there are foods that give you little but calories (empty calories), and others that give you calories plus nutrients. How many calories you need depends on how much energy you use.

---

[7] For more information on calories and exercise, see: Frank Konishi, *Exercise Equivalents of Foods* (Carbondale, Ill.: Southern Illinois U.P., 1974).

[8] Extracted from *Food*, A Publication of Food and Nutrition by U.S. Department of Agriculture, 1979. For more information, write Consumer Information Center, Pueblo, Colo.

7-3 *The U.S.D.A. Daily Food Guide, The Basic Four Plus One. (From* Food, *a Publication on Food and Nutrition of the U.S. Department of Agriculture)*

Generally older people need fewer calories than younger people, women need fewer calories than men, and inactive people need fewer calories than active people.

If you are gaining unwanted weight, cut down first on the portions from the fifth group (Fats, Sweets, Alcohol). If you are still gaining weight, cut down on the size of the portions from the other groups. Remember, *cut down*, do not cut out any one of the first four food groups. Learn to select a variety of the lower calorie foods within each group. If you wish to gain weight, increase the intake from all food groups. Emphasize foods from groups one through four and enjoy in moderation the foods from the fifth group.

Remember the Guide gives you only the basics. You have to choose foods to meet *your* special needs. Nutritionists and other health authorities agree that a wide assortment of foods from the first four food groups provide the best known diet. They also agree that a nutritionally sound diet combined with regular exercise is the key to lifelong health (Figure 7-4).

The USDA's Daily Food Guide Serving Recommendations

The USDA's Daily Food Guide Serving Recommendations for each food group are included here. It gets a little complicated when you eat foods that span several groups such as a hamburger, chicken-vegetable soup, or macaroni and cheese. Sometimes there is no way to precisely determine portions of the different food groups in such combinations of foods. It all depends on how much you eat and the amounts of each food group used in the recipe. In such cases, you just have to estimate for yourself.

Milk-Cheese Group

Basic Servings Daily
(Based on servings of fluid milk; for milk product equivalents see below)

Children under 9	2 to 3 servings	Adults	2 servings
Children 9 to 12	3 servings	Pregnant Women	3 servings
Teens	4 to 6 servings	Nursing Mothers	4-6 servings

What's a Serving?
Includes milk in any form: whole, skim, lowfat, evaporated, buttermilk, and nonfat dry milk; also yogurt, ice cream, ice milk, and cheese, including cottage cheese.
Count one 8-ounce cup of milk as a serving.

7-4 *Nutritionists and other health authorities agree that a wide assortment of foods from the first four food groups provides the best diet known. A nutritionally sound diet combined with regular exercise is the key to lifelong health. (Courtesy Allied Corporation)*

Common portions of some dairy products and their milk equivalents in calcium are:

1 cup plain yogurt	= 1 cup milk
1 ounce Cheddar or Swiss cheese (natural or process)	= $\frac{3}{4}$ cup milk
1-inch cube Cheddar or Swiss cheese (natural or process)	= $\frac{1}{2}$ cup milk
1 ounce process cheese food	= $\frac{1}{2}$ cup milk
$\frac{1}{2}$ cup ice cream or ice milk	= $\frac{1}{3}$ cup milk
1 tablespoon or $\frac{1}{2}$ ounce process cheese spread; or 1 tablespoon Parmesan cheese	= $\frac{1}{4}$ cup milk
$\frac{1}{2}$ cup cottage cheese	= $\frac{1}{4}$ cup milk

235

Note: You'll get about the same amount of calcium in each of these portions, but varying numbers of calories.

Milk used in cooked foods—as in creamed soups, sauces, puddings—can count toward filling your daily quota in this group.

What's in It for You?

Milk and most milk products are relied on to provide calcium for healthy bones and teeth (they're the major source of this mineral in the American diet) and riboflavin and to contribute protein and vitamins A, B_6, and B_{12}. They also provide vitamin D, when fortified with this vitamin.

Fortified (with vitamins A and D) low-fat or skim-milk products have essentially the same nutrients as whole-milk products but fewer calories.

Meat-Poultry-Fish-Beans Group

Two Basic Servings Daily

What's a Serving?

Includes beef, veal, lamb, pork, poultry, fish, shellfish (shrimp, oysters, crabs, etc.), organ meats (liver, kidneys, etc.), dry beans or peas, soybeans, lentils, eggs, seeds, nuts, peanuts, and peanut butter.

Count 2 ounces of lean, cooked meat, poultry, or fish without bone *as a serving*. One egg, $\frac{1}{2}$ or $\frac{3}{4}$ cup cooked dry beans, dry peas, soybeans or lentils, 2 tablespoons peanut butter, and $\frac{1}{4}$ to $\frac{1}{2}$ cup nuts, sesame seeds, or sunflower seeds count as 1 ounce of meat, poultry, or fish.

What's in It for You?

These foods are valued for the protein, phosphorus, vitamins B_6, B_{12}, and other vitamins and minerals they provide. However, only foods of animal origin contain vitamin B_{12} naturally.

It's a good idea to vary your choices among these foods as each has distinct nutritional advantages. For example, red meats and oysters are good sources of zinc. Liver and egg yolks are valuable sources of vitamin A. Dry beans, dry peas, soybeans, and nuts are worthwhile sources of magnesium. The flesh of fish and poultry is relatively low in calories and saturated fat. Seeds (sunflower, sesame, for example) contribute polyunsaturated fatty acids which are an essential part of a balanced diet.

Cholesterol, like vitamin B_{12}, occurs naturally only in foods of animal origin. All meats contain cholesterol, which is present in both the lean and fat. The highest concentration is found in organ meats and in egg yolks. Fish and shellfish, except for shrimp, are relatively low in cholesterol. (Dairy products also supply cholesterol.)

Is Getting Enough Iron a Problem? It can be, particularly for young children, teen-age girls, and women of childbearing age.

Remember—meats are reliable sources of iron. So are whole-grain and enriched breads and cereals, dry beans, and dry peas, but the body can make better use of the iron these foods provide if they are eaten at the same time as a good source of vitamin C (orange juice, for example) or along with meat.

Vegetable-Fruit Group

Includes all fruits and vegetables.

Four Basic Servings Daily Recommended
Include one good vitamin C source each day. Also frequently include deep-yellow or dark-green vegetables (for vitamin A) and unpeeled fruits and vegetables and those with edible seeds, such as berries (for fiber).

What's a Serving?
Count ½ cup as a serving, or a typical portion—one orange, half a medium grapefruit or cantaloupe, juice of one lemon, a wedge of lettuce, a bowl of salad, and one medium potato.

What's in It for You?
This group is important for its contribution of vitamins A and C and fiber, although individual foods in this group vary widely in how much of these they provide. Dark-green and deep-yellow vegetables are good sources of vitamin A. Most dark-green vegetables, if not overcooked, are also reliable sources of vitamin C, as are citrus fruits (oranges, grapefruit, tangerines, lemons), melons, berries, and tomatoes. Dark-green vegetables are valued for riboflavin, folacin, iron, and magnesium, as well. Certain greens—collards, kale, mustard, turnip, and dandelion—provide calcium. Nearly all vegetables and fruits are low in fat, and none contains cholesterol.

Bread-Cereal Group

Four Basic Servings Daily
Select only whole-grain and enriched or fortified products. (But include *some* whole-grain bread or cereals for sure!) Check labels.

What's a Serving?
Includes all products made with whole grains or enriched flour or meal; bread, biscuits, muffins, waffles, pancakes, cooked or ready-to-eat cereals, cornmeal, flour, grits, macaroni and spaghetti, noodles, rice, rolled oats, barley, and bulgur.

Count as a serving 1 slice of bread; ½ cup to ¾ cup cooked cereal, cornmeal, grits, macaroni, noodles, rice, or spaghetti; or 1 ounce ready-to-eat cereal.

What's in It for You?
These whole-grain or enriched foods are important sources of complex carbohydrates, the B vitamins and iron. They also provide protein and are a major source of this nutrient in vegetarian diets. Whole-grain products contribute magnesium, folacin, and fiber, in addition.

Most breakfast cereals are fortified at nutrient levels higher than those occurring in natural whole grain. In fact, some fortification adds vitamins not normally found in cereals (vitamins A, B_{12}, C, and D). However, even these cereals, if refined, and other refined products (enriched or not), may be low in some other vitamins and trace minerals, which are partially removed from the whole grain in the milling process and are not added. For this reason, it's a good idea to include some less refined or whole-grain products in your diet.

Fats-Sweets-Alcohol Group—Extra Foods

What's a Serving
Includes foods like butter, margarine, mayonnaise and other salad dressings, and other fats and oils; candy, sugar, jams, jellies, sirups, sweet toppings, and other sweets; soft drinks and other highly sugared beverages; and alcoholic beverages such as wine, beer, and liquor. Also included are refined but unenriched breads, pastries, and flour products. Some of these foods are used as ingredients in prepared foods or are added to other foods at the table. Others are just "extras."

No serving sizes are defined because a basic number of servings is not suggested for this group.

What's in It for You?
These products, with some exceptions such as vegetable oils, provide mainly calories. Vegetable oils generally supply vitamin E and essential fatty acids.

Fats and oils have more than twice the calories, ounce for ounce, as protein, starches, or sugars, but keep hunger pangs away longer.

Pure alcohol has almost twice the calories per ounce as protein, starches, or sugars. However, few alcoholic beverages are 100 percent alcohol. Generally, the higher the alcohol content, the higher the calories, ounce for ounce.

Unenriched, refined bakery products are included here because, like other foods and beverages in this group, they usually provide relatively low levels of vitamins, minerals, and protein compared with calories.

People are Asking Questions About . . .

Sugar
For Example . . .
Does eating too much sugar cause diabetes, heart disease, and other disorders?
Is our increasing consumption of sugar in foods a factor in the widespread overweight and obesity seen in this country?
We don't know everything about the role of dietary sugar in health, but we do know quite a bit.
Dietary sugar consists of a group of sweeteners. There's sucrose (cane and beet sugar), other caloric sweeteners such as corn or glucose sirups, and sugars that

7-5 *Because sweets are well liked, and contribute calories without bulk or fiber, it is easy to eat more of them—and more kcalories—than we realize. (Courtesy Geiger of Austria)*

occur naturally in foods—lactose in milk and fructose in fruit. The most common sweetener is table sugar (sucrose).

From 1960 to 1977, annual per capita consumption of caloric sweeteners increased about 22 pounds, mostly as a result of sweeteners added to commercially prepared foods and increased consumption of sweetened foods such as soft drinks. In addition to obviously sweet foods such as candy, sirup, jam, jelly, pie, and cake, many other commercially prepared foods and beverages contain substantial amounts of sugars and sweeteners, even though they may not taste sweet. Catsup, salad dressings, and peanut butter are examples.

Sugars and sweeteners play important roles in food preparation. Besides making foods taste good, they add texture and color to bakery products like breads and pastries and help thicken, firm, or preserve puddings, jellies, and the like.

Commonly eaten sugars and sweeteners offer little nutritionally except calories. When sugars and sweeteners make up a substantial share of your calories, they may replace other foods which offer vitamins, minerals, and protein in addition to calories. Because sweets are well liked, and contribute calories without bulk or fiber, it is easy to eat more of them—and more calories—than you realize (Figure 7-5).

More calories than you need make you fat. It doesn't matter where they come from, sugar or other sources.

Sweet foods, especially sticky sweets, are a major cause of dental cavities. Between-meal sweets (even cough drops) are worse offenders than the same foods eaten with meals. The total amount of sugar eaten is not as important as how many times, how long, and the form of sugary food (liquid or solid, for example) to which your teeth are exposed, and whether or not you clean your teeth after eating sugary foods.

Apart from sugar's role in tooth decay and its potential contribution to obesity, there is little evidence that directly links sugar with various disorders. However, scientists are still studying this issue. If you're concerned about the level of sugar in your diet, here are some points to keep in mind:

1. Check the ingredient label for sweeteners and sugars in products. Sugar is not the only word to look for on labels. Watch for such words as *sucrose, glucose, dextrose, fructose, corn sirups, corn sweeteners, natural sweeteners,* and *invert sugar.* Remember that ingredients are listed on the label in the order of predominance, with the ingredients used in largest amounts listed first.
2. Substitute fruit juices or plain water for regular soft drinks, punches, fruit drinks, and ades which contain considerable amounts of sugar.
3. Go easy on candy, pies, cakes, pastries, and cookies.
4. Fruits are often canned in heavy sirup, which is a high-sugar product. Buy fruit canned in its own juice, other fruit juice, or light sirup.
5. Many cereals are presweetened. Check the label. Buy *unsweetened* kinds, so *you* can control the amount of sugar added.
6. Experiment with reducing the sugar in your favorite recipes. Be prepared for products that may look and taste different.

Guidelines for Good Dental Health:
1. Reduce consumption of sugars and foods high in sugar.
2. Avoid between-meal snacks of sweet or sticky foods. Replace with foods such as nuts, fresh fruits, raw vegetables, and milk.
3. Brush or floss teeth or rinse your mouth after meals and snacks—particularly after eating sweet or sticky foods.

Fat

People who eat a high-fat diet—especially a high *saturated*-fat diet—often have higher levels of blood cholesterol. High levels of cholesterol (a fatlike substance) in the blood are linked to formation of fat deposits in the linings of arteries, a condition associated with heart disease. In contrast, diets with lower levels of fat and relatively more polyunsaturated fat (most vegetable oils) are linked to lower levels of blood cholesterol and possibly less risk of heart disease. Cholesterol occurs naturally only in foods of animal origin.

Fats in the diet come from two sources—(1) fats occurring naturally in foods such as whole milk, cheese, nuts, seeds, meat, poultry, fish, chocolate; and (2) fats and oils added in preparing foods such as fried foods, pastries, gravies, and salad dressings.

All fats, no matter what the source (whether liquid oils, shortening, margarine, the marbling in meats, or the fat in milk and cheese) have the same calorie value; however, saturated and polyunsaturated fats in diets differ in their effect on blood cholesterol.

If you want to cut down on the level of fat in your diet, here are some suggestions:

1. Include more of these foods in your meals: fruits (except avocado and olives), vegetables, breads, cereals, dry beans, and dry peas.
2. Cut down on fatty meats. This includes regular ground beef, corned beef, spareribs, sausage, and heavily marbled cuts, such as prime rib. Keep in mind that prime beef contains more fat than choice, and choice more than good grade.
   Include more fish, shellfish, chicken, and turkey in your diet. These foods are generally lower than many meats in fat content.
   Leaner cuts of meat include the following:

   Beef—flank, round, rump
   Lamb—leg, loin
   Veal—all cuts

   Pork cuts—such as lean ham, loin, Boston butt, and picnic—are moderate in fat content.
3. Limit nuts, peanuts, and peanut butter, which contain considerable amounts of fat.
4. Reduce the use of whole milk and whole-milk products, such as most cheeses and ice cream, in favor of skim or lowfat milks and their products, such as uncreamed cottage cheese, which are lower in fat content.

Sodium

Excess sodium in the diet is believed to contribute to high blood pressure (hypertension) and stroke in some people.

If you want to limit sodium intake, limit the use of table salt (sodium chloride) and salty foods. This means cutting down on:

1. Foods prepared in brine, such as pickles, olives, and sauerkraut.
2. Salty or smoked meat, such as bologna, corned or chipped beef, frankfurters, ham, luncheon meats, salt pork, sausage, smoked tongue.
3. Salty or smoked fish, such as anchovies, caviar, salted and dried cod, herring, sardines, smoked salmon.
4. Snack items such as potato chips, pretzels, salted popcorn, and salted nuts and crackers.
5. Bouillon cubes; seasoned salts (including sea salt); soy, Worcestershire, and barbecue sauces.
6. Cheeses, especially processed types.
7. Canned and insant soups.
8. Prepared horseradish, catsup, and mustard.

Read labels. You may be surprised to learn that some processed foods which contain no table salt and don't taste salty have lots of sodium. Look for the word *soda* or *sodium* or the symbol *"Na"* on labels. Examples are *sodium* bicarbonate (baking *soda*), mono*sodium* glutamate, most baking powders, di*sodium* phosphate, *sodium* alginate, *sodium* benzoate, *sodium* hydroxide, *sodium* propionate, *sodium* sulfite, and *sodium* saccharin.

Fiber

Dietary fiber is plant material that is not digested in the gastrointestinal tract of man. There are some indications that eating fibrous foods may prevent constipation and help to prevent some chronic diseases of the large intestine. In addition, fiber is a plus in weight reduction because bulky foods fill you up.

The types or amounts of fiber in foods that are the most beneficial to health are not known. However, plant foods—whole-grain breads and cereals, bran, dry peas and dry beans, nuts, fruits, and vegetables—particularly those that are unpeeled or have edible seeds—are considered good sources.

Nutritional Variations During the Life Cycle

Americans have been having a love affair with protein and vitamins for many years. A fallacy held by too many Americans is that a lot of protein and a multivitamin pill each day is all that is needed for good health. The Dietary Goals for the United States established by a Senate Committee working with nutritionists and other scientists recommended that the daily diet include the following:

protein, 12 percent of kcalories
complex carbohydrate, 48 percent of kcalories
sugar, 10 percent of kcalories
fat, 30 percent of kcalories[9]

Diets too high in protein and low in complex carbohydrates create a condition called *ketosis*. Large dosage of certain vitamins can be toxic. Often the first symptoms of either of these conditions are very similar to flu symptoms: headache, nausea, body ache.

Nutritionists are hoping to re-educate the American public to switching to diets which are lower in protein with more fish and fowl than red meat and thus lower in fat, and higher in complex carbohydrates found in vegetables, seeds, nuts, and whole grains. Vitamins and minerals are needed in very small amounts. A diet which contains a mixed variety of foods as recommended in the Basic Four food plan supplies all of the vitamin and mineral requirements.

Each age has its nutritional needs. The baby and child are growing and developing rapidly and, therefore, demand a balanced diet. The teen-ager has the same needs, but because this period of growth is intensified, his food intake should be at a lifetime high. The late teens and early twenties are especially significant for women. Not only is the body completing the growth and development cycle but it is also preparing for, or is actually engaged in, pregnancy. For the girl who has not built up sufficient nutritional reserves, the period of pregnancy and lactation is especially demanding. Some cases of physical and mental handicaps in infants have been attributed to poor nutrition of the mother both before and during pregnancy. After age twenty-five the body needs are less, and, most often, so are the physical activities of many people. This is the period when eating habits must be carefully analyzed or the pounds begin to creep on. If a bride and groom add only a pound a year each, together they will be a hundred pounds overweight when they celebrate their golden wedding anniversary! Nutritional needs should be based on a varied diet including the six essential nutrients daily for a lifetime; however, the amounts should be limited as the birthdays increase. The previous statement emphasizes that the amount of food eaten should decrease as one grows older. But the variety of food consumed remains important for the entire life cycle. Many of the problems, both physical and mental, of the elderly stem from malnutrition throughout the lifecycle.

Eating Patterns

One of the cherished ideals of most Americans is the family pattern of gathering together for meals and camaraderie. Memories of the Thanksgiving turkey, 4th

[9]Eleanor Noss Witney and Eva May Nunnelley Hamilton, *Understanding Nutrition*, 3rd ed. (St. Paul, Minn.: West Publishing, 1984), p. 29.

of July picnics, and birthday cake and ice cream celebrations are woven into the American ideal life. For some, the evening family dinner is the most important event of the day when all members gather at an appointed time for some of "Mom's good home cooking." These meal ideas are often reflected in various advertising media trying to sell products for the "good life."

Many "Moms" still prefer to believe that they serve three meals a day—breakfast, lunch, and dinner with some snacks in between. The pattern more often is this:

Little or no breakfast, but two or three snacks during the morning.
Maybe some lunch.
Big snack in late afternoon.
Dinner (often eaten at different times and places by individual family members).
Snacks around the television set often followed by a refrigerator raid on the way to bed.

For the college student, classes, sports, jobs, and social activities all take preference to eating with the family or living group. We are now a nation of grazers who grab food on the run from the family refrigerator, the vending machine, or the neighborhood drive-through.

The popularity of the low-cost, franchised, self-service food vendors has contributed to changes in eating patterns. These were purposely located in the suburban areas to attract family business. Interestingly, the "small fry" lunch business is one of the biggest factors of their early success. Children clustered around the stand are a familiar sight in many neighborhoods. Thus, an entirely new eating pattern has been fostered, a diet high in fat, high in sugar, high in calories, a diet that nutritionists warn when eaten exclusively could give a customer scurvy because of the lack of vitamin C. Since no one is forced to eat at these places, the owners must be selling what people want.

The complicated pace of modern life, combined with the rise of women in the work force, the number of varied lifestyles and the decline of domestic help, has accelerated the inventiveness of food technologists. Grocery stores are now repositories for an amazing variety of frozen, dried, dehydrated, canned, and cellophaned food-stuffs. Emphasis has been placed on ease of preparation. "Ready-to-eat," "add-water-and-stir," and "heat-without-thawing" are the favored instructions. Nutritional value does not seem too important *if* dinner can be on the table in ten minutes and the cooking vessels are disposable.

Advertising, particularly through the medium of television, has had an impact on eating patterns. Not only is television time snack time but the television commercial thrust often directs all viewers to indulge themselves in some tasty treat. The foods advertised are generally not apples, oranges, beets, or squash but some miracles of food technological manipulation, which are high in price, but low in nutritive value. Novelist Vance Bourjaily noted:

This country is full of people who have forgotten what good food is. Eating in most countries is a basic pleasure, but people in the U.S. don't eat for pleasure. To them, eating is just something done in response to advertising.[10]

Nutrition—Fact and Fallacy

As the field of nutrition research is expanded, countless articles on foods and nutrition are churned out for the popular press. Some of these are based on valid, documented research, whereas others are based on the commercial appeal of the article itself. It has been noted that, excluding sex, more is written in the popular literature about food and nutrition than about any other subject. How can one evaluate these articles to determine which are worthy of thoughtful study and which are the work of a food faddist out to make a "fast buck"?

The best solution is to acquire a basic nutrition education. Learn the compositions of food and the relationship of the essential nutrients to body functioning and maintenance. Understand the caloric requirements at varying ages. Use this knowledge to evaluate the written material.

Learn, also, to determine the credentials of an author. All are experts, because they tell you so. Some are accredited: they are the Home Economist with B.S., M.S., physicians with the M.D. after their name, the nutritionists or biochemists with either Ph.D. or D.Sc., the Registered Dietician with R.D., or others with some combination of these degrees. The others are amateurs, some well informed, some well meaning, and some are simply hucksters. Before accepting any nutritional or diet advice, challenge the qualification of the author. Investigate his credentials, and above all, apply the nutritional education you have acquired through credited nutrition, physical education, or health classes. Be an aware consumer.

Fad Diets

Fad diets are those that promise miracles. They are usually based on one food or a strange combination of foods. They are offered to help you "crash" weight off in a very limited time. The variety of these diets stretches the imagination. There are diets based on grapes, apples, grapefruit, wine, "booze," milk, water, potatoes, rice, meat, chicken, eggs, sauerkraut, pickle juice, *ad infinitum*. Some call for all vegetables and no meat, others for all meat and no vegetables. For some you count calories, for some you count protein, for some you count carbohydrates, and for some you do not count anything. One thing that they do have in common is that they are almost impossible to maintain for any length of time, because of their unusual and unsatisfying nature. The weight lost from such a regime is usually quickly regained. Fad diets can be dangerous to your health, causing illness and in some extreme cases, death.

[10]"Living Off the Fat of the Franchise," *Pasadena Star News*, August 19, 1979, p. 16.

A fad diet should never be embarked upon without competent medical supervision. Common sense should always prevail whenever diets are planned. Compare any fad diet to the Basic Four and be aware of the nutritional discrepancies. Medical histories are written about persons who have ruined their health by do-it-yourself diets. Skeletons are skinny, but one has yet to win a beauty contest!

Health Foods

Pushing from another direction come the health foods promoters. Building on the fear of poor-quality foodstuffs, they often twist basic nutritional information into an exploitation for profit. Of course, there are many reputable health foods stores operated by people who are honest and knowledgeable. It is important to understand the facts about health foods stores in order to evaluate them. They have grown in popularity because a number of people have become alarmed about the proliferation of low-nutrition foodstuffs that crowd the marketplace. Health foods stores generally specialize in certain kinds of foods. Some will sell special grain bakery products, some chemicals, vitamins, and minerals; some sell organically grown vegetables, some sell raw milk. The merit of these foods can be debated. Often the prices in these stores are very high. Because of a low volume turnover, the quality sometimes can be quite low. The best criteria of judging the products sold in any market is a basic knowledge of food values and of quality foods. The only valid way of judging the status of a market is by reading the labels of products sold and of judging the merit of each product to decide if the food merchandised is truly better for your purposes.

Food quackery, miracle diets, and unethical "fat doctors" are all big business in the United States today. Many people are being exploited by these unscrupulous merchants in the business of selling the promise of health. As an educated person, one should be alert to nutritional misinformation in whatever form it is dispersed. When one is uncertain of the validity of material or the credentials of the people involved, there are a number of reliable sources that can help. Among those offering accurate information are the following:

Registered dieticians connected with city, county, and state health offices or with social welfare offices.

Teachers in the health and home economics fields on the elementary, secondary school and college level—including university extension agents.

The Federal Food and Drug Administration regarding labeling and practices related to food.

The Federal Trade Commission for questions about advertising or doubtful statements made on mass media.

Your family physician.

Diet Groups

Psychologists and physicians concerned with obesity generally agree that diet groups are among the more successful techniques known to date in treating overweight people. Each group has certain fees, rules, procedures, and diets.

They are all based on the human foible "misery loves company." Many successful dieters have learned that the diet is not enough; it must be combined with motivation, will power, and the support of other human beings. Group dieting provides all of these elements. Various groups have had outstanding success with vast numbers of dieters who have lost weight and maintained their loss.

Choosing the right diet group is important. There is a wide variety from which to choose. The main difference seems to be in the degree of maturity, sophistication, and involvement they anticipate from the dieting participants. The basic diet is essentially the same for each group and is based on a variety of meats, fruits, vegetables, grains, and dairy products, and the lowering of the intake of fats and sugars. The goal of each group is to help the individual lose weight safely and to maintain the loss through establishing new, healthful patterns of eating.

It should be noted that authorities on nutrition and obesity point to four major shortcomings of the diet clubs:

There is a lack of professional supervision or medical guidance.

Club lecturers and leaders lack a scientific knowledge of nutrition.

The need for exercise while reducing is often overlooked or the exercises suggested are not strenuous enough to be effective.

The diets tend to be standardized and thus too rigid for some participants, such as teen-agers and senior citizens.[11]

For those considering joining a diet club, the following recommendations are made:

First, consult your doctor for a health diagnosis, especially if you are more than 10 percent overweight.

Learn if the diet club asks for medical approval before you join; if so, who are their professional consultants?

Learn if their program was developed by professional doctors and nutritionists or by a nonprofessional.

Learn how the club keeps up with new developments in nutrition and diet updates.

Learn how the club leader follows your reaction to the diet. Is there concern about fatigue or stomach trouble, circulatory problems, or diabetes?

As an intelligent individual, you should check out the diet club's reputation with your doctor or local medical society.

Diseases Attributed to Malnutrition

Malnutrition (lack of proper nutrition, inadequate or unbalanced nutrition) is a very serious problem in the United States as well as in many other parts of the world. Statistics show alarming increases of deaths from diseases such as heart

---

[11] Theodore Irwin, "Clubs—Good or Bad," *Parade*, July 25, 1971, p. 7.

disease, atherosclerosis, cerebrovascular disease (stroke), diabetes, arterial hypertension, and gout. These are called degenerative diseases because they each involve the breakdown of individual body cells which results in the degenerative breakdown of the whole person as well. One degenerative disease can lead to another. For example, a diabetic can become a victim of hardening of the arteries, a heart attack, high blood pressure, and finally suffer a stroke. Are all these diseases of the elderly? No. The shocking facts are that these degenerative diseases are striking down the young as well. The incubation period for atherosclerosis is estimated to be twenty years, so anyone past his twentieth birthday could be in the process of developing this disease. How are these diseases related to malnutrition? Research studies at the University of California, Berkeley, have shown that the food variety typical of many Americans' diets contains a high quantity of fats and sugars. In this country we are averaging 141 pounds of sugar per person a year and about 150 pounds of meat. Our total intake of food is 584 pounds.[12] Without proper exercise, this diet leads to overweight and obesity. The obese are considered malnourished.

Overweight

What is obesity? It is simply the state of being too fat. This does not refer exclusively to the grossly overweight; obesity is the term that best describes the condition of those who carry too much fat on their frame. Some nutritionists estimate that about half the total population of the United States is overweight.[13] The U.S. Public Health Service reported that there are enough statistics available to "indicate a substantial prevalence of obesity at every age in both sexes." The data specifically indicated that American women gain most weight at two periods of life: when they are pregnant and, later, after menopause. Men gain most weight between ages twenty-five and forty, but gain faster after age forty. Many of today's overweight adults were overweight as children, and the national statistics indicate that this trend continues.[14] According to one study, close to one fifth of our children are overweight by the time they graduate from high school.[15]

How did this serious nutritional disease strike a country that prides itself in both abundant resources and technological advancement? Look back into history for some of the answers. The United States, along with many other affluent countries of the world, evolved from a heritage of most people working long and arduous hours to create shelter, protection, clothing, and food. As the countries advanced economically, scientifically, and technologically, the majority of the people were required to expend less physical energy to accomplish their work. For example, farmers drove trucks and tractors, and housewives used machines

[12] Food Consumption, Prices, Expenditures, *Statistical Bulletin,* **656,** USDA, Summer, 1984.

[13] Theodore Berland, "Ten Misconceptions About Overweight and Dieting," *Better Homes and Gardens,* June 1972, p. 49.

[14] "Obesity and Health," *Public Health Service Pub. No. 1485* (Washington: U.S. Government Printing Office, 1966).

[15] Jean Mayer, *Overweight, Causes, Cost and Control* (Englewood Cliffs, N.J.: Prentice-Hall, 1968). p. 36.

such as the washer, dryer, vacuum cleaner, and mixer. Mass transportation and communications made it easier to get around and sometimes even eliminated the need to go anywhere.

Our pioneers walked across the continent; we ride. Driving has been called one of our most fattening activities. Jean Mayer, Harvard nutritionist, put it well when he said:

The modern American man is incredibly inactive. He gets up, and, after briefly standing in front of his mirror using his electric toothbrush and his electric razor, sits down at the breakfast table, goes on to sit in his car, in his office, at coffee break, at lunch, in his office, in his car, at dinner, and in front of the television set and after lying in a warm bath for a while, goes on to lie in bed.

Mayer also estimated that the luxury of a telephone extension, by eliminating walking, helps everyone who owns one to accumulate an extra five thousand calories a year—enough to put on fifteen pounds of fat in ten years.[16]

As the need for physical energy to accomplish the tasks of living diminished, foods also become more plentiful and easier to acquire and to prepare. The typical American diet of meat and potatoes has been enhanced by ethnic contributions such as spaghetti, dumplings, and grits, along with pita, pizza, tacos, and soul foods. Technological genius contributed crackers, potato chips, breakfast cereals, carbonated beverages, heat-and-serve dinners, and endless cookies, cakes, and candies. More foods were consumed by a population doing less physical labor. For these reasons, the problem of obesity has become our number one nutritional disease. Obesity is the disease that is often the forerunner of all the degenerative diseases, including heart disease, atherosclerosis, cerebrovascular disease, diabetes, arterial hypertension, and gout. The incidence of obesity is increasing in all countries enjoying prosperity and is striking down citizens of increasingly younger ages. To illustrate this point:

In 1971, more than 100 autopsies were performed on American soldiers killed in South Vietnam, using advanced methods of determining heart disease. It was found that 45 percent of the autopsies showed evidence of medium heart damage. In another 5 per cent of the autopsies, there was evidence of severe artery damage. The average age of the soldiers was 22 years.[17]

It has been stated that the overweight, particularly obese children, are the unprotected minority in our society. In the United States at this time, overweight is much more common among the poor than among the rich. This is probably because of food prices and diet choices. For many, the fat problem begins in childhood. University of Pennsylvania researchers speculated that overweight resulted from faulty nutrition habits established for the children by their families.

[16] Ibid., p. 79.
[17] J. J. McNamara et al., "Coronary Artery Disease in Vietnam Casualties," *Journal of the American Medical Association*, May 17, 1971, p. 51.

It has been established that in the upper, more affluent, classes, there is greater social pressure to be thin.[18]

Income, Education, and Weight

A study showing the relationship between income, education, and body weight was conducted by a University of Michigan research team. The results showed that women in higher-income groups were 20 percent leaner than women in lower-income groups. As men got to the middle-income group they were 20 percent fatter than the lower-income males. As men got into the upper-income group they were leaner. Dr. Stanley Garn, the director of the team, explains that men do not get the leanness message until they go beyond the middle-income range. Low-income males remain lean because they are frequently involved in active physical work; as they get into the middle group their work becomes sedentary, thus the weight gain.

A similar relationship was found between education level and body weight. Women who did not go to high school were 30 percent fatter than women with 12 or more years of education. Men with a college education were 10 percent fatter than men with no high school education.[19]

Often success or failure can be determined by the shape you are in. Many people including employers discriminate against the overweight. Dr. Rudolf Noble, an obesity specialist at the University of California, found that among 1,000 overweight patients, 14 percent said that they were unable to find jobs because of their weight. Dr. Noble believes that, even though employers say they do not hire overweight people because of health reasons and insurance rates, the real issue is appearance.

In California, as in other states, it is against the law for employers to discriminate on the basis of race, national origin, religion, sex, age, and physical handicap. Lloyd Zimpel of the State Fair Employment Practices Commission says obesity is considered a physical handicap only if it is "a stable, permanent condition, not amenable to medical treatment." (In other words, hopeless.) Since the law regarding physical handicaps is recent, Zimpel said to date there had not been many legal challenges. He did cite one case of a woman who weighed 300 pounds. She was employed on a temporary basis and wanted permanent Civil Service status. She was turned down because "she weighed too much." When she appealed this decision, she lost, because two doctors said that her overweight was not a permanent condition. "She could lose weight if she wanted to."[20]

Metabolic, genetic, or glandular disorders are rarely the cause of obesity. Eating more food than is required by the body for energy and activity are considered to be the most common cause of overweight. Current research is revealing both

---

[18] "Poor Eating Habits," *Parade*, October 8, 1972, p. 10.
[19] "Income Status and Fat," *Los Angeles Times*, August 31, 1977, Pt. IV, p. 4.
[20] Harriet Stix, "A Lean Job Market for the Overweight," *Los Angeles Times*, April 6, 1975, Pt. IX, p. 1.

physical and psychological causes of overweight. Although the causes of extreme overweight may be complicated, the cures for overweight are certainly not simple or easy. All have to do with the limiting of food intake, increasing exercise, and modifying eating behaviors.

Weighing. There is a device on the market that will help everyone control his/her weight problem, *if* that person will use it. It is called a scale. If you use a scale faithfully, three things can happen:

It can tell you how much weight you need to gain or lose.
It can motivate you to get a sensible diet from your doctor and stick to it.
It will help you maintain the weight you have achieved by your hard efforts.

J. Mark Hiebert, president of Sterling Drug Company, New York City, believes so much in the use of the scale that he requires his executives to weigh in each weekday lunch time in the company dining room. Over the scale is a sign reading, "To Gain Is to Lose." Daily weights are posted on a chart. Some of these people have been following this procedure since 1960. To gain more than two pounds is to risk a warning of banishment from the dining room by the president. Over a five-year period, seventy-six executives maintained their best weight, seventeen lost from four to twelve pounds; only eight have gained three or more pounds.[21]

Medical specialists generally agree on the importance of a regular weighing-in program. They suggest that you make it a habit to weigh on your own scale, unclothed, at the same time each day without fail. They recommend that you keep a chart and tape measure handy. In addition to regularly recording your nude weigh-in figure, keep track of your key dimensions as indicated on the tape measure. (Male problem area is the midriff just below navel; for most women, it is the hip and thigh area.) Displaying your weight chart can sometimes give you a psychological impetus to stick to your diet. Perhaps most important is to learn to consider a three-pound weight gain with the same alarm that you would a three-degree temperature rise (see Chapter 6 for ideal weight charts).

Eating Disorders

The opposite of obesity is the psychological problem diagnosed as *anorexia nervosa*, which causes its victims to stop eating to the point they may die of starvation if untreated. Anorexics are almost always teen-age girls between the ages of thirteen and nineteen, although both boys and adults of either sex can be affected. According to New York psychologist Steven Levenkron, the incidence of anorexia nervosa in the United States has increased over 1,000 percent from 1973 to 1978.

The symptoms are not pretty: loss of 20 percent of body weight; loss of menstrual period, which doctors fear may lead to sterility if prolonged; loss of hair (a starvation symptom); lanugo (a bodily growth of downy hair); a heartbeat of 50 per minute (72 is normal); blood pressure down to 80/50. If untreated or ineffectively treated, 10 percent of the victims will die.

Until recently, it was thought that anorexia nervosa was a sickness of the upper classes. This appears no longer true. The ideal of thin has worked down to middle-class families. The thin ethic is claiming the daughters of policemen and auto mechanics as well as the more affluent.

Levenkron explains the causes of anorexia nervosa:

We're living with the Twiggy[22] image. It permeates fashion and adolescence. These girls keep dieting way past thinness. That's the message fashion and advertising deliver over and over to females. The message to males is "firm and sturdy." Why shouldn't it be the same to females? Combine a lack of family nurturing and a society which says thin is excellence and you have an epidemic of anorexia.... Another symptom is a fastidious approach to eating. Anorexics eat slowly, go in for food fadism such as eating only vegetables, then eliminating the vegetables from their diet. I have a girl in the hospital now who ate only pickles. There is also body consciousness, and no matter how thin they are, they still feel they are overweight.

Asked about the startling increase in anorexics in recent years, Levenkron acknowledged that part of the increase might be due to better identification of the illness. "But mostly it is that we have more Twiggy babies, kids brought up with the ideal of thinness."[23]

The practice of food bingeing and then purging the system to avoid weight gains, clinically described as *bulimia*, has recently been recognized as a very common practice particularly among college students. Case studies reveal that bulimics often consume over 10,000 calories on a binge and purge themselves five to ten times a day.

This eating disorder primarily affects women and teen-age girls. Enlargement of the salivary glands, erosion of dental enamel, and menstrual irregularities are symptoms of the disorder. Use of laxatives and diuretics may lead to changes in bowel habits and dehydration. All can result in muscle weakness and possible renal and cardiovascular failure.

There is no doubt that innumerable women control their weight at their desired level through fasting, vomiting, or purging to compensate for overeating. The disorder, although known since Roman times, is attributed to society's premium for thinness in women. Bulimia is less common in men because obesity is more acceptable to them.

It is recognized that people who indulge in the gorge-purge syndrome may have underlying emotional disturbances or conflicts. Bulimia is considered a very serious health problem. While the condition can exist over many years, it can be life-threatening. No medication has proved helpful in solving the disorder. Therapy that educates the bulimic to understand the underlying causes for the ad-

---

[21] "Contemporary," *Denver Post*, June 20, 1971, Pt. 3. p. 1.

[22] Twiggy is a model, who was the fashion ideal of the late 1960s, early 1970s when she was fourteen years old. She was 5'7" and weighed less than 90 pounds at the height of her career.

[23] Ursula Vils, "Treating Teens Who Starve for Thinness' Sake," *Los Angeles Times*, October 22, 1978, Pt. VIII, p. 1.

diction and positively supports the modification of eating behavior has offered the greatest success for recovery.[24]

Individual Choices

The grim reality of a worldwide food shortage, the predicted overpopulation of the earth's surface, and the dwindling acreages available for agriculture are factors that substantiate the necessity of new eating patterns. It is difficult to know what foods will be available in the future. Educated guesses predict that plant protein will replace animal protein in the diet. Soybeans seem to have the highest potential for becoming a staple in the American diet of the future.

It is not anticipated that pills will fulfill the nutritional needs of the future. Food in a variety of forms, old and new, will continue to be recognized as the primary source of nutrients no matter how many "magic formulas" are invented.

Snack foods have become an important part of the diet. They simply must be planned. The individual must learn to live nutritionally with a combination of manufactured foods and unprocessed foods. A variety of foods is the best insurance to good nutrition.

Research and industry are continually making progress toward understanding human nutritional needs. Food technology has brought a proliferation of food-

[24] Alexander R. Lucas, "Bulimia: Nightmare of a Food Addict," *Journal of the American Medical Association*, January, 1984, p. 16.

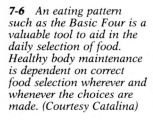

7-6 *An eating pattern such as the Basic Four is a valuable tool to aid in the daily selection of food. Healthy body maintenance is dependent on correct food selection wherever and whenever the choices are made. (Courtesy Catalina)*

stuffs and food processes into our lives. Each mature person must assume the responsibility for his personal nutritional needs at each stage of his life cycle. If we need to develop new guides to eating, these guides should be tailored to the individual needs, periods of life, and activities.

Accredited nutritionists generally agree that a diet that contains a variety of foods, including fruits, vegetables, breads and grains, meats, fish, and dairy products will be a good one. It is also believed that the more refined, processed, and mutilated the food becomes, the less nutritious it will be. Foods such as corn chips, puffed cereals, and dehydrated mashed potatoes fall into this group. Convenience foods and easily prepared foods may be of lower food value. Foods obtained from vending machines or franchised fast food stands are often high in fats and sugars.

Our diet must be based on the essential nutrients and tailored to fit personal needs at each stage of life. This basic knowledge will provide an intelligent perspective with which to evaluate the barrage of conflicting and confusing advice used in the promotion of foods, diets, and nutrition information. An eating pattern such as the Basic Four is a valuable tool to aid in the daily selection of food. Healthy body maintenance is dependent on correct food selection wherever and whenever the choices are made (Figure 7-6).

Suggested Activities

1. Read labels on various foods to learn just what they contribute to your diet.
2. Collect articles and advertisements on foods and nutrition from magazines and newspapers. Analyze credentials of author, accuracy of information, and emotional appeal of copy. Compare findings with those of class members.
3. Collect and display cartoons about eating habits and problems.
4. Discuss individual eating habits of class members. Include food likes and dislikes. Try to determine why students eat as they do.
5. Keep track of your food intake for a period of three to seven days. Analyze nutritional status of your diet. If possible, arrange with college computer department to analyze individual class members' diets.
6. Invite to class guest speakers such as nutritionists, doctors, physical fitness instructors, and community business people involved with foods or nutrition or dieting.
7. Investigate community resources related to nutrition or weight control.
8. Collect pictures that show how fashion has decreed changes in body shape. Use catalogues of great paintings, historic fashion books, and old magazines for sources. Use current fashion magazines to see if you agree anorexia nervosa is promoted by fashion and advertising. See how many queen- and king-size fashion advertisements you can find. Discuss the availability of various size ranges in men's clothing. How does this relate to the nutritional status of the United States population?

8 *Your Skin, Nails, and Hair*

Healthy skin, nails, and hair are an important part of individuality at every age (Figure 8-1). Each year huge sums of money are spent for promises of unblemished skin, perfect nails, and magnificent hair. Big businesses have been created to manufacture, promote, and sell both products and services for the care and maintenance and embellishment of skin, nails, and hair.

The consumer is faced with a very difficult task of selecting the products and regimes of care that will promote the health and attractiveness of these organs and appendages. In the past, the Food and Drug Administration has had very little authority over cosmetics. Legislation requiring the truthful listing of ingredients on labels met with great opposition from big business lobbies who feared that the public would buy far fewer cosmetics and grooming aids if they found out the ingredients of most of them are basically the same. Legislation was passed in 1975, requiring all ingredients of beauty potions to be listed on the container. The listing of ingredients seems to have made very little impact on consumer buying habits.

Some of the key ingredients and their functions are listed in Appendix C.

Clever promotional advertising of skin care and cosmetic products is often based on emotional appeal. The truth about skin, nails, and hair is frequently distorted to create more dramatic advertising copy. Packaging is another factor. A pretty bottle, a masculine name, or a promise of sexual appeal and romance sells many cosmetics made of inexpensive ingredients for a large dollar profit. Studies show that personal costs of grooming products increases with an increase in income. Status is purchased with the bottles displayed in the bathroom. The girl who got through college using discount store cosmetics often finds great satisfaction in using the expensive products of Lancôme, Estee Lauder, or Chanel.[1] However, those who have great wealth often buy low-cost cosmetics since they do not need to purchase status symbols.[2]

The material in this chapter is presented to help you understand the structure, function, and care required for skin, nails, and hair. It is based on anatomy, physiology, and chemistry plus the social expectations of our culture. It is factual, not emotional. It is presented as basic information so that you may better evaluate the products in the marketplace and separate the advertising promises from your physical requirements.

[1] "Search for Beauty Big Business," *Los Angeles Times*, June 5, 1972, Pt. IV, p. 1.
[2] Eleanor Carruth, "In Cosmetics the Old Mystique Is No Longer Enough," *Fortune*, October 1973, p. 175.

254

8-1 *Healthy skin, nails, and hair are an important part of individuality at every age and reflect personal care. (Courtesy Camp Beverly Hills)*

Anatomy of the Skin

The skin can be divided into two layers. The outer layer (epidermis) that you see and the inner supporting layer (corium or dermis) that you cannot see (Figure 8-2). The outer layer's primary function is to provide physical protection for the inner layer. The outer layer creates a barrier that seals in all the body fluids while keeping out things that are harmful to the body. The outer layer can absorb a limited number of chemicals or drugs, but these are all of a type that will be taken into the general circulation system. The cells of the epidermal layer are not fed by capillaries of the blood system. The nutrient fluid flows through small spaces and channels between the cells.

The outer layer consists of several rows of living cells covered by multiple sheets of densely compacted dead cells. This layer is called the *keratin* or horny layer. It is constantly growing. The living cells are born at the base of the outer layer. They quickly die, and these dead cells are then pushed toward the outer surface of the skin by the arrival of the new cells. The top surface of dead cells is continually shed. If you should accidently remove a section of outer skin by a scrape or cut, it will grow back as good as new. As long as the injury is limited to the outer layer, complete replacement of skin always occurs. The damaged area heals without a trace of scar tissue.

The inner layer supports the outer layer, nourishes it, and supplies it with moisture. In the dermal layer are found the blood supply, the lymphatic channels,

255

the nerve supply, and a variety of nerve endings called *end organs.* Hair roots, sweat glands, and sebaceous glands are also located here and communicate with the outer layer by means of tubular ducts. (The surface ends of the sebaceous glands are commonly called *pores.*)

The inner layer of the skin is quite different from the outer layer and plays a much greater part in determining the skin's contour. This layer cannot replace itself and grows only until physical maturity is reached. Damage to the inner layer results in degeneration and the formation of scar tissue. Any damage to the inner layer, no matter how slight, will result in a permanent structural change. In addition to contour, this layer is also responsible for tone and resiliency; its condition determines whether the appearance of the skin is taut and unlined or wrinkled, loose, and sagging. The tissue of the inner layer is all living. It consists of bundles of tough supporting tissue interlaced with elastic fibers. Blood vessels

8-2 *The anatomy of the skin.*

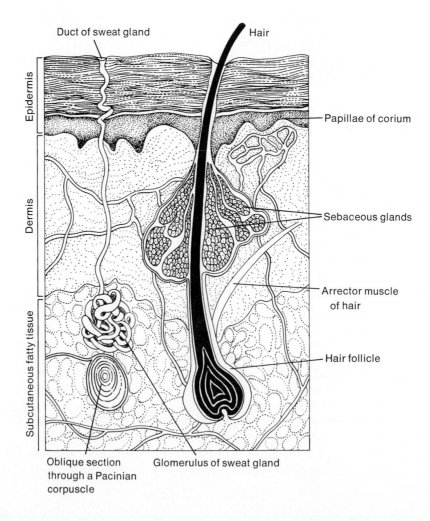

Duct of sweat gland

Hair

Epidermis

Dermis

Subcutaneous fatty tissue

Papillae of corium

Sebaceous glands

Arrector muscle of hair

Hair follicle

Oblique section through a Pacinian corpuscle

Glomerulus of sweat gland

transport water and nutrients to the entire skin. They play an important secondary role in setting the color tone of the complexion.[3]

The skin is one of the largest organs of the human body. The skin of an average adult contains nerves, blood vessels, and glands packaged in an average skin thickness of two millimeters and a total skin area of approximately twenty square feet (1.8 square meters). The average adult skin weighs about 8½ pounds (3.82 kg).

The skin differs from other body organs because of its location. It is continually on view so that its condition is obvious. One can function minus some internal organs such as one kidney or the appendix and no one need ever know. But the skin organ must remain intact, and if damaged, must be repaired. Skin flaws in most locations are noticeable and can seriously detract from appearance.

Functions of the Skin

The skin is the most versatile of all organs for it serves many functions. It acts as a container for the body that protects it from injury and invasion by bacteria. The temperature-regulating function of the skin can either cool the body, conserve body heat, or with the help of the sweat glands and blood vessels raise body temperature to fever height. Sunlight helps the skin manufacture vitamin D for the body. The skin allows us to feel the world outside; touch helps us to know warmth and cold, to recognize conformation and texture. Pain and itch are also understood through the skin.[4]

Skin Color

Skin color is determined in the inner and actively growing layer of the *epidermis,* technically called the *stratum spinosum.* The cells in this area contain varying amounts of the brown pigment, *melanin.* This pigment is produced by *melanocytes* in the area where the *stratum spinosum* of the epidermis and the *dermis* meet. The melanin granules are then picked up by the cells of the *stratum spinosum,* especially those of the basal layer. As the cells are crowded toward the surface, the melanin granules are fragmented to dust. In blacks and other dark-skinned people, the skin color is caused by the greater amount of melanin in all layers of the epidermis. Only the albinos, found in all races, have a skin that does not have melanin.

Undertones in skin coloring are created by the presence of the orange pigment *carotene* found in the epidermis; or by the cast of the circulating blood that shows through the skin. The *hemoglobin* of the blood is responsible for this reddish-blue color. The intensity of this color depends upon the state of contraction or dilation of the superficial blood vessels and upon the extent of oxygenation of the blood.[5]

[3] James E. Crouch, *Functional Human Anatomy,* 2nd ed. (Philadelphia: Lea & Febiger, 1973), pp. 68–77.

[4] Milton S. Ross, M.D., *Skin Health and Beauty* (New York: Funk and Wagnalls, 1969), p. 5.

[5] Ibid., p. 226.

The difference in color among individuals and ethnic groups is the result of the concentration of the pigments melanin and carotene and the thickness of the skin. Thinner skins allow the hemoglobin color of the circulating blood to shadow through. Freckles are spots created by pigment concentrations.[6,7]

The color of the skin, which varies greatly from one person to another, is also a unique feature of our individuality. The portrait artist trying to duplicate skin tones uses every color of his palette. Nature works with a combination of varying darks and lights created by the shadows of the body contours and reflecting light. She also creates skin color by the pigmentation of the skin.

The skin color of most of the world's population is brown. Only people of Northwestern European descent are very light-skinned as a group. Exceedingly dark, or black skin, is almost as rare as "white" skin, although it is geographically distributed more widely.

Scientists questioning the variation of skin coloring have yet to discover a truly satisfactory answer. Downs and Bleibtreu discussed reasons for skin color variation in depth and presented interesting, thought-provoking conclusions. They observed that in a very general way, the distribution of human skin color runs from dark to light as we move away from the equator toward the North. They believed that this very broad generalization was challenged by the rarity of white skin, along with light eyes and hair, found in the northwestern geographical location (prior to relatively recent expansion).

They concluded, in general, that skin color probably has something to do with the way human beings maintain core temperature, but extremes of skin color appear to confer advantage in one area while taking it away in another. Perhaps this explains why in the total world population, so few are extremely dark, and so few extremely light, and the vast majority of people are somewhere in between.

Downs and Bleibtreu emphasized that skin color was not a good indicator of race. Separate populations with similar skin color are not necessarily more closely related than people with differing skin colors.

They pointed out that all skin tends to change color when exposed to the sun. Since in many cultures, people do not cover themselves as do Americans and Europeans, many "dark-skinned" people are considerably lighter than they appear to be. Downs and Bleibtreu concluded that this was particularly important in societies with definite hierarchical rankings. Almost universally lower-class people must labor outdoors in fields and thus they tend to be darker than upper-class people of business or leisure. Protecting upper-class people, especially women, from exposure to the sun is a major concern in many groups. As an example of this, some African tribes seclude girls in a dark hut from puberty until marriage. The Japanese developed large hats to be worn by upper-class women along with enveloping scarves whenever they were forced to be outside. The parasol, in addition to being a symbol of rank, was used by ancient Egyptians, Assyrians, Greeks, Burmese, Siamese, and Chinese to protect the elite from the sun. Euro-

[6] Crouch, op. cit., pp. 69–71.
[7] Henry Gray, FRS, *Anatomy of the Human Body*, ed. by Charles Mayo Gross, A.B., M.D. (Philadelphia: Lea & Febiger, 1973), pp. 727–728.

peans and Americans until mid-twentieth century considered it unladylike to appear outside with very much skin exposed and disapproved of outdoor sports for young women.

In more recent times in Europe and America, paleness has been associated with those who must remain inside to work in a factory or office. The upper class or affluent with more time and money can afford longer vacations to sunny climates, belong to golf or tennis clubs, or may own a swimming pool. Today, the darker "tanned" skin is often a sign of upper-class status.[8]

Environmental Concerns

For the skin, the earth's environment can be considered hostile. It is exposure to sunlight, extremes of weather, and substances in the air that damage the skin. Shelmire reported the results of an investigation on the dramatic skin changes caused by the environment. The skin on both the buttocks and faces of a number of subjects ranging in age from newborn to mature adults was examined. The face was studied because of its exposure, the buttocks because of its enclosure. The texture and the contour of the newborn skin on both face and buttocks was almost exactly the same. The findings in the middle-aged group were that the skin areas were remarkably different. In most cases, the older buttocks skin was in excellent condition and closely resembled the skin of the newborn. The older facial skin, almost without exception, looked damaged. The conclusions drawn were that the texture and contour of skin exposed to the environment are permanently damaged in a very short period of time.[9]

Sunlight

The most harmful of the environmental factors is sunlight. Shelmire and Ross agreed that a few months of intense sun exposure could produce more damaging skin changes than a lifetime of normal wear. They noted that sunlight is capable of penetrating the skin; it affects not only the surface but the living tissues of both epidermis and dermis. The structural changes caused by the sun are both immediate and delayed. The immediate changes are a direct response to the irritative effects of the sun. The first indication of this change is an expansion of the inner layer's blood vessels that changes the skin's color to a bright red— sunburn. This is followed by pigment increase and cellular buildup in the outer layer. Both of these responses are designed to protect the inner layer or dermis.

[8] James F. Downs and Herman K. Bleibtreu, *Human Variations: An Introduction to Physical Anthropology* (Beverly Hills, Calif.: Glencoe, 1969), pp. 181–188.
[9] Bedford Shelmire, Jr., M.D., *The Art of Looking Younger* (New York: St. Martin's, 1973), pp. 22–23.

At this point the skin changes are temporary and will disappear if sunlight exposure is avoided for a short time. If the sun exposure is repeated, the pigmentation and cellular buildup will become more lasting—suntan. This process can still be reversed if sun exposure is eliminated.

The delayed skin changes caused by sun exposure are more serious and appear later in life. They are both permanent and cumulative and are caused by the destructive effects of light on the living tissues of both skin layers. The outer layer changes, which were once temporary and correctible, increase in degree and become irreversible. The final result of sun damage is a skin that has dark areas of accumulated pigment, rough red spots, and skin cancer. The delayed inner layer changes are caused by severe damage to the skin's supporting tissue, elastic fibers, and blood vessels. The skin appears to be thick, tough, wrinkled, spotty, and aged looking.

Shelmire stated that sunlight is never beneficial to adults under any circumstances. Some sun is required by children for vitamin D metabolism. He stated that the extent and severity of the permanent light-induced changes that appear in the skin are determined by three factors: skin type or complexion, intensity of exposure, and time or duration of the exposure.

Your skin type is the factor over which you have no control. Fair skin that freckles easily is the most susceptible to light. Darker skins are generally thicker and have more protective pigment. Black skin is not completely immune to sun damage. Shelmire concluded that the same changes seen in fair skin will also occur in dark skin with intense, prolonged exposure.[10,11]

It should be noted that a sunlamp is considered to be just as damaging as natural sunlight for the skin. All the problems brought on by the natural sun are also created by artificial sun. The extreme rapidity with which second- and third-degree burns can be suffered with the concentrated light of the sunlamp makes it an extremely dangerous device.

There are two methods of protecting your skin from the sun. One is physical, the other chemical. Physical protection means mechanical shielding; that is, putting something opaque between your skin and the sun. It includes staying indoors, using clothing, hats, gloves, and umbrellas.

Chemical protection means a substance put on the skin that blocks out the damaging part of the sun's rays. Chemical screens offer a simple method of protecting the skin against sun. They can be used by either sex, at any age. They work selectively, blocking out the light rays responsible for damaging and aging skin.

Shelmire cautioned that one should never buy a sun screen that does not list the name of the chemical screen on the label. This is not required by law at this writing, but a reputable manufacturer will voluntarily list ingredients. Shelmire divided sun screens according to their efficiency and degree of protection and ranked them as follows:

[10] Ibid., pp. 25–28.
[11] Ross, op. cit., pp. 10–11.

Group 1—*Superior:* para-aminobenzoic acid (PABA)
Group 2—*Good:* benzophenone derivatives
                  p-aminobenzoic derivatives such as the iso-amyl and glyceryl
Group 3—*Also rans:* digalloyl trioleate
                  cinoxate[12]

There is controversy among scientists and doctors as to how much, if any, intentional suntanning should take place within a lifetime of an individual. There is further controversy as to how to acquire a tan. Some experts allege that a moderate tan, properly acquired, will not cause noticeable injury within the average life span. Others maintain that the only healthy tan is no tan at all, that a suntanned skin is a damaged skin and that damaged skin is one that will wrinkle and sag prematurely and be more vulnerable to skin cancer. All agree that the effects of the sun on the skin are cumulative. In other words, a fair-skinned baby who burns on the beach, and burns again during teen years while playing tennis, surfing, and bike-riding, and burns again as a young adult golfing and gardening is accumulating damage that may result in prematurely deeply wrinkled skin at the age of 40. If unprotected exposure to the sun is prolonged enough, such a person could develop skin cancer as a result of the exposure (Figure 8-3).

Check your skin regularly for any changes. If you have the slightest doubt, see your doctor or a physician who specializes in skin diseases.

The Food and Drug Administration has acted to help protect the sun-exposed public. Believing that a better-informed consumer and a better-regulated suntan

[12] Shelmire, op. cit., p. 30.

8-3 Sunlight damage to skin is cumulative. Protection from sunlight should begin at an early age. (Courtesy Danskin, Inc.)

lotion industry will help protect against solar overkill, the FDA has regulations that require all sunscreen labels to bear a number that identifies the sun-protection factor (SPF) of each product. The numbers 2–4 offer the least protection and permit suntanning; the number 15 offers the most protection from sunburning and permits no suntanning. The SPF needs to be coordinated with the individual skin type and the kind of sun exposure to be effective.

Extremes of Weather

Extremes of weather, such as humidity and temperature variations, also create skin damage. This is usually done by producing a state of severe moisture depletion. This problem is most common in winter and is aggravated by wind and the extreme dryness of heated rooms. Unprotected skin exposed to cold, blustery weather followed by a dry overheated room atmosphere will be damaged by a critical loss of moisture.

Moisture depletion causes the skin to feel rough, dry, wrinkled, unattractive, and easily irritated. Moisture depletion affects only the outer layer of skin. It can be prevented by the use of skin moisturizers and room humidifiers. Senior citizens are more susceptible to moisture depletion than young people.

The environmental extremes of either heat or cold can cause skin irritation. If the exposure is unusually severe or prolonged, permanent and irreversible damage to the living cells of the skin may result. Extreme cold can cause frostbite.

Heat damage caused by exposing the skin to intense heat can produce skin damage very similar to that caused by sunlight. The elevated temperatures that are so damaging are ones that are usually man produced. Procedures involving extreme heat such as the "facial sauna," hot towels, and steam from "standing over a hot stove" bring skin to dangerous temperature levels. The skin performs best when held at body temperature, 98.6 degrees. When the temperature is raised or lowered greatly, skin problems may arise.

Air pollution of the environment also damages skin. In many ways this irritant is more difficult to avoid than those already discussed. The exact damage caused to the skin by air pollution is not yet known. It is known that among the most common pollutants are sulfur-containing compounds. These are partially converted to sulfuric acid on the skin surface. Most students who have had some experience with this corrosive chemical in chemistry lab know how powerful it is. Many studies are being conducted at this time to learn the effects of air pollution on the body, which, of course, includes the skin. At this time, physical protection of the skin is the only practical known preventative against air pollutants. This includes both proper cleansing and moisturizing of the skin, discussed later in this chapter.

Many products used in both industry and the home can be damaging to the skin. When working with any product with which you are not familiar, it is best to read and follow the directions carefully, to protect the skin if possible, and to always proceed with caution and common sense.

If you have doubts about any product that will come in contact with your skin, from hair coloring to shoe polish, it is wise to try a "patch test." Apply a little of the product to a very small area of skin on the leg, arm, or behind the ear. Wait twenty-four hours. If nothing happens, proceed. You may want to insist on a "patch test" when someone else is going to apply an unknown product to your skin. Hair stylists, doctors, and other professionals are familiar with this procedure and often recommend it.

This hostile environment in which we live is constantly weathering and aging the skin. Much of the damage can be prevented by protecting your skin. Remember, if you really care, the skin of your face can look as good as that on your *derrière*.

Black Skin Problems

Most diseases of the skin that occur in whites also occur in blacks. However, certain problems of the skin are more prevalent among blacks. These include:

Dryness—dry skin is not only uncomfortable but also more easily seen because this condition gives the skin a greyish appearance. Blacks tend to use a great many oils and greases on the skin to lubricate it and cause the scale to disappear. This practice can create other skin problems such as acne.

Pigmentary disturbances—black skin produces more pigment and produces it faster than white skin. Because of this difference, pigmentary disturbances may be more apparent in blacks. The most common problems are too much color or too little color. This pigmentary activity has advantages; blacks rarely develop skin cancer, and black skin does not show aging changes as early as white skin.

Lichenification—this condition consists of thickened, hyperpigmented areas of skin with accentuated normal skin markings.

Dermatosis papulosa nigra—this condition occurs almost exclusively in blacks and most frequently in women. The brown to black lesions that characterize this condition resemble moles in the skin of whites, but they are different. The lesions are seborrheic keratoses resembling flat warts. They are not painful and they do not become malignant. They are often removed for cosmetic reasons.

Keloids—when a cut or wound heals, usually a scar about the size of the wound appears in its place. The scar sometimes extends and spreads beyond the limit of the original wound. Such scars are known as keloids: they are more prevalent in black skin.

Pityriasis alba—a harmless disease with oval or round patches of light skin (hypopigmentation) covered by fine scales.

Tinea versicolor—hypopigmentation which becomes evident after exposure to sunlight.[13]

The Face

The skin of the face ranges in thickness from the average of 1 to 2 mm to the sensitive eyelid area where the thickness is only 0.5 mm. The face is one of the most oily areas of the body. Both males and females have hair on their face, only the male hair is usually more visible.

The skin type of the face is generally referred to as oily, dry, normal, or a combination of these. The areas of the forehead, nose, and chin are most often oily. The eye area is generally dry because there are no oil glands located there. The rest of the face can be any type. The skin type can change with age, physical condition, or the weather.

Large pores, which are often found on the cheeks or nose, are duct openings of oil glands that have become widened and permanently stretched. This damage was caused by plugging by fat and scale and the force of material extruded from the gland, all of which caused a variation in the natural elasticity and vascularity of the skin. Blackheads and pimples are pores clogged with matter created by infection, excessive cholesterol in the diet, or improper cleansing of the skin.

Facial Skin Care

Facial skin care involves three processes. These processes are needed to correct the three main problems of a healthy skin, which are

dirty surface film
thickening cellular buildup
moisturizing

The skin care processes should correct these conditions and make the skin appear as attractive as possible. The steps that are needed to achieve these results are:

cleansing
thinning
moisturizing

These three activities carried out regularly and properly are all that is required for healthy skin care. The materials needed are not expensive. The time required is minimal. Any claim for a skin care regime that requires more than these three steps is not entirely honest.

[13] *Facts About Black Skin*, American Medical Association pamphlet, 1979.

Cleansing

Cleansing is the most important corrective procedure. Its purpose is to completely remove the dirty surface film. Cleansing is the same for men and women.

The ideal cleansing agent removes all dirty surface film, is nonirritating, and can itself be easily and completely removed. There are four types of general purpose skin cleansers. They are:

oils and greases
cold creams
rinsable cleansers
soaps

Cleansers containing oils, greases, and cold creams are much alike. Cold creams are really water-containing greases. These products all depend on oily or greasy substances for their cleansing action. Each is used in the same way. These types of cleansers are almost always nonirritating; however, they do a poor job of removing surface grime and are almost impossible to remove from the skin. Oils, greases, and cold cream leave a film of contaminated cleanser on the skin's surface. They are not satisfactory cleansers.

Rinsable cleansers and soaps also have much in common. Rinsable cleansers, sometimes called face washes, are creams or lotions containing a soaplike substance. Both cleanse in much the same way. Looking at the requirements for an ideal cleanser, we find that this group does an excellent job of removing the dirty surface film and can be easily removed with water. On the other hand, soap and soaplike products are potential skin irritants. This irritation happens generally when the product is not completely removed or is left on the skin for a long period of time. This problem of skin irritation can often be avoided if the skin is cleansed no more than is necessary and the cleansers are always completely rinsed away with several changes of water. Rinsable cleansers and soaps should never be used in the manner of cold creams and simply tissued off; they must always be carefully rinsed away with ample amounts of water.

When choosing between a soap and a rinsable cleanser, consider your personal requirements. A soap generally is less expensive and cleans better. It is easier to remove. Soaps are also more irritating than rinsable cleansers. This is usually noticeable by a feeling of dryness. To select the soap or rinsable cleanser that is best for you, there are several key points. Shelmire recommended the following as guidelines:

Soap Selection

Composition

Conventional soaps and detergents are two entirely different types of cleansers, but both are sold in bar form and called "soap." Conventional soaps are all the same chemical formula but detergents are formed from a great variety of ingredients. Detergents often contain the following on the label: "soapless," "non-alkaline," "lathers in hard water," "leaves no bathtub ring." Detergents are excellent cleansers, but they are more harsh than conventional soaps. Detergents are found in many products such as shampoos and medicated soaps. Adolescent skins often tolerate detergents better than more mature skin. Because detergents are more drying and irritating to sensitive skin, conventional soaps are recommended for cleansing face and also hands.

Purity

Any soap that has been adulterated with other substances will not cleanse as well as pure soap. "Cream" ingredients added to soaps are in reality waxy, or greasy materials. While these "fatted" soaps may be milder and good for bath soap, they do not cleanse as well as pure soap.

Additives

The main additives found in soaps are deodorant chemicals and heavy fragrances. Both should be avoided as both can cause skin irritation.

Rinsable Cleanser Selection

Label Information

Read the label carefully. If the instructions do not tell you to "rinse off," do not buy it. Do not believe the claim that the product will both cleanse and moisturize. A cleanser should leave the skin clean and that's all. Any moisturizing film left on the skin by the product should be considered contamination. Cleansing and moisturizing are two separate processes. They are diametrically opposed to each other. They cannot be performed simultaneously.

Physical Form

Free-flowing lotions are preferable. Lotions spread more evenly over the skin surface and are easier to rinse off. They clean better.

Additives

These include various kinds of medications, antiseptics and heavy perfumes. None of these ingredients promote cleaning. All can be irritating. Any medication would not be on the skin long enough to benefit it. Antiseptics are required only for an acne condition, then under a doctor's care. Strong fragrances are extremely popular in this product, but cause many problems.[14]

Face and neck cleaning routine. The skin of the face and neck should be cleaned at least once a day and preferably at night, because this is the time of most dirt buildup. It is recommended that you not overclean your face because this, too, can cause skin problems. Twice a day is the maximum number of times you should completely clean your face, unless, of course, you are under a doctor's care. Your age and activities and skin type will help you determine your face-cleaning routine. The neck should be included in this care. The active, young, oily-skinned person and the heavily madeup city dweller will need more frequent face cleaning than the inactive resident of a rural, leisure world.

The cleaning routine should be accomplished quickly and efficiently. Wet the skin thoroughly with lukewarm water. Lightly massage the soap or rinsable cleanser into the skin. Use only the fingertips; their texture is abrasive enough.

---

[14] Shelmire, op. cit., pp. 52–59.

Cleanser should be applied evenly to all areas of the face and neck, including the creases and folds. This entire process should not last longer than sixty to ninety seconds. Rinse off completely. If you wish to dawdle during this process, do it at the rinse stage; you cannot rinse too much. Remember that any cleaning that is continued after dirt is removed can harm the skin. So clean quickly and completely and rinse, rinse, rinse. The choice between a soap and a rinsable cleaner should also be related to your age and your skin type. Most children are schooled and scrubbed with soap, which because of its cleansing ability and ease of rinsing is an excellent choice. Young oil glands are more active, and since most children are not too concerned about being overly clean, the natural skin moisturizer can compensate for any soap-caused dryness.

In later years, when the skin becomes more sensitive and less able to hold moisture, soap can become an irritant. Indication of this is usually a feeling of dryness and itching. Fair-skinned individuals encounter this problem earlier than other complexion types. A gradual changeover from soap to a rinsable cleanser is advisable.

No product can ever give your skin the same deep cleansing that soap can. For this reason, soap should always remain a part of your skin-cleansing routine. How frequently you use soap to cleanse your face should be determined by your skin condition. Some people can continue to use soap all of their lives; others must limit soaping of the face to once a week and use rinsable cleansers the rest of the time.

Whatever product is used to cleanse the skin, it must be completely rinsed off. Water is the best rinse; it can never harm the skin. Remember that the first nine months of your life were spent completely immersed in water in the womb and that your skin at birth was in perfect condition. So learn to rinse the skin completely by splashing it with several changes of clean water and then one more to be absolutely certain that all traces of cleanser are removed.

The water used to rinse away the cleanser should always be lukewarm and never extremely hot or cold. It is a false premise that hot water will open the pores and that cold water will close them. Pores just do not work that way. Extremes of heat and cold in the rinse water can cause some of the same problems discussed under extremes in environmental conditions.[15]

Thinning

The primary purpose of thinning is to remove excess, dead surface cells and their contained pigment from the skin. It also opens pores blocked by cellular buildup and helps prevent the formation of blemishes. Simply, the skin needs to be trimmed occasionally much like the nails and hair. The skin's texture and contour are both improved by thinning. Thinned skin feels smoother, appears more translucent, and has a lighter and more uniform coloring. The pores appear smaller after thinning and the number of blackheads is reduced. The outer layer of the skin is more easily moisturized after the hard dry cells are removed.

[15] Shelmire, op. cit., p. 59.

Men thin the bearded area of their face as they shave. Women who shave their legs achieve the same. The concept of thinning belongs to ancient cosmetic history. The Greeks, Romans, and Egyptians all used pumice and other gritty materials to polish the skin.

Very young skin does not need thinning. Undamaged skin may be thinned simply by rubbing with a terry washcloth rung out with lukewarm water. The entire face and neck should be gone over, using a circular motion on the forehead, chin, and cheeks; a horizontal or vertical motion on the nose, facial edges, and the neck. Apply moderate pressure. The process should take about two minutes. Repeat twice a week. Thinning should be done right after cleansing and before moisturizing. Be gentle, but firm. Experiment gradually until you are familiar with how much abrasion your face can tolerate.

Older skin may require heavier thinning. Two types of cosmetic products are available for this. The first type includes sponges, brushes, and other textured surfaces to be used alone or with soaplike cleansers. The second type are abrasive particles in some kind of cleansing base. Both cosmetic thinners work on the same abrasion principle as the terry washcloth.

The thinning discussed here is of a mechanical type. It should not be confused with the chemical thinning that dissolves or peels away the outer layer of skin. Chemical thinning should not be a part of weekly skin care. It is best done by professionals.

Thinned skin does look better. Remember, it is fresh and tender and, therefore, must be protected. Thinned skin is extremely vulnerable to environmental damage, particularly sunburn. All skin thinned by either mechanical or chemical techniques needs extra protection.

The greater part of skin care is directed to the face and neck; the skin of the ears, and also the hands, deserves attention. These exposed areas should be cleansed and moisturized like the face. Thinning is usually not required because the skin covering these areas is normally quite thin and the cell buildup does not seem to affect their appearance.

Facial skin care is very easy. It should not seem complicated, tiresome, or expensive. Daily cleansing and moisturizing, and twice a week thinning take only a very few minutes. This simple routine will help you achieve a healthier, younger-appearing, and more attractive face for a lifetime.

Moisturizing

The purpose of skin cleaning is to remove the grimy surface film that is potentially harmful. During the cleaning process the surface film is removed from the skin. This film contains dirt and grime but it also contains beneficial natural oils that help protect the skin. Just as it is necessary to clean the skin, it is important to replace these natural moisturizers.

Oils and greases are both excellent substitutes for the natural moisturizers that cleaning strips away. Every man-made moisturizer or protector uses oil and/or greases as the main ingredient.

Moisturizer softeners and protectors work in exactly the same way regardless of their commercial form. They spread along the skin's surface as a film and moisturize the skin by slowing the evaporative water loss from the epidermis. Moisturizers cannot penetrate the skin as many cosmetic advertisements claim. This action is not even desirable. It is the presence of the protective film on the surface of the skin that creates the moisturizing effect.

Moisturizers also protect the skin by forming a physical barrier between the skin and the harsh, polluted environment. Moisturizers are lubrications that give the skin a better "slip" and smoother feel.

It is absolutely essential that some form of moisturizing protection be worn on the face at all times. This is true for both men and women. Those who do not use this type of product will find that their faces become wrinkled and weatherbeaten at an early age.

Products for men that have this protection quality have been masculinely rejected and limited in production in the past. Their importance is becoming more recognized with the vast growth of the men's cosmetic industry. Aftershave lotions and creams are types of moisturizers. So important is the moisturizing-protection step in skin care that the products for this purpose should be considered irrespective of gender. Married men often secretly use their wives' moisturizers, but the single man should buy moisturizers for himself and feel comfortable doing so.

Women usually use two types of moisturizer, one for overnight use and the other, a lighter type, for day use. In addition to protecting the skin, this product usually helps create a smooth base for other types of cosmetics. All moisturizing products that create a thin, invisible film are as effective, and perhaps more so than the heavy, greasy "kidstuff" type that are unattractive, unpleasant, and rub off easily.

Shelmire recommends the following considerations in selecting a moisturizing product:

Foreign Materials

Select a light lotion or cream that is not adulterated with foreign materials such as pigments and powders. A moisturizing agent is separate from a cosmetic foundation. Do not buy products that combine the two steps.

Useful Ingredients

A very great number of oils and greases can serve as moisturizer-protectors. The fact to remember is that all moisturizers of the same consistency will perform in about the same manner. Extravagant claims for exotic oils and expensive price tags do not improve the function of the very common vegetable, animal, and petroleum products that are the oils and greases that are the principal ingredients of all moisturizer-protectors on the market today.

Useless Ingredients

The number of useless ingredients placed in cosmetic products is beyond counting. Common sense can help you determine that the incredible variety from Queen Bee jelly, placenta extract, hormones, vitamins, proteins, milk, honey, seaweed, cucumbers, strawberries, herbs, and family or laboratory secret ingredients are more for product promotion than for moisturizing. Hormones are not moisturizers. They do not make more water available to the skin's surface but they do change the metabolism of the living tissue, which causes it to expand and plump up. Hormone therapy should only be employed under the supervision of a physician.

Advertising promotions of special qualities such as "organic" ingredients are emotional rather than factual. Remember everything that contains the element carbon is defined as organic. Therefore, mineral oil, cod-liver oil, and crude oil are all organic just as everything growing in your garden is.

Humectants

Creams and lotions often contain a humectant; that is, a smooth substance such as glycerine. A small amount of a humectant in a moisturizer will improve the skin slip and make it feel softer. Too much humectant will cause the skin to dry. Beware of products labeled "rich" in humectants.[16]

Moisturizing products are among the most expensive skin care items, yet they are probably the least sophisticated. Their basic technology is very simple. All that is required of them is that a thin film of oil or grease is deposited on the skin's surface. Inexpensive mineral oil and Vaseline (petroleum jelly) work as well as the most costly product. True, their container is not as fancy and their smell is quite ordinary, but the price is certainly right. Remember as you survey the marketplace for moisturizers that no matter what the manufacturer claims, the ingredients are all basically the same. You are paying for the commercial pitch and packaging.

Skin Care from the Neck Down

Care of the body skin does differ from that of the face, both because of our cultural habits of washing it and because of its structure. As a culture, Americans believe in bathing frequently in a tub or shower. The range in number of baths varies from one or two per week to several per day. This number of daily baths far exceeds the bathing frequency customs of many other cultures.

The skin covering the body has fewer oil glands than the face. Constant scrubbing of the body with soap and water washes away the natural protective moisturizing oil film. If this is not replaced, itching, burning, and flaking often result.

Most "body odor" comes from specific areas of the body and not the skin as a whole. These areas include underarm, the genital region, and the feet. The odor of sweat is thought to be one of the secondary sex characteristics. The underarm sweat glands become most active after puberty and remain so during the years of greatest sexual activity. Sexual excitement and emotional states cause this kind of sweating. It seems that nature intended this odor to be attractive. In many cultures, including those of Western Europe and South America, bathing is not a frequent occurrence and body odor is considered romantic.

[16] Shelmire, op. cit., pp. 65–70.

In the United States at this time, body odor is considered offensive and reason for ridicule or disgust. Because of this, we have developed the practices of frequent bathing and the use of a variety of deodorants and antiperspirants. These practices, which promote cleanliness, can be detrimental to skin health.

Bathing can cause skin discomfort, particularly if harsh soaps or perfumed products are used. The areas most frequently scrubbed vigorously with such products are the neck, chest, arms, back, abdomen, and thighs. Sweat glands in these areas are formed so that they do not harbor odor-forming bacteria. Overwashing the skin in these areas can cause it to dry out and become flaky and itchy, since there are very few oil glands in these locations.

Because the face and scalp are formed with an abundance of oil glands, they cannot be overwashed. These oil glands protect the face and scalp from soap and water but also from wind and weather.

Deodorants used underarm or in the crotch area can cause the swelling and plugging up of sweat glands and result in severe infections. Antiperspirants can also produce small tumors or granulomas at the gland openings, which are brought about by the presence of certain metallic ingredients commonly used in the products. This is not to imply that deodorants are not to be used; it is simply a statement of precaution.

Skin irritation can be caused by both the dye and the fragrance used in facial and toilet tissue. Those with sensitive skins should select white tissues without added perfumes.

In general, the face and scalp are oily and frequently need washing; the body is dry and may need oiling. The less we tamper with natural processes, the better it will be for us. The skin has a remarkable physiology. Its processes should be assisted and not hindered.[17]

The daily bath or shower is very therapeutic for many people. Some describe it as relaxing, others as refreshing or invigorating. Water temperature, time, and technique all create the varying end results.

Whether you prefer a bath or a shower, try making some changes in your techniques to help the condition of your skin. Soap carefully the underarm, groin, anal area, and feet, and simply rinse the other areas of the body unless they are actually soiled. Remember that hot showers wash away more body oils than baths.

Thinning of the body skin is beneficial. Use the same techniques mentioned under face care. Brushes and sponges can help with thinning the various areas of the body.

Calluses and corns are caused by localized pressures. Calluses on the feet, hands, and elbows can be thinned during the bath by pumice stone or other abrasives. Corns are better attended to by a physician.

Dry the body carefully, paying special attention to the skin folds and enclosed areas such as groin, underarms, and toe webs. Moisturize the body by use of oils during or after the bath, or by body lotions. Bath powders are good for absorbing

---

[17] Ross, op. cit., pp. 8–10.

excessive body perspiration. Cornstarch is an excellent, inexpensive, nonperfumed powder substitute that is often used in hospitals to make bedridden patients more comfortable.

The fairly common vaginitis in women and "jock itch" in men are often caused by fungus molds that thrive in moist, warm conditions. Improper drying after bathing promotes the growth of such fungus and molds. Wearing tight, nonbreathing, and nonabsorbtive garments such as nylon underwear, bathing suits, ski pants, or panty hose contribute to both of these itchy, uncomfortable problems.

Nails

The nails are flattened, elastic structures of a horny texture located on the ends of toes and fingers. Each nail is convex on its outer surface and concave within. It is implanted by a portion called the *root*, into a groove in the skin. The exposed portion is called the *body*, and the distal extremity, the *free edge*. The nail firmly adheres to the epidermis and is accurately molded to its surface. The part beneath the body and root of the nail is called the *nail matrix*. This is where the nail is produced. Under the greater part of the body of the nail, the matrix is thick and raised in a series of longitudinal ridges. The color of the nail is produced by the vascular quality of the ridges and seen through the transparent tissue. Near the root of the nail, the area is less vascular and irregular, the tissue of the nail is not firmly attached, but only in contact; this portion is whiter in color and called the *lunula* because of its moonlike shape. The cuticle is attached to the surface of the nail a little in advance of the root (Figure 8-4).

The nails grow about 1 mm per week in length. This growth is caused by a proliferation of cells at the root of the nail. The thickness of the nail is determined by the cell formation underlying the lunula.[18]

Nail Care

Manicure refers to the care of the hands and fingernails. *Pedicure* is the cosmetic treatment of feet and toenails. The equipment and techniques used are generally the same for nails of both hands and feet. General guidelines for both procedures are these:

1. File and shape nails. Hold file at a slant. File from the corner to the center of the nail. Sawing back and forth across the entire nail tends to split nails. Avoid filing deep into corners of the nail, this causes nails to break. On feet, filing deep into corners can also promote ingrown toenails.
2. Soak nails in warm, soapy water. This helps to soften cuticle.
3. Thin any callused areas with pumice stone or other abrasive.

[18] Gray, op. cit., pp. 1104–1105.

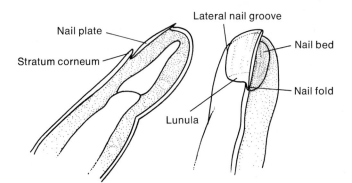

Nail plate

Stratum corneum

Lateral nail groove

Nail bed

Nail fold

Lunula

8-4 *The anatomy of the nail.*

4. Moisten the skin around the nail with oil. Gently push back the cuticle. Avoid cutting the cuticle. This area can be damaged and infected, which can cause loss of the entire nail. Trim away hangnails or bits of torn skin. Badly neglected cuticles may take several weeks to loosen and push back.
5. Buff or polish nails as desired.
6. Clean nails as part of a daily routine or as they need it.

Nail Problems

Fingernails reflect your physical and emotional condition. If you notice ridges or depressions in the nail, it is wise to consult a physician. Nail-biting is a nervous habit that reflects, among other things, emotional tension. Splitting, cracking, or peeling nails reflect poor diet, damaged nail tissue, or both. Diet should be checked to see if it needs improvement. Do not believe the claims of gelatin manufacturers. Massive intake of gelatin, although not harmful, will not grow nails because it is taken into the general system and can not be directed to nails exclusively.

Damaged nails can be caused from all kinds of abuse. Physical injury can be caused by smashing, cutting, stubbing, or bruising. Chemical damage can be caused by exposure of the nail to a variety of products that dry out or dissolve such as those used for cleaning, painting, and dyeing. Cosmetic products, especially when they are used continuously, can damage the nails. Nail polish, false nails, including acrylic nails, and other such things seal the nail and can cause trouble. Even the healthiest nails should have a period of freedom from such devices.

Ingrown toenails are usually caused by the nail's cutting too deeply at the corners of the toes. Growing longer toenails and wearing larger shoes sometimes helps. This is a problem that should be treated by a podiatrist if it persists.

Infection, fungus, and disease can all damage nails sometimes to the point of destroying the cells that produce nails. The nails often can recover and replace themselves when damaged, but if the cell-producing matrix is damaged severely, the nail will never return.

The shape, size, and condition of nails are another part of your individuality. Others often use the condition of your nails to make judgments about you. Clean, healthy, cared-for nails on both the feet and hands are most attractive and desirable.

To Stop Nail Biting

Nail biting plays no favorites. It usually begins when one is a small child and continues into adulthood in both sexes. The habit is caused primarily by stress, anxiety, and poor nail care and it continues by habit.

We all experience stress and anxiety in our lives which usually manifests itself in some form of bodily disorder. A person who is experiencing a stressful situation may find himself unconsciously biting his nails. Some common instances when this occurs are while watching a suspense movie, thinking idly, studying, or driving the car. It is difficult to set stress or anxiety aside but if a person truly wants to stop the habit of nail biting he must become aware of the situations that make him vulnerable to it. Changing patterns such as doodling with a pencil and paper while watching a movie or finding another time or place to study have proven effective in stopping nail biting. Only you can determine what is contributing to the stress in your life. Many books and courses are available to help you learn to take control of your emotions by generating stressful moments into productive ones for a healthier well-being.

Care of your nails plays a very important role in deterring nail biting. Well-groomed nails are essential. Very soft, thin nails are most susceptible to snags, splitting, and breaking. Keeping a very fine file with you at all times will help to correct a bothersome snag much better than grinding and chewing on the nail. Using a hand lotion frequently will soften the rough cuticles that often become a target for chewing. Keeping the nails coated with a fortifier while they are growing out will help the nails from splitting by adding strength. Be aware that polished nails can be very annoying and create a challenge to pick at or chew if they are not perfectly groomed. Another preventative for nail destruction is to wear gloves while working in water and doing other chores such as yard work.

If you are not familiar with giving yourself a proper manicure, treat yourself to one; men too can enjoy this privilege. It may be just the incentive you need to start yourself on a program of healthier and more attractive looking nails.[19]

Hair

Hair is much more widely distributed over the body than most realize. Because much of it is soft and fine, it is not noticed. Only the palms, soles, sides of the fingers, lips, nipples, umbilicus, and portions of the male and female genitalia are actually hairless. Conspicuous hair is located on the head and, after puberty, in the axillary and pubic regions.

[19] Contributed by Pat Solderblom, student at Mt. San Antonio College, Walnut, Calif.

Men are more hairy than women. They grow longer facial hair and they have a stronger growth of hair on their chests and backs and usually on their legs and arms. The pattern of growth of body hair is very much a sexual characteristic. The hair growth on the head of both men and women is very much the same.

It has been established that early man was very hairy. Exactly why he lost so much of his hair is not known. Why special areas of dense hair remain is also puzzling. The function of hair on the human body is most obviously for protection. This is true of the hair located on the head, and the eyebrows and eyelashes. The hairs found across the open passages of the nose and ears act as sieves against insects, dust, and irritants. Pubic hair and armpit hair also have somewhat of a protective purpose acting as padding against friction; however, the fact that they both appear at puberty gives them a sexual significance. Both pubic and underarm hair grow in areas where scent glands are located in the skin. The secretions of these glands need exposure to air to develop their full odor. The tufts of hair provide a holding surface where this oxidation can take place.[20]

Anatomy of Hair

A hair consists of a *root*, the part implanted in the skin; and a *shaft*, the portion projecting from the skin surface. The root of the hair ends in an enlargement, the *hair bulb*, which is whiter in color and softer in texture than the shaft, and is lodged in a *hair follicle* in the dermis. When the hair is very long, the hair follicle extends into the *subcutaneous cellular* tissue. The hair follicle extends from the skin's surface in a funnel-like shape to its deep extremity where it takes the shape of the hair bulb. Opening into the hair follicle are one or more *sebaceous glands*. (The oil secreted by these glands gives hair its sheen.) At the bottom of each hair follicle is the *papilla*. This small peg of tissue pushes up through the center of the follicle into the bottom of the hair bulb. When a hair is plucked out, the papilla stays behind and manufactures a replacement. The papilla is rich in minute blood vessels; it supplies amino acids that are synthesized into protein to feed the continuous formation of cells on the outer surface of the papilla (Figure 8-5). These new cells are continuously being created from below and pushing the older cells up. As they rise, the cells undergo structural differentiation into the variously shaped cells that make up the hair shaft. After a hardening process, *keratinization*, the shaft emerges out of the mouth of the hair follicle as a hardened shaft or visible hair.[21,22]

As long as the hair's substance is continually being formed at the papilla, the individual hair grows longer and longer. When the follicle can no longer support the weight, the growth ceases. In an adult this takes from two to four years, after which time the hair falls out. As a preliminary to this event, the proliferation of the papillary cells stops abruptly and the detached hair gradually works its way

[20] Wendy Cooper, *Hair* (New York: Stein & Day, 1971), pp. 16–17.
[21] Ibid., p. 23.
[22] Gray, op. cit., pp. 1105–1108.

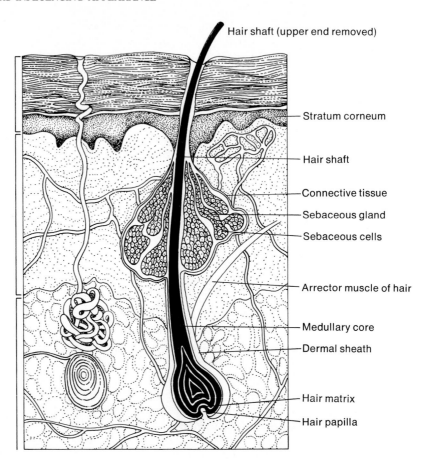

Hair shaft (upper end removed)

Stratum corneum

Hair shaft

Connective tissue

Sebaceous gland

Sebaceous cells

Arrector muscle of hair

Medullary core

Dermal sheath

Hair matrix

Hair papilla

8-5 *The anatomy of the hair.*

upward toward the mouth of the hair follicle. Even before the old hair drops out, production has started and new hair begins to arise from the renewed papilla.

In children and young adults, the discarded hair will be replaced and often will actually increase in the number of individual hairs produced. This is how the hair on a baby's head thickens as the child grows. As long as the scalp is thick and pliable and moves freely over the skull, the hair growth will be healthy. If the hair follicle is damaged or the *matrix* cells lose their vitality for any reason, hair will not grow. In maturity or in illness, the scalp is sometimes drawn tightly over the skull. This causes constriction of the blood vessels and atrophy of the hair roots. Massage can help to loosen the scalp and improve circulation. This can promote hair growth.

The Hair Shaft

The portion of the hair that extends beyond the skin is called the *hair shaft*. It is composed of united cells arranged in different layers, the *cuticle*, the *cortex*, and the *medulla* (Figure 8-6).

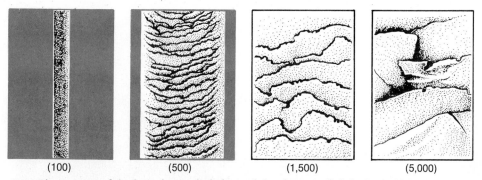

(100) (500) (1,500) (5,000)

8-6 *The portion of the hair that extends beyond the skin is called the hair shaft. It is composed of united cells arranged in different layers. Sketches show microscope sections of a healthy hair magnified 100, 500, 1,500, and 5,000 times.*

The cuticle, or the outer hair membrane, is made up of delicate overlapping cells. In the finer hairs, these cells resemble flat bands. In the coarser hairs they may be likened to shingles on a roof. The scales are derived from *epithelial* cells that have become hardened and are very closely related to fingernails or toenails. This is not living tissue, but dead cells.

The cortex, or middle portion of the hair, which is the largest part of the shaft, is made up of elongated cells. The pigment of the hair is found here.

The medulla, which is the inner layer or central pith of the hair, is composed of rows of polyhedral cells. The short, fine hair on the body surface and sometimes long, coarse hair do not have this layer.

Forms of Hair

Straight, wavy, curly, or crinkly forms of hair are determined by the shape and cross-section of the hair follicle and the direction of the hair follicle in the skin. Straight hair grows from follicles that are perfectly straight throughout their length.

Wavy hair grows from curved follicles; the degree of waviness is dependent upon the amount of curvature. Loosely waved hair is usually deceptive in appearance. Because of its shallow curvature it may appear straight. Sometimes the weight of the hair will pull the hair wave into a straight position.

Curly, woolly, or kinky hair is also caused by the curvature of the follicle. The more the curl the more is the curvature. In the most extreme curl, the follicles are almost coiled.

Health of Hair

The hair of a healthy person is continually growing. If it does not appear to grow it is probably breaking or sloughing off and thus maintaining its same length. Healthy hair should have a natural sheen or lustre. It should have resiliency. Wet hair can be stretched one fifth of its total length (Figure 8-7).

8-7 *Good diet and health practices are reflected in healthy skin, nails, hair, teeth, and a zest for life. (Courtesy Cotton Incorporated)*

Some heads are covered with a downy growth that never gets very long. Other people have coarse and wiry hair. Still others have such fine hair that the scalp can be seen in spite of the fact that they have the normal number of hairs per square inch. In each of these cases there is nothing that can be done to change the amount or texture or promote better hair growth. A scanty head covering can be a normal hair growth for that individual.

A great variety of conditions can disturb the health of the hair. Some of these factors are poor diet, nervousness, ill health, diseases, wearing tight hats or wigs, harsh chemicals, overprocessing and exposure to the elements, snapping in the wind, and swimming in salt water or a chlorinated swimming pool.[23]

Growth of Hair

Hair grows in phases. An active growing period is followed by an intermediate period that is followed by a resting period. The rate of growth is not easily measured. Hair grows at different rates on different parts of the body and the

[23] Winifred Fayant, *Successful Beauty Culture* (Philadelphia: Brownell, 1969), pp. 127–133.

rate of growth varies with sex, age, and health. Cooper noted that recent observations have established that hair grows faster on people between the ages of fifteen and thirty. Women between the ages of sixteen and twenty-four have the fastest rate. This may be as much as eighteen centimeters, or seven inches of hair growth per year. The rate of growth slows down as we age. Hair-growth patterns are slowed down during illness and, in the female, during pregnancy. Often during convalescence after severe illness, the growth pattern of hair is accelerated.

Shaving or cutting does not really promote hair growth, but it may make the growth appear coarse because of blunt ends. Hair often grows faster in hot weather.

Although hair is continually growing, it is also continually sloughing off; therefore, the estimated average of lifetime hair growth is twenty-two to twenty-eight inches or fifty-five to seventy centimeters. Some intriguing exceptions have been reported. Perhaps the longest hair length record claimed was by an Indian monk, named Swami Pandarasannadhi, who was reported to have hair twenty-six feet long.[24]

Some daily hair loss is natural. It is estimated that between forty to sixty hairs fall out daily. At varying times of the year and in different states of health, the dropout may seem to be excessive. If this symptom persists, consultation with a physician or cosmetologist is wise.

Racial Differences

Hair is a physical sign of racial differences. Its texture, color, and distribution vary widely between races. Almost all Mongolians, including Chinese, Japanese, American Indians, and Eskimo, have straight, coarse, dark hair on their heads and only sparse facial and body hair. Negroes have slightly more body hair and crinkly or woolly hair on the head. Caucasoids have an in-between form of wavy, curly, or straight, fine hair and more body hair than any other race except the Ainus of Northern Japan.

The pattern of hair growth, as well as its form and color, varies racially and seems to have adaptive value. Crinkly hair bunches into spirally wound locks. Really woolly hair clumps together into small spiral twists leaving bare skin between the clumps. These characteristics seem to allow for greater sweating. The Bushmen of the Kalahari and the Pygmies of the African rain forest both have tight spirals. The wiry matlike hair of some desert tribes seem to be designed to give maximum insulation.

Hair Color

The geographical distribution of hair color tends to follow skin color. The darker the skin, the blacker is the hair. The lighter the skin tones, the lighter is the hair shading ranging from brown to blond. Hair color depends on the concentration of the pigment, melanin. A heavy deposit of melanin in the hair cells results in black hair. Less melanin produces a hair color range from dark brown to light brown to blond. The more dilute the melanin, the weaker is the color.

---

[24] Wendy Cooper, op. cit., pp. 27–28.

Red hair is the product of a supplementary gene that produces a red pigment. If the hair melanin content is low or deficient, the hair will be light red in color. If the red-hair gene is present with strong melanin, the red either will not show or will act as a highlight in black hair or will produce reddish-brown or chestnut shades.

Hair-color genes can be slow in appearing. Often light-haired babies will have dark hair as adults. The darkening of hair can also be caused by structural changes.

The graying of hair is caused by a process of decolorization and structural changes. Existing hair, such as a lock clipped for sentimental reasons, will always keep its color. Therefore, it is not correct to think of gray hair as faded hair. As the existing colored hair grows out, hair lacking pigment grows in. This replaced hair is white or gray. Heredity governs the time when gray hair appears. In some families, it is shortly after puberty; in other families it never seems to occur.[25]

Other Hair Characteristics

The hair whorl or manner in which hair grows wheel-like around the crown of the head is an inherited characteristic. Some people have a clockwise whorl and others a counterclockwise whorl. A very few have a double hair whorl.

The character of the hair is dictated by the genes. The woolly gene is the strongest and dominates all others. The crinkly gene dominates the curly, the curly dominates the wavy, and the wavy dominates the straight. Male hair tends to be wavier than female hair in the same family.

The tendency to go bald is an inherited characteristic. Researchers believe that there are specific genes that cause baldness which are carried by both male and female. Although baldness is more common in men, the right combinations of genes can produce balding and thinning in women. Although many conditions cause baldness, an overproduction of male hormones (androgens) is believed to be a factor. There are two kinds of male baldness, *alopecia prematura* (early baldness) and *alopecia senilis* (old-age baldness). It is estimated that one man in five starts to go bald soon after adolescence and is very bald by the age of thirty. Another one in five retains a full head of hair past sixty. The rest range in more gradual hair loss. The greatest amount of baldness in both men and women comes after fifty. Reasons and cures for baldness vary tremendously. The reasons are quite possibly valid, the cures quite likely invalid.[26]

Hair Removal

The problem of *hypertichosis* (too much hair) can be as vexing as baldness. This hair growth is dependent on genetic characteristics and endocrine factors.[27]

Removal of this superfluous hair is governed by social custom. The practices change or evolve from one area to another and from one generation to another. Within the limits established by social custom, the personal decision to remove

[25] Wendy Cooper, op. cit., pp. 31–33.
[26] Wendy Cooper, op. cit., pp. 47–53.
[27] Ross, op. cit., p. 242.

the extra hair, to tolerate it, or to cultivate it seems to be an expression of individuality. Throughout the history of the world an amazing variety of styles and customs have been fashionable. In the United States, current ideas of social acceptability of body hair vary between men and women. Most men accept body hair as part of their masculinity and most women shun it as not being feminine. Men generally limit their efforts and concern to removing or designing beards, moustaches, and sideburns. However, some men do remove body hair, sometimes from the eyebrow or from underarm, or from the back, if it grows long and heavy there. Women, most often, remove hair from face and eyebrow; from leg (ankle to knee or ankle to hip), from the body or bikini line, from underarm, and sometimes from forearm.

The most common method of hair removal for both men and women is shaving. The instruments for shaving and the preparations used vary with the individual. The technique is principally to slice the hair off at skin level. Most men shave their faces; most women shave their legs and underarms. It is generally believed that shaving and cutting do not influence hair growth and texture, although evidence indicates that light, down hair (*lanugo,* as on the upper lip) sometimes becomes coarsened on some areas following shaving (also with cutting or use of depilatories discussed later). The bluntness of the hair tips after cutting and shaving has mistakenly been thought to indicate a change in texture. The hair will be normal again after it has grown a short distance from the skin.[28]

Tweezing or plucking the hair is another form of removal. This method is used for removing a small number of hairs, sometimes those that grow longer than others in areas such as the chin, throat, and back of neck. Eyebrows are most often shaped by plucking. Plucking is accomplished by using tweezers to pull out the hair from the follicle. The hair is snapped off in the area of the hair bulb, which is often visible on the plucked hair. The skin is usually softened by cleansing prior to plucking. Extremes of heat or cold applied for purposes of plucking are not recommended because of the damage they may cause to skin structure.

Electrolysis is the permanent removal of hair caused by electrically destroying the hair follicle. In discussing electrolysis, Ross emphasized that patients should locate competent electrolysis service through a dermatologist. He cautioned that anyone anticipating this type of treatment should understand the time and costs involved. Ross stated:

The patient should appreciate that treatment cannot be thought of as a course of five or six treatments or even a dozen. The treatment course must be evaluated in units or blocks of time within the span of one or two years for limited zones. There is usually more hair present than average observation reveals. . . . Roughly speaking, a chin moderately covered with hair will take about one year of weekly treatments of about a half-hour each. An upper lip may take about the same or longer.[29]

Waxing is an ancient practice of hair removal that is still popular today. It may be performed in a barber or beauty shop or at home. Wax depilatories may

[28] "Hair Removal Techniques," *What's New in Home Economics,* April 1974, p. 17.
[29] Ross, op. cit., p. 243.

be purchased wherever cosmetics are sold. The wax is melted and coated on powdered skin where hair is to be removed. When the wax is hardened, it is peeled quickly from the skin. The superfluous hair is stuck into the wax as it hardens and is thus removed. Hair is removed from arms, legs, eyebrows, upper lips, and chins this way. Some men use this method in preference to shaving. The hair regrows in one to three weeks. Waxing is generally free from allergy or lasting irritation. Redness and whealing may follow the immediate treatment.

Cream depilatory products dissolve the hair. These products do not leave the bristly feeling stubble that shaving does. Depilatories are strong chemicals and are thus not recommended for use on the face. There is high risk of allergy and irritation with these products.

Hair removal can also be achieved by abrasion or rubbing by a pumice stone. This method is simple and cheap. Singeing, particularly the hair of the forearm, is practiced by some. For obvious reasons, it is not recommended. Hair on the forearm is often better bleached rather than removed.

Hair Care and Processing

The hair cannot be considered separately from the skin. It is dependent upon the skin for development, nourishment, and growth. Hair is subject to the same deteriorations and diseases that affect the skin. The proper functioning of the sebaceous glands is extremely important to the well-being of the hair. The scalp, the skin on the head that produces the most luxuriant growth of hair, has many sebaceous or oil glands, one or two per hair follicle. For this reason the scalp and hair become oily frequently and must be cleaned. How often this cleaning occurs depends on the individual. Healthy hair and scalp cannot be overwashed. Diseased or injured scalp must be promptly treated, best by a professional cosmetologist or physician. If left untreated, scalp injury or disease can produce permanent hair loss because of structural damage to the hair follicle and/or papilla.

Washing or shampooing the hair is a personal grooming process that should be done as often as necessary. The frequency of shampooing depends on the amount of oil and dirt that accumulates on the hair and scalp. Some people shampoo as often as they bathe, which could be more than once a day. Other people with very little oil production and very clean environment shampoo as infrequently as once a month. Others, particularly in Mexican or South American cultures, depend on methods of cleaning the hair that do not involve wetting it with water. (This usually is done by brushing or rubbing the hair to remove oil; sometimes an absorbent ingredient such as corn meal is brushed through the hair.)

Washing is considered the most common method of cleansing hair and scalp. The criteria for selecting a shampoo are the same as those listed for a facial cleanser. Shampoo should remove the dirty surface film on the hair, be nonirritating to the skin, and can itself be easily and completely removed. Both soaps and detergents do this job satisfactorily. Soaps based on tallow or animal fat are easier on the hair because their chemical composition is similar to that of human hair and the secretions of the sebaceous glands. Detergents will make the hair cleaner than soap, but because of their chemical composition, they can dry and lighten the hair.

Creme rinses are wetting agents. They make the hair more pliable and softer by removing all the natural oils. (If you should creme rinse a pond full of ducks, they would all sink!) Creme rinses are good for hard-to-manage or wiry hair. They make fine hair too soft. A very good rinse that has been used for many years is diluted vinegar or lemon juice. The acid of these ingredients neutralizes the alkalinity of the soaps used for washing and leaves the hair free from soap deposits.

There are many hair care products on the market. They all make claims for improving the quality of the hair. It should be remembered that the shaft of the hair is dead cellular material. Therefore, it cannot be fed or nourished. It can be coated, swollen, or made rough or smooth. Read the manufacturer's claims carefully to understand what this product is designed to do and then consider whether hair is actually able to do these things. Often a very good type of conditioner, particularly for dry or very long hair, is some type of oil or grease. Several very inexpensive and long-lasting products are available. Brushing these through the hair will help improve the sheen. The value of brushing the hair is more dependent on the length of hair and amount of oil produced by the sebaceous glands. Brushing does stimulate the oil gland production and also helps to distribute the oil the length of the hair shaft. Whether this is desirable or not depends on you.

The kind of brush used in hair care is a matter of individual preference. Nylon-bristle brushes are most common and less expensive; they are stiff when new and maintain this quality. Natural bristle brushes are expensive and soft. Combs come in a variety of styles. The kinds to avoid are the ones with sharp teeth that can scratch and cut the scalp.

When brushing or combing the hair, care should be taken not to break the hair or pull it out. Hair should be treated gently. Start brushing the hair at the scalp. Rub the brush back and forth on the scalp to stimulate the oil glands. Brush the full length of the hair to distribute oils out to the ends. If a snarl or tangle is located, take it out with brush or comb, working from the end of the hair away from the scalp a bit at a time. Do not use brute strength to pull out a snarl. You will pull out too many hairs. (A helpful hint to remember is that chewing gum can be dissolved from hair by vegetable cooking oil. Just sponge the oil on with a cotton ball and gum soon disappears—works equally well on kids and pets.)

Backcombing, also called roughing or ratting the hair, is explained by all three names. When combed in a backward direction, the hair shaft is made rough. This is caused by pushing out the cells forming the hair. The rough hair is then matted or ratted with other hair to create the illusion of more bulk or volume, which some hairstyles require.

The haircut is vital to styling the hair (Figure 8-8). The hair may be cut by scissors or razor. The scissor cut takes a more talented operator. It gives a blunt cut that is best for fine hair. The razor, which tapers or slices the hair shaft, is best for coarse hair. Often a combination of scissors and razor is used to achieve a particular style. Hair is cut wet when using the razor to avoid pulling. Hair is more compact when wet, care must be taken to avoid overcutting wet hair. Thinning shears are used to thin and shape the hair to fit the contour of the head.

Since people with curly hair have often desired straight hair and those with straight hair frequently want curls, many processes have been invented that gratify both of these desires. The basis of these procedures, whatever the latest names are, is pretty much the same. Permanents are used to curl the hair. Chemical solutions are placed on the hair that break down the sodium bonds and allow the hair to be molded in the shape of the rod on which it is wrapped. Straightened hair is treated in the same manner except it is combed out straight. When the pattern is strong enough, in both permanent and straightening process, a neutralizer that restores the sodium bond is applied. Thus, the newly created pattern is set in the hair where it will remain. Permanent waving and straightening of hair must be repeated because of new, untreated growth and haircuts.

Overprocessed hair has been allowed to go beyond the point where the sodium bond restoration can occur. The result is damaged hair that is soft and spongy when wet and dry and brittle when not wet.

Hot combing, pressing, hot rollers, blow drying, and curling irons all create a temporary hair pattern. The heat of the device is used to force the cells of the hair shaft into new patterns. These processes are all temporary because no chemical breakdown of the cells occurs. Shampooing or simply wetting with water will return the hair to its natural shape.

Coloring of the hair is accomplished by two methods. A temporary color change is accomplished by coating the hair shaft with color. This type of color change is usually called *tinting*. It will often last for several shampoos but must be renewed frequently. This type of hair coloring often rubs off on combs, brushes, clothing, and bed linens. Permanent hair color change is a chemical process. The hair is lightened to a dark, medium or light yellow stage by bleaching. Chemicals force open the cells of the hair shaft and strip out or bleach the pigment. Exactly how hair will lighten is not predictable. This is dependent on the individual pigmentation of the hair. The red hair pigment that sometimes is not visible is

8-8 *Each year both men and women spend large amounts of personal income on skin, nail, and hair grooming products. Understanding the physiology of the skin, nails, and hair will help separate the emotional appeal from the physical requirements in the promotion of these products. (Courtesy Altra)*

the complicating factor. Lightened hair that often looks red or brassy is considered unfinished. Toners are used to create more attractive, fashionable colors. The paler the toner desired, the lighter the bleaching process must be. This chemical alteration of the hair weakens the hair. If improperly done, the cellular arrangement of the hair shaft can be completely destroyed and break off at scalp level. If the chemical process has not burned the scalp so severely as to destroy the hair follicle, the hair will grow out. This condition can be not only dangerous but emotionally painful as well. Often the very blond "cotton candy" hair one sees is close to this extreme state of hair damage.

Wet hair is elastic. This is the physical characteristic that is employed in setting the hair for various styles. Wet hair is stretched and placed in a pattern either by wrapping around an object such as a roller, or by shaping the hair into a pin curl or molding it into a wave. Moisture is needed to establish the pattern and heat is needed to set or dry the hair into the pattern. The quick dry accomplished by the hair dryer is best because the hair is under more tension. Hair allowed to air dry relaxes and the set obtained is looser and not as lasting as the quick-dry set.

Setting lotions, gels, and mousses coat the hair. They give it more body, more texture, and make it appear thicker. They also can cover the natural sheen or gloss of the hair. Certain products are not compatible with certain hair. They make it gummy or sticky and dirty looking. Hair sprays put an interlocking film on the hair that helps hold it in place. Some sprays coat the hair and make it less susceptible to moisture. The basic ingredient of hair spray is lacquer.[30]

Suggested Activities

1. Collect cosmetic and grooming product advertisements. Evaluate the advertisements to determine what part of the appeal is factual and what part is emotional. How much copy is honest information based on the physiology of skin, nails, and hair? How much is a distortion of the facts? Report findings to other class members.
2. Read the labels of the skin, hair, and nail products you use. How much information is available to you? How helpful are the directions in the use of the products? Discuss your findings with the class.
3. Collect news articles pertaining to legislation regulating cosmetic products. Discuss trends that appear to be emerging in this area.
4. Write for more information:

The Skin Cancer Foundation   American Academy of Dermatology
475 Park Avenue South   820 Davis Street
New York, N.Y. 10016   Evanston, Ill. 60201

[30] Chester Specht, President, Lake Salon, Inc., personal interview, Pasadena, Calif., January 1985.

III

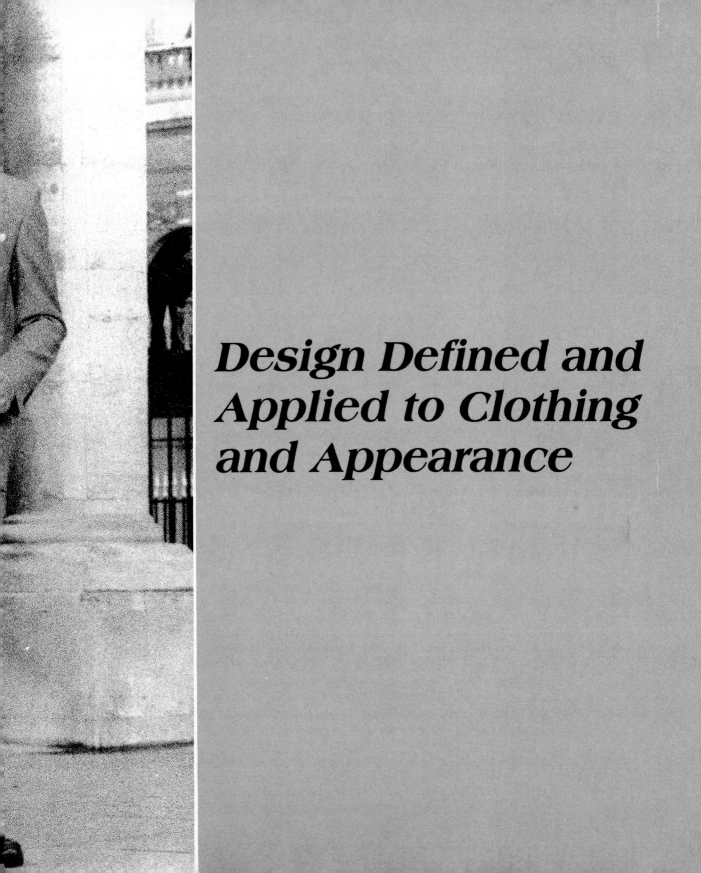

Design Defined and Applied to Clothing and Appearance

9 Design

You are a very creative individual. Perhaps you are wondering why a chapter on design would start with that statement. To illustrate, think about the garments you are wearing right now. Who selected them? Who assembled them and arranged them on your body just as they are right now? Who selected your jewelry and other accessories and who planned their placement on your body? Who arranged your hair? Who decided how your face would be adorned? If you made all of these decisions and executed the positioning or arrangement of all the articles mentioned, and if you do this each time you get dressed, you are a very prolific creative designer. Since *you are a designer*, the challenge of this area of study is to understand design better and incorporate these understandings into all of your design work.

Design decisions are made in the selection of most of the consumer goods. We evaluate the design of many objects including cars, appliances, houses, furniture, toys, artwork, as well as all wearing apparel. We do this in an unconscious manner when we think or say, "I really like this item, but I do not care for that one" or "This looks good on me, but that one does not."

This section of your text will help you develop a vocabulary that will allow you to express your design opinions. It will present guidelines for making design decisions in a more professional manner. It is the goal of the authors to help students make design a vital part of their everyday life. To reach this goal, learn to apply the material presented in these chapters to all design that surrounds you wherever you may be and wherever you may go.

Design may be defined as the arrangement of lines, form-shape-space, colors, and textures into a coherent whole. This definition can be applied to any kind of design including that of houses, cars, refrigerators, gardens, bouquets, and of course, clothing. The elements of design—line, form-shape-space, color, and texture—are called *fundamental* or *plastic*. They are fundamental because they are basic to every design. They are plastic because they may be formed in infinite variety.

Because the design elements have no practical meaning with reference to clothing unless the discussion integrates the application of the organizing principles, the authors preface the design section with an analysis of design principles, followed by chapters on the design elements.

There are two general divisions of design . . . *structural* and *applied*. Structural design is created by the construction detail form as the design is assembled. Applied design, also called decorative design, is created after the form is complete and is the result of surface enrichment.

Structural and Applied Design of Clothing

Structural design is inherent in all garments because they are created by construction details when put together, including seams, collars, pockets, and the color and texture of the fabric. Any detail that is an integral part of the garment is structural design. This structural detail may be either very elaborate or very plain. In clothing, structural design is most important because it is the fundamental component of the garment. Garments that rely on structural design for their interest and appeal are usually pleasing, and are often expensive because of this detailing (Figure 9-1).

Applied design may be added to some garments. Applied design is surface enrichment added to the garment (Figure 9-2). It consists of trims such as sequins, beading, embroidery, appliqué, rickrack, and piping. It sometimes includes buttons without buttonholes and flaps without pockets. Applied design is sometimes used as a less expensive method to achieve design interest. In mass production, applied design may be used to cover shoddy workmanship. Ready-made garments that do not have appropriate or effective applied design in decorative buttons, bows, scarves, and trims can often be enhanced by eliminating these details entirely or by replacing them with more suitable trims. Existing garments in the wardrobe can be radically transformed by the use of applied design.

9-1 *Structural design is created by construction details when the garment is put together. Details that form an integral part of the garment are structural design. Designer and model Cynthia Thompson. (Courtesy David Estep)*

9-2 Applied design is surface enrichment added to the garment. Lace, appliqué, beads, pearls, and fox fur enrich the surfaces of a silk satin wedding gown. (Courtesy Priscilla of Boston)

9-3 Applied design decoration should be related to the structural lines of the garment. (Courtesy Allied Corporation)

Applied design can be evaluated by use of the following criteria:

1. Applied design should reinforce the basic design concept created in the construction of the garment. This is achieved when the placement of the trim is related to the structural lines of the garment. Decoration placed without consideration of the basic garment lines often produces a disorganized impression that lacks unity (Figure 9-3), or a feeling that the items do not belong together.
2. Applied design is most attractive when it is related in size and texture to the textile of the garment (Figure 9-4). Compatible combinations of textures include:

fine embroidery—finely woven fabrics
sequins—shiny, fine textures
rickrack—medium-weight cottons
embroidered tapes—medium-weight cottons and wool
raffia—homespun cottons and linens
crewel embroidery—heavy woven and knitted fabrics

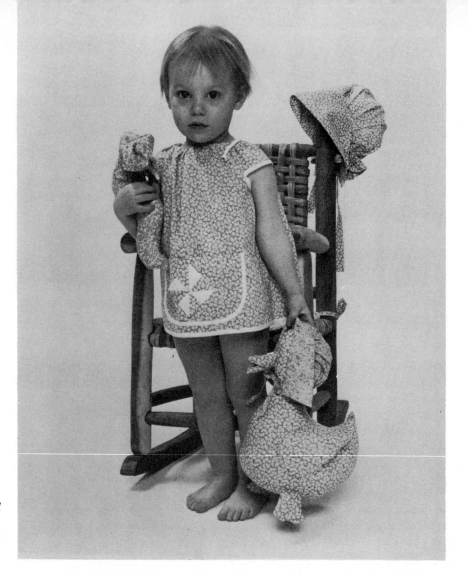

9-4 *The size of the applied design is related to the size of the area that it occupies. (Courtesy Mountain Laurel)*

3. Applied design, when used in limited areas, will produce an organized impression. Overuse of decoration usually detracts from the total effect of the garment. For example, applying bands of peasant embroidery at the neck, at the hem of sleeves, and on the yoke is overdoing it and obvious; a disunified impression may result. When trims are very eye arresting, they are most effective concentrated in one or two areas (Figure 9-5).

4. Applied design should create an interesting color harmony with the garment fabric. Colors can be selected to match, blend, or contrast. When the garment fabric is a print, repetition of a predominant color used in the print will often unify the applied design.

5. The applied design should be related in size to the size of the area that it occupies. Small areas such as cuffs and collars can accommodate trims of limited size; large areas such as yokes, the skirt, and bodice can adequately utilize large-scale trims (Figure 9-6).

292

9-5 *Applied design used in limited areas produces an organized impression. Eye-arresting trims are most effective when they are concentrated in one or two areas. (Courtesy Catalina)*

9-6 *The size of the applied design is related to the size of the area that it occupies. (Courtesy Folkwear, Inc.)*

The Principles of Design

The arrangement of the elements of design into a completed coherent composition is the work of each artist. In order to create a "pleasing" design, thoughtful arrangement of materials is made to produce certain desired effects. Each design is a creative statement of the individual artist. Each design exhibits techniques of handling the fundamental elements: line, form-shape-space, color, and texture. How the design is organized depends on the individual artist. How the design is evaluated depends on the frame-of-reference of the evaluator.

In our culture, many people recognize and use, as a basis of their artistic judgment, certain guides that are referred to as the *Principles of Design* (or Art Principles). Our discussion includes the design principles commonly referred to as balance, proportion, emphasis, rhythm, and unity. It should be kept in mind that these principles are intended to give coherence to the elements of design and to help to achieve an ideal. The Principles of Design are often used as a device to judge the validity of any work of art including garment design.

It is emphasized that the Principles of Design are *value judgments.* They are subjective evaluations that are determined by and are expressions of cultural ideals of this period. They are personal "points-of-view."

There is some disagreement among scholars as to the specific design principles and their interpretation. The principles most often used in garment evaluation are the ones included in this chapter.

The Principles of Design Related to the Individual and Fashion

The same elements and principles are used in clothing design as in any other design form. In judging garments for personal wear certain special requirements should be considered. These include:

individual physical characteristics
the personality of the wearer
the intended use of the garment

The organizing principles of design can be used to evaluate apparel designs at point of purchase or during home construction. The principles can be of help when selecting separate garments and when coordinating several garments and accessories into a complete outfit. Although the individual items of dress can be evaluated by the design principles both on and off of the body, the final analysis should always occur with the complete outfit on the individual so that both the clothing arrangement and physical form are viewed as one complete design.

The art principles should not be considered as rigid, unbreakable formulas; they should be thought of as guidelines. The fact that the principles of design are flexible is attested to by the diversity of styles in which they are seen. Designers may deliberately break a principle in order to express a fashion statement of the period. Fashion reflects conditions of the time in which it exists. An example of how a design principle was broken was demonstrated in the fashion of the early 1970s. During this time, a very popular "layered look" was achieved by using stripes, plaids, abstracts, and textured fabrics together in a single outfit. The combined fabric designs often lacked any unifying idea. This was a period of political, social, and economic discord. Thus, the current events of the times were mirrored in fashionable apparel (Figure 9-7).

Faulkner explained how the design principles are utilized by the artist:

An artist does not apply a design principle as he works, rather, the organization emerges as the work develops—the artist may, in the process of creation, wish to review his work critically from time to time, to withdraw somewhat from it and examine what he has done with an objective eye. It is at such moments of removal and evaluation that the artist consciously or unconsciously uses the principles of organization as he checks.[1]

We can use the design principles for creating, discussing, and evaluating garment designs, on and off the individual, providing there is an understanding of the terminology and a consensus as to the importance of the particular design principles. To establish this basis, a discussion of each of the design principles—balance, proportion, rhythm, emphasis, and unity—follows.

Balance

Balance may be defined as equal distribution of weight (actual or visual) from a central point or area. It is a state of equilibrium. The purpose of balance is to bring into being a satisfying relationship of all design parts. When the design elements: line, form-shape-space, color, and texture are in balance, a pleasing harmony is established. There are several kinds of balance of shape and form including:

formal balance, also called symmetrical balance or bilateral symmetry
informal balance, also called asymmetrical or occult balance
radial balance

Formal Balance (symmetrical balance)

Formal balance occurs when identical objects are equidistant from a center (real or imaginary) and the objects appear to equalize each other. Formal balance can also be explained by saying that when measured from the center, one half of the design is the exact mirror image of the other half (Figure 9-7). An example of formal balance is found in the front or back view of the human body. Because of the shape of the human body, it is also an example of vertical, formal balance. Many examples of formal balance may be found in clothing including:

a formal tuxedo shirt with equal rows of tucks or ruffles from the center buttoning

9-7 *Formal balance occurs when one half of the design is the mirror image of the other half. (Courtesy Pendleton Woolen Mills)*

---

[1] Ray Faulkner and Edwin Ziegfield, *Art Today* (New York: Holt, 1969), p. 377.

a buttoned blazer jacket, if the pockets are the same on either side
a pair of jeans, buttoned or zipped

In interior design, formal balance is said to have stability, dignity, and formality. In dress design the feeling of dignity or formality created by formal balance is also influenced by color, texture, and cut. Formally balanced designs often give an impression of stability; this is because of the equal or balanced placement of the parts that compose the design.

In apparel, formal balance may emphasize body irregularities. This is because equal distribution of design parts from a center (real or imaginary) gives the eye of the observer "benchmarks" with which to judge or compare the body conformation. Formal balance often encourages comparisons of one side of the body with the other.

Creating an outfit using formal balance is easy, it is safe, but it may not be very exciting. This is the kind of balance found most often in ready-to-wear. When using formal balance in garments, it is a good idea to add interest and flair with unusual colors, textures, or accessories.

Informal Balance (asymmetrical balance)

Informal balance occurs when objects arranged on either side of a center (real or imaginary) are equal (in weight or mass), but not identical (Figure 9-8). The side view of the normal-weight human body is an example of informal balance as the weight or mass of the front-side anatomy is balanced by the weight or mass of the back-side anatomy. Horizontal informal balance may be observed in the side view of the normal human body conformation. The weight or mass of the head and torso on one end of the long body is informally balanced by the weight and length of the hips and legs on the other end. Many examples of informal balance may be found in clothing including:

A side-closing Cossack-inspired shirt, often used as a uniform style. In this garment the mass of one side is informally balanced by the button closing on the other.

The unbuttoned blazer jacket styled so that two small pockets on one side of center are informally balanced by one large pocket on the other side. The buttons will also be informally balanced by the buttonholes.

Remember that informal balance is more a matter of visual impact than of exact physical weight distribution. In our example of the human body, the head and torso may actually weigh less than the hips and legs; however, the mass of the head and torso appears to be balanced by the weight and length of the hips and legs. This gives this human-body formation informal balance. Often the interior designer will arrange a wall of pictures and art objects together, the grouping will achieve informal balance visually, but it will not necessarily be an actual weight balance. This same concept is often used in clothing design. A jacket may appear balanced even though it has one self-fabric pocket on only

9-8 *Informal balance (left) occurs when elements on either side of the center are equal, but not identical. The garment on the right represents formal balance. Designer and model Cynthia Thompson (left) and Eleanor Dolgin (right). (Courtesy David Estep)*

one side of center; this is because the visual impact of the pocket is negligible (Figure 9-9). However, if a jacket had one large pocket on one side of center that was of strongly contrasting color or texture, the garment could not appear to be balanced. In this example, informal balance could be achieved by accessorizing. A scarf that appears equal in visual mass or importance to the contrasting pocket could be tied at the neck in such a manner as to complete the informal balance of the jacket design (Figure 9-10).

9-9 *Informal balance is more a matter of visual impact than equal physical weight distribution. If the visual impact is negligible, the effect will not appear unbalanced. (Courtesy the Joseph & Feiss Company)*

Informal balance can be used to correct the appearance of body irregularities. This is because the eye of the observer is not given exact duplicates with which to compare one side of the body with the other. If one side, or one part of the body, is not the same as the other (which is true of most human bodies), informal balance in clothing may create illusions that will make the body appear symmetrical.

Informal balance gives the designer more freedom of expression than does formal balance. Informal balance is more difficult to use because of the many variations that are possible. The artist must use different objects and create a visual stability in order to achieve informal balance. When properly executed, informal balance is intriguing and dynamic because it has an element of surprise.

9-10 *The pockets contrast with the garment owing to a color contrast. The pocket on the upper side of the garment creates an illusion of a heavier look, giving an unbalanced impression.*

Consumers should be aware that informal balance in apparel design generally is more expensive than formal balance. As home sewers know, garments having informal balance are more difficult to construct. This is because the right and left sides of the garment are cut and handled differently. Assembling this type of garment is more time consuming, which adds to the cost of manufacturing.

Formal balance combined with informal balance in clothing. Sometimes both formal and informal balance are combined in a single garment (Figure 9-11). This could happen in a dress when the bodice design is in formal balance and the skirt design is in informal balance. Such an arrangement is often lacking in harmony and relationship of the various parts. A design with this problem can appear pleasing when there is an interesting transition between the parts that unifies the two opposite effects.

Radial Balance

Radial balance occurs when the major parts of the design radiate from a central point. The central point is the focal point. Pleats, seams, gathers, darts, or motifs radiate from the focal point creating a sunburst effect (Figure 9-12). Garments using this type of balance are limited. Radial balance is found frequently in necklines where the neck or head is used as the focal point. It is used in evening gowns to achieve a body-clinging effect in the bodice area. Radial balance is also used in the bra section of some swimsuits. Because of the intricate detailing involved in this type of construction, it is usually found only in expensive clothing.

Vertical and Horizontal Balance

We have mentioned examples of vertical and horizontal balance using the human body. Formal vertical balance is achieved in clothing when each detail of the garments and accessories on one side of an imaginary vertical line bisecting the body is a mirror image of the other side. (Each detail is balanced by the same detail on the other side of the imaginary line.) Informal vertical balance is achieved in clothing when the details of the garments and accessories on one side of an imaginary vertical line bisecting the body differ from those on the other side yet appear to have the same visual weight.

Perhaps because of the length of the body, or perhaps because of the view we get of the face and torso when we look in the mirror, we seem most frequently concerned with vertical balance in dress. This should not be our major concern. Horizontal balance is of greater importance in clothing selection.

Horizontal balance is achieved above and below the body "landmarks" (waist, hip, bust/chest) where horizontal garment interest is located. Because of the visual interest attracted to the area emphasized by the horizontal line, and because of the effect caused by this body division, horizontal balance should be considered as each outfit is selected (Figure 9-13). Horizontal balance on the human body can only be informal because of the anatomical differences between the upper and the lower sections of the body.

9-11 *Formal and informal design are combined in one garment. The arrangement is successful because the beaded design is repeated by the drape and hem lines of the skirt. (Courtesy J. P. Stevens & Co., Inc.)*

9-13 *Vertical balance is achieved on either side of an imaginary line that bisects the body. Horizontal balance is achieved above and below the body "landmarks" where horizontal garment interest is located. Vertical and horizontal balance should be considered as each outfit is selected. (Courtesy Pendleton Woolen Mills)*

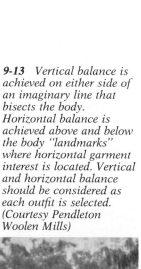

9-12 *Radial balance occurs when the major parts of the design radiate from a central point. Here the gathers radiate from a focal point creating a sunburst effect. (Courtesy J. P. Stevens & Co., Inc.)*

The horizontal division in clothing may not always result in horizontal balance. Some outfits are top-heavy whereas others are bottom-heavy. The classic man's business suit is an example of a top-heavy garment. The width of the shoulders combined with the length of the jacket creates a bulk in the upper torso that is not balanced visually with the length of the pants. An unadorned crop-top worn with full long pants of contrasting color is an example of a bottom-heavy outfit. The small top is not balanced visually with the mass of the pants.

The shape, width, length, color, and texture of each garment should each be evaluated for its effect on the body. The visual impression that the clothing is in balance both vertically and horizontally will give the outfit a look of stability and harmony.

Proportion

Proportion may be defined as the pleasing relationship of areas. Proportion is the design principle concerned with the relation of the size of the parts to the whole and to each other. Proportion is sometimes referred to as scale. Proportion includes the relationship of height, width, depth, and the surrounding space of each design. It is the differences in proportion that make individuals look different from one another.

Study the proportion of the five rectangles in Figure 9-14. Which looks the longest? the broadest? Which division of spaces would give the most slender illusion for a garment? the broadest? the shortest?

No. 1 represents the shape of a garment having no waistline, such as a jumpsuit (having no waistline definition).

No. 2 represents an empire line, with the high waistline under the bust.

No. 3 represents a natural waistline, waist-length jacket, and pant.

No. 4 represents a waistline dropped to hip level, jacket, and pant of equal length.

No. 5 represents a long jacket with a short skirt or pant, ¾-length coat over pants.

Basic Laws of Proportion

Proportion is usually based on an ideal. In Chapter 4 we learned that most cultures have their own ideals of what is beautiful. These ideals often pertain to proportion. A slender or a stout body, a tiny or prominent nose, layers of constricting clothing or near nudity, the tiny bound foot or the normal size shoe all

9-14 *Study the proportion of the five rectangles in this figure. Which looks the longest? the broadest? Which division of spaces would give the most slender illusion for a garment? the broadest? the shortest?*
No. 1 represents the shape of a garment having no waistline, such as a shift.
No. 2 represents an empire line, with the high waistline under the bust.
No. 3 represents a natural waistline, a classic shirtdress, waist-length jacket, and skirt.
No. 4 represents a waistline dropped to hip level, jacket and pant of equal length.
No. 5 represents a long jacket with a short skirt, 3/4-length coat over skirt, long tunic.

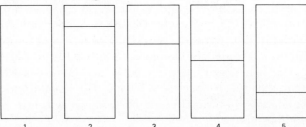

1   2   3   4   5

reveal the differences in the taste proportions of people. When something is out of proportion we usually react: a little girl wearing a dress with a huge print, a tiny young woman who carries a massive handbag. Proportions idealized in the Western world are based on mathematical formulas established by the early Egyptians and later by the Greeks. Their historic buildings such as the pyramids and the Parthenon and many of their sculptured figures were based upon the proportions of 3:5:8; 5:8:13.[2] That is, the smaller space (3) has the same relationship to the larger space (5) as the larger space has to the whole (8). The same would be true of the 5:8:13 relationship. These proportions are sometimes referred to as the *Golden Mean* or the *Golden Section*. Actual measurements of the eye-satisfying pieces of ancient architecture and sculpture revealed these equations. The Golden Mean equations are used to establish pleasing horizontal divisions. They are useful in many ways in various kinds of designs. Once understood, the proportions of the Golden Mean are often achieved artistically or visually rather than by actual measurement.

Proportion Applied to Clothing Design

The principle of proportion is used effectively in clothing design and selection. The Golden Mean equations are used to produce garments that may be divided visually into 3:5, 5:8, 8:13 horizontal sections. Sometimes these divisions may not be precisely measurable, but they are within certain limitations. This is because garment design is a creative expression and we can accept certain variations *if* they are eye-pleasing (Figure 9-15).

For example:

In the classic shirtmaker dress, the horizontal divisions appear at the natural waistline and at the hemline. Proportion will be most pleasing if the bodice, skirt, and total body represent the 3:5:8 ratio (Figure 9-16).

In long-panted garments for either men or women, the shirt or jacket proportion should represent 3 (or 5); the pant area, 5 (or 8); and the shirt or jacket and long-pant area combined, 8 (or 13) (Figure 9-17).

There are fashion periods when proportion may be inverted. That is, the largest division of the garment appears on the top section of the body. This happens when styles that do not use the natural body divisions are fashionable. When the waistline of a garment is lowered, the proportion is inverted. When a jacket hemline is lowered, proportion is inverted. The proportion of such garments will be visually pleasing if the space divisions are those established by the *Golden Mean*.

There are also periods of fashion when garments are designed in "poor proportion." Examples of this are found in the many miniskirted styles. These garments represent "poor proportion" because many of them could be visually divided into two equal halves. However, when the miniskirted styles were judged on the body, the principle of proportion was effective. The short garment was

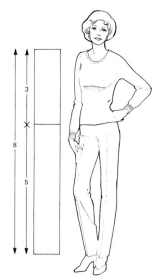

9-15 *Proportion of the* Golden Mean *represents a ratio of 3:5:8. The smaller space has the same relationship to the larger (3:5) as the larger space has to the whole (5:8). The relationship of the sweater length to the pant is in pleasing proportion. The sweater is related to the pant in a 3 to 5 proportion.*

[2] Harriet T. McJimsey, *Art & Fashion in Clothing Selection* (Ames, Iowa: Iowa State U.P., 1973), p. 127.

9-16 In the classic shirtmaker dress, the horizontal divisions appear at the natural waistline and at the hem line. Proportion will be most pleasing if the bodice, skirt, and the total body represent the 3:5:8 ratio. (Courtesy Pendleton Woolen Mills)

9-17 In long-panted garments for either men or women, the shirt or jacket proportion should represent 3 (or 5); for the pant area, 5 (or 8); for the shirt or jacket and long-pant area combined, 8 (or 13). (Courtesy Traci Scherek for Traci Ltd., St. Paul, Minnesota)

proportionally balanced by the length of the leg exposed and the use of colored stockings and flat shoes that completed this fashionable style (Figure 9-18).

Proportion of texture relates the dimension of the surface interest to the size of the wearer. Surface interest or texture refers to nap, pile, slubs, plissé, flocking, and other textile treatments that give dimension. It also includes fur.

The length, depth, bulk, or visual illusion created by the texture of a garment must be considered in relationship to the space the texture occupied in the garment design and to the body conformation of the wearer. Pleasing proportion is achieved when the texture of the clothing supports the garment design and is in keeping with the size of the person wearing the garment (Figure 9-19).

9-18 *In the late 1960s miniskirted styles ignored the principle of proportion; however, when these styles are judged on the body, the length of the exposed leg and use of colored stockings and flat-heeled shoes makes a visually pleasing effect. (Courtesy Celanese Fibers Marketing Company)*

Proportion of fabric design considers the dimensions of the individual motifs, their position in both fabric and garment, and the background spaces. The scale of the garment design must be in proportion with the size of the person wearing it (Figure 9-20).

305

9-19 *Pleasing proportion of fabric design is achieved when the texture of the cloth supports the garment design and is in keeping with the person wearing the garment. (Courtesy Geiger of Austria)*

9-20 *The proportion of fabric design relates to the size of the individual motifs, the background, placement on the garment, and finally the size of the wearer. (Courtesy American Enka)*

9-21 *Proportion is an important principle to remember when clothing is selected for children and young people. The size relationship of each detail should be in scale with the total garment and the body size. (Courtesy Cotton Incorporated)*

Proportion of color involves using color in unequal amounts. When several colors are used together, one color should dominate. When garments of different colors are combined into one outfit, the line of color transition becomes a visual division that will have impact on the proportion of the entire outfit. In other words, garment lines are emphasized by color change and, therefore, are important proportion considerations.

Proportion and body conformation should be considered carefully. The human body size can be divided into three general categories: small, medium, and large. Each individual should strive to develop an accurate self-image of where he fits in these groupings. This body size identification should be a guide in selecting all clothing including fabric designs, textures, trims, and accessories (it can also be applied in other areas of living). The small or petite person should limit himself or herself to items that are of small or medium scale (Figure 9-21). The medium or middle-sized person may select from the small, medium, or large scale. The large person should be limited to the large or medium scale.

The reason for this size limitation is the principle of proportion (Figure 9-20). When a person wears clothing that is too large in actual fit, in texture, and fabric design and selects accessories that are too large, such as hats, purses, and jewelry, the size relationships are out of proportion. The petite stature of the individual is overwhelmed by the clothing and accessories. When a large person selects clothing that is too small in fit, in texture, or fabric design, or trims and selects accessories that are too small, such as hats, purses, and jewelry, the size relationships are out of proportion. The large stature of the individual is contrasted to the small scale of the clothing and accessories and body size is emphasized. The large-sized body needs to have body mass broken up in structural line and prints. The medium or middle-sized person has more freedom to select clothing and accessories in a wider scale range. However, such a person should be sensitive to the principle of proportion and evaluate the effect of the size relationships of the articles he/she selects to each other and to his/her own body conformation (Figure 9-22).

Sometimes we may wish to create illusions to correct parts of the body that are out of proportion with the rest of the body. This can be achieved by studying the size relationships of all parts of the body and learning to bring them all into the visual illusion of proper proportion. (See Appendices A and B.)

Emphasis

Emphasis is dominance or a concentration of interest in one area of a design that prevails as the center of attention and is more eye-arresting than any other part. All areas may be interesting, but not all areas should have equal strength of interest. This implies the use of subordination in other parts so that some area may be emphasized.

Placement of emphasis should not be at any area the individual wishes to minimize. The face or personality area should be emphasized most often (Figure 9-23). This is the part of the person that is most unique and individualistic.

9-22 *Individuals should be sensitive to the principle of proportion and evaluate the effect of the size relationships of the articles selected to each other and to their body conformation. (Courtesy the Joseph & Feiss Company)*

9-23 *The placement of interest near the face is achieved by the use of a V-shaped neckline, floral headpiece, and flowing veil. (Courtesy Priscilla of Boston)*

Emphasis at the personality area may be achieved by color and texture contrasts, necklines, jewelry, scarves, neckties, hats, hairstyles, and makeup. Only one area must be the most important or dominant, and all other ornamentation is subordinate to it.

Sometimes interest may be concentrated at the waistline, bust/chest, hip area, hands, legs, or feet. Hands are emphasized by long sleeves, especially when cuff-linked, by bracelets, and rings and by well-manicured nails. Poor grooming of the hands, or dirty or chewed nails can bring negative emphasis to this area.

Legs and feet are made dominant by unusual hem lengths, design detail at the hem, textured or colored hosiery, and elaborate footwear. Color contrasts, texture, or cutwork in shoes is very eye-arresting and should be evaluated carefully.

Parts of the torso, such as the waist and hips, become areas of interest when garment lines or ornamentation fall at these areas. Emphasis is achieved by the use of color, line, texture, decoration, or trim, or by the absence of fabric that reveals the skin. The methods used to obtain emphasis are:

repetition or concentration
unusual lines or shapes, textures
decoration on a contrasting background
contrast or opposition
progression

Repetition or concentration may be achieved by grouping rows of stripes, tucks, gathers, ruffles, buttons, or trim in one area, or by concentration of jewelry, such as rows of beads, chains, or pins. Repeated cutout areas of fabric and concentrated areas of bareness located in the midriff, front, or back produce areas of concentrated interest. Emphasis gained by repetition or concentration as well as the other four methods implies that these devices are used in one area and that other areas are subordinated to this. Repeating rows of trim in many different areas will not accentuate any one area but often produces confusion because of a lack of emphasis.

Unusual lines and shapes by virtue of their uniqueness are eye-arresting. Unusual shapes of collars, sleeves, pockets, jewelry, outsized buttons, belts, and trims can be used to localize interest (Figure 9-24). Textures and fabric designs that depart from the ordinary may be the focus of attention (Figure 9-24). Elaborate, complex, or eye-arresting fabric design is best displayed by simple garment design, so that the fabric and garment design do not compete with each other for attention. Because of high labor costs the majority of ready-to-wear garments feature simple cut and uncomplicated lines in combination with unusual textures and prints, which emphasize the fabric (Figure 9-25).

The placement of decoration on a plain, contrasting background permits the decoration to be dominant. The use of a figured pin such as a cameo or mosaic on a print dress does not allow the jewelry to dominate. Trims, embroidery, appliqué, jewelry, buttons, and belt buckles, when used on a contrasting background, are emphasized and become areas of interest.

9-24 *Unusual lines and shapes, by virtue of their uniqueness, are eye arresting. The draped collar is emphasized by contrasting edging. (Courtesy Traci Scherek for Traci Ltd., St. Paul, Minnesota)*

9-25 *The simple cut and uncomplicated line emphasize the beauty of the fabric. (Courtesy Priscilla of Boston)*

9-26 *Shape contrasts are emphasized when color differs from the color of the background. Panel shapes are outlined by contrasting embroidery. (Courtesy Folkwear, Inc.)*

Contrasts of color, line, shape, and texture will create emphasis. Some unifying factor must be used to connect these contrasts, or the result may be confusing.

When contrasts are kept close together in placement, the continuity of the idea comes into better focus. An example is the use of color contrast in hat and neck scarf rather than in neck scarf and shoes. The scarf and shoes are relatively far apart, which weakens, or destroys, the effect of the color contrast. Contrasts that are used too many times also lose their impact.

Shape contrasts in designs are more strongly emphasized when their color (intensity, value or hue) differs from that of the background. Yokes, collars, cuffs, and panel shapes will be more noticeable when their edges are outlined in a contrasting trim or when these sections are of themselves an intensity, value, or color contrast (Figure 9-26).

Texture contrasts provide a means of emphasis. The combination of texture creates excitement in an outfit. The use of all shiny, all dull, or all heavy textures in the same garment produces monotony; variations are more interesting.

Progression means a continuing change in size. Emphasis can be achieved by progression in ruffles, contrasting bands, buttons, and other trims. Progression may be achieved by intensity change from bright to dull, by value change from light to dark, or by the use of related color harmonies.

Rhythm

Rhythm may be defined as "a pleasing sense of organized movement that gives continuity to a design." Rhythm provides a transition from one unit to another and leads the eye in a fluid movement throughout the design. The pathway along which the eye is led may be actual or implied. Without rhythm, a design may appear spotty or disconnected. Rhythm results from a regular repeat, or a gradual change, giving the feeling of continuity throughout the design. Rhythm in visual design resembles rhythm in music or audio design.

Rhythm in Clothing Design

Individual garments and assembled outfits need rhythm to unify their composition. When rhythm is lacking the separate parts of the design appear spotty or disconnected. Rhythm is achieved in garment construction by the following combinations of lines, shapes, colors, and textures:

Rhythm by repetition or regular repeats of (Figure 9-27)

motif	other trims
shapes	color
buttons	texture
tucks, pleats	fabric design
laces, edgings	

9-27 *Rhythm is achieved by repetition or regular repeats of the motif in the fabric design. (Courtesy Jantzen)*

Rhythm by progression or gradation or an orderly sequence of gradually increasing or decreasing changes in sizes of (Figure 9-28)

motif
buttons
trims
flounces, ruffles, or tiers
colors, values, intensity, or shading from one color to another
textures
fabric design

Rhythm by radiation or organized movement emanating from a central point of (Figure 9-29)

gathers   darts
folds   pleats
tucks   lines

9-28 Rhythm results from gradation or an orderly sequence of gradually increasing sizes of the embroidered geometric motif. (Courtesy Folkwear, Inc.)

9-29 Rhythm is created by radiation, line from a central point, and by gradation of color. (Courtesy Danskin, Inc.)

Rhythm by continuous flowing lines of (Figure 9-30)

trims
bands of color
fabric design

9-30 *Flowing lines of bias-cut panels create rhythm, a path for the eye to follow. (Courtesy Maria Rodriguez Designs)*

Rhythm in an outfit is often more successful when it is sensed rather than too obvious. Rhythm need not always be in a regular series, but may be in a feeling of echoing some line, shape, color, or texture occurring in the main theme of the look. Accessories may be used to create rhythm by picking up lines, shapes, colors, or textures and repeating them with variation of the basic theme. Rhythm in clothing design is most interesting when it is not too predictable.

Fabric designs with widely placed motifs may lack rhythm. These designs should be evaluated critically when they are cut and constructed into garments. Often the garment design will interrupt this type of fabric design and produce strange effects when worn on the body. Decorative applied designs should be incorporated so that they support the rhythm of the garment design.

Unity

Unity, also called *harmony*, in design is achieved when the fundamental elements, line, form-shape-space, colors and textures, have been used to express a single concept or theme. Unity is created when all parts of the design are related, consistent, and orderly. When a design has unity, it gives an overall impression that attracts and holds the attention of the observer (Figure 9-31).

Unity should not imply dullness. Unity is best when achieved with variety. Variety may be achieved by manipulation of any or all of the fundamental elements composing the design. Care must be taken to make certain that the central idea of the design is emphasized and that the variation of theme is supportive to the main theme. When unity of design is achieved, all parts of the design give a sense of belonging to the composition (Figure 9-32).

Unity in Clothing Design

The term *total look* has been coined to describe unity in dress. A total look is achieved when each part of the design, including garments, accessories, jewelry, hairstyle, and facial ornamentation, expresses a single theme that is consistent with the age and time and the personality of the wearer and with the time and the place it is to be worn.

The total look of the cowboy is achieved when riding clothes are accessorized with appropriate hat and boots and worn by a lean, athletic, outdoor person in a Western setting. The clothing may be worn on the streets of the big city, but it will separate the wearer from the local residents. This same total look would be appropriate for a country/western dance but not a prom.

The total look of the *femme fatale* includes body-revealing garments of sensuous fabrics, accessorized with furs or feathers, worn by a voluptuous woman in an

9-31 *Unity expresses a single concept or theme. Unity results when lines, shapes, colors, and textures express a single idea. (Courtesy Pendleton Woolen Mills)*

9-32 *Unity is successful when a degree of variety is used. A contrast of textures and fabric design is one method used to avoid monotony and provide interest to the total composition. (Courtesy Pendleton Woolen Mills)*

intimate setting. This look may be appropriate for evening wear and selected indoor sports but is not appropriate for city streets or football games.

Some other stereotyped total looks include the:

construction worker	jogger
tennis player	macho man
corporate executive	feminine woman
priest	

One of the most common problems of dressing is the creation of unity of all elements of the outfit. Without unity the effect will be chaotic and haphazard. Too frequently garments are combined with accessories that are not quite appropriate. This often happens with shoes. To illustrate this point, consider the classic tennis shoe. It is sporty, casual, and informal. It does not belong with more formal clothes such as tailored suits or party dresses. Sandals are also casual footwear. They should be limited to casual clothes and to warm-weather dressing. They look out-of-place with tailored outfits and in cold winter weather. Heavy shoes such as boots, oxfords, wingtips, or saddle shoes go with sporty, tailored clothes; they look ridiculous with tuxedos and formals. Perhaps these examples seem too obvious to you. Make a study of the footwear worn on your campus. See if you do not agree that often the shoe selection spoils the unity of the total look presented by many.

Hairstyles often spoil the total look also. For women, the elaborate styles appropriate for elegant evening wear are not a part of the total look of casual campus fashion. For men shaggy hair and untrimmed beard may be accepted for campus lifestyle, but when dressing in traditional business wear for job hunting, they will be a jarring factor in the total look of the young businessman.

When fashion evolves from one look to another, some people have problems in establishing the unity of the new look. A major fashion change requires modification of hairstyles and facial adornment, changes in accessories, including jewelry, purse design, and shoe shape, in addition to the newly styled garments. Too often, only part of the new fashion look is acquired and the other details are ignored; therefore, the total look is destroyed. For examples of this problem look around your campus or community. It will be possible to observe people who have developed a look collected over several fashion periods. Some women cling to styles such as the high stiletto heel of the 1950s combined with the miniskirt and long straight hair of the 1960s and worn with the brighter makeup and nail polish of the 1980s. Some men combine the "Fonzie" hair style of the 1950s with the moustaches of the 1960s with the John Travolta three-piece suit of the late 1970s with the jogging shoe of the 1980s.

Each time you put yourself together by selecting garments, accessories, hairstyle, and facial adornment, you become a designer creating an artistic composition. By applying the organizing principles of design presented in this chapter, you can evaluate the effect of your total look. These guidelines should not be confining, but should give you more confidence to experiment and to express your individuality through dress.

Suggested Activities

1. Recall some purchase, other than clothing, in which the design evaluation was an important part of the decision to buy the item.
2. Study your reflection in a mirror; apply each of the principles of design to the clothing you are wearing. Repeat this with several kinds of outfits.
3. Study the clothing of your classmates. Apply the principles of design to the clothing they have selected.
4. Collect pictures of a variety of clothing styles. Determine how the principles of design have been used in each garment design. Evaluate the individual designs to determine why you like, or dislike, them.
5. For class discussion, ask students to create a "total look" for assigned occasions. Evaluate the outfits, using the principles of design.

10 *Line*

The design elements of form-shape-space and line should be studied together because they must function interdependently. In order to understand this relationship, begin with a definition of terminology:

Form is a three-dimensional object. The human body is an example of form. The body can be viewed from different directions (front, back, or either side), and thus the contours of the form are revealed.

Shape refers to the outside dimensions of contour of an object. When the silhouette of the body is observed, the shape of the body is seen. Shape encloses space.

Space is the background area found within the shape. Space divisions are an important part of design. If the space is too crowded, the eye is distracted or fatigued. The human eye seems to need uncluttered space for visual relief.

Line indicates the dimensions of length and width. The edges of a line define and create shape. Lines combine to enclose spaces. Lines create shape and form. Lines imply direction.

Because of the integral relationship of form-shape-space and line, the discussion of any one of these elements involves the others. Understanding the role of form-shape-space and developing the skill to analyze line direction help one learn to predict the effect or impact of each design. These design elements combine with color and texture to produce all designs. They are important in all areas of creativity including clothing selection and personal appearance.

To better understand the definitions of form-shape-space and line, apply the above definitions to the book you are holding. The form of the book is three-dimensional, it has length, width, and depth. The shape of the book is defined by the outside dimensions. It is a rectangle. This is also the silhouette of the book. Look at the front cover of the book. The space is the background area found within the shape or silhouette of the book. This area is divided by the printing and illustrations. This division of space is extremely important to the visual effect created by the dimensions of the book. Line has the dimension of length and width. Lines create the shape and form of the book. The lines that divide the space of the cover of the book lead the eye as it looks at the book.

Practice applying the definitions of form-shape-space and line to any object you see. Every design contains these elements. Now apply the same elements of design to clothing both on and off the body. Remember that form-shape-space

317

10-1 Form-shape-space-line are important considerations in clothing selection. Form is revealed by the three-dimensional body contours. These body contours give the garment shape and create the silhouette. The space of the garment is the background area within the shape or silhouette. The division of this space determines the effect of the garment on the body. Lines are used to create form and shape and to divide the space within the shape of the garment. (Courtesy Traci Scherek for Traci Ltd., St. Paul, Minnesota)

and line are interrelated. They are present in every design. They work together with color and texture to create the visual impact of a design.

When applied to clothing selection the importance of form-shape-space and line becomes obvious. The three-dimensional form of the body within the garment creates contours. These body contours give the garment shape. The silhouette or outside dimensions of the garment may be body-concealing or body-revealing dependent on the design details of the garment, but the illusion of the shape of the garment is always dependent upon the form of the body within the garment. The space of the garment is the background area found within the shape or silhouette. It is the division of this space with construction details, decoration, texture, color and/or fabric design that is critical to the style of the garment. Lines are used to create the form and the shape of the garment and to divide the space within the shape of the garment. Lines lead the eye in a definite direction (Figure 10-1).

When selecting clothing it is customary to try the garments on. Generally they are accepted or rejected quickly. This first appraisal of the garment on the body is very often a mental computerization of form-shape-space and line along with color and texture. These elements are all responsible for determining how the garment looks on the body. The home sewer must develop the skill to visualize the dimensions of form-shape-space and line on the body to avoid disappointments in the finished garments.

Shape—The Silhouette in Clothing

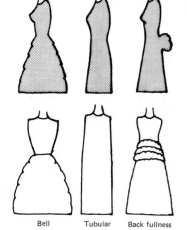

The shape of the body plus the lines of a garment create an overall form that defines the silhouette of the garment. Often the silhouette gives the first impression because it is seen from a distance and because it is contrasted to a background. The silhouetted form of the clothed body reveals the shapes of various parts of the body and the garment, such as sleeve, shirt, or pant.

Designers throughout the history of costume have developed only three basic dress silhouettes. They are the straight or tubular, the bell or bouffant, and the back-fullness or bustle. A study will reveal that each of the basic silhouettes has been used repeatedly with an interesting range of variations (Figure 10-2). The tubular silhouette has dominated fashion since 1900. The bell silhouette, probably because it reveals feminine curves, comes and goes in fashion but remains popular in classics such as the shirtmaker dress or blouse and gathered skirt combination. The bustle or back-fullness silhouette has more limited appeal but is found frequently in traditional wedding gown styles (Figure 10-3).

Bell   Tubular   Back fullness
or bustle

10-2 *Throughout history there have been only three basic silhouettes: the bell, the tubular, and the back fullness, or bustle. They recur, but not in predictable cycles. The bell and tubular silhouettes, because they follow the contour of the body, are more predominant in fashion.*

1895   1910   1924   1938

1942   1947   1954   1962

1970   1975   1980   1985

10-3 *Styles of the past century illustrate the repeated use of the three basic silhouette shapes. Fashions change gradually in one direction until the extreme has been achieved, then fashion takes a new emphasis. This is illustrated by both silhouettes and hem lengths of the past century.*

10-4 *There are only two kinds of lines—straight and curved. Lines create visual impressions and illusions. The effects that lines produce are related to many other factors. Study the lines in this picture carefully. How many kinds of lines can you find? How many different effects of line are represented? (Courtesy Catalina)*

Lines

Lines create visual impressions. Lines can be used in a garment to make you look taller, shorter, heavier, or thinner. Lines, and the optical effect that they create, can make hips look small or large, shoulders look broad or narrow, and waists look thick or thin. The effects that lines produce are related to other factors, such as:

the shape of the body wearing the design
the color of the fabric
the degree of contrast that enables the lines to be noticed
the comparison of adjacent shapes or spaces formed by lines
the fabric drape, hand, weave, print, texture
the effect that the viewer has been preconditioned to expect

There are only *two kinds of lines*—straight lines and curved lines. Straight lines can take three directions—vertical, horizontal, or diagonal. A curved line may be extreme, approaching a full circle, or it may be very gentle or subtle, almost straight (Figure 10-4).

Straight Lines

Straight lines are in opposition to the natural curve of the body. The use of straight lines in clothing design is very often softened by the texture of the fabrics selected. For example, when a soft fabric such as a matte jersey is used, the straight lines drape on the body curves; stiff fabrics such as organdy or taffeta maintain the straight line because they stand away from the body (Figure 10-5).

Straight lines in clothing are achieved from:

fabric design, weaves or prints (stripes, plaids)
structural lines or cut and seaming
structural design forming pleats, tucks, gathers, or creases
trims such as rows of buttons, braids, laces, or embroidery

Each direction of a straight line (vertical, horizontal, diagonal) creates an optical effect or illusion that must be judged on the individual to learn exactly the effect in a particular garment design. Important to note, visual illusions are not experienced by all people to the same degree, and some people may not perceive them at all. Perception of illusion varies among individuals because of experience, association, imagination, attitude, cultural differences, and eyesight.

10-5 *The use of straight lines in clothing design is very often affected by the texture of the fabrics selected. When soft fabric is used, the straight lines drape on the body curves creating a rounded effect. When stiff fabrics are used the straight line is maintained.* (Left: *courtesy Maria Rodriquez Designs.* Right: *Photo courtesy of the Butterick Fashion Marketing Company)*

What we have been conditioned to expect plays an important part in how we perceive. Illusions are errors of the visual sense, the intellect, or judgment. Lines, forms, shapes, spaces, colors, and textures may form illusions that will distract the eye or make accurate judgments impossible. We can use illusions to produce certain effects, but we cannot be certain that the effect will be recognized in the same manner by everyone.

Vertical Lines

Vertical lines *generally* add height or length to the body and make it appear more narrow. This is the favored line direction for those who wish to appear taller and more slender. Vertical lines are found in the following examples:

fabric design with vertical movement
construction lines
tall hats
long, narrow neckties
pointed collars
stovepipe pants
vertical placement of trims and buttons
vertical slash pockets
vests
jumpers
sleeveless garments
classic pump shoe
single column of color, including garments, hose, and shoes
accordion-pleated skirts, also knife pleats
dress shirts
hairstyles

Vertical lines *usually* lead the eye up and down the body. When a vertical line is emphasized in garment design, the eye of the observer measures the length of that area (Figure 10-6). Noticeable vertical lines that divide skirt/pant and bodice/shirt areas can reduce the apparent visual width of these spaces. To illustrate, a plain skirt, undivided by visible vertical seaming, usually appears broader than a skirt having one or more vertical seams in the front and back sections. The angle and spacing of two or more visible vertical seams in the same garment will vary the effect of slimness and length.

A most important fact to consider about *vertical lines* that are repeated in quantity (such as in a striped-print pattern) is that they *can add width*. The visual effect of the vertical line is dependent on the spacing and the background color contrast (Figure 10-7).

Closely spaced, parallel, vertical lines may lead the eye in an upward direction, but as the space between the lines is increased, the eye may begin to measure width. This widening effect may also occur if there is variation in the distance between the two lines. As noted previously, to judge the effect of vertical lines,

10-6 *Vertical lines usually lead the eye up and down the body. When a vertical line is emphasized in garment design, as in this center front button placket, the eye of the observer measures the length of that area. (Courtesy Simplicity Pattern Company)*

10-7 *Noticeable vertical lines such as this skirt button closure divide the areas and reduce the apparent visual width of these spaces. The vertical lines in this jacket are spaced so that the eye is led across the body thus adding width to the shoulder area. (Courtesy Pyke Manufacturing Company)*

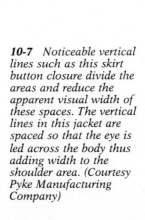

it is best to study the garment on the body (Figure 10-8). Double-breasted garments almost always add width because of the space between the vertical lines, in addition to the bulk of the double layers of fabric (Figure 10-9).

Horizontal Lines

Horizontal lines *generally* add width or breadth and shorten the body. Horizontal lines are used often in clothing (Figure 10-10). The following are areas in which these lines appear:

fabric fullness
fabric designs with horizontal movement
construction lines
hats that are flat and/or wide-brimmed
necklines including bateau, turtle, square
contrasting collars and cuffs
chokers

10-8 *To judge the effect of line, it is necessary to study the garments on the body. Here the vertical line movement of the garment design is reinforced by the fabric design vertical line in both pants and jacket. (Courtesy Ermenegildo Zegna Corporation)*

bow ties
some sleeve shapes (puffed, bell)
trims
pocket flaps
patch pockets
double-breasted garments
midriff (especially bare)
hems wherever they occur (sleeve, jacket, skirt, pant, and so on)
contrasting belts
wide belts
large shoulder-strap bags
shoes, especially those with straps, including sandals
color-contrasting stockings (create a horizontal band of leg color between garment hem and shoe)
hairstyles

Horizontal lines *usually* carry the eye across the body (Figure 10-11). When a horizontal line is emphasized in a garment, the eye of the beholder measures the width of that area. For example, widths of waists are measured by belts; widths of hips are measured by hemlines of jackets or sweaters; widths of legs may be measured at the level of the pant hem; apparent widths of bust/chest may be

10-9   Double- and single breasted garments create different effects on the body in both men's and women's wear. Double-breasted garments almost always add width because of the space between the vertical lines, in addition to the bulk of the double layers of fabric. (Courtesy Hartmarx Corporation)

10-10   Horizontal lines generally add width or breadth and shorten the body. Bow ties create a strong horizontal at the neckline which underscores the width of jawline. (Courtesy the Joseph & Feiss Company)

10-11 *How does your eye read this group of horizontal stripes?*

10-12 *Ankle-strap shoes create horizontal lines that measure the width of the leg and shorten the length of the leg. This is especially true when the shoe color is a strong value contrast to the stocking color. (Courtesy Cotton Incorporated)*

increased if the hemline of the sleeve ends at the fullest part of the bosom or chest (Figure 10-12).

Just as repeated vertical lines may sometimes add width, some horizontal line spacing can produce the *illusion of length*. This is because horizontal lines spaced closely together can create an illusion that leads the eye of the observer in an upward direction (Figure 10-13).

Diagonal Lines

Diagonal lines assume the characteristic of the vertical or horizontal line as the degree of slant approaches each extreme. The degree of slant determines the illusion created (Figure 10-14). The diagonal line approaching a horizontal is

10-13 *Plaids must be studied from a distance to determine which line direction will be emphasized. Study the figure on the left and decide which direction you read this plaid. Some horizontal lines that are spaced closely together create the illusion of length. This appears to happen on the shirt,* right, *until the horizontal lines grow farther apart. Then the spacing between the horizontal lines adds width and makes the shoulder area appear wider and emphasizes that area. This would be a good shirt to wear to balance narrow shoulders and wide hips. (Courtesy Jantzen)*

10-14 *Diagonal lines assume the characteristic of the vertical or horizontal line as the degree of slant approaches each extreme. Study these two bathing suits and determine the difference in the illusion created by the design of the diagonal lines. (Courtesy Catalina)*

10-15 *The same skirt silhouettes with different space division create varying visual effects on the body.*

found in the wide, bouffant skirt. This diagonal line assumes the characteristics of the horizontal line. The very subtle slant of the diagonal found in the A-line skirt or flared pants approaches the vertical line. This diagonal line assumes the characteristics of a vertical line. The diagonal lines of an A-line skirt will help to subordinate hip width. This silhouette brings the greatest width at the skirt hem area, thus making the hip width appear narrower by comparison to the hem width (Figure 10-15).

The use of diagonal lines in clothing design is often very pleasing. It is one of the best lines to incorporate when trying to camouflage poorly proportioned parts of the body. Diagonal construction lines generally result in informal balance.

A zigzag line is a series of connected diagonal lines (Figure 10-16). A zigzag line forces the eye to shift direction abruptly and repeatedly in an erratic and jerky movement. This type of line is found most often in fabric design. Because of the eye activity caused by zigzag lines, they tend to increase the apparent mass or size of the area covered by them.

Curved Lines

Curved lines *generally* follow the contour of the body and are flattering. When the curved line becomes exaggerated toward a full circle, it becomes very active and may easily be overdone in a design. A restrained curve is graceful, flowing, and gentle. A gradual transition in the change of direction of a curved line adds a pleasing quality to the design. Just as straight lines can conform to the body contour through fabric textures, so do curved lines. The effect of curved lines is emphasized if the body conformation is extremely curvy (Figure 10-17).

10-16   Zigzag lines are a series of connected diagonal lines. A zigzag line forces the eye to shift direction abruptly and repeatedly in an erratic and jerky movement. Because of the eye activity caused by zigzag lines, they tend to increase the apparent mass or size of the area covered by them.

Curved lines are found in the following areas:

fabric designs	yokes
construction designs	lapels
necklines	hems
collars	trims
sleeves	scallop detail
pockets and pocket flaps	body shirts
hats	
hairstyles	

10-17 *Curved lines generally follow body contours and are becoming to them. Curved lines may add fullness to the body. (Right: Courtesy Catalina; Left: Courtesy Folkwear, Inc.)*

10-18 *Internal lines in a garment are emphasized by trim in a contrasting color. (Courtesy Folkwear, Inc.)*

Emphasis of Line

In using line concepts, one needs to understand how they are affected by the principle of emphasis. Lines are emphasized by both repetition and contrast. Internal lines in a garment are emphasized by trim or piping in a contrasting color (Figure 10-18).

When applied to clothing selection, emphasis of line works in the following manner:

Line emphasis through repetition examples:

A very tall, slender body is emphasized when the garment design features vertical lines that lead the eye of the observer up or down the body.

331

A square jawline is emphasized with a square neckline.

A full hip-thigh region is emphasized by repetition when the pant leg width is the same as the horizontal shape created by the hip-thigh area.

Line emphasis through contrast examples:

A short, chubby body is emphasized when the garment fabric design features broad vertical lines that are spaced so the eye of the observer is led across the body.

A square face shape is emphasized by a round hair or hat style.

A small cinched-in waistline may emphasize the size of a large hipline.

Clarity of Line

The outline or silhouette of a garment and the body within it is more evident when there is contrast with the background. Not all internal structural lines are noticeable in a garment design because of a lack of contrast to emphasize them. Some garments do not show a definite line direction. The internal lines may not be noticeable in garments made of printed fabrics, especially dark prints, or those having a great deal of color contrast. In some garment construction, dark or napped fabrics may conceal structural lines. Internal lines usually become less noticeable as the distance from which they are viewed increases.

10-19 *The garment lines are made more noticeable by construction details such as top-stitching. (Courtesy J. C. Penney Co.)*

Garment lines are made more noticeable by construction details such as (Figure 10-19):

panels of contrasting color, fabric, or texture
welt seams
lapped seams
top stitching
piping
trimming

When line direction is emphasized, the principle of balance becomes an important factor to consider. The feeling of equilibrium and stability must be achieved if harmony of design is to result.

Suggested Activities

1. Select a garment illustrated on full-length body. Using a ruler and a red-inked felt pen, draw over all the vertical lines in the garment design to make them more obvious. Change ink color and repeat each for the horizontal lines, diagonal lines, and curved lines. Determine the effect on the body of the various lines.
2. Study the line direction of clothing of class members and of yourself as reflected in a mirror. Try to determine the line directions that best create the desired body illusions of classmates and yourself.
3. Try to become more aware of the importance of form-space-shape and line as you move about in your daily life. Try to see these design elements everywhere. Try to determine how your eye reacts to them. Try to determine if any moods or feelings are created for you by these elements of design.

11 *Color*

Color has been an important part of the human experience for as long as the *Homo sapiens* has been known to exist. It is a vital part of our lives today. Try to imagine a world without color. Mentally attempt to remove color from the landscape, from exterior and interior design, from food, from clothes, and from people. If everything we see and know were suddenly to lose its color, our patterns of living would be greatly altered. Most of us would experience extreme mental depression. Color is that important.

A complete understanding of color in all of its dimensions is not, at this time, a part of our knowledge. There is much to be learned, and research in color is continually being conducted. Because of the fascination that it holds, a great deal is known about color, far more than could possibly be covered in a text such as this. Therefore, it should be understood that the purpose of this chapter is to explore the use of color in its relationship to clothing selection and personal adornment. Students wishing to expand their study of color are referred to other sources.

Color and Fashion

Color is a part of the fashion mystique. Just as there are fashionable garments, accessories, hairstyles, and facial adornment, there are fashionable colors. A particular color may be high fashion one season and passé the next. Because color is one of the least expensive factors to change in the production of clothing, the garment industry frequently changes color before changing style. Each fashion season presents a variety of "new" colors that differ from those of the past season. Fashion colors are rarely pure spectrum hues but variations of them. One of the ways "new" colors differ from "old" colors is in name. What's in a name you might ask? A lot as far as fashion colors are concerned. The wrong name can spell disaster for a product. Recently a paint company saw its classic paint color named "Ivory" sink to the bottom in sales. A name change to "Oriental Silk" brought sales zooming to peak profits.[1] Another paint company took note of this and renamed its entire stock of hundreds of paints. This task enlisted the imag-

[1] Donald Pavey, *Color* (London: Marshall Editions, 1980, distributed by Viking, New York), p. 134.

334

ination of the entire staff from president to stockboys and girls who came up with names like "Charade Pink," "Corsair Blue," "Sicilian Olive," and "Cochise Tan." These name changes updated the product and gave the company a competitive edge.[2]

Fashion Color Prediction

There are several groups worldwide whose purpose is to forecast the colors that will be used in business and industry in the future. These include The Colour Group (Great Britain), Canadian Society for Color, the Color Science Association of Japan, and The Color Association of the United States (CAUS).

CAUS was founded in 1914, and is the oldest group in America. Working with an 18- to 24-month lead time, it currently issues five forecast cards annually to over 700 subscribers. Forecast cards for women's and men's apparel are issued twice a year. One forecast card for environments is issued every year.

The CAUS colors are selected by three professional committees, one for women's wear, one for men's wear, and one for environmental colors. Each panel is made up of eight members who contribute their time and expertise as an industry service. All work with color in some aspect of the American fashion, textile, and design industries. Members of the panels, all three of which meet separately for working sessions, come to the CAUS office with their ideas and their individual color selections. These are bantered about until each committee reaches a consensus. The Association then authorizes and supervises the dyeing of the forecast shades and subsequently publishes the three separate forecast cards. Forecasts are printed and swatched to serve as working tools for stylists and designers.[3]

The strength of the CAUS forecasts has always rested with the color sensitivity of the members of its forecasting panels. The color sages note that the color climate is very nebulous . . . it is a feeling about color that is in the air. Current color authorities get cues from various influences, including the hues, values, and chroma/intensities that have been popular, political and societal situations, museum and art exhibits, celebrities and public personalities.[4]

From the thousands of color choices available, a limited palette is selected to be used for items to be sold at a particular time. Mass production of a limited range of colors keeps costs down. Many fabricators build their range of colors around a group of steady-selling colors plus a limited group of fashion colors. This explains why you can choose from about twenty shades each season and not be able to match a fashion color exactly the next year. Lower-priced items

[2] Rodney Jones, Vice President, Ameritone Paint Company, personal anecdote.
[3] Margaret Walch, "Forecasted Shades for 1984/85 Reflects A Merging of Taste in Interior Design and Fashion Apparel," *The Designer*, Fall 1982, p. 52.
[4] "The Bluing of America," *Time Magazine*, July 18, 1983, p. 62.

such as apparel follow color fashions quickly. Larger-ticket items such as home furnishings and cars have a slower color fashion change.

What Is Color?

In 1666, Sir Isaac Newton conducted the first recorded experiments on light. By passing light through a prism that refracts or bends the light rays into a spectrum of colors, he illustrated that color is contained in light, and that color does not exist in the absence of light. Light is a part of the electromagnetic field that is visible. In the nonvisible area are x-ray, radar, radio waves, and others. Within the visible area, variations in wave lengths enable us to see different colors.

In his work, Newton counted seven hues in the spectrum—red, orange, yellow, green, blue, indigo, and violet. Newton's work is revealed to us when we see a rainbow. The rainbow is a breakdown of light into hues that have the same fixed arrangement. This order always remains the same because each hue has a different wavelength (or rate of energy radiating from the sun). The longest wavelength is red, followed by orange, yellow, green, blue, indigo, and violet (the shortest wavelength). We see this predictable arrangement again and again in the spray of a waterfall, a crystal chandelier, the sparkle of a diamond, even in a soap bubble.

How Do We See Color?

Physiologists are discovering the exact process by which color is seen by the human eye and translated to the human brain. This is an extremely complicated process. The color reflected from an object is determined by the composition of the object. Light striking an object may be reflected, absorbed, or transmitted. Object transparency or opacity will determine the pattern of the reflected light. Colors not reflected are absorbed by the object and are not visible. For example, a green fabric is green because its dye absorbs all colored rays of light except green, which it reflects. In this manner, all other colors are reflected. If all light is absorbed by the surface, the surface appears black. If all light is reflected, it appears white.

Color Systems

Many systems are used to organize color. These color systems are based upon the different interests of the people who work with color. The painter and the dyer are interested in the mixing of pigments or colorants. The physicist is interested in the aspects of light and measuring the wavelengths of the spectrum. The physiologist studies the eye-brain color effects and physiological responses. The psychologist examines the emotional responses to color.

The various systems have differences with respect to the following:

primary or principal colors or hues
color terminology
color complements and notations

The various systems have similarities with respect to the following:

All are based on the spectrum, a series of colors arranged in a fixed order.
All have color wheels that are formed by twisting a band of color representing
the spectrum into a circle.

The color systems frequently used are the Prang (sometimes referred to as Brewster) and the Munsell, which are capsulized here.

The Prang Color System

The Prang color system is based on the mixing of pigments (Figures 11-1 and Color Figure 1). It is the oldest, simplest theory and is most often used by students and artists for mixing paint colors. It is based on three primary hues placed equidistant on a color wheel. When two neighboring primary hues are combined, a secondary hue visually halfway between the two may be produced. The tertiary hues are formed when primary and neighboring secondary hues are combined:

3 Prang primary colors: red, yellow, blue
3 Prang secondary colors: orange, green, violet
   red + yellow =   orange
   yellow + blue =   green
    blue + red =   violet
6 Prang tertiary colors: red-orange, yellow-orange,
    yellow-green, blue-green,
    blue-violet, red-violet

11-1 *Prang Color System.*

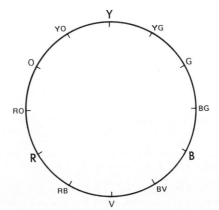

The Munsell System

The Munsell system is based on five basic hues that are placed equidistant around a color wheel. The basic hues are combined in equal amounts of the same visual intensity of two neighboring hues to produce the first intermediate hues. The second intermediate hues are formed by mixing the neighboring first intermediate hues.

5 Munsell principal hues: red, yellow, green, blue, purple
5 Munsell intermediate hues: yellow-red, green-yellow, blue-green, purple-blue, red-purple

Then ten hues are subdivided into ten equal steps for each hue, making a total of one-hundred Munsell hues, designated by hue number.

The Munsell color system uses a three-dimensional irregular sphere having as its vertical axis the scale of values. The value scale is in ten steps from white at the north pole to black at the south pole. The horizontal axis carries the chroma or saturation. The saturation is greatest at the outer end and decreases to neutral at the center. In the Munsell system, each value and chroma change has a numerical notation, thus making it valuable in exact duplication of color. Equal numerical differences are equal visual differences (Figures 11-2, 11-3, 11-4, and Color Figure 7).

11-2 Munsell Color System.

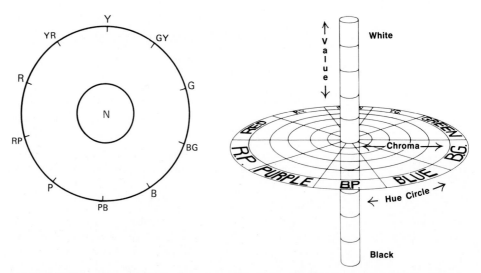

11-3 The dimensions of color—the color solid: every color has its own particular place in a three-dimensional solid. Think of our Earth as the solid, rotating on its axis. The North Pole is white, the South Pole is black, and the axis is the gray scale. Then take a rainbow of the most intense colors, join the two ends to form a circle, and place these around the Earth's equator. These are the hues. By adding white, black, or gray (black plus white) in varying amounts to any hue, you create the color family of that hue. A color containing equal visual amounts of pure color and white is located halfway between the equator and the North Pole on a line drawn between the pure hue and white.

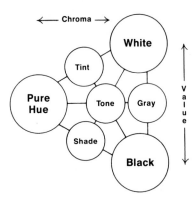

← Chroma →

White

Tint

Pure Hue

Tone   Gray

Shade

Black

V a l u e

11-4 *The hue family: to see all the colors in a hue family, slice the Earth in half from the North to the South Pole. You now see the entire gray scale, plus all the tints, tones, and shades of the two hues you cut through at the equator. Pure hue plus white makes tints. Pure hue plus black makes shades. Adding both white and black to a pure hue makes tones. Suppose one of the pure hues exposed is orange. A medium tint would be peach; a medium tone would be beige or buff; a medium shade would be brown. If the hue is red, a tint is pink, a tone is rose, and a shade is maroon. A group of colors selected exclusively from one hue family is known as monochromatic harmony.*

Dimensions of Color

To discuss color, a knowledge of color terminology is necessary. Describing color is very difficult because each color has so many variations. Each person sees color in an individual manner related to the acuity of the eye and to past experiences with color.

In fashion, descriptive terms are often used to denote a particular color. These terms may be understood only by association. It must be remembered that fashion merchants sell color. "Watermelon pink" sells better than a "hue of red, medium value, and bright intensity." However, the person who has never seen a slice of watermelon would be unable to understand the color described by this fashion terminology.

The terms *hue, value,* and *chroma* are used to describe the three dimensions of color. By using these terms, we can more effectively communicate the dimensions of color we see.

Hue

Hue is the name of a color family such as red, blue, or green. The term *hue* is often erroneously used interchangeably with the word *color.* Hue refers to only one dimension of color.

Warm and Cool Hues

Hue may be described as being warm or cool. Warm hues are those found in sun and fire; they are red, yellow, and orange. Cool hues are those found in water and sky; they are green, blue, and violet. Warm hues can have a cool cast and conversely cool hues can reflect warmth, for example, red purple will be cooler than red yellow.

The warmth or coolness of a hue carries with it an illusion of visual weight. The warm hues, yellow-orange-red, are known as *advancing* hues because they create an illusion of moving forward. Warm hues make objects, shapes, or areas appear larger, more important, and closer than other colors. Warm hues emphasize the body size and contours.

The cool hues of blue, blue-green, and violet are *receding* colors. Cool hues make objects, shapes, or areas appear smaller, less important, and farther away than other colors. Cool hues minimize the apparent body size and shape.

To illustrate this color phenomenon, two people of the exact same dimensions are dressed in exactly the same style garments except that one outfit is a warm red, the other a cool blue. When viewed from a distance, and in the same color environment, the person wearing the warm hue will appear to be closer and larger; the person wearing the cool hue will appear to be farther away and smaller.

Psychological Effects of Warm and Cool Hues

In a factory the temperature was maintained at 72°F. The walls were painted a cool blue-green. The employees complained of the cold. The temperature was maintained at the same level, but the walls were painted a warm coral. The employees stopped complaining about the temperature and reported they were quite comfortable.[5]

The psychological effects of warm and cool hues seem to be used effectively by the coaches of the Notre Dame football team. The locker rooms where half-time breaks are taken have reportedly been painted to take advantage of the emotional impact of certain hues. The home-team room was painted a bright red, which kept team members agitated or even angered. The visiting-team room was painted a tranquil blue-green, which had a calming effect on the team members. The success of this application of color can be noted in the records set by Notre Dame football teams.

Color Psychology and the Marketplace

Color psychology is applied to the selling of products in the marketplace. The wrong choice of color in packaging can spell financial disaster for products that must sell themselves on the shelf at the supermarket. The customer is faced with hundreds of similar products from which to choose. It is estimated that the customer's gaze rests on each package on the supermarket shelf a scant .03 seconds. In that instant the package must attract attention, convey the contents, and plant the desire to have it. For example, a synthetic cleaning cloth was packaged in blue and white; after the colors were changed to a deep blue and red and yellow, the sales were boosted 30 percent.[6] Detergent boxes tend to have pure white backgrounds or designs in bold primary colors to lend the image of strength and cleanliness. Low-tar and low-nicotine brands of cigarettes use white background area with light-colored letters to convey purity. White cans of diet

---

[5] Ray Faulkner and Edwin Ziegfield, *Art Today* (New York: Holt, 1969), p. 320.
[6] Pavey, op. cit., p. 170.

cola convey the image of low calories. Vacuum cleaners for the home are often light-colored, giving the idea to women that they are lightweight and easily handled, whereas a similar model intended for a man for his shop is a bold color, indicating heavy-duty.[7]

Although these are interesting examples of color response, a more scientific study of the emotional effects of color was tested by Felix Deutsch, a physician. He found that color does bring about a reflex action upon the vascular system, if only through the feelings and emotions. This effect is not achieved by any specific hues, either warm or cool. Cool hues may stimulate some people and calm others. Deutsch explained that emotional changes are brought about by association. Green may remind one of mountains and nature; red may recall fire, warmth, the sun. These associations lead to memories that explain our psychological responses toward color.[8]

Carolyn Bloomer, author of *Principles of Visual Perception*, concurs that our response to color is an individual one:

> While some colors appear to affect people in general psychological ways, other human responses to color are arbitrary, personal or socially influenced. Cultural tradition determines the symbolic meanings of colors. In our culture, for example, white represents purity, but for the Chinese it is the color of death. Clergy of the Judeo-Christian tradition wear black, but the Buddhist monks wear saffron orange.[9]

Value

Value describes the lightness or darkness of a color. As an example, when white is added to the hue red, a white-red or pink results. This new color is described as having a *higher value*, that is, it is *lighter* than the original hue. When white is added to a color, the result is called a *tint* of the original hue. When black is added to red, a black-red results. This new color is described as having a *lower value*, that is, it is *darker* than the original hue. Black added to a hue creates a *shade* of the original hue. There are limitless possibilities for degrees of color values. For example:

original hue		tint	shade
green ___ plus white ___		lime	
green ___ plus black ___			olive
orange ___ plus white ___		peach	
orange ___ plus black ___			rust
red ___ plus white ___		pink	
red ___ plus black ___			maroon

[7] *Time Magazine*, July 18, 1983, p. 62.
[8] Faber Birren, *Color and Human Response* (New York: Van Nostrand Reinhold, 1978), p. 47.
[9] Carolyn Bloomer, *Principles of Visual Perception* (New York: Van Nostrand Reinhold, 1976), p. 119.

Value and Clothing Selection

The application of value in clothing selection is most important. Exciting and dramatic effects and clever body camouflaging can be created by the use of value in clothing selection.

Value Related to Body Size and Conformation

The extremes of value, very light or very dark, will usually emphasize the body appearance. The middle or grayed values will camouflage the body conformation. Light or very high values reflect the light, which makes the object, shapes, or areas appear larger and stand out. Very dark or very low values will outline or silhouette the object, shapes, or areas and make the body contours stand out. Middle or grayed values are not eye-arresting; they do not make the object, shapes, or areas important or well defined but tend to blend them into the background. The strength of the effect of hue value depends on the amount of contrast it has to the background against which it is viewed. For illustration, consider a skier dressed in white ski togs with a snowy white background. There would be very little value contrast between the skier and the snow, so the skier would tend to blend into the background. However, if the skier were dressed in black, or a value close to black, the skier would contrast sharply to the white background. Most of the environment in which we live and work consists of middle values. Therefore, when we wear grayed or middle-value clothing, we tend to blend into the background. White is the lightest value; black is the darkest value. White and black garments are generally strong contrasts to their background, especially during daylight hours. Because night lighting is low in value when compared to daylight, darker-value clothing worn in the evening usually blends into the background. The effect of the value of the color against a background is important for those who do not wish to reveal their body conformation (Figure 11-5).

The Attention Power of Value Contrast—Emphasis

The placement of value contrast on the body is of importance because the eye of the observer will be attracted to this area of sharp contrast. Wherever the value contrast is placed on the body, the area will be emphasized. It follows that if you do not wish to emphasize a part of the body, you should avoid placing value contrast there. As an example of this, imagine an outfit of dark pants and pastel cardigan sweater. The length of the sweater will determine the line of value contrast. If the hemline of the sweater falls at the largest part of the hipline, this will be the point of emphasis. So dramatic is this effect that it is almost like placing a sign at the hipline saying, "Here, world, look at this!" Value contrast at the hipline would be avoided if the pants and sweater were of the same color or of different, yet close-in-value, hues. Value contrasts that emphasize are found in many clothing designs, including:

contrasting belts
contrasting buttons and trims
contrasting shoes/stockings

garments constructed of contrasting fabrics in areas such as yoke, sleeve, bodice/shirt, skirt/pant

11-5 *The extremes of value, very light and very dark, will usually emphasize the body size. The middle or grayed values will camouflage the body conformation. Avoiding color breaks by keeping various garments comprising an outfit in the same color family and close in value will make a petite figure seem taller. This same color technique will also camouflage body irregularities such as wide waist or hipline. (Courtesy Susie's Casuals)*

White or very light-colored shoes are in direct contrast to dark, suntanned legs or dark stockings; this emphasizes the size of the feet because of the value contrast. This also happens when the light shoe is contrasted against the dark surfaces on which we often walk. Because of the advancing quality of light values, white, light or shiny hose also seem to increase the size of the leg and feet.

Value and Skin Coloring

Value contrasts may be used to enhance personal coloring. The value of hues used in clothing has an effect on the coloring of the skin, especially on the face. Dark values generally drain color from the skin. Pale or very fair-complexioned people will find that dark values may make them appear more colorless. Those with a great deal of color in their skin may find that dark values help to tone down their complexions. Light values generally lend color to the skin and are a good choice for those who desire a richer complexion appearance, but they should be avoided by those who desire to tone down their coloring. The opposite effect is sometimes utilized. Those with very light personal coloring, including hair,

343

eyebrows, and skin, may like the effect created by contrasting their paleness with strong, dark-value-colored garments. Those with dark personal coloring may be pleased with the effect of wearing light-value-hued clothing.

Certain cosmetics are applied to vary the value of tones found in the skin as discussed in detail in Chapter 14, Facial Design. Eye shadows are used to darken the eye area. Eyebrow pencils darken brows. Corrective cosmetic work is done with light or white pencils or creams. The principle of dark value to make an area appear to recede and light value to make an area appear to advance is incorporated over and over again in facial makeup.

Chroma or Intensity[10]

Chroma is the term used to describe the purity of a color. Chroma is expressed as the strength or weakness, the brightness or dullness, or the degree of saturation of a color. High-chroma colors are pure, strong, brilliant, saturated colors. Low-chroma colors are weak, grayed, and dull.

On the color wheel each hue is usually shown at its fullest chroma, which means the yellow you see on the color wheel is yellow at its greatest saturation, its greatest brightness, its most brilliant, its fullest intensity. The same is true for each hue on the wheel.

The Interrelationship of Value and Chroma

Each color can be described in terms of hue, value, and chroma. A tint of a saturated, high-chroma red such as pink is light in value yet may be as high in chroma (intensity) as a shade of red that is darker in value, such as "dusty rose." Many dark colors are both low in value and low in intensity. Maroon is a shade of red and is low in intensity. Browns are usually low-value and low-intensity yellow-red. Tans are actually high-value, low-intensity yellow-red. When both white and black (gray) are added to a hue, the result is a change in chroma. For example, green plus white and black produces chartreuse; orange plus black and white produces buff. When describing color technically, all three dimensions of hue, value, and chroma are required.

Color Chroma and Clothing Selection

Color chroma is an effective tool for creating both camouflage and flair in the wardrobe. Clever use of chroma can extend the basic wardrobe by creating a wide range of accessory effects with the same basic clothes. Because of the eye-holding power of chroma, often the accent will be remembered, but the background garment will go unnoticed. Small amounts of high-chroma color can be used to direct and hold the eye of the observer to any area of the body that is to be emphasized. Thus, the use of chroma is an important technique in creating illusions with clothing.

[10]*Chroma and intensity* are often interchangeable. Because chroma is the more accurate term, it appears more frequently in color literature.

Color Chroma Related to Body Conformation

Bright, strong, high-chroma colors are conspicuous and make the body appear larger. Dull, weak, low-chroma colors are less conspicuous and make the body appear smaller.

The intensity of colors can be manipulated by placing them against various backgrounds. Colors appear more intense when placed against those less colorful or gray or black backgrounds. Thus, a red will appear redder, brighter, stronger, or more intense when placed against a dull color or white, gray, or black background. In clothing selection, remember the higher the chroma of the color, the more attention it attracts. High-chroma colors will emphasize the body conformation.

Colors can be made to appear less intense by placing them next to their neighbors on the color wheel (*analogous* colors). Thus, red will appear less red, duller, weaker, or lower in chroma when placed next to an analogous color such as orange or magenta. This effect can be observed in various fabric designs.

Colors will appear more intense when they are placed next to or near their opposites on the color wheel (*complementary* colors). Thus, red will appear redder when placed next to its complement, green.

Chroma Related to Personal Coloring

When the use of colors of high chroma is considered, the relation to personal coloring must be carefully analyzed. Hues that have a chroma greater than that of the hair color will rob the hair of some of its color. Most eye coloring, except brown and hazel, is intensified by a hue that matches it in chroma. Brown eyes benefit most from contrasting shades of high intensity. Hazel eyes are like chameleons and reflect the color of their environment in direct relation to its brilliance.

High-chroma colors bring out or force their complement. This means that a high-chroma green will force the red complement in any area of color close to it. This happens very often with skin coloring. A brilliant green dress can make a blushing or ruddy complexion look crimson. The complements of violet and yellow have the same effect. A violet garment may bring out the yellow in a sallow or olive complexion almost to the point of making it look jaundiced. This effect does not always have to be negative; a bright orange pin can intensify blue eyes, or a green gown can brighten rosy cheeks. Sometimes the chroma of a color is increased by combining it with a neutral such as black or white. A very intense color may have a more subtle effect if it is placed next to an analogous color. Bright orange appears less firey when placed next to yellow than it does next to its complement blue. These tricks of chroma of color should be evaluated whenever color and designs are selected.

Attraction Power of Chroma—Balance of Color

The classic rule of color balance, sometimes called *the law of color areas*, defines the ratio of high-chroma color to lower-chroma colors in an outfit. The law of color areas states that bright, saturated colors should be used in small areas and less intense color or neutrals should be used in larger areas.

Fashion sometimes ignores this dictum and features entire garments of very high chroma. However, the law or rule is a good one to consider carefully for several reasons, including these:

Entire garments of high-chroma color have such strong impact that the personality of the wearer can be overpowered.

The illusion of body conformation can be manipulated by following this guideline.

Small, high-chroma areas near the face attract and hold the eye of the observer there.

A small amount of high-chroma color, when selected to accent eyes, hair, or skin, has more impact than a larger area.

Nature's Guide for Using Color

People who are color shy and tend to limit their dress to neutrals can use nature as a guide for ideas for color harmony. Nature uses a broad color palette, filling the whole world with exotic colors and harmonies that could lead us to do more experimenting in the personal use of color. Consider the natural coloring of flowers, birds, and animals. Lovely blossoms are light and bright and usually contrast to dark foliage. A snow-capped mountain set against a deep blue sky framed by evergreens or a field of wild flowers forming a mosaic of color provides an excellent example for combining hues, values, and intensities. Certain birds and animals wear protective middle-value coloring that blends in with their environment and hides them from their predators, while other birds and animals have bright colors to attract attention. If putting colors together is difficult for you, try some of Mother Nature's color harmonies; they are free for observing and for using.

Color Harmonies

Color harmonies are recipes used to achieve pleasing combinations of hues. Preference for a particular color harmony depends on social and cultural factors that are learned. Personal likes and dislikes cause a variety of responses to different color harmonies. No hard and fast rules should govern the use of color harmonies, but traditionally organized patterns of color merit study, if only as a point of departure for personal improvisation. It must be kept in mind, however, that successful harmony depends on many factors, including the color pattern of the individual, the size of the area in which the color is used, its location, and the selection and combination of the value and chroma of the hue.

The traditional color harmonies are divided into related and contrasting groups. Related colors and related color harmonies are composed of groups of color having at least one hue in common. Yellow is related to orange and to green because it is common to the composition of these hues. Contrasting colors or color harmonies have no hue in common. Thus, red, blue, and yellow are contrasting hues.

Summary of Hue, Value, Chroma, for Clothing Camouflage

Problem	Hue	Value	Chroma
If you wish to increase body size choose	warm hues (reds, oranges, yellows)	light, high values, tints, strong value contrasts	pure, strong, brilliant, saturated, high-intensity colors
If you wish to decrease body size choose	cool hues (blues, blue-greens, blue-purples)	low, middle values, shades, weak or no value contrasts	weak, grayed, low-intensity colors

Note: Yellow-green to green is considered neutral.

Related Color Harmonies

Related color harmonies have one hue in common. They may be monochromatic or related.

Monochromatic Harmony: One hue is used in its various tints, tones, and shades for monochromatic harmony; for instance, light pink, rose, maroon, and watermelon. If value and chroma gradations are too close together, the effect may be unpleasing because of ambiguity of colors, giving the impression of mismatch. These schemes require noticeable differences to achieve the variations necessary to avoid a fatiguing and monotonous effect (Figure 11-6).

11-6 *Monochromatic Color Harmony.*

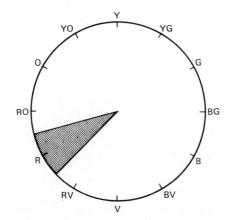

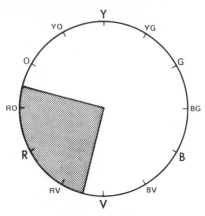

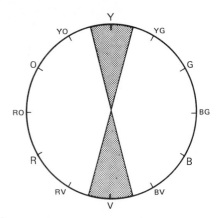

11-7 *Analogous Color Harmony.*   **11-8** *Complementary Color Harmony.*

Analogous Harmony: Colors appearing next to each other on the color wheel, such as yellow-orange, yellow, and yellow-green, make up an analogous harmony. When one of the hues is allowed to predominate and when values and chromas are varied, striking effects can be achieved. This harmony creates movement and excitement because of the vibrating effect of adjacent hues. A variation of this harmony that produces a dramatic effect combines three analogous hues with an accent of the complement of the middle hue. Thus, yellow-orange, yellow, and yellow-green would be used with violet to produce an analogous scheme with a complement (mutual complement). Up to five neighboring hues on a sixteen-to-eighteen-color wheel may be grouped for an analogous scheme (Figure 11-7).

Contrasting Color Harmonies

Contrasting color harmonies have no hue in common. Some contrasting color harmonies are complementary, split complement, triad.

Complementary Harmony: Any two hues opposite each other on the color wheel produce a complementary harmony. Blue and orange, red and green, yellow-orange and blue-violet are examples. Simple complementary schemes of two hues can be extended by using tints, tones, or shades of the selected hues (Figure 11-8).

When complementary hues are used in their full strength (high chroma) and in equal quantity, they intensify each other and produce sharp contrasts. This causes a vibration that is often painful to the eye. Red will seem redder when placed next to its complement green than when red is used with yellow. Green appears greener next to red than when used next to yellow. This phenomenon is called *simultaneous contrast*. The effect the vibrations cause by these complements can be lessened by using a smaller amount of intense color or by substituting a tone or shade of the desired hue.

Remember the effects of complements when worn next to the skin. A reddish skin will appear redder if green is worn next to it. If the skin is pink, green brings

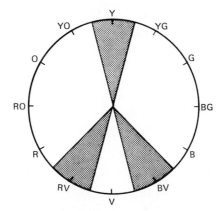

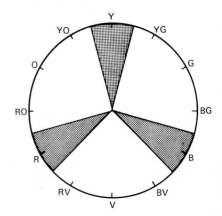

11-9 *Split Complement Harmony.*   **11-10** *Triad Harmony.*

out the pinkish hue. Blue-green will also bring out pink in the skin. If the skin has yellow tones that are not desired, avoid wearing violet, red-violet, or blue-violet.

Split Complement Harmony: The hue is used with the colors on each side of its complement. Thus, yellow would be joined with red-violet and blue-violet (Figure 11-9).

Triad Harmony: Three hues placed equidistant on the color wheel are used as yellow, red, and blue (Figure 11-10).

Influences on Color

A color is never seen alone. It is always seen next to another color. For this reason, it will always relate to another color. Two colors placed next to one another will interact with each other. For example, a medium blue will appear lighter against a darker background, darker against a lighter background, clearer against a grayer background, grayer against a clearer background, redder against a green background, and greener against a red background. Color under one set of conditions may appear very different under another set of conditions.

Light Source
A factor affecting color is the light source under which it is viewed. The type of light will affect the depth of the color. Incandescent light, fluorescent lights, sunlight, and candlelight all have different effects on color. Sometimes this effect can be predicted and sometimes it cannot. The best way to test color is to view it under the light source with which it will be used most often. Generally, bright

sunlight changes the intensity of a color. As the intensity of daylight changes from morning to night, the degree of the color alteration also changes. Artificial lights come in different color tones such as yellow, white, rose, and so on. Each of these lights has a different effect on color. The incandescent light bulbs commonly used in the home give warm-hued light. Fluorescent lights are available in both warm and cool hues. Generally, a warm-hued light source intensifies red, yellow, and orange, whereas it grays cool colors such as blue and violet. A cool-hued light source usually intensifies green, blue, and violet and grays red, yellow, and orange.

Distance

The distance from which a color is viewed can change its effect. Because of the amount of color used and the hue combination, proximity to the colors influences their appearance. In some allover designs of tweeds, tiny stripes, or checks, the mixture of colors blends together to form new combinations when viewed from a distance; the individual colors making up the design lose their original color identity. When this blending occurs, more accurate color matching of fabrics and accessories can be achieved by observing them from a distance rather than at close range.

Texture

Texture changes color. The same dyes used on different textures will produce a range of colors. Shiny fabrics such as satin reflect the light so that the colors become brighter or more intense. Dull textures, such as flannel, absorb the light and cause colors to become less intense. Shoes, stockings, garments, hats, and scarves are all made of materials of different textures; for this reason they can seldom be perfectly color matched. The textures involved reflect or absorb light differently, thus changing the value or chroma of the color.

Personal Color Pattern

When colors are selected for personal adornment, individual coloring should be a main consideration. Skin, hair, eye, and tooth coloring (in order of importance) should be evaluated carefully. Colors should be selected to enhance personal coloring. All colors worn should have the same undertones as are found in the individual coloring. Undesirable tones in the skin can be subdued by using analogous colors in the personality area. Desirable skin coloring can be enhanced by using complementary colors. The value and chromas of the colors worn should vary and be in pleasing harmony with the personal coloring.

Body Area and Shape

The size and shape of the individual should influence color choice. Warm hues, light values, and bright chromas create the illusion of increased body size. Cool colors, medium values, and low chromas help decrease the apparent body size. Low value and less intense colors in major areas of clothing with high-chroma colors as the accents in the personality area will focus the eye of the observer away from the body and thus create a camouflage.

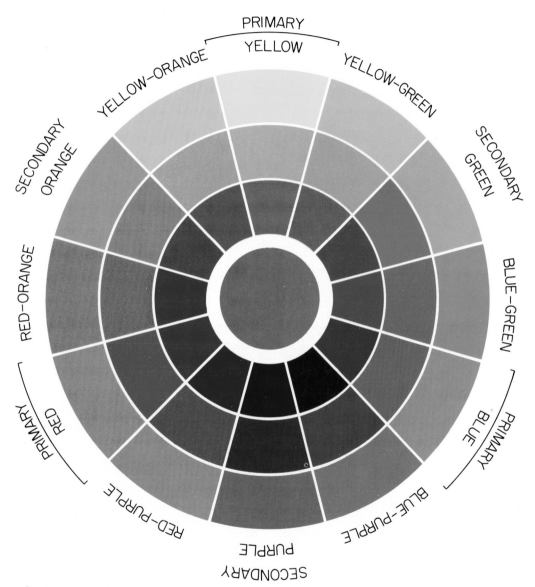

Color Figure 1 *The Prang color wheel consists of three groups of colors, primary, secondary, and intermediate. The primary colors—yellow, red, and blue—when paired, make the three secondaries— orange, green, and purple. The primary colors, paired with secondaries, yield six intermediate colors. (From* Introduction to Interior Design, *third edition by Frederick Stepat, Daniel DeVan, Darlene M. Kness, Laura Szekely, and Kathryn A. Camp Logan. Copyright © 1980 by Macmillan Publishing Company. Reprinted with permission of the publisher.)*

Key I Group

Key II Group

Color Figure 3 Magenta and orange are the color indicants of the Color Key Program. Magenta is kinder to Key I personal coloring because it has the same blue undertone. Orange is kinder to Key II personal coloring because it has the same yellow undertone. Caution: remember that individual color preferences have nothing to do with this test. You do not need to wear magenta or orange to use the Color Key Program. (Courtesy Cam Smith Solari, Photographer)

Color Figure 2 The Color Key Program is based on the mechanical separation of all colors of the spectrum into two groups labeled Key I and Key II. All colors in the Key I group have a blue undertone. All colors in the Key II group have a yellow undertone. These are the same undertones that are found in personal color patterns. (Courtesy Cam Smith Solari, Photographer)

Color Figure 4 *Examples of Key I personal coloring reveal blue (or rose) undertones to skin, hair, eye, and tooth coloring. The Color Key Program works for men and women of all races, all ages. (Courtesy Cam Smith Solari, Photographer)*

Color Figure 5 *Another way to test for your Color Key group is to study the colors you usually select. Most people will find the colors they like the best are those in their true Color Key grouping. (Courtesy Cam Smith Solari, Photographer)*

Color Figure 6 *Examples of Color Key II personal coloring reveal yellow (or peach) undertones to skin, hair, tooth, and eye coloring. Color Key remains the same as the hair greys, skin tans, and the body ages. (Courtesy Cam Smith Solari, Photographer)*

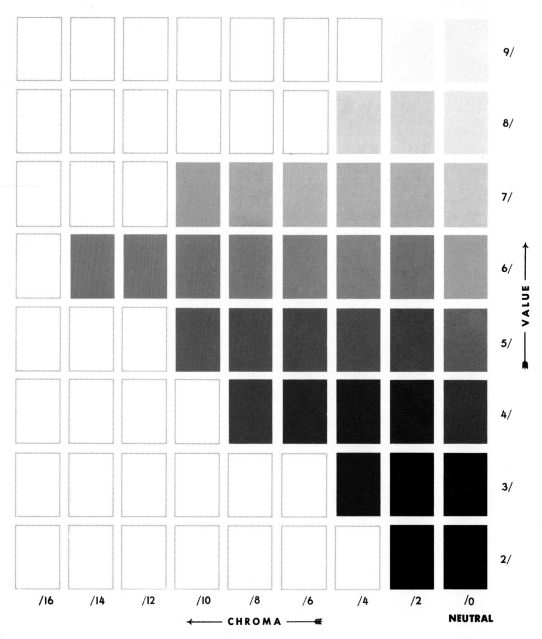

9.5/

9/

8/

7/

6/

5/

4/

3/

2/

VALUE

/16   /14   /12   /10   /8   /6   /4   /2   /0

← CHROMA →

NEUTRAL

Color Figure 7 *One page from the Munsell Color Co., Inc., color-order system. Variations in value (brightness) and chroma (saturation) are shown for a single hue. (Courtesy Munsell Color Co., Inc.)*

Age

As one ages, the skin and hair coloring becomes less intense. Harsh, bright colors and clear pastels are generally less attractive on the older person. Just as nature softens personal coloring by the aging process, so the mature individual should soften color choices. Vivid colors contrast with fading skin and hair coloring and thus emphasize age.

Personal Reactions

Recent research has delved into psychological reactions to color. Although there are still many questions to be answered in this area, it has been established that response to color is highly individual. One reacts to color in a certain manner because of personal color preferences and the experiences and associations he has had with that color. Each man, woman, and child has a degree of color sensitivity. Some people are more aware of color sensitivity and react more violently to it than others. People may actually become physically ill, excited, soothed, or depressed by exposure to certain colors. It is not completely understood why these intense emotional responses to color are evoked or why they vary so much with the individual. Attitudes toward color may be the result of some childhood experience (either pleasant or unpleasant), lack of experience or association with color, or a psychological phenomenon. Each individual has certain colors and combinations of colors that are more pleasing to him than others. For this reason any dogmatic approach to color for the individual is misleading. The individual needs to experiment with color in relation to both his physical and psychological self and discover color and color harmonies that are most pleasing to him.

Computerized Color

One of the dreams of the colorist is a giant step closer to reality with the development of a computer-based color control system. Since the development of modern dyeing techniques decades ago, the term *echo repeatability* has represented the optimum—the ability to reproduce colors exactly from batch to batch. Minute differences in dye batches have made realization of this ideal impractical until recently.

The Compucolor Color Control System now makes it possible for a textile manufacturer to find a dye formulation for any color sample he wishes to match. This computer allows the user to duplicate a color effect simply by placing a swatch of the fabric to be matched under the system's spectrophotometer and pressing a button. The computer then presents a complete analysis of the sample color. The manufacturer can echo-repeat the exact color, hue, and shade with the information supplied by the system.

With this computer breakthrough, matching color in the future may not be the problem that it has been in the past. However, so long as individuality is expressed in color selection, the complexity of color will continue to intrigue and amaze.[11]

[11] George Lorditch McBeth, "Color and Photometry," Division of Kollmorgen Corporation, Newburgh, N.Y.

Personal Color Selection

Many people are intimidated by color. They have not been exposed to working with color and therefore their ability to see color is limited. They have a belief that color is difficult to work with and that selecting and combining colors is beyond their talent. Once again astute business people have capitalized on this human foible to create a cottage industry that has an estimated income of $250 million a year. The *color consultant* is in the business reaping this profit.

"Having my colors done" has been a status symbol which could be considered both a fad and a fashion of the 1980s. A color consultant, for a fee ranging from $25.00 to $800.00, will make a color analysis of the individual and work out a pattern of colors that from that time forward are to be that individual's *colors*.[12]

In this information age, when people are in the habit of seeking instant answers, rather than taking the time to study and think out solutions, the color consultant joins the other "experts" such as the nutritionist, the financial planner, the exercise coach, and the interior designer. These outsiders are trusted to make decisions of a very personal nature which are based on both the psychological and physiological needs of the individual. If the training and the talent of the "expert" are valid, then the confidence is warranted, but this is not always the case.

Color Consultant is a title that requires no formal training. A color consultant can open a business without any qualification other than the desire to be in business. Training is available and some color consultants have invested up to $2500.00 and many hours under the tutorage of various private businesses turning out color consultants. Some public schools offering vocational training have very recently added a color consultant certificate to their curriculum.

Each color consultant uses one of a variety of systems to analyze the individual's personal color pattern, including skin, hair, eyes, and sometimes teeth, gums, and inside lining of lips. The personal color pattern is then related to a selected group of colors that may be identified by the seasons of the year, the time of day, the name of jewels, or personality type. Once the individual's color pattern has been related to the group of colors those become his/her *colors*. Often the client is given a pack of fabric swatches or paint chips to carry along to use as an aid in making future color decisions.

It is true that we do look better in some colors than others, depending on a lot of variables including time of day, light source, and our personal health. We learned in Chapter 8 that our skin color is based on three factors: the pigment melanin, which determines its darkness or lightness; the pigment carotene, which gives it peach or yellow undertones; and the translucence of the skin, which is related to the hemoglobin in the underlying blood vessels which produces a rose or blue cast. Personal color typing by all of the various systems is based on these factors. However, there is at this time no scientific method to determine how personal coloring consistently relates to one group of colors or another.

---

[12] Judith Rasband, *Color Crazed*, A Report to the Consumer, Provo, Utah, 1983.

The color consultant makes a personal judgment of how the individual's personal coloring relates to the various color groupings. Another color consultant may not make the same judgment. Both are being honest, but because we do not all see color the same way and because of a myriad of factors influencing color (discussed in this chapter), the judgments of color consultants can conflict. Some people fall into color classifications more easily than others because their personal color pattern is more obvious. Examples of this would be golden blonde hair with peach skin tones, yellow-gray eyes, and creamy-white teeth, or a person having jet black hair with rose-blue skin tones, red-brown eyes, and bright white teeth. The majority of people are much harder to classify because their personal coloring is much more subtle.

While color consultants and their systems may be helpful tools to selecting and combining colors, they do little in teaching people to be sensitive to color. They do not teach basic color principles. They do not take into consideration all physical requirements of color; for example, a color may be beautiful next to facial skin tones, but the body size and shape may make the color in that value and intensity unsuitable. They also ignore the psychological reaction of an individual to color; that is, a beautiful color may make the individual uncomfortable because of a past association.

Color should be fun. We should use any tools available to help us learn more about color and how to use color in our lives. The color consultant does offer an opinion and system of working with color, and this advice should be considered along with other color knowledge. If what the color consultant tells us makes us feel better about ourselves, gives us more color confidence, makes us feel more attractive, and gives us the ability to build our wardrobes with more of a personal signature, then the money spent on "having my colors done" was a good investment. Build on this color information, keep an open mind, and make color your own; use it as part of your individuality.

Personal Color Analysis Methods

Draping Fabrics

This method requires a very large number of fabric samples or drapes in many hues, values, and chroma/intensities. The collection should contain both standard or staple and fashion colors that have been identified by color name(s). Natural daylight (or daylight-type artificial light) will produce the most satisfactory results. The individual to be tested should be devoid of makeup; if hair has been highlighted or colored, it should be covered.

Method: Seat the person in front of a mirror and drape the colored fabrics individually over the shoulders. Determine which hues, values, and chroma/intensities are the most flattering to the person. Develop a list of these colors and if possible, provide the person with color swatches.

Caution! The effectiveness of this method relies upon the interest, experience, judgment, and the ability to perceive color or acuity of the eye of the person(s) doing the analysis. Circumstance such as different color surroundings, different times of day, and different judges may give different results.

Personal Color Aid

This method involves matching colored swatches of fabric, paint chips, or paper to the subject's skin, hair, and eye coloring to create a Personal Color Aid.

Method: Devise a paper mask with two ½-inch squares cut about ½-inch apart. Place one of the cut-out squares next to the forehead and match the skin color by placing a color swatch under the remaining square. When the correct match is found, affix the color match to masking tape trimmed to 1 inch. Repeat this step with the hair and eye. Glue the personal color matches to a 1 × 6 inch strip cut from a file card. The skin, hair, and eye colors are placed adjacent to each other with no card space exposed. The *personal color stick* is then compared to a specially prepared Munsell personal color chart, which contains many examples of skin, hair, eye color, and reds that have been separated into warm and cool groups. The individual selects from a range of harmonious reds that fall between personal skin, hair, and eye colors. Additional 1 × 6 inch file cards are prepared for skin, hair, and eye color and reds of the same hue but differing in value and intensities.

Color sticks can be included using hue families that are not found in the personal color pattern. The sticks are then punched at the end and held together with a brass paper tack, so that it can be fanned out. This color aid can be used when shopping by holding the aid next to the garment in question to determine whether it is in harmony with the personal color pattern. The Color Aid was developed by the Agricultural Extension Service at the University of California, Berkeley.[13]

The Color Key Program[14,15]

The Color Key Program is based on a mechanical way of selecting and identifying colors that complement an individual's natural coloring. All colors of the spectrum have been divided into two palettes labeled Key I colors and Key II colors. All colors in the Key I palette are technically perfect and visually pleasing for use in multiples with each other. The same holds true for the Key II colors. The reason for this is that the colors in each palette have a common color denominator, which is the same undertone found in personal color patterns.

---

[13] Further information can be obtained by writing: Consumer Color Charts 4018, Agricultural Sciences Publications, University of California, 6701 San Pablo Avenue, Oakland, Calif. 94608.
[14] The Color Key Program is used by permission of Color Key Corporation, P.O. Box 190, Long Beach, Calif. 90801. *Teaching aids including a slide/cassette lesson are available from this address.*
[15] The Color Key Program, Color Key, Key I Colors and Key II Colors are registered trademarks of Color Key Corporation, Member of Grow Group, Inc.

Study the two Color Key dictionaries (Color Figure 2). Note that each palette contains some reds, purples, blues, greens, and yellows. Can you see how the groups differ? Key I colors have a blue undertone, whereas Key II colors have a yellow undertone. This is even evident in the blacks, grays, and whites. In Chapter 8, in the discussion of pigmentation of skin and hair, it was noted that skin color was created by the pigment melanin and that undertones in skin coloring are the result of the presence of the yellow-orange pigment carotene, or the reddish-blue cast of the blood's hemoglobin. Hair coloring is created by concentrations of melanin and the gene-related red pigment. Hair coloring generally follows skin coloring, although the enzymes or genes responsible for hair coloring are different from those responsible for skin and eye color. The undertones found in the two color groups are the same undertones that are found in the personal coloring of each individual. When a person is correctly color coded, the colors in his own group are usually more satisfying and more becoming than those in the opposite group. The preferred color group represents color proportions that are related to the individual's own natural coloring.

Most people can select, or have identified for them, the correct color group based on their personal coloring, including skin, hair, eye, and tooth color. Past experiences with color, individual preferences, the acuity of the eye, and the strength of the undertones present in the personal color pattern all influence the individual's ability to select a preferred color group. For those who have trouble with the selection, there are several solutions. For many, the study and application of Color Key in their daily life will make the preference for one group or the other obvious. For a few, their personal color pattern may be a combination of yellow and blue undertones, or it may be of such value and chroma that differentiation is difficult. For this minority, either Key I Colors or Key II Colors may be selected.

When you choose the group of colors you prefer—Key I colors or Key II Colors—do not be influenced by a single color choice but select the entire palette. Remember that the choice of one group does not mean you dislike the other; it means that you prefer one group of colors over the other. You may find colors in your group that you dislike. However, do not let a color prejudice for or against one color confuse your choice of the entire Color Key palette (Color Figure 5).

Colors selected from the correct group will present you at your best because they have the same undertones as your personal coloring. Study the color groups carefully. Note that each group has both warm and cool tints, tones, and shades. In the Key I Color palette all colors are represented except orange. The hue families missing in the Key II Color palette are turquoise and magenta. These colors are the indicant of The Color Key Program. To fully understand the effect of Color Key, use fabrics or towels of orange and magenta (Color Figure 3). Place the different-colored fabrics across the shoulders, under the chin, in a manner so that necklines are concealed. Alternate the colors and study the effect of each on the individual coloring. Of course, this should be done in daylight (daylight bulbs are available at photography supply stores). The color of artificial light may interfere with this test. If your personal coloring falls within the Key I Colors, the magenta drape will be kinder to your skin. Facial lines, shadows, freckles, pigmentation, or blemishes will be softened; circles under the eyes will be less noticeable; and hair, eye, and tooth color will be complemented. This is because the magenta drape has the same blue undertones that your personal coloring has. If your coloring falls within the Key II Colors, the orange drape will be kinder to your skin. This is because the orange drape has the same yellow-orange undertones that your personal coloring has. For this test to be most effective, the face should be devoid of cosmetics. Cosmetic hair coloring may be in the wrong color group, which may interfere with this test. For best results, cover tinted hair. If you cannot determine your own color group, try to get the opinion of a group of people (your classmates, for example), rather than depending on the opinion of one person.

How Does The Color Key Program Relate to Your Personal Coloring?

The Color Key Program works for men and women of all races—yellow, red, brown, black, or white (Color Figures 4 and 6). In selecting color, the skin, hair, tooth, and eye coloring should be considered carefully. In the white race people in the Key I group, because of the prominence of blue in their skin tone, have a rose-pink complexion. They look better when associated with Key I Colors. People falling within Key II groups because of the prominence of yellow in their coloring, have a peach-pink skin tone. They look better in Key II Colors. Skin tones are consistent even as the skin weathers, tans, and ages. After the initial sun- or windburn, the skin darkens in its own group. As the skin ages, the undertones become darker, lighter, or remain consistent as the body chemistry adjusts. Aging will never cause a change in the color group of the skin.

Color Key skin tones in the yellow, red, brown, or black races is distinguishable not by the darkness of the skin but by the undertones. Skin tones within the Key I Colors have a predominant blue undertone that gives the skin an umber cast. The skin tones within the Key II Colors have a yellow undertone that gives it a golden cast. It is important to note that very often olive skin tones of Latins and Orientals are in the Key I Color group.

Eyes are a fascinating index to personal coloring. Eye color although it may darken or fade with age, or be altered by disease or the use of contact lenses, remains in the same color group from infancy on. Blue and brown eyes are found in either group. Bright blue eyes are Key I Colors; gray-blue eyes are Key II Colors. Red-brown eyes are Key I Colors, and yellow-brown eyes are Key II Colors. The colors comprising the hazel eye and unusual eye colors, such as green and violet, must be observed carefully in order to define their composition, which will then determine the group to which they belong.

Hair colors are also color coded. All colors are represented in both groups. It is the undertone of the hair color that establishes in which group it belongs. The blue or smoky undertones of Key I Colors claim the platinum and ash blondes, auburn reds, jet blacks, snow whites, and the smoky blue or purple tints. The golden undertones of the honey and strawberry blondes, rust reds, chestnut, off-blacks, and cream whites belong to Key II Colors. Remember this especially when you help nature with the color of your hair. Always choose an artificial hair coloring in your color group. When you gray, you will do so in your own group, snow white—Key I Colors, and cream white—Key II Colors.

Keep in mind that the colors from your own group are your most flattering because they are related to your natural coloring. Try not to be influenced by fashion to change your Color Key group, as you will not look your best in the other group. Colors not of your group will tend to make you look older by emphasizing facial wrinkles, shadows, and blemishes.

Color Key Combinations

Use your knowledge of Color Key for every purchase where color must be considered. All cosmetics should be selected in your color group. Accessories such as shoes, handbags, hosiery, and jewelry should be coded along with the entire wardrobe. All items of exterior and interior design and decoration can be coded.

All of the colors found in one group may be successfully combined with all the other colors of that group when values and chromas are manipulated. Applying this knowledge, you can develop endless varieties of color harmonies individualized by you. Each combination selected from your group will flatter your personal coloring and present you at your best.

Color palettes are crossed; that is, colors from both groups are combined only when emphasis or impact is desired. When you see this in the marketplace, it does attract attention but usually does not wear well. It is interesting to note that restaurants that use this type of decor are usually those that cater to a large-volume business where it is important to attract the customer, serve him quickly, and replace him with the next customer in a fast, efficient manner. The crossed color group decor helps speed the customer on his way because it becomes physically uncomfortable after a short time to remain surrounded by such jarring color combinations.

Combining colors from the two groups can be done effectively in clothing combinations if the purpose is to attract attention. This is sometimes done in theater costumes. When the color group of the clothing is different from that of the set, the character attracts and holds the attention of the audience. In fact, it is very difficult to watch any other part of the stage.

Usually, crossing color groups is harsh and inharmonious. The combination of the two groups, whether it is in a fabric or combination of garments, does not wear well visually or psychologically.

If you apply The Color Key Program to your wardrobe planning, you will find that your clothing budget will seem to go farther. This is because everything you buy will go with everything else. Sweaters, coats, and jackets will blend with bags, dresses, shirts, skirts, and pants. Shoes and bags will mix with gloves, hats, and scarves. In clothing selection, texture and design may limit some combinations of apparel, but a Color Key selected wardrobe will be in color harmony.

Textures have an effect on color. Textures such as patent leather or satin that reflect the light make the color appear lighter. Textures such as velvet or corduroy that absorb the light make the color appear darker. Artificial light will also affect the color. This effect of light on color varies with the kind of light, the colored surface, and other surroundings. Even the professional designer who deals constantly with color cannot make decisions about color without testing. However, regardless of the textures and the lighting, if you have selected the items in your color group they will remain flattering to you.

Be aware that there are no "unkeyed" colors in this system. The beiges of Key I Colors are different from those in Key II Colors as are the blacks, browns, navies, and whites. For example, the snow white of most synthetic fabrics has a blue undertone that makes it a Key I Color. The cream white of 100 percent undyed wool always belongs to Key II Colors. This is because as white wool is worn and ages, it becomes more yellowed and thus very flattering to a person having Key II coloring.

Special Color Key considerations for women. When choosing hosiery, check to see if it is in your color group. Beige or natural-colored hosiery should be coded by matching skin tones. Often very inexpensive hosiery has a red tone to it that becomes redder as the stockings are laundered. This red-blue undertone is in the Key I Color group and should be avoided by people within the Key II Color group. If your natural-colored stockings are always carefully coded, you will never find yourself with the "wrong stockings."

All cosmetics should be in your color group. Foundation colors should match the skin or be slightly darker. Eye liner, mascara, brow pencil, and shadows are coded in the same tones as hair coloring. Eye makeup may vary in value and chroma or intensity, but their undertones must be coded. Rouge, blusher, lipstick, and nail enamel also should be coded. Cross keying the reds used in these cosmetics creates unflattering effects that make the facial wrinkles and blemishes more pronounced or emphasize the pigmentation of the face making it appear more florid or sallow. Careful selection of nail enamel will enhance the beauty of the hand by complementing the skin tones. Key Color I nail polish is rosy-pink or has a bluish undertone. A Key II Color nail enamel is peach-pink or has a golden cast. Properly coded nail enamel always blends with all your chosen wardrobe and therefore eliminates forever the frustration of a speedy polish change.

Color Key considerations for both men and women. Each of us desires to have bright, healthy, white teeth. However, snow-white teeth are only found in faces with Key I coloring. Tooth enamel of Key II Colors is creamy white. This is a very important point to remember when having any type of corrective dentistry done. Cross keying of tooth enamels will most always appear false and, therefore, unattractive.

Jewelry can also be coded. Rose and white gold, silver or platinum are considered to be in the Key I Color group; yellow gold falls within the Key II Color group. Precious stones, such as the diamond, emerald and ruby can belong to either group. A person who is truly sensitive to color will want to carefully consider this aspect before selecting jewelry.

Relationship of Color Key Groups to Personal Coloring

The Color Key Program is related to the individual's personal color pattern. All of the people of the earth, male-female, young-old, black-white-red-yellow-brown, may be coded. The theory mechanically relates all hues with those found in the individual's skin, hair, and eyes. A summary of the personal coloring attributes of Key I Colors and Key II Colors follows:

SKIN COLORING

Key I Colors
White race: Prominence of blue undertone in skin gives rose-pink, or olive-blue complexion tone.
Brown, yellow, red, or black races: Prominence of blue undertone in skin gives umber or smoky cast to skin.

Key II Colors
White race: Prominence of yellow undertone in skin gives peach-pink skin or olive-gold complexion tone.
Brown, yellow, red, or black race: Prominence of yellow undertone gives golden cast to skin tone.
Note: skin tones are consistent even as skin weathers, tans, or ages.

HAIR COLORING

Key I Colors	*Key II Colors*
blue or smoky undertones	golden or yellow undertones
platinum blondes	honey blondes
ash blondes	strawberry blondes
auburn reds	rust reds
jet blacks or bluish blacks	chestnuts
snow whites	off-blacks (brownish)
smoky blue or purple tints	cream whites

EYE COLORING

Key I Colors	*Key II Colors*
bright blue	gray-blue
red-brown (chocolate)	yellow-brown (chestnut)
blue-green	green

TOOTH COLORING

Key I Colors	*Key II Colors*
snow white	creamy white
blue white	yellow white

When it is difficult to determine the grouping of the skin or the hair or the eye, study the combination of skin-hair-eye-teeth coloring factors to determine the correct group. Mismatches are often made with makeup choices, hair coloring, and even with contact lenses which interfere with Color Key determinations.

Suggested Activities

1. Determine your personal colors by using one of the methods described in this chapter.
2. Study your own wardrobe and determine your color preference. Identify clothing in the wardrobe that is disliked or not worn; determine the color of this clothing. Is color the reason for the displeasure with these garments?
3. Create a color collage by collecting pictures from various sources, including magazine advertisements, which represent Key I Colors and Key II Colors. Pictures may be of anything but should include pictures of people of varying ages representing the blondes, brunettes, and redheads of each group as well as people of different races representing each group. This activity may be done by individual students or as a class project.
4. Prepare a montage of color combinations in your personal colors that can be used as a basis for your wardrobe planning. Textures and fabric designs should be incorporated into the montage.
5. Make a written or visual presentation describing the various color systems and their organization. Include The Color Key Program, Prang, and Munsell. Determine which system is most functional for the selection of items of clothing and personal adornment.

12 *Texture*

Texture is the element of design that describes surface appearance and feel. Fabric, metal, leather, and straw—each has a distinctive texture. The descriptive words used to characterize textures are comparative: both burlap and sailcloth are *coarse* textures, but their degree of coarseness differs. Textures are also comparative to other textures with which they are combined and to the person wearing them. Some adjectives used to describe textures are smooth, heavy, fine, crisp, glossy, and nubby.

Texture is a sensory impression understood by sight as well as touch. The visual aspect of texture is perceived by the eye because of the degree of light absorption and reflection on the surface of the material. Lustrous textures are seen in satins and dull textures in fuzzy wools. Texture has the definite physical dimensions of weight, size, bulk, and shape. These physical dimensions are also visually perceived (Figure 12-1). The opaqueness of butcher linen and the transparency of handkerchief linen are recognized by sight.

Hand is the term used to refer to the tactile aspects of fabric; that is, the coarseness, softness, or rigidity is recognized by feel. Hand determines how some fabrics will respond to a given style. Some textures virtually speak to the designer as to how they should be used. Firm gabardine, linen, and worsteds call for crisp tailorings; matte jerseys, and chiffon are effective in draped designs (Figures 12-2, 12-3, 12-4, 12-5). Softly tailored garments need pliable fabrics such as crepe, shantung, or lightweight wool flannel. Texture is fully comprehended by touch, but it is not always necessary to feel an object to understand its tactile qualities, as sight can recall the memory of touch.[1]

Each fabric has many textural characteristics that can be described as:

feel	soft-crisp
feel	smooth-rough
see and feel	thick-thin
see and feel	clingy-rigid
see	shiny-dull
see	opaque-transparent

[1] Lorenz Eitner, *Introduction to Art: An Illustrated Topical Manual* (Minneapolis, Minn.: Burgess, 1961), p. 41.

12-1 *Texture is a sensory impression understood by our eyes as well as by our touch. The texture of this fur can be readily understood visually. (Courtesy Susie's Casuals)*

12-2 *The tactile aspects of fabrics determine how they will respond to a given style. Challies, having a soft hand, responds to designs featuring gathers for gentle fullness. (Courtesy Folkwear, Inc., Marcy Malloy photo)*

12-3 *Jersey fabric, having a soft and supple hand, is a fine choice for a draped style. (Courtesy Susie's Casuals)*

12-4 *Firm fabrics call for crisp tailoring. (Courtesy American Enka)*

12-5 *Fine linen is combined with lace to create a delicate feminine image. (Courtesy Hamilton Adams Imports)*

Components That Determine Texture

Texture is determined by the arrangement of the component parts in fabric. These are the fiber, the yarn, the weave (or other methods of making fabric), and the finish given to the fabric.

Fibers are hairlike strands of raw materials that are spun into yarns and woven into cloth. Fibers of wool produce soft textures; fibers of linen produce crisp textures. Both of these textures are the result of the inherent characteristics of the raw materials used. The short, fuzzy fibers of cotton will produce fabrics that will absorb light and be dull; the long, smooth filaments of reeled silk will make fabrics that reflect light, giving a shiny appearance.

Yarns are composed of fibers that are short lengths twisted together or long filaments laid or twisted together. The methods used in joining fibers and filaments into yarns results in the formation of distinctive textures. A yarn given a low twist will produce a shiny texture, as found in satin; a highly twisted yarn will form a rough texture, such as crepe. Yarns organized by thick slubs form shantung; and those that are looped or coiled produce stretch fabrics. Yarns having a little twist can be brushed after weaving to produce a nap or fuzzy texture.

Fabric is formed by putting yarns together by some method, such as weaving, knitting, crocheting, felting, bonding, and braiding. Some fabrics, called film fabrics, which are often used for rainwear or which simulate leather, are formed by chemicals that are extruded in sheets instead of filaments. The way yarns are put together to form fabric determines the texture. A satin weave of loosely twisted yarns, woven so that the yarns float across many threads, produces visual effects that will reflect light and give a shiny texture. The diagonal design formed in gabardine, denim, covert, and drill is the result of a twill weave. The pattern of knits is formed by the way the loops of yarn are formed. Knits absorb light and are dull textured unless a plastic or metallic yarn is used.

The *finish* given to cloth after it is constructed can impart or change texture as well as other qualities. The no-iron finish that makes a fabric smooth and wrinkle-free usually stiffens the texture and makes it less pliable than fabrics not given this finish. Crisp fabrics are produced by the addition of a sizing mixture that gives stiffness to the finish. Embossed fabrics, which are characterized by their three-dimensional designs, are formed by passing the fabric through rollers having embossed designs. Flocked fabrics have short fibers attached to the surface by means of adhesives.

The texture of fabrics is affected by the characteristics of the raw material used and by the production processes involved, from fiber to the final stage when the finish is applied. Texture determines how the cloth should be used. Garment designs that do not respect the texture characteristics cannot be satisfactory.

Fashions in Textures

Textures as well as silhouettes and colors enter and leave the fashion picture. The style of garments determines which textures will be used. Changes in fashion bring changes in texture (Figure 12-6).

Because texture and garment styling must be compatible, the fashion reappearance of textures as well as garment designs occurs periodically. Tailored styling trends require crisp, firmly woven fabrics to enhance the precise line. Body-clinging styles require textures that express this quality in soft and drapable fabrics. Fashion requires bulky, fuzzy textures at times and smooth, soft, or firm textures at other times.

Designers often determine their styles by what the available fabric textures suggest. They manipulate the material to determine the hand and how it will react to draping, pleating, folding, or tucking. This technique helps them to decide how a garment should be designed. Many designers drape the fabric as they are creating a garment. People who make their own clothes may find that they are more successful when they select the fabric first and then find the pattern.

12-6 *Textures as well as silhouettes have periods of popularity. Garment design determines which textures will be required for innovative styles. (Courtesy Maria Rodriguez Designs)*

12-7 *Some textures are classics; they remain popular year after year. These textures are neither very rough nor smooth, very thick or thin, but they belong to the middle group. They are not extreme. Medium weight herringbone shown in this jacket is an enduring texture. (Courtesy the Joseph & Feiss Company)*

Some textures are classics; they remain popular year after year. These are usually textures that are not extremes, that is, they are neither very rough nor very smooth, very thick nor very thin. They belong in the middle textural range. Broadcloth, percale, lightweight flannel, and lightweight linen have all been fashionable for a long time. These textures are not particularly exciting, but their appeal is lasting because people do not tire of them as quickly as they do of the extreme textures. Because of their plain surfaces, these textures can support intricate structural design (Figure 12-7).

Selection of Texture

When selecting textures, keep in mind your physical proportions, and skin and hair textures, as well as your personality. Texture selection should create combinations that will provide contrast and at the same time carry out a predominant theme or idea. The result should be unity or a total look of textures and the other design elements.

Effect of Texture on Physical Proportion

Textures have the physical properties of weight, size, bulk, shape, light absorption, and reflection. Textures can produce illusions that change apparent body size (Figure 12-8). Textures can make you look heavier or thinner.

When considering textures, try garments on (or place yardage across the area of the body where they are to be worn) and stand away from a mirror to study the physical effects produced by the fabrics.

Fabrics may be grouped together by common characteristics such as softness, coarseness, or stiffness. Most fabrics possess a combination of characteristics that must be evaluated in regard to the effect they produce when incorporated into a garment design and placed on the body. For example, a fabric may be soft, bulky, and shiny. A person may want the softness but not the shine or bulk, as

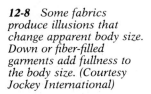

12-8 Some fabrics produce illusions that change apparent body size. Down or fiber-filled garments add fullness to the body size. (Courtesy Jockey International)

these two characteristics may not be becoming to a particular body type. In this situation it will be better to find another soft fabric that is not bulky or shiny. Thoughtful selection of textures can help produce physical illusions desired by the individual.

Proportion of Textures

All fabrics have proportion or scale. The size relationship of the pattern formed by the texture determines the scale.

Obvious proportion differences are seen by comparing the surface or the wale of corduroy in fine-, medium-, and wide-wale varieties. The small-scale pattern of some tweed fabrics is not so easily discernible as the large-scale patterns of tweed fabrics having coarser yarns. Rep fabrics that have a thick filling yarn vary from fine, as in broadcloth, to heavy, as in bengaline. Nap length of wools determines their scale. The size of the yarn and the needles used in knitting produce the differences in the scale of textures in knits. When the scale formed by the pattern of texture is tiny, the pattern is lost when seen from a distance, and it is perceived as an overall effect. The textural effect of very large-scaled patterns such as wide-wale corduroy, Erin Isle knits, and wool fleece remains identifiable when viewed from a distance.

The selection of scale of textures should be analyzed in relationship to the size of the person wearing them. A contrast in texture will emphasize form.[2] The small-sized body wearing large-scale textures can get lost in the texture because of the extreme contrast between fabric surface and figure dimensions. Petiteness is emphasized by the large-scale texture. Very heavy people who wear large-scale textures will appear heavier owing to repetition of size.

Soft and clingy fabrics. Fabrics that are soft and drapable cling to the body, show every contour, and reveal any body irregularities. Unless additional treatment is given in the inner construction of garments made from these fabrics, their use should be limited to those people who wish to reveal their body (Figure 12-9).

The fashion fabric quality of softness and the way it clings to the body can be changed by the addition of underlining or bonding. The degree of firmness of the underlining will determine how stiff the outer fabric will be. It is possible to camouflage the body contour with these textures if they are underlined to provide the firmness needed to lessen the clingy quality of the fashion fabric. (This should be done with care since stiff, supportive fabrics can spoil the effect of the fashion fabric.)

Stiff fabrics—bulky fabrics. Textures that are stiff stand away from the body and hide body irregularities. Excessively stiff fabrics appear to add bulk and weight to the body. Very stiff fabrics can be worn to advantage by persons who

[2] June King McFee, *Preparation for Art* (Belmont, Calif.: Wadsworth, 1961), p. 263.

12-9 *Soft drapable fabrics may cling to the figure and reveal body contours unless gathered or pleated fullness is used.* (Left: Courtesy Edward Dalmacio. Right: Courtesy Folkwear, Inc.)

are average-to-tall in height, having either average or thin bodies. These textures will be avoided by persons having very small bodies who do not wish to appear dwarfed by the contrast. Overweight people will look heavier in these fabrics because they stand away from the body, creating the illusion of additional thick-

369

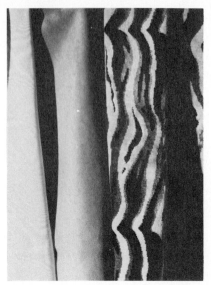

12-10 Stiff and bulky fabrics stand away from the body. Excessively stiff fabrics appear to add bulk and weight to the body. (Left: Courtesy Edward Dalmacio. Right: Courtesy Jones of New York Sport)

ness. A moderate amount of stiffness in fabrics is desirable for the overweight figure because the cloth does not cling to the body and reveal its exact contours (Figure 12-10).

Some textures add volume to the body by virtue of their weight and bulky nature. These fabrics, like those in the stiff classification, may by contrast be overpowering on the very slight, very thin, or petite body. The tall, slender person can use these textures more effectively.

Shiny textures—dull textures. Shiny textures reflect light and make the person wearing them appear larger. The fabric color is intensified by shine. Pile fabrics such as velvet, plush, velour, corduroy, and velveteen both reflect and absorb light. In these fabrics shadows occur because of multiple reflections of light on the pile. Those who do not mind appearing larger can wear these textures effectively (Figure 12-11).

Fabrics that absorb light and are dull do not enlarge the body. These textures are suitable for all body types, provided they do not possess other qualities such as bulk, softness, and crispness that would contribute undesirable characteristics.

12-11 Shiny textures reflect light and make a person wearing them appear larger. These include satins, glittery, and wet-look textures. (Courtesy Edward Dalmacio)

12-12 Textures that are not extreme such as medium-weight flannel, tweed, and broadcloth do not call attention to body irregularities. (Courtesy Edward Dalmacio)

Textures that are not extreme. People who do not wish to call attention to their body irregularities will select textures that are not extreme—very thin or thick, very soft or stiff, or very shiny (Figure 12-12). Because textures found in the middle group may not be structurally as interesting as the more extreme textures, other features such as color and line are often used to add interest to garments designed of such fabrics.

Texture Related to Skin and Hair

Skin and hair have texture. Both have degrees of fineness and coarseness that must be kept in mind when selecting fabrics, jewelry, and other textures to be worn next to the face.

The extreme contrasts of coarse skin and hair textures with very fine fabrics can produce uncomplimentary effects in both skin and hair appearance. People having coarse or aging skin should select the middle range of textures, which are neither very fine nor very coarse. Fabrics such as piqué, crepe, jersey, medium knits, dull silk, linen, and lightweight wool are considered medium textures.

People with fine, smooth skin and hair can use fine textured fabrics such as voile, sateen, satin, organdy, polished cotton, batiste, dimity, China silk, finely woven silk, and smooth plastics. They can also wear the middle and rough textures effectively. If skin and hair differ in texture, careful analysis should be made to find textures most flattering to both.

Frames of glasses and jewelry worn next to the skin, should be analyzed for textural qualities. Shiny metals and smooth stones are best used by individuals who have smooth and fine-to-medium-fine skin. In the medium range of textures in jewelry are coarse stones, Florentine-finish metals, and tortoise shell.

Hair textures are not usually as important a consideration as skin textures. However, materials used for hats should be complementary to hair textures. Smooth felt, shiny leather, satin, and finely woven straw will emphasize coarseness of hair textures. Most furs, velour felt, coarse leather, felt, and medium-textured straws fall into a medium-textured category, which can be worn by all.

Expressing Personality Through Texture Selection

The ability to select textures that reflect the self-concept of an individual is achieved when there is an understanding of the character or idea projected by the textures (Figure 12-13). The distinctive individual qualities of some textures typify particular moods and feelings. A variety of fabrics must be examined carefully in order to be able to identify the character they usually project. For example, the response learned by feeling burlap differs from that of feeling velvet.

Personal preferences will undoubtedly play a large part in the selection of textures that the individual feels comfortable wearing. One should not overlook the possibility of using different and exciting textures to mirror personal qualities, enhance appearance, and give personal satisfaction. Texture is an element of design that can be effectively used to express individuality.

Harmony in Texture Combination

Combinations of texture related to weight (thickness and thinness) and those related to firmness (crispness and softness) do not present particular problems, but combinations related to the image, feeling, or personality of textures should be analyzed carefully (Figure 12-14). Delicate lace and fine embroidery harmonize with fine, sheer fabrics (Figure 12-15). Coarse cotton lace and heavy crewel embroidery are too great a contrast for the same fine, sheer fabrics. Cotton lace combines well with percale, velveteen, and piqué. Crewel embroidery has qualities in common with homespun, heavy knits, and monk's cloth. Sequins convey formality for evening wear and are better applied to silks, satins, taffeta, and laces rather than to straw purses, heavy knits, and medium-weight cottons. Heavy tweed pants and jersey tops have a similar character, whereas heavy tweed pants and smooth satin shirts do not.

12-13 *Personality is reflected in texture selection when the character or idea projected by the textures is understood. These four garment textures project differing personal qualities which complement each wearer.* (Top left: *Courtesy the Joseph & Feiss Company.* Top right: *Courtesy Hamilton Adams Imports.* Bottom left: *Courtesy Folkwear, Inc.* Bottom right: *Courtesy Priscilla of Boston*)

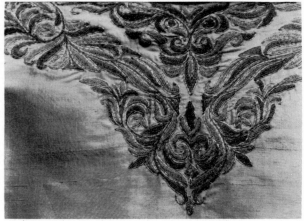

12-14 *Laces are available in a wide variety so that they can be selected to harmonize with many textures. (Courtesy Edward Dalmacio)*

12-15 *Embroidery thread must be compatible in weight and texture with the ground fabric. Silk shantung cloth is enhanced by using embroidery floss having similar qualities. This Kashmir embroidery is enhanced by the use of gold threads to outline the motifs.*

Some fashion periods feature strong texture contrasts used together. Such combinations as glitter fabrics and denim for day wear, heavy boots with summer cottons, sheer blouses with jeans produce change for the fashion moment. Contrasts are necessary to avoid sameness and monotony; however, a predominant texture idea should be evident so that unity is achieved.

When making decisions regarding textural combinations, stand away from them. Distance will diminish the effect the combinations present up close. They may blend together and appear too similar in texture, or obviously they may not belong together because they are too unrelated. Good design requires texture contrasts that are varied enough to be interesting.

Contrast of Textures with Accessories

The selection of accessories for an outfit provides an excellent way to use contrasting textures. An all-smooth or all-coarse, all-dull or all-shiny textured ensemble would be unified, but it also might be monotonous and unrelieved. For example, the combination of a hopsacking dress, straw basket, and raffia shoes carries out a textural theme but lacks contrast and, therefore, seems uninteresting. Variety in texture combination lends excitement, but a thoughtful selection is required (Figure 12-16). A soft wool sports coat with gabardine slacks accessorized with smooth leather suede shoes, a felt hat, and a silk scarf brings into the outfit a variety of compatible textures. A comfortable pair of faded blue jeans combined with a pastel-colored T-shirt is a marvelous texture background for a handsome leather belt.

For women, purses and shoes do not have to be of identical texture to be used together. It is more important that they express the same feeling. Gloves can provide a variety of texture accents in knits, crochet, fabric, and many types of leather.

Hosiery is available in a wide assortment of textures from the traditional fine-knit and mesh to coarse-ribbed, net, and crocheted. Coordination of these textures with the garment is essential. For both men and women the heavier textured hosiery is best worn with medium-to-coarse fabrics, because it conveys the image of these materials. The same textured hosiery usually clashes with fine textures because of the extreme contrast. Women should note that the heavier textured hosiery will enlarge the appearance of the legs and call attention to them, even more so when the color of the stockings contrasts with that of the skirt.

Suggested Activities

1. Try on garments of varying textures and study the effect they have on your body shape. Determine which textures please you the most.
2. Analyze the garments in your wardrobe for texture. Which textures seem to predominate? Can you find garments that illustrate how texture supports structural design? Can you find garments that illustrate how texture detracts from structural design?

12-16 *Accessories provide an excellent way to use contrasting yet compatible textures. The result to be achieved is the design principle of unity with variety. (Courtesy Geiger of Austria)*

3. What textures are being promoted in current fashion? What textures are now out of current fashion? Can you find garments in your wardrobe that are not being worn because of their texture?

4. Collect fabric swatches for a collage showing pleasing textural combinations suitable for yourself. Give reasons for your selection based upon the effect you wish to project.

5. Collect pictures from fashion magazines and catalogues that show textures and combinations of textures that are pleasing to you. Use this information as a basis of future garment purchases.

13 *Fabric Design*

Design in fabric is achieved by many different techniques. It may be created as the fabric is being made or it may be applied to the finished goods. The selection of fabric with any kind of a design requires a careful appraisal of all the components that combine to form the finished product. These components include pattern or allover design, shape and arrangement of individual motifs, background areas, color and color combinations, texture and texture combinations, and end use of fabric.

Pattern and Motif

A *pattern* is an overall design. A *motif* is an individual unit of a pattern. *Fabric design* is often created when motifs are repeated in a prescribed manner to create an overall pattern. Motifs are classified according to design style as geometric, realistic, stylized, and abstract.

Geometric Motifs

Geometric motifs include plaids, checks, stripes, and circles (Figure 13-1). Some geometric motifs are formed with yarns dyed before weaving whereas other geometric motifs are formed by printing on woven cloth. Patterned fabrics made from yarns dyed prior to weaving ensure that the pattern will be "on grain." This means that the design formed by the colored yarns is in a horizontal (filling or weft) and vertical (warp) pattern, as these yarns form the grain of the fabric. When such fabrics are fashioned into garments, the pattern should be placed on the body so that the design looks straight and hangs evenly.

Plaids, checks, and stripes printed on a fabric after it is woven are often crooked; that is, the pattern is not straight with the grain formed by the vertical and more often, the horizontal threads. Printed fabrics often create problems in construction because the finished product will appear either to be crooked or mismatched on the body or to hang unevenly. It is important when purchasing fabric or garments of printed geometric designs to check to see if the pattern runs true with the horizontal grain and if the motifs are aligned (Figure 13-2). If they are not, the fabric or garment should be rejected because it will always result in an unsatisfactory garment.

13-1 *Geometric designs include plaids, checks, stripes, and circles. (Center and right: Courtesy Edward Dalmacio)*

13-2 *These geometric motifs were printed on the fabric. They were not printed straight with the grain. Note how the design does not align with the torn edge. (Courtesy Edward Dalmacio)*

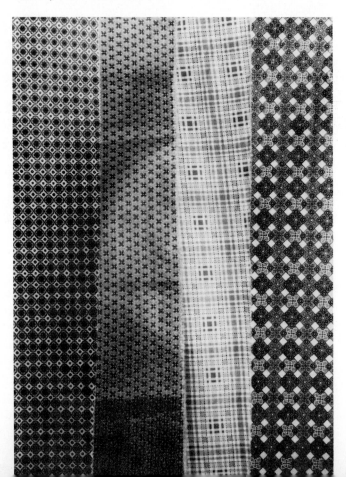

13-3 *Realistic motifs duplicate nature or man-made objects. The blouse at the right uses realistic motifs that appear three-dimensional owing to shading. The blouse at the left uses abstract motifs. (Courtesy J. C. Penney Co.)*

Realistic Motifs

Realistic motifs duplicate nature or some man-made object. These motifs include florals that look as if they grow in a garden, lemons that hang on a tree, toys that belong in the nursery, and animals that abound in the forest. Motifs such as these do not show much imagination or creativity on the part of the fabric designer and are, therefore, less enduring than motifs that result from an artist's interpretation (Figure 13-3). The realistic treatment of subjects is obvious, and frequently the obvious becomes monotonous.

13-4 Three realistic designs that do not respect the flatness of the fabric. Shading makes the designs appear three dimensional. (Courtesy Edward Dalmacio)

Realistic designs often attempt a three-dimensional form in order to copy reality. Because of the perspective achieved, these designs do not respect the flatness of the fabric. Devices that are used to make a design appear three-dimensional are shading, overlapping of objects, diminishing sizes, and texture. The artist attempts to make the motif and pattern appear to advance and not remain flat by the use of these techniques (Figure 13-4).

Imitation of reality is not generally the effect one wishes to achieve in garment fabrics. Because these motifs are obviously reproductions of nature or man-made objects, they are not particularly suitable for apparel although they appear in fashion periodically.

Stylized Motifs

Stylized motifs are variations of natural forms. Stylized floral or leaf motifs show imagination, not imitation, on the part of the artist who designed the fabric. Realistic floral forms are often used as inspiration, then creatively interpreted into infinite varieties of interesting shapes by fabric designers. Stylized motifs are successful for fabric design because they are two-dimensional and they relate to the flatness of the fabric (Figures 13-5, 13-6, 13-7).

Abstract Motifs

Abstract motifs include splashes of color and shape; they are nonobjective and have no counterpart in nature or man-made objects. The effect produced by them is much like that found in paintings by Mondrian and Pollock. These motifs are very pleasing when used in fabric design (Figures 13-8, 13-9).

Warp prints and ikats belong in the classification of abstract motifs. These fabrics use groups of multicolored warp yarns woven with solid filling yarns. The effect produced is a blur of soft, hazy colors, often in random groupings (Figure 13-10).

13-5 *Stylized motifs are variations of natural forms that show imagination rather than imitation on the part of the designer.*

13-6 Left: *A butterfly was used as an inspiration for this design and interpreted in an unusual stylized composition.* Right: *Japanese calligraphy in a bold stylized print says, "I love you." (Courtesy Cotton Incorporated)*

13-7 *Floral forms were stylized for an overall design for a kimono. (Courtesy Folkwear, Inc.)*

13-8 *Abstract motifs have no counterpart in nature. The motifs include splashes of colors and shapes. (Courtesy Edward Dalmacio)*

13-9 *This overall abstract design has motifs of varying shape and size. (Courtesy WilliWear)*

13-10 *Ikats are often abstract designs. The effect results in blurred hazy motifs.*

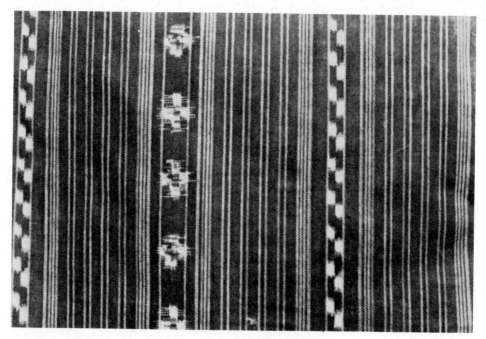

Combinations of Different Motifs in a Pattern

When different motifs are combined in a fabric, they should be related to each other in shape and size if unity is to be achieved. This does not imply that they should be alike, for this would produce monotony. Some variation and some similarity produce interest. Totally unrelated shapes and sizes destroy harmony (Figure 13-11). When many different motifs are combined, there will be greater coherence to the total effect of the design if one shape or size dominates and the others are subordinated. Different motifs can be made cohesive by use of a predominant color (Figure 13-12).

13-11 *Harmony is destroyed by the use of many unrelated motifs to form the pattern in fabric design. The realistic, geometric, and stylized motifs do not form a cohesive effect. (Courtesy Edward Dalmacio)*

13-12 *Several motifs are used in this fabric. One shape predominates while the others are subordinated; a single background color is used against the white motifs giving a cohesive effect.*

13-13 *A photographic lace print is emphasized by value contrast. Each detail is clearly discernible.*

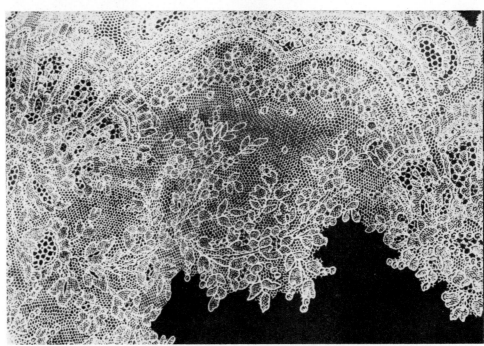

Motif shape is emphasized by value or chroma contrast from the background areas (Figure 13-13). If there is little value or chroma difference, the motif is not easily discernible. To illustrate, bright pink polka dots on a pale yellow background will not appear as bold as black polka dots on a bright white background (Figure 13-14).

13-14 *Motif shape is emphasized by value or chroma contrast from the background areas. Note the differences in the importance of the motif against backgrounds of varying contrast. (Courtesy Edward Dalmacio)*

Pattern and Pattern Arrangement

Pattern is made up of the arrangement of motifs into an overall design. These may be considered formal—showing a regular methodical repetition of the motif, or informal—having irregular placement of motifs.

When motifs are placed, the background areas, sometimes called negative spaces, become as important in the design as the motifs themselves. The background areas should show thoughtful spacing of the motifs, whether the arrangement is formal or informal. If the background space is greater or smaller than the area occupied by the motif, the spacing will be more interesting than if it is equal to the motif. When the background area is greater than the motif, it helps to give it strength (Figure 13-15). However, too much background space generally makes the motif lose its importance. Not enough background space makes the motif appear crowded and prevents the single motif from dominating in the design (Figure 13-16). Equal divisions of the motifs and background areas lack variation and may be displeasing to look at, particularly when strong color contrasts are used.

In order to avoid spottiness, the arrangement of the pattern should show some rhythmical movement from one motif to another. This should not be overdone so that the pattern fatigues the eye. For example, repeating checks or stripes of great value contrast are often difficult to look at or sew on because there is a great amount of agitated line movement. Fabrics that have such movement can be tranquilized by combining them with a solid-color fabric.

13-15 *When the background area is greater than the motif it helps to give the motif strength. (Courtesy Edward Dalmacio)*

13-16 *These two fabrics illustrate how too little background space makes the motif appear crowded and prevents the motif from dominating the design. (Courtesy Edward Dalmacio)*

Fabric Design Related to Garment Construction

Apparel constructed of a distinctly patterned fabric should show coordination of the fabric to garment cut and design. Gross distortions often result when little thought is given to the placement of the fabric design. Some of the most displeasing effects, perhaps because they are so obvious, occur in garments made from plaid fabrics. Unmatched seams, and too many seams will break the continuity of the plaid motif. Darting, particularly in the bodice, often distorts the fabric design and forms unbecoming angles. Curved seams that do not repeat the angularity of the fabric make the matching of seams, as in the princess line or raglan sleeves virtually impossible. These all result in distortions of the design (Figure 13-17).

13-17 Left: *Note how the continuity of the plaid is distorted by the use of diagonal darts in the bodice in the top part. The bodice in the lower part utilizes horizontal darts which do not disrupt the geometric design as greatly. (Courtesy Edward Dalmacio)*

13-17 Right: *In the example at the top the center skirt seam matches horizontally; however, no thought has been given to matching the plaids vertically. Lower example, the skirt shows both vertical and horizontal matching. (Courtesy Edward Dalmacio)*

Motifs whose shape, size, and spacing demand continuity must be matched both vertically and horizontally (Figure 13-18). Often these fabric designs are broken by too many seams and unmatched units. Motifs should not appear in unbecoming places on the body. When widely spaced, realistic motifs are arranged informally, it is of particular importance that their placement on the body be considered. Such motifs as roses with realistic thorns rising from the seat of the skirt are painful to see. Flowers blooming at the bustline or a large cabbage rose isolated over the abdomen call unnecessary attention to these areas of the body.

Geometric fabric patterns with angular lines, such as plaids, checks, and stripes, suggest designs with straight lines that are tailored and sophisticated. Dots and curvilinear patterns imply curved or transitional lines. One-way designs such as flowers with stems must be positioned correctly so that the motifs are placed in the same direction on all parts of the garment.

Fabrics having surface interest, napped fabrics such as velveteen, velvet corduroy, pile fabrics, satin, and some knits must also be arranged during cutting so that all garment pieces are placed in the same direction. Failure to do so results in color change owing to the way that light strikes the fabric surface.

13-18 *Plaids must match both horizontally and vertically in order to give continuity to the design.* Left: *Note the carefully matched seams at the seams of the sleeves to the armholes, center front closure, and patch pockets.* Right: *The plaid skirt was constructed on the bias. The center front seam matches on both horizontal and vertical grain. (Courtesy Pendleton Woolen Mills)*

Either the pattern of the fabric or the structural lines of the garment should be allowed to dominate. If the garment lines are most important, they are best combined with a plain fabric. If the fabric design is most important, the lines of the garment should remain simple. If both have equal appeal, there will be a lack of emphasis and the total impression of the design composition will lose impact (Figure 13-19).

Effects of Fabric Design on the Body

The scale or size of the motif, its arrangement, and its colors are three factors that strongly influence the effect a fabric design has upon the body. Ready-to-wear garments are best judged on the body; yard goods can be draped over the body to suggest effects. Light source and viewing distance should also be considered when selecting fabric designs.

The scale of the pattern should be related to the size of the wearer. Very small overall patterns can be worn by almost all people without producing unfavorable effects. Usually these patterns blend into a nondistinct design and do not increase or decrease apparent body size, providing they are of middle value and intensity (Figure 13-20). Generally, plain, undecorated fabric is body-revealing; a small overall pattern is body-concealing.

Small, distinct motifs, spaced so that the motif dominates the design, look best on the small or average-size body. Those who do not wish to call attention to a body that is tall and large or short and full will avoid this group because the extreme contrast of the body to the scale of the pattern will emphasize the body size.

Fabrics that call attention to body proportion include those with bold designs, large-scale plaids, or big motifs on large amounts of background area. Men and women who have pleasing proportions and who are medium to tall in height are enhanced by larger-scale designs. A small body may seem smaller in large-scale designs because of the contrast in scale between body size and design. A person with a large, well-proportioned body wears the large-scale fabric designs best because he or she has the frame to exhibit the entire design.

Plaids come in small-, medium-, and large-scale units. The larger the scale of the unit, the wider the body will look. Small plaid units usually do not adversely affect the apparent size of the small or average-size body. Medium-scale plaids usually can be worn by all, but very large-scale plaids are best suited to the average or tall body type. Large, full bodies and small bodies are best in medium-scale plaids with close value contrasts. The greater the contrasts of colors or values and intensity in the plaid, the greater is the apparent width of the body (Figure 13-21).

13-19 *The fabric design and the garment cut do not show coordination. The large floral motifs are grossly distorted by the center back seam. (Courtesy Edward Dalmacio)*

13-20 *Small overall patterns that blend into nondistinct designs do not increase or decrease apparent body size provided they are of middle value and intensity. (Courtesy Edward Dalmacio)*

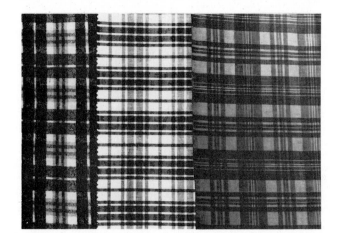

13-21 The greater the contrasts of color or value and intensity in the plaid the greater is the effect upon increasing apparent body width. (Courtesy Edward Dalmacio)

Circular motifs, such as polka dots, add width and fullness to the body (Figure 13-22). Border designs placed at the hemline, waistline, sleeve, or hipline also increase body width.

Motifs showing a strong vertical movement usually add height to the body, and those showing horizontal movement usually add width. This is particularly true when there is great contrast in values, intensity, and colors and when motifs are arranged so that they appear isolated from each other (Figure 13-23).

Sharp color contrasts used in prints will enlarge the visual appearance of the body. The use of light values and bright intensities adds weight, whereas medium to darker values or dull intensities usually do not call attention to body size.

For those wishing to reveal body conformation, the solid-colored fabrics provide the least design distraction and are, therefore, the best for this purpose. On the other hand, for those who wish to conceal body contours, printed fabrics of low-value contrasts are recommended because they seem to break up the body boundaries and distract the eye. These fabrics tend to camouflage.

13-22 Circular motifs such as polka dots may add width or fullness to the body. (Courtesy Edward Dalmacio)

13-23 The motif shows strong horizontal movement adding width to the body. (Courtesy Pendleton Woolen Mills)

13-24 *A predominant color is used to unify the total effect in an outfit that combines different fabric designs. (Courtesy Cotton Incorporated)*

Use of Different Prints in One Outfit

To unify two or more prints in one outfit requires careful analysis of the fabric designs. Some garments are designed for the use of coordinated fabrics. These fabrics go together because some factor unifies them to create a total effect. Techniques used to combine different-patterned fabrics include these:

1. Using the same predominant color in different prints (Figure 13-24).
2. Using fabrics with the same motif but with different background colors.
3. Using a patterned fabric that is greatly subordinated with a patterned fabric that has a more pronounced design (Figure 13-25).
4. Using ribbons, tapes, or solid color between the joinings of two fabrics (Figure 13-26).

Whichever technique is used in combining two different fabric patterns, one should be dominant in the design; and a unifying theme, such as color or motif, should unite the two fabrics. The inclusion of patterned fabrics in the wardrobe

13-25 *When using different patterned fabrics in an outfit, a coordinated effect can result when one of the patterns is subordinated. (Courtesy Folkwear, Inc.)*

provides variety and interest. Fabric design selections should be made so that the design relates to the physical characteristics and personality of the wearer.

The cut and construction of the garment should reinforce the essence of the design of the fabric. This is done by repetition of straight or curved lines and by the limited use of seams, which results in continuity of distinct and large-scale designs.

Women's accessories such as fabric-patterned shoes, handbags, scarves, and gloves have limited use in the wardrobe. They are shown to best advantage when worn with apparel of solid colors.

Coordination of different fabric designs in the same costume requires skillful selection if a harmonious effect is to be achieved. A unifying factor, such as color, motif repetition, or use of one dominant pattern, will help to combine successfully the two fabric designs.

392

Fabric Design and Light Source

When choosing fabrics, the light source is very important because it affects the appearance of color. Daylight, phosphorescent, and incandescent light may each produce different effects. When possible, the fabric should be studied in both natural and artificial light. Some stores have a setup of light sources for checking the effect.

Colors in two or more different fabrics that are to be combined may appear to match under one light source and not under another. This effect is known as *metamerism*. If possible, match the fabrics under the light conditions in which they will be worn. For example, fabrics selected for a wedding pageant should be studied at the site of the wedding ceremony and reception. When the clothing will be worn under various lighting conditions, check the fabrics under both daylight and incandescent light; if they match under both of these light sources, they will probably match under all other conditions.

Fabric Design and Distance

Distance also influences the appearance of a fabric design. Certain combinations of colors may take on different hues when viewed from various distances, and often tiny patterns will seem to blend into the background. Examples of this are fine checks, narrow stripes, and dainty floral patterns. For example, a red-and-white check can become pink when seen at a distance. Large motifs can appear spotty, blotchy, or without rhythm or unity when viewed from afar. Stand

13-26 When using different prints in the same fabric, placing bands of color at the joinings of the fabrics will help to unify the print. (Courtesy Geiger of Austria)

away from mirror and squint to evaluate the effect that distance has on fabric design.

Fabric Design and Texture

Both fabric design and texture are very important factors in clothing selection decisions. The visual impression created by these two elements can greatly influence the appearance of a garment on the figure. Fabric design and texture are interrelated and yet separate. Fabric design includes all elements of the design that make a visual impression—the construction method, the color, and the pattern. Texture is the surface interest of the fabric. Although it is a component of the fabric design, it is important enough to be considered separately.

Suggested Activities

1. Collect fabrics that have the same motif (such as circles and dots) but vary in size. Study the effects of the background space upon the impact of the motif.
2. Collect fabrics that vary in color value and intensity and study the relationship of design to color effects.
3. Study the effect of fabric design on garment construction. Find garments or pictures of garments illustrating how fabric design is supported by construction details, or distorted by construction details.
4. Develop a checklist of fabric design details that are important for you to look for when you shop either for yardage or for ready-made garments.
5. Try to determine your design preferences. Are there some kinds of fabric designs that make you physically or emotionally uncomfortable? Are there other fabric designs you prefer? Can you determine why you feel this way about various fabric designs?
6. Add to collage (Suggested Activities, No. 4, in Chapter 12) using prints suitable for your wardrobe.
7. Collect pictures from fashion magazines and catalogues that show fabric design and combinations of fabric design that are pleasing to you. Decide which of these would be best for you. Use this information as a basis of future garment purchases.

14 *Facial Design*

Each face is unique. No two faces are exactly alike, not even those of identical twins. The arrangement of features becomes even more individualized with the animation of facial expression. As one matures, the facial contours develop characteristics caused by the total lifetime environment of the individual. Lines are etched on the face by both years and experiences. The faces of the very young are enjoyed for their unmarked beauty, whereas the faces of the mature are made more interesting by the patterns achieved by years of living.

It is the face that identifies one. We recognize our friends and acquaintances not by their hands or feet but by their faces. The face is where the personality is expressed. It is our most individual signature. It is the face that should most often be emphasized in dress.

Bringing emphasis to the face, or personality area, is easily achieved in a number of ways:

—Facial ornamentation, including the use of cosmetics and, for men, the styling of beards, moustaches, and sideburns.
—Face-framing details, including hair design, hats, jewelry, eyeglasses, necklines, scarves, and any other type of ornamentation used in the personality area.

The facial adornment details are subject to the most rapid fashion change. This is because most of them are comparatively inexpensive and, therefore, often faddish. It is also because the viewer's eyes are held by these details more than any other part of an outfit and we may simply grow tired of seeing them. One should be sensitive to this phenomenon and change facial adornment with fashion. The person who clings to such details as the hairstyle or eyeglass design of a decade ago is advertising both age and a lack of awareness. Old college yearbooks graphically illustrate this point. The Sweetheart of Alpha Xi Delta pictured in the twenty-year-old annual looks rather funny by today's beauty standards. So does the same middle-aged sweetheart if she is still wearing the hairstyle, makeup, and jewelry of her college days.

Because styles and popularity of the various face details change so rapidly, it is impossible in a textbook to be specific about what might be currently fashionable. It is better for students to understand the underlying principles for choosing each detail so that no matter what the mode of the day, they may select facial adornment that will be the most becoming to them.

All adornment, including facial design, incorporates the design elements and the design principles, particularly balance, proportion, and emphasis. Application of these to each fashion variation is the key to selecting individual facial details. In choosing the items that bring emphasis to the personality area, one must constantly remember that these are only a part of the total look. These details should be evaluated with the entire outfit so that the finished product presents a unified image. Thus, each of the facial details should be selected so that its line-form-shape-space, colors, and textures harmonize with and complete the total look.

Head, Face, and Neck Conformation

The size and shape of the head, face, features, and neck should be considered in relationship to the conformation of the total body. By analyzing the body as suggested in Chapter 6, by studying pictures of oneself in many poses, and by viewing oneself in a mirror from many angles, one can become familiar with the shapes and lines of the head, as well as face and neck conformation.

The head must appear to be in proportion with the body if a pleasing relationship is to be realized. A person having a small head appears out of proportion and balance although the head size may contrast with the rest of the figure in a manner that emphasizes body length. A large head distorts the proportional relationship of the body and may make one appear shorter or top heavy. Try to determine your head size in relationship to your body. Is it small, well-proportioned, or large? Hair and hat styles can be used to affect pleasing relationships as discussed later in this chapter.

Face shapes are difficult to determine. Reference books often define faces by the geometric shapes. Nature never seems this exacting. Because the face is composed of so many planes and shapes, it is easier to describe a face than to label it as a particular geometric shape. Some people do not have a definite face shape.

Study your features, both individually and in their relationship to your face and head. Pull the hair back from your face and study your head and face both in profile and full face. Start with the forehead profile; does it recede, stand straight, or bulge forward? Full-face: Is your forehead wide or narrow? What is the hairline position on your forehead? How are the eyes set in your head? Are they deep set or do they bulge out? Are they wide set or close together? Analyze your nose for length, shape, and size. Study your mouth; does it droop or pout? Are your upper and lower lips formed with the same amount of fullness? Is your mouth evenly centered? Examine your chinline. Does you chin recede or jut forward? How many chins do you have? Facial photos, both full-face and profile, may help you make this objective analysis.

After studying each feature individually, analyze it in relationship to the others and to your entire face. Try to determine which are the predominant lines in the shape of your features and face.

Study your neck in relationship to your total body and your head. Does your neck appear to be long or short? Is it thick or thin? How is your head carried on your neck?

Next, decide what you really like about your face, features, and neck. Learn to emphasize these areas. Decide which areas of your head, face, and neck formation you wish to minimize. Develop an eye for balance, proportion, and emphasis to achieve the "looks" that are best for your face and body.

Ideals and Standards of Beauty (Male and Female)

Ideals of physical attractiveness are based on personal opinions that have been influenced by current fashion, local environment, and the culturization of the individual. Roach and Eicher observed that in all societies some forms of human appearance are singled out as having desirable aesthetic qualities, whereas other qualities are rejected. Cultural ideals for physical beauty evolve when a consensus on what is considered most beautiful is developed. They noted that ideals of beauty exist as goals and may be achieved by only a few people. They believed that cultural standards for beauty are distinguished from ideals, because a standard was real and could be measured and thus achieved by many people. Roach and Eicher gave the example of a standard length for a woman's dress at a particular time being ten inches from the floor; any variation from this standard could be measured. They concluded that there is no exact standard to use in measuring ideal facial form. Therefore, facial beauty is an ideal that must be judged by each individual in his own frame of reference.[1]

Beauty can be created. An individual's idea of attractiveness combined with the fashion of the day, environmental concepts, and skillful application of the art elements of line-form-shape-space textures and colors can create a concept of beauty.

For many the term *beauty* denotes the female. In our culture, most people are more comfortable describing males as handsome or attractive. How you feel about this terminology is a matter of personal opinion. However, the authors do recognize that the techniques of enhancing the facial appearance of male and female, although similar in many aspects, are very different in others.

[1] Mary Ellen Roach and Joanne B. Eicher, *The Visible Self: Perspectives on Dress* (Englewood Cliffs, N.J.: Prentice-Hall, 1973), pp. 93–94.

Plastic Surgery

Since World War II, cosmetic surgery has continually become more common-place. Requests for this service come from people on all social levels and of all racial backgrounds. It was reported that one in five requests for cosmetic surgery comes from men. Most people request face-lifts, including eyelid surgeries; other popular surgeries are nose jobs, breast reductions or augmentations, ear corrections, and hair transplants.

The two most often expressed motives for desiring plastic surgery are to look younger to obtain or maintain a job, and to look younger to obtain or maintain a mate. Publicity given plastic surgery in the popular press and on television has extended knowledge of the practices and the possibilities of this cosmetic surgery to the general public.

Changes in attitudes toward personal vanity have also contributed toward the increased use of cosmetic surgery. Vanity is now considered healthy. Most people no longer consider it a sin to want to look better. Dr. Franklin Ashley, a prominent plastic surgeon, feels that personal vanity should play an important part in one's life. He observed:

You owe it to your friends, and your family and yourself, especially if you're in the business community. I think most people who have any intelligence and are fairly broadminded have come to the conclusion that people have the right to do whatever they can to improve themselves. Within the lifetimes of many young people, plastic surgery will be an everyday occurrence.[2]

Cosmetics for Men and Women

Medicated Cosmetics

Medicated cosmetics are big business. They are directed to all age groups but especially to teen-agers. Self-medication is almost an American tradition. The cosmetic industry has taken advantage of this and has consequently pushed into the province of patent medicine. Products ranging from baby powder to after-shave lotions boast of "special medicated ingredients." The teen-ager plagued with acne at a time when social acceptance is so important is a natural consumer of such products; the cosmetic industry directs much of its advertising and packaging specifically toward him/her. It is not surprising then that medicated cosmetic products are usually preferred by this group because of a conditioned response in teen-agers developed by the advertising industry.

What advertising-heavy, research-light cosmetic companies seldom broadcast

[2] Beth Ann Krier, "Why They Want Beauty Surgery," *Los Angeles Times*, June 24, 1973, Pt. II, p. 1.

is the biological truth. The intact human skin has a phenomenal, built-in defense system against infectious bacteria. Constant degerming and chemical interfering with this natural restorative process of the skin can and often does lead to more, not less, trouble. If the skin is broken, simple cleansing with mild soap and water is most often recommended. If it is not seriously wounded, the skin usually heals more quickly through its own recuperative powers. A wrong medicated cosmetic may further injure the skin.

Next time you are shopping for cosmetics, pause and read the labels of the medicated products. Can you find the answers to these questions: Medicated with what? To cure what? And for whom?

Collagen and Hormones in Cosmetics

Collagen and hormone creams have been introduced into the cosmetic market with great fanfare. Extravagant claims of skin rejuvenation have been made for the various creams and lotions containing hormones. These products are generally very expensive.

Scientists have not discovered completely why the skin wrinkles as it ages. However, we do know that as the epidermis (outer layer of the skin) ages, it usually becomes thinner and dryer. Locally applied creams containing collagen and hormones may possibly counteract nature by thickening the skin somewhat and by holding water to the skin, but so will other simple emollient creams. The fatty layer below the dermis provides support for the skin. As a person ages, the fatty layer often diminishes, particularly in some areas of the face, resulting in wrinkling and changes in facial contour. No cream will restore fat to the subcutaneous layer.

There has been some concern about the amount of hormone concentration in various cosmetic products. The Federal Drug Administration has established limits of hormone content that it regards as being safe. These limits apply to individual products. It is within the realm of possibility that a consumer could use a variety of products, all containing hormones, such as face creams, body oils, and hand creams, and exceed the amount thought to be safe. An excessive use of hormones could produce systemic effects, and this possibility must be kept in mind when such products are used.

In summary, cosmetics containing hormones should be carefully evaluated. They are generally expensive and directed toward the mature or "aging" consumer. Some may cause side effects if large amounts of various products are consistently used. They cannot rejuvenate the skin.

Hypoallergenic Cosmetics

Hypoallergenic cosmetics are designed to prevent allergic reactions in people who have allergies or extrasensitive skin. They are limited as to fashion colors and glamour products. Unfortunately, many hypoallergenic cosmetics are not exactly what they claim to be. To remedy this situation, legislation has been proposed to establish a standard scientific basis and definition for "hypoallergenic."[3]

Legislation now requires all manufacturers of cosmetic products to print the exact ingredients on the label. All cosmetic products are made of essentially the same basic ingredients, which the law now exposes. It is primarily the packaging and promotion that distinguishes one cosmetic from another and establishes its price range. Perutz concluded in her work that consumers are not really interested in dissecting the cosmetic industry. She stated:

Nothing is bought through physical necessity; no one is dependent on cosmetics, as on food and drugs, for the continuation of life. Almost every product exists at different price levels, and there are few women in America who can't afford a lipstick. When people pay five dollars or fifty dollars for a cream, they don't want to know the cost of making it. Elizabeth Arden has a subsidiary company's inexpensive line selling at Woolworth's; but though many people know that exactly the same products are sold in different packaging they insist on buying the more expensive variety.[4]

Most consumers are gullible when it comes to cosmetics; they invest a large amount of money and hope in a beauty jar. The success of Egmont Desperrois, a French chemist in charge of research at the cosmetics house of Orlane, is an example of this. In 1968, he introduced a cream advertised as "Creme B21." It contained various amino acids. The creme sold at $40 a bottle. In three weeks he sold 20,000 bottles, in one year, 180,000 bottles. In 1974, this same product was introduced in the Mexico City market at $110 a jar, and demand exceeded the supply.[5]

Facial Ornamentation—Men

One can imagine that thousands of years ago the ancient hunter smeared paint over his nakedness. Did paint make him feel greater than he was? Did the strongest hunter of the tribe wear the most paint?

Later, man may have discovered that the fat of animals protected his skin from the elements and made it harder for an enemy to grasp him, so he oiled his face and his body. The strongest tribesman may have gotten the most fragrant oils. Thus "cosmetics" may have been created—by man and for man, not woman.

But woman was not to be denied. Having her babies and biding her time, she used his paints and his oils.

Along came the contemporary man with his health kicks, head shops, and

---

[3] "Truth in Labeling Cosmetics," *Consumer Register*, Vol. 4, No. 2 (April 15, 1974).

[4] Kathrin Perutz, *Beyond the Looking Glass, America's Beauty Culture* (New York: Morrow, 1970), pp. 22–23.

[5] "Beauty at Any Price," *Parade*, August 18, 1974, p. 4.

14-1 *The contemporary man cares about his looks. Sales of men's grooming products are at an all-time high. (Courtesy Jockey International)*

Cardin suits in the 1960s and set off a new wave of men's cosmetics. Call them toiletries or grooming aids if that soothes your psyche. But the fact remains that men are rediscovering the joys of smelling good, taking better care of their skin and hair, and helping nature to make them look better (Figure 14-1).

Macho men along with the not-so-macho types are using colognes, moisturizers, treatment masks, peeling creams, bronzers, eye makeup, cheek and lip color. Sales of these men's products hit the billion dollar mark in 1977, and have not stopped climbing yet. More and more men are going to skin-treatment salons, especially as increasing numbers of these places are established as part of hair-styling salons. They also are getting permanents and hair coloring and hairpieces.

Men are getting nose jobs, eye jobs, and face-lifts. They are exercising and dieting. They want to feel good and look even better.

Instead of smelling like "Old Spice" or "Aqua Velva" after-shave lotions, they are more likely dousing themselves with a so-called prestigious designer fragrance. Bill Blass, Ralph Lauren, Geoffrey Beene, Hermes, Yves Saint Laurent,

Lagerfeld, Calvin Klein, and Guy Laroche are among the big name designers profiting from men's fragrances.

Avon, the world's largest cosmetic firm, now has men doing the "Avon Calling." Avon, incidentally, was the first of all cosmetic companies to introduce a product solely for men. In 1896 it sold California Cream Shaving Soap. Today Avon lists over forty cosmetic products for men ranging from shaving soap to colognes or body splashes.

Aramis, launched by Estée Lauder in 1964, has pioneered the proliferation of men's toiletries and grooming aids. This fast-moving, innovative line currently has more than eighty products including three new skin-care systems geared to various types of skins, beards, and climates. In 1978 Lauder added "Devin," with about a dozen products for men from antiperspirant to cologne and moisturizer with a country air fragrance.

At this time, colognes and after-shave lead the sales of men's toiletries and grooming products. Skin treatment products now represent the fastest growing area of this market.

Skin care specialist Georgette Klinger introduced her first products for men and established her first men's salon in New York City in 1972. Today the men's salon business in her New York, Chicago, Beverly Hills, and Bal Harbour, Florida, locations accounts for about 15 percent of her total business. Klinger claims her men's and women's businesses are both growing at the same rate, approximately 25 percent a year.

A new line, which has omitted the fragrance, or promise of the ultimate in sex appeal, is Sheldon Simon's "Therapeutic Skin Care Program for Men." It has five products to be used each day including preshave base, shave foam, facial soap, facial scrub, and facial conditioner. The soap and the scrub come in three formulas, for dry, normal, and oily skin. Others who have jumped on the men's skin-care products bandwagon include Jovan, Monsieur Rochas, "Polo," Pierre Cardin, Yves Saint Laurent's "Pour Homme," Fabergé with "Brut" and "Macho," Geoffrey Beene, Givenchy, Lagerfeld, Chanel, Scannon, Royal Copenhagen, and Paco Rabbane.

Cosmetic industry spokesmen say there are no up-to-date factual figures on industry-wide sales of cosmetics and/or toiletries and grooming products—only estimates and projections. One of the most respected sources of estimates is *Beauty Fashion*, a trade magazine. This magazine estimated total cosmetic industry sales of about $8 billion with an 8 to 10 percent growth per year. Of this amount, about $1.5 billion was in men's cosmetic products.[6]

At this time, it cannot be predicted with any certainty that the majority of men will eventually use as many or as elaborate facial cosmetics as women. However, it is certainly within the realm of possibility. The techniques for applying cosmetic products would be the same for men as women if the final effect were to be an androgynous one.

[6] Patricia Shelton, "For Men," *Los Angeles Times*, Fashion 84, July 13, 1984, p. 5.

Facial Routine

For most men, facial ornamentation begins with a clean face. Oily faces may need special care to control the oil. This was discussed in Chapter 8.

For many men, shaving is an important part of the daily routine. Shaving instruments and methods are best determined by the quantity and texture of the beard and the sensitivity of the skin.

There is one product on the market, a bronzer, that has gained wide acceptance among many men. The purpose of the bronzer is to give the skin a healthy, suntanned glow. It also helps to moisturize and protect the skin from dirt and grime. It is very similar to the cosmetic foundation used by women. Bronzer should be applied to extend into the hairline, under the jawline, and around the ears if they are exposed. The bronzer color selected should blend with the natural skin tones. It should be completely removed during the skin-cleansing routine.

Facial ornamentation for men refers most often to beards, moustaches, and sideburns. All these require a good deal of thought as to their design and a great deal of time for their upkeep and care. The design of a beard, moustache, or sideburns should enhance the face. It should emphasize the eyes and mouth. It should minimize or conceal facial faults or problem areas. In selecting the style of beard, moustache, or sideburns, the head should be studied from all angles to see exactly how hair growth affects the facial planes. The rule of line should be employed. Facial lines repeated in beard, moustache, or sideburn lines emphasize by repetition. Extreme facial lines emphasize by contrast.

Beards, moustaches, and sideburns seem to carry the same kind of nonverbal messages as eyebrows. They can make the individual appear evil, suave, jolly, sexy, or sad. Untrimmed facial hair looks messy and unkempt. Overtrimmed moustaches can create the illusion of a dirty upper lip.

The color of facial hair may vary from that of the hair on top of the head. If the contrast is great, this should be a consideration in selecting a becoming style of beard, moustache, or sideburns.

Facial Ornamentation—Women

The use of facial cosmetics is almost as old as woman herself. As soon as civilization progressed past the point of survival, self-adornment became important, and, of course, this holds true today. A study of the various cultures shows that, although the standards of beauty vary tremendously, facial makeup plays an important part in the lives of most women the world over.

The use of cosmetics in the United States has had a varied history. Their acceptance and popularity has been related to both social and religious beliefs. The majority of today's population accepts the use of cosmetics and enjoys their benefits.

Some girls will reject cosmetics, saying that the men in their lives prefer the natural look. The wiser girl will acknowledge this preference for a natural look but will use subtle cosmetics to enhance her beauty, for this is what the art of makeup is all about. Cosmetics may be applied to improve on nature without distorting the original. Professional makeup artists term this "the natural look." If the cosmetics are properly applied for this look, they are never obvious. Others, including models and actresses, use a more exotic cosmetic approach termed "high fashion," "fantasy," or "character." For these special effects, the makeup may be very obvious.

A wise woman learns to use the cosmetics that are best for her. She knows her face. She uses cosmetics to accent her best features and to camouflage the problem features. She studies the fashion trends of cosmetics in the current magazines and changes her routines to stay abreast of the time. She is also willing to practice and learn new techniques so that when she presents herself she is at her best.

This same wise woman has made a commitment to herself and to those around her. She takes the time and makes the effort to always appear at her best. Makeup is a vital part of her grooming. It is as important to her private life as it is to her public life. She may sometimes vary her routine, using very casual makeup for daytime activities, sports, or picnicking, and more formal makeup for glamorous evenings, but nonetheless, she is made up.

This commitment means that she will always manage to have the time to properly cleanse and make up her face, comb her hair, and dress before making her appearance. This means that she can never be a "slug-a-bed," snoozing the last second away, because she must allow time to prepare herself to face the world. Look around your early morning classes; check the early morning lady chauffeurs. It will be obvious which women have enough self-pride to present themselves at their best to this early audience.

A phenomenon of the female psyche is that many women report that they actually get more accomplished on the days they are faithful to their early morning beauty routine than they do on the days they skip the ritual. Work seems to go faster, studying becomes more effective, and emergencies are easier to cope with. This same woman is never embarrassed by her appearance, for she is prepared to receive whomever knocks at her door, whether it be her best beau or the Avon Lady.

Properly applying makeup takes time. It begins with completely cleaning and moisturizing the face. The artwork follows. The popular magazines and newspapers frequently print interviews with models and actresses who claim to take only ten minutes to make up. This cannot be true. If a picture accompanies the article, try to analyze all the makeup the woman has on. She probably spent about six times that ten minutes applying makeup to her face! Of course, how long it takes depends on your skill at applying makeup. But a much more honest time allotment might be thirty minutes for most days, sixty minutes for a special occasion. This estimate includes time for cleansing, moisturizing, grooming, and doing cosmetic artwork.

The best way to learn about makeup is to have a personal consultation with a professional cosmetologist. Most cosmetic firms train their representatives to help patrons learn to use their company's products. Many of these firms advertise free personal demonstrations. These advertisements are located in the yellow pages of telephone books, in newspapers, in magazines, and in brochures mailed out by department stores. These demonstrations are not only fun to take advantage of but are also informative. Of course, it should be remembered that the demonstrators are trying to sell you their products, but you need never buy more than you actually wish, and you can always take time to consider your purchase for a while. Most stores that feature cosmetics also have specially trained people to help you learn to use them, and often these people have free samples for you to try.

Fashions in makeup change as quickly as fashions in clothing. Many magazines and newspapers carry beauty columns and regularly feature picture stories on new makeup techniques. For additional ideas, study the models used in any type of advertising copy; they are all professionals in the beauty business and must keep up with the new fashion trends. When you see a look you like, analyze the makeup carefully. Choose what is best for you and evolve your own look from what is currently popular.

To achieve the best makeup look for yourself, you must have a complete understanding of your face. You should decide which features are your best and those features you wish to camouflage.

Facial Shapes

Motion pictures and television have both had great influence on the cosmetic industry and on makeup fashion. As these industries pioneered and grew in their craft, they created makeup artists who developed products, techniques, and styles of beauty that were copied both by the cosmetic manufacturer and the average woman. In the black-and-white days of motion pictures and television, makeup techniques were invented to meet the special lighting requirements of these media. Some of these makeup ideas were accepted as basic principles, when actually they were devised to meet the special needs of the film-making business. Because most filmwork is now in color, there has been a tremendous change in makeup products and techniques used in this industry. These new ideas can be incorporated into the beauty routines of all interested women.

In his discussion on face shapes, Kehoe revealed the recent thinking of professional studio makeup artists. *Coordinative Compatibility* is the new concept that has been developed. It discards the old principle that facial shapes are geometric (such as square, round, oblong, and the like) and that the ideal face is oval-shaped and all women should use makeup to create this face shape. *Coordinative Compatibility* introduces a new method of facial accents.

Kehoe explained that the idea of the oval-shaped face being the so-called perfect face was based on the photographic effect experienced in black-and-white photography. The oval face, because it presented the most pleasing planes, was the easiest to light and photograph. Studio makeup artists therefore developed ways of making all faces appear oval. These makeup concepts worked fine for black-and-white movies and later for black-and-white television. However, many manufacturers of street makeup and fashion writers said that these principles should also be applied to street makeup, which was a fallacy.

The concept of *Coordinative Compatibility* was explained by Kehoe:

First, we coordinate as a whole the elements of the face and hair; second, conform them to the present modes of daytime or evening make-up and wardrobe combinations; third, with make-up, accomplish the most important new point in beauty: use the individual's own features as they are to create an overall pattern of concept of beauty. This means, in short, that we create a perfect symmetry of beauty for each individual woman.

He continued:

Primarily, make-up does two things in combination. It emphasizes the best and most important features, and, in doing so, it tends to minimize the less desirable ones.[7]

Each face has three fundamentals: the eyes, the lips, and the complexion. Makeup is used to accent each of these.

The eyes are the most important feature of the face. They are the focal point we look at when talking to another person. They reflect the thoughts and emotions of that person. They are the center of interest in the face. More makeup products are produced for the eyes than for any other part of the face.

Next important are the lips. From this feature come the words, the smile, and the kiss. In rest or in motion, they should appear soft and expressive.

Supporting the eyes and lips is the complexion. It should appear soft, smooth, clean, and fresh. Color accents used should appear natural. The style, cut, and color of the hair should be coordinated with the makeup. By following basic makeup principles, each woman can achieve a look based on her own facial features. Her individual beauty will be revealed.

Makeup Products and Techniques

All makeup should be carefully applied and well blended so it does not appear artificial—unless that is the intent. Makeup that appears as "makeup" is unnatural looking. A natural makeup is not apparent; it is so well applied that it complements the woman wearing it in every way.

The type of cosmetics used and the sequence of makeup application varies with the individual and may change as new products come on the market. However, the following sequence is a good guide. A discussion of each term, the products used, and the techniques required follows:

[7] Vincent J-R Kehoe, *The Technique of Film and Television Make-up for Color and Black & White* (New York: Hastings House, 1969), pp. 58–59.

SEQUENCE OF COSMETICS APPLICATION

1. Moisturizer
2. Corrective Color Tint
3. Countershading
4. Foundation
5. Shading
6. Cheek Color
7. Eye Color
8. Eyebrows
9. Powder
10. Lashlines
11. Mascara
12. False Lashes
13. Lip Color

Corrective Tint. Corrective tints may be used under all makeup to counter the strong pigmentation of some skins. The corrective tint is a high-intensity color product. It employs the color principle that some colors neutralize each other in the following manner:

Corrective Tint Color	Skin Color Neutralized
aqua-green	red tones
mauve-rose	ruddy-sallow tones
apricot	yellow tones

The corrective tint is spread in a thin film all over the face and edges and blended into the hairline and under the jawline. This product also acts as a moisturizer.

Countershading. Countershading is the technique used to cover birthmarks, pigment spots, freckles, shadows, unwanted lines, and blemishes on the face. For some women this is the first step of the makeup routine that begins after the face has been cleansed and moisturized. The purpose of countershading is to cover the problem areas with a film of a light-colored product designed for this purpose. The color principle involved is that a white or light color will make the area covered appear to advance and thus minimize the problem. Countershading should not attempt to obliterate completely the shadow or blemish but should cover it, and the edges of the countershading should be blended into the skin.

The area of the eye socket should be carefully studied. Here, there is a natural shadow that has a deeper tonality than the rest of the face. This is a gray tone. In both countershading and shading this is an important color source. All the natural shadows of the face are variations of this same grayed color. To countershade, select a light tone with this gray characteristic. To shade, select a darker tone with this gray characteristic. (Shading is explained later.)

Foundation. Foundation is exactly what the name implies. It is the basis on which other artwork is done. Foundation also helps moisturize the facial skin as well as protect it from dirt, grime, and weather. The correct foundation color is based on the natural skin color, texture, and condition. Foundations come in a variety of forms so the techniques for applying them vary. It is important to remember that the foundation should be applied smoothly and thinly. It should extend past the edge of the jawline to avoid a masklike appearance. If you have enlarged pores or other such problems, learn to fill in the opening with foundation by "fingering-in." If the foundation sits on the edge of the pore, it will make it seem larger.

Also learn to make "erasers" to correct any artwork mistakes. Use an orange-wood stick, twist a small amount of cotton around the end, pour a small amount of foundation in the palm of the hand, and work the foundation into the cotton twist. This "eraser" can help you make any color corrections you wish to make.

Shading. Shading is the technique used to create shadows. It can be used to correct or reshape various areas such as the width of the nose, the frontal bone, the eye spacing, the cheek hollow, or the jawline. Colors used for this were noted in the discussion of countershading. (See Figures 14-2, 14-3 for shading directions.)

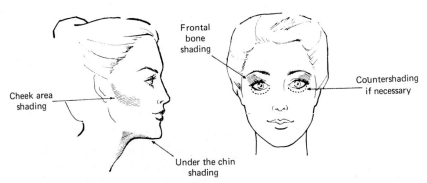

14-2 *Facial contouring.* Left: *Some women have a small portion of flesh under the chin. This can be minimized with a grayed-tan shade for light-hued skins or a grayed-brown for deeper or olive-hued skins.* Right: *Heavy frontal bones above the eyes can be shaded to appear narrower. Conversely, this area can be countershaded to appear wider.*

14-3 *Shading the eyes. (A) If the area between the brows is too wide, (B) it can be made to appear narrower by countershading the eye sockets near the corners. (C) If the area between the brows is too narrow, (D) it can be made to appear wider by shading the inside area of the eye sockets near the corners and extending the shading slightly over the edges.*

Color Contouring. Bright, high-intensity colors are used to accent and highlight the face. Cheek color, eye color, and lip color are all of this type. It should be remembered that a bright color always draws attention and highlights the area where it is applied. The use of color need not be limited. Touching the forehead, chin, or nose with color can be very flattering and break the overall flatness of the skin tone. Women with oily skins should avoid this, however, because their natural oil will create reflective highlights.

Cheek Color. A thin, transparent film of moist cheek color should be blended on the "apple," or bulge, of the cheekbone. This provides a color highlight and gives the effect of higher cheekbones.

Eye Color. Eye color products come in every form and color imaginable. The choice is a personal one. Whatever product you select, it should stay on your skin without disappearing or gathering in the lines formed as your eye opens and closes. (Powder can help set this, but even that will not help a poor-quality product.)

Eye color should coordinate with personal coloring. When the eye shadow repeats the eye color, the latter is reinforced.

Application of eye color depends on the structural formation of the eye, the lid, the socket, and the frontal bone. Color principles should be employed. Light eye color advances the area whereas dark eye color recedes the area. For street wear, it is recommended that the strongest concentration of color be near the lashline and carried in a slightly outward direction. This color should never be blended over the frontal bone where shading has been placed (except for special or fantasy effects). The eye color should not extend over the area where countershading has been placed at the corner of the eye. Rather, it should be swept in an upward direction. (See Figures 14-4, 14-5.)

Remember that the natural eye colors are the most subtle. Exotic effects can be obtained by using unnatural eye colors, including silver, pearl, or gold.

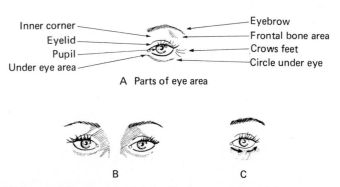

14-4 *The eyes: (A) Parts of the eye area, (B) the shadow area around the eyes, and (C) application of countershading under eye.*

14-5 *Eye shading and makeup.* Top Left: *Frontal bone highlighted.* Top Right: *Frontal bone shaded.* Center Left: *Eye color on lid area and extended slightly at corner.* Center Right: *Accent in hollow of eyelid.* Bottom Left: *Two shades of eye color on eyelid.* Bottom Right: *Highlight color.*

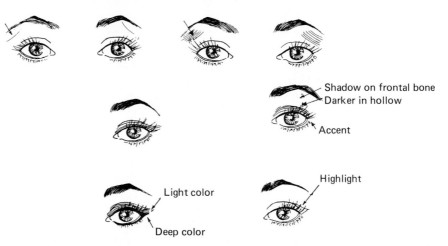

Shadow on frontal bone
Darker in hollow
Accent
Highlight
Light color
Deep color

Lashlines. The lashline serves to outline and emphasize the eyes by making the base for the eyelashes appear to be heavier in hair growth. The colors best suited for this purpose are natural colors. Lighter-skinned women look better in a brown-toned eyeliner, whereas the darker-skinned need black eyeliner.

When applying lashlines, use the natural lashes as a guideline. Start your lines where the hair grows. The contour of lashlines changes quickly with fashion, but whatever the current style, the eye should *not* be completely encircled. This closes the eye and makes it appear smaller. Allow the ends of your lashlines to open. (See Figure 14-6.)

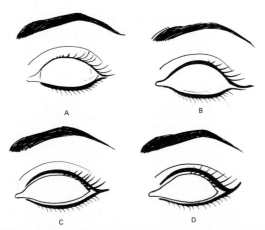

A
B
C
D

14-6 *Eyelining: (A) The lower lashline should begin where the lashes start to grow and extend beyond the outer corner of the eye in an upward sweep. (B) The upper lashline can be fine or heavy. It begins at the inner corner of the eye and continues to the outer corner, where it follows the lower lashline without meeting it. (C and D) Two* incorrect *methods of drawing lashlines. They should not meet, nor should the lower line take an exaggerated upward sweep.*

The Oriental Eye. The eyes of Oriental women often have a lovely almond shape and single-fold eyelid. Eye color and lashlines for these eyes need to be applied differently. Because of the way the single eyelid folds back into the eye socket, any eye color placed on the lid is not visible. Eye color will be more effective if placed just above the fold line. Because the space between eye and brow is often quite narrow, eye color usually should be limited to one color. Lashlines can be applied to emphasize and exaggerate the almond shape of the eye. Because of the single eyelid fold, false lashes may not be satisfactory.

Powder. Powder is used to set the makeup (not cake or compacted powder). It is an essential step in makeup. It keeps the artwork on you and not on your clothing or your best beau.

The best powders are called *neutral* or *transparent* as they can be used with any shade of foundation without changing its color or appearing heavy or powdery. A good powder should be light in weight, have little or no perfume, and should never turn color, streak, or build up and cake if worn over an extended period of time.

Powder that comes in a shaker bottle is easy to use and not as messy as that which comes in a box. A brush is better than a cotton ball for applying powder as the cotton can leave fuzz or linters on the face. Remember that the brush should *always* be clean.

Sprinkle the powder onto the palm of the hand and work it into the brush. Shake the brush to remove excess. If you have the right amount of powder, it will not fall from the brush if inverted at this point. Lightly brush the powder onto your face. Do not rub as this will abrade your skin. Brush the powder all over your face where foundation has been applied, over the eye color, cheek color, and eyebrows. Sweep off excessive powder using a downward stroke that follows the growth pattern of facial hair. The powder will set and soften your makeup. Powder should be applied in this manner several times during the makeup process. Retouch during the day in the same manner. Brush powder into the shiny areas. Compacted powder may be used for touchups but will not set makeup.

When you finish with the powder you may feel a little pale. It takes about thirty minutes for the oils of the skin to blend with the makeup. After this length of time you will find that the powder has taken on the tones of your skin.

The powder finish has been named the *matte* look. If you wish the *dewy* look, blot the face carefully with a small sea-sponge wrung out with cold water. This absorbs extra powder and gives a moist, young look to makeup. This step may also be repeated throughout the day and is especially refreshing during hot weather.

Eyebrows. The eyebrow should be a soft complementary shade and shape for each individual woman. Eyebrows that are incorrectly done can give undesirable expressions to the face. For example, a woman may look mean, tired, or surprised just because of the tilt or exaggeration of her brows.

The color of the brows is dependent on the hair color. Women with light-colored hair should have light-colored brows. Black should be used only by those who

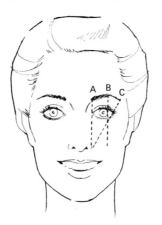
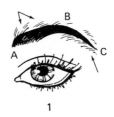

14-7 *To determine the eyebrow dimensions use a straightedge such as pencil or nail file to locate the following points: 1. Measure from side of nose straight up past tear duct to point A. This is the starting point of eyebrow. Pluck extra hair growing between A points of both eyes or pencil eyebrow to reach point A. 2. Measure from cheek straight past outside of edge of iris to point B. This locates the highest part of brow. The brow should be angled or curved at this point depending on other lines in face. 3. Measure from nostril straight past edge of eye to point C. This is the end point of brow. Point A and point C should be straight across from each other. The space between the eye and the brow in the area between B and C should be about the width of the iris.*

14-8 *Eyebrow. 1. The brows usually need plucking in this area. 2. The correct shape. The pencil is sketched on in small hairlike strokes where needed.*

have jet-black hair. Too dark a brow becomes too important to the overall composition of the face; too light a brow lacks expression. To get the exact shade right for you may take a combination of colors; use more than one pencil.

Before drawing brows with pencil, brush them with an eyebrow brush (a toothbrush will do). Brushing helps to groom and clean brows; it also guides them into the desired line. After sketching in brows, brush them again to work in color and soften their effect, then set and soften eyebrow with powder. (See Figures 14-7, 14-8.)

The eyebrow is the picture frame for the eye. If it is too broad, heavy, or low, it may distort the appearance of the eye. If it is too high, thin, or narrow, it will make the eye appear smaller and expose too much of the frontal bone. Heavy brows seem masculine; skinny brows seem hard. Both types seem to add age to the face.

Mascara. Mascara is used to darken the lashes and make them appear fuller. Black or dark brown are the colors most suitable for this product. Other fashion colors do create special effects but their use should be limited. Straight lashes can be curled before using mascara with a handy curler obtainable at most places where cosmetics are sold. After the mascara has dried the lashes should be separated. Several coats of mascara, each applied after the other has dried, will give a darker, fuller appearance.

False Eyelashes. False eyelashes are used by many. Their design changes with fashion. They add glamorous emphasis to the eyes and can change the appearance of the entire profile. Eyelashes vary greatly in price. The inexpensive ones are just as satisfactory as the higher-priced ones and are especially recommended for beginning experiments. The color, shape, and thickness of the lashes are a matter of personal choice. Some choose them for impact, whereas others wish only to assist nature slightly. If the latter is your intent, choose lashes that are close in color to your own and in a believable length and thickness. Measure your eye as the upper lashes grow from inner to outer edge. Snip off the extra lashes. It is easier to fit a too short pair, so do not worry about this in your first attempts. Measure both eyes, as they often differ.

Surgical glue, which can be purchased at any drugstore, is the best adhesive. It is chemically pure, dries quickly, and is inexpensive and lasts a long time. Spread the glue carefully along the back of the false lash, allow about ten seconds for the glue to set, and then place the lash against the base of your own lashes. Use a blunt pusher, such as the back of a hairpin or eyebrow tweezer, to reinforce the sticking. You will probably have white glue showing, but it becomes transparent as it dries so give it time. As a final step, pinch false lashes into your own lashes with your thumb and forefinger.

False eyelashes should be comfortable. If they are not, they may be glued incorrectly or they may need to be trimmed shorter. They will seem heavy at first, but you will adjust to this feeling before long. Clumps of lashes are sometimes used on the bottom lashes. These may be glued on separately or purchased as transparent strips. They are applied under your own bottom lashes. Practice should perfect this technique.

False lashes may be cleaned with rubbing alcohol. Just pop them in a small container and shake. Dry them on a tissue. They should last for about six weeks of daily wear.

Eye Makeup and Glasses. Women who wear glasses often misunderstand the importance of their eye makeup. Glasses shade and shadow the eyes, but the eye area is visible. Therefore, eye color needs to be more emphatic when glasses are worn. Use slightly more eye color and slightly higher-intensity eye colors. Be very careful to create an eyebrow shape that is compatible with the frame shape of the glasses. Your glasses are a facial accent; they call attention to the eyes. You cannot hide the eyes behind glasses so emphasize them.

Lip Color. Lip color is used to both accent and moisturize. Although the lip color should coordinate with clothing and/or accessories, it is more important that it complement both skin color and tooth color.

A word of caution about long-lasting or permanent lip colors. These colors contain high concentrations of dyes that are very drying to the lips and may promote chapping or cracking. With this type of lip color the wax or emollients that were a part of the original formula are often licked or eaten off, leaving just the dye stain on the lips, which does not moisten or protect this sensitive area.

Changing the shape of the mouth is tricky. The change of just a fraction of an inch can make a tremendous difference. Exaggerated changes of either over-painting or underpainting the lip will usually result in a quite unnatural look. If the mouth line looks false, it usually detracts from the rest of the face and spoils the total look.

If lip color changes color on your lips or if your lips are of different colors, as often happens with dark-skinned women, use a lip undercoat that is available at cosmetic counters. Lip color is best applied by brush. The lips should be defined working from center to corner, and then filled in. To check your lip print for evenness, carefully press the mouth with a tissue.

Remember that the mouth, to be beautiful should balance the bottom part of the face. The shape and size of the your mouth should fit the rest of your face. In the past, many black women worried about the large size of their mouths; this should not be a concern today. The black woman should consider this feature as part of her proud heritage and enhance the wide lips as part of her individuality.

When the mouth is in motion, particularly when speaking, attention is directed to the teeth. To be attractive, teeth must be clean and they must be in good repair. Not all teeth can be chalk white. The same pigments that determine your skin undertones also determine the color of your teeth, so teeth come in as wide a range of colors as skin does. When choosing lip colors, choose those that are most complementary to your tooth color as well as your skin color.

Facial Expressions

The techniques of cosmetics help to emphasize and express the beauty that each woman possesses. It should always be kept in mind that the face is a mirror of oneself. Facial expressions reflect how one feels about oneself and the world around one. Happiness and peace are expressed in smiles, and any smiling face is a beautiful face. In the words of Chanel: "We are born with one face, but . . . laughing or crying, wisely or otherwise . . . eventually we form our own, along our own lines. A good face is composed of thoughtful laughter."[8]

No Makeup

Many women, for personal reasons, do not use cosmetics. These women must work a bit harder if they are to present themselves at their best. Their hair must always be shiny clean and attractively arranged, their skin immaculate, their teeth clean and repaired, and their eyebrows groomed. Their clothing should be carefully selected to enhance their delicate coloring and not overpower their personality. They should try always to wear a pleasant expression that reflects a zest for life and inner harmony.

[8] Gabrielle Chanel, "Collections by Chanel," McCall's, July 1968, p. 43.

14-9 *Hairstyles, jewelry, necklines, applied and structural design, all help bring emphasis to the face or personality area. (Courtesy American Enka)*

Face-Framing Details—Men and Women

Hair Design

Hair design is one of the most important dress details, for it is truly face-framing (Figure 14-9). Hair design is an integral part of the total silhouette. It should be in harmony with the age and activities of the wearer as well as with the conformation of the face and body. Two important factors in selecting a hair design are the amount of time an individual plans to devote to hair care and the amount of skill the individual has in handling hair. For those with limited time, patience, or skill, a simple, easy-care hairstyle is a must. For those who have both the time and the talent, a more complicated hairstyle is possible. Everyone should learn to care for his or her own hair.

The texture and condition of the hair will often limit the styles that can be achieved. This must always be an important consideration. Permanents add body to fine, limp hair and give it the illusion of increased volume. Straighteners soften and release or relax curl. Both permanents and straighteners change the texture of the hair, making it more manageable. There are many hair conditioners on the market; their general purpose is to improve the health of the hair by reconstructing the hair shaft chemically. It should be understood that there is a direct relationship between diet and the health of the hair, and a well-balanced diet is nature's best hair conditioner.

Natural hair coloring is closely keyed to skin coloring. Nature has a wide variety of skin and hair combinations, all of which are pleasing. Modern technology has made it both tempting and easy to alter nature's color scheme. However, anyone considering changing hair coloring should give the project careful study before beginning. Trying on wigs of various colors is a good, safe way to experiment.

One first needs to analyze and understand one's own coloring in order to select a new hair color that will be complementary. Second, one needs to select the correct agents for both hair and scalp. Third, and perhaps most important, directions must be carefully followed in applying hair coloring or disaster may result. Although changing hair coloring can be exciting and make one feel glamorous, many people have been bitterly disappointed, and even disfigured, because they did not understand the importance of the foregoing. Shocking, ludicrous hair colors, or subtly mismatched hair and skin tones, are both detractors of beauty. Damaged, weak, brittle hair with a "straw" or "cotton candy" appearance may result from wrong solutions. Painfully blistered scalp, even baldness, may be the product of an incorrect coloring technique.

Hair changes color naturally throughout the different stages of life. The vivid colors of youth generally begin to lighten or dull by the midtwenties. Graying hair, because it is associated with aging, distresses many, often quite early in life. This natural lightening process should be remembered when one decides to assist nature with hair coloring. As one matures, dark hair coloring should be lightened. The use of harsh, intense hair colors emphasizes the aging of the face and skin, whereas soft, pastel colors have a softening effect. The color of the hair has a definite effect on the illusion created by the style. Masses of dark hair appear to have more volume than light hair and for this reason usually require more thinning and shaping. Light hair shows off the intricacy of the design, whereas dark hair conceals the design.

In selecting a hair design, the facial features and head conformation are important. The hair can be styled to emphasize interesting facial features and minimize others. Thus, eyes may be emphasized by bangs, the mouth by sideburns or *guiches*, and so on. If you wish to narrow a wide face, comb the hair forward; if you wish to widen a narrow face, pull the hair back. Generally, the hair length should end above or below a feature that is to minimized, such as the jawline or cheekbone.

A short neck is lengthened by a short haircut or upswept styling. A long neck appears shorter with a longer hair style that ends an inch or two below the jawline. A small head appears larger when the hair is fluffed out. A large head may be made to appear smaller by the use of a controlled hairstyle.

Severe hairstyles, those that are smoothly drawn back from the face, reveal each contour of the head. In this type of hairstyle, imperfect features are emphasized. Center parts also emphasize features as they give the eye of the beholder a line with which to measure the formal balance of the face. Soft, informally balanced hairstyles are much kinder to the wearer. Because of their free form, they may be used to perfect the contour of the head. They have an irregular shape and, therefore, disguise the imperfections of the features.

The lines of the hairstyle should be analyzed carefully with consideration to head, feature, and body conformation. Remember that repeating a line emphasizes that line; going to the extreme of the line also emphasizes it. Therefore, if you wish to minimize a very round face, select a style that is neither completely round nor straight. To minimize a long face, avoid very straight lines and very round lines. To minimize a triangular face, avoid fullness at the widest and narrowest points of the face.

The best friend your hair can have is a professional hairstylist. Styling, shaping, and coloring are best done by trained specialists. If you give the stylist a chance to understand both you and your hair by having your hair done several times before doing any drastic changing, you will be wise. Shopping around for the stylist and salon that suits your needs is an excellent idea. Try to let the professional hairstylist take over. Relax and enjoy the appointment and do not make too many suggestions. Take advantage of the skill you are paying for, and you should discover a variety of becoming hairstyles and enjoy a pleasing period of pampering.

Wigs and Hairpieces

Wigs and hairpieces have found new popularity and acceptance. Some hairstyles could not be achieved without them. Modern technology has improved the quality and styling of both wigs and hairpieces, and public acceptance has made them fashionable.

Wigs and hairpieces may be styled in many different ways. They can be used by both men and women to cover balding or thin hair. They give freedom to many women, who may engage in vigorous sports or other activities confidently, knowing there is a fresh, attractive hairdo sitting on the closet shelf.

A wardrobe of wigs can provide a variety of hair colors and lengths. Many celebrities depend on this instant glamour and change. However, hairpieces added to one's own hair must be carefully color-matched so that they blend in and are not obvious.

Styles for both wigs and hairpieces should be selected by the same principles used in choosing a style for one's natural hair. One may be more adventuresome with the false hair, of course, but the end result should be becoming to the individual. Proper maintenance of hairpieces is important to ensure both attractiveness and long service. Wigs and hairpieces should be cleaned and restyled regularly.

Necklines

Necklines, including collars and lapels are also face-framing details of clothing. They should be selected with the same considerations as other parts of the outfit.

14-10 *Necklines,*
including collars and ties,
are also face-framing
details of clothing. They
should be selected with the
same consideration as
other parts of the outfit.
(Courtesy Pendleton
Woolen Mills)

Since the neckline of a garment forms only part of the frame for the face, it must be selected with careful thought for the other elements completing the frame, such as hair design or hat style (Figure 14-10).

The shape of the neckline is determined by the lines of the garment design. Again, the old rule holds true: do not repeat in the neckline a face shape you do not want to emphasize; do not emphasize shapes by using the extreme of their lines in a neckline. Square faces or jawlines are emphasized by square necklines or very round necklines such as the turtleneck. Round faces are emphasized by round necklines and also square necklines, and so on. The shape of the collar and lapels creates the same illusions.

The size of the neckline, collar, and lapels should be related to the size of the body, head, and features. It is possible for a person to have a small body and a large head with broad features, or a large body and small head with tiny features. The scale of the face-framing details should be selected to complement both the body and the face. Usually, the best way to create unity between disproportionate areas is to select elements that will create a transition in size between the two.

Thus, by selecting collars, lapels, or jewelry of a medium scale, the disproportionate face and figure are unified.

The neckline is often the most eye-arresting area of a garment. This effect can be created by either color or bare skin (Figure 14-11). Bright or contrasting colors used at the neckline area attract attention. This is an excellent way to create the illusion of a more slender body, as the eye of the beholder is held by the neckline interest rather than by the body silhouette. In this manner, the size of the body is camouflaged.

Décolleté, or open, necklines are always eye-arresting, and, of course, the more daring the cleavage, the more emphasis will be placed there. In selecting gar-

14-11 Décolleté necklines are always eye arresting. The more daring the cleavage, the more emphasis will be placed there. In selecting garments with an extreme neckline, the effects created by the movement of the body within the garment should be carefully studied. (Courtesy American Enka)

ments with an extreme neckline, the effects created by the movement of the body within the garment should be carefully studied. A garment cut low in front, back, or underarm may be impossible for some body types to wear without revealing much more than was intended. Study this in the dressing room before making such a purchase. A garment that inhibits movement for any reason becomes a kind of straitjacket, which never has been nor ever will be *in vogue*. Any garment that is to be worn dining should also be analyzed for its effect from the table up. The line of the table can cause some very unusual illusions.

Hat Styles

Hats have several functions. They may be worn to provide warmth and protection, to cover a wilted hairstyle, or to add the finishing touch to an outfit. Whatever the reason or occasion for wearing a hat, the hat should be flattering to the wearer.

When selecting a hat, view it from all angles. All hat stores and departments have full-length mirrors. Use them! Study the hat in relationship to the total body, the head, and the face. Choose only the hat that is becoming, no matter what its purpose—rain, sun, or special occasion.

Hats go through fashion cycles just as do other accessories. The size, shape, and decoration of the hat are keyed to the latest trends in garments. The statement made by the hat should correspond to the rest of the outfit and to what is being said by current fashion (Figure 14-12).

Hairstyles are closely correlated to hats, both in popularity and styling. When elaborate or bouffant hairstyles are fashionable, hats become less popular. A person must decide between hat and hairdo. If the hair design was difficult to achieve, one is usually reluctant to crush it under a hat. The hair design must be appropriate for the hat. Casual hairstyles do not complement sophisticated hats and *vice versa*. Usually the hairstyle must be subordinate to the hat.

The lines and shape of the hat can create illusions about the height of the wearer. Any hat lines that lead the eye in an upward direction will give the illusion of height. Lines that lead the eye across terminate the height at that point, whereas lines that lead the eye downward give the illusion of shortening the body.

A hat style that fits closely to the head and completely covers the hair emphasizes facial shape and features. The asymmetric brimline is the most flattering to all face shapes because of its irregularity. Hats that are worn on the back of the head allow the hair to soften facial features. Because hat designs are continually changing, it is best to discuss here only the basic principles of hat selection rather than to discuss specific hat styles.

The color of the hat should be selected to add flair and interest to the outfit. Repeating the hat color in the costume loses color impact. Matching hat and outfit color creates the illusion of height because a column of color is created.

Texture is probably the most limiting element of a hat. The textures of the

14-12 *Headcoverings and hats go through fashion cycles just as do other accessories. The size, shape, and decoration of all accessories should be keyed to the latest trends in garments. The statement made by the accessories should correspond to the rest of the outfit and to what is being said by current fashion. (Upper Left: Courtesy Jones of New York. Lower Left: Courtesy Catalina. Right: Courtesy Traci Scherek for Traci Ltd., St. Paul, Minnesota)*

materials used in making the hat determine the season that it may be worn. For women, straws, veiling, and flowers are spring and summer textures. Velours, felts, furs, and satins are fall and winter textures. For men, straw and Panama are spring and summer textures; felt and fur are fall and winter textures. Wearing a summer-textured hat in the blustery weather of winter is ridiculous. It would be better not to wear a hat than to wear one that is so inappropriate.

Jewelry

Jewelry has two broad classifications, referred to as "real" and "costume." Real jewelry is made from natural, or genuine, stones mounted in precious metals. Real stones are subclassified as precious and semiprecious. Among the precious gems are diamonds, pearls, sapphires, and rubies. These are very expensive because of their rarity and the skill required to cut them to achieve maximum beauty. Semiprecious stones include amethysts, agates, opals, turquoises, and corals. Real stones are mounted in gold, silver, or platinum; these metals are referred to as *fine* or *precious* metals. Scientists have developed man-made stones that closely resemble such natural stones as diamonds, rubies, and sapphires. Only close inspection by an expert can reveal the differences. Cultured pearls are not really man-made, as they result from the same processing as natural pearls.

Costume jewelry was made popular by Coco Chanel in the 1920s. Chanel continually used imitation jewelry in her collections, and the rest of the world has followed her lead. Costume jewelry may be made of wood, metal, paste, plastic, glass, or feathers. It has the single purpose of completing the outfit; its monetary value is not important. Its color, shape, or design in relationship to the garment is the important factor. Some costume jewelry may rival "real" jewelry in price because of its original design and beauty.

Whatever its value, jewelry is acquired permanently for the pleasure it gives. Each person needs to develop his or her own philosophy about jewelry. Selecting jewelry is a very personal matter based on individual values. Jewelry should be pleasing to look at and should add distinction to the clothing it adorns. This is really the only criterion for choosing jewelry; if it pleases you, then it is right (Figure 14-13).

Fashions in jewelry change. Some designs are ageless, whereas others are enhanced by updating. Often the settings of wedding and engagement rings signify the date of ceremonies. The length of a necklace may date it. The design of a bracelet may be stylish for only a short period of time. Generally, the more valuable the jewelry, the more ageless it is. However, the quality of the original design is a more important factor than its age. Resetting or restyling important jewelry is part of wardrobe upkeep, and can be very interesting as well.

In collecting costume jewelry, the fashion of the moment is most important. Costume jewelry may be faddish. It is sometimes short-lived because it appeals to a mass market and is usually inexpensive. When it is passé, it should disappear from your collection. Out-of-date costume jewelry will not add flair to any outfit. Some pieces of jewelry, such as handcrafted or ethnic items, do not fit this category and can be favorites for years. A fashion-sensitive individual can easily judge what should be kept and what should be discarded.

College women should sort out their jewelry collections. Some of the jewelry may now be too infantile in either scale or design. Evaluate each piece. It is important to understand that jewelry designed for a child can never enhance a woman. Some of the collection may be plain junk that should be discarded or put in a memory box.

College students should put away high school rings and pins. These belong to your past and have no part of your current life. If the pin or ring has sentimental importance, it is best worn on a chain around your neck and out of sight. Clinging to high school jewelry in college is considered immature by most college students.

Fraternity jewelry belongs to the college campus. Most fraternities and sororities have regulations for wearing their insignias, and, of course, these should be followed. When a girl accepts a fraternity pin, she should learn how she is supposed to wear it. Often, the uninformed wear fraternity pins on jackets or coats, which is considered bad form by most national fraternities.

College jewelry, with the exception of rings, should be put away at the end of

14-13 *Jewelry should be pleasing to look at and should add distinction to the clothing it adorns. This is really the only criterion for choosing jewelry. If it pleases you, then it is right. (Courtesy Bleyle)*

college days and worn only for alumni/alumnae gatherings. College jewelry, especially sorority and fraternity pins, has no place in the business world. Again, if the jewelry is of great sentimental value and you feel you must wear it, conceal it under your clothing—it will be closer to your heart anyway.

Eyeglasses

Eyeglasses are both eye-arresting and face-framing, and, therefore, must be considered a fashion accessory. An individual's face shape, coloring, and personality; his interests and activities; and when and how much he will wear his glasses are all important factors in selecting frames for eyeglasses.

The size of the frames should be related to the size of the face. (Fashion sometimes dictates otherwise.) Personal coloring will limit some choices of frames. The fair blonde usually looks best in lighter-hued frames, whereas the brunette looks best in darker frames. If you can afford it, a wardrobe of frames is desirable, but this is usually too expensive for most people. Those who wear glasses only part of the time are freer to select "kooky" or extreme frames than those who wear glasses constantly. The latter should choose the less extreme or less faddish styles.

Styles of frames for eyeglasses come and go, as they are a part of the total fashion picture. Be careful not to be dated by your last visit to the ophthalmologist. Consider changing your style of frames every three years.

If you must wear glasses, learn not to hide behind them. Too many people plop their glasses on their noses and think, "Now no one can see me!" Remember always that glasses bring attention to the personality area. Make them a fashion accessory and consider them in relationship to your total look.

Suggested Activities

1. The classic face is said to have regular features. Some arrangements of features are more pleasing than others. Often what pleases most depends on the fashion of the moment. Individuality is created by the unique arrangement of features in each face. Consider some public personalities. These women have all been called beautiful: Barbra Streisand, Grace Jones, Diana Ross, Cher Bono, Diahann Carroll, Raquel Welch, Linda Evans, Nastassja Kinski, and Connie Chung. These men have been considered handsome: Robert Redford, Toshiro Mufume, Carl Louis, Tom Selleck, Greg Louganis, Mikail Baryshnikov, and Prince Charles of England. You can add others that you believe belong on this list. Try to determine why these people are considered so special. Each has a very different look, yet is considered attractive by a large segment of the population. What sets them apart?

2. Investigate cosmetic pricing. Compare several brands sold at different types of stores. As a consumer are you concerned about cosmetic legislation? How, and to whom, should you express this concern?

3. In this chapter we have discussed many of the face design details common to men and women. How do you feel about this? Do you feel that the cosmetic and grooming needs of men and women are similar or very different? Why do you feel the way you do?

4. Collect pictures from magazines that feature "makeovers" for men and women. Study the details of the "makeovers." Decide if any of the techniques used are ones you would choose to adopt and explain why.

IV

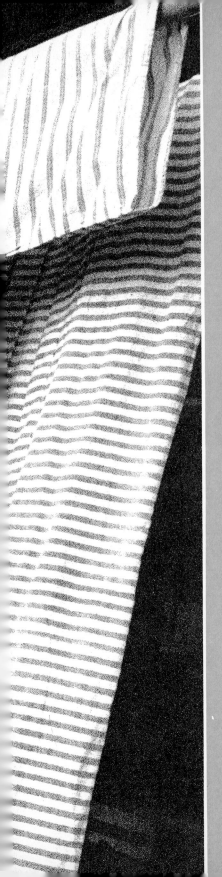

Consumer Clothing Considerations

15 *Wardrobe Strategies*

The purpose of your text is to help you understand and develop your own unique individuality. This aim would be defeated if a dictatorial wardrobe plan were presented. The following wardrobe strategies draw from all the material previously presented and require that the student apply this information to the guidelines for personal wardrobe planning and collecting.

The popular literature is full of schemes for developing the perfect wardrobe. These plans are usually based on "power" or "investment" clothes which the writer claims will have you "dressed for success." The plans are probably excellent ideas for the authors of these articles but not necessarily a panacea for the rest of us. If we all followed their advice we would all look alike, and how successful do you think a nation of clones would be? When anyone gives advice for selecting clothes it is usually based on his or her personal value system, lifestyle, psychological and physical needs. Therefore, that person's wardrobe plan will be appropriate only for people with that same value system and lifestyle and with the same psychological and physical needs. With the wide variety of occupations and leisure activities pursued today, how can a limited clothing plan work for everyone in every geographical and climatic location?

Imagine what people in the following occupations would wear for a regular day at work:

a computer programmer
a department store manager
a lawyer
a nursery school teacher
a TV reporter
a fashion editor

Now imagine what they would wear if they worked in:

New York City
Miami, Florida
Los Angeles, California
St. Paul, Minnesota
Corvallis, Oregon
Houston, Texas
Omaha, Nebraska

429

Could the same clothing plan work for people in each of these occupations in each of these geographical and climate zones? What additional factors can you add to the list of considerations which also would make identical clothing plans inappropriate?

Personal preference
Design (line-form-shape-space, color, and texture)
Fit
Lifestyles
Values
Individuality
Fashion/fad
Local custom
Physical requirements
Weather

Next review Chapter 2, Individuality—A Search for Identity. Answer these questions:

What *image* do I want to project with my clothing?
Is this image always the same? Or do I want to present a variety of looks to suit my different *roles*?
How can I reveal my *personality* with the clothes I wear?
How does my *self-concept* limit the choice of clothes I feel comfortable in?
What are the *values* that influence my wardrobe choices?
What is my *attitude* toward clothing?
What are my *interests* that concern clothing?
What *activities* requiring special clothing are part of my lifestyle?
How can I express my *individuality* with the wardrobe I collect?

Clothing must fit the individual psychologically. All the clothing requirements numerated by answering the above questions must be incorporated into planning your wardrobe.

Now review the work you did in Chapter 6, Your Body, and the Design Guidelines in Appendices section A and B, Summary of Design. Answer these questions:

What do I like best about my body that I would like to *emphasize*?
What do I consider a problem about my body that I would like to *minimize*?
Do I like to *conceal* my body?
Do I like to *reveal* my body?
How do I like my clothes to *fit* my body?
How does my body compare to the current *fashion ideal*?

Clothing must fit the individual physically. All the clothing requirements numerated by answering the above questions must be incorporated into your wardrobe planning.

15-1 *A wardrobe plan must fit your lifestyle, the pattern by which you live, including all the things you do each day, each week, each month, each year. If a sports activity like skiing is part of your lifestyle, then you need the appropriate clothing for that sport. (Courtesy Levi Strauss & Co.)*

Your *lifestyle* is the pattern by which you live. It includes all the things that you do each day, each week, each month, each year (Figure 15-1). It is affected by:

your family, friends, and colleagues
your education, occupation, and recreation
your financial status
your housing and transportation
your nutritional status
your geographic location, local customs, weather
your psychological and physical needs
your personal preferences

431

As the years pass, we live through the cycles of life, and our lifestyles evolve through different patterns. When planning a wardrobe, individual lifestyles must be the basis of our plan. Understanding our own lifestyle requirements will enable us to know the variety of garments we need for our activities. Because abrupt changes in lifestyle result from such things as the completion of school and full-time employment, job transfers, parenthood, or retirement it is important to anticipate these changes and incorporate them into wardrobe planning.

Your *fashion position* also has a great deal to do with the kind of wardrobe that will be best for you (Figure 15-2). Are you a fashion leader or a fashion follower? Do you enjoy wearing a look of new trendy clothes or are you more comfortable in clothes you have grown accustomed to wearing? Are you a conservative dresser who likes to use clothing to blend in with the crowd, or are you part of a subculture that uses clothing to identify yourself and sometimes to shock or poke fun at the establishment? Are you sometimes one kind of a dresser and sometimes another? Or perhaps you would prefer to describe your style of dressing in completely different terms. The answers to these questions will give

15-2 *Your fashion position also has a great deal to do with the kind of wardrobe that will be best for you. Determine your fashion position and then develop a wardrobe based on this information. (Courtesy Traci Ltd.)*

you more understanding of the wardrobe plan that will best suit your individual requirements.

Planning and Collecting

Wardrobes often just happen. The term *wardrobe* is defined as "a stock of clothing or costumes belonging to a person."[1] This stock of clothing, in most cases, was accumulated over a long period of time and consists of wearables, nearly wearables, and nonwearables. Some garments are worn frequently, some are saved for special occasions, and some are pushed to the back of the closet and ignored. Many people keep a neat closet or at least clean it up once-in-a-while, but very few have a workable, coordinated wardrobe that completely suits their lifestyle. Most of us go on adding to and subtracting from our personal stock of clothing and costumes with little forethought or planning.

A planned wardrobe can work very much like a planned budget. Assets should be built upon and liabilities should be disposed of. By careful wardrobe analysis, groups of clothing can be organized and coordinated so that they can be worn for a variety of needs and occasions. If your wardrobe plan is successful, you will never be guilty of the old bromide: "I haven't a thing to wear." Perhaps this last statement is too strong for you to accept. However, if you carefully consider what has been stated, it should become obvious that it is a valid claim.

There are times, of course, when new garments are needed for special occasions. For example, the first weekend spent at a ski resort could be such an occasion. This type of event would be out of the ordinary for the individual and would, therefore, represent an expansion of his/her lifestyle. If it were a one-time-only activity, some warm clothing in the existing wardrobe could "make do" for one weekend; if skiing became a regular activity, however, then the appropriate gear should be added to the wardrobe because the lifestyle has been expanded to include this activity. Participation in a wedding party is another type of special occasion. If the wedding is to be informal, some apparel in the existing wardrobe may be appropriate; if the wedding is to be a formal pageant, then the bride would prescribe the apparel, which would then have to be obtained for the big event.

This type of functional wardrobe is the result of thoughtful planning and prudent buying. It does not happen all at once; it is continually developing and evolving. A wardrobe plan does not start with a complete new beginning—very few of us could or would want to throw out all our clothing and start anew with an empty closet. A planned wardrobe starts with analyzing your needs, evaluating present clothing, examining available resources, and developing a clothing-collecting plan. Any wardrobe plan must begin with your lifestyle and your closet.

[1]*The Random House Dictionary of the English Language,* unabridged (New York: Random, 1966), p. 1608.

Wardrobe Planning—Step One

Lifestyle Chart

The Lifestyle Chart (Table 15-1) has been designed to help you understand the patterns of your everyday living. By filling in one chart with your current activities you can determine your current wardrobe needs. Fill in a second chart for a future time, perhaps five years from now, or a time when you will have reached certain personal goals. This will help you anticipate the clothing needs required by changes in your lifestyle.

Fill in the charts with various colors to represent your weekly activities. Include the following:

school	dressy
work	formal
casual/at home	sports
casual/out	sleep

(additional activities may be added)

The amount of time you spend in the various activities will give you a graphic idea of the percentage of your wardrobe you may choose to devote to the kinds of clothing required by these activities. The information learned from these lifestyle charts is part of the basis of information you need to develop your individual wardrobe plan.

Wardrobe Planning—Step Two

Analyzing Existing Wardrobe

The next step in wardrobe planning is evaluation of existing clothing. Divide all garments into groups. In the first group, place all the garments you wear frequently. In the second section, place all the garments you wear occasionally. In the third group, place all the garments that need repairing or updating. In the last section place all the garments that you have not worn in the past year. Divide all accessories into the same categories. Carefully analyze each of the separate groups of clothing. Determine the characteristics of the garments placed in each group. Answer each of the following questions for each garment:

Lifestyle:

For what activities do you wear this garment?
Do these activities fit your lifestyle now?
Will these activities be part of your lifestyle in the near future?

Table 15-1. Lifestyle Chart

Directions: Fill in the chart using color to represent your weekly activities such as school or work, casual at home or going out, sports, formal dress, sleep, and so on.

	Mon.	Tues.	Weds.	Thurs.	Fri.	Sat.	Sun.
A.M. 5							
6							
7							
8							
9							
10							
11							
P.M. 12							
1							
2							
3							
4							
5							
6							
7							
8							
9							
10							
11							
A.M. 12							
1							
2							
3							
4							

Source: Adopted from Alice Meyer and Clara Pierre, *Clotheswise Successful Dressing for Your Lifestyle* (New York: Dutton, 1982), p. 12.

Design:

What are the predominate lines?
What is the style? Is it fashionable?
What is the color? Is it fashionable?
What is the texture? Is it fashionable?
Is the design classic or timeless?

Fit:

How does it fit your present body conformation?
Is it physically comfortable?
Is it psychologically comfortable?

Care:
The care it requires:

Does it keep its shape/or wrinkle?
Is it hard to press?
Does it soil easily?
How is it cleaned?
Is it expensive to maintain?

Quality:

How much did you pay for it?
How long have you had it?
Does it represent the look you prefer?

Individuality:

Does it have flair or signature?
What do you especially like (or dislike) about it?

Repeat this process with accessories.

Wardrobe Planning—Step Three

From the information gathered from the groupings and questions, you should be able to determine the following:

The various characteristics that make garments pleasing, practical, and appropriate for you.

The variety of clothing needed for your lifestyle.
The garments that need mending or recycling.
The garments that should be passed on to friends, relatives, or to charity.
The accessories that work for you.

From this information you should be able to develop the criteria for selecting the new garments and accessories to complete your wardrobe.

The kinds of garments that need to be added to your existing wardrobe are the ones required to meet your personal needs. These needs are depicted on your lifestyle chart, which graphically shows the activities of your life that demand certain kinds of clothing.

The measure of a well-planned wardrobe is the special invitation or unexpected occasion. If your wardrobe is planned for your lifestyle, you will have the right thing to wear for everything you might be called upon to do. A good example of this was the quickly planned swearing-in ceremony of Gerald R. Ford as the thirty-eighth president of the United States. Mrs. Ford, who had worked as a fashion coordinator prior to her marriage, reached into her closet and came up with the right outfit to wear for this historic ceremony.[2]

Exploring Resources

Wardrobe planning entails exploring all available resources. The first question that most often comes to mind is how much of the income can be allotted for clothing purchases and upkeep. Studies show that about 6 percent of the total family income was used for clothing expenditures in 1984. The United States Department of Agriculture studies estimate that consumers spent $588 per person on clothing and shoes in 1984. This was an increase of $46 over the 1983 amount (in current dollars). Of this increase 35 percent was attributed to higher prices and 65 percent to increased buying.[3]

To be realistic, all resources must be examined in planning for clothing. The existing wardrobe contains items on which to build. The items found in the first group of the wardrobe analysis, the garments you wear frequently, will provide this foundation. These basic favorites should be augmented by planned additions so that they will interweave with other clothing and be extended into several varying combinations. If these favorite garments are of a style that enables them to be worn for most of your activities, they may become the "fundamental components" of the wardrobe. Additions to these favorites should be fairly easy to coordinate and can be called "wardrobe extenders." If your favorite garments seem too limited in their use, they can also become "wardrobe extenders." You can plan to add new purchases of "fundamental components" to combine with your already acquired "wardrobe extenders."

An important resource is home sewing. This resource is possible only if you

[2] *Time*, August 14, 1974, p. 28.
[3] Joan C. Courtless, U.S. Department of Agriculture, Outlook '85 Conference, Washington, D.C., December 3–5, 1980.

have developed the skills and have the time to sew. (Sewing is a skill that can be acquired by both men and women.) It is estimated that about 62 percent of clothing costs can be saved by sewing clothes at home.

Resourceful shoppers have found a valuable source for garments in the used-clothing market. In some areas there are shops that sell high-quality, seldom-used clothing in excellent condition. These stores sell clothing donated by or purchased from people who wear their clothes just a few times and then replace them. Some localities also have outlet or discount houses and stores that sell factory samples and factory rejects. The latter are clothes that have some manufacturing error that keeps them out of the usual retail market. The error may be as minor as a small fabric flaw or it may be a noticeable construction mistake such as an incorrectly inserted sleeve that can be reworked if you have the skill.

Another money-saver is the recycling of your own clothing. Adding trims, removing tired looking decorations, dyeing, and remodeling can revitalize garments. Some clothing can be recut for use as children's garments when the fabric has wear-life remaining.

Wardrobe costs should include the price of upkeep. The methods utilized for garment cleaning will often affect the clothing budget and these will need to be planned. Whether to buy a "real" suede jacket, which requires leather-cleaning techniques at about seven times the cost of regular professional dry cleaning, or a washable "pseudo" leather garment is more than a decision of fashion. Fake fur coats, which require "fur coat cleaning methods," can drain a clothing budget rapidly. Economical, washable fabrics can replace the "dry-clean-only" textiles in wardrobes of people with limited clothing dollars. Light-colored clothing with "dry-clean-only" labels will require more expensive upkeep than darker colors, particularly if they are worn in areas such as large cities where the environment is sooty or grimy. These are some of the kinds of clothing factors to be considered before making a purchase.

Many people overlook the simple economics of quality versus quantity. High-quality clothing of fine workmanship and materials is often overlooked from the standpoint of dollar savings. A good-quality major clothing item of classic style can be worn for many years and, therefore, will be less expensive in the long run than two or three garments of lesser quality that will need replacing during the same number of years. For example, a topcoat that costs $100 and lasts only two years costs $50 per year. A topcoat that costs $200, if worn for eight years, costs $25 per year. The less expensive topcoat thus costs more in the long run. Garments that need frequent replacement do not contribute to wardrobe-building. Quality versus quantity is a personal value judgment. Some people prefer many changes of clothing and would be unhappy with a limited, long-lasting wardrobe.

It would appear that rising costs of living have mandated a change in consumer buying practices. Inflation of clothing costs resulting from higher costs of fibers, labor, and production creates the necessity for a coordinated, flexible, and extendable wardrobe. This type of wardrobe depends on classic styles and coordinated colors and textures. Building on such basics, the wardrobe becomes a continual and ongoing project.

Family clothing budgets must be extended to cover the needs of each individual. Major purchases should be staggered so that family members do not require expensive items of clothing, such as winter coats, all at the same time. Single persons living on a limited budget need to do the same kind of balancing but often must trade off a major clothing purchase with something such as a car repair. Both families and single persons are better off if they plan for clothing expenditures in advance. Because emergencies do arise, it is always a good idea to have a "crisis fund" built into each budget.

Wardrobe Planning—Step Four

Fundamental Components + Wardrobe Extenders = the Collected Wardrobe

The final step in wardrobe strategy is putting all the preliminary budgeting, analysis, and planning into action. The existing wardrobe (which now has been thinned out, repaired, or recycled) should be grouped to fit into the two categories of fundamental components and wardrobe extenders.

Fundamental Components

"Fundamental components" form the basic framework of the wardrobe. They will be the garments worn most often. Wardrobe "Fundamental components" are placed into this category because of the following characteristics (Figure 15-3):

Style or Design	Simple, basic, classic.
	Structural design rather than surface enrichment.
Color	Staple or basic low-value colors such as beige, brown, gray, white, black, or navy.
	Fashion colors[4] such as hunter green and plum.
	Classic middle-value colors such as red, blue, orange, green.
	All "fundamental components" should be in the same Color Key palette (see Chapter 11, Color).
Texture	Middle textures, not extremes of roughness or smoothness.
	Background textures[5] that are not eye-arresting.
Trims	Contrasting trims and surface enrichment that are not eye-arresting. Subtle, self-trims are acceptable.
Quality	The highest quality you can afford is generally a wise investment for these wardrobe fundamentals. (This is a value judgment that must be made on an individual basis.)

[4] Fashion colors become dated with the change of fashion.
[5] Textures also become dated with changes of fashion.

15-3 *Wardrobe "fundamental components" are placed into this category because the style or design is simple, basic, classic; the color is staple or basic low value; the texture is not extreme. These two outfits would be classified "fundamental components" for a conservative executive career-type wardrobe. (Courtesy The Joseph & Feiss Company)*

Wardrobe Extenders

"Wardrobe extenders" add flair and a fashion signature to the "fundamental components" (Figure 15-4). These items, which may be long-lived, such as a silk scarf that has classic status, are always acceptable, and recur as fashion periodically; or they may be a fleeting fad worn with good humor on one or two occasions and then discarded.

Suggested "wardrobe extenders":

Men		Women	
sweaters/jackets	belts	sweaters/jackets	belts
special occasion	ties	special occasion	ribbons/ties/scarves
garments	scarves	garments	hats
knit shirts	hats	knit shirts/blouses/tops	purses
sport shirts	shoes	vests	shoes
vests	jewelry	pants/slacks/shorts	jewelry/hair
pants/slacks/shorts		skirts, varied lengths	ornaments

15-4 *"Wardrobe extenders" add flair and fashion signature to the "fundamental components." Here the same tie and shirt are worn in a variety of ways including business and casual wear. (Courtesy Jones of New York)*

Characteristics of "Wardrobe Extenders":

Style or Design	Special, unique, interesting, exciting.
Color	Flair or accent varying in value and intensity.
	In the same Color Key pallete as "fundamental components," color combinations unlimited.
Texture	Any texture pleasing to the individual, scaled in keeping with his/her size.
Trims	Any trims pleasing to the individual, scaled in keeping with his/her size.
Quality	As pleases the individual. There will probably be a wide range from costly to inexpensive "treasures."

Achieving Variety

Evaluate the existing "fundamental components" in your wardrobe to decide what major purchases will be required. These "fundamental components" should be planned so that they can be worn together as well as with a variety of "wardrobe extenders" (Figure 15-5). What additions would provide added individuality and needed refreshment to your wardrobe?

To illustrate the variety that can be achieved from following a wardrobe plan based on "fundamental components" and "wardrobe extenders," "Tic Tac Dough" game show host Wink Martindale has never worn the same outfit twice in the more than 1,000 segments. Martindale has 115 suits, dozens of shirts, hundreds of ties that his wardrobe manager mixes and matches to create new combinations.[6]

It has been stressed that each wardrobe must be suited to the individual and to the unique requirements of each lifestyle. Because many career-oriented adults have similar wardrobe requirements, we have included photos of a sample wardrobe for both men and women to illustrate the kinds of "fundamental components" to be considered. People who live in regions with extremes in seasonal weather will find warm-weather and cold-weather variations necessary (Figure 15-6).

It is recognized that some students and others with a very simple lifestyle may require only a few garments; the wardrobe suggested here is one based on current social standards and business world requirements. Students should recognize the proven phenomenon of American "upward mo" (yuppie). It carries with it

[6] Los Angeles Times, *Listen*, August 12, 1983, Pt. IV, p. 6.

15-5 *"Fundamental components" should be planned so that they can be worn together as well as with a variety of "wardrobe extenders." Factors determining whether garments go together include style, color, texture, trim, and quality. (Courtesy Jantzen)*

15-6 *People who live in regions with extremes in seasonal weather need to plan for these weather variations. Casual clothes can fulfill the requirement of "fundamental components and wardrobe extenders." How would you classify these two warm-weather outfits? (Courtesy Camp Beverly Hills)*

an implication of homogeneity. Successful professionals begin to look uniformly young, uniformly fashionable, uniformly striving.[7] (See Figure 15-7.)

Wardrobe strategy must be ongoing. The wardrobe should be evaluated on an annual basis in the same manner just discussed. As your lifestyle evolves so must your clothing. Once the pattern has been established, "fundamental components" can be combined with "wardrobe extenders" to create a kaleidoscope of outfits to meet the dress needs of every occasion in your life. Adding to, subtracting from, recycling, and creating new combinations from your stock of clothing and costumes is what wardrobe-collecting is all about. This plan is flexible enough to work for single people and families. It allows for wide variation to meet the special needs of each lifestyle. It provides a wardrobe to complement and accent each expression of individuality.

Fundamental Components + Wardrobe Extenders = the Collected Wardrobe

[7] Charles T. Powers, "One Tough N.Y. Avenue Now in Vogue," *Los Angeles Times*, August 16, 1979, p. 1.

15-7 *Students should recognize the proven phenomenon of American mobility (yuppie). Young professionals dress in a manner that reveals their degree of success. (Courtesy The Joseph & Feiss Company)*

Appropriate Dress

Learning how to dress appropriately for a variety of occasions is a difficult task for anyone who moves, either geographically, socially, or economically, from familiar and comfortable surroundings. These kinds of moves are often encountered as one accomplishes professional goals. Appropriate dress is important for any individual who is upwardly motivated, and it is equally important for the spouse also. In many businesses couples are both considered a part of the corporate image (Figure 15-8).

The best way to learn how to dress appropriately for any occasion is to embark on a study plan which would need to include sensitive observation of practices of dress in the new or aspired-to surroundings. Studying the photos in society sections of the local newspapers, walking the various shopping areas and observing what is being worn and what is being offered for sale, reading current etiquette books and dress advice magazines and newspaper columns can all help. Watching people, especially those who seem to have it "made" is really the best. People-watching should become a daily habit. Good advice is to dress like the person whose job, status, or lifestyle you would like to have. Of course to follow this advice adjustments sometimes must be made for the economics involved.

Power Dressing

Consider this statement:

The way in which we are clothed, by choice or by necessity, is, of course, far more than a matter of protection or adornment, far more than a measure of our culture, our earnings, our tastes. Fashion, as it is called, is often a question of politics, a barometer of the most profound social and economic change or longing. It reveals not only who has the power but who lacks it, who represents the dominant society and who is defying that dominance.[8]

[8] Gloria Emerson, "Your Clothes: What They Tell About Your Politics," *Vogue*, September 1979.

15-8 *Learning how to dress appropriately for a variety of occasions is a difficult task for anyone who moves, either geographically, socially, or economically from familiar and comfortable surroundings. Appropriate dress is often critical for the spouse also. In many businesses, couples are both considered a part of the corporate image. (Left: Courtesy Catalina. Right: Courtesy The Joseph & Feiss Company)*

Very often we immediately stereotype "power dressing." Most of us would describe the traditional man's business suit complete with stiff-collared shirt and tie, oxford-type shoes and executive-length matching socks and the female version of the business suit, as "power clothes." In many cases they certainly would be. When doctors or lawyers wear these outfits to professional meetings they show their power. But what about the Indian chief at a ceremonial powwow. His adoption of the business suit in lieu of the traditionally prescribed headdress, garments, face and body paint would cause him loss of power!

Power can be defined as being in charge, in control, in command or having authority. Clothing can help to reveal this status only if the garments selected are appropriate to the situation, the time, the place, the activity and the age and the body conformation of the wearer (unity). Our same business suit is only a power garment when it is appropriate to the occasion. It loses power when worn to the beach, a football game, a rock concert, a black-tie affair, or an aerobics class. It also would be an inappropriate choice when applying for a job where no one in authority dressed in business suits. Power dressing is achieved only when the outfits worn are accepted by the people in control of the situation and considered by them to be appropriate for the wearer and the occasion (Figure 15-9).

Dressing for the Job Interview

What to wear to a job interview is always a concern. While the choices of clothing must vary, the best guideline remains constant. Dress as though you already have the job. This means you need to find out what the company dress standards are in advance of your interview.

If you are seeking an executive-type job with a conservative company, the traditional business suit is generally the safest. For women, the business suit may be softened and feminized; understated dresses and jackets or coats also work well. Both men and women should be certain all accessories are well co-ordinated and shoes repaired and polished.

If you are applying for a job in a creative field such as fashion, interior design, promotion or entertainment, the dress requirements are very different. Your clothing should reveal not only your creativity but also your awareness of what is current and a quality befitting the salary level you are seeking. (Refer to Chapter 17, Family Clothing Needs and Buying Guides.)

If you are applying for a nonexecutive or entry-level job in fields such as construction, manufacturing, distribution, or transportation, it is important not to overdress. Your clothing should reveal that you are ready to work, that you do not think of yourself superior to the person who will be your supervisor or the person doing your interview.

Whatever the job, it is wise to do your "homework" before the interview. This means finding out all you can about the company and the job requirements

15-9 *Power dressing is achieved only when the outfits worn are accepted by the people in control of the situation and considered by them to be appropriate for the wearer and the occasion. Think of how this family on an autumn mountain outing would look if the parents were dressed in conservative businesswear, the boy in a school uniform, and the teen-aged daughter in a party dress with heels and hose. Dressed in such a manner, the family would lose power and be treated in a manner different from that accorded to those dressed appropriately for the outing. (Courtesy Altra)*

including what the dress code will be. If possible, go to the job location and discretely observe the employees entering or leaving work before you choose the outfit you will wear for the interview.

It is also imperative that the clothing you select for the interview be comfortable both physically and psychologically. Once you have decided on what you want to wear, a dress rehearsal is in order. Put the entire outfit together. Make sure all parts of it are coordinated in design. Inspect it for loose buttons, tears, and spots and press it. Try it on and sit, stand, move around to make certain you are truly comfortable. Make any adjustments or repairs needed in advance of your interview date. If you are doing a series of interviews it would be wise to keep this assembled outfit ready for each appointment. The purpose of this advance planning is so that you can concentrate on your interview and not be distracted by your clothing.

Listed here are some of the cautions that apply to any job interview:

Never chew gum. Gum chewing is extremely offensive.

Be clean, well-groomed, manicured.

Hair should be styled appropriately. For men this includes trimming beards and moustaches. For women this often means controlling long romantic locks.

For most jobs women should wear stockings. Remember women do not make it to the board room without stockings. (Men probably don't either.)

Try to wear something that will help you to be identified and set apart from the other applicants, a flower, a special piece of jewelry, an interesting color combination.

For women, use makeup in keeping with the outfit.

For both men and women, jewelry needs to be thoughtfully selected and kept appropriate.

The most important thing to establish in an interview is credibility. The interviewee needs to help the prospective employer understand that he/she is knowledgeable and serious about accepting the responsibilities of the job. Clothing can be selected to help establish this credibility.

Dressing the part is only a portion of the job interview. Eye contact, intonation of voice, verbal skills, posture standing and sitting, combined with business manners, including the handshake are another portion. Preparedness both in required skills and/or education plus the self-confidence to sell oneself complete the package.

Dressing on the Job

The dress code that you sleuthed out for your job interview should continue to be your guide after you have landed the job. You need to continue to be sensitive to the kind of apparel that seems to win approval and be worn by the people who run the company and those who appear to be favored for advancement. You need to decide what you want from this company too; if you are planning on advancement, your wardrobe strategies may need to conform to what has been established.

Companies that fit into the ultraconservative classification, including most banks, some law firms, most brokerage firms, and some corporations, want employees to dress conservatively. Most of these companies are endeavoring to extend a corporate image that says "trust us." They want employees to dress in a manner that will inspire this confidence. They also want their employees to dress in a manner that will not attract attention. Quiet or dark colors such as navy, gray, brown, and beige work well. Matched business suits, of good quality and well-tailored are the basic uniform. Women can sometimes vary this look with dresses. Accessories should be in keeping with the quality conservative image. Immaculate grooming is essential.

For men the rules are specific: Traditional business dress and understated accessories in the best quality you can afford.

For women the rules are more elaborate and include a lot of negatives:

NO plunging necklines	NO sweaters
NO cling	NO bare legs
NO loud colors	NO ankle-strap shoes
NO see-through fabrics	NO short skirts
NO glittery fabrics	NO tight skirts
NO pants	NO tight anything

The ranks of business where anything goes are a minority but very much a part of many creative fields such as the entertainment industry, including music, television, movies, and the theater. Some public relations firms, some advertising agencies, some interior design firms, some fashion magazines, some boutiques are among the businesses that could be ranked in this grouping. These organizations want their employees to project unique, creative, attention-grabbing images. For employees in these firms anything goes—wild, funky, punky, bizarre, wonderful dress. Everyday can be Halloween fantasy.

In the middle of the road are the companies that make up the bulk of American business, from the huge urban conglomerates to the small town family-owned stores. Here in the middle are located most law firms, advertising agencies, marketing firms, insurance companies, retailers, educational institutions, libraries, and governmental agencies. These organizations want to project a comfortable, reliable, trustworthy, professional, businesslike image. Appropriate apparel for positions in these firms is a casual variation of the conservative look. Garments acceptable in these places of business have a wide range, so look around. Remember always that this is a place of work and employees are expected to project this in their dress.[9]

Many people are employed in jobs that require a uniform. This uniform was selected to project a very specific corporate image. Companies such as the airlines disapprove of any personalization of their uniform. Other employers such as hospitals have much looser rules. Do remember what the basic purpose of the uniform is when you decide to embellish it. Too much of a personal signature may interfere with the function of the uniform, by drawing attention to you in a manner that will be criticized by your superiors.

Workers who perform skilled labor make up a large part of the work force in this country. While sometimes they are assigned a uniform, more often they are not. Clothing choices for these jobs generally should be body-covering and protective. Safety is always an important clothing consideration for workers in these jobs. Long-sleeved shirts and long pants with sturdy shoes or boots are usual choices. Weather can determine other garments. Cold, wet climates and warm, high humidity can change clothing choices from winter to summer. Once again, the garments selected should be in keeping with the tasks required in the job. Anything that draws too much attention to the worker will be subject to criticism.

For women entering professions such as civil engineering or forestry, which formerly were the province of men only, clothing choices must be seriously considered. Clothes for field work are usually determined by the factors mentioned for skilled workers. Clothes for the office and conferences can be a more personal choice. The type of firm would determine the garments most suitable for these appearances. It is not necessary to look like "one of the boys"; in fact it probably is very important not to. Natasha Josefowitz, lecturer and author, has noted, "you [women] can dress like a man, but you can never pass."[10]

[9] Emily Cho and Jermine Lueders, *Looking, Working, Living Terrific 24 Hours A Day* (New York: Ballantine Books, 1982), pp. 38–47.

[10] Lecture to California Community Colleges' Home Economics Annual Meeting, March 1, 1983, Sacramento, Calif. Natasha Josefowitz, *Paths to Power* (Reading, Mass.: Addison-Wesley, 1980).

Whatever your employment, whether it is president of your own company or the lowest entry-level position; whether it is a part-time summer job or the professional position you have worked long and hard to attain, your work clothes are important. Clothes are the instant communicators, signaling to others your competence, judgment, and confidence in one quick impression.

Clothes for Personal Life

The clothing you select for your personal life can have great variety just as your lifestyle may have. The only guidelines that would apply for the clothes that you select for your personal life are the ones that have been stated several times: the garments should be appropriate to the situation, the time, the place, the activity, and the age and body conformation of the wearer. The clothing that you select should give you the power to make you appear in control. These garments should be your most comfortable and fit you both physically and psychologically (Figure 15-10).

Our bodies and how we handle them, or our physical selves, combined with our personalities and other nonvisible characteristics, create our personal signature or image. This image should be a true reflection of our individuality. The better we understand our individuality, the better we can present this image to the world, and the better we can select our clothing to conform with our image.

People do not have to know more about your private life than you want to tell them, but they will "read" everything about you, correct or incorrect, by the way you dress. Of course, people interpret what they read by the alphabet that they know, from their own personal computer or frame of reference. How they react to you is based on this information. This response will be based on their feeling that they have "read" you accurately. You will enhance your position if you communicate your image message clearly and consistently.

Cho explained:

Over and over again, research studies and psychological experiments have shown that both men and women judge attractive people as more skilled, brighter intellectually and more socially likable.

(Proving yet again the truth of that old saying, "Them that has, gets.")

If you change the impression your clothes make, you'll set off a whole series of changes in people's responses to you. When people respond differently, how *you* feel about yourself will change. And before you know it, there you are in the winner's circle, where things keep getting better and better.

Your image can be a wonderful, magical tool to open doors for you, to help get you where you want to go.

If, on the other hand, you stop caring about how you look, you'll lose that

15-10 *The clothing you select for your personal life can have great variety just as your lifestyle may have. The only guidelines that would apply for the clothes that you select for your personal life are that the garments should be appropriate to the situation, the time, the place, the activity, and the age and body conformation of the wearer.* (Upper Left: *Courtesy Maria Rodriguez Designs.* Lower Left: *Courtesy Ermenegildo Zegna Corp.* Right: *Courtesy Folkwear, Inc.*)

delight in living that people are instinctively attracted to. Being poorly dressed over time leads to a chronic feeling of inferiority and inadequacy.[11]

When dressing for your personal life and leisure activities you possibly contact many more people than you do in your place of work. It is equally important that your appearance continue to project the messages you intend to send.

Dressing for Special Occasions

15-11 *The rules are well defined for "black tie" occasions. It often is a good idea for men who do not attend many formal functions to rent because tuxedos quickly become dated. (Courtesy Caumont Cherchez Ltd., Allan Curtis)*

Social invitations present the opportunities to dress for special occasions. What to wear can present a true dilemma especially if the occasion is one that is unfamiliar.

This is once again the time for research. If you are in a familiar setting and you know the host or hostess well, a simple telephone call can put you at ease. However, if you are in a new location, and or if you do not know the host or hostess, you will have to search out the answers yourself. Here are several resource suggestions; perhaps you can think of others:

1. If the invitation is printed, look up this type of invitation in a current etiquette book and check the type of clothing suggested.
2. Discuss the invitation with several people whose judgment you trust.
3. Study the society pages of the local newspaper to see what kinds of clothing seem to be fashionable.

If your research still leaves you in doubt, be safe and underdress. That is, dress conservatively in dark clothes that will not shout for attention. If the occasion is business-related, wearing something similar to what you regularly wear to work is safe; remember even though it is called an office party, you will still be working for the company and judged in this context.

If it is a black-tie occasion, the dress rules are well-defined. For men, a tux with a black tie is in order. In the major cities of the United States black-tie parties are very fashionable. Tuxes can be rented with all the appropriate accessories, and for men who do not attend many formal functions, this is a good option because tuxedos quickly become dated (Figure 15-11). For women, black-tie always means an escort. Think about it, who is supposed to wear the black tie? Any exception to this should be carefully explored. It is possible for a man to escort more than one woman. Women can wear either short or long gowns depending on local custom. This is an opportunity for women to pull out all the stops and dress in "drop dead" glamorous evening wear (Figure 15-12).

For some, the special invitations do not seem to offer a chance to dress up, especially if one is socializing with familiar friends who have settled into the

---

[11] Cho, op. cit., p. 30.

15-12 *A formal invitation is an opportunity for women to pull out all the stops and dress in glamorous or romantic formal wear. (Courtesy Priscilla of Boston)*

habit of casual dressing for everything. Since dressing is one of our most personal expressions, you may be finding yourself frustrated at not being able to break out of this mold. Expressing individuality with dress is an indication of maturity. Think about this, any occasion can be made special by dressing up.

Travel Wardrobes

By planning your wardrobe based on your lifestyle you will always have a travel wardrobe ready to go. This is true because when people travel they continue to do things that are a part of their lifestyle. People who love sports usually select holidays that include these favorite activities just as people who love art and music plan vacations that include enjoying museums and concerts. Of course, there are exceptions; a trip to Uncle Paul's and Auntie Alice's may concentrate more on relatives than your favorite leisure, just as a first trip to Western Europe may include touring more churches and art museums than subsequent trips. But chances are if these excursions allow you any free-choice time, you will elect to do something that you consider fun and that is part of your lifestyle pattern. We tend to enjoy the same things when we travel that we do when we are home; therefore, the clothing that we wear at home can be the basis of our travel wardrobe.

453

When planning any trip to an unfamiliar place, one of the most important things to do is to do enough "homework" to be familiar with such things as the weather and dress customs as well as the points of interest to you and range of activities you will be experiencing. When traveling to foreign countries, both the monetary rate of exchange and health conditions should be researched along with a variety of personal considerations.

A planned travel wardrobe is an essential part of the preparation and if done well will contribute greatly to the success of the trip. Each travel wardrobe must fulfill the following criteria:

Be attractive and comfortable.
Be appropriate for a wide variety of occasions.
Be easily packed.
Be easily maintained.
Be easy to carry.
Meet climate changes.

Clothes in the existing wardrobe should be the basis for planning. Apart from the money-saving factor, clothing that has been worn has already been tested for both psychological and physical comfort as well as maintenance. Shoes that are known to be comfortable are a much wiser choice than new ones. When purchasing needed new items for the trip it is a good idea to allow some weartime to test them for comfort and service before departing.

Clothing selected for travel should be "fundamental components" that can be accessorized with lightweight "wardrobe extenders." If the "fundamental components" are all the same color, a great variety of outfits can be devised with a minimum of garments. Heavy items like shoes, coats, and sweaters will all interweave with the "fundamental components." Variety and flair can be added with "wardrobe extenders." This *one-color* clothing plan may seem boring to you now, but when traveling over an extended time the responsibility of a lot of personal possessions can become a burden. Remember that as you move about you will be making many entrances where no one has ever seen you or your wardrobe.

Do be aware that the clothes we wear are part of our local scene. There are still parts of the United States of America as well as parts of the world where certain garments and personal adornment are offensive and sometimes illegal. (See Chapter 4, Clothing, the Communicator of Culture.)

Select garments and fabrics that travel well. A simple test before buying is to crush the fabric quickly in your hand and release it. If wrinkles appear in this brief time you know this fabric would not sit or pack well. Knits usually travel very well and will shed wrinkles easily. Good travel fibers are wool, polyester, acrylics, nylon, and permanent-press blends. Select fibers/fabrics that are easy care or will not show soil. Avoid garments with sharply pressed pleats or very full gathers as they do not pack easily.

You should be able to maintain your travel wardrobe yourself. It is not only expensive, but very time-consuming to depend on outside services. Stores specializing in luggage usually have ingenious travel accessories such as portable clotheslines, inflatable hangers, and travel irons.

Plastic bags of powdered detergent can be tucked in the suitcase for use along the way. Many hotels provide drying racks for "drip drying"; of course, towel racks are often pressed into service for this purpose.

Shoes should be selected with care. Even though you have eliminated the need for a variety of shoes by selecting a one-color wardrobe, you should plan to take several pairs of shoes for both foot comfort and for the variety of activities you plan. At least one pair should be selected for solid comfort and be sturdy enough to endure miles of walking and sightseeing. Also include lightweight sandals for warm weather and dressier shoes for special events.

Packing

When traveling by car it is often easy to pack just the car and take all kinds of items. This type of travel wardrobe is really not a planned one. Often in this case the wardrobe does not work and you have hauled around a lot of unnecessary paraphernalia. The experienced traveler will travel by car with the same type of wardrobe that is required when traveling on public transportation; that is, one that a person can handle alone. The maximum should be one suitcase and one "under-the-seat" bag. Sophisticated travelers usually get along with even less than this. With the wide variety of styles currently available it is easy to select luggage to meet your individual needs and preferences.

Lightweight luggage is really imperative. It should be sturdy and comfortable for you to carry. It should be designed to accommodate the things you want to take with you. Be sure to examine the closures carefully and make certain they will take the stress to which they are bound to be subjected. Luggage should resist soil and be easy to wipe clean. Luggage with wheels or separate wheels that accommodate several bags are helpful for travelers who are willing to trade a little hindrance in mobility for a lot of saved energy. Garment bags work well for short trips and are preferred by many. However, they are difficult for some to carry and do not always receive kind treatment from baggage handlers.

Both men and women should consider some type of shoulder bag to carry such important documents as passport, travelers checks, camera, sunglasses, and personal items. This bag should be constructed of lightweight materials, easily cleaned inside and out, and should be comfortable to carry. It should have a number of zippered compartments to accommodate belongings. It should be of the same color as selected for wardrobe components. Women will want to take a smaller handbag that can be used for dressy occasions. Also to be considered are money belts or other items designed to secure money, jewelry, or passports on your person. Ask for these items at a luggage store.

Here is a tested way of packing a suitcase. Pack in layers. Place the heaviest, bulky, odd-shaped items on the bottom and arrange them so they will be balanced as you carry the case. Level this layer with items that can be crushed into the small spaces, things like socks and underwear. Smooth this layer by laying out as flat as possible items that wrinkle very little like sweaters, T-shirts, sweat suits. Next take the garments you want to keep wrinkle-free, such as a suit jacket or blazer. Place the collar and shoulders next to the side of the suitcase (which side will depend on the size of the garment). Grasp the garment under the arm, behind the pocket area and pull the garment to establish the straight grain line of the fabric. Make this line your fold line. Lap the fronts of the garment and the sleeves over each other and smooth out any wrinkles. You may want to stuff socks in the sleeve fold by the armseye to prevent wrinkling in this area. The coat hemline will extend out of the suitcase. If you are taking a second suit, layer the jacket in the same manner. Next layer in pants by placing the waistline at one side of the suitcase. Smooth out wrinkles and align pant leg creases; allow pant leg to extend over side of case. Repeat this step until all pants (and skirts) are layered in. Shirts, blouses, and dresses can be layered using the same technique. Remember to fit the garment in the case in the direction that it seems to fit the best. Alternate the direction that garments hang over the edge so that when you have finished with the large garments you have them hanging over all four sides of the case. Roll small accessories, underwear, nightwear, and fit these on top of garments to cushion the extended parts of the garments when they are folded over garment by garment to fit into the case. Small items can be placed on top of the folded-over clothes.

Remember when using this method of packing, fit garments into case smoothly, do not button garments; lap fronts of garments by establishing the underarm grain line. This will prevent wrinkled fronts, curled lapels, and pockets. Also note that a suitcase must be full to prevent garments from sagging to the bottom of the case when it is carried by the handle. Most suitcases have ribbons or tapes

15-13 *When traveling on commercial transportation carriers take a small under-the-seat bag that contains all the items it takes to make you comfortable. This type of packing can prevent the distress that is experienced when luggage is lost or delayed. (Courtesy Hartmarx Corporation)*

which can be used to secure garments in position, but these will only work when there is enough in the case. Fill any extra spaces with small crushable items or clothing or tissues. Also include plastic bags which can be used to hold items that might snag, soiled laundry, or damp bathing suits.

In the small under-the-seat bag place the items it takes to make you comfortable. This would include your teddy bear if that is really important to your well-being. Generally things like cosmetics, toilet kits, hair care gear, medicine, change of clothing, nightwear, reading and writing materials are placed in this bag. The purpose of this bag is to prevent the distress that is experienced by many travelers when luggage is lost or delayed when checked through on commercial transportation carriers (Figure 15-13).

When traveling overnight or on very long trips it is a good idea to take a change of clothing that is very comfortable in your carry-on. The jogging/sweat suit is ideal. This outfit can be worn during the trip, changing just before or after departure. The long hours of sitting, sleeping, and eating in cramped quarters leave even the most fastidious feeling grimy. Just before or just after arrival change back to the original clothes. You will arrive at your destination looking clean and crisp.

Suggested Activities

1. Fill in two Lifestyle Charts (Table 15-1) as directed in the text. Compare your clothing needs now with those projected at a future date.
2. Analyze your wardrobe as described in this chapter.
3. Summarize your "wardrobe strategy." Divide the existing clothing found in your wardrobe into "fundamental components" and "wardrobe extenders" insofar as possible. Plan for additions to these two groups. Include your color plan. Find pictures in pattern books and fashion magazines or sketch them yourself to illustrate your plan. Estimate the costs for the additions.
4. Make up a two-year clothing budget plan in order to accommodate the needed additions for your plan. Examine your resources and explain how the costs will be met.

16 *Fit in Clothing*

The way clothing fits your body is an important factor to consider in selecting clothing. It determines whether an appearance of quality and attractiveness is achieved by the apparel. Even the most carefully constructed garment made of the finest fabric cannot give the appearance of quality if it fits poorly.

On the stage, actors often wear ill-fitting clothes to depict both comical and pathetic characters. In the role of the comic, the clown often wears oversized pants and shoes, which can be counted upon to draw laughs. The actor in a role of the pathetic character chooses too tight or too loose clothing to evoke pity. Although these are examples of extremes in clothing fit, they illustrate the point. Improperly fit garments can never appear attractive or give the look of quality clothing. Proper fit gives one a feeling of physical comfort and self-confidence.

Apparel worn by models in fashion showings is usually carefully fitted to the model so that the garments will be presented in the best manner possible. If our personal standards of fit are the same as those used by professional models, our clothes will help us achieve a more attractive appearance (Figure 16-1).

16-1 Apparel worn by models in fashion photography is usually carefully fitted to the model so that the garments are presented in the best manner possible. Studying this type of picture will help us learn to recognize good fit and good structural and applied design. Note how this shirt fits the body. Note the matching of the fabric design in all areas. (Courtesy Eagle Shirtmakers)

16-2 Both men and women should study all combinations of garments for fit in motion as well as standing still. (Courtesy Pendleton Woolen Mills)

Fit in Motion

To determine whether an article of clothing fits, you must observe it from all angles in front of a triple, full-length mirror, while wearing the same underclothing and height of the shoe heel that will be worn with the garment. This is very important because underclothing and shoe style can change the fit and hang considerably in both men's and women's garments. In fact, it is so important that *haute couture* houses make special underclothing for each gown to ensure that the outer garment fits correctly.

Remember that a garment is worn and seen in motion as well as standing still. Check to determine if it looks attractive and feels comfortable while you are sitting, standing, walking, and bending. If it is an active sports garment, such as a bathing suit, tennis outfit, or ski pants, bend, twist, and reach to decide if it is comfortable or whether it strains when these movements are made. Women's wraparound skirts and dresses should be carefully observed while walking and sitting in order to make sure that underclothing is not revealed.

Both men and women should study all combinations of garments for fit. Shirts should stay tucked in; vests should meet or extend over pants; sweaters, coats, or jackets should accommodate garments worn under them; sleeves should be appropriate length (Figure 16-2).

Fit Determined by Style, Use, and Preference

The design of a garment, how and when it is to be used, and your own personal requirements for wearing comfort will determine how a particular garment should fit. The amount of ease, drape, length, shoulder placement, and closeness to the body should be examined. Some garments are designed to be somewhat loose on the body; others are intended to fit more snugly. The amount of ease desired is always a matter of personal preference. Some people prefer ample ease, whereas others feel more comfortable in closely fitted garments. It must be remembered, however, that a very tight or a very loose-fitting garment will affect the appearance of the body shape. Often a very thin person will look thinner wearing a very loose-fitting garment because of the extreme contrast (Figure 16-3). A moderately close-fitting garment, when worn by a thin person, generally does not effect a thin look because there is no extreme contrast. A heavy person in a somewhat loose fit looks less heavy because of the lack of contrast between the silhouette created by the garment as compared with that of the body. You can experiment with this principle by comparing sleeve widths on the arm and shorts styles on the legs. Legs and arms look larger in close-fitting styles than in loose-fitting lines. Tight-fitting garments will also reveal body irregularities by emphasizing their contours (Figure 16-4). Body irregularities can be minimized by the use of adequate ease and of textures that do not cling to the body.

16-3 Some garments are designed to be loose on the body. The amount of ease desired is always a matter of personal preference. It must be remembered that a very tight- or overly loose-fitting garment will affect the appearance of the body shape. (Courtesy Catalina)

16-4 A tight-fitting garment will reveal body irregularities by emphasizing contours. (Courtesy Angie Lovett)

Sizing of Clothing for Women

Shops and stores generally have clothing grouped together by categories known as Misses, Juniors, Women's, and Half-sizes. In some lines, there are groupings of Teen, Petite, Contemporary, Queen, and other subdivisions. In addition, specialty stores carry sizes labeled Slim, Chubby and Short, Regular and Tall. All of these are figure divisions rather than age groupings.

The standard for the clothing industry is the Misses sizes, 10–20, which are intended for the woman of average height and proportions. The larger, or Women's, sizes feature styles intended for the mature woman of average height and are not often youthful in design. They are cut for the figure with larger-than-average bust, waist, and hips. Half-sizes are also for the mature woman with larger-than-average bust, waist, and hips, but they are cut for women about 5'4" and under. The Junior clothes are sized in odd numbers, such as 9 and 11, and are often youthful in style.

Size numbers do not represent the same sizes for every manufacturer. A woman may wear a size 12 in an inexpensive dress and a size 8 in an expensive costume. For this reason, you may have a range of sizes in your closet.

Sweaters and blouses are sold according to bust measurement: small, medium, or large sizes 32–38 for Misses, and sizes 38–44 for Women's. Skirts and slacks may be sized according to the waist measurement in sizes 22–44, or classified by sizes 9–15 or 6–14. These garments also come in proportioned lengths.

Currently there is no established, mutually agreed-upon plan for apparel sizing based upon the metric system. There are those who hope that a more consistent method of sizing, based upon body measurements, will emerge. However, people do not come in consistent sizes, and manufacturers have their own favorite cuts and ease allowances that distinguish their garments from those of other manufacturers. It is likely that body type, rather than body measurements, will continue to be used to differentiate sizing when the metric system is used.

Sizing of Clothing for Men

Suits are sized by chest and waist measurements. They are proportioned in short, regular, long, and extra long lengths and for average and portly builds.

Coats and jackets are sized by height and chest measurements. Trousers, slacks, shorts, and jeans are sized by the measurement of the waist and the length of the inseam. The inseam measurement is from the crotch to the ankle on the inner part of the leg.

Sport shirts are measured by the neck circumference and are sold in small ($14-14\frac{1}{2}$ neck), medium ($15-15\frac{1}{2}$ neck), large ($16-16\frac{1}{2}$ neck), and extra large ($17-17\frac{1}{2}$ neck).

Dress and work shirts are sized by the neck circumference and sleeve length. The neck measurement is taken from the circumference at the base of the neck, and for long sleeves the length is taken from the center back neck base across the shoulder to the wrist with the arm slightly bent. For example, a man with a 15½″ neck and a 32″ sleeve would require a shirt size 15½-32.

Judging the Fit—Women

Many women are not aware of what constitutes a properly fitted garment. To judge fit, first make a general observation of the grain direction of the fabric. If the grain is not correct, do not buy the garment. The cloth must be cut on true grain; that is, the lengthwise grain is intended to be exactly perpendicular to the floor at the center front and center back, and the cross grain is parallel to the floor across the chest, upper back, and hip area. There are exceptions to this, such as the bias cut, which may appear in the entire garment or special sections of it. Bias-cut provides flare or drape at the bias area. If a garment is designed to be cut on lengthwise grain and it is off just a little, the garment will not hang properly, and correcting alterations are impossible to make. The garment should not be purchased.

Examine each area of the body for diagonal wrinkles. These indicate a fitting problem. Follow the diagonal wrinkles to their source, and you will usually find their cause. Horizontal wrinkles usually mean that the garment is too long or too tight for that section of the body.

Check the neck, shoulder, and upper sleeve area. It is important that these areas fit properly because they are seen as part of the personality area and they are the most difficult and costly to alter. Notice where the armhole-seam and shoulder-seam length coincide with the body. Some garments are designed with extended shoulder length so that the set-in sleeve begins at the edge of the shoulder. This is found in most tailored shirts and shirtdresses. This type of sleeve does not have extra fullness in the sleeve cap because it is not needed with the extended shoulder. Sleeves that are set in at the ball-and-socket joint should have extra fullness eased into the sleeve cap to accommodate the upper arm muscle.

In the same area notice if the lower armhole is cut deeply enough to be comfortable but not so low that the hemline of the garment is raised when the arms are raised. The shoulders must fit comfortably. The length and slant of the shoulder seam should coincide with the body underneath. The area across the upper back section must have enough width so that a person can move her arms forward sufficiently to drive a car or to place arms forward on a table without undue strain at the back armhole seam.

The area just below the collar at the back should be free of a horizontal bulge; a bulge would indicate that the collar was set too high for the wearer's back length. The collar at the neckline should fit the back and sides of the neck snugly unless this section is designed definitely to stand away from the body. A scoop-neck dress must fit snugly around the chest area so that it does not gap when the wearer bends forward or moves her arms.

Sleeve width should be adequate to cover the heavy upper arm muscle without silhouetting the bulge. When the arms are at the sides, no diagonal wrinkles should appear in the sleeve area. Sleeve lengths vary. Wrist-length sleeves reach or cover the prominent wrist bone unless the garment is designed to accommodate a cuff that is intended to show below this area. Elbow darts or fullness should be located at the elbow bend. If a long sleeve is designed with one dart, the dart is directed to the elbow joint; if it has two darts, the space in the middle of the two darts should meet the elbow. A three-darted sleeve should have the middle dart pointed to the elbow. The arm should be slightly bent when you check this area.

The fullness in the bust area is provided for by the use of darts, gathers, or curved seams. Large-body curves require darts that are deep at the base; small-body curves need darts that are proportionately smaller at the base. Therefore, a person with a large bust will need deeper darts than the smaller-busted person. The reason for this is that deep darts create more fullness than shallow darts. This dart principle applies to any curved area of the body, such as the hip and shoulder. Darts must *point* to the area of greatest fullness. They should not extend beyond the area of the greatest curve. Bust darts are directed to the point of the bust. If they come above or below this area, they do not release the fullness where it is needed. The underarm bust dart usually comes within $1\frac{1}{2}$ to 2 inches (3.75–5.0 cm) of the bust point. Waistline darts directed to the bust usually end about $\frac{1}{2}$ inch (1.25 cm) below the bust point, and long diagonal French darts that begin at the hip side seam end just short of the bust point.

When princess styling is used in garments, the fullness required at the bust area is provided by means of curved seams. The fullest part of the curve must coincide with the fullest part of the bust. This styling is often impossible to alter because the fabric is cut into a curved shape.

If bust fullness does not meet the fullness provided in the garment, sometimes all that may be needed is an adjustment of the brassiere straps. If this does not help, the darts must be altered (this cannot be done if the dart has been slashed or the fabric distorted). One of the most common fitting problems is the incorrect placement of bust darts.

Vertical ease across the bust and waist must be adequate so that the dress does not draw across this area. Some dresses are worn so tightly that the dress acts as a foundation garment and reveals folds of flesh, which is neither attractive or fashionable.

The waistline of a fitted garment or of one that has a seam at the natural waistline should meet the waist at its smallest area. If the waistline of the dress hits above or below this area, the garment will never be comfortable.

Gathers are used to give fullness. Gathers below the bust or above the hip area should be placed to allow fullness where it is needed. Gathers over the abdomen will add visual fullness to an area where it may not be flattering.

Vertical fullness at the hip and thigh area is adequate if it allows room for movement and provides space so that the skirt does not ride up toward the waist.

If a skirt is too tight, it will move up and cup in the seat area. A straight skirt should have at least 2 inches (5.0 cm) of ease in the hip area; you should be able to pinch ½ inch (1.25 cm) out of each side seam. Another method of testing is to lift the skirt upward above the hipline; it should slide down into place easily. Front and back hip darts are directed to but do not extend beyond the fullest part of the body curve.

Women who are swaybacked or slightly hollow above the buttocks may find a horizontal fold of fabric below the waistline. If there is a waistline seam, the extra fabric can be lifted and eliminated at this point.

Side seams should fall straight down toward the ankle from the hip. The center front and center back are also perpendicular to the floor. This can be checked by using a plumb line much like the one masons use when building. Place a weight at the end of a string. Hold the string at hip level at the sides, center front, and back. Because of gravitational pull, the weight will fall, making the string perpendicular to the floor. The seams should follow the string. If the side seam pulls forward, the thigh may need more room than the skirt front allows or the back may be flat below the waist, not filling in the area allowed at the skirt back. A dress with a waistline seam or a skirt can be raised at the waist back to bring this seam in a line perpendicular to the floor. A dress without a waistline seam could be altered only from the side seams. The front side seam would need to be let out or the back side seam made deeper, or both. Inadequate seam allowance usually makes this alteration impossible. If side seams are directed toward the back of the string, there is probably not enough skirt back fullness to accommodate the *derrière*.

Skirt length is determined by fashion, a woman's legs, and her age. A skirt should be equidistant from the floor on all sides unless the style dictates otherwise (Figure 16-5).

AREAS TO CHECK FOR FIT IN A WOMAN'S DRESS (SEE FIGURE 16-5)

1. Collar or neck edge lies flat and fits neckline snugly as designed.
2. Shoulder length is correct for body and style.
3. Horizontal grain is parallel to floor at bust, hip.
4. Length grain is perpendicular to floor at center and at side seams.
5. Darts point toward and end before the fullest part of curve, bump, or bulge.
6. Adequate sleeve width.
7. Waisted dresses meet natural waistline.
8. Pocket openings and pleats lie flat while standing.
9. Adequate seat room.
10. No horizontal fold below waist back.
11. No diagonal wrinkles unless part of design.

Pants

When checking the fit of slacks, sit down to see if the crotch length is long enough. If it is too long, the pants will be baggy in the seat. If it is too short, the

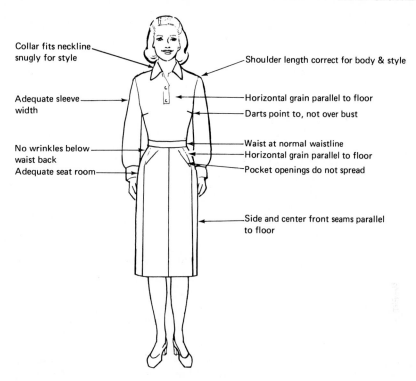

16-5 *Areas to check for fit in a dress or blouse and skirt.*

Collar fits neckline snugly for style

Shoulder length correct for body & style

Adequate sleeve width

Horizontal grain parallel to floor

Darts point to, not over bust

Waist at normal waistline

No wrinkles below waist back

Horizontal grain parallel to floor

Pocket openings do not spread

Adequate seat room

Side and center front seams parallel to floor

back waistline of the pants will drop down. If slacks are too tight in the thigh or hip, "smile" wrinkles will appear in the crotch area and below. If the slacks have a crease down the front as design detail, this should hang in a straight line. No diagonal or horizontal wrinkles should appear in the pants while in a standing position.

Judging the Fit of Women's Suits

Fit is judged by how the garment feels on the body. Designer Paul Schnell of Ernest Strauss believes that the properly fitted suit is not felt by the body of the wearer. As the body moves within the garment it should have no feelings of garment stress, strain, or tightness. To achieve perfect fit Schnell advises purchasing a suit slightly large and having it altered to your exact body conformation.[1]

A suit should fit gently over the waist and hip. The garment should fit smoothly over the body. Wrinkles are formed in garments either because there is not enough fabric (tight fit) or there is too much fabric (big fit). Such wrinkles often occur in a suit shoulder, bust, sleeve cap, back neck, small of back, hip/crotch area.

The collar and lapels form the focal point and frame the face. They must fit

[1] Jean Cox Penn, "Suit Pursuit," *Los Angeles Times*, December 22, 1978, Pt. III, p. 4.

smoothly and mold to the neck and body. The collar and lapels should lack bulk. The top collar and lapel should turn slightly over the under collar and facing so seam edges are hidden (Figure 16-6).

Sleeves should hang free of folds when the body stands at ease with arms relaxed at side. Full-length sleeves should come to the wrist bone when the arm is slightly bent. When the arms are lifted the body of the garment should stay in place and not strain across any part of the torso.

Linings should be attached to the fashion fabric at the sleeve hem, armhole, and side seams. To check this, gently separate the lining from the garment at these points. The lining should be stitched around the perimeter of the garment

16-6 *The collar and lapels form the focal point and frame the face. They must fit smoothly and mold to the neck and body. The collar and lapels should lack bulk. This photo also illustrates the fine matching of plaids in the sleeve–body area and the pocket area. Such matching is always a sign of quality. (Courtesy Jones of New York)*

with concealed stitches. Linings must not pull, twist, or strain. They should not be visible from the right side of the garment. Linings should be slightly larger than the garment so that they permit body movement without straining fashion or supportive fabrics. Check for a small pleat or tuck at the center back neckline and waistline and for a slight lap or fold at the hems of sleeves and jacket. Lining fabrics should be opaque to conceal construction details. They should be smooth and slippery for ease in putting on and removing garments. They should be attractive. Often darker colors are best because they do not show soil quickly and therefore need less maintenance.

Supportive fabrics or interfacings should not shadow through either lining or fashion fabrics. Sleeve and jacket hems should be interfaced to help keep these edges in shape and to help keep hem stitching from showing. All hems should be invisible from the right side of the garment unless the hem stitching is part of the decorative detail.

Center and side vents and pleats should remain closed when the body is standing at ease. Pockets and pocket flaps should not bulge but should lie smoothly and follow body contour or design line. Remove basting from pockets and vents after purchase. These bastings are used to hold the pockets and vents in place during construction and display. When they are not removed they prevent the garment from functioning properly when worn. They make the garment look funny too.

Coats should fit with sufficient ease so that they may be worn over a suit or a dress with sleeves. Armholes must be deep enough to accommodate the garments worn underneath. Suit jackets usually should allow for a sweater or blouse to be worn under them. Full-length coats need to be about one inch (2.5 cm) longer than the dress length if you wish the dress to be hidden as the body moves.

Fitting a Bra

The way you shop for a bra is the same as you should shop for other articles of clothing: trying on each style and judging how it fits your body contours. It is important to keep in mind that bra size can change from year to year, from month to month, even from day to day. Breast size changes as body weight fluctuates up or down, after childbirth, with certain medications and during the premenstrual and menstrual cycles. Some women may even need different size bras to accommodate breast swelling owing to hormonal increases every menstrual cycle.

To determine correct bra size: first, measure your rib cage under your bust. This is a snug but not tight measurement. Then add five inches to that sum for your correct body size. If it is an odd number (like 33) go on to the next highest number (in this case 34). Next, measure around the fullest part of your bust. If this measurement is one inch more than your body size, your cup size is an A; two inches more, a B; three inches more, a C; and four inches more a D.

Proper fit is equally important. The correct way to try on a bra is to slip the bra over your shoulders and lean forward, grasping both sides of the bra, easing your breasts into the cups. Straighten your body up and, without letting go of the fabric, slide both hands toward the back of the bra and hook it—making sure the back band is low. Adjust straps to smooth out the top of the bra cups. If the bra is the proper size and fits correctly, it should not restrict your movements nor cause discomfort in any way.

Bra Checkpoints:

1. The straps should not pull or bite into the flesh of your shoulders. Their only function is to hold the bra in place and to form smooth tops of the bra cups. The straps should not be shortened to achieve the proper fit of the cup. The uplift comes from the design of the cups themselves and the back of the bra construction. Tight straps do not raise cups, they simply hike up the back of the bra. Tip: Drop one bra strap. If you lose support on one side, you are wearing the wrong size bra. The larger-breasted women should look for wider straps with minimal stretching in the front and little stretch in the back for freedom of movement. Buckles on adjustable-strap bras should be slipped to the back so they do not cause lumps under tight-fitting clothes. Smooth, nonadjustable styled straps eliminate this problem.

2. The back of the bra aids uplift. It should be low enough to support from underneath. If the back of the bra hikes up, you are not getting the necessary support and comfort. You might also be getting an unsightly bulge above or below the back fastening. Back-closure bras offer more support than front closure.

3. The undercup or bra band should be snug, not tight, with sufficient give for easy breathing. If you can slide your finger easily under the bra band, the fit is correct. A too tight band may curl up.

4. The cups: Wrinkles in the cups could mean the bra is too large (obviously) or too small (surprisingly). If the cup is too small, the breast tissue is pushed against the rib cage or to the sides, rather than flowing to the end of the cup where it belongs. This is why the cup that is too small wrinkles. If the cup is not filled out, a smaller or lined cup may be needed. If the breast overflows, a larger cup or a style with more coverage may be the answer.

5. A bulge above the bra edge in the front or at the underarm means the bra is either too tight, too small in the cup size, or not the right style for your body.

6. Gapping can mean a too small bra. A well-fitted bra should stay close to the body, clinging to the breast bone, with no gaps between the cups. Too much tissue for the bra cup pushes the bra away from the chest cavity. Gapping can also be caused by a bra that is simply the wrong design for your body type. Be aware that there are wide differences in the cut or style of bras. Most manufacturers design bras of all sizes but there are variations with each brand. The only way to know which brand fits your body is to try the bras of different brands until you find the designs that fit you best.

If you wear only one type of dress, you probably need just one type of bra. Today women are becoming more aware that a wardrobe of bras can be matched to a wardrobe of clothing. Smooth seamless bras go under sweaters and other knits; lace bras under sheer fabrics; a plunging bra (perhaps with a front closure) with tops that plunge; a sturdy bra for active sports; a convertible bra for halters, backless, or strapless clothes; a strapless underwire bra for B and C cup wearers; bandeau strapless for A and AA cup wearers; a bra with more shape (perhaps Fiberfil) under heavier fabrics like tweeds. Color coordinated bras complete the wardrobe; they come in black, nude, and all the colors of the rainbow.[2]

Judging the Fit—Men

Coats and jackets should hang straight from the shoulder to the hem edge, free from wrinkles and bulges. The collar should fit smoothly and snugly at the neck area showing $\frac{1}{2}$ inch (1.25 cm) of the shirt collar in back. The area below the collar should lie flat showing no horizontal fold. Should a fold appear, the collar is set too high for the back length of the wearer or the back width is too tight. The shoulder line should lie smooth and straight from the neck to the sleeve, ending as close to the natural armline as possible. Armholes should not be so deep as to raise the jacket hem when the arms are raised, and not so high as to bind. The sleeve length should expose $\frac{1}{2}$ inch (1.25 cm) of the shirt cuff. Lining wrinkles should not shadow or leave imprints on the outside of garment. Jackets that feature pleats, flaps, and vents at the sides and/or back should lie flat at these areas while the wearer is standing. When the jacket is buttoned at the waist, look for an X-fold that radiates from the center button. The front does not need to be perfectly smooth at this area, but if folds are pronounced, the waist is too tight. The bottom of the jacket should be even with the thumb in traditional styles. This means that the trouser seat will be covered (Figure 16-7).

Pants should fit snugly at the waist. No wrinkles should be evident at the seat and crotch area nor in the thigh or calf areas when standing or walking. Pant length should meet the top of the shoe in front without a break or fold in the fabric at the instep. The hem is canted (slanted so that the hem is lower on the shoe in back).

A traditional dress shirt that fits correctly shows $\frac{1}{2}$ inch (1.25 cm) of the collar above the jacket. This type shirt sleeve should extend $\frac{1}{2}$ inch (1.25 cm) below the jacket sleeve. The sleeve armholes should be wide enough for freedom; the collar should fit the neck comfortably, and tabs lie flat. Check shoulder, back, and chest for ample fullness. Dress shirt and dress shoes *must* be worn when checking suit for fit.

These points should be checked for fit: (see Figure 16-8).

---

[2] Allison Leopold, "The Answer to All Your Questions About Bras . . . ," *Vogue,* March 1980, p. 362.

SUIT AND SPORT JACKETS

1. Collar hugs neck, shows $\frac{1}{2}$ inch (1.25 cm) shirt collar at back.
2. No wrinkles across shoulder back or bubbles under collar area.
3. Full-cut armholes for movement.
4. No wrinkles across chest area.
5. Lapels lie flat to chest, do not gap.
6. Front hangs straight when buttoned.
7. Sleeve shows $\frac{1}{2}$ inch (1.25 cm) shirt cuff.
8. Vents, pleats, and flaps hang straight, do not spread while standing.
9. Jacket covers trouser seat or is longer in some styles.

TROUSERS, SLACKS

1. Waist fits comfortably.
2. Pleats, if any, lie flat.
3. No wrinkles when standing.
4. Crease is straight with grain at front.
5. Adequate seat fullness.
6. Length to top of shoe in front, no break, correct cant.

16-7 *Coats and jackets should hang straight from the shoulder to the hem edge and be free from wrinkles and bulges. The collar should fit smoothly and snugly at the neck area (Courtesy,* Left: *Ermenegildo Zegna Corp.;* Right: *The Joseph & Feiss Company)*

16-8 *Areas to check for fit in a man's suit.*

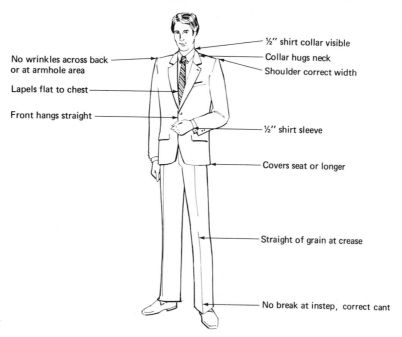

No wrinkles across back or at armhole area

Lapels flat to chest

Front hangs straight

½″ shirt collar visible

Collar hugs neck

Shoulder correct width

½″ shirt sleeve

Covers seat or longer

Straight of grain at crease

No break at instep, correct cant

To Alter or Not to Alter

Some alterations are possible, others are not. Professional alteration costs are always high, and this may boost the price of the garment considerably. Some men's clothing stores do not charge for alterations, but almost all women's stores do. Inquire as to cost before consenting to any alterations. If major changes need to be made in the areas of the shoulder, sleeve, and neckline and in lined garments, it may be wise not to buy the garment. It may not be possible to alter certain garments for several reasons. Some alterations interfere with design lines that cannot be changed. Some alterations may change the general proportions and scale of the individual sections so that they do not look aesthetically right for the body. Some manufacturers may not have allowed the necessary seam allowance needed for letting out seams. Many garments have slashes in darts and seam allowances that were used for matching seams. Lack of fabric would make it impossible to let out these areas. Fabric construction and finishes may not permit alterations. Some fabrics leave holes when former stitching lines are removed. Removing a press mark in hems and seams is a major problem with some fabrics such as durable press, crease-resistant finishes, taffeta, and some synthetics and blends in wovens and knits.

If you understand how to make alterations, it is possible to have the needed changes pinned at the store and do them yourself (be aware that you may be charged for this service). Changing hem lengths and taking in seams are minor alterations that usually can be done without difficulty by a person who has some knowledge of sewing.

Personal weight change is often noticed first by a difference in the way clothing fits. It is difficult to keep up with the necessary clothing adjustments when great weight changes occur, but it is especially important that this be done. Both comfort and appearance will be enhanced if alterations are made. Remember that clothing that fits too tightly or too loosely will exaggerate body defects and call attention to them.

Suggested Activities

1. Analyze class members' clothing for fit. Use the criteria given in the text for judging various garments.
2. Bring to class and model garments that do not fit correctly. Analyze the fit problems. Consider grain line. Decide what alterations could recycle the garments and which alterations would be impossible to make.

17 Family Clothing Needs and Buying Guides

If you have thoughtfully analyzed your wardrobe and worked out a plan to put into use the "fundamental components" and "wardrobe extenders" idea suggested in Chapter 15, Wardrobe Strategies, you are well equipped with information related to satisfying your personal clothing needs. Each one of us has specific requirements that we expect our clothing to satisfy. The amounts and kinds of garments we buy will, we hope, serve our individual social, emotional, physical, and aesthetic needs. The types of clothing we purchase depend on such factors as age, geographic location, local customs, sex, occupation, lifestyle, and income. Within the family, meeting each person's clothing needs is complicated because of the individual requirements of each of the several family members. An understanding of these individual requirements is essential if satisfactory clothing purchases are to be made.[1]

It is important to have reliable information regarding the workmanship and fiber quality of the specific items that are to be purchased in order to obtain maximum value for the amount of money spent. Ever-increasing apparel prices make it necessary for the average consumer to be knowledgeable about both personal clothing needs and practical guides for buying clothes.

The clothing needs and buying information included in this chapter are intended to help the consumer obtain maximum value for money spent on clothing. The articles of clothing described encompass only the major and most often purchased garments rather than the entire family wardrobe. Listed within this chapter are books and pamphlets that can be referred to for more comprehensive buying guides for all kinds of clothing.

Recognizing Quality in Wearing Apparel

The quality of a garment is determined by the characteristics of each of its components. Every element, from the fiber used to construct the fabric to the last finishing detail, will influence the final appearance of the garment. To the discerning eye, quality is evident in the external appearance of a garment; it is

[1] Refer to Life Stages and Clothing Behavior in Chapter 2.

473

also evident in the details that are not seen from the outside, such as interfacings, linings, and construction techniques. These elements affect not only how the garment looks but how it will retain its shape and wear.

Fabric Components

The construction of a fabric will determine its wearing qualities. Fabric is made from yarns. Yarns are made from fibers. A variety of natural and man-made fibers are currently used in producing fabric yarns.

Fibers

Each fiber has qualities that give particular characteristics to the fabrics constructed from it. Each fiber has positive and negative characteristics; at this time there is no one "perfect fiber." Some plus and minus qualities of fibers are:

Cotton. Cotton is the most commonly used fiber in the world. Fabrics of cotton are available in a wide price range. Cotton fabrics have the desirable characteristics of comfort, easy care, good durability, softness, moisture absorbency, air permeability, and pliability. They are easy to launder yet may be dry cleaned if the garment construction so requires. Cotton fabric requires ironing, unless it is designed to have a crinkled appearance. Special finishing processes must be given cotton fiber in order to produce cotton fabrics that are water repellent, stain and spot resistant, flame retardant, shrinkproof and/or durable press.

Linen. Linen fabrics range from rough to very smooth and from coarse to very sheer. They are both strong and cool. Comfort is enhanced by the wicking properties of linen. Wearing apparel made of linen is popular because in addition to being cool, the garments maintain their clean appearance and are easily laundered or dry cleaned. However, linen does wrinkle easily unless treated to be wrinkle-free. Ramie, also called China Grass, is an ancient fiber that is finding new popularity today. It has many of the same properties as linen.

Silk. Silk, the ancient fiber with a romantic history, has always been considered a luxury fiber. Fabrics made of silk combine strength, flexibility, durability, warmth, moisture absorbency, softness, drapability, and luxurious appearance. No other fabric can match the beautiful drapability of silk, although some of the synthetics appear to closely resemble silk. Some silk garments, such as blouses, can be hand washed following explicit instructions. However, pressing of silk garments requires expert iron techniques to remove all the small wrinkles. Dry cleaning of silk garments is most often recommended. Silk garments are generally expensive to buy and expensive to maintain.

Wool. Fabrics made from wool fibers range from very thick, heavy, and stiff to the sheerest gossamer. They have the desirable properties of warmth, comfort, elastic recovery, absorbency, flexibility, and resistance to wrinkling. Wool fabrics can be tailored to fit the body. Garments made from wool look and feel good. A major problem with wool fabrics is a tendency to shrink if not handled properly. Some wool garments such as sweaters can be carefully hand washed, but dry cleaning is generally required for most other wool fabric garments. Machine washable wool fabrics have a finish that allows for this type of laundering; this same finish robs wool fabric of many of its desirable properties. Mohair, cashmere, camel hair, alpaca, llama, and vicuna are speciality fibers which are often classified as wool fibers because they share many of the same properties.

Rayon. Rayon was the first man-made fiber. Early marketing of rayon promoted it as artificial silk. This resulted in a poor reputation for rayon among older consumers. Younger users appreciate rayon for the many fine properties that it has. There are several divisions of rayon including acetate, triacetate, and viscose. Rayon fabrics vary in weight from very heavy to very sheer and in hand from very soft and limp to very firm and stiff. Rayon can stretch when wet and shrink when dry. It is important to handle rayon carefully during laundering to reduce garment distortion. For this reason rayon garments are often dry cleaned. Rayon is easily pressed. Rayon is often combined with other fibers because it contributes absorbency, comfort, and softness to the resulting fabric.

Synthetic Fibers. This group of fibers includes nylon, polyester, acrylic, modacrylic, olefin, spandex, and other less well known man-made fibers. Each synthetic has its own characteristics. Man-made fibers were developed in the chemical laboratory to compete with or replace natural fibers. Shortages of their fundamental components may lessen the use of these fibers in the future. Fabrics made from synthetic fibers are generally inexpensive, strong, durable, and easy to care. Generally they are machine washable, machine dryable and do not require much pressing. The biggest problem with the group is that they are not absorbent and therefore can be very uncomfortable; the wearer feels hot in warm weather and clammy in cold weather. This disadvantage may be compensated for by using synthetics to make fabrics with open weaves or knits. Often synthetic fibers are blended with natural fibers to create a more desirable fabric.

Fiber Blends. Several factors are responsible for the development of textiles composed of blends of two or more fibers. These include industry's need to develop fibers to replace those that are in short supply or those that are high priced. Two or more fibers are sometimes used in a fabric in order to take advantage of the outstanding characteristics of each. For example, cotton and polyester have been used together for years; the correct percentage of each fiber is combined to make a fabric that possesses the best characteristics of cotton and polyester. Wools are blended with nylon to create a stronger fabric and to compensate for the diminishing wool supply. Ramie, grown in Southeast Asia, is blended with cotton in imported apparel to circumvent the quota imposed on cotton garments.

The fiber content label required by federal law to be in each garment must indicate the percentage of each fiber present in the textile. The chief characteristics of the fabric are those of the predominant fiber. Understanding the textile information given on garment "hang tags" can help the consumer know what to expect in garment performance and care before purchase.

Tables giving more important information on the natural and man-made fibers are found in Appendix D and Appendix E. Included are their principal uses, major characteristics, and tips for their care. Study these charts to learn what you can expect from fabrics made of the various fibers in terms of their qualities, and the care involved for their upkeep.

Yarns

Fibers are twisted together to make yarns. Yarns may be made of short or long fibers. Higher-quality yarns are made from the longer fibers. The twist placed into the yarns may be low; this results in fabrics that reflect light, such as satin and sateen, because low twist gives yarns luster. Low-twist yarns are comparatively weak, and high-twist yarns create the strongest fabrics. However, extremely highly twisted yarns are weak; these are used for crepe and novelty yarns, the former a texture variation appreciated for its aesthetically pleasing appearance.

Fabrics or Textiles

Yarns are made into fabrics by many different processes. Weaving and knitting are the most common methods currently used; however, textiles may also be made by felting, molding, flocking, and bonding. Weaving is the interlocking of two or more separate yarns. There are many different types of weaves. Some are strong, such as twill weave, and some are weak, such as basket weave. Knitting is the joining of loops of one continuous yarn. The size and strength of the yarn determine fabric strength.

The characteristics of the completed fabric are determined by the type of fabric construction, along with the other components, fiber, and yarn. These characteristics, in turn, determine the end use of the textile. A fabric woven from low-twist yarns composed of short woolen fibers will be soft and weak, but it can be molded by heat and moisture into a tailored garment. A textile knitted of a fine, continuous nylon filament would be smooth, lightweight, clinging, and wrinkle-free, yet would melt under high ironing temperatures.

Fashion Fabric

The fashion fabric is the exterior layer of a garment. It must have eye appeal to attract the attention of the buyer and it must be attractive on the body. The wearing qualities depend on the fiber used and the yarn and fabric construction (Figure 17-1).

The quality of the fashion fabric is also dependent on the dyes or the dyeing methods used to add color. Some dyeing techniques cause colors to fade when exposed to sun, atmosphere, cleaning, or wear. The labels on the garment should give information regarding colorfastness but they are not required to do so. The consumer can check for colorfastness by rubbing a white piece of cloth over the fabric in question to see if any of the color crocks (rubs) off. For further testing,

17-1 Fashion fabric must have eye appeal to attract attention of the buyer and it must be attractive when it is tried on. (Courtesy Brando Crespi Association)

moisten a bit of the fabric and again rub it against white cloth. These methods may help to identify a possible colorfast problem.

Finishes are added to the fabric in the final steps of production. A variety of finishes are used for specific purposes; they often affect the performance of the fabric. For example, a finish used to prevent wrinkling may make ironing difficult if wrinkles are set by the heat in the dryer; soil-resistant finishes sometimes stiffen the fabric so that a familiar textile takes on new characteristics; durable-press finishes create some abrasion and spot-removal problems. These fabrics are easy to care for but do not wear as long as they would without this finish.

Supportive Fabrics

Fabrics used on the inside of a garment fulfill one of several purposes. If they are supportive and build shape and design into small areas of the garment, they are called *interfacings*. If they are supportive and add stability and durability to the fashion fabric, they are called *underlinings*. If they are decorative and enclose construction details, they are called *linings*. The fabrics used for interfacings, underlinings, and linings are a significant factor in the quality of the garment.

Supportive fabrics should be fastened securely and finished appropriately for the design of the garment. They should not wrinkle or distort the fashion fabric in any manner. These construction features may determine how long a garment will maintain its shape and fit, and how long it will wear.

Fashion trends that present a soft unconstructed look utilize few if any supportive fabrics. Interfacings, underlinings, and even facings may be eliminated to present a supple and fluid fashion image.

Construction Details

Some fashion fabrics have design or texture direction. This must be taken into consideration in the construction of a garment, or the beauty of both fabric and design will be distorted. Fabric designs such as twills, plaids, large checks, stripes, or distinctive motifs must be cut and sewn together so that the design is not distorted. The fabric design must be matched in the construction of the garment. This includes center front and center back, side seams, and sleeve and bodice joining. Bias-cut seams should be made to "chevron" or match at their joining. Plaids and stripes must match both horizontally and vertically in order not to break the continuity of the design. Darts must be placed so that the integrity of the fabric design is maintained. Motifs such as flowers intended to be whole must not be quartered or halved. Matching is costly, and may be difficult to find in low-priced garments.

If the design is in the texture, such as a twill weave, the garment must be constructed so that the diagonal line flows in one direction or chevrons at the seams. In some fabrics—velvet, velveteen, corduroy, some satins, and some knits, a change in color depth will be obvious unless the grain of the fabric pieces runs in the same direction.

Sewing machine stitch length should be appropriate to the fabric used. Generally small stitches indicate quality, but some fabrics such as synthetics, blends, or permanent-press require longer stitch length in order to avoid seam-puckering. Thread color should match the fashion fabric. Transparent thread is a sign of low-quality construction. Thread endings should be secure so that they will not pull out. Pucker is the result of poor sewing techniques, and pressing cannot correct this problem. Check for pucker on lengthwise seams of fabrics of synthetic fibers, blends, and permanent-press garments.

Many ready-to-wear garments have narrow overlocked seams, which are satisfactory. An adequate seam width in most woven fabrics is about ½ inch (1.25 cm) so that it can stand the stress of wear without pulling or fraying out. The seam should be pressed open smoothly unless design detail indicates otherwise. Seams should not show signs of pucker or pulling. Only fabrics that tend to ravel need an appropriate seam finish to prevent this. These include slippery-feeling fabrics such as acetate, some rayons, and smooth synthetic fibers. Seam finishes include pinking, edge stitching, and overlocking of cut edges. Cut edges may be completely hidden by seams that are bound, French, flat-felled, and "Hong Kong" finished.

Garments made of knitted fabrics may have $\frac{1}{2}$-inch (1.25 cm) to $\frac{5}{8}$-inch (1.56 cm) seam width if seams lie flat. Some knits have a very small seam allowance since the knit may tend to roll and produce a bulky seam. Knits that do not ravel do not need a seam finish.

Unless hems are a design feature, they should be invisible from the right side of the garment. Hem width depends upon the fabric and the garment style. The hem finish should be appropriate for the fashion fabric and not stitched so that a ridge shows on the right side of the garment. Some fabrics such as matte jersey, felt, and synthetic leathers do not need hems that are turned under.

Sleeves should be set in smoothly without signs of puckering (unless a design detail). There should be comfortable ease in the fit of a sleeve so that it does not draw or pull when on the body. The grain line for a set-in sleeve should be parallel and perpendicular across the center upper arm. (See Chapter 16, Fit in Clothing.)

The collar must be placed on the garment so that both sides are symmetrical, unless indicated otherwise by the design. The undercollar should not be visible from the right side. The collar should have well-defined edges and a good shape.

The amount of ease or fullness in a garment often indicates quality. The overall fit of the garment should leave adequate and comfortable room for movement. A garment should never bind or constrict the body. Adequate ease should also be found in the fullness of gathers, pleats, and tucks.

Finishing Details

All fasteners should be properly placed and securely attached. Quality in a garment is indicated by the choice of fasteners, such as buttons. Buttons should be in harmony with the texture, color, and design of the garment.

Buttonholes must be properly placed and correctly sized to accommodate the buttons. Bound buttonholes are a sign of quality in women's clothes, but not all fabrics are suitable for them. Machine buttonholes should have close stitches, and the thread ends should be secured to prevent raveling.

Zippers should zip easily. Unless otherwise indicated by design, the zipper should be well covered by the fashion fabric. It should be installed in such a manner as to stay closed; often a hook and eye are placed at the top of the placket to ensure this. In some quality garments the zipper is "hand-picked" (sewn with small backhand stitches to make it nearly invisible).

Decoration and trim should be in keeping with the quality of the garment. The placement and quantity of the applied design should add to the beauty of the garment. Check all applied design to see that it is appropriately placed and securely attached.

Coats and jackets should have a firmly attached lining that is caught at the shoulder seams in order to prevent it from pulling and showing below the hemline. A pleat of about $\frac{3}{4}$-inch (1.87 cm) at the center back should release extra fullness for movement.

Pressing is extremely important to the appearance of the garment. The presser is one of the highest-paid workers in the garment industry because a garment

17-2 *Pressing is extremely important to the appearance of the garment. (Courtesy Hartmarx Corporation)*

can be ruined by improper pressing. Each detail of the garment should be pressed into position. There should be no overpressing effects on the right side of the garment, such as hem and dart impressions or pocket imprints. The garment should be smooth, well shaped, and ready to wear (Figure 17-2).

Relationship of Price to Quality

The price paid for a garment is often equated with the quality one expects to receive. You have heard the statement, "You get what you pay for." High-priced garments are expected to be high-quality garments, but this is not always true. Although the price tag may be an indication of overall quality, several factors influence the pricing of garments.

A garment may be expensive because the fabric is costly. High-quality virgin wool, finely woven silk, and linen are more expensive than most cottons, synthetics, and blends. Garments made from these fibers will cost more at the outset. The costs of wool and silk fibers have increased between 25 and 75 percent in the past few years and the price tags on these garments reflect these increases. In order for garments to be sold in a particular price range, the manufacturer may use high-quality fabrics or high-fashion fabrics and cut corners on the amount of fabric used, the construction, or the finishing details.

The exclusiveness of the design will influence the price. If only a few garments of one design are cut, this will be reflected in a higher price. The design of the garment will affect its price. Garments composed of many pattern pieces and odd-shaped pieces require more seaming and special handling than garments having few, simple seams. Fabric designs that require matching of pattern pieces require more labor and are thus more expensive.

The amount of handwork involved also affects the price. Linings stitched in by hand, fabric-covered snaps, zippers inserted by hand, and hand hemmings all result in high labor costs. On women's garments, the price of the trims used, such as fur, lace, and ribbon, contributes to the final cost of the garment. For instance, the use of four high-quality buttons priced at $6 each will add $24 alone to the total cost of a garment. Inserting a zipper in the neck of a sweater increases labor costs two or three times; the zipper itself costs just a few cents, but the cost of sewing it into the sweater makes the difference in the pricing (Figure 17-3).

Sweaters that have full-fashioned sleeves and cuffs rather than sleeves and cuffs that are knitted separately and stitched on are high-quality garments. Full fashion can be identified by decreased and increased stitches in the sleeve near the cuff, near the armhole, and in the body of the sweater near the armholes. Full-fashioned construction in knitwear will be more expensive. It is a more labor-intensive process, as home knitters well know.

17-3 Signs of quality are important clues for the consumer to check before buying.

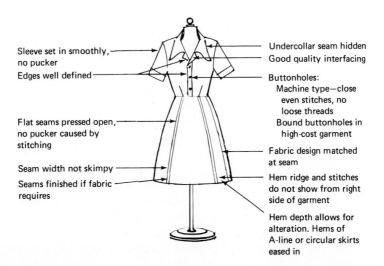

Sleeve set in smoothly, no pucker

Edges well defined

Flat seams pressed open, no pucker caused by stitching

Seam width not skimpy

Seams finished if fabric requires

Undercollar seam hidden

Good quality interfacing

Buttonholes:
Machine type—close even stitches, no loose threads
Bound buttonholes in high-cost garment

Fabric design matched at seam

Hem ridge and stitches do not show from right side of garment

Hem depth allows for alteration. Hems of A-line or circular skirts eased in

Manufacturing Costs

How much does it cost to produce a garment? The calculation ticket for a tailored cotton dress that sells retail for $72.90 is as follows:

Fabric

2½ yards cotton at 54″	$6.50
¼ yard plain fabric at 36″	.50
Zipper	.15
Thread	.15
Labels	.10
4 Buttons	.60
Total materials	8.00

Labor

Cutting	$ .65
Sewing	3.50
Total Labor	4.15
Total Cost	12.15
Mark-up Factor 200% (overhead and profit)	24.30
Cost per garment quoted wholesale price to store	36.45
Keystoned retail price	72.90

Clothing for the Business World—Women

The phenomenon that has brought 51 percent of all women in the U.S. into the paid work force has changed the very fiber of our society. The increasing number of women who work outside the home has had far-reaching effects on lifestyles, on marriage, on family, and importantly, on consumer expenditures, priorities, and buying patterns.

A PRADS survey revealed interesting data. The women were divided into two classifications: career women, defined as professional and technical workers (just over 15 percent of the working women force) and working women, defined as the rest of the women work force.

According to the survey, career women do not spend a large amount of their salary on clothes. In fact, they spend *less* on clothes than the nonworking wives of professional and top executive men. Career women, like other working women, look for value for their dollar. One third to one half of their clothing purchases are at markdown or discount prices. Only 11 percent claim to shop at designer shops. New York career women were the most conscious and knowledgeable about designers. The New Yorkers spent two times more on clothing than did the Midwestern career woman. The majority of career women shop in department stores. The second choice for New Yorkers was discount houses, and for Midwesterners it was chain stores. The main reason for these store selections was the variety of merchandise. The majority of fall and winter clothing purchases are made in September and October. The majority of spring and summer clothing purchases are made in April and May.

The survey revealed that career women spend:[2]

> 9% of take-home pay for all clothing purchases
> Of this expenditure:
> 39% is used for accessories, shoes, intimate apparel
> 2.5% for cosmetics

When a man prepares for a business appointment, interview, or new job, his clothing choices are limited. He may wear a designated uniform, casual clothes, or a business suit. If he is unsure of the most appropriate attire he probably will opt for the suit. If this choice is incorrect, he may be kidded a bit, but he will not be penalized or ridiculed. Chances are if the suit was really wrong, our businessman would quickly remove the jacket and tie, roll up the sleeves of his dress shirt, and feel fairly comfortable.

When a woman prepares for a business appointment, interview, or new job, her clothing choices are almost endless. She might have a designated uniform, which makes the choice simple. Or she might wear casual clothes, which could mean shirt and skirt, short or long, or pants or shorts or culottes. She may wear a dress, which could be body-concealing or body-revealing—the dress could be austere or ornate. It could be in or out of fashion. She could decide to wear a nondescript coat or a flamboyant fur. She could wear a sequined sweater or a novelty knit. She could wear a blazer or a bolero jacket. She could wear sandals, flats, heels, or boots. The choices are almost limitless. But if she makes the *wrong choices* her career may end before it begins. She may think of herself as executive material when those around her categorize her abilities in the same manner they categorize her apparel choices, which could be kitchen, club, bedroom, golf course, nursery, sandbox, or garden. Many women have found discrimination on the job because of clothing choices. Yet very few women realize that their clothing choices are the source of their trouble.

For this reason, many wardrobe consultants advise that a business woman consider tailored clothing as an essential part of her business wardrobe. A suit or dress may be traditionally tailored or softly tailored. It may be accessorized in many ways to suit the individuality of the wearer.

Clothing for the business world constitutes a major purchase. The investment in time considering the choice should be comparable to the investment in dollars. The design details including line, color, and texture should be selected in keeping with the psychological and physical requirements of the wearer and the clothing requirements for the job.

---

[2] "Chipping Away at the Myth," *Retailweek*, November 1, 1978, pp. 44–54.

Recognizing Quality

Quality is important. Quality depends on appropriate fabric, correct fit, detailed construction, and good styling. Quality is not always determined by dollars. Learning to recognize quality in any price range is the hallmark of the prudent consumer. Buy the best quality you can afford is the recommendation of most wardrobe consultants. Of course, this is a personal value judgment, but it is advice that should be carefully considered. Quality garments speak for themselves and for you in positive terms. Cheap garments look cheap. No one is fooled except the wearer, who by wearing cheap garments advertises a great deal about herself and her taste and judgment. The nonverbal messages sent by cheap clothes are generally perceived in a negative manner.

Selecting a Quality Tailored Garment

Quality is especially important in tailored garments. A tailored garment is molded to fit the body. This is achieved by building up layers of supportive fabrics, which are shaped and formed by various construction techniques into the lines of the garment as they fit the body. A properly tailored garment maintains this built-in shape both on and off the body throughout the life of the garment. Inferior fashion fabrics and supportive fabrics will not tailor properly. They do not hold their shape. They do not wear well. They do not stand up when dry-cleaned. They do not have the look of quality. To test for both fabric quality and tailoring quality, gather a section of the garment in your hand and quickly crush it. A good quality garment springs back into shape quickly and smoothly. The fashion fabric of a high-quality tailored garment is made of wool, linen, or silk. The interfacings may be tailor canvas attached by tiny pad stitches which give the collar area shape. If these are present they may be seen as tiny pricks in the undercollar and behind the lapels. This type of tailoring is very expensive and has been replaced by fused interfacing. Whichever type is used, the interfacings should be used in the collar, the lapels, and down the front, and in the sleeve and lower jacket hem to preserve the shape of these areas.

Feel the collar and lapels. They should lack bulk. The top collar and lapel should turn slightly over the undercollar and facing so that the seam edges are hidden. Look for a good roll in the collar and lapel area. Sleeves should be set in smoothly, be padded so that the shoulder area is smooth with no indication on the outside where pads begin and end. In high-quality tailored jackets the buttonholes are bound if the fabric is suitable for binding, or they are closely stitched with a rounded shape at the end. Buttons are of high quality appropriate to the style of the garment and sewn with adequate shanks so that the buttons do not sink into the fabric when buttoned.

Linings of closely woven, smooth, and somewhat slippery fabrics should be opaque to conceal construction details. Linings are attached to the body of the garment at the sleeve hem, armhole, side seams, lower hem, and back vent. To check this gently separate the lining from the garment at these points. Lining stitches should be tiny and concealed. Check to see that the lining does not twist, pull, or strain. Inspect the lining at the center back for a small pleat or tuck laid in near the neckline and waistline. This extra fullness is needed for body movement and to relieve strain from the fashion and supporting fabrics. A small lap of lining should be found at the sleeve and lower hem area.

Supportive fabric or interfacings should not shadow through either lining or fashion fabric. All hems should be invisible from the right side of the garment unless stitching is part of the decorative detail.

Unless yours is an unlimited budget, it is wise to avoid fashion details that will date or limit the wear life of a tailored suit. This is especially true of your first few purchases. To work as a business garment basic colors and classic designs are most practical. Flair and evening wear suits can be added as both wardrobe and income grow. For longest wear life, avoid high-fashion colors and textures and eye-arresting details and silhouettes.

Maternity Fashions

Maternity wear can be found in styles appropriate for the employed woman. Several manufacturers are expanding their line in suits and sophisticated styles to meet the needs of the professional employed woman. The profile of the new "mother-to-be" is an older woman in a dual career family who postponed childbearing in her twenties while she was getting started in her career. Now in her thirties she is planning to establish a family before her biological clock makes her ineligible. A maternity chain estimates that the average customer spends $800 to $1,000 during her first pregnancy on maternity fashions alone. A department store chain claims that the pregnant customer is the best customer who comes into the store. These more mature and affluent customers are also willing to spend more on the new baby's needs.[3]

Clothing for the Business World—Men

A greater amount of available money, increased leisure time, and the influence of youth are three factors that have made men more fashion-conscious in recent years. Many men are now doing their own shopping. Men want to coordinate their suits, shirts, ties, socks, and shoes themselves. This trend is bringing about changes in merchandising. Because tastes in men's clothing are changing so rapidly, stock cannot be ordered six months ahead as was done in the past. Greater style choices are now available. Boutiques for men's fashions have sprung up in both department stores and small independent shops. Fashion shows of male

[3] Doris Byron Fuller, "Baby Boom Puts Style on the Bottom Line," *Los Angeles Times*, September 8, 1983, Pt. I, p. 1.

17-4 *A beautifully tailored classic trench coat is a sound investment for an aspiring young man in the business world. (Courtesy Hartmarx Corporation)*

apparel have become regular features in some department stores and men's apparel, along with women's, is now being modeled in restaurants (Figure 17-4).

Author Michael Korda says the man who is interested in being a winner must dress like one. "Dress as if you expected to be promoted to the board of directors at any minute, and perhaps you will be." The dress standard that applies in a particular business or company will be worn by the senior officers in that organization. By adopting those standards one cannot go wrong. Korda advises that a plain dark gray or dark blue suit with or without a multipattern or stripe is appropriate for business day or evening wear. It is the kind of suit that you would expect your banker or clergyman to wear. He cautions against contrasting stitching, piping, pockets with buttons, overly wide lapels, and exaggerated suppressed waists.[4]

Men's Dress Shirts

Shirt styles include many variations of collar shapes, neckband widths, cuff designs, sleeve lengths, body shapes, colors, and fabrics.

Stitching. Shirts having 22 stitches to the inch mean quality construction. Inspect for pulled stitches, loose thread ends, puckered stitches, and puckers stitched into the seam. Nothing can help these problems; they are a sign of inferior quality. Two basic types of stitching construction are used in the manufacture of men's shirts—single-needle or double-needle construction. The single-needle construction results in stitching that is easier to control during the sewing process. It is more time-consuming to construct because two separate steps are used for each seam; thus, the shirt will be more expensive. The double-needle construction is done quickly with a high-speed machine that is difficult to control. The stitches show on the right side. Today most shirts are double-needle stitched, some utilize the single needle at the shoulder (which is a tricky area to control) and the double-needle along the body of the garment.[5]

Sizing. Dress shirts are sized by collar and sleeve length. To determine the correct size, measure the base of the neck with one finger inserted under the tape. The sleeve length is measured from the center back of the neck to the wrist. A shirt labeled 15/33 means that the neck is 15 inches and the sleeve length is 33 inches.

Collars. Collars may be rounded or pointed in varying degrees of length of tips and of spread between the tips. Longer collar tips with a close spread are flattering to round-shaped faces; short-spread collars that are round are becoming to long, thin-shaped faces. Collars are available in three constructions, low, medium, and

---

[4] Michael Korda, "The Look of Success," *Sky*, February 1978, p. 44.
[5] Donald Dolce with Jean-Paul DeVellard, *The Consumer's Guide to Menswear* (New York: Dodd, 1983), pp. 55–56.

A. Barrel

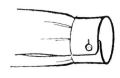

B. Convertible

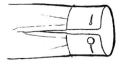

C. French

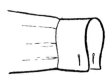

17-5 *Three cuff styles found on men's dress shirts. (A) The barrel cuff is single; it laps and buttons. (B) The convertible cuff is single; it may use either buttons or cuff links. (C) The French cuff is double; it requires cuff links.*

high slope. Slope is the collar height as it sits on the neck. The downward-slope collar is cut with a downward slant from neck back to center front. It is lower at front and exposes more neck. It is best for the man with the heavy neck because it will make his neck seem longer and his overall image seem slimmer. The high-slope collar sits high on the neck and gives the effect of more collar; it is good for the man with a long neck. Collars are fused so that they remain permanently stiff, or they may have stays to keep the collars flat. Some shirts have collars with removable stays. Others have soft collars that button down. Neckbands are narrow, medium, or deep to conform to neck lengths and widths.

Cuffs. Cuffs may be barrel, convertible (single), or French (double) (Figure 17-5).

Body Shapes. The regular body shirt is the roomiest and is cut straight from the sleeve to the tail without any curve. This shirt is preferred by men with portly physiques or men who like lots of ease in their shirts.

The contoured body is curved in at the waist. It is found in traditional styles and is favored by slim men and those who like a trim look (Figure 17-6).

The tapered body narrows from the sleeve to the tail. It is ideal for the man with narrow hips because there is no excess fabric at this area.

Shirt body shapes

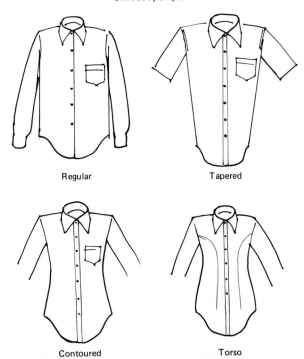

Regular

Tapered

Contoured

Torso

17-6 *Body shapes found in shirts.*

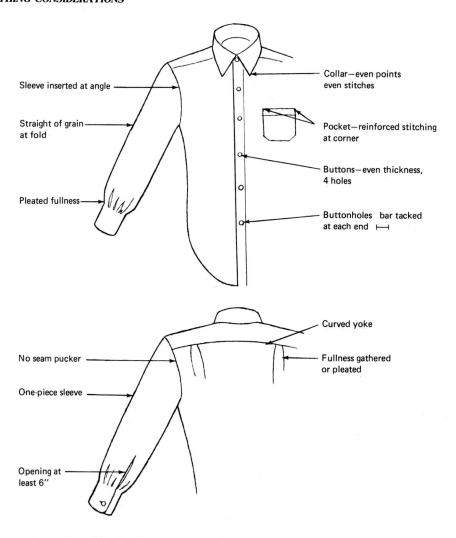

Collar—even points
even stitches

Sleeve inserted at angle

Pocket—reinforced stitching
at corner

Straight of grain
at fold

Buttons—even thickness,
4 holes

Pleated fullness

Buttonholes bar tacked
at each end

Curved yoke

No seam pucker

Fullness gathered
or pleated

One-piece sleeve

Opening at
least 6"

17-7 *Points to check
when buying shirts.*

One type of body shirt is known as the torso shirt. It is the most shaped of all the styles. The shaping is accomplished by darts and several curved seams in both the front and the back. This style is best for slender physiques.

Construction features to check when buying shirts (Figure 17-7):

1. Even collar points.
2. Uniform stitching on collar.
3. Cut on grain—the fold at the top of the sleeve should be on grain.
4. Sleeves cut in one piece rather than two.
5. Sleeve inserted at an angle for greater room for movement and comfort.
6. Fullness at the cuff pleated rather than gathered.
7. Cuff placket on grain and at least six inches in length for ease in ironing.
8. On higher-priced shirts, a row of stitching in the inside center of cuff holds interlining in place.

9. Seams free from pucker.
10. Matching of patterns, plaids at center front, pockets, and collar points.
11. Pockets evenly stitched and reinforced at corners.
12. Four-holed buttons of uniform thickness.
13. Buttonholes with close stitching, backstitching at each end.
14. Deep yoke, curved at back, fullness at back pleated into yoke in more expensive shirts, and gathered into yoke in less costly shirts.

Neckties

A necktie can cost from $5 to over $100. Quality construction is evident by the fashion fabric used, the interfacings, linings, and the stitchings. A tie made of silk, the strongest of natural fibers, is lightweight, durable, fairly free of wrinkling, and easy to knot. The interfacing helps the tie retain its shape and is attached at each end of the fashion fabric. This cannot be seen, but it can be felt. The lining (called pocket tipping) runs from the widest point of the tie for about 6 inches and from the narrow end for about 4 inches. A length of thread in a loose slip stitch runs from the top to the bottom of the tie between the folds on the back side. Two bar tacks about $\frac{1}{4}$ inch long connect the back seam to the inner seam at the top and bottom. These can be seen on the back side placed horizontally across the seam[6] (Figure 17-8).

[6] Ibid., pp. 65–69.

17-8 *A necktie of quality is constructed with quality-silk fashion fabric, woven interfacings, and compatible lining. The construction techniques used are visible for inspection. High-quality ties form a good knot, keep their shape, and stand the strain of frequent use. (Courtesy The Joseph & Feiss Company)*

Men's Suits, Sport Coats, Trousers

There are three categories of men's suits based on construction:

ready-made
made-to-measure
custom-made (also called made to order)

The ready-made suit is a mass-produced factory-made garment. It may contain some handwork or no handwork. The Amalgamated Clothing Workers Union created a grading system that indicates the amount of handwork that is found in a suit. The scale goes from 8, which represents the highest quality, down to X, which indicates no handwork. Automation and innovative supportive fabrics are presently being used to produce ready-made suits of good quality and reasonable prices. Ready-made suits are the largest segment of the suit business. Quality and cost cover a wide range.

Made-to-measure suits are manufactured from an existing suit pattern that has been modified to fit the body type of the individual customer. The customer selects the fabric and details. The suit is made in a factory which also produces ready-made suits. Made-to-measure suits fit the customer better than ready-made and offer some degree of quality control.

Custom-made suits are made to the special order of the individual. All designs and fabrics are selected by the customer. Measurements are carefully taken and the suit is fitted several times during the construction process. The custom-made suit is the most personalized suit. For some men a custom-made suit is the only one that will fit properly. The cost of custom-made suits is comparable to the higher price range of ready-made ($250–$300) and up to the thousands of dollars depending on the reputation of the tailoring establishment. Tailors in America traditionally came from Europe and had been trained since boyhood. Second generation Americans have not followed this trade and today it is difficult to find a European tailor. Most of the tailoring business is now being taken over by Orientals. When selecting a custom tailor it is wise to inquire about costs and quality before making a commitment to buy.[7]

Style choices in suits include straight, boxy, fitted, or flared silhouettes (Figure 17-9). They may be double- or single-breasted, regular- or high-waisted, or have vents at the jacket sides or back. The various pocket styles are bound, welt, patch, or flap. Lapels are notched, peaked, or shawl, either narrow or wide. Jackets may be fully lined, partially lined, or unlined. Trousers come with or without cuffs, beltless, or with belt loops.

Fabric choices are as varied as styles: cottons, silks, wools, synthetics, and blends. Finishes can be wash-and-wear or durable-press. Durable-press garments must fit without requiring letting-out alterations, because the seams, when let out, will not press flat.

The quality and price of a suit will depend on the outer fashion fabric, the

[7] Ibid., pp. 16–18.

17-9 Quality in a sports jacket depends upon the fashion fabric used, the inner materials, and the construction. Unfortunately many of these details are hidden by facings and linings and may not become evident until the garment has been worn and cleaned. (Courtesy The Joseph & Feiss Company)

materials used for interfacings and linings, and the amount of handwork involved in making the suit. Unfortunately, much of the quality is hidden by facings and linings and cannot be seen. Quality may not become evident until the garment is worn and cleaned. Check the following construction features for quality when buying:

SUIT AND SPORT JACKETS

1. Plaids and patterned fabrics match at center back, side seams, across the front, at pockets, welt, and flaps.
2. When lapel is crushed, it pops back into place when hair canvas has been used for interfacing.
3. Buttonholes with even, close stitching, reinforced at the ends.
4. Buttons firmly attached with adequate shanks to prevent buckling when buttoned.
5. Pockets lined in a durable fabric; reinforced openings.
6. Exposed seams turned and stitched or bound.
7. Lining not seen below the coat hem.
8. Armholes taped to prevent stretching; shields in armholes.

TROUSERS, SLACKS

1. Belt loops firmly stitched.
2. Interfacing at waist of noncrushable fabric to prevent wrinkling.
3. Pockets of generous size, reinforced at ends. Linings of closely woven, durable fabric; pocket facing deep enough to keep lining from showing.
4. No piecing in crotch in high-quality garments; facings extended to reinforce crotch line.
5. Inseam with adequate allowance for letting out.

Infant Wear

Clothing requirements from birth to six months of age are few. The principal needs of the newborn infant are for warmth, comfort, and cleanliness. Clothing should be soft, light in weight, easy to maintain, and simple to put on and take off. The type of clothing needed will depend upon the geographic location and heating conditions of the home (Figure 17-10).

The baby's principal activity for the first few months is sleeping. This need for sleep gradually tapers off, and by the time the baby is one year old, it will sleep only half the time. Babies sleep in diapers, shirts, and short jackets, called sacques. The use of these garments eliminates the need for a complete change when diapering. Some babies sleep in gowns or sleepers. A sleeper is a garment that covers the legs and feet as well as the rest of the body. There are two main types of sleepers, pants (resembling pajamas) and bag. One pants style has a top and bottom joined together at the waist with grippers. The feet are completely enclosed. This style can sometimes be obtained with two pairs of pants (Figure 17-11). Another style is one-piece with a zipper down the front and leg. The bag style resembles a long nightgown sewn together at the bottom. It usually has a generous hem, which can be let down as the baby grows. A garment called a "sleep-and-play set" can be used for all baby activities; it is made of two-way-stretch terrycloth or cotton knit (Figures 17-12, 17-13, 17-14).

Shirts and diapers form the basic wardrobe for the baby. Cotton shirts can be found in styles that slip on or that have double-breasted front openings with snaps, which are easier to put on and take off than those with buttons. Both styles are available with or without sleeves. Some shirts have waterproof tabs for pinning the diaper to the shirt. Check to be sure the tabs are anti-wicking to prevent urine from being drawn up from the diaper to the shirt.

Diapers are available in a wide variety of fabrics, shapes, and sizes. It is more economical to purchase a larger size, one that can be used for as long as the baby requires diapering. Gauze diapers are considered the best; they are not bulky, they dry quickly, and they are soft and absorbent but not as durable as bird's-eye. Regulation-style gauze measures twenty-seven by twenty-seven inches (67.5 × 67.5 cm), but these diapers are also available in prefolded styles, which save time and storage space. Stretch gauze diapers are easy to use. They fit smoothly and their stretchability is not affected by washing. Bird's-eye is ab-

17-10 *For the creeper set, a two-piece no-iron knit: knee-saving for the child and labor-saving for the mother. (Courtesy Kiddie Kover, Jayvee Brands)*

17-11 *"All-boy" styling of no-iron batiste polyester and cotton. (Courtesy Kiddie Kover, Jayvee Brands)*

17-12 *Baby's clothing should be light in weight, soft, and easy to put on and take off, like this boy's sleeper in polyester with zipper-down leg. (Courtesy Kiddie Kover, Jayvee Brands)*

17-13 *A baby's clothing should provide warmth, comfort, and cleanliness. A soft velour terry sleeper zips down the leg for easy diaper changing. (Courtesy Kiddie Kover, Jayvee Brands)*

17-14 *A sleep-and-play set of wash-and-wear fabric featuring plastic-covered soles and zippered front for easy dressing. (Courtesy Kiddie Kover, Jayvee Brands)*

sorbent, but it is bulky and does not dry as fast as gauze. This fabric is available in various weights, the heaviest being the most absorbent. Flannelette diapers are soft and warm but not as absorbent as gauze or bird's-eye. They are bulky and do not dry quickly. Cotton knit diapers are tubelike in shape and fit more like panties. Diaper liners can be used with any style diaper; they reinforce the diaper, giving greater protection. Diaper liners are available in fabric or disposable types.

Disposable diapers, which were formerly used only for travel, have become regular diaper wear for many babies. These are made of several layers of cellulose material. Some brands feature a hydrophobic liner (which remains dry) that draws moisture away from the baby's skin to the adjacent layers, thus keeping the baby dry. Diapers with an outer plastic covering eliminate the need for waterproof pants. The plastic layer must be removed before disposing of the diaper in the toilet.

Diaper costs vary. Buying your own supply of fabric diapers and laundering them at home is the least costly way. The use of diaper liners, a diaper service, or disposable diapers may increase diaper costs considerably. These conveniences must be evaluated in terms of the time and money available.

The stretch "sleep-and-play sets" previously mentioned are but one type of the many garments made of stretch fabrics that are now available for babies and young children. These garments, of nylon, cotton, and rayon, have replaced many of the traditional clothes. They reduce the need for concern with the baby's exact size. They eliminate binding, because they stretch gently with the baby's growth. Most garments are one piece and have front openings. It is easy to care for stretch apparel, and no ironing is required. Stretch apparel is available in shirts, pajamas, and play sets.

The suggested needs for the first six months are:

3 dozen diapers	*For the crib*
3–4 long- or short-sleeve shirts	1–2 blankets
3–4 cotton receiving blankets	5–6 sheets
6 sacques or kimonos	2 mattress pads
1 wrapping blanket	*For the bath*
1 sweater and cap	3 towels
1 dress-up outfit	3 face cloths
2 waterproof pants	
2 stretch coveralls	

Creeper Age

The creeping baby needs clothes for protection. Dresses, although pretty and feminine, are an impediment to creeping because they get in the way and do not offer adequate protection (Figure 17-16). Overalls shield tender knees from floor and carpet burns. Reinforcements in the knees of pant legs provide for greater durability. Snappers or grippers on the crotch of overalls save time when diaper changes are necessary. Garments of firmly woven or knitted fabrics with appropriate seam finishes give good service for rough wear and many launderings.

In cold weather zones, a snowsuit, mittens, and hood are necessary. Snowsuits having a closely woven outer fabric provide good protection against the cold and wind. Linings should be durable in both fabric and construction. Twill, poplin, and taffeta fabrics are made of cotton, nylon, or polyester; these fabrics are light in weight and have little bulk. Look for labels that indicate water repellency and the type of care required. Washable snowsuits should be so labeled. This will mean that both linings and outer fabric can be laundered.

During the creeping stage, soft-soled shoes may be worn if protection from the cold is needed. Shoes should be about $\frac{1}{2}$ inch (1.25 cm) longer than the toe, and stockings should be $\frac{1}{2}$ inch (1.25 cm) longer than the foot.

Training pants are often worn when toilet training begins. This occurs at about eighteen months of age, but the time will depend upon the child. Training pants are worn until toilet training is accomplished. These pants are made of two-way stretch fabrics that fit snugly at the hip. Center panels of two, three, and four layers provide for absorption and protection.

Toddler Age

The toddler age starts when the child begins to walk, which generally occurs when the child is between one to one-and-one-half years old. About this time, he graduates from the infant's to the children's department (Figures 17-15, 17-16).

The principal clothing concern in the toddler age is the selection of shoes. When walking begins, flexible-soled shoes with rough soles of $\frac{1}{8}$ inch (0.31 cm) thickness are worn. They may have either a slight heel or no heel, and they should be full and puffy in the toe area. Shoes should be $\frac{1}{4}$ inch (0.63 cm) wider than the foot and $\frac{1}{2}$ inch (1.25 cm) longer than the big toe. Greater length and width than this in a shoe will not be comfortable. The toe area should be wide enough to permit the toes to spread when the body weight rests upon them. The toe area should be deep enough to avoid flattening and pinching. The instep should be ample enough to allow the blood to circulate. If the instep is too tight, the developing foot presses the bones of the arch out of shape and cramps the foot. The shoes should fit snugly at the heel in order to grip the foot firmly and prevent heel rotation when walking. The heel is the part that balances and controls the foot.

As the child grows and begins to run about, the soles of the shoes should be about $\frac{1}{4}$ inch (0.63 cm) thick and the heel $\frac{1}{4}$ to $\frac{3}{8}$ inch (0.63–0.93 cm) high. The inside line should be straight, and the length should be about $\frac{3}{4}$ inch (1.88 cm) longer than the foot.[8] Some parents dress their children in tennis shoes or sneakers exclusively. If these shoes do not have support they should not be worn all of the time. However, those tennis shoes and sneakers that have supports built into them, making them similar to a regular shoe, may be worn.

Shoes that fit well help to build good body skills in balance, climbing, and running. As they are outgrown, shoes need replacing and, in a rapidly growing child, this may be as often as every pay day.

[8] Household Finance Corporation, "Better Buymanship—Use and Care of Shoes," Chicago, 4th rev. ed., Bulletin No. 5, pp. 12–13.

17-15 *Toddler's jumpsuit of machine-washable corduroy features feminine trim. (Courtesy Kiddie Kover, Jayvee Brands)*

17-16 *Two-piece toddler garment of machine-washable cotton jersey features plastic-covered toe and sole covers. (Courtesy Kiddie Kover, Jayvee Brands)*

From Three to Six

Clothing for children from three to six years of age must provide for the activities of sleep, rough play, school, and occasional dress-up. Because of growth and increased activity, these ages bring an increase in clothing expenditure to almost double that of children under two years. Consequently, it is wise to purchase quantity rather than quality in clothing for children in this age group. Features to look for when shopping include self-help, safety, room for growth, and comfort for the child (Figure 17-17).

Self-Help Features

Control of the large and small muscles develops between the ages of two and six years. Usually a child can partially dress himself by the third year if the clothing selected helps him with this task. By the fourth year he needs little assistance. The selection of clothing with self-help features is a means by which we can teach children independence. To encourage children to dress themselves, the following ideas are suggested:

1. Place hooks and rods for hangers at a level that can be easily reached by children.

2. Lay clothing out in the order in which the garments are to be put on.
3. Mark shoes for the right and left foot.
4. Mark the front or back of the garments.
5. Select garments having:
    Front openings.
    Large armholes.
    Large necks on slipovers.
    Zippers rather than buttons.
    Large buttons and snaps rather than small ones.
    Stretch fabrics with no closures.
    Pants that slip down easily.

Growth Features

Buying clothing with growth features will enable a garment to be worn over a longer period of time. Growth features include the following (Figure 17-18):

1. Long straps on overalls.
2. Tucks near the hemlines of dresses and slips.
3. Stretch fabrics.
4. Deep hems on skirts and pants.
5. Two-piece garments.
6. Indefinite waists.

17-17 Features to consider when shopping for growing youngsters include room for growth, safety, and comfort. (Courtesy Mountain Laurel)

17-18 Practical clothing with growth features means long straps on overalls, indefinite waists, and two-piece garments. (Courtesy The Rowland Company)

Safety Features

Flame-Retardant Clothing. Fibers of cotton, rayon, and silk catch fire easily and burn rapidly. Most synthetic fibers, such as acetate, nylon, acrylic, and polyester, do not burn easily, but they melt, causing a sticky substance to adhere and burn deeply into the flesh. Blends of natural and synthetic fibers can both burn readily and melt. Wool is both difficult to ignite and slow to burn.

The construction of a fabric also affects the way it burns. Open and loose weaves are more flammable than are tightly woven fabrics. Sheer and lightweight fabrics ignite more rapidly and burn faster than heavy, durable weaves. Fuzzy-surfaced fabrics with a brushed nap catch fire easily and burn at a fast rate.

The design of clothing affects burning; loose-fitting garments that permit air to reach both outer and under surfaces of the garment permit fire to spread rapidly. These include loose-fitting sleeves, ruffles, and flaring skirts.

More children than adults suffer from burns caused by clothing, and there are more severe burns from sleepwear than from any other garments, according to data collected by the National Bureau of Standards.[9] This serious problem has brought about legislation requiring children's sleepwear to meet flame-retardant standards.

In current use are inherently flame-resistant fabrics achieved through fiber and fabric construction techniques rather than by chemical finishes. These fabrics include:[10]

1. Vinal/vinyon blend. Trademarks are Kohijin, Cordelan.
2. Modacrylic. Sold under the brand names SEF and Kanecaron, Verel.
3. Blends of Cordelan and modacrylic with polyester or nylon.

Information on flammability standards is found under the topic Legislation of Textiles, further on in this chapter.

Researchers at the Johns Hopkins University School of Public Health found that burn deaths decreased as the fashion for blue jeans and slacks replaced skirts. In the last 15 years, burn fatalities decreased 55 percent for girls and only 12 percent for boys under 10 years of age. Inflammable, frilly dresses appear to be the culprit.[11] Parents often buy larger sizes of clothing with an eye to growth or have a child wear "hand-me-downs" that are too large. This is a dangerous practice, because loose-fitting garments may catch on things such as branches of trees and parts of bicycles, causing serious accidents.

Other safety features include:

1. Reinforcement at the knees to prevent skin burns.
2. No drawstrings at the neck.
3. No unnecessary ribbons or bows that can get caught.

[9] "Sleepwear to Be Safer," American Apparel Manufacturing Association Newsletter, August–September 1973.
[10] *Family Economics Review,* U.S. Department of Agriculture, Summer 1977, p. 3.
[11] Dr. Neil Solomon Column, *Los Angeles Times,* June 3, 1979, Pt. IV, p. 23.

17-19 Comfort features for children include garments that hang from the shoulders. (Photo courtesy The Butterick Fashion Marketing Company)

4. No cuffs on pant legs and no long skirts that may cause children to trip.
5. Bright colors that permit motorists to see children.
6. Shoes that protect the foot.

Comfort Features

Children, as well as adults, feel more comfortable in certain types of garments. Fabrics that are soft and absorbent contribute to comfort. Other comfort features in children's garments include (Figure 17-19):

1. Garments that are sized correctly and fit the body and limbs.
2. Straps that stay up on the shoulder.
3. Pants and panties that do not restrict the waist or leg. Red marks on the body mean that the garments are too tight.
4. Bows that do not come untied.
5. Lightness in weight.
6. Textures that are not scratchy.
7. Seasonally appropriate clothing.
8. Clothing that offers protection from bruising, such as long sleeves and long pants.
9. Garments that hang from the shoulder.
10. Shoes and stockings that are the correct size.

499

Ages Six to Eleven

Clothing needs for children in elementary school vary in some respects from those of preschoolers, although many requirements remain the same. This period is a very active one physically; sports rate high in interest for both boys and girls. Clothing plays an important role in social development too, as definite ideas about clothing likes and dislikes are developing during this period. This is an age when belonging to a group, and wearing what the group wears, is very important. (Refer to Chapter 2.)

Playing is the chief pastime of elementary-age boys and girls. Leadership ability and popularity are frequently found among those children who have developed skills in games and sports. Durable clothing must be provided that will withstand the strains of vigorous exercise. Garments should be cut so that they are comfortable and do not restrain activity. Dresses and shirts should have adequate fullness across the back; pleats at the center back or yokes with fullness will provide for strenuous arm movement without tearing the garment. Dresses that hang from the shoulders provide more freedom than fitted dresses. The armhole of shirts and dresses should be at least one inch below the armpit for comfort.

The Teen Years

A large proportion of teen-agers are wage earners. Whether teen-agers get their money from allowances or jobs, the buying potential of this group is sizeable. National and local advertising is geared to the youth market. Department stores feature teen-age boutiques and devote a large share of space to clothing and accessories for this group. Many stores have fashion boards of young people for the purpose of promoting sales to the teen-age market. Magazines, such as *Glamour, Mademoiselle,* and *Seventeen,* are directed at the teen-age market and do much to promote fashion among the older girls of this group. They provide hints on beauty and grooming together with product advertisements.

The qualities in clothes that are most important to teen-agers are fit and style. Construction is not often considered. It is likely that teen-agers do not consider construction of the clothes they buy because they are not aware of what qualities to look for. Many adults, as well as teen-agers, do not realize the importance of fabric, cut, and construction to the total appearance of the garment and to the amount of wear that can be expected from it.

Because growth during the early adolescent period is so rapid, a minimal wardrobe is advisable at any one time. Two-piece outfits, such as sweaters, blouses, pants and skirts, may extend parts of the wardrobe over a longer period of time, because different parts of the body grow at different rates. If the shoulders and bust grow faster than the hips, a new top may be worn with an older skirt,

17-20 *Garment fit and style are two important qualities of the teenager. Two-piece garments may extend the wear life for some garments because different parts of the body grow at different rates. (Courtesy Altra)*

whereas a one-piece dress might have to be discarded because of growth in only one section of the body (Figure 17-20).

Teen-agers create new styles. This age group has introduced and popularized many styles. Many fashion designers get ideas for their new designs from observing youth. Teen-agers are also great followers of fashion and fads. These fads usually involve only accessories but, even so, the cost of adopting and discarding the latest fads can be significant over a long period of time.

Dressing for Exercise

Dressing for exercise serves several purposes. Adequate body covering for modesty and for safety are obvious considerations. Most sports have a prescribed style of clothing. Dressing in variations of these traditional uniforms can give even the most novice participant an air of authority. A good guide to follow when beginning a new sport is to dress in the most traditional manner so as not to call attention to total inexperience—at least you will *look* as if you know what you are doing. As skills increase the individualizing of the uniform is more acceptable. Once true expertise has been attained, untraditional clothing can call attention to the fact that you really are a "pro."

For all sports, except swimming, a good pair of shoes particularly adapted to the exercise or sport is necessary. The correct footwear makes exercise more enjoyable and prevents such problems as strains, blisters, sprains, and sore legs and ankles. For jogging and games that include a lot of running consider the following when purchasing a pair of shoes:

1. The sole must be adequately cushioned to absorb the impact of running on a hard surface. A shallow to deep ripple or waffle works best.
2. The heel should have a slight elevation to take some of the strain off the Achilles tendons. A wide heel that tends to stabilize the foot works well for many people. If the back of the shoe comes up high on the heel it tends to distribute the pressure on the Achilles tendons more evenly.
3. An adequate arch support is necessary.
4. The width as well as the length of the shoe should fit the foot. Soft materials used in construction of the top of the shoe can be adjusted to accommodate the width of the foot by loosening the laces.

Two pairs of socks help avoid blisters, especially when you are beginning to exercise. If your thighs chafe, cut down the friction by rubbing them with vaseline prior to the workout. Wear loose clothing that does not restrict your movements. For men, jockey shorts give enough support and are recommended for long-distance running, but for short-distance, racketball, and other vigorous sports, an athletic supporter should be worn. Women need a good supportive bra, not only for comfort but also to avoid straining on the ligaments supporting the breast. Covering the nipples with Band-Aids for long-distance running will prevent friction from the shirt causing irritation and bleeding.

Wash all clothing that comes in contact with your body after each workout. This simple hygiene can save your skin from irritation and rashes.

In any weather avoid the rubberized or impervious suits and belts advertised to give you fast weight loss. They are dangerous. The pounds you sweat off during a workout are pounds of water. This weight is regained as soon as you quench your thirst after the workout. They are unsafe because these rubber suits block the body's natural cooling system by trapping perspiration. They are particularly unsafe on hot humid days. The body tries to cool off by perspiring but the perspiration is trapped by the rubber suit and cannot evaporate. The body temperature climbs dangerously high and the symptoms of heat exhaustion or sunstroke may develop.[12]

Clothing and Energy Conservation

Since the nation's thermostats have been regulated to meet national energy conservation goals, we have been made more aware of the protective function of clothing. Physiological principles can be applied to increase body comfort.

[12] Kenneth H. Cooper. M.D., M.P.H., *The Aerobics Way* (New York: Pocket Books, 1977), pp. 58–60.

17-21 Warmth without weight can be best provided by down-filled garments. (Courtesy Altra)

As rivers freeze and room temperatures hover around the prescribed 68 degrees, the need to minimize loss of body heat is essential. Wearing several layers of thin clothing gives better insulation than wearing one heavy garment. The spaces between the layers trap the body-warmed air. Sweaters can be worn under as well as over dresses and shirts. Smocks, vests, interlined and padded garments, will help to raise body temperature. Warmth without weight can best be provided by down-filled garments (Figure 17-21). Much body heat is lost through the head. Wearing a cap or scarf will keep the warm air in. Sleepwear can consist of cotton flannel nightwear, including sheets, bed jackets, shawls, sweaters, and bed socks. Natural fibers are warmer to use than man-made, as the latter hold the outside temperature, and thus are cold in winter and warm in summer.

While exercising outside when it is cold, wear a hooded sweat shirt or cap that comes over your ears. If the temperature is around zero use a surgical or dental mask, a knitted ski mask, a loose muffler or a terry-cloth "veil" over the mouth and nose to warm up the air before it goes into your lungs. Loose-fitting mittens keep hands warmer than gloves. A towel or scarf around the neck will help keep body heat in.

Avoid putting on too many clothes when exercising in cold weather. They will hamper your movements and make you perspire excessively, which may make it more easy to chill after exercise.

Dressing for Warm Weather

On the other side of the calendar, when the temperatures soar, you can "keep your cool" by using clothing of natural fibers constructed in open weaves or knits. These are more absorbent than man-made fibers. An important factor in keeping cool is garment style. Still air acts as an insulator keeping body heat in. Select garment styles that will not trap air pockets near the body. Garments that have openings at the neck, waist, wrist, and ankles will carry heat away from the body.[13] Men will be cooler when omitting a tie and using short-sleeved shirts and short pants.

Light colors reflect the sun's rays and will be cooler to wear than dark hues which absorb the sun's rays. Skirts are cooler than slacks.

Legislation of Textiles

Protection is provided to the consumer through various legislative acts pertaining to textiles and fur products. These provisions require accurate labeling in regard to fiber content and care, and to protection from the use of dangerously flammable fabrics.

Wool Products Labeling Act

This act requires that the percentages of wool, recycled wool, and nonwool fibers used in a garment be specifically identified. Originally enacted in 1939, the act was amended in 1980 to allow the substitution of the term "recycled wool" for the previously required terminology "reprocessed and reused wool." The new terminology does not indicate whether the recycled wool was previously worn or scrap wool. The terms wool, new wool, and virgin wool indicate that the fibers are being manufactured for the first time. The name of the manufacturer or distributor must be included. In June 1984 legislation was introduced to require the label to include the country of origin, where the product was manufactured or processed, either in the U.S. or elsewhere (S. 1816). For the first time, items made in the U.S. would be included in the labeling requirement.[14]

---

[13] Marjorie S. Stewart and Willodean D. Moss, "100 Ways to Save Energy," *Journal of Home Economics* (May 1978) p. 34.

[14] Joan C. Courtless, Agricultural Research Service, Outlook '85, "Recent Trends in Clothing and Textiles," 1985 Agricultural Outlook Conference, Washington, D.C., December 3–5, 1984.

Fur Products Labeling Law

Giving misleading names to furs is prohibited by this law. The label must indicate the animal from which the fur was taken, the country of origin, and whether the pelt has been used, damaged, or is scrap fur. The label must also indicate if the fur has been dyed or bleached.

The Textile Fiber Products Identification Act

This legislation requires labeling to disclose the following:

The percentage of each fiber present, designated by generic name.
A listing of fibers in order of predominant weight.
The manufacturer of the product.
If imported, the textile fibers used and the name of the country where the product was processed or manufactured. In June 1984, legislation was introduced to amend the Textile Fibers Identification Act to include in the label country of origin (where it was processed or manufactured) whether it be in the U.S. or elsewhere (S. 1816).

Textile Care Labeling Act

A permanently attached care label on wearing apparel must indicate at least one safe method for cleaning. It will identify in detail washing or dry-cleaning instructions using a standardized language, and require that the instructions be supported by test results, current literature, or past experience. To insure consistent, complete, and accurate information, the legislation provided for a glossary of terms to be used on the label. (The glossary of terms can be found in Appendix G.) Piece goods labels can be attached to the bolt rather than provided individually to the customer. Excluded are remnants up to 10 yards long and trims up to 5 inches wide. First enacted in 1972, revised in 1980 and again in 1983, the amended rule became effective January 1984. Complete information on care labels can be found in Chapter 19, Care and Maintenance of the Wardrobe.

Flammability Standards

Flammable Fabrics Act

This standard provides a minimum of protection for consumers from highly flammable wearing apparel manufactured and sold since 1954. This standard excluded interlining fabrics, hats, gloves, and footwear.

The Consumer Products Safety Commission is proposing updating the CS191-53 standard to provide increased protection from burn injuries for all apparel items except shoes. Called the General Wearing Apparel Standard, it would provide new test methods to be used to measure the rate of flame spread. Fabrics would be categorized into four classes according to ease of ignition and rate of heat transfer and garments would be classified into three classes according to how tightly or loosely they fit the body. Specific fabric requirements would then be assigned to garment styles depending upon their tightness or looseness on the body. That is, garments that fit loosely or flare away from the body would be required to be made from fabrics that do not burn easily.

Flammability Standards for Children's Sleepwear

Infants' and children's sleepwear in sizes 0–6x and 7–14 must meet the Department of Commerce's standards for flame resistance. These garments must maintain this property for fifty washings. The standard covers nightgowns, pajamas, robes, and other garments intended for use as sleepwear in the sizes given above. Diapers and underwear are excluded from this standard. The use of inherently flame-resistant fabric achieved through fiber and fabric construction techniques has replaced the use of chemical finishes. (Refer to Safety Features, under From Three to Six, earlier in this chapter.) Labels must be readily visible and manufacturers must advise consumers of any agents or treatments known to cause deterioration of the effectiveness of flame resistance.

Consumer Aids

An abundance of factual data and information is available to the consumer regarding specific clothing purchases. When the shopper knows what features to look for in clothing, better judgments of value and quality can be made. The following list includes several books and pamphlets that can be obtained by writing to the addresses given.

Consumer Product Safety Commission. The Federal Consumer Product Safety Act of 1972 established a Federal regulatory agency, the Consumer Product Safety Commission. This commission issues and enforces safety standards governing design, construction, content, performance, packaging, and labeling of consumer products. If you feel a product is unsafe, contact the organization: Toll-free hot line—800-638-2666. Address: U.S. Consumer Product Safety Commission, Washington, D.C. 20207.

Guide to Federal Consumer Services. Department of Health, Education and Welfare, Office of Consumer Affairs. Lists agencies and services in Federal programs that help consumers. Describes where and how to get help.

Consumer Product Information is a booklet of publications, including those pertaining to clothing and fabric. Published quarterly, it may be obtained free by writing to the Superintendent of Documents, Washington, D.C. 20402. There is a nominal charge for the pamphlets listed in the booklet.

Consumers' Research publishes the *Consumers Bulletin*, which contains the results of, and evaluations of, tests conducted by Consumers' Research of branded and trademarked items. It also publishes the *Consumer Bulletin Annual*. These may be obtained from Consumers' Research, Inc., Washington, N.J. 07882.

Consumers Union, in its magazine, *Consumer Reports*, discloses the results and evaluations of its tests of branded and trademarked items. The December issue of the magazine is an annual buying guide in the form of a paperback book. Both the magazine and the book are available from Consumers Union of the United States, Inc., 256 Washington Street, Mount Vernon, N.Y. 11055. *Consumer Reports* may also be found on newsstands.

Professional Organizations Concerned with Consumer Clothing Problems

International Fabricare Institute provides services to its members through its test laboratories, courses, and publications. Table 17-3, designating the life expectancy of clothing and household items was developed by the International Fabricare Institute Research Center, Silver Springs, Md. 20910. Fabricare Institute is listed in telephone books of major cities to aid the consumer.

The American Home Economics Association, a professional organization for home economists, supports programs for the protection of the consumer and to the direction of programs in consumer education. The association promotes informative and descriptive labeling and advertising of consumer goods and services; the Association's interest in developing quality and safety standards is of benefit to the consumer.

Suggested Activities

1. Invite a retailer or a buyer to speak to the class on the subject of "how to buy quality in ready-to-wear clothing."
2. Bring examples to class of satisfactory and unsatisfactory clothing buys. Analyze these examples with class members.
3. Collect several samples of fashion fabric and supportive fabric. Analyze the fabric in terms of its fiber content, fiber length, yarn twist, and fabric construction (weave, knit, and the like). Can you predict wear quality from this examination?
4. Set up a bulletin board exhibit of construction fabrics, giving qualities and suggested end uses for them.
5. Arrange a display of children's garments to show growth, safety, and self-help features.
6. Collect "hang tags" from newly purchased garments. Compare information given on "hang tags" with data given in this chapter.

18 **Shopping**

In an urban society such as ours, the selection of consumer goods is an important task. Very few households produce the major share of items required by the family or its individual members. Since a substantial portion of income is spent on purchased goods, an examination of shopping practices is desirable. It seems that many have developed shopping habits but not shopping skills. Although the primary concern of this text is clothing selection, much of the information given in this chapter can be applied to shopping for any item found in the marketplace.

Merchants employ a variety of selling techniques to assist and influence the customer. The packaging of products, the displaying of merchandise, the pricing of items, the store's image and advertising methods, even the floor plan, are all thoughtfully designed to attract customers and sell goods. The merchant must constantly utilize many merchandising methods to attract, hold, and increase the number of customers and sales.

The individual, in turn, has the privilege of selecting from a vast array of stores and merchandise. The customer is always in the lead position in a relationship with a merchant, but too often individuals fail to press this advantage to the fullest. The customer has the prerogative to select or reject what the merchant is selling. The exercise of this prerogative is what we commonly call *shopping*. The shopper should understand merchandising and selling so that full value is received for the money spent.

Promotion and Advertising

Advertising means different things to different people. To some it may mean the weekly specials at the supermarket. To a teen-ager it may mean peer identification with products promoted and worn by a popular celebrity. To a business person it may mean selling campaigns. To a child it may mean singing commercials on a favorite television program. These concepts all represent different forms of advertising.

The primary purpose of advertising is to move goods and services. It does this not only by making people aware of products and services but also by creating in the consumer a desire to have them. Advertising also attempts to convince the consumer that one brand is more desirable than all the others.

Advertising is sometimes designed to put pressure on the individual to make purchases irrationally or emotionally rather than intelligently. To become a wise shopper, one must develop the skill to distinguish between advertising that is informational and factual and that which appeals only to the emotions.

The average American consumer is exposed to approximately 1,500 advertisements each day through television, radio, newspapers, brochures, magazines, outdoor signs, cards, personal letters, and product packaging.[1] Of these 1,500 advertisements, it is estimated that only 75 are noticed and only 30 remembered. Of this latter number, only 5 can be considered informational advertising. The vast majority of advertisements are designed to sell a product by emotional persuasion.[2]

Motivational research, developed by psychologists, is the technique used by advertising agencies to discover the human factors that persuade customers to buy. The results of this research are utilized to learn the anxieties and desires of consumers. With this knowledge, the advertising agencies are able to develop more effective appeals in their advertising programs. Very often, advertising is used not to sell a particular product directly but to sell an idea that fulfills a need. This includes emotion-charged advertising that is directed to the hidden fears of the consumer or advertising that promises to satisfy the concealed hopes of the consumer. For example, products for personal hygiene generally advertise "social security" rather than the qualities of the soap, deodorant, or toothpaste; cosmetic ads offer a promise of beauty, while perfume and scent ads assure romance.

Arthur A. Winters, whose advertising agency specializes in fashion advertising, comments:

> The basic difference in the salesmanship of fashion advertising is emotion. The appeals are emotional, the approach more imaginative. Effective advertising will use a knowledge of the particular set of emotions concerned with the desire and need for individuality, romance, recognition, acceptance, compensation, career *etc*. . . . Fashion advertising is extremely effective when it lets the woman know exactly how she will feel, and what will happen when fashion follows one's own inner concept.[3]

Most advertisements use a variety of techniques of emotional persuasion to appeal to our basic needs and values (Figure 18-1). These techniques may be social, psychological, physical, or economic in nature. Numerous advertisements are directed toward the human desires for:

1. Emotional security—youthfulness, glamor, belonging, sex appeal, prestige, or status.
2. Convenience and comfort—ease of care, upkeep, or use.

18-1 Advertising directed to comfort. (Courtesy Heidi Kessler and Mt. Sports, Ltd.)

YOUR BEST PALS FOR SUMMER HIKES the SIERRA DESIGNS 60/40 PARKA and a GERRY DOWN VEST are ALL YOU NEED FOR ANY WEATHER.

MOUNTAIN SPORTS
821 PEARL ST.   443·6770

[1] Suzy McNeil, "Fashion, Fiber, Fabric," *California Apparel News*, December 14, 1973, p. 13.

[2] Leland J. Gordon and Stewart M. Lee, *Economics for Consumers*, 5th ed. (New York: American Book, 1967), p. 162.

[3] Jeannette A. Jarnow and Beatrice Judelle, *Inside the Fashion Business* (New York: Wiley, 1981), p. 377.

3. Safety and health—best for yourself and those you love.
4. Financial gain—wise buy, bargain, economical, shrewd investment, snob appeal.[4]

It is revealing to compare the style of advertising for various price ranges of clothing. Advertisements for high-priced designer clothes often incorporate line drawings or action photographs that reveal little of the garment detail. Often only the designer or brand name appears and sometimes the name of one retailer. There is no detailed descriptive copy accompanying these drawings. These advertisements appear in newspapers and fashion magazines. The concept for this type of promotion is that the *avant garde* or established designer patron does not need selling or persuading to wear innovative styles; such a patron needs only to be notified that new garments are available.

Fashion advertising in newspapers and magazines for medium-priced clothing features detailed illustrations or clear photographs. The accompanying copy contains extensive descriptions written to persuade the customers that they will appear fashionable in these styles, or that they will achieve the lifestyle they desire by wearing this apparel.

Low-priced clothes usually sell themselves. Advertising is limited. Often the type of retail outlet selling clothes in this price range is known and its customers are usually after body coverings. Low-priced clothes are fashionable, but they are in the styles that have been proven. Medium- to low-priced clothing is frequently advertised on television.

Although the main purposes of advertising are to sell a product or gain acceptance of an idea, scores of different approaches have been developed. For the consumer, recognition of the underlying purposes of an advertising campaign can assist in establishing the credibility of the information presented. Specific purposes of advertising are:

1. To increase the use of a product (frequency of use, frequency of replacement, variety of uses, units of purchase, extended length of buying season).
2. To attract a new generation.
3. To present a special merchandise offer.
4. To coordinate a family of products (which are to be used together, such as detergents, bleaches, conditioners, and softeners for laundry).
5. To introduce or increase knowledge of the organization behind the product.
6. To render a public service.
7. To dispel wrong impressions.
8. To meet competition.
9. To reach the person who influences the purchaser.

The vehicles that carry the advertising are spoken of as the *media*. Chief advertising media may be classified as:

[4] Gordon and Lee, op. cit., pp. 179, 385.

Newspapers
Magazines
Radio, television
Direct-mail advertising

Outdoor advertising
Transportation advertising
Point-of-sale displays, motion pictures
Premiums and special offers

Because more and more women are working outside the home, the Bureau of Advertising made a survey to determine if this factor affects the influence advertising has on them. They found that among both working and nonworking women, newspaper advertising plays a major role as a shopping aid. It saves the women time and helps them to decide where to buy.[5]

Advantages and Disadvantages of Advertising

Advantages

Advertising makes people aware of new products and services and of the stores in which they can be purchased. These products may be time- and/or labor-saving, such as no-press garments and laundry equipment, which can ease the burden of wardrobe maintenance.

Informative and descriptive advertisements enable people to make some comparisons between products without leaving their homes. Newspaper ads are an important source of such shopping information. The size of the Sunday newspaper, weighted down with ad for fillers attests to the importance of this media for shopping information.

Although a great many newspaper, catalogue, and direct-mail ads do use informative and useful copy, most radio and TV commercials do not. The majority, in a study of four hundred TV commercials provided no information on price, performance, safety, or any other of fourteen attributes that would aid viewers in making an intelligent buying decision.[6]

Advertising is necessary to the economy because it moves goods and services, which in turn provide employment in all phases of manufacturing, distribution, promotion, and selling. Advertising helps create a higher standard of living because it engenders the mass production of goods, and this mass production makes it possible to sell the goods at prices most people can afford to pay. Advertising pays for a large part of the expenses involved in the publication of newspapers and magazines, and it sponsors the radio and television programs, cultural and sports events that provide much of our entertainment.

Disadvantages

Advertising influences some people to overextend their budgets and misuse credit. It tempts people to buy products they cannot afford and do not need, thus creating a serious financial burden for the gullible.

[5] "Survey on Working Women...," *California Apparel News*, June 14, 1974, p. 50.
[6] A. Kent MacDougall, "National Advertisers Worry About Mounting Clutter of Product Pitches," *Los Angeles Times*, Pt. V, p. 1, November 29, 1981.

Advertising encourages obsolescence by making consumers dissatisfied with what they own. It is obvious in the area of fashion apparel that the promotion of frequent changes of styles creates psychological wardrobe obsolescence often long before signs of garment wear appear.

False or exaggerated claims, misrepresentations, and promotion of dangerous products by some advertisements are all detrimental to the consumer and can result in serious injury when harmful products are unknowingly purchased. A few of these examples are allergy-causing cosmetics, drugs with harmful side effects, and ineffective sun protection products.

To make a revealing evaluation of advertising, clip several kinds of clothing and cosmetic advertisements from magazines and newspapers. Underline in red all copy based on emotional and nonrational appeals and underline in black all copy that is informative. Jot down to what needs and values the appeals are directed, such as emotional security, health, convenience, comfort, status, power, prestige, or financial gain. You will then readily see the type of appeal of the advertisement to the consumer.

Consumers are in a better position to make intelligent decisions regarding the purchase of goods and services when they understand the motivational appeals made by advertising. They should be able to distinguish factual and informative copy from that which appeals to the emotions and from that which makes ambiguous claims.

Types of Stores

The type of store with which people prefer to do business is based upon personal attitudes and values. Some consumers consider shopping as recreational; increasing numbers use it as a psychological bondage; others regard it as an undesirable chore; and many view it as a bargain hunt. There are shoppers who are willing to pay higher prices to be in pleasant surroundings with soft carpets and subtle lighting, and to enjoy the advantages of service and convenience. These extra services include trained, courteous sales help, credit, liberal return policy, free delivery, dining facilities, and attractive rest rooms. Other shoppers consider these to be frills of little importance, and they prefer to look for values at shops with lower overhead and fewer services. Most shoppers select stores that carry the quality of merchandise they wish to have at prices they can afford to pay. Many shoppers patronize certain stores for the image the company has created. Store location, ease of accessibility, and type of parking facilities are also important considerations for many customers.

Store Image

The image that a business projects is recognized as being a very important factor in attracting a specific clientele into a specific store. Potential customers can evaluate a store's image with a "blink of the eye." They know almost immediately whether or not they will feel comfortable with this image. If shoppers identify with a store's image, or if they would *like* to identify with it, they will investigate the store further. People tend to shop in stores that cater to their own socioeconomic level.

There are many different kinds of store images; their number is limited only by the imaginations of the business community. Some could be classified as:

High-fashion
Fashion
Trendy
Opulent
Thrifty
Conservative
Casual
Ultramodern
Old-fashioned
Family-oriented
Singles-oriented
Career-oriented
For all types of physical and age categories
For all kinds of specialties
For all the newest fads and fancies

Store image is created by a combination of many aspects of the business operation, which form the appearance, the atmosphere, and the mood of an establishment. Some factors influencing the exact image a store projects include the following:

1. Location, including its exact placement in the community, surrounding environs, neighboring businesses, and both vehicle and pedestrian traffic patterns.
2. The physical appearance of the business building; the architecture, colors, the style of fixtures, and decor used throughout the building, including dressing rooms and rest rooms.
3. Music, merchandise displays, window design, packaging of purchases, and furnishing of shopping bags.
4. Store personnel; their general appearance, clothing, attitude, manners, competence, and willingness to provide service.
5. The methods of advertising and billing used.
6. Community involvement of the store.
7. The appearance and the socioeconomic level of the store's patrons.
8. The kinds and quality of merchandise sold by the establishment.

Shopping Centers

Suburban shopping centers built by real estate developers, usually feature one or more large, well-established department stores (known as anchor stores) in addition to many small satellite specialty shops, boutiques, travel agencies, and restaurants.

The shopping centers are usually located near dense urban areas adjacent to or near freeways, expressways, thruways, or turnpikes. They feature spacious parking areas. Some of the centers seem akin to the old Greek *stoa*, which must have been the precursor of today's shopping mall. Families turn out *en masse* on weekends, many of them apparently more intent on recreation than serious shopping. Some centers provide entertainment areas for children as well as theaters, banks, college extension classes, restaurants, and museums. They offer "a little something for everybody." The controlled environment of an enclosed mall is designed to attract shoppers all year round in any kind of weather.

Recent central city redevelopment is responsible for relocating shopping centers back to where they began. With diverted traffic patterns, streets have been transformed to oases of flowers, trees, and grass amid high-rise structures that accommodate multilevel parking. Apartment houses, hotels, and convention centers surround these shopping areas.

Retail competition between suburban shopping malls and redesigned civic centers is fierce. The problems are many for both types of operations. Often the consumer can make good buys by shopping comparatively between the two areas. However, if either or both operations are bankrupt, the consumer suffers losses on many levels. It is hoped that wise city planning will help alleviate overbuilding in retail developments and will create shopping centers that can make a profit while serving a wide variety of customer needs.

Department and Chain Stores

Department stores merchandise many different items in various departments all under one roof. A department store may be a one-family operation, but more likely it belongs to a corporation comprised of a large group of stores. These include Associated Dry Goods, Allied Stores, Federated, and Carter Hawley Hale. Each organization has a Board of Directors who are responsible to stockholders. The latter expect to make a profit from money they have invested in the organization. Department stores cater to customers on every social and economic level. Each store or chain of stores creates an image and develops a reputation for a particular level of quality, quantity, and price range of its goods and services. The large department store organizations are able to purchase merchandise in greater quantities, thus enabling them to obtain goods at lower prices than the small stores. The big end-of-season clearances, frequent sales, and markdowns have become a way of life in the department store since it is in competition with stores selling the same merchandise at lower prices.

At one time the department stores offered the customer a large staff of well-trained, knowledgeable sales help. Unfortunately this situation is seldom true today except in the higher-priced department stores. Owing to money-saving cut backs, well-trained and knowledgeable sales help is becoming rare, particularly in stores catering to customers in the moderate- and lower-income groups.

Department stores provide many types of services, a few of which are free delivery, free clothing alterations for men, assistance in planning weddings, and interior design. It is to the customer's advantage to utilize these services as their costs are not charged to the individual customer but rather are included in the prices of everything in the store. Department stores also offer other services as a convenience for their customers, but these are services for which the individual customer pays. Some of them are custom-made window coverings, furniture reupholstering, barber shop and beauty salon services, and, available recently from some stores, in-the-home services such as carpet and upholstery cleaning. Harrod's, a famous London department store, takes care of all one's life needs. It will plan and carry out your wedding celebration and take care of your funeral as well. Department stores have gained public confidence and customer loyalty because of their reputation for accepting return merchandise and standing behind the products and services they sell. Major conventional department stores are considered the backbone of the fashion industry in the U.S.A.

Large national chain stores, such as Montgomery Ward and Company and Sears Roebuck and Company feature basic, traditional styles at affordable prices. These stores do not claim to be in the high-fashion business. Career and sportswear in many styles appeal to price-conscious shoppers. Wards and Sears also have outlet stores that carry sale items, returned goods, and slightly damaged merchandise. Savings from 20 to 75 percent can be found in these outlets.[7]

J. C. Penney and Sears have recently worked to change their image. Penney's seeks to attract a wider range of customers with upscaled goods. Sears seeks to be the one-stop shopping center for the entire family and has entered into banking, insurance, investments, as well as selling soft and hard goods.

Personal Shoppers

If you are too busy to shop, or if you are not interested in spending time looking for just the right items, take advantage of the personal shopper service offered by most major clothing stores. Dawn Mello, president of Bergdorf Goodman, gives this advice: "Most stores have specialists with whom you can work. It's just a question of making a phone call. If you have a very good shopping consultant, you tell her how much you want to spend and she will put the clothes together the way the designer did it, but she'll understand you, your body. . . . We have women call and say, 'Look, I'm going to be there at four o'clock this afternoon, I have no time, and what I'd like is to have three outfits together. I'm thinking in terms of a suit, but I need an evening dress and I really need something to wear on weekends. Can you put some things together in a size 10? By the way, my favorite designers are usually so and so.' When the woman arrives, it's there for her to choose. After awhile, as your personal shopper gets to know you, she calls you not only when new merchandise arrives but also when things go on

---

[7] Annette Swanberg and Leigh Charlton, *Chic on a Shoestring* (New York: Doubleday, 1984), pp. 165–167.

sale, which is of interest to everyone.'' She continued to stress the point that this service was available to all customers in all price ranges.[8]

Specialty Shops

A specialty shop creates a distinctive lifestyle image (Figure 18-2). It usually carries a limited selection of its specialty and caters to a small clientele. Very often it specializes in only one category of merchandise or in related items such as dresses within certain price, size, and style ranges, lingerie, handbags, hosiery, or men's haberdashery. Owing to this more limited selection, the shopper is not faced with hunting through floors of merchandise in order to find his/her style choice. This type of shop builds its reputation on its merchandise selection and personal services. Very often the sales personnel are well trained and have more information about the merchandise than sales persons in department stores. They may keep a card on customers' preferences listing colors, sizes, and styles, enabling the store to serve the customer more personally when new merchandise

[8] "Is Fashion Working for Women?" A Vogue Symposium, *Vogue*, January 1985, p. 274.

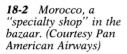

18-2 *Morocco, a "specialty shop" in the bazaar. (Courtesy Pan American Airways)*

arrives and to notify him or her when markdowns will be forthcoming. If the specialty shop carries several categories of merchandise, the salesperson who is well acquainted with all of the merchandise in the store can help the customer put together a totally coordinated outfit.

In men's specialty shops the coat and suit department usually has a wide selection of merchandise from which to choose. It is to a customer's advantage that the shop's alteration personnel work exclusively on tailored garments because the alteration of suits and coats requires special skills in order to result in the proper fit.[9]

Salespersons in specialty shops are usually paid on commission; that is, the more they sell, the more they earn. It is to their benefit to serve the customers well by helping them select satisfactory merchandise, thus encouraging future business with the shop.

Because of the personal services that the specialty shop offers, plus attractive store decoration and atmosphere, the price of the merchandise may reflect the added costs necessary to run such a business. Be sure to inquire about the return and refund policy before closing a sale. Some of these shops do not have a liberal return and refund policy. Some accept returns but give credit toward future purchases rather than refunding money.

The Boutique

The *boutique* is a small shop that features a strong fashion image. The recent success of this type of retailing is the result of the trend toward individuality in dress. These shops feature a look. They carry a few carefully selected garments and accessories. Prices range from a few dollars to $1,000 or more. Boutiques may have their own designer or use a free-lance designer. They sell garments obtained from large manufacturers, but they do not depend upon mass-produced ready-to-wear. Custom-made or custom-designed clothes can be purchased in most boutiques.

The boutique appeals especially to the young and the young in spirit. The background music, the fashion-conscious salespeople, the invitation to browse, refreshments, and styled interiors all contribute to making shopping an exciting adventure. The display equipment is often movable and can easily be arranged to accommodate new ideas and groupings.

Many department stores have boutique departments. These are small areas of floor space with all the features and attractions of independent boutiques. The atmosphere in a boutique department is one of a small shop that caters to individual tastes. Carefully selected items are displayed together, and the shopper can often purchase an entire coordinated outfit in one area (Figure 18-3).

[9] Donald Dolce and Jean-Paul DeVellard, *The Consumers' Guide to Menswear* (New York: Dodd, 1983), p. 147.

18-3 *Japanese department stores offer high-quality products and services of all kinds. Many feature child care facilities for use while Mother shops. (Courtesy Consul General of Japan)*

The Franchise Store

Travel agencies, auto dealerships, real estate companies, and quick-food service, gasoline stations, and ice cream stands have been in the franchise business for a long time, but this type of business is now reaching into fields such as fashion retailing. Yardage shops for the home-sewing customer were among the first to enter franchise fashion retailing. Shops such as "The House of Nine,"

Ralph Lauren's "Polo Shops," Givenchy's "Nouvelle Boutiques," and Yves St. Laurent's "*Rive Gauche*" are franchise shops. The franchiser offers a well-established name, expert business guidance, and brand merchandise. The franchisee invests in the parent company and subsequently pays a percentage of all sales to the franchiser.

Off-Price Stores

A new genus of stores labeled "off-price" has become the fastest growing segment of the retail industry. Not to be confused with the discount houses and factory outlets located on the fringe of garment districts or in low-rent areas which sold seconds, overcuts, and slightly damaged merchandise, the "off-price" stores sell brand-name and designer apparel at prices pegged 20 to 70 percent lower than those demanded by department stores.[10]

Off-price retailers buy apparel at less than wholesale prices, then set the retail selling price below that set by conventional retailers. These stores are in direct competition for the same shopper the department store is after, the middle- and upper-income consumer. It is estimated that 10 percent of all apparel and footwear sales will be sold by off-price stores nationally.[11]

Marshalls, T. J. Maxx, Loehmans, Burlington Coat Factory, B. F. Shoes, and J. Brannan are situated in small shopping malls or near large shopping centers. The merchandise is obtained from a variety of sources. Excess production, close-outs, and canceled orders of clothing are purchased directly from factories, from buying services that specialize in the business, or from jobbers. These are middlemen who take merchandise that manufacturers or department stores cannot sell. If the retailer cannot purchase the garments at discount prices he will still sell the merchandise for less in hopes of making it up by selling larger volume. Obviously, stores selling merchandise at regular prices have been most unhappy over this situation. Some department stores show their displeasure by no longer doing business with vendors who sell to discounters, while others have brought antitrust suits against them.

Discount Stores

Clothing obtained by discount houses comes from a variety of sources and is available at lower prices for many reasons: manufacturers' closeouts, discontinued lines, unsold merchandise, garments manufactured in excess of what is sold, past season merchandise, stock liquidation caused by the need for immediate cash because of financial trouble, and returns of orders refused by the stores because they do not arrive on time. Seconds, irregulars, and samples used by salesmen may be sold at near wholesale prices.

Although women have been rummaging for designer fashions at discount out-

[10] "Prices War: Retail vs. Discounters," *Los Angeles Times*, September 20, 1983, Pt. I, p. 1.
[11] "Off-Price Stores Assault Retailers," *Los Angeles Times*, December 6, 1983, Pt. IV, p. 10.

lets for years, men generally have not. But as clothing prices continue to climb, fashion-conscious men should give these glorified warehouse stores a try.

Men's discount stores operate much the way women's do, with few frills. Some women's stores now carry men's garb also. Independent stores and small chains have done most of the menswear discounting, but some larger retailers are suiting up for the contest.

Discount stores, either chain or independent, operate on a high-volume, rapid-turnover principle. They offer fewer services to the customer than department stores do, and they charge for all services, including delivery. Most discount stores are self-service, although there are sales personnel available for assistance. Low prices are the chief feature of discount houses. However, before making a purchase, the customer should be able to judge quality and know the regular retail price of the merchandise he is interested in to ensure a good buy. Sometimes it is difficult to return unsatisfactory merchandise to discount stores; many of them have a posted policy against returns of any kind. A wide variety of merchandise is available from discount stores, and there are many excellent buys. Parking space is usually plentiful. These stores often cater to the evening and Sunday shopper.

Membership Stores

A membership store, either chain or independent, is a combination of a department store and a discount store. Memberships are sold to and restricted to a particular group of people, who then have the privilege of shopping in the store. Membership stores work on the large-volume, rapid-turnover, reduced-prices policy. They generally offer fewer services than department stores but stand behind their merchandise better than do discount stores.

Used Clothing Market

Resale and thrift shops, flea markets, swap meets, church rummage sales, and garage sales have become a way of life for thrifty, treasure-hunting individuals in pursuit of a bargain or a Sunday outing. The U.S. Department of Agriculture reports that one-fifth of the clothing worn by moderate-income families consists of hand-me-downs, handmade, or secondhand store apparel.

Especially helpful for pregnant women, dieters, and fast-growing children, whose clothing cannot keep pace with changing body dimensions, people are turning to sources that sell top-condition used clothing. These sources are popular with young families and retirees living on limited incomes.

Wearing used clothing has become chic among high school and college students. "The right Hawaiian shirt can instantly convey an air of blissed-out tropic cool; a baggy '50s sport coat, collar up, can transform anybody into Elvis or James Dean for a day."[12] Students give a word of warning however:

---

[12] "Dressing up on the Cheap," *Newsweek on Campus*, November 1984, p. 22.

Associate yourself with another era. But in so doing, always make sure that the era is far enough in the past so your intentions are clear . . . the '50s are cool, the early '70s are not (yet). Anything that makes you look like Lucy or Ricky Ricardo is cool. Anything that makes you look like Betty or Gerald Ford is not.[12]

The traditional thrift shop often handles worn, and/or out-of-date clothing that has been obtained by donations. Some thrift shops are run by organizations such as the Assistance League, Salvation Army, or Heart Association to raise money for charitable causes. At times almost new, high-quality clothing worn by wealthy men and women who update their wardrobes frequently can be obtained at nominal prices.

Another type of shop that has become popular is the so-called "transitional" shop. People bring in clothes they no longer use, and leave them on consignment. When they are sold, the shop and the former owner share in the proceeds. These stores can be located in the "Yellow Pages" under "Used Clothing" or "Thrift Stores."

Mail Order

Mail order now represents big business, selling $40 billion worth of merchandise through 6,000 catalogue companies.[13] This business built on the rural customer in the 1930s now does over half of its business in metropolitan areas.

This lucrative business makes 6 percent profit for the mail-order firm as compared to a 3.5 percent profit made by the conventional retailer. Armchair shoppers willingly forego crowded stores and parking lots, harassed sales people, using valuable time, and inconvenient shopping hours. Filling out mail orders has even been eliminated through the use of toll-free telephone numbers and credit card charges. In some cities cable TV lets shoppers see the items for sale before purchasing.

Mail order has evolved. The 1984 Robinson's Christmas catalogue featured a romantic 700-year-old castle in Scotland, available as a gift at the cost of $5,750,000. Of course this price includes the grand furnishings, priceless tapestries and art, heliopad, tennis courts, gym, and central heating. Subject to prior sale, of course. Offerings now have little resemblance to the kind of merchandise first sold by the Montgomery Ward catalogue over 100 years ago, which was a one-page publication featuring bed ticking, hoop skirts, and ladies' watches for $8.[14]

The "Sears Christmas Wish Book" does not offer luxury vacations nor ultra-expensive furs, but its claim to fame is that it sells more. This giant of the catalogue industry, begun in 1896, is the nation's largest both in dollar volume sales and in the number of catalogues produced. Sears mails over 300 million catalogues a year. Besides the Christmas publication it produces a total of forty yearly catalogues.[15]

---

[13] "Sears Tops in the Catalogue Business," *Los Angeles Times*, November 24, 1983, Pt. IV, p. 21.

[14] "Is the Store Becoming Obsolete?" *Time Magazine*, November 27, 1978, p. 94.

[15] "Sears Tops in the Catalogue Business," op. cit.

When using mail order, never send cash. Instead use credit cards, checks, or money orders. Read the fine print regarding delivery date, returns, refund and sale merchandise policy. Because you cannot inspect the merchandise, or try it on before purchasing, read the descriptions carefully and check the fabric content. Generally if you are a hard-to-fit size, mail order isn't for you. However, some mail order companies do specialize in hard-to-find items such as wide or narrow shoes, 100 percent natural fiber clothes, and clothing for people with special needs. By patronizing catalogue companies who are members of Direct Mail/Marketing Association, a professional organization, you should obtain satisfactory service.[16]

Techniques for Intelligent Shopping

Intelligent shopping should result in receiving value and satisfaction for the money spent. The following techniques are recommended:

1. Plan purchases rather than buy on impulse.
2. Know value and quality.
3. Shop comparatively for major purchases.
4. Know your requirements and do not be influenced by others.
5. Be cautious of sale items.
6. Understand the uses and costs of credit.
7. Return unwanted merchandise immediately.
8. Demand replacement of or satisfaction for defective merchandise.

Plan Purchases Rather Than Buy on Impulse

Planned purchases make it possible for the consumer to bring unity into the wardrobe by having outfits that coordinate. This type of shopping also enables the consumer to budget clothing expenses over a longer period, thus cutting back on the excessive use of credit and the costly carrying charges that sometimes follow.

Impulse buying means the unplanned purchase of an item. If the purchase is an item of apparel that does not coordinate with the existing wardrobe, it represents an unnecessary, and wasted, expense. As a rule, impulse buying should be avoided. However, there are exceptions. A shopper may come across an item that is not on the shopping list but is exceptionally tempting, appears to be suitable, and is likely to be unavailable at a later date. When this occurs, the shopper should take the time to evaluate the item quickly to determine if it will:

---

[16] The Association may be addressed at 6 East 43rd Street, New York, N.Y., 10017.

Be suitable for one's lifestyle.
Work into the existing wardrobe.
Require buying additional items.
Depict the desired image.
Be suitable in price and design, including line, shape, texture, and color.

Stores take advantage of impulse buyers by placing eye-catching displays in prominent areas near store entrances, elevators, escalators, and cash registers. Surveys show that 70 percent of the purchases made in self-service stores are made on impulse. In full-service stores, 35 percent of all purchases are made on impulse.[17]

Know Value and Quality

The informed consumer knows value and quality. This knowledge can be acquired from this text, buying guides, magazine and newspaper articles, and government bulletins that describe how to evaluate fabric and workmanship in garment construction. Merchandise should be carefully inspected before purchases are made. The buyer should be able to compare values on the basis of quality, style, and price in order to get the best buys possible for money spent. An informed shopper also reads and understands labels and guarantees.

Shop Comparatively

Watch the advertisements and visit several stores before purchasing major or expensive items. Price differentials on the same quality merchandise are found in various shops in the same locality. The markup on merchandise varies because different stores have different overhead expenses, sales volume, and merchandise turnover. It is a questionable use of time, energy, and transportation to shop comparatively for minor items.

Know Your Requirements

Shoppers should know what items they actually require and should not let their purchasing decisions be affected by the opinions or attempted persuasions of salespeople or friends. Many people find it difficult to make up their own minds so they succumb to the recommendations of others. When a person asks a salesclerk if a garment looks good, the answer is going to be the obvious one, yet customers continue to ask. If in doubt, it is best to put off the purchase, think it over, and decide later.

The consumer who is aware of clever selling techniques will be less inclined to make unnecessary purchases. Perhaps more selling pressure is exerted at the cosmetic counter than anywhere else. When a woman goes in to buy a lipstick and leaves with several other items, a clever salesperson has been successful.

---

[17] Gordon and Lee, op. cit., p. 385.

Flattery is often used to make sales. Another approach used in the clothing department is to show a customer a garment that is not on display; this often makes the shopper believe that he is getting special attention, which promotes the sale. Still another technique, called the "multiple sale," occurs after a customer has purchased one article of clothing and is then talked into buying a related item, such as shoes, hosiery, jewelry, or perhaps even another garment. The sales method of "trading up" takes place when the customer is sold an item of higher cost than the one originally considered.

Be Cautious of Sale Items

Because an item is on sale, many people think it is a bargain. This is not always true. The fact that an item is on sale may mean that it is not wanted by either the store or the manufacturer. A sale item may be a bargain or not. If the sale merchandise is wearing apparel, decide whether it is a style that is out of fashion or will become obsolete in a short time. Avoid trendy seasonal colors or details such as trims (sequins, beads, metallics) that quickly tend to go out of fashion. For items such as undergarments and sleepwear, sales can benefit the budget.

Some sales are not legitimate. This occurs when merchants mark up the "regular" price on the merchandise to make the sale price look good by comparison. Traditionally many stores offered several legitimate sales a year, usually in the following months: "End of Season Clearance Sales" on clothing in January— after Christmas is over and before inventory begins; the end of April just before the arrival of summer stock; after July 1, before the arrival of winter stock; and in October or November to clear the way for Christmas merchandise. Currently, owing to competition from "off-price" stores, department stores tend to have frequent sales year round. Some stores feature sales of "special purchase" merchandise that is not their regular store stock. This may be of lower quality than that usually carried, and, therefore, should be inspected carefully.

Understand the Uses and Costs of Credit

Credit costs money, and in many instances, consumers who do not use it still pay for this service indirectly. Stores that offer credit run the risk of losses on bad debts, and frequently these losses are passed on to the consumer in the form of higher prices on merchandise. The carrying charges imposed on accounts that extend beyond thirty days should be clearly understood by the buyer. In most states, revolving or budget accounts are charged 1 to $1\frac{1}{2}$ percent per month on the unpaid balance. This amounts to from 12 to 18 percent over a twelve-month period. For example, if you were to buy a $240 coat and make twelve payments of $20 per month, the interest charged on the $240 would amount to $53.20 at 1 percent and $59.30 at $1\frac{1}{2}$ percent. Since September 1, 1969, the federal government has required all stores to inform their customers in writing as to exactly what the stores credit charges are and how they are computed.

Return Unwanted Merchandise Immediately

It is the consumer's responsibility to return unsatisfactory merchandise promptly. This merchandise should be in the best possible condition. Returned goods involve an expense for the store, as it must be either reticketed and returned to the stock or sent back to the manufacturer. When returning unwanted merchandise, be friendly, courteous, and firm. If a salesclerk does not have the authority to make the exchange, ask to see the department or store manager or the department buyer. A friendly smile and polite attitude usually get far more satisfaction than a rude or hostile approach. If you feel you are being treated unfairly, ask for the name of the store representative you are dealing with and his superior. Repeat this process until satisfaction is obtained even if it means writing letters to the company president. If this fails, follow recommendations suggested below.

Demand Satisfaction for Defective Merchandise

Satisfactory adjustments for defective merchandise should be demanded. Reputable stores will accept the return of these goods without question, whereas other stores may be less responsible. Some stores advertise an "all sales final" policy, which should serve as a warning to the shopper to inspect all goods carefully before purchase. If the store does not give proper satisfaction and the customer believes he is being cheated, the best recourse is to discuss the matter with the local Better Business Bureau. If this fails to get the desired results, a local consumer protection agency should be consulted if one is available. Some states have consumer laws that are expressly intended to resolve consumer-merchant conflicts. If all else fails, the consumer may seek redress in a small claims court.

Clothing Selection Process Summary

The garments and accessories you choose for your wardrobe express your value system and lifestyle. A discussion of the selection process may help you to understand how personal clothing selection is. It may also give you some insight into why various garments evoke different emotional responses, both when they are acquired and when they are worn. Finally, it will help explain why a criticism of one's apparel cuts so deeply.

A new garment is usually acquired for a specific *purpose*. This purpose may be a party, a new job, a new school, or a new date, or it may be a replacement for a worn garment.

The *resources* available for the purchase of the new garment will, of course, determine how much money can be spent. For some shoppers, this will be a large sum spent in the most exclusive shop in town. For others, it may mean a few dollars spent at a thrift shop. Still others may choose to have the garment custom made. Some may choose to make the garment themselves, either because they enjoy creative sewing or because it may be the only way they can afford a new garment.

The buyer's *self-concept* determines what kind of garment will be purchased. The *psychological self-concept* affects how the garment we select will be styled: elaborate, understated, bizarre, conservative, fashionable, or nondescript. The *physical self-concept* affects how the garment we select will fit: body-revealing, body-concealing, or a combination of both.

The *elements of design*: that is, the line-form-shape-space, shape, texture, and color of the garment, will project a particular look and mood. The image the garment projects and the feelings it evokes may be perceived differently by the individual who wears the garment and by those who see the garment being worn by the individual.

The *theme* is the central idea of the garment. It will suggest all the accessories to be added to complete the outfit. It will also suggest complementary hairstyles and facial adornment. It will delimit where and when the garment should be worn. The theme may also reflect the age of the wearer. The theme of any garment should be in keeping with the lifestyle of the wearer. When the theme is expressed in each detail of the outfit unity has been achieved.

To summarize, the guidelines for selecting garments are these:

Purpose
Resources
Self-concept
Design
Theme/Unity

The garment is well selected if it:

Serves the purpose for which it is intended (Purpose).
Was priced within available resources (Resources).
Fits both psychologically and physically (Self-concept).
Pleases the individual (Design).
Presents a "total look" (Theme/Unity).

Suggested Activities

1. Determine several store policies in regard to pricing.
   (a.) Shop four stores in the same neighborhood for one identical item. (Identical in style, quality, preferably brand, model number.) The item can be apparel, cosmetics, or grooming equipment, such as a dryer or a curling iron.

(b.) Then shop three department stores at three different shopping centers for that same item. Note the names of the stores, their exact locations, what brand or brands were compared, the manufacturers' names, and what price was charged for that item at each store. Discuss your results with the class.

2. Visit, analyze, and compare several shopping centers. Determine their differences and similarities in regard to what they offer the consumer. Consider the following:

Types of shops that predominate
Degree of "fashion" represented
Services offered
Number and diversity of shops and services
Greatest attraction for shoppers
Greatest disadvantage for shoppers
Cleanliness and attractiveness
Proximity to other centers
Access to public transportation and parking facilities
Other observations of importance to you

3. Do the following shopping comparison and report findings to your class:
   (a.) Read several articles on comparison shopping.
   (b.) Compare similar garments in three different price ranges.

For example:	slacks/dress	$50	$130	$250 and above
	suit	80	150	250 and above
	top coat	80	180	250 and above

   (c.) Write a report on your comparison shopping experience. Include the following information:

Hangtag or label information:
  price
  brand-name/manufacturer
  designer
  fiber content
  care instructions
Store names, addresses, and locations:
  store image
  type of merchandising
  type of store
  type of service
Garment presentation:
  display appeal or impact
  coordination of accessories
Garment construction:
  fashion fabric

supportive fabrics
linings
number of pieces in design
matching of pieces including fabric design
seam widths/seam finishes
handwork quality
finishing details and trims
manufacturing shortcuts
pressing

(d.) Summarize your findings and recommend the garment you believe to be the best buy for the price.

4. Analyze advertising for informative content vs. emotional appeal as suggested in this chapter, under the heading Disadvantages of Advertising.

19 *Care and Maintenance of the Wardrobe*

Knowledge of appropriate care and maintenance of the wardrobe is very important for several reasons. "Wear life" of the contents of the wardrobe can be greatly extended by proper care and maintenance. This extension of wearability helps to stretch the shrinking clothing dollar. Scarcity of raw materials, cutbacks in the production of apparel products composed of petrochemicals, and the precarious energy situation may curtail the production of clothing. This could make extended wearability a necessity. Management of the wardrobe through care and repair also keeps the clothing fresh and ready to wear, which can save time and reduce stress by helping to avoid frantic last-minute dressing hassles.

Daily and Periodic Care

Daily and periodic care helps to extend the "life" of clothing and ensures that it is always ready to be worn when needed. After wearing, inspect garments for rips, loose buttons, hooks, and other breakdowns. Either make the necessary repairs right then or put the garments aside for a more convenient time for mending and pressing.

Spots given attention when they are fresh are far more easily removed than those that have aged and set into the fabric. Commercial spot- and stain-remover preparations give excellent results, but reading and following the directions for their use are essential for obtaining good results. Be sure that the fiber content of the garment and the cleaning agent are compatible.

Daily care may involve brushing, airing, and pressing before storage. This is of particular importance for the care of wools. Garments made of wool need a rest between wearings in order to regain their shape, so give them at least a day off after wearing them.

Good hangers are important for the support of garments. Wire hangers that usually are returned with clothes from the dry cleaners do not provide adequate support for most garments. Wire hangers often cause distortion of the fabric in the shoulder and sleeve cap area. Padded hangers can be purchased, or wire hangers can be padded at home by covering them with tissue paper and fabric scraps or crocheting. Skirts and pants can be clamped to wire hangers with pins or snap-type clothespins.

529

One way to avoid wrinkles forming while garments are stored in the closet is to allow sufficient room so that clothes are not crowded or packed in tightly. They should be permitted to hang straight. Some garments crush less if stuffed with tissue paper. Allowing sufficient hanging space may entail some reorganization, such as finding another place to store garments that are infrequently worn. A double row of rods running halfway through the closet can double the available space for short lengths such as shirts, skirts, folded pants, and jackets, thus leaving the remainder of the rod space for full-length garments.

Closet Arrangement, Care, and Maintenance

"Getting your Closet Done" has become a popular innovation in home remodeling. . . . Many closet reconstruction firms have sprung up throughout the country to fill the needs for wardrobe reorganization. (Note the before-and-after illustrations Figure 19-1.) A relatively small space can be organized to provide adequate hanging and flat storage space. Shoes, which are often relegated to the floor to gather additional scuffs and dust and become separated from their mates can be given shelf storage and easy accessibility. Hanger accommodation is multiplied by utilizing shorter spaces for blouses, shirts, and jackets. Knitted garments such as sweaters are best stored flat to prevent stretching. Handbags, belts, and scarves also deserve their "space." Organization such as this would not only take the hassle out of getting dressed in the morning; it would also serve to keep clothing in ready-to-wear condition.

Check footwear for scuffs and touch it up with polish if needed. Saddle soap all leather shoes occasionally to preserve and soften the leather. Shoe trees help to maintain the shape of shoes that are fully enclosed. Open or sandalback styles can be stuffed with paper to help keep their shape. Metal shoe racks are available, and these can help in holding the toe shapes. Run-down heels need prompt attention to prevent the entire shoe from becoming permanently distorted. Heels in need of repair present an unsightly appearance that detracts from the total image. Leather footwear that has become wet needs special care. Stuff the foot with newspapers and dry slowly. Do not hasten the process by placing wet articles near or on direct source of heat. Leather becomes stiff when dried improperly.

Reliable cleaners are sometimes difficult to locate. The symbol of The International Fabricare Institute displayed in a cleaning establishment is one of the best guides to quality work. Shoe, purse, zipper repair, and other such businesses are also hard to find. Word-of-mouth recommendations of satisfied customers are usually the most helpful references.

19-1 *"Getting Your Closet Done" has become a popular innovation in home remodeling. A relatively small space can be organized to provide adequate hanging and flat storage space. (Courtesy California Closet Company)*

Permanent Care Labeling

A permanently attached care label is required on all textile items of wearing apparel. A ruling by the Federal Trade Commission was first made effective in 1972, revised in 1980, and most recently amended in 1983, effective January 1, 1984. The revision was ordered to restore consumer confidence in garment care labels by providing information known to be reliable to be used on labels. At least one safe method for cleaning must be given even though other methods may also be satisfactory. Until the 1983 ruling, garment care labels were inconsistent, incomplete, and inaccurate. To insure clarity, a glossary of terms to be used on the labels was provided for use by manufacturers, importers, and consumers. This glossary can be found in Appendix G. The care instructions indicate whether the garment should be washed or dry-cleaned and only the process listed on the label has been checked for safe use.

Washing instructions are as follows:[1]

Method must be indicated—by hand or machine. Water temperature must be given if hot water cannot be used safely.

Bleaching guides must be given unless any bleach can be safely used. If chlorine bleach cannot be used the label must state "only nonchlorine bleach when needed."

Drying instructions must indicate machine or some other method. If garment cannot be dried at high temperatures, the temperature settings must be given.

Ironing instructions need not specify the temperature needed unless a hot iron would damage the item. If ironing is not needed on a regular basis the label does not mention ironing.

Warnings must be given if a garment would harm another garment being washed in the same load. For example, a noncolorfast garment must bear a label stating that the garment must be washed separately or with like colors.

Dry-cleaning instructions are as follows:

"Dry-cleaning" means that any dry-cleaning method may be used with any dry-cleaning solvent.

"Professionally dry-clean" means that the dry-cleaning process is modified either by an attendant or through use of a machine that permits modifications or both.

If all solvents cannot be used, the instructions must specify the solvent to be used.

Any modifications must be stated on the label.

---

[1] Federal Trade Commission Manual for Business. "Writing a Care Label," Bureau of Consumer Protection, March 1984.
Federal Trade Commission, "What's New About Care Labels," Bureau of Consumer Protection, April 1984.

Piece Goods Labeling

For piece goods the label can be attached to the bolt; the manufacturer then does not have to provide the retailer with individual labels for the customer as was formerly required. Excluded from the piece goods labeling are remnants up to 10 yards long and trims up to 5 inches wide.

Exempted:

Apparel not used to cover or protect a part of the body, including leather, suede, fur and footwear, gloves, hats, ties and belts, need no care labeling whatsoever.

Totally reversible clothing can carry a temporary label.

Products that can be cleaned by the harshest procedures (i.e., washed, bleached, ironed, or dry-cleaned by any normal method) can bear instructions on a temporary label stating "Wash or dry-clean by any normal method."

If a product such as nylon or wool hosiery would be harmed in appearance or usefulness by a permanently attached care label, a temporary label may be used.

Certain other exceptions do exist, for example, products sold to institutional buyers for commercial use such as rental services, hospitals, or nursing homes.

Dry Cleaning

Whether a garment is washable or dry-cleanable depends upon several factors—the fiber content, fabric construction, type of dye, finish, garment construction, and trim or decoration. A fabric made of cotton fiber may be washable, but the trims or lining used might not withstand washing, thus making the garment dry-cleanable only. This is a factor to consider at the time of purchase.

The choice of using a coin-operated, self-service cleaner or a professional dry cleaner will be guided by the 1984 care-labeling information attached to the garment. Cleaning instructions labeled "dry-clean" can be cleaned by any normal dry-cleaning method. Labels that state "Professional dry-cleaning" should be taken to a professional dry cleaner, not placed into a coin-operated machine.

When the consumer has the choice of using either a coin-operated, self-service cleaner, or a professional dry-cleaner, personal choice will probably depend on budget, the value and condition of the garments, and the past performance experienced with each.

The chief advantage of using the self-service establishments is the low cost per cleaning load. The major disadvantage is the lack of professional help in removing spots and stains. Pressing or touch-up must be done by the individual after cleaning. Many garments that are still serviceable may not be worth the price asked by the professional dry-cleaner. These might include backpacking clothes, sweaters, children's woolen outerwear, and simply designed garments.

When you utilize self-service cleaning, separate the light- and dark-colored garments and the fragile and heavy clothing, and do these in separate loads. Check pockets and brush lint from cuffs and pockets, and remove buttons, belts, and trims unsuited to cleaning. After drying is completed, remove the garments immediately and hang them on hangers.

A professional dry-cleaner should detach noncleanable accessories; remove spots and stains (he can do this even better if you tell him what caused them); and clean, dry, and finish clothing under conditions that are best suited for the garments. Commercial pressing equipment and a skilled presser should restore garments to the best possible condition.

Wet Cleaning—Laundering

Although in most of the world home laundry is still done by hand, economically advanced countries take advantage of automatic laundry appliances for the task of soil removal. Modern washing and drying equipment represents sophisticated engineering and technology and eliminates much drudgery and guesswork (Figure 19-2).

Washing machines are available in many models and price ranges. Some equipment has cycles for prewashing and presoaking as well as special cycles for delicate fabrics. There are also automatic dispensers for discharging the proper amount of detergent, bleach, and softeners at the right time. You can select the proper amount of water for the size of the load, control the water temperature for wash and rinses, and choose the correct speed for agitation and spin dry for each kind of load, depending on the amount of soil and type of fabric.

Dryers can be regulated by selecting the temperature that is best suited for the various fabrics and finishes. Some drying equipment has computer controls that stop the dryer automatically when the clothes reach the right amount of dryness. Automatic-dampening devices are found on some models, as well as signals that warn you to remove the clothes from the dryer before they wrinkle (Figure 19-3).

Coin-Operated Equipment

People who do not own laundry equipment may use coin-operated machines, either in living units or in commercial establishments. Most commercial equipment has fixed cycles, and the selection for agitation and water temperature is limited.

Commercial, multiload dryers utilize one temperature, and it is not recommended that synthetics and knits be used in these dryers. Durable-press garments should be removed from these dryers as soon as they are dry to prevent heat set wrinkling. Persons who use coin-operated equipment should use a disinfectant

19-2 *For some people, doing the family laundry means washing the clothing in a nearby stream, as this Indian family must do. The drudgery of the task is reduced by the camaraderie of the group. (Courtesy Qantas)*

in the machine before washing their clothes or in their wash to prevent the spread of bacteria. (Refer to Disinfectants.)

Laundry Products

Supermarket shelves display a large variety of laundry products that give excellent performance in cleaning clothes. The number of choices available can make selection a confusing experience. Some laundry products, such as soap or detergent, are essential; other aids, including bleaches, fabric softeners, enzyme

535

products, and fabric finishers, aid in getting better results and may be considered necessary for certain laundry problems. Regardless of which products are selected, it is important to read and follow all the label instructions carefully. Use a standard measuring cup to get the exact amount since guesswork may result in serious, irreparable damage to fabrics. Some products cannot be used in combination with other products because chemical reactions may result in formation of new compounds that may damage the fabrics or give off harmful fumes, which can endanger human health.

Soaps and Detergents

In a washing machine, clothes are cleaned by agitating soiled fabrics so that the dirt is broken up into small particles. The soap or detergent then surrounds the dirt particles with a film that holds the dirt in suspension in the wash water so that it does not settle back into the clothing.

19-3 Bombay, India. Public washing ghats *are rented out for doing the family wash.*

Soaps are natural cleaning agents composed of fats, oils, and alkali along with compounds used to increase sudsing, soften hard water, and generally improve cleaning. Soaps are rarely used in home laundry today. The chief reason for the decline in popularity of soap as a cleansing agent is its reaction to hard water. When the components of soap combine with the lime and magnesium salts found in hard water, a curd or scum is formed. This curd is almost insoluble and it clings to the fibers and fabrics. The resultant laundry is boardlike—stiff, and grayed (tattletale gray). Breaking down and removing this soap scum are difficult and further complicate home laundering.

A detergent is a synthetic, or man-made, cleansing agent. There are many varieties of detergent on the market today. Some are designed for specific purposes such as rug shampooing, dishwashing, or laundering, whereas others are made for general household tasks.

Basically, there are two types of detergents. Heavy-duty, also called all-purpose or "built," contains an alkali for increased cleaning power. The heavy-duty detergent is for use with sturdy fabrics with medium to heavy soil. The second type of detergent is called mild, light-duty, or "unbuilt"; it does not contain alkali. The mild detergents are designed for use with more delicate fabrics such as silks and wools, which are damaged by alkalis. Interestingly, the packaging of these detergents often helps identify their strength. Heavy-duty detergents are usually wrapped in bright, high-chroma colors, whereas pastels are used for the mild ones.

Either detergent type may be high- or low-sudsing. This means that the detergent may be formulated to give a large volume of suds or a small amount. Unfortunately, many people equate the cleansing ability of a detergent with its sudsing level. This is a completely misunderstood concept. *Suds do not clean;* it is the formula of the detergent that establishes the cleansing power. Front-loading washers require low-sudsing detergents.

One difficulty that is often encountered with the use of detergent in home laundering is a yellowing or graying of fabrics. This may happen when an insufficient amount of detergent is used for the amount of soil, water, or wash load. Hard water and inadequate rinsing of the clothes may also result in this discoloration. However, there are products on the market designed especially to recondition such damaged clothes.

The personal decision of whether to use soap or detergent as your cleansing agent should be based directly on the quality of the water available to you. If the water supply is over three grains of hardness, the use of a detergent will be more satisfactory than the use of soap. Water over four-to-ten grains of hardness requires the use of larger amounts of detergent. (A discussion of water conditions follows later in this chapter.)

Ingredients of soaps and detergents. Each product has its own formula but these basic ingredients may be found in the detergent:

Builder—to soften water and disperse soil.
Surfactant—to lift dirt from clothes.

Processing aid—to improve manufacture and powder properties, e.g., pourability.

Corrosion inhibitor—to protect interior washer parts from corrosion.

Antiredisposition agent—to prevent dirt from going back into fabric.

Fabric whiteners—to make fabrics appear whiter or brighter.

Suds control agent—to raise or lower level of foam generated by a detergent formulation.

Perfume—to cover chemical odor of base product and perhaps leave a pleasant residual odor on laundry.

Oxygen bleach—a mild bleach to help remove stains that are susceptible to oxidation, e.g., fruit stains.

Enzyme—to help remove proteinaceous stains, e.g., egg, chocolate, etc.[2]

Disinfectants

Bacteria can survive on garments whether they are washed in hot water or cold, although more survive in cold water. People who use coin-operated laundry equipment can pick up bacteria on their laundry from the machine. Illness of one family member can be transferred to others by bacteria on clothing whether the laundry is done at home or elsewhere. The problem of eliminating bacteria is further compounded because more people are using warm or cold water for their entire family wash rather than hot. The most effective way to eliminate bacteria in cold water washing is to use a disinfectant. Liquid chlorine bleach added to the wash cycle will reduce bacteria to a safe level. Use 4 oz (½c) for a front-loading machine; use 8 oz (1 cup) for a top-loading machine.[3] (Note: Chlorine bleach cannot be used on spandex, silk, wool, colors not fast to bleaching, or on some wash-and-wear finishes.)

Bacteria can remain in the washer and be transferred from load to load. Coin-operated machine users should sanitize the washer by using the disinfectant only (no clothes) and hot water on a 15-minute cycle,[4] before doing laundry.

Bleaches

Bleaching agents are used to remove color from stains and to make certain compounds of the natural soils soluble.[5]

Liquid Chlorine Bleach. Chlorine bleaches are the most effective. However, they cannot be used on all fabrics, especially on those with a wash-and-wear chlorine retentive finish. Refer to the garment care label. Chlorine bleaches cannot be used on silk, wool, mohair, spandex, colors not fast to bleach, and certain flame

---

[2] *Learn Your Laundry Lessons the Easy Way*, U.S. Borax and Chemical Corporation, 1975, p. 9.

[3] U.S. Department of Agriculture, "Sanitation in Home Laundering," Home and Garden Bulletin No. 97, Washington, D.C., U.S. Government Printing Office (1967), p. 5.

[4] "Detergents in Depth, '78," Third Biennial Symposium, Soap and Detergent Association, 1978, p. 76.

[5] "Fabrics, Fashions and Facilities," report of National Home Laundry Conference, Los Angeles, November 1965—Chicago: American Home Laundry Manufacturers' Association—p. 67.

retardant finishes. Liquid chlorine bleach must always be diluted, 1 part bleach to 4 parts water, before being added to the wash water. Bleach is added after the suds have had time to act, about five minutes. The optical brighteners used in detergents must be allowed to act for a few minutes as the bleach interferes with their performance. Once the optical brighteners have become attached to the fabrics, they will not be affected by the bleach. Avoid using chlorine bleach without a detergent. The detergent acts as a buffer to protect fabrics. In hard water, chlorine bleaches intensify the discoloration of fabrics.[6,7]

If fabrics of chlorine-retentive finish are yellowed by chlorine bleaches, this can be removed by soaking the fabric in a solution of two tablespoons of sodium sulfite or hyposulfite (obtainable at a photographic supply shop) and $\frac{1}{2}$ cup (4 oz.) of white vinegar per gallon of hot water.

Oxygen Bleaches. Oxygen bleaches are safe for all washable fabrics including cotton, silk, wool, wash-and-wear, rayon, spandex, and resin-treated and colored fabrics. They do not perform as effectively for soil and stain removal as the chlorine bleaches. They will not restore whiteness to the same degree as chlorine bleach, but they help to maintain whiteness when used consistently. Oxygen bleaches, found in granular form, are two types: (1) perborate oxygen—most effective in very hot water and (2) potassium monopersulfate—used with lower temperatures with good results. The latter type is more effective than the perborate type.

Fabric Softeners

Fabric softeners are used to make clothes fluffy, minimize wrinkling, and eliminate the static electricity that causes clothes to cling. These products are used either in the wash water, the rinse water, or as a dryer product.

Liquid fabric softeners should be diluted with water to avoid staining when added directly to laundry load. Fabric softeners to be used in dryers are specially treated papers or sponges. The heat of the dryer releases the softening ingredients. When using the dryer-type fabric softener, the low heat setting should be used, because high heat may cause spotting of some synthetic fabrics garments such as solid color polyester shirts and pants. Should spotting occur, it can usually be removed by rewashing. The dryer-type fabric softener can be used in the last rinse water if the clothes dryer is not used.

Excessive use of liquid softeners coats the fibers of cloth, which results in a lack of absorbency. This creates problems for textile products that are used to absorb moisture such as towels, diapers, and active sports clothes. It should be noted that fabric softeners have been known to cause skin irritations for some people.

Antistatic products are available that can be sprayed directly on clothing to eliminate static electricity instantly. Static electricity is what causes the clinging

[6] "Lighten Your Laundry Load," HE-65, Iowa State University Cooperative Extension Service, Ames, Iowa, March 1965, p. 9.

[7] *The Maytag Encyclopedia of Home Laundry*, 2nd ed. (New York: Popular Library, 1969), p. 78.

of clothing to the body. It is a particular problem with certain synthetic fabrics. The lack of humidity in dry weather increases the problem. Spraying clothing lightly with water also eliminates the problem, but may result in a rather "wet look."

Starches and Fabric Finishes

Starch products that come in spray cans are the easiest to use but the most expensive of the starch products. They can be used on either damp or dry articles, and clothes can be sprayed as they are pressed, or the entire garment can be sprayed, rolled in a towel for a few minutes, and then pressed.

Fabric finishes also come in aerosol containers. These impart less stiffness than starch, and their chief advantage is that they can be used at lower pressing temperatures, which are required for many modern fabrics.

Laundry Procedures

Clothes that are to be laundered need some attention prior to being put in the machine if satisfactory results are to be achieved. Remove all items from the pockets and take off pins, detachable ornaments, and unwashable belts and buttons. Zip up zippers and turn dark clothing inside out to prevent lint from collecting on the outside. Inspect for and complete needed repairs so that little rips will not become a major mending task after laundering.

Sorting

Laundering would be simplified if all clothes could be put into the machine together, but various fabrics and colors do not mix. Sorting is done in washing loads to keep similar fabrics together. Improper sorting causes lint to collect, color transfer, shrinkage, and graying. Often dark-colored fabrics such as terry cloth look faded when actually the color has dimmed because of lint buildup. Light-colored lint from one garment attaches to the surface of dark-colored garments causing a faded look. Sort as follows:

Dark colors—Separate dark-colored clothing to keep them free of lint and to prevent any color transfer to light-colored garments.
White and light-colored synthetics—Color pickup from other garments is avoided if these garments are handled separately.
Fabrics to be bleached—White and light-colored synthetics and cottons to be bleached during washing are put together.
Colored clothes—Brilliant colors should be washed separately to avoid color transference. These may require cold or warm water.
Terry and velvet cut towels—If these are dark, intense colors, they will be dulled by lint from other colors. They should be washed separately.
Knits and delicate garments—These require gentle handling.
Durable-press—Durable-press can be washed in the regular manner if an au-

tomatic dryer is to be used. However, if these garments are to be line dried, wrinkles caused by wear and washing may not be removed. In the latter case, the garments must be washed in warm water and given a cool rinse.

Pretreatment of Spots and Stains

Spots, stains, and excessively soiled garments may need treatment before washing. Wash-and-wear, durable-press, and synthetics do not give up oil-borne stains readily. The problem is compounded for cold-water laundry procedures. Those sections of the garment that are most readily soiled, such as the collar and cuff areas, should be treated with a concentrated liquid detergent and allowed to stand for fifteen minutes to an hour before washing. Specially formulated pretreatment products are also available.

Heavily soiled garments require presoaking. This can be done in the washing machine on a presoak cycle, if there is one, or on the rinse cycle. If the latter is used, turn the dial to rinse, let the machine fill, and turn it off. Detergent or an enzyme-acting laundry aid should be added to warm water; hot water may set stains. Allow the clothes to soak for fifteen to twenty minutes, or follow the directions on the package.

Some stains require special preparation for their removal. Commercial products are available that remove stains safely and effectively. It is necessary to read and follow label instructions, to know the fiber content of the garments, and to know the nature of the soil in order to satisfactorily treat the stain. Always test the product on a hidden area of the garment to determine whether the fabric will be damaged by the product.

Oil spots can sometimes be removed by applying dry cornstarch directly to the spot. This absorbs the oil and can be brushed out easily without leaving a ring. Water spots on silks, rayons, and acetates may come out by rubbing or slightly scratching the area with your fingernail.

A stain removal guide can be found in Appendix F.

Washing Water

Hard water creates problems in the laundry, and the minerals present in the water will prevent the soap or detergent from cleaning effectively. Soap used in hard water causes a curd to form that adheres to the fabric, giving it a yellowish or gray appearance. When detergents are used, an increased amount of detergent should overcome the problem of water hardness unless the water is excessively hard.

Water hardness of zero-to-three grains is considered soft, and soap may be used satisfactorily. Between three to nineteen grains of hardness requires an increased amount of detergent; over nineteen grains is so hard that increased detergent alone will not give satisfactory cleaning performance, and the use of a packaged water conditioner will be necessary.[8] Consult your city water department to learn the degree of water hardness in your community.

[8] Ibid., pp. 76–77.

Water Temperature

The fiber, construction of the garment, fabric dyes, finishes, and the amount of soil will influence the degree of water temperature needed to clean clothes.

Hot water—140°F (60°C) used for white cottons, white linens, and heavily soiled clothing.

Warm water—100–110°F (37.78°–43.33°C) used for colored cottons, delicates, and spandex. Wash-and-wear, durable-press, and synthetics and blends that will be dryer-dried can use this temperature.

Cold water—Wash-and-wear, durable-press, synthetics, and blends if no dryer is available. Washable woolens and knits used with gentle action. Bright colors or sensitive colors that have a tendency to fade.

Cold water washing has become the practice in many homes as a means of lowering the increasing utility bills and as an energy conservation measure. In fact, 95 percent of the energy used in laundry is used in heating the water and 5 percent is used to run the machines. Certain fiber constructions and finishes have always been cleaned more efficiently in warm or cold water rather than in hot water.

Using cooler water temperatures sometimes results in undissolved detergent residue on the fabrics, particularly in hard water. This occurs when the detergent is poured on top of the clothing or the dispenser tray for detergent on top of the machine. These techniques can be used to avoid this problem:[9]

1. Predissolve the powdered detergent in hot water first.
2. Add dry detergent to the empty washer, fill with water, and then add the laundry load.
3. Use unbuilt liquid detergent.

Decreasing the water temperature also decreases the soil removal, particularly in permanent press. To compensate for using colder water, either use a smaller wash load or use more detergent or wash for a longer period. Pretreating oily soils with a liquid detergent will help to remove these soils.

Loading and Cycle Selection

Overloading the washer causes wrinkles to form and does not result in effective cleaning. Use the correct cycle for the load.[10]

Rinse

Wash-and-wear, synthetics, and durable-press require a cool rinse to prevent wrinkles from forming before they are spun. If these clothes are to be tumble-dried, a cool rinse is not important because the heat of the dryer will remove the wrinkles. A warm rinse is preferred for most other fabrics, as a better job of

9 "'Detergents in Depth," op. cit., p. 44.
10 *How to Read a Hangtag* (Newton, Iowa: Maytag Company), p. 14.

soil removal occurs. Cottons, linens, and sheets treated with durable-press finishes can take a warm rinse. A thorough rinsing is necessary to remove loosened soil and detergent residue that can build up in clothes and cause grayness.

Drying

Overloading the dryer may cause wrinkles to form. Fabrics made of natural fibers should be removed when a little moisture remains to prevent a harsh feeling and a wrinkled appearance. Garments should be removed from the dryer as soon as the cycle is finished and hung or folded to avoid wrinkling.

Dryer settings depend upon the fiber and fabric finish. A low setting should be used for man-made fibers and a medium setting for durable-press, wash-and-wear, and cottons. If a dryer has a wash-and-wear setting, the temperature will be raised sufficiently to release the wrinkles, followed by a cooling period.

Energy conservation can be achieved by hanging the clothes to dry as our grandmothers did. If the clothes are hung in fresh air, they usually have a marvelous fresh aroma when dry. Air-dried clothes are stiffer than machine-dried laundry. This is because of the lack of softening action caused by the tumbling motion of dryer (Figure 19-4).

Ironing and Pressing

Modern textile technology has progressed a long way toward eliminating the need for ironing or pressing. Personal standards will influence the amount of smoothness expected of the clothes. Many items need some "touching up" with the iron.

Never press a garment that has a stain. This may heat set the stain, making it impossible to remove it. The garment should be cleaned before ironing or pressing.

Equipment Needed:

Ironing board—A well-padded, balanced board is necessary to obtain a good finish on fabrics. Insufficient padding results in an unsightly shine. A tight-fitting lint-free cover is also essential.

19-4 Energy conservation may lead to more open-air clothes drying. Here cotton kimonos are hung out to dry on bamboo poles. The photo was taken at a Japanese inn where kimonos are furnished to all guests. (Courtesy Japan National Tourist Organization)

Sleeve board or sleeve roll—These are long, narrow items that are used to press sleeves and small shaped areas so that a crease line is eliminated. A substitute can be made by rolling up a magazine, tying the ends with a string, and covering the roll with a small Turkish towel.

Iron—A steam iron is more versatile and easier to use than a dry iron. Some are equipped with a spray; some with reversible cords for left-handed people. Sole plates with a nonstick finish are a convenience. Some people prefer the weight of the standard dry iron; the choice is a personal one.

Steamers—These come in various designs for home use. They are small and lightweight. Some manufacturers guarantee "No Shine," "No Scorching," "No Press Cloth"; some simply claim that no other pressing equipment is needed.

Pressing mitt—This aids in pressing difficult areas such as sleeves and shoulders—rounded and shaped areas. It is also handy for small areas that need a "touchup."

Press cloths—These aid in preventing a shine when "touching up" is needed on the outside of the garment. They can be made of cotton drill or wool.

Strips of heavy wrapping paper—Paper placed in under the seam will prevent a seam impression from showing on the outside of heavy fabrics, particularly wool. Hems that are stitched with a tailor's hem stitch slightly below the edge of the hem can accommodate the paper strip, thus preventing the unsightly imprint from forming on the outside of the garment.

Ironing Temperature

The ironing temperature should be selected for the fiber of the fabric. Cotton and linen require a high temperature on dampened clothes unless a wrinkle-resistant finish has been used. Silks and wools need medium temperatures. Wool needs steam or a dampened press cloth. Blends and synthetics require low temperatures.

Techniques

Ironing is a sliding motion following the grain of the fabric on flat surfaces. Items such as cotton garments, tablecloths, and men's shirts are ironed. Wools and contoured garments are always pressed. *Pressing* is a lifting up and pressing down motion, not a back and forth motion. Correct pressing technique eliminates shine.

Special Fabrics Needing Special Care

Acrylics—Lay knits out flat to dry. Some woven acrylics and acrylic blends do not respond well to moisture while ironing. These garments tend to "grow" or stretch or become elongated when moisture and heat are applied. . . . Bulky knits will also stretch during wear. Once stretched, it is usually impossible to restore the original shape."[11]

[11]International Fabricare Institute, *Bulletin FF283*, Silver Spring, Md., 1980.

Crepes—Some crepes stretch or bubble with moisture. Try a hidden seam allowance to determine whether moisture can be used.

Dark-colored clothes—Press on the wrong side to avoid shine.

Flame-retardant finishes—Follow the manufacturer's directions carefully.

Heat-sensitive fibers—These will glaze and melt when subjected to high ironing temperatures. Use low temperatures and a soft pressing pad to permit seams and edges to sink into the pad, which will prevent glazing (flattening of the surface). Heat-sensitive fibers used in clothing are:

Acetate
Nylon
Polyester
Acrylic
Modacrylic (requires extremely low temperatures)

Knits—Avoid overdrying knits made of synthetic yarns. They will shrink, distort, become harsh, and collect static electricity. Use lowest heatsetting and dry to damp dry level.

Leather—Do not attempt to clean or steam leather or suede garments at home; take the leather garment to a professional leather cleaner (not the local dry-cleaner). Leather cleaning is a more expensive process than fabric dry-cleaning. Suede garments can be brushed with a soft brush or another piece of suede (do not brush suede when it is damp or wet). Smooth leathers can be wiped with a damp cloth to remove dust. Wearing a scarf at the neckline will protect leather from body oils and skin preparations. To store garments, place on a wooden or padded hanger, store in a cool ventilated place. Do not store in plastic bag.[12]

Wool—Use a steam iron or a dampened press cloth and press on the wrong side of fabric. Avoid using too much hand pressure on the iron as the steam, hem, and facing imprints will show through to the outside. Should overpressing occur, causing a shine to form or a seam to show through, hold the steam iron (or dampened press cloth with the nonsteam iron) over the area and allow a little moisture to form, then press out the mark on the underside, under the seam or facing. Brush outside area lightly to raise the nap.

Silks—Silks are damaged by deodorants and perspiration. Discoloration and deterioration of the fibers can cause permanent damage. Chloride salts in perspiration cause most of the damage. Immediate dry-cleaning is necessary in these cases in order to save the garment. Alcohol stains from perfume or beverages will often result in permanent color loss. The International Fabricare Institute warns that silk should never be rubbed while wet with water as the surface yarns tend to break. This will change the light reflection on the fabric and results in a color loss.[13]

—Label instructions most often recommend dry-cleaning. Silk cannot be made colorfast without damaging the fiber, therefore colors will run. Bright colors

---

[12] California Fabricare Institute, "Focus on Fibers, Fabric and Fashion," Cupertino, Calif., Vol. 6, #4, Winter 1983, p. 1.

[13] International Fabricare Institute, "Professional Consumer Newsletter," Silver Spring, Md., No. 4, 1984.

and prints should be dry-cleaned. Chiffon, satin, and crepe should be dry-cleaned only. Silks that can be washed are light, solid colors (not iridescent) and broadcloth, crepe de Chine, pongee, some Honans, and many blends. Use lukewarm water and a mild soap (castile or a natural shampoo). Rinse, do not wring but wrap in a towel to blot out the moisture. Hang away from the sunlight, on a towel over the shower rod, until slightly dry. Press on wrong side with a dry iron. Iron temperature should not exceed the synthetic setting.[14] It is wise to test the shrinkability of silk before washing by snipping a piece of fabric from a hidden seam. Then draw exact dimensions on paper, wash, press, and place on drawn outline to check for shrinkage.

Address List

The International Fabricare Institute
12251 Tech Road
Silver Spring, Md. 20904

Federal Trade Commission
6th and Pennsylvania Ave., N.W.
Washington, D.C. 20580

The Maytag Company
Consumer Education Department
Newton, Iowa 50208

Suggested Activities

1. Check the labels of garments in your wardrobe. Do you find any garments that you feel are mislabeled? Do you find any instructions that make the garment a noncleanable? Discuss your findings with your class.
2. Read the labels on the laundry products used in your home. Check both ingredients and instructions. Are the products correctly suited to the laundry procedures recommended?
3. Using the Glossary of Standard Terms in Appendix G, write care labels for a garment you have recently made or purchased.
4. Bring to class garments that did not dry-clean or launder satisfactorily. Try to determine what the problems were and what caused them. As a consumer, what is your recourse for such clothing failures?

---

[14] "'Sew with Silk," *Vogue Pattern Magazine*, January–February, 1979, p. 22.

20 *The Future of Clothing*

Since the beginning of civilization people have attempted to predict the future. They have sought to foretell destiny from the intricate patterns of the star-filled heavens, from the entrails of animals, from the residue of tea leaves, from the turn of the tarot cards, and from thousands of other signs and omens.

Of course, it is unknown exactly what forces will shape the future. We can look back in time and evaluate what has come about. We can survey the present to find out what is now happening. We can make predictions about the future. The study of historic costume has revealed much about the trends and factors that shaped times past. The apparel worn today makes a strong statement about our total society as well as our individual lifestyles.

Guesses about the future of clothing can perhaps help us to anticipate some of the sociological, psychological, and technological changes that are in store for us.

Historical Patterns of Dress

Johnston astutely observed a historically repeating pattern of dress in times of transition. She detected three forces that motivate people in their manner of dress. Some cling to tradition, hanging on to the old ways of dressing (Figure 20-1). Others hunt desperately for alternatives; these are the persons who grab at the bizarre and escape into fantasy (Figure 20-2). The third force, the future of dress, pushes through spontaneously. A large number of people become very confused trying to integrate and translate all the current conflicting forces of society into a personal style of dress. (An example of this kind of ambiguous clothing statement might be found in the combining of "thrift shop treasurers" with new-tech neon-bright layered socks and plastic shoes worn by high school and college students in the mid-1980s.) Johnston believed that confusion between clinging, escape, and change always leads to extravagant and exciting periods of dress.

She briefly summarized the history of dress by noting that one of the earliest, most important changes in dress took place during the shift from hunting to farming. Along with agriculture came the knowledge of how to weave cloth of wool and linen. Many were reluctant to give up the animal skins of their former hunting period and so they went to great trouble to produce a fake fleece on their

547

20-1 *Many people throughout the world cling to traditional ways of dressing. Some examples of traditional dress are shown (Upper Left) by women at the marketplace in Solola, Guatemala (Courtesy Guatemala Tourist Commission); (Lower Left) the fishermen and women of Hakkito, Japan (Courtesy W. Stanley Larsen); (Upper Right) Filipino girls in their national costume (Courtesy Qantas); and (Lower Right) Egyptian children on their way to the Cairo Zoo. (Courtesy Qantas)*

20-2 *Some people hunt for dressing alternatives as they face the uncertainty of the future. Some grab at the bizarre in dress and escape into fantasy. (Designed by Cynthia Thompson. Modeled by Elizabeth Keegan. Courtesy David Estep)*

newly invented looms. They took loosely woven cloth and pulled tufts of real sheep or goat wool through it to create a shaggy cloth garment called a *kaunake*. It had the look, the feel, and the smell of the real skin. This garment, designed to simulate the garments worn in the hunting period, helped people endure the Neolithic transition (see Figure 3-3).[1]

Challenges of Today

Like our early ancestors, we, too, are resisting change. Although plastics are meant to be poured, molded, or bonded, we seem emotionally unready to leave weaving behind, so we go to the excruciating trouble of spinning plastic threads and weaving simulations of fur, cotton, linen, silk, and wool, much the same as the Neolithic farmwoman was weaving 10,000 years ago. We are not yet ready to accept a molded plastic tunic. We can only accept the new in the guise of the familiar (Figure 20-3).

In this last part of the twentieth century, things are happening that may force us to accept new clothing forms at an accelerated pace. If and when this happens, mankind will be on the threshold of a new and different period of civilization, one that is being hailed as the postindustrial or informational age. If we make this transition, we will be the first of twenty-one major civilizations that have

[1] Moira Johnston, "What Will Happen to the Grey Flannel Suit?" *Journal of Home Economics*, November 1972, p. 8.

graced the history of mankind, to jump the void from one age to another.[2] The forces that are mandating change are technological advancement, particularly automation and computerization; accelerated social change; worldwide shortages of food, petrochemicals, and other natural resources; inflation; population growth (estimated to be 6.4 billion by the year 2000, and 11 billion by 2050);[3] extremes of incredible affluence and abject poverty; and continuing international, political, and geographical strife. Mass media and mass transportation have broken down national isolation and are forcing the establishment of a global village. Population growth is creating a lack of environmental space as well as shortages of all kinds. New ways and new methods must be used if we are to survive.

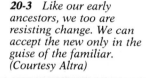

20-3 Like our early ancestors, we too are resisting change. We can accept the new only in the guise of the familiar. (Courtesy Altra)

Since clothing changes have always been related to civilization changes in the past, it seems safe to assume that they will be related to civilization changes in the future.

New Clothing Methods Available Now

If we were psychologically ready to change our form of dress, the methods to do so are already available to us. There are currently five ways to make a garment without stitching it. The first is *fusing*. This method has been adopted for the construction of interfacings and underlinings of jackets, chest pieces for suits, and the entire front of suits.

The second alternative is *molding*. A French company by the name of Giffo has already marketed a process called "Jetset," whereby a raincoat has been molded together, including buttons, pockets, and all other construction details, without benefit of seams. Because the molding process involves a considerable expense at this time, the range of sizes was limited to two European sizes, 38/40 and 42/44, and only three colors are available. Decorative ridges around the hem of the coat serve as hemline adjusters. To shorten the coat, the owner simply needs to cut between the ridges with common scissors. Paco Rabanne first designed the coat in 1968, and it sold for $15 retail under the "Ariel" rainwear label. Because of cost factors, the mold method is limited in style, size ranges, fabrications, and colors. This limitation has made it unacceptable for mass production, which demands more volume.

Flocking and *spraying* are two other forms of clothes production now being studied. These methods involve charging particles electrostatically so that they are attracted to, and coat, a mold. After the particles set, and the mold is collapsed and the resulting form is the finished garment.

The fifth method of joining fabric is called *alternative seaming techniques*, by which a seam is made by point-to-point fusing rather than by solid welding or stitching. These seaming techniques can be accomplished by ultrasonics, dielectrics, radio-frequency energy, or just plain heat.

[2] Dan Moore, "A New Direction, a New Dimension," California State Department of Education, Consumer and Homemaking Symposium, Hilton Hotel, Los Angeles, Calif., February 28, 1984. Moore is executive vice-president, Industry Education Council of California.

[3] "Worldwide Limit of Two Children per Family Proposed by U.S.," *Los Angeles Times*, August 21, 1974, Pt. 1, p. 1.

Each of these methods is limited in the variety of styles, silhouettes, colors, and sizes it can produce. Therefore, at this point of development, it could not be put into mass production unless society were willing to sacrifice individuality in clothing for what would best be termed a "uniform."

After all these years, Isaac Merrit Singer's 1850 invention, the sewing machine, has been radically re-engineered. His invention was truly ahead of its time. Technologically it was advanced enough to stitch the first astronaut's lunar suit, but since then, new developments have produced sewing machines with calculators, motors for computers, and a 2,525-pound device for stitching heavy conveyor belts. In addition, there now is a machine for binding books, a machine that knits, a machine that eliminates sparks from static electricity so that bags of gunpowder may be sewn up safely, and a button sewing machine that can make a lockstitch without employing a bobbin.

Industrial sewing machines can sew one hundred stitches per second. Twelve stitches per inch is average, which means that these new machines can sew at least eight inches per second. The problem now is that the machines are capable of sewing faster than the operators can control the fabric going through the machines.[4]

Automation and the Clothing Industry

Until very recently the $40 billion apparel business was one of the least automated and most labor-intensive in the United States with the majority of the nation's 15,000 mostly family-owned clothing firms relying on outdated equipment. There have been some big changes in the basic tools which will have great impact on the future production of clothing.[5]

Laser Beams

Garments are individually cut by laser beams faster and more accurately than by any other method. The laser, a pure form of light that is as bright as the center of the sun, burns a line through the fabric that is sharper than any cut of a knife. The laser, on instruction from computer tape, cuts one garment at a time with the same accuracy that could only be achieved before in custom clothing. It cuts costs in inventories because it is now just as economical to cut one garment at a time as it previously was to cut thousands. There is no knife to get dull. With computers there is no loss from human error.

Heat Transfer Dye

Two things that have always raised the cost of garments made from printed fabrics were the necessity to print great quantities of one pattern in order to have it available if needed and the potential loss of fabric caused by inaccuracies and shrinkage in the postprinting treatment of material. With the recently developed method of printing fabric, mistakes are made on paper, not on the fabric. There

---

[4] Marylou Luther, "Styles Thread Maze of New Technology," *Los Angeles Times*, March 7, 1971, Section E, p. 1

[5] Jennifer Seder, "Apparel Industry and the Laser Age," *Los Angeles Times*, Fashion 79, August 10, 1979, p. 4.

is no shrinkage since the dye is applied to the fabric in a dry method. There is no commitment of fabric to print beyond what is needed. The print can be stored away on paper, eliminating the need to store the more expensive fabric itself. Because the print is actually done on a fine-grade paper, there is a greater variety and clarity from printing techniques than has been achieved by other methods. Currently, it is only synthetic fibers that can accept the heat-transferred dyes from paper. Wider application from this method is anticipated when it is perfected for use on linen, silk, wool, and cotton.

Computer-Programmed Machines

An electro-optical device has been developed that is so color-sensitive that it can distinguish between the color of a leaf growing on a plant and a leaf used for camouflage. Applied to the fashion industry by the American textile firm, Sci-Tex, the machine (known as Response) is capable of breaking down the pattern into bits of information to be fed into a knitting machine by a computer. In minutes, the knitting machine runs off the printed fabric. Once the knitting machine is turning out a pattern, a designer can inject into the computer, by way of an electrosensitive pencil used on a television screen, a change in colors, and enlargement, or scaling down, of the pattern. It can even switch to a reverse of a mirror image of the pattern already in the machine, all by pushing buttons.

A major technological advance is a computerized grading and marking system, which singlehandedly breaks one of the clothing industry's most severe bottlenecks—grading and marking of patterns. In the past it took days, sometimes weeks, for skilled workers to take one design in a sample size and, by hand, grade it (or reinterpret it) for a full-size range and then draw up markers (patterns) for each size. With the use of the grader and marker, the entire process takes about one hour. The system also indicates where each separate piece of a design should be placed on a marker in order to get the most economical use out of the fabric. It is estimated that it reduces fabric waste by as much as 5 percent a year.

In addition to saving fabric costs, this equipment also eliminates manual labor costs. It is generally believed that Camsco, Inc., of Dallas developed the first computerized grader and marker in 1971. The firm was started not by apparel people, but by a group of former engineers and technicians from the aerospace industry who figured out that the same advanced electrical systems used to power missiles and chart flight patterns could also chart apparel patterns. Hughes Aircraft (Industrial Products Division) also developed a grader and marker, and now the company has an Apparel Systems Department.

What's new for the future? Presently the graders and markers have the ability to alter patterns within the systems so that mid-season changes can be incorporated easily without having to go through a redesigning process. Machines that watchdog production and loading are being developed. Several apparel companies, such as Levi Strauss, have their own research and development centers, which have developed such things as semi-automated back pocket hemmers and automated sewing equipment for the designing of back pocket labels.[6]

[6] Ibid., p. 4.

Photometric Measuring Devices

Photometric measuring devices can determine the dimensions of the body. This information can then be fed into a computer that can cut the desired garment to these specifications.[7]

Robotics

The use of robotics is on the rise in all industrialized countries as automation makes rapid advances in manufacturing systems. Studies reveal that in 1970 there were 200 robots in the United States. In 1990 General Motors alone expects to have 14,000 robots installed. The textile industry has been slow to develop the use of robotics because of labor problems and costs. It is anticipated that robots will be used increasingly in the textile industry because of its labor-intensive nature. How soon robots are used will depend on the cooperation of textile machine manufacturers, robot manufacturers, plant-design engineers, and the textile industry and unions.[8]

Resistance to Automation

As automation comes to the industry, it is the giants such as The Lee Company, Catalina, Jantzen, and Alex Coleman that have the capital to invest large amounts in equipment change-over. Resistance to automation in the United States apparel marketplace is still significant. The reason? Partly because of inexpensive labor available offshore in such countries as Brazil, China, and India; partly because most manufacturers are too small to afford costly systems and partly because they feel the long production runs needed to justify the costs are not consistent with the fickle world of fashion. Designer Stan Herman warns, "These small firms are the heart and soul of our industry. But you know in this business we're used to cutting corners to get by. And the money commitment decision to so hard to make when you work on such small markups, as most of these firms do. It's sad, but understandable."

The changes for the future of the apparel industry seem to become obvious. As with the *couture*, the small, piecemeal, hand-crafted, manually produced facets of clothing production are being forced to yield to computerized machines. The costs of labor and materials join with the expense of retooling to automated equipment, forcing the small producer either to bankruptcy or to sell out to the industry giant, which is often a part of an enormous industrial conglomerate. The dollars and cents of profit sheets become more important than the art of clothing.[9]

Fashion Computer Command Center

The old cash register has been replaced in many department and clothing stores by an electronic cash register that turns the humble checkstand into a corporate command center. This machine has an almost limitless capability to help a store

---

[7] "The Future of Fashion," *Pasadena Star News*, May 22. 1974, p. 1.
[8] Martin Gurian, "Implications of Robotics," *The F.I.T. Review*, October 1984, pp. 4–8.
[9] Seder, op. cit., p. 4.

manager control inventory. The prices of thousands of items on store shelves can be changed by pushing a few buttons. A store manager can find out in the afternoon whether the sale advertised in the morning paper is attracting customers. The machine can run an instantaneous credit check every time a customer uses a charge card. Control of inventory can be exercised more easily and accurately so that less cash is tied up in items stored on warehouse shelves. New fashions can be experimented with and promptly reordered if they are "hot."

The Technology and Industry of Fashion—Some Points of View

The 11th Annual Symposium of The Costume Society of America hosted in New York City by the Fashion Institute of Technology was entitled "The Technology and Industry of Fashion." Four leaders in various aspects of the fashion field discussed both the present and future of textile technology and its link to fashion apparel.

Robert Beaulieu, textile industry consultant and professor, FIT, traced the history of the world through textile development. He stated that the textile industry is the largest industry in the USA today, employing 2.5 million workers. It produces products ranging from water dam liners and airport runways (replacing steel) to the gossamer fabrics used for wedding veils. He believes that the textiles industry *was* strategically important to the future of the country, yet it was being allowed to die or slip away because of the lack of both industry and government support for the new technology needed to keep the American textile industry competitive in the world market. He stated that what was needed was a new system of thinking which would totally integrate textiles production and apparel construction. Textiles should be produced with the end product, function and aesthetic design, preplanned.

He stated that the biggest problems today are both management and labor in the textile industry. Too many managers have MBA's without having any textiles training. They therefore do not fully understand their charge. Cheap labor on the world market makes the cost of American labor a critical concern. Automation of the textile industry is replacing many textiles workers. The reality of such a large segment of the population with obsolete work skills has the potential of causing social problems similar to those created in Western Europe by the Industrial Revolution of the nineteenth century which resulted in the birth of Marxism.

Beaulieu observed that Sweden and Japan are coleaders in textile technology. He stated that the competition for dominance between these two was so intense that they were more than "friendly" enemies—they were on a warlike footing.

He described some of the research of the Swedish Industry Textile Research in body measurements. They were looking for a critical measurement that could be used to predict all other body measurements. They confirmed that all human anatomy did not move the same, that variations occurred with sex and age. They discovered that the critical measurement for a young woman was the chest. With this measurement they could then predict all other measurements within 3 percent. Machinery now can reproduce the body measurements using television cameras to take the critical measurement and computers to calculate the other measurements. They hope to develop "ego-centers" where measurements will be taken and garments produced from a design that the consumer selects from a stylebook. The individual's critical measurement would be kept on file for all future garment orders.

He reported that Swedish inventors have produced totally automated equipment which can produce textiles. They are working on robots that will be able to produce garments. To date they have not been able to duplicate the human hand-eye coordination in a machine. They predict that soon robots will produce garments sewn with liquid fiber thread. Multipurpose machines will do each operation so that breakdowns will not be shutdowns. This technology is already for sale.

The Swedish auto company, Volvo, is buying this type of technology. This company is looking forward to total automation. Volvo is investing only in products that are necessary for life. They are preparing for a future that differs vastly from the past.

Beaulieu concluded that when automation is completed the advantage of cheap labor is removed. He felt that at that point the textile industry would move back to the United States and Western Europe. He stated that what will happen in the future is buried in the past. If the planet survives, so will the textile industry.

Alexander Julian, creator of the firm, "Colors" and the first American garment designer to design his own fabrics, took a very different approach. He felt the future of apparel was with the aesthetic. He predicted a return to the cottage industry of creating beautiful fabrics and garments in a traditional manner for a limited group of consumers. Although this designer has been successful in the broad marketplace of American fashion, his commitment is to color and beauty regardless of the cost.

Phil Shroff, of Monsanto Fibers and Intermediates, discussed the emerging trends in textiles with the technology and contemporary design using man-made fibers. He noted that synthetics brought American fashion into the mainstream. This has bred a need for a new kind of designer, one who can combine technical understanding with creativity. This type of designer needs to understand what the machines can achieve and needs to be able to create to this capacity. He labeled this new kind of designer a "fashion technologist." He countered Alexander Julian by saying that man-made fibers combined with technology could create whatever fabrics the heart desired. These beautiful and complex fabrics could be produced at prices that would be competitive in the world market. He concluded that the behavior and developmental designer was influenced by political, sociological, and economic factors plus the consumer psychic.

The last speaker, Didier Raven, publisher of *American Fabrics and Fashions*, compared problems in the textile industry with problems in the publishing industry. He noted that there had been a resurgence in the magazine industry due to many technological changes. He noted the textile industry needed to change in order to remain competitive or else we may have a future without clothes to be curated. He felt that free trade would disappear and remarked that Japan has no free trade. He described a ten million dollar media campaign sponsored by the textile industry which would include a major lobby day in Washington D.C. He concurred with Beaulieu, saying that the fate of the textile industry would affect all of us. The standard of living which we enjoy is threatened. He noted that third world countries are producing *services* rather than goods and that the task of industrial nations was to provide goods for the rest of the world. He felt the textile industry's problems were bigger than robotics or automation. He opined that the electronics, auto, steel, and shoe industries had been lost from the United States. He questioned whether the loss of the textile industry could be stopped. His solution was nationalistic: he cited England's major retailer, Marks & Spencer, noting that they sell only items made in the British Commonwealth. His message was "buy USA."[10]

Career Apparel

More and more employees are suiting up each workday in company supplied clothing. Today's wrinkle-free synthetic textiles are comfortable, fashionable, and utilitarian. But more importantly, companies usually foot the bill to supply and maintain these corporate fatigues. Once as synonymous with blue-collar workers as the lunch box, uniforms have expanded from industrial garb to career apparel for white-collar type jobs.

To the United States garment rental business, uniforms represent about $1.5 billion of business annually and this amount is growing. David MacKenzie, executive director of the California Laundry and Linen Supply Association, reported that less than 20 percent of the whole United States working population is now in uniform. However, the industry feels that there is a potentially large market for career apparel. They are currently trying to develop better products for clerical and office workers.

Increased protective clothing requirements from such government agencies as the Occupational Safety and Health Administration and the Federal Food and Drug Administration are triggering demand. Some states, like California, have stringent rules for employers to follow in requiring employees to wear uniforms. The California Industrial Welfare Commission takes the position that if uniforms are required as a condition of employment, the employer shall provide and maintain them. The term "uniform" includes wearing apparel and accessories of distinctive design or color.

[10] The Costume Society of America 11th Annual Symposium "The Technology and Industry of Fashion," Fashion Institute of Technology, New York, N.Y., June 12 1985.

An increasing variety of firms such as banks and insurance companies are avoiding the problem of setting dress codes by providing a wardrobe of color-coded mix-and-match separates. In an era of casual clothes and skin-tight jeans, they found corporate-furnished apparel eliminated embarrassing confrontations. More importantly, companies have been discovering that readily identifiable personnel become corporate image extenders, particularly in a service-oriented business. Career apparel is a way to eliminate the confusion between employee and customer. Herb Yager of Saul Bass/Herb Yager and Associates observed that "the notion of putting a corporate design on a person is a very touchy subject. People typically respond to uniforms as dehumanizing." Yager's firm has worked on corporate image programs for organizations ranging from American Telephone & Telegraph to the Girl Scouts. He said there was tremendous resistance at the phone company when the image program was extended to experiment with uniforms. "Unless there is a functional reason for a uniform, people tend to resist it." Work apparel is a more acceptable term than uniforms.

Clothing and cleaning costs are now considered part of the fringe benefits package of many employers. The wearing of company-supplied clothing cuts personal wardrobe costs. It allows employees the option to use the money they would spend for business attire for other things.

Many other companies use modified versions of uniforms, such as smocks or aprons. Supermarket workers, restaurant personnel, medical professionals, and a variety of other job-holders wear uniforms. The bulk of the uniform rental business is derived from the industrial sector in which companies clothe everyone from janitors to service managers. Most color code the various job categories so personnel can be easily identified.

It is felt by many that the growth of career apparel has risen with the general rise in the standard of living and work environment. With more women joining the work force at all levels, work apparel suppliers are attempting to deal with fashion consciousness. Women are generally very particular about what they wear. Some men will accept a set of coveralls or a work shirt and pants, but many women will not. Women want more personalized clothing, which brings in problems with sizing and fitting.[11]

From London comes another version of career apparel. It has been developed by Michael Goddard, head of Denman & Goddard Ltd. Called the *Executive Clothing Plan*, it allows a firm to dress its upper executives in Savile Row style at comparatively low cost. The gimmick is that the suit remains the property of the company and is rented to the executive for a nominal fee. The executive gets a custom-made fringe benefit, and the company has a well-dressed employee, and its accountants can count the suit as a revenue item, or it can be written off 100 percent the first year.

Denman & Goddard give as an example a £500 ($1,100) suit that is leased to an executive for two years at £50 a year. The net cost to the firm, £400, can be

---

[11] Nancy Yoshihara, "The Uniform: Suitable in Confusing Era," *Los Angeles Times*, April 29, 1979.

set against corporation tax. If the firm were instead to pay the executive an extra £400 in salary, the sum would also be allowable against corporation tax but would leave the executive with only £268 after taxes and less if he were in a higher-income bracket. And £268 is not enough to buy a Denman and Goddard suit.

"A firm's position is enhanced if its senior men are well-dressed," Goddard says. "Depending on the job, a suit could be a tool of work. Why spend money on expensive status symbols like big cars when I can get you started for far less?"[12]

The economic forces of tax write-offs and employee fringe benefits seem to be combining with the technology of computerized clothing. Corporate images and status symbols combine to influence even the most conservative institutions. Entrepreneurs in the businesses of providing career clothing are preparing for a bonanza. Career apparel, recognizable or not, appears to be the clothing of the future.

The Future?

Planning for the future has become a critical function of many institutions around the world. There has been a proliferation of groups created to cope with the future. Toffler in *Future Shock* challenged all concerned individuals to become sensitively concerned with the changes the future demands so that mankind can undertake the control of this change and the guidance of his evolution.[13]

Toffler listed a number of future-oriented organizations that are currently working on a myriad of problems. Included were "think tanks," such as the Institute for the Future and the National Commission on Critical Choices for Americans; academic study groups such as the Commission on the Year 2000 and the Harvard Program on Technology and Society; futurist journals published in England, France, Italy, Germany, and the United States; university courses in forecasting and related subjects in dealing with the future; convocations of international futurists that meet in Oslo, Berlin, and Kyoto; and societies such as Futuribles, Europe 2000, Mankind 2000, and the World Future Society.

Toffler reported that futurist centers are to be found in West Berlin, Prague, London, Moscow, Rome, Washington, D.C., and in the remote jungles of Brazil. The futurists in these centers differ from the technological planners who concentrate on a time period comprising only the next fifteen, twenty-five, or fifty years.[14]

Futuristic planning is now spawning new ideas. Experiments and recommendations such as the following give us clues as to what to expect in the future:

1. *New food sources:* Waste materials scientifically transformed into protein-rich yeast cells that can be made palatable.[15]

[12] Mary Blume, "Haute Finance: Lease a Suit," Fashion 79, *Los Angeles Times*, August 24, 1979, p. 4.
[13] Alvin Toffler, *Future Shock* (New York: Bantam books, 1970), p. 487.
[14] Ibid., p. 459.
[15] "Scientists Turn Waste into Protein," *Los Angeles Times*, July 21, 1974, Pt. II, p. 1.

2. *New energy sources:* Kelp beds create ocean energy farms that produce petroleum-like products that can be used for food and fuel, including electricity.[16]
3. *New population controls:* The United States recommends a world goal to limit average size of family unit to two parents and two children who reach productive age.[17]

Such programs are continually being expanded and other ideas are put into action. In an article that traced the fuel source history of the world from Paleolithic times, Hardy concluded that historical shortages of animal food, manpower, and wood proved beneficial in the long run. To secure alternative sources of power, people came to grips with their environment. The discoveries they made in the process of adapting the new power sources to society's needs bred a host of technological refinements. The energy shortages that we currently face should stimulate new inventions and discoveries as well as a new social order.[18]

Nowhere are the dreams of the future more fascinating than those that will be closest to mankind—the clothing that he will wear. It is certain that a fashionable body covering of some kind will be worn because it always has been. Total nudity has been rejected by all cultures. If there were any particular pleasure in nudity, social or personal, it would have been adopted by some society. Yet, with very few exceptions, people in even the oldest cultures and warmest climates have found a way to cover themselves. Records show that even the Polynesians who lived on the climatically perfect Pacific Islands wore loincloths and embroidered jackets before the missionaries came. Acceptance of nudity depends upon the mores of a culture, and although acceptance is possible, it is not at all probable.

The dress a woman wears in 1999 may feed her dog in 2000. The shirt a man puts on his back at that time may change color every time he changes his tie and jacket. The pants they both wear to protect against cold may also air-condition them from heat. This kind of brave, new fashion is just a test tube away according to Corrin N. Corbin of E.I. du Pont de Nemours & Company, Inc., the nation's largest producer of man-made fibers. Corbin has challenged the scientists of his company to develop fibers that will solve problems instead of create them. Some of the textile experimentations include:

A fiber that will open up to let air circulate through it when the weather is hot, and close up to hold in body heat when it is cold.
A climatized fiber that will take the wearer comfortably from a cold morning through a hot afternoon to a cold evening.

[16] "Kelp Will Be Grown in Ocean Energy Farm," *Los Angeles Times*, August 13, 1974, Pt. II, p. 1.
[17] "Worldwide Limit of Two Children per Family Proposed by U.S.," *Los Angeles Times*, August 21, 1974, Pt. 1, p. 1.
[18] Andrew Hardy, "The Energy Crisis of 1593 Led to the Industrial Revolution," *Smart Money*, January 1974, pp. 6–7.

The fibers and fabrics of 2000 must not only look good and feel good but must also satisfy the needs of a changing society. One of those needs will be to provide ecologically sound products. These are Corbin's goals. He explained that du Pont is not only in the fiber business but is also in the business of supplying base materials, and that these base materials should improve the quality of life. He prophesied that pharmaceutical companies could develop a pill that would make a woman feel beautiful, safely; if this happens, she is not going to need a $200 dress. He hopes to guide his company to meet that kind of competition.

Du Pont currently produces 2.8 billion pounds of fiber each year. This converts into approximately 10 billion yards of fabric. Corbin wants future production to concentrate on fibers with a meaningful afterlife. He hopes that today's trash compactor will become tomorrow's old apparel converter, producing useful products, such as logs for fuel, or pet food, from recycled clothing fibers.[19]

Dr. James Bonner, biology professorr at Cal Tech and internationally recognized authority on the evolutionary patterns of the future, has a fashion view of the twenty-first century that he admits is as much influenced by the science fiction of Buck Rogers and Flash Gordon as it is by scientific certainties. He predicts that tomorrow's clothes, in addition to providing body coverage, will be used primarily to flaunt status. His reasoning, "We'll all be rich so we won't need clothes to denote bank accounts or birthrights, but we'll all be members of a power hierarchy and will need and want clothes to identify our position in the planetary pecking order. In a sense, we will return to the dress of ancient times. We will wear highly decorated, flowing mantles, or capes, not only to adorn ourselves but also to symbolize our power or authority. At every level of society, there always have been, and there always will be, those who lead and those who are led." Since we will not be able to tell who's who by wealth, we will need to identify our place of leadership by clothes.

The professor believes that by the year 2001 we will be well on our way in the exploration of other planets, but he sees only a small percentage of people wearing pressurized lunar suits. He thinks that because life in the hostile environments of other planets will be difficult and unpleasant, most people will not want to colonize other planets. However, those who do will be workers, probably farmers or miners, and they will wear something similar to blue jeans and denim shirts, which may be in the form of body stockings or leotards. These colonists will find life on the other planets much like that in California in the 1880s: a rough, tough new existence that allows no time for clothes-consciousness.[20]

Pierre Cardin agrees that the body stocking is the garment of the future. He sees it for off-duty wear and feels that the body stocking will be found in most wardrobes. He believes it would take time to gain acceptance, but would eventually be accepted because it is the ultimate clothing for relaxation. Pierre Cardin conceives the body stocking in this manner:

[19] Marylou Luther, "Fabrics of Future: Wearable and Edible," *Los Angeles Times,* July 5, 1974, Pt. IV, p. 1.

[20] Marylou Luther, "21st-Century Fashions: View by a Futurist," *Los Angeles Times,* October 10, 1971. Pt. E, p. 1.

20-4 *Many agree that the body stocking will be the garment of the future. (Courtesy Danskin)*

It will feel like a second skin. It will eliminate the need for undershorts and it will, of course, be of knitted or stretch fabrics. At home you lounge around. The body stocking will allow you to do it in perfect comfort.... It can be decorated with a shirt on top, a sweater, anything. You can even put a loose coat over it ... (the body stocking) will be one piece with a big diagonal zipper.

Cardin continued, stating that the only term that described the garment he had in mind better than body stocking was the French *double peau*, which translates double skin. Cardin was practical about body variations. He predicted, "Everyone will wear the *double peau*. Because everyone wants to relax. At the beach everyone is seen in brief trunks and no one is concerned" (Figure 20–4).[21]

Another view of clothing of the twenty-first century was formed by a group of French couturiers, including André Courreges, Emmanuelle Khanh, and Paco Rabanne, who participated in a fashion history exhibit at Paris's Museum of Decorative Arts. These designers felt that future fashion would be unisex, seasonless, and totally synthetic.

[21] Jack Hyde, "Overview: Pierre Cardin Peers into the Future," *Menswear*, November 17, 1972, p. 42.

The prototype of future fashion created by Michele Rosier consists of a one-piece unisex jumpsuit with built-in heating and air conditioning to maintain a comfortable body temperature all year round. The transparent, phosphorescent garment will be worn over skin-tone bikini underwear. Topping it will be a helmet equipped with a transistor radio and telephone.

Designer Christiane Bailly added an interesting fashion accessory to the jumpsuit model for women. It is an electric beam that at different currents will alternately attract or repel male suitors. Other futuristic fashion predictions made by this group were these:

By the year 2000, natural fibers such as cotton and wool will be obsolete; we will wear synthetics, plastics, Plexiglas, and metal.

We will all be bald by the turn of the century due to insufficient nourishment, so wigs and helmets will enjoy almost universal vogue. Transportation in the cities will have ground to a complete halt. Sidewalks will be converted to conveyor belts and footgear will consist of noiseless roller skates.[22]

Whether you view the future with bright-eyed optimism, defeatist pessimism, or pragmatic logic, it is safe to predict that future dress will reflect the evolvement of mankind. Clothing will continue to satisfy the psychological and sociological, as well as physical, needs of people. Apparel of the future will depend upon what resources are available and what technological advancements and social patterns have evolved. Clothing will fit the lifestyles of the future and reveal personal values just as it does now (Figure 20-5).

[22] "Fashion of the Future," *Parade*, January 13, 1974, p. 6.

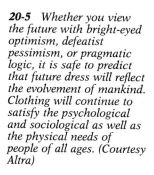

20-5 *Whether you view the future with bright-eyed optimism, defeatist pessimism, or pragmatic logic, it is safe to predict that future dress will reflect the evolvement of mankind. Clothing will continue to satisfy the psychological and sociological as well as the physical needs of people of all ages. (Courtesy Altra)*

In the decades ahead, there will be more changes taking place than we can possibly imagine. Our planet may be overpopulated, underfed, and depleted of natural resources, or we may learn to solve these current problems and progress to a glorious new level of civilization. Whatever the future holds, the authors predict that the people of Earth will continue to adorn themselves in a manner that sets them apart and expresses their unique individuality.

Suggested Activities

1. Set up a file for articles from the popular press that predict the future. These can be found in the news, fashion, and business sections of newspapers and magazines. Try to predict your future lifestyle.
2. Discuss with class members clothing projections for the future.
3. Watch science-fiction movies and try to determine how plausible the costumes are. Think of yourself wearing such garments.
4. Attend exhibits in your local libraries and museums that predict the future. If you live in a remote area, plan to attend these when you travel.
5. Explore the future with students and instructors in other disciplines. The biologist, the psychologist, the agriculturist, the physician, the businessman, the economist, the scientist, the home economist, and the food technologist all have their own points of view based on their research and reading.
6. Communicate with a futurist organization; try to get on its mailing list. Attend any functions the organization might sponsor in your area. If possible, arrange to have a futurist speak to your class or on your campus.

Appendices

Appendix A

Design Guidelines for Men

To Appear Heavier	To Appear Thinner
Hairstyle—Short hair—thicker style at sides—away from head.	**Hairstyle**—Short style—close to head.
Long style—wide style—even length.	Long style—also close to head—tapered from face.

Garment Design

Suit—Natural shoulder—straight hanging fitted slightly at waistline. Suit should fit easy or loosely. Choose thick fabrics such as corduroy, tweeds, flannel. Choose horizontal line movement.

Jackets—Double-breasted jackets good, wide lapels, long roll line. Avoid short jackets. For tall, patch and flap pocket good.

Dress Shirts—Widespread, short-pointed collar. Fabric patterns good. Avoid vertical line movement.

Ties—Choose wider style—bold patterns. Use wide knot. Choose style within current fashion.

Casual Shirts—Any bold patterns. Avoid clinging knits.

Pants—Avoid too tapered leg. Cuffs cut length. Should be long as dictated by fashion.

Socks—Same color as pants or darker. Executive length.

Vests—Colorful and contrasting will add bulk. Easy or loose fit.

Shoes

   Dress—Heavier styles—thick soles and built-up heel. Contrasts to pant color will cut height.

   Casual—Any style.

Topcoat—Raglan sleeve and double-breasted good for tall. Horizontal line movement good.

Garment Design

Suit—2–3 button styles—avoid wide lapels that widen shoulder area. Choose smooth fabrics. Avoid heavy fabrics as well as lightweights that wrinkle or seersucker. Avoid pocket flaps and side vents. Choose vertical line movement.

Jackets—Shorter jackets will add height as will fitted jackets.

Dress Shirts—Regular-point collars with low slope best as make neck look longer. Vertical line movement in fabric designs.

Ties—Keep patterns subdued, but not drab. Tie should reach belt line. No bow ties. Avoid large knot. Choose style within current fashion.

Casual Shirts—Avoid body contouring knits. Choose colors to match pants. Open throat. Avoid turtleneck.

Pants—Tapered leg. Pleats over stomach will camouflage "pot." Cuffless ones add length. Should be as long as dictated by fashion.

Socks—Matching pants or darker. Executive length.

Vests—Matching one good—will cover waistline and reinforce vertical line. Avoid fancy or contrasting ones that focus attention at midsection.

Shoes

   Dress—Avoid heavy looking shoe. Select tapered toe. Matching pants or darker.

   Casual—Choose styles that fit over foot or barefoot sandal.

Topcoat—Single breasted. Set-in sleeve best design. Choose vertical line movement.

Design Guidelines for Men (*Continued*)

To Appear Heavier	To Appear Thinner
Patterns—Color—Textures Distinctive patterns such as plaids, checks, and stripes. Choose horizontal line movement. Use thicker, heavy bulky textures. Mix and match color as desired. Color key wardrobe.	**Patterns—Color—Textures** Vertical line movement to add height and slenderize. Solid colors best. Choose one color varying values and chroma in various pieces of outfit. Muted plaids, tweeds. Use only two different patterns in one outfit. Keep textures flat and smooth. Color key wardrobe.

To Appear Taller	To Appear Shorter
Hairstyle—Shorter style—close to head. Longer styles should taper from face to middle of back.	**Hairstyle**—Wear shorter style—full at side. Wear longer styles cut evenly around head.
Garment Design Suit style—2 or 3 button styles. Single breasted with long lapel line. Avoid wide lapels. Choose slightly built-up shoulders. Choose smooth texture. Choose vertical line movement or solids.	**Garment Design** Suit style—2 or 3 button suits with wide button spacing and moderately rolled lapels. Textured fabrics. Horizontal line movement. Checks and plaids good. Edwardian and double-breasted good. Shoulders squared. Loose waist fit. Flap pockets give horizontal movement.
Jackets—Bottom of jacket even with thumb knuckle for best length. Vertical line achieved with center or side vents. Avoid horizontal line created by pocket flaps. Choose smooth textures. Vertical line movement or solids.	Jackets—Blazer or battle jacket styles good. Horizontal line movement in texture and fabric design.
Dress Shirts—Choose collars that are regular spread, tab, or long pointed. Choose vertical line movement in fabrics.	Dress Shirts—Choose widespread collar. Solids, checks, Jacquards, oxford, cheviot weaves all good.
Ties—On narrow side as dictated by fashion. Vertical or diagonal line movement. Tied four-in-hand rather than fat Windsor.	Ties—Avoid long, thin ties but choose widths from current fashion. Wide knot good.
Casual Shirts—Match color to pants. Open throat.	Casual Shirts—Go wild if you wish. Large scale. Hawaiian prints. Have fun.
Pants—Tapered for longer leg look. Avoid cuffs. High-rise waist treatment for longer leg look. Smooth textures. Solids or vertical line movement.	Pants—Tapering leg. Avoid low rise and too tight fit. Be certain they cover ankle to top of shoe.
Socks—Matched to pants or darker. Executive length.	Socks—Matched to pants or darker. Executive length.
Shoes Dress—Choose heavier styles such as brogues and wing tips. Color match pants or darker. Elevated heel if desired.	Shoes Dress—Choose heavier shoe—wing tip, moccasins. Avoid built-up sole and heel. Contrast shoe color with pants.
Casual—Choose shoes that fit up on foot such as loafer or barefoot sandal or thong.	Casual—Any fashionable style.

Design Guidelines for Men (*Continued*)

To Appear Taller	To Appear Shorter
Topcoat—Choose knee length. Solid color. Smooth texture.	Topcoat—Any well-tailored coat. Single- or double-breasted. Raglan sleeve good. Avoid vertical stripes.
Patterns—Color—Textures	**Patterns—Color—Textures**
Accentuate vertical line by choosing patterns that elongate. Avoid strong horizontal lines in garment design or color coordination. One color outfit, varying values and intensities good. Choose muted small-scale plaids, tweeds, or herringbones. Keep textures smooth, flat. Color key wardrobe.	Choose most designs except narrow, vertical stripes. Mix colors freely. Use heavy, bulky textures. Color key wardrobe.

Appendix B

Design Guidelines for Women

Body Feature	To Appear Taller	To Appear Shorter
Neck	Necklines—Open, such as V, square, low, round.	Necklines—Covering, such as turtleneck, jewelry neckline. Scarves tied around throat excellent.
	Hairstyle—Short, close to head, or upsweep piled high on head. Longer hair pulled back from face.	Hairstyle—Shoulder length or longer.
	Earrings—Close-to-ear styles.	Earrings—Dangling type.
	Necklaces—Longer, past base of neck.	Necklaces—Short to base of neck, chokers.

Body Feature	To Appear Wider	To Appear Narrow
Shoulders	Garment Design—Puff sleeve, cap sleeve, or drop shoulder; jacket dresses, sweater sets, use of horizontal structural detail.	Garment Design—Sleeveless, dolman, high set-in sleeves; garments that create vertical lines in this area such as vests, jackets, jumpers—princess line.
	Color—High value, high chroma—color contrast, value contrasts.	Color—Use of different colors such as dark jumper, lighter blouse. Middle values to low values.
	Textures—See through, medium to bulky.	Texture—Avoid bulky sweaters, choose flat to medium textures.
	Fabric Design—Horizontal line movement and designs that achieve horizontal movement. Solid color designs.	Fabric Design—Vertical line movement designs that lead eye in vertical direction. Color variation in designs.

Body Feature	To Appear Fuller	To Appear Smaller
Bust	Garment Design—Easy fit such as in dolman sleeve, gathered bodice, structural or applied design to locate fullness in this area. Layering of garments such as blouse, vest, jacket, or sweater sets. Horizontal line movement. End short sleeve at bust level.	Garment Design—Avoid tight-fitting designs. Choose moderate amount of ease. Dolman sleeve creates fullness at bustline. Sleeve length should end above or below fullest part of bust. Vertical line movement as found in button closings, zippers, or other structural or applied design good.
	Color—High value, high intensity combinations of colors changing at bustline.	Color—Middle values, middle intensities.
	Textures—Soft draping fabrics. Bulky knits, reflecting satins.	Textures—Flat to medium thickness, avoid bulky, shiny, see through.

569

Design Guidelines for Women (Continued)

Body Feature	To Appear Fuller	To Appear Smaller
Bust	Fabric Designs—Allover patterns, horizontal movement, solid color designs.	Fabric Designs—Allover patterns in scale. Avoid too large prints. Vertical line movement. Solid color designs.

Body Feature	To Appear Longer, More Slender	To Appear Shorter, Wider
Arms	Garment Design—Sleeveless with armscye cut up into shoulder area. Full-length sleeve ending past wristbone, fit to arm.	Garment Design—Cap, short, ¾ or bracelet length. Ease or width good as in puffed or bell sleeve.
	Color—Best in same color as basic garment.	Color—Contrasts in color trims such as cuffs.
	Texture—Flat, smooth, same as basic garment.	Texture—Contrasts used in cuffs.
	Fabric Design—Not eye-arresting. Same as basic garment. Vertical line movement.	Fabric Design—Stripes, allover designs. Horizontal line movement.

Body Feature	To Emphasize	To Subordinate
Waist	Garment Design—Snug fit at waistline with soft fullness above and below waistline. Use contrasting belts or trim. Caution: Emphasized waistline can create an "umbrella" effect if hips are large.	Garment Design—Easy fit at waistline or avoid belting. Overblouse or sweater good.
	Color—Strong color contrasts of upper and lower garments. Belt color contrasts.	Color—Avoid color changes of waistline. Use self-fabric belts.
	Texture—Eye-arresting texture in belts or jewelry used at waistline.	Texture—Avoid bulky textures. Use flat, smooth, opaque textures.

Body Feature	To Appear Fuller	To Appear Smaller
Hip	Garment Design—Tight fit body-revealing styles. Full gathers. Eye-arresting detail at hipline such as belting, jewelry. Garments that make shoulders appear narrow, such as sleeveless dress, can make hips appear larger. Choose ¾ length sleeve.	Garment Design—Easy fit, A-line, princess styling. Designs that balance shoulder and hip width. Waistline not accented. No design detail at hipline. Avoid ¾ length sleeve.
	Color—Changes of color at hipline as in cardigan sweater and pants.	Color—No color change at hipline. Jackets, sweaters, blouses end above or below fullest part of hip.
	Textures—Choose bulky, heavy textures.	Textures—Choose smooth to medium textures.

Design Guidelines for Women *(Continued)*

Body Feature	To Appear Fuller	To Appear Smaller
	Fabric Design—Allover designs in scale, solids, horizontal line movement.	Fabric Design—Allover designs in scale, solids, vertical line movement.
	Accessories—Handbag large scale carried by strap at hip.	Accessories—Clutch handbag in scale.

Body Feature	To Appear Taller	To Appear Shorter
Leg Foot	Garment Design—Choose shorter fashionable dress length. End jackets and sweaters between waist and hip. Choose longer fashionable pant length. Avoid shoe styles that come up over instep or around ankle.	Garment Design—Choose longer fashionable dress length. End jackets, sweaters, or overblouses at hip or below. Choose shoe styles that cover instep—ankle straps.
	Color—Select hosiery to match dress and shoe for longest effect. Hosiery and shoe same color for next longest look. Avoid strong color contrasts with garment—hosiery and shoe. Medium intensities better than extremes.	Color—Use color contrasts in skirt, stocking, shoe area.
	Texture—Smooth—fabrics that cling and reveal leg often lengthen it.	Texture—Medium to stiff textures will stand away from body and create shortening illusion.
	Fabric Design—Not too common in hosiery. If fashionable, select vertical line movement. For pants, skirts choose vertical line movement.	Fabric Design—Not too common in hosiery. If fashionable, choose horizontal line movement. For pants, skirts choose horizontal line movement.

Body Feature	To Appear Heavier	To Appear More Slender
Leg Foot	Garment Design—Choose closely fit pants, straight figure-revealing or bulky skirts. Horizontal line movement in structural design.	Garment Design—Choose pants with ease so they do not cling to leg. Choose A-line or gored skirts to stand away from leg and not outline it. Vertical line movement.
	Choose shoes with horizontal line movement in toe, instep styling—ankle straps.	Choose shoes with vertical or diagonal line movement—pointed toe—V cut instep. Avoid ankle straps.
	Color—High or low value stockings such as white or black. Also high chroma stockings.	Color—Middle value stockings. Avoid high chroma stockings.
	Garments in same high-low value. High chroma will make area appear larger.	Garments in middle values, middle chromas.

Design Guidelines for Women (*Continued*)

Body Feature	To Appear Heavier	To Appear More Slender
Leg Foot	Textures—Choose bulky, heavy textures. Fabric Design—Choose horizontal line movement.	Textures—Choose smooth to medium textures. Fabric Design—Choose vertical line movement.

Body Feature	To Appear Taller	To Appear Shorter

Total Body Illusion	Hat Styles—Upturned brim. Extension such as feather leading eye upward. Hat worn tilted upward.
	
	Hairstyle—Upsweep—chignon—or close to head.
	
	Garment Design
	    Necklines—V or Y line that lead eye upward. Vertical line movement in construction details and trim.
	
	Color—One-color outfit including shoes and stockings. Middle values and chromas. Color accent near face.
	
	Texture—Smooth, flat.
	
	Fabric Design—Vertical line movement—solid colors.
		Hat Styles—Wide and flat worn straight on head (brim should not extend past shoulder).
		
		Hairstyle—Flat to head at crown. Short cuts wide at end length. Longer styles past shoulder.
		
		Garment Design
		    Necklines—Turtle, T or jewelry—collar extends on neck. Horizontal line movement in construction details and trim.
		
		Color—Several bands of different hues varying in value and chroma (including shoes and stockings). Color accent within garment silhouette.
		
		Texture—Bulky—heavy—not smooth.
		
		Fabric Design—Allover patterns toward large scale. Horizontal line movement. Varied colors.

Body Feature	To Appear Heavier	To Appear More Slender
Total Body Illusion	Hat Styles—Ornate; wide brim; veiling when in fashion. Hairstyles—Elaborate creating much visual interest. Fluffed away from head—in proportion with body. Garment Design—Use of varied line direction—diagonal and zigzag good. Busy effect in construction details and trim. Layering of garments such as blouse, vest, jacket. Color—Combinations of colors varying high to low value and chroma. Texture—Stiff, shiny, bulky, see-through, away from body qualities. Fabric Design—Allover patterns—scaled in proportion to total body. Horizontal line movement.	Hat Styles—Simple—fitting close to head. Ornamentation flat to hat. Hairstyles—Simple—flat smooth—close to head but in proportion to body size. Garment Design—Simple, not much detail. Vertical line movement in construction details and trim. Color—Single color outfits best. Use of muted color combinations. Texture—Flat, smooth. Fabric Design—Small allover patterns scaled in proportion to total body. Solid color designs. Vertical line movement.

Appendix C

Skin Care and Cosmetic Ingredient Functions

Anti-Caking Agents:
Calcium carbonate, hydrated silica, magnesium carbonate, silica
Function:
Keep loose powders free-flowing

Antimicrobials:
Benzoic acid, borax, boric acid, cetyltrimethylammonium bromide, citric acid, dehydroacetic acid, formaldehyde, imidazolidinyl urea, methylparaben, propylparaben, sorbic acid, triclosan, 2-bromo-2-nitro-1,3-propanediol
Function:
Preservatives that help destroy and prevent growth of microorganisms such as bacteria

Antioxidants:
BHA-butylated hydroxyanisole, BHT-butylated hydroxytoluene
Function:
Preservatives that help prevent deterioration of such ingredients as fragrance oils and emollients which can result in off-odor, off-color, or product separation which can occur if these ingredients react with oxygen in the air

Antiperspirant:
Aluminum chlorohydrate
Function:
Helps inhibit the flow of perspiration

Binders:
Aluminum distearate, kaolin, zinc stearate
Function:
Hold loose powders together when compressed into a solid cake form

Color Additives & Opacifiers:
Any ingredient prefixed by FD&C, D&C, or Ext. D&C are color additives certified by the FDA. Others include bismuth oxychloride, chromium hydroxide green, chromium oxide greens, ferric ferrocyanide, guanine, iron oxides, kaolin, mica, talc, titanium dioxide ultramarines, zinc oxide, zinc stearate
Function:
Impart color and/or increase coverage

Deodorants:
Cetrimonium bromide, cetylpyridinium chloride, triclocarban, triclosan, zinc phenosulfonate
Function:
Mask or decrease perspiration odors and/or help prevent their development

Emollients:
Beeswax, candelilla wax, caprylic/capric triglyceride, carnauba, castor oil, cetyl lactate, diisopropyl adipate, dimethicone, ethylhexyl palmitate, hydrogenated vegetable oil, isodecyl oleate, isopropyl lanolate, isopropyl myristate, isopropyl palmitate, isopropyl stearate, lanolin, lanolin alcohols, lanolin wax, microcrystalline wax, mineral oil, myristyl myristate, oleyl alcohol, ozokerite, paraffin, petrolatum, propylene glycol dicaprylate/dicaprate, sesame oil, stearyl alcohol, talc, wood wax alcohols
Function:
Skin conditioners which help prevent or relieve dryness and protect the skin by softening, conditioning, lubricating, and minimizing moisture loss

Emulsifiers:
Ceteth-2, glyceryl stearate, glycol stearate, laneth-10 acetate, lecithin, oleth-10, PEG-6, PEG-32, PEG-32 stearate, PEG-40 hydrogenated castor oil, PEG-40 stearate, PEG-75 lanolin, polysorbates 20, 60, & 80, PPG-12-buteth-16, PPG-14 butyl ether, PPG-33 butyl ether, propylene glycol stearate SE, sorbitan sesquioleate, sorbitan stearate, stearamide DIBA stearate, steareth-2
Function:
Enable oil and water to mix together to form a smooth lotion or cream

Film Formers:
Acrylate/acrylamide copolymer, ethylene/vinyl acetate copolymer, nitrocellulose, polyvinylpyrrolidone (PVP), PVP/VA copolymer, toluene sulfonamide/formaldehyde resin
Function:
Provide a continuous film to decorate (nail enamels) or to control (as in hair sprays)

Skin Care and Cosmetic Ingredient Functions (*Continued*)

Foamers & Foam Stabilizers:
Lauramide DEA, lauric DEA, linoleamide DEA, PEG-15 cocamine
Function:
Create good, long-lasting foaming properties

Fragrances:
Fragrance oils (these are a complex blend of oils that provide a particular scent)
Function:
Impart a scent to a product, the skin, or the air[1]

Hair Conditioners:
Hydrolyzed animal protein, quaternium-18, -20, -23, stearalkonium chloride, stearamine oxide
Function:
Improve ease of combing, control fly away hair, and impart sheen

Humectants:
Animal protein derivative, butylene glycol, glycerin, propylene glycol, sodium lactate, sodium PCA, sorbitol, triethylene glycol
Function:
Skin conditioners that attract water, thereby further helping to maintain the skin's moisture balance

Mineral Suspending Agents:
Pentasodium pentetate, tetrasodium EDTA, trisodium HEDTA
Function:
Ingredients that bind minerals commonly found in hard water which would otherwise deteriorate the product

pH Adjusters:
Citric acid, phosphoric acid, triethanolamine
Function:
Control how acid (low pH) or alkaline (high pH) a product is

Propellants:
Butane, isobutane, propane
Function:
Force a product out of an aerosol container in the form of a spray, mist, or foam

Soaps & Detergents:
Ammonium laureth sulfate, ammonium nonoxynol-4 sulfate, amphoteric-2, dioctyl sodium sulfosuccinate, magnesium lauryl sulfate, nonoxynol-12, pareth-25-12, sodium cocoate, sodium laureth sulfate, sodium lauryl sulfate, sodium oleate, sodium tallowate, TEA-lauryl sulfate
Function:
Cleansing materials that break up and hold oils and soil so they may be removed easily from skin or hair surface

Sunscreens:
Amyl dimethyl PABA, octyl dimethyl PABA
Function:
Absorb ultraviolet light from sun's rays to help prevent or lessen sunburn while allowing the skin to tan

Thickeners/Solidifiers/Liquidifiers:
Bentonite, butyl acetate, butyl alcohol, carbomer-934, -940, -941, CD alcohol 19, cellulose gum, dibutyl phthalate, ethyl acetate, gum damar, hydroxyethyl cellulose, hydroxypropyl cellulose, isopropyl alcohol, magnesium aluminum silicate, magnesium silicate, methylcellulose, mineral spirits, SD alcohols, toluene, water
Function:
Make a product become thicker (less watery), thinner (more watery), or even solid (as in a lipstick)

Ultraviolet Absorbers:
Benzophenones-1, -2, -4, -9, -11, -12, UV absorbers-1, -5
Function:
Ingredients that help prevent deterioration of those ingredients which might be affected by the ultraviolet rays found in ordinary daylight

---

[1] Courtesy Avon Products, Inc. If you do not find the ingredient you are looking for on this list, write to Avon Consumer Information Center, 9 West 57th Street, New York, N.Y. 10019.

Appendix D

The Uses, Characteristics, and Care of Natural Fibers[1]

Some Principal Uses	Major Characteristics	Care Tips
Cotton:		
apparel	absorbent	1. If labeled "Do not bleach," never use chlorine bleach.
upholstery	medium strength	
draperies	wrinkles unless treated	2. Remove durable press garments from dryer as soon as tumbling is completed.
curtains	shrinks unless treated	
bedding	easily laundered	
toweling	subject to mildew	3. Use moderately hot iron.
thread		4. Press while damp.
slipcovers		5. Press dark garments on wrong side.
Linen:		
toweling	lint-free	1. Avoid repeated pressing of sharp creases for longer wear.
table linens	strong	
garments	absorbent	2. Use high ironing and pressing temperatures.
	wrinkles unless treated	
	subject to mildew	3. Iron while damp on wrong side.
	costly	4. Protect stored items from mildew.
Silk:		
apparel	soft hand	1. Usually dry-cleaned.
lining	lustrous	2. If labeled "hand washable," do not use chlorine bleach, or built soaps or detergents.
drapery	strong	
upholstery	resilient	
	accepts dye well	3. Use mild soap or detergent.
	costly	4. Protect from prolonged light exposure.
		5. Protect from moths and carpet beetles.
Wool:		
apparel	absorbent	1. Is usually dry-cleaned.
blankets	resilient	2. If washed, use cold water with mild soap or detergent.
carpets	has insulating capacity	
		3. Avoid chlorine bleach and built soaps and detergents.
		4. Protect against moths and carpet beetles.
		5. Press with steam, wrong side of fabric.

[1] Sources: Maytag Company and American Home Economics Association. *Textile Handbook* (Washington, D.C.: American Home Economics Association, 1970).

575

Appendix E

The Uses, Characteristics, and Care of Man-Made Fibers[1]

Some Principal Uses	Major Characteristics	Care Tips
Acetate:		
(Apparel)	Luxurious feel and appearance	Most acetate garments should be
Blouses	Wide range of colors and lusters	dry-cleaned but if laundering is indi-
Dresses	Excellent drapability and softness	cated, use the following guide:
Foundation garments	Relatively fast-drying	
Lingerie	Economical	1. Handwash in warm water with
Linings	Shrink-, moth-, and mildew-resistant	mild suds.
Shirts		2. Garment should not be twisted or
Slacks	Special dyes were developed for	wrung out.
Sportswear	acetate since it does not accept the	3. Don't soak colored items.
(Fabrics)	dyes ordinarily used for cotton and	4. Press while damp on wrong side
Brocade	rayon. This dye selectivity makes it	with cool iron. If finishing on the
Crepe	possible to obtain multicolor effects	right side, use a pressing cloth.
Double knits	in fabrics made from a combination	
Faille	of fibers—cross-dyeing. In cross-	NOTE: Acetate is adversely affected
Knitted jerseys	dyeing, yarns of one fiber (for exam-	by acetone and other organic sol-
Lace	ple, acetate) and those of another fi-	vents such as nail-polish remover
Satin	ber (such as cotton or rayon) are	and perfumes containing such sol-
Taffeta	woven into a fabric in a desired pat-	vents.
Tricot	tern. After such a fabric has been	
(Home Furnishings)	dyed in one bath, this pattern will	
Draperies	appear in different colors or shades	
Upholstery	according to the distribution of the	
(Others)	respective fibers. Solution-dyed or	
Cigarette filters	spun-dyed acetate provides excellent	
Fiberfill for pillows,	color fastness to sunlight, perspira-	
comforters, mattress pads,	tion, air contaminants, and washing.	
jackets, and other quilted		
products		
Acrylic:		
(Apparel)	Soft, warm, and lightweight	1. Wash delicate items by hand in
Dresses	Shape-retentive	warm water. Static electricity
Infant wear	Resilient	may be reduced by using a fabric
Knitted garments	Quick-drying	softener in every third or fourth
Skirts	Resistant to sunlight, weather, oil,	washing. Gently squeeze out
Slacks	and chemicals	water, smooth or shake out gar-
Snow and ski wear		ment, and let dry on nonrust
Socks		hanger. (Sweaters, however,
Sportswear		should be dried flat.)
Sweaters		2. When machine washing, use
Work clothes		warm water and add a fabric sof-
(Fabrics)		tener during the final rinse cycle.
Fleece fabrics		3. Machine dry at a low tempera-
Face fabric in bonded fabrics		ture setting. Remove garments
Pile fabrics		from dryer as soon as tumbling
		cycle is completed.

[1] Courtesy Man-Made Fiber Producers Association, Inc.

The Uses, Characteristics, and Care of Man-Made Fibers *(Continued)*

Some Principal Uses	Major Characteristics	Care Tips

(Home Furnishings)
    Blankets
    Carpets
    Draperies
    Scatter rugs
    Upholstery
(Others)
    Hand-knitting yarns
		4. If ironing is required, use a moderately warm iron.

Aramid:
    Hot-air filtration fabrics
    Protective clothing
    Military applications (helmets, bullet-proof vests)
    Structural supports for aircraft and boats
    Sail cloth
    Tires
    Ropes and cables
    Mechanical rubber goods
    Marine and sporting goods
	No melting point
	High strength
	Low flammability
	High tenacity
	High modulus
	Good fabric integrity particularly at elevated temperatures
	Inertness to moisture
	
	    The above characteristics have made possible the manufacture of fibers having a truly unique combination of high strength and toughness at levels never before attained in nature or by industry with any material.	

Modacrylic:
    (Apparel)
    Deep-pile coats, trims, and linings
    Simulated fur
    Wigs and hairpieces
    (Fabrics)
    Fleece fabrics
    Industrial fabrics
    Knit-pile fabric backings
    Nonwoven fabrics
    (Home Furnishings)
    Awnings
    Blankets
    Carpets
    Flame-resistant draperies and curtains
    Scatter rugs
    (Others)
    Filters
    Paint rollers
    Stuffed toys
	Soft
	Resilient
	Easy-to-dye
	Abrasion-resistant
	Flame-resistant
	Quick-drying
	Resistant to acids and alkalies
	Shape-retentive
	
	    The low softening temperatures of modacrylic fibers allow them to be stretched, embossed, and molded into special shapes. The fibers may be produced with controlled heat shrinkage capacities. When such fibers of different shrinkages are mixed in the surface of a pile fabric, the application of heat develops fibers of different lengths, providing a surface that resembles natural fur.
		Dry-cleaning or fur-cleaning process is suggested for deep-pile garments. For washable items, however, use the following as a guide:
		
		1. Machine wash in warm water and add a fabric softener during the final rinse cycle.
		2. If dryer is used, use low setting and remove articles as soon as tumbling cycle has stopped.
		3. If ironing is required, use low setting. Never use a hot iron.

The Uses, Characteristics, and Care of Man-Made Fibers *(Continued)*

Some Principal Uses	Major Characteristics	Care Tips

Nylon:
(Apparel)
  Blouses
  Dresses
  Foundation garments
  Hosiery
  Lingerie and underwear
  Raincoats
  Ski and snow apparel
  Suits
  Windbreakers
(Home Furnishings)
  Bedspreads
  Carpets
  Draperies and curtains
  Upholstery
(Others)
  Air hoses
  Conveyer and seat belts
  Military uses
  Parachutes
  Racket strings
  Ropes and nets
  Sleeping bags
  Tarpaulins
  Tents
  Thread
	Exceptionally strong
	Elastic
	Abrasion-resistant
	Lustrous
	Easy to wash
	Resistant to damage from oil and many chemicals
	Can be dyed in wide range of colors
	Resilient
	Low in moisture absorbency
	Filament yarns provide smooth, soft, long-lasting fabrics.
	Spun yarns lend fabrics light-weight warmth.
		1. Most items made from nylon can be machine washed and tumble dried at low temperatures. Use warm water and add a fabric softener to the final rinse cycle.
		2. Remove articles from dryer as soon as tumbling cycle is completed.
		3. If ironing is required, use warm iron.

Olefin:
(Apparel)
  Knitted sports shirts
  Men's half hose
  Men's knitted sportswear
  Sweaters
(Home Furnishings)
  Carpets, indoor and outdoor
    (largest single use)
  Carpet backing
  Slipcovers
  Upholstery
(Industrial)
  Dye nets
  Filter fabrics
  Laundry bags and sandbags
  Nonwoven felts
  Ropes and cordage
  Sewing thread
	Able to give good bulk and cover
	Abrasion-resistant
	Quick-drying
	Resistant to deterioration from chemicals, mildew, perspiration, rot, and weather
	Sensitive to heat
	Soil-resistant
	Strong
	The fiber possesses a dry hand and a unique wicking characteristic ability to draw body moisture from the skin and up through fabric interstices to the outer surface which give olefin a desirable comfort factor for apparel applications.
	Very light in weight (olefin fibers have the lowest specific gravity of all fibers).
		1. Machine wash in lukewarm water and add a fabric softener to final rinse cycle.
		2. If machine drying, use very low setting. Remove items from dryer immediately after tumbling cycle. Gas-fired dryers of the commercial or laundromat type should be avoided.
		3. If touch-up fibers which include olefin fibers, use lowest possible temperature setting. Do not iron articles containing 100% olefin fibers.
		4. Stains on carpeting containing olefin fibers will usually blot away with an absorbent tissue.

The Uses, Characteristics, and Care of Man-Made Fibers *(Continued)*

Some Principal Uses	Major Characteristics	Care Tips

Polyester:
(Apparel)
  Blouses and shirts
  Career apparel
  Children's wear
  Dresses
  Half-hose
  Insulated garments
  Lingerie and underwear
  Permanent-press garments
  Slacks
  Suits
(Home Furnishings)
  Carpets
  Curtains
  Draperies
  Sheets and pillow cases
(Others)
  Fiberfill for various products
  Fire hose
  Power belting
  Ropes and nets
  Thread
  Tire cord
  Sails
  V-belts
	Strong
	Resistant to stretching and shrinking
	Easy to dye
	Resistant to most chemicals
	Quick-drying
	Crisp and resilient when wet or dry
	Wrinkle-resistant
	Abrasion-resistant
	Able to retain heat-set pleats and creases
	Easily washed
		1. Most items made from polyester can be machine washed and dried. Use warm water and add a fabric softener to the final rinse cycle. Machine dry at a low temperature and remove articles as soon as the tumbling cycle is completed.
		2. If ironing is desired, use a moderately warm iron.
		3. Most items made from polyester can be dry-cleaned. However, pigment prints, commonly applied to polyester double knits, do not withstand dry-cleaning well.

Rayon:
(Apparel)
  Accessories
  Blouses
  Coats
  Dresses
  Jackets
  Lingerie
  Linings
  Millinery
  Rainwear
  Slacks
  Sports shirts
  Sportswear
  Suits
  Ties
  Work clothes
(Home Furnishings)
  Bedspreads
  Blankets
  Carpets and rugs
  Curtains
	Highly absorbent
	Soft and comfortable
	Easy to dye
	Versatile and economical
	Fabrics made from rayon fibers have a good drapability.
	
	A stretching process, applied in spinning, may be adjusted to produce rayon fibers of extra strength and reduced stretch. Such fibers are designated as high-tenacity rayons, which have about twice the strength and two-thirds of the stretch of regular rayon. An intermediate grade, known as medium tenacity rayon, is also made and its strength and stretch characteristics fall midway between those of high-tenacity and regular rayon.
		Most rayon fabrics wash well, but some types of fabric and garment construction make dry-cleaning advisable. For washable items, however, use the following as a guide:
		
		1. Fabrics containing rayon can be bleached; some finishes, however, are sensitive to chlorine bleach.
		2. Use mild lukewarm suds, gently squeeze suds through fabric and rinse in lukewarm water. Do not wring or twist the article.
		3. Smooth or shake out article and place on a nonrust hanger to dry.
		4. Press the article while damp on the wrong side with the iron at a moderate setting; if finishing on the right side is required, a press cloth should be used.

The Uses, Characteristics, and Care of Man-Made Fibers *(Continued)*

Some Principal Uses	Major Characteristics	Care Tips
Rayon *(Cont.)* Draperies Sheets Slipcovers Tablecloths Upholstery (Others) Industrial products Medical/surgical products Nonwoven products Tire cord		
Spandex: Articles where stretch is desired Athletic apparel Bathing suits Delicate laces Foundation garments Golf jackets Ski pants Slacks Support and surgical hose	Light in weight Soft and smooth Resistant to body oils Stronger, more durable, and more powerful than rubber When spandex is used in sewing, the needle causes little or no damage from "needle cutting," as compared with the older types of elastic yarns. Able to be stretched repeatedly and still recover to original length Able to be stretched over 500 % without breaking Abrasion-resistant Supple Spandex does not suffer deterioration from perspiration, lotions, or detergents. Lends lightweight freedom of movement in men's, women's, and children's apparel.	1. Hand or machine wash in lukewarm water. 2. Do not use chlorine bleach on any fabric containing spandex. Use oxygen or sodium perborate type bleach. 3. Rinse thoroughly. 4. Drip dry. If machine drying, use low temperature setting. 5. Ironing, if required, should be done rapidly and the iron should not be left in one position too long. Use a low temperature setting.
Triacetate: Apparel where pleat retention is important Dresses Fabrics such as faille, flannel, jersey, sharkskin, taffeta, textured knits, and tricot. Skirts Sportswear	Shrink-resistant Wrinkle-resistant Resistant to fading Easily washed Fabrics made from triacetate fibers maintain pleat retention and a crisp finish. Fabrics made from triacetate fibers develop their most valuable characteristics by heat treatments that are included as a part of their normal finishing.	1. Pleated garments are best hand laundered. Most other garments containing 100% triacetate can be machine washed and dried. 2. If ironing is desired, a high temperature setting may be used. 3. Articles containing triacetate fibers require very little special care due mainly to the fiber's resistance to high temperature.

Appendix F

Stain Removal Guide[1]

This chart applies only to washable items. It does not apply to garments which should be dry-cleaned. Some stains are not easily seen when the fabric is wet. Air dry the articles to be certain the stain has been removed. Machine drying might make the stain more difficult to remove. Prewash products may be more convenient to use in treating stains than the process of rubbing detergent into the dampened stain.

Stain	**Bleachable Fabrics:** White and colorfast cotton, linen, polyester, acrylic, triacetate, nylon, rayon, permanent press.	**Non-Bleachable Fabrics:** Wool, Silk, Spandex, non-colorfast items, some flame-retardant finishes (check labels).
Stain	**Removal Procedure**	**Removal Procedure**
Alcoholic Beverages	Sponge stain promptly with cold water or soak in cold water for 30 minutes or longer. Rub detergent into any remaining stain while still wet. Launder in hot water using chlorine bleach.	Sponge stain promptly with cold water or soak in cold water for 30 minutes or longer. Sponge with vinegar. Rinse. If stain remains, rub detergent into stain. Rinse. Launder.
Blood	Soak in cold water 30 minutes or longer. Rub detergent into any remaining stain. Rinse. If stain persists, put a few drops of ammonia on the stain and repeat detergent treatment. Rinse. If stain still persists, launder in hot water using chlorine bleach.	Same method, but if colorfastness is questionable, use hydrogen peroxide instead of ammonia. Launder in warm water. Omit chlorine bleach.
Candle Wax	Rub with ice cube and carefully scrape off excess wax with a dull knife. Place between several layers of facial tissue or paper towels and press with a warm iron. To remove remaining stain, sponge with safe cleaning fluid. If colored stain remains, launder in hot water using chlorine bleach. Launder again if necessary.	Same method. Launder in warm water. Omit chlorine bleach.
Carbon Paper	Rub detergent into dampened stain; rinse well. If stain is not removed, put a few drops of ammonia on the stain and repeat treatment with detergent; rinse well. Repeat if necessary.	Same method, but if colorfastness is questionable, use hydrogen peroxide instead of ammonia.
Catsup	Scrape off excess with a dull knife. Soak in cold water 30 minutes. Rub detergent into stain while still wet and launder in hot water using chlorine bleach.	Same method. Launder in warm water. Omit chlorine bleach.
Chewing Gum, Adhesive Tape	Rub stained area with ice. Remove excess gummy matter carefully with a dull knife. Sponge with a safe cleaning fluid. Rinse and launder.	Same method.

[1] Courtesy Maytag.

Stain Removal Guide (*Continued*)

	Bleachable Fabrics: White and colorfast cotten, linen, polyester, acrylic, triacetate, nylon, rayon, permanent press.	Non-Bleachable Fabrics: Wool, Silk, Spandex, non-colorfast items, some flame-retardant finishes (check labels).
Stain	**Removal Procedure**	**Removal Procedure**
Chocolate and Cocoa	Soak in cold water. Rub detergent into stain while still wet, then rinse thoroughly. Dry. If a greasy stain remains, sponge with a safe cleaning fluid. Rinse. Launder in hot water using chlorine bleach. If stain remains, repeat treatment with cleaning fluid.	Same method. Launder in warm water. Omit chlorine bleach.
Coffee, Tea	Soak in cold water. Rub detergent into stain while still wet. Rinse and dry. If grease stain remains from cream, sponge with safe cleaning fluid. Launder in hot water using chlorine bleach.	Same method. Launder in warm water. Omit chlorine bleach.
Cosmetics (Eye shadow, lipstick, liquid make-up, mascara, powder, rouge)	Rub detergent into dampened stain until outline of stain is gone, then rinse well. Launder in hot water using chlorine bleach.	Same method. Launder in warm water. Omit chlorine bleach.
Crayon	Rub soap (Instant Fels, Ivory Snow, Lux Flakes) into dampened stain, working until outline of stain is removed. Launder in hot water using chlorine bleach. Repeat process if necessary. For stains throughout load of clothes, wash items in hot water using laundry *soap* and 1 cup baking soda. If colored stain remains, launder with a detergent and chlorine bleach.	Same method. Launder in warm water using plenty of detergent. Omit chlorine bleach. If colored stain remains, soak in an enzyme presoak or an oxygen bleach using hottest water safe for fabric; then launder.
Deodorants and Antiperspirants	Rub detergent into dampened stain. Launder in hot water using chlorine bleach. Antiperspirants that contain such substances as aluminum chloride are acidic and may change the color of some dyes. Color may or may not be restored by sponging with ammonia. Rinse thoroughly.	Rub detergent into dampened stain. Launder in warm water. Antiperspirants that contain such substances as aluminum chloride are acidic and may change the color of some dyes. Color may or may not be restored by sponging with ammonia. (If ammonia treatment is required, dilute with an equal amount of water for use on wool, mohair, or silk.) Rinse thoroughly.
Dye (Transferred from a non-colorfast article)	May be impossible to remove. Bleach immediately using chlorine bleach. Repeat as often as necessary. Or use a commercial color remover.	Use a commercial color remover.
Egg, Meat Juice, and Gravy	If dried, scrape off as much as possible with a dull knife. Soak in cold water. Rub detergent into stain while still wet. Launder in hot water using chlorine bleach.	Same method. Launder in warm water. Omit chlorine bleach.
Fabric Softener	Rub the dampened stain with bar soap (such as Ivory or Lux) and relaunder in the usual manner.	Same method.

Stain Removal Guide (*Continued*)

	Bleachable Fabrics: White and colorfast cotten, linen, polyester, acrylic, triacetate, nylon, rayon, permanent press.	Non-Bleachable Fabrics: Wool, Silk, Spandex, non-colorfast items, some flame-retardant finishes (check labels).
Stain	**Removal Procedure**	**Removal Procedure**
Fingernail Polish	Sponge white cotton fabric with nail polish remover; other fabrics with amyl acetate (banana oil). Launder. Repeat if necessary.	Same method.
Formula	Soak in cold water, then launder in hot water using chlorine bleach. If stain persists, soak in an enzyme presoak.	Soak in warm water using an enzyme presoak. Launder in warm water using plenty of detergent.
Fruit Juices	Soak in cold water. Launder in hot water using chlorine bleach.	Soak in cold water. If stain remains, rub detergent into stain while still wet. Launder in warm water.
Grass	Rub detergent into dampened stain. Launder in hot water using chlorine bleach. If stain remains, sponge with alcohol. Rinse thoroughly.	Same method. Launder in warm water. Omit chlorine bleach. If colorfastness is questionable or fabric is acetate, dilute alcohol with two parts water.
Grease and Oil (Car grease, butter, shortening, oily medicines such as oily vitamins)	Rub detergent into dampened stain. Launder in hot water using chlorine bleach and plenty of detergent. If stain persists, sponge thoroughly with safe cleaning fluid. Rinse.	Rub detergent into dampened stain. Launder in warm water using plenty of detergent. If stain persists, sponge thoroughly with safe cleaning fluid. Rinse.
Ink (Ballpoint)	Sponge stain with rubbing alcohol, or spray with hair spray until wet looking. Rub detergent into stained area. Launder. Repeat if necessary.	Same method.
Ink, Drawing	May be impossible to remove. Run cold water through stain until no more color is being removed. Rub detergent into stain, rinse. Repeat if necessary. Soak in warm sudsy water containing one to four tablespoons of ammonia to a quart of water. Rinse thoroughly. Launder in hot water using chlorine bleach.	Same method. Launder in warm water. Omit chlorine bleach.
Ink from Felt Tip Pen	Rub household cleaner such as 409 or Mr. Clean into stain. Rinse. Repeat as many times as necessary to remove stain. Launder. Some may be impossible to remove.	Same method.
Iodine	Make a solution of sodium thiosulfate crystals. Use solution to sponge stain. Rinse and launder.	Same method.
Mayonnaise, Salad Dressing	Rub detergent into dampened stain. Rinse and let dry. If greasy stain remains, sponge with safe cleaning fluid. Rinse. Launder in hot water with chlorine bleach.	Same method. Launder in warm water. Omit chlorine bleach.
Mildew	Rub detergent into dampened stain. Launder in hot water using chlorine bleach. If stain remains, sponge with hydrogen peroxide. Rinse and launder.	Same method. Launder in warm water. Omit chlorine bleach.

Stain Removal Guide (*Continued*)

	Bleachable Fabrics: White and colorfast cotten, linen, polyester, acrylic, triacetate, nylon, rayon, permanent press.	**Non-Bleachable Fabrics:** Wool, Silk, Spandex, non-colorfast items, some flame-retardant finishes (check labels).
Milk, Cream, Ice Cream	Soak in cold water. Launder in hot water using chlorine bleach. If grease stain remains, sponge with safe cleaning fluid. Rinse.	Soak in cold water. Rub detergent into stain. Launder. If grease stain remains, sponge with safe cleaning fluid. Rinse.
Mustard	Rub detergent into dampened stain. Rinse. Soak in hot detergent water for several hours. If stain remains, launder in hot water using chlorine bleach.	Same method. Launder in warm water. Omit chlorine bleach.
Paint and Varnish	Treat stains quickly before paint dries. If a solvent is recommended as a thinner, sponge it onto stain. Turpentine or trichloroethane can be used. While stain is still wet with solvent, work detergent into stain and soak in hot water. Then launder. Repeat procedure if stain remains after laundering. Stain may be impossible to remove.	Same method.
Perfume	Same as alcoholic beverages.	Same as alcoholic beverages.
Perspiration	Rub detergent into dampened stain. Launder in hot water using chlorine bleach. If fabric has discolored, try to restore it by treating fresh stains with ammonia or old stains with vinegar. Rinse. Launder.	Same method. Launder in warm water. Omit chlorine bleach.
Ring Around the Collar	Apply liquid laundry detergent or a paste of granular detergent and water on the stain. Let it set for 30 minutes. A prewash product especially designed for this purpose may be used. Follow manufacturer's directions. Launder.	Same method.
Rust	Launder in hot water with detergent and RoVer® Rust Remover. Follow manufacturer's instructions. RoVer is available from authorized Maytag dealers and parts distributors; specify Part No. 57961.	Same method. If colorfastness is questionable, test a concealed area first.
Scorch	Launder in hot water using chlorine bleach or RoVer Rust Remover. (See Rust.) Severe scorching cannot be removed; fabric has been damaged.	Cover stains with cloth dampened with hydrogen peroxide. Cover with a dry cloth and press with an iron as hot as is safe for fabric. Rinse thoroughly. Rub detergent into stained area while still wet. Launder. Repeat if necessary.
Shoe Polish (Wax)	Scrape off as much as possible with a dull knife. Rub detergent into dampened stain. Launder in hot water using chlorine bleach. If stain persists, sponge with rubbing alcohol. Rinse. Launder.	Scrape off as much as possible with a dull knife. Rub detergent into dampened stain. Launder in warm water. If stain persists, sponge with 1 part alcohol and 2 parts water. Rinse. Launder.
Soft Drinks	Sponge stain immediately with cold water. Launder in hot water with chlor-	Same method. Launder in warm water. Omit chlorine bleach.

Stain Removal Guide (*Continued*)

	Bleachable Fabrics: White and colorfast cotten, linen, polyester, acrylic, triacetate, nylon, rayon, permanent press.	Non-Bleachable Fabrics: Wool, Silk, Spandex, non-colorfast items, some flame-retardant finishes (check labels).
	ine bleach. Some drink stains are invisible after they dry, but turn yellow with aging or heating. This yellow stain may be impossible to remove.	
Tar and Asphalt	Act quickly before stain is dry. Pour trichloroethane through cloth. Repeat. Stain may be impossible to remove. Rinse and launder.	Same method.
Urine	Soak in cold water. Rub detergent into stain. Launder in hot water using chlorine bleach. If the color of the fabric has been altered by stain, sponge with ammonia; rinse thoroughly. If stain persists, sponging with vinegar may help.	Same method. Launder in warm water. Omit chlorine bleach. If ammonia treatment is necessary, dilute ammonia with an equal part of water for use on wool, mohair, or silk.
Wine	Same treatment as for alcoholic beverages. Wait 15 minutes and rinse. Repeat if necessary.	Same treatment as for alcoholic beverages.
Yellowing Of White Cottons And Linens	Fill washer with very hot water. Add at least twice as much detergent as normal. Place articles in washer and agitate for 4 minutes on regular cycle. Stop washer and add 1 cup of chlorine bleach to the bleach dispenser or dilute in 1 quart of water and pour around agitator. Restart washer at once. Agitate 4 minutes. Stop washer and allow articles to soak 15 minutes. Restart washer and set 10 minute wash time; allow washer to complete normal cycle. Repeat entire procedure two or more consecutive times until whiteness is restored.	
Yellowing of White Nylon	Soak 15 to 30 minutes in solution of $\frac{1}{8}$ cup of chlorine bleach and 1 teaspoon of vinegar thoroughly mixed with each gallon of warm water. Rinse. Repeat if necessary.	

Appendix G

Terminology for Garment Care Labels[1]

To insure clarity in garment care labels, a glossary was provided to the manufacturer, the importer, and the consumer by a ruling of the Federal Trade Commission effective January 1984. The care instructions must include one safe method of cleaning the garment even though other methods can also be satisfactory.

Glossary of Standard Terms

1. **WASHING, MACHINE METHODS:**
   a. **"Machine wash"**—a process by which soil may be removed from products or specimens through the use of water, detergent or soap, agitation, and a machine designed for this purpose. When no temperature is given, e.g., "warm" or "cold," hot water up to 150°F (66°C) can be regularly used.
   b. **"Warm"**—initial water temperature setting 90° to 110°F (32° to 43°C) (hand comfortable).
   c. **"Cold"**—initial water temperature setting same as cold water tap up to 85°F (29°C).
   d. **"Do not have commercially laundered"**—do not employ a laundry which uses special formulations, sour rinses, extremely large loads, or extremely high temperatures or which otherwise is employed for commercial, industrial, or institutional use. Employ laundering methods designed for residential use or use in a self-service establishment.
   e. **"Small load"**—smaller than normal washing load.
   f. **"Delicate cycle"** or **"gentle cycle"**—slow agitation and reduced time.
   g. **"Durable press cycle"** or **"permanent press cycle"**—cool down rinse or cold rinse before reduced spinning.
   h. **"Separately"**—alone.
   i. **"With like colors"**—with colors of similar hue and intensity.
   j. **"Wash inside out"**—turn product inside out to protect face of fabric.
   k. **"Warm rinse"**—initial water temperature setting 90° to 110°F (32° to 43°C).
   l. **"Cold rinse"**—initial water temperature setting same as cold water tap up to 85°F (29°C).
   m. **"Rinse thoroughly"**—rinse several times to remove detergent, soap, and bleach.
   n. **"No spin"** or **"Do not spin"**—remove material at start of final spin cycle.
   o. **"No wring"** or **"Do not wring"**—do not use roller wringer, nor wring by hand.

2. **WASHING, HAND METHODS:**
   a. **"Hand wash"**—a process by which soil may be manually removed from products or specimens through the use of water, detergent or soap, and gentle squeezing action. When no temperature is given, e.g., "warm" or "cold," hot water up to 150°F (66°C) can be regularly used.
   b. **"Warm"**—initial water temperature 90° to 110°F (32° to 43°C) (hand comfortable).
   c. **"Cold"**—initial water temperature same as cold water tap up to 85°F (29°C).
   d. **"Separately"**—alone.

[1] Source: *Writing a Care Label*, Bureau of Consumer Protection, Federal Trade Commission, March 1984.

e. **"With like colors"**—with colors of similar hue and intensity.
f. **"No wring or twist"**—handle to avoid wrinkles and distortion.
g. **"Rinse thoroughly"**—rinse several times to remove detergent, soap, and bleach.
h. **"Damp wipe only"**—surface clean with damp cloth or sponge.

3. DRYING, ALL METHODS:

a. **"Tumble dry"**—use machine dryer. When no temperature setting is given, machine drying at a hot setting may be regularly used.
b. **"Medium"**—set dryer at medium heat.
c. **"Low"**—set dryer at low heat.
d. **"Durable press"** or **"Permanent press"**—set dryer at permanent press setting.
e. **"No heat"**—set dryer to operate without heat.
f. **"Remove promptly"**—when items are dry, remove immediately to prevent wrinkling.
g. **"Drip dry"**—hang dripping wet with or without hand shaping and smoothing.
h. **"Line dry"**—hang damp from line or bar in or out of doors.
i. **"Line dry in shade"**—dry away from sun.
j. **"Line dry away from heat"**—dry away from heat.
k. **"Dry flat"**—lay out horizontally for drying.
l. **"Block to dry"**—reshape to original dimensions while drying.
m. **"Smooth by hand"**—by hand, while wet, remove wrinkles, straighten seams and facings.

4. IRONING AND PRESSING:[2]

a. **"Iron"**—Ironing is needed. When no temperature is given iron at the highest temperature setting may be regularly used.
b. **"Warm iron"**—medium temperature setting.
c. **"Cool iron"**—lowest temperature setting.
d. **"Do not iron"**—item not to be smoothed or finished with an iron.
e. **"Iron wrong side only"**—article turned inside out for ironing or pressing.
f. **"No steam"** or **"Do not steam"**—steam in any form not to be used.
g. **"Steam only"**—steaming without contact pressure.
h. **"Steam press"** or **"Steam iron"**—use iron at steam setting.
i. **"Iron damp"**—articles to be ironed should feel moist.
j. **"Use press cloth"**—use a dry or a damp cloth between iron and fabric.

5. BLEACHING:[3]

a. **"Bleach when needed"**—all bleaches may be used when necessary.
b. **"No bleach"** or **"Do not bleach"**—no bleaches may be used.
c. **"Only non-chlorine bleach, when needed"**—only the bleach specified may be used when necessary. Chlorine bleach may not be used.

6. WASHING OR DRYCLEANING:

a. **"Wash or dryclean, any normal method"**—can be machine washed in hot water, can be machine dried at a high setting, can be ironed at a hot setting, can be bleached with all commercially available bleaches, and can be dry-cleaned with all commercially available solvents.

7. DRY-CLEANING, ALL PROCEDURES:

a. **"Dry-clean"**—a process by which soil may be removed from products or specimens in a machine which uses any common organic solvent (for example, petroleum, perchlorethylene, fluorocarbon) located in any commercial establishment. The process may include moisture addition to solvent up to 75% relative humidity, hot tumble drying up to 160°F (71°C), and restoration by steam press or steam-air finishing.

---

[2] If ironing is not mentioned, it is not necessary.
[3] If bleaching is not mentioned, all bleaches can be used when necessary.

b. **"Professionally dry-clean"**—use the dry-cleaning process but modified to ensure optimum results either by a dry-cleaning attendant or through the use of a dry-cleaning machine which permits such modifications or both. Such modifications or special warnings must be included in the care instruction.

c. **"Petroleum," "Fluorocarbon,"** or **"Perchlorethylene"**—employ solvent(s) specified to dry-clean the item.

d. **"Short cycle"**—reduced or minimum cleaning time, depending upon solvent used.

e. **"Minimum extraction"**—least possible extraction time.

f. **"Reduced moisture"** or **"Low moisture"**—decreased relative humidity.

g. **"No tumble"** or **"Do not tumble"**—do not tumble dry.

h. **"Tumble warm"**—tumble dry up to 120°F (49°C).

i. **"Tumble cool"**—tumble dry at room temperature.

j. **"Cabinet dry warm"**—cabinet dry up to 120°F (49°C).

k. **"Cabinet dry cool"**—cabinet dry at room temperature.

l. **"Steam only"**—employ no contact pressure when steaming.

m. **"No steam"** or **"Do not steam"**—do not use steam in pressing, finishing, steam cabinets, or wands.

8. LEATHER AND SUEDE CLEANING:

a. **"Leather clean"**—have cleaned only by a professional cleaner who uses special leather or suede care methods.

Glossary

abstract having no counterpart in nature or among man-made objects.

acrylics a quick-drying synthetic fiber (see Appendix E).

aerobics body exercises which demand oxygen and can be continued over a long period of time.

aesthetic pertaining to a sense of the beautiful; characterized by a love of beauty.

analogous color harmony colors next to each other on the color wheel.

anchor stores well-established department stores situated in shopping centers for the purpose of attracting other business firms and shoppers.

androgynous being both male and female.

anthropology the science that deals with the origins, physical and cultural development, racial characteristics, and social customs and beliefs of mankind.

archaic ancient, old, from antiquity.

art nouveau a style of fine and applied art current in the late nineteenth and early twentieth centuries, characterized chiefly by curvilinear motifs derived from natural forms.

art principles also called *principles of design*, guides used to judge design, including balance, proportion, emphasis, rhythm, unity.

assumptions opinions or ideas we take for granted as true or factual.

attitudes how we think, feel, and behave.

balance equal distribution of weight (actual or visual) from a central point or area; a state of equilibrium.

bias a diagonal line across a woven fabric; a bias line stretches and hangs differently from lengthwise or crosswise grainlines.

bifurcate, bifurcated divided skirt, early form of culotte.

birds-eye a fabric woven with small diamond-shaped allover design.

black tie a notation on formal invitations which signifies that men are expected to wear tuxedoes or dinner jackets with black bow tie. Fashion sometimes varies the tux look, but the classic tux is black; black accessories are worn with white shirt. Women are expected to wear long gowns or formals. Depending on local custom, short cocktail dresses may sometimes be worn. White tie is more formal than black tie, and not nearly so common.

body image an individual's perception of his own physical being.

body language lay term for *kinesics*, or body communication.

body proportion the size of each part of the body compared to every other part and the relationship of the individual parts of the body to the total body mass.

bolero a jacket ending above or at the waistline, with or without collar, lapel, or sleeves, worn open in front.

bolt a cardboard form around which yardage or piece goods are wrapped.

boutique a small store that features a strong fashion image; especially one that sells fashionable clothes and accessories for women.

campus fashion styles worn on high school or college campuses; they are often unique to a specific campus or geographical area.

cant term used to describe the angle at which men's pants are hemmed. The length at the top of the arch of the foot is tapered to the length at the back of the heel, making a slanted hemline.

carotene orange pigment found in the epidermis.

celebrity a person who has been accepted by a notable percentage of the masses as being over them and beyond them in terms of life accomplishments.

chain store one of many stores belonging to a corporation that owns and operates the stores from a central location.

chic 1) attractive and fashionable in style. 2) style and elegance, especially in dress. 3) stylishness, modishness, fashionableness.

chroma also called *intensity;* term used to describe purity of a color, its strength or weakness, brightness or dullness, or degree of saturation.

classic styles that endure.

clothing, dress, costume, body covering anything put on the body such as a textile or jewelry, and anything that is done to or applied on the body such as hair arrangement, painting, tattooing, or scarring.

color wheel shape formed by twisting a band of color, representing the spectrum, into a circle.

complementary harmony effect produced by using any two hues that appear opposite each other on the color wheel.

conservative traditional in style and manner, avoiding showiness.

contrasting color harmony effect produced by groups of colors having no hue in common.

Cooper's droop body sag caused by stretching the ligaments of Cooper, which support the mammary glands or breasts.

corium inner layer of skin; also called *dermis.*

corrective tint a high, intense color product used under makeup to counter strong pigmentation in skin.

countershading covering a problem area of the skin (such as birthmarks, pigment spots) with a light color to advance the area and thus minimize the problem.

couture a French term for an establishment devoted to the creation of fashion where the designer, rather than working to meet the requirements of the individual customer, develops his own ideas. The *couture* sells clothing to an exclusive clientele.

couturier a French term for designer.

creative having the quality or power of creating, resulting from originality of thought or expression.

crepe a light, crinkled woven fabric of any of various fibers.

culotte women's pants of any length cut to look like a skirt; divided skirt.

culture the product of the creative human response of a group in meeting their needs for obtaining food, shelter, clothing, and so on.

cummerbund wide fabric belt, sometimes pleated lengthwise, fastened in back; worn with men's "black tie" tux and also worn by women.

curved line a continuous bending line without angles.

　　extreme curve a bent line that approaches becoming a circle.

　　gentle curve a line with a slight degree of bend.

custom made for the individual. Sometimes called made-to-measure.

décolleté, décolletage low-cut, revealing neckline.

department store a business establishment for retail sale characterized by having many departments under one roof; it must have at least twenty-five employees and merchandise that includes home furnishings, apparel, and household linens.

dermis inner layer of skin, also called *corium.*

design the arrangement of lines, form-shape-space, colors, and textures.

　　applied design also called *decorative design;* it is created after the form is completed and is the result of surface enrichment.

　　elements of design lines, form-shape-space, colors, and textures.

　　structural design design created by the construction detail form as the design is assembled; any detail that is an integral part of the design.

diagonal lines lines having an oblique direction.

discount store a store that sells merchandise below regular retail prices and offers fewer services than do conventional retail stores.

dry-clean a process of removing soil in a machine that uses a common organic solvent.

eating disorders eating problems that can lead to diseases such as anorexia nervosa and bulimia.

ectomorph body type that is long and lean.

elegance tasteful fineness or luxury as in dress, style, design.

emphasis the dominance or concentration of interest in one area of design that prevails as the center of attention and is more eye-arresting than any other part.

endomorph body type that has a genetic tendency toward softness in outline.

epidermis outer layer of the skin.

evolution any process of formation or growth, development.

fabrics cloth made up from yarns by weaving, knitting, netting, and so on.

face-framing details details that include hair design, hats, jewelry, eyeglasses, necklines, scarves, ties, and any other type of ornamentation used in the personality area.

facial ornamentation decoration of the face including the use of cosmetics, and for men, the styling of beards, moustaches, and sideburns.

fad a fashion that is short-lived.

fad diets eating plans usually based on one food or on strange combinations of foods that are not nutritionally balanced.

fashion broadest definition: a general social phenomenon that affects and shapes mankind as a whole.

> narrower definition: the style accepted by a large group of people at a particular time.

anti-fashion resisting fashion change.

avant-garde those who are extremely far ahead of fashion years.

fashion cycle the movement of fashion from its introduction to acceptance, peak of popularity, and then decline. Usually a period from seven to nine years.

fashion fabric the exterior layer of a garment, the layer that is visible when wearing the garment.

fashion-follower one who waits for fashions to be completely established before embracing them.

fashion leader one who quickly adopts new styles.

fashion plate a picture showing the prevailing or new style in clothes. A person who consistently wears the latest style in clothes.

fashion position personal relationship to fashion, that is, fashion leader, fashion follower, old-fashioned, *avant-garde.*

fashion trends the directions in which fashion is moving.

fashionable observant, or conforming to the fashion.

fashionmonger a person who studies, follows, and helps to popularize current fashion.

fossilized fashion the difficult-to-explain phenomenon of a fashion that remains constant, for example, the priest's robe.

old-fashioned styles of another period, usually in the immediate past.

fibers the raw material from which yarns are made. Cotton, silk, wool, nylon, rayon, and so on are fibers.

flame-retardant finish a finish that resists burning.

flat-felled seam an enclosed cut edge forming a flat seam having two rows of stitches.

form a three-dimensional object.

formal balance also called *symmetrical balance;* occurs when identical objects are equidistant from a center (real or imaginary).

footwear boots, shoes, slippers.

frame-of-reference personal point of view resulting from sum of lifelong experiences, personal "computer."

franchise store a store in which the franchisee invests in the parent company and pays it a percentage on all his sales. In return he gets a well-established name, business guidance, and brand merchandise to sell.

French seam a seam within a seam. The cut edge of a seam is completely enclosed, resulting in a durable seam finish. One row of stitches is visible.

fundamental components garments that form the basic framework of the wardrobe. Their style/design, color, texture, trims, are not all eye-arresting, so that they form the background of an outfit.

grain, grainline the direction of threads or yarns in relation to the selvage of woven threads; lengthwise threads are intersected with crosswise threads to form a weave.

genetic alteration change determined by heredity.

Gothic pertaining to a style of architecture originating in France, twelfth to sixteenth centuries.

halo effect the first impression, which becomes lasting and unchanged.

hand-tactile aspects the sense of touch revealing softness, coarseness, rigidity, and so on.

hang tag a name given to labels suspended from garments for sale; these labels state information prescribed by Federal law including fiber content, and care instructions on new merchandise.

haute couture high fashion, very new, expensive, and often bizarre.

heat sensitive melting or glazing at low temperatures.

health foods foods promoted as having special nutritional value.

Hong Kong seam finish seam in which the cut edge is enclosed by another strip of fabric.

horizontal lines lines at right angles to the vertical, parallel to the level ground.

hue name of a color family such as red, blue, green.

humectant a substance that absorbs or helps another substance retain moisture.

in vogue French term meaning in fashion.

individuality personification of characteristics that make a person distinctive.

informal balance also called asymmetrical balance, occurs when objects are arranged on either side of a center (real or imaginary), are equal (in weight or mass), but are not identical.

intensity also called *chroma;* term used to describe purity of a color, its strength or weakness, brightness or dullness, or degree of saturation.

interest feeling of concern or intrigue; that which appeals.

interfacings fabrics used between two layers of cloth to build support and shape in small areas of a garment such as the collar, cuffs.

ironing smoothing the fabric by a sliding motion following the grain of the fabric.

isometrics body exercises that contract one set of muscles without producing movement or demanding large amounts of oxygen.

isotonics body exercises that contract muscles and produce movement, but do not require large amounts of oxygen.

keratin horny layer of the epidermis.

keystone something on which associated items belong; a term used in RTW for costing from wholesale to retail price.

kilocalories, kcalories, or kcals thousands of calories; the unit used to measure the energy produced by food.

kinesics the science based on the behavioral patterns of nonverbal communication.

knits fabrics constructed by the interlacing of yarns with needles into a series of connected loops.

liberal open-minded or tolerant; not bound by traditional or conventional ideas.

lifestyle the pattern by which one lives.

line that which indicates the dimensions of length and width.

linings fabrics used on the inner side of an area to cover the construction details of a garment; used in coats, jackets, dresses, pants.

melanin brown pigment in the epidermis; it gives color to the skin.

membership store a combination of a department store and a discount store where shopping is restricted to a particular group of people.

mesomorph body type in which the musculature is visibly pronounced.

metamerism colors in two or more fabrics appearing to match under one light condition and to mismatch under another.

monochromatic color harmony a group of colors selected from one hue family.

mores prevailing uses and traditions.

morphology the study of the physical structural aspects of the organism as well as the externally observable and objectively measurable attributes of the person including aesthetic attractiveness.

motif individual unit of a pattern.

motivational research technique used by advertising firms to discover the human factors that persuade customers to buy.

New Look term given to Christian Dior's collection of 1947 and the fashions that it inspired. Still used to refer to that collection of forty years ago.

obesity overweight.

obsolescence the process of becoming outdated.

off-price store store that sells brand-name and designer-label garments for less than regular retail prices.

overlock seam machine stitching that covers cut seam edges protecting them from ravel.

pattern overall design made up of motifs.

personality distinctive individual qualities of a person.

personality types artificial classifications of personalities into types such as romantic, athletic, macho, based on composites of various personalities.

physical fitness no medical definition. Authorities agree that fitness involves being strong and flexible, having adequate endurance to do the tasks desired.

piece goods yardage used for sewing.

posture the term used to describe the position of the limbs and the carriage of the body as a whole.

pressing smoothing the fabric by the lifting up and pressing down motion of an iron.

prêt-a-porter French term for ready-to-wear.

principles of design also called *art principles;* guides used to judge design, including balance, proportion, emphasis, rhythm, unity.

progression a successive passing from one member of a series to the next; succession; sequence.

proportion the pleasing relationship of areas, sometimes referred to as scale.

psychological pertaining to the mind as a function of awareness, feeling, or motivation.

psychology the study of individual behavior.

Punk term describing styles of antisocial behavior emanating from London in the late 1970s. Exemplified by bizarre hairstyles, colorful makeup, and clothing.

purdah the excluding of women from public observation. It includes wearing a veil that covers the body from head to foot. The face may or may not be covered.

radial balance balance occurring when the major parts of the design radiate from a central point.

raiment clothing; apparel; attire.

realistic duplicating nature or some man-made object.

related color harmony pleasing effect produced by groups of colors having at least one hue in common.

remnant a small amount of piece goods left at the end of the bolt.

Renaissance the activity, spirit, or time of the great revival of art, literature, and learning in Europe, fourteenth to seventeenth centuries.

rhythm a pleasing sense of organized movement that gives continuity to a design.

RTW abbreviation for ready-to-wear.

ruche, ruching trimming made by pleating a strip of lace, ribbon, net, and so on, and stitching through the middle.

saddle soap a mild soap made with unsaponified oil used for cleaning and conditioning smooth leather.

scarification the act of making scratches or small cuts on the skin that produce permanent scars.

self-concept, self-image the general notion that each person has of himself.

shading makeup used to create shadows and correct or seemingly reshape areas of the face.

shape term referring to the outside dimensions or contour of an object.

shirtwaist blouse styled like a tailored shirt.

shirtwaist dress dress with top styled like a tailored shirt, usually buttoned from neck to waist.

silhouette the outline or the outside dimensions or contour of an object.

simultaneous contrast the sharp contrast produced when complementary hues placed next to each other are used in their full strength and in equal quantity. They intensify each other and cause vibrations. Red will appear redder next to green (complement) than when used next to yellow (analogous).

social psychology the study of the influence of group behavior on the individual.

sociocultural relating to a combination of social and cultural factors.

sociological focusing on the cultural and environmental factors rather than on psychological or personal characteristics.

sociology the study of group behavior.

somatotypes body types; three basic somatotypes: endomorph, mesomorph, and ectomorph.

space the background area found within the shapes.

spectrum rows of colors formed in a fixed order by diffraction.

SPF sun protection factor; a number that identifies the sun-protection factor on the label of sun-screen products.

sportswear a classification of dress that includes spectator sports apparel.

status social or economic placement.

stereotype a standardized mental picture that is held in common by members of a group.

style a distinctive characteristic or way of expression. Style in dress describes the lines that distinguish one form or shape from another.

stylized variations of natural forms, such as flowers or leaves, that do not look three-dimensional and do not imitate realistic forms.

sumptuary laws laws regulating personal expenditures on food and dress, often perpetuating distinctions in social class.

supportive fabrics fabrics used on the inside of garments such as linings, interlinings, interfacings.

surcoat the outer coat worn over a robe.

surface language a pattern of immediate impressions conveyed by appearance.

taste a subjective judgment of what we think is appropriate or beautiful. Because of the individualness of this judgment, standards of taste are not universal.

tattoo an indelible mark or figure made on the body by inserting a pigment under the skin.

texture surface appearance or feel.

theme a subject of discourse or composition; topic.

toiles French term for muslin copy of designer original garment.

tone effect of adding white and black to a pure hue.

total look a term coined to describe an outfit that expresses a single theme or idea; unity in dress.

trait term used to describe a consistent manner of behavior.

trotteur a hobble skirt, very narrow, tapered ankle-length.

underlining fabric used to lend support, durability, and stability to the fashion fabric. It is cut in the same shape as the fashion fabric and is handled as one in the construction of the garment.

unity also called *total look*, achieved when the fundamental elements—line, form-shape-space, colors, and textures—have all been used to express a single concept or theme.

value lightness or darkness of a color.

values qualities of importance or worth; a motivating force in behavior and decision making.

vertical lines lines in a position or direction perpendicular to the plane of the horizon.

wardrobe extenders garments and accessories that add flair and fashion signature to the wardrobe.

wet-cleaning process of removing soil with water and soap or detergent.

wicking property ability to draw up moisture.

WWD abbreviation for the fashion trade paper *Women's Wear Daily*.

yarns strands formed by fibers twisted together.

yoke a shaped piece of a garment, fitted about or below the neck and shoulders or about the hips from which the rest of the garment hangs.

Selected Readings

Arts of Asia Magazine, Vol. 12, No. 4. July–August 1982. Arts of Asia Publications, Ltd., Hong Kong.

Barthes, Ronald. *The Fashion System*. New York: Hill and Wang, 1983.

Cho, Emily, and Hermine Lueders. *Looking, Working, Living Terrific 24 Hours a Day*. New York: Ballantine Books, 1982.

"Cleanliness Facts." Soap and Detergent Association, 475 Park Avenue South at 32nd Street, New York, N.Y. 10016.

Cordwell, Justine M., and Ronald A. Schwartz, eds. *The Fabrics of Culture*. The Hague: Mouton Publishing, 1979.

Davis, Marion L. *Visual in Dress*. Englewood Cliffs, N.J.: Prentice-Hall, Inc., 1980.

Fraser, Kennedy. *The Fashionable Mind, Reflections on Fashion 1970–1981*. New York: Alfred A. Knopf, Inc., 1981.

Gentleman's Quarterly. *Fashion Handbook*. New York: Esquire, Inc., 1984.

Hamilton, Eva May, Eleanor Noss Whitney, and Frances S. Sizer. *Nutrition: Concepts and Controversies*, 3rd. ed. St. Paul, Minn.: West Publishing Co., 1985.

Hollander, Anne. *Seeing Through Clothes*. New York: The Viking Press, Inc., 1978.

Horn, Marilyn, and Lois Gurel. *Second Skin*, 3rd. ed. Boston: Houghton Mifflin Company, 1981.

Jarnow, Jeannette A., and Bernice Judelle. *Inside the Fashion Business*, 3rd. ed. New York: John Wiley & Sons, Inc., 1981.

Joseph, Marjorie L. *Essentials of Textiles*, 3rd. ed. New York: Holt, Rinehart and Winston, 1984.

Kaiser, Susan B. *The Social Psychology of Clothing and Personal Adornment*. New York: Macmillan Publishing Company, 1985.

Lauer, Robert H., and Jeanette C. Lauer. *Fashion Power*. Englewood Cliffs, N.J.: Prentice Hall, Inc., 1981.

Lurie, Alison. *The Language of Clothes*. New York: Random House, Inc., 1981.

The Maytag Encyclopedia of Home Laundry, 5th ed. Western Publishing Co. Inc., Information Center, Maytag Company, Newton, Iowa 50208.

Melinkoff, Ellen. *What We Wore, An Offbeat Social History of Women's Clothing, 1950–1980*. New York: Quill, 1984.

Meyer, Alice, and Clara Pierre. *Clotheswise Successful Dressing for Your Lifestyle*. New York: E. P. Dutton, 1982.

Naisbitt, John. *Megatrends*. New York: Warner Books, 1982.

Renbourn, E. T. *Materials and Clothing in Health and Disease*. London: E. K. Lewis and Company, Ltd., 1972.

Rudofsky, Bernard. *Are Clothes Modern?* Chicago: Paul Theobald, 1947.

Solomon, Michael R. *The Psychology of Fashion*. Lexington, MA: Lexington Books, 1985.

Sones, Melissa. *Getting Into Fashion, A Career Guide*. New York: Ballantine Books, 1984.

Sproles, George B. *Fashion, Consumer Behavior*. Minneapolis, Minn.: Burgess Publishing Company, 1979.

Tate, Sharon Lee, and Mona Shafer Edwards. *The Fashion Coloring Book*. New York: Harper & Row, Publishers, 1984.

Thompson, Jacqueline. *Image Impact for Men.* New York: A. & W. Publishers, Inc., 1983.

Toffler, Alan. *The Third Wave.* New York: William Morrow & Company, Inc., 1980.

Von Furstenberg, Egon. *The Power Look.* New York: Fawcett Books Group, 1984.

Vreeland, Diana. *D.V.* New York: Alfred A. Knopf, Inc., 1984.

Watkins, Susan M. *Clothing, The Portable Environment.* Ames, Iowa: Iowa State Press, 1984.

Wenck, Dorothy A., Baren Martin, and Sat Paul Dewan. *Nutrition, The Challenge of Being Well Nourished,* 2nd ed. Reston, Va.: Reston Publishing Company, 1983.

Whitney, Eleanor Ness, and Eva May Nunnelley Hamilton. *Understanding Nutrition,* 3rd. ed. St. Paul, Minn.: West Publishing Company, 1984.

Wingate Isabel, Karen Gillespie, and Betty Addison. *Know Your Merchandise.* New York: McGraw-Hill Book Company, 1984.

Author Index

Subject Index